PROGRAMMING WEB COMPONENTS

Programming
Web
Components

Reaz Hoque
Tarun Sharma

McGraw-Hill
New York • San Francisco • Washington, D.C. • Auckland
Bogotá • Caracas • Lisbon • London • Madrid • Mexico City
Milan • Montreal • New Delhi • San Juan • Singapore
Sydney • Tokyo • Toronto

Library of Congress Cataloging-in-Publication Data

McGraw-Hill
A Division of The McGraw-Hill Companies

Copyright © 1998 by The McGraw-Hill Companies, Inc. Printed in the United States of America. Except as permitted under the United States Copyright Act of 1976, no part of this publication may be reproduced or distributed in any form or by any means, or stored in a data base or retrieval system, without the prior written permission of the publisher.

1 2 3 4 5 6 7 8 9 0   DOC/DOC   9 0 2 1 0 9 8 7
1 2 3 4 5 6 7 8 9 0   DOC/DOC   9 0 3 2 1 0 9 8

P/N 029236-1
PART OF
ISBN 0-07-912316-3 (PBK)

P/N 029240-X
PART OF
ISBN 0-07-913776-8 (HC)

The sponsoring editor for this book was Michael Sprague and the production supervisor was Tina Cameron. It was set in Century Schoolbook by Douglas & Gayle, Limited.

Printed and bound by R. R. Donnelley & Sons Company.

McGraw-Hill books are available at special quantity discounts to use as premiums and sales promotions, or for use in corporate training programs. For more information, please write to Director of Special Sales, McGraw-Hill, 11 West 19th Street, New York, NY 10011. Or contact your local bookstore.

 This book is printed on recycled, acid-free paper containing a minimum of 50% recycled de-inked fiber.

DEDICATION

I would like to dedicate this book to my wife, Reshma, for her support. Reshma, I can never thank you enough for being understanding when I spent all those long nights and weekends on this book. Thanks for your support and encouragement during the times I thought I would break down; you made me believe in myself. I love you.

I would also like to thank my parents and my brother for loving me and encouraging me to be what I am.

—TARUN SHARMA

I would like to dedicate this book to those who are not as lucky as I am. I truly appreciate being surrounded by some great people and some great opportunities.

—REAZ HOQUE

CONTENTS

Contents

Contents

Contents

Contents

Contents

INTRODUCTION

In today's fast-growing Internet world, we need a way to save time and run as fast as the competition. Therefore, we need to make sure that what we create is reusable and scalable as well as capable of being distributed across all platforms. With the growth of Java and component-based architecture such as ActiveX and JavaBeans, we can now "glue" software pieces together and build killer applications that not only run on a browser but also work as standalone applications, independent of all platforms. We can build the connection between different software easily and without being explicit. The end user doesn't have to know that an Excel spreadsheet is accessing a database that actually resides in a corporate data warehouse. All users care about is getting things done faster and more easily.

Imagine you're building a house. If someone has already built the components, such as panels, windows, bricks, and so forth, all you need to do is put the pieces together. This method saves you time and gives you the option to pick and choose what components are best suited for the house. Component-based software programming is yet to mature as much as the technology of building houses, but we can see trends of this architecture coming of age. Now we don't have to code every single function to create our software application because we can buy components from other vendors and tie them together or modify them to fit our own needs and growth.

JavaBeans and ActiveX are two of the most exciting components on the Web today. JavaBeans supplies the critical link between the cross-platform potential of the Java language and the need for interoperability at a component level. ActiveX, on the other hand, takes existing OLE/COM technology and extends it to a higher level. It uses Windows' wealth of functions and features to create live, scalable applications both on the Web and on the network. Both of these components will play a big role in creating killer network-centered applications, and this book tells you how to use them. Moreover, we, as the authors of the book, take an objective role in presenting the two technologies. There are obviously some advantages and disadvantages to the two technologies, but it's up to you to decide which technology to use after you read the book. This book also shows you how to bridge the two technologies as an example of distributed computing. We use JavaSoft's ActiveX and JavaBeans bridge wrapper to tie the two technologies together.

Two different types of people are affected by components—users and developers. There are several reasons why developers would want to use the ActiveX Packager from JavaSoft for wrapping JavaBean components. The key reason for using any tool or technology is that productivity increases, and application building is a breeze using prefabricated components. They reduce development time, giving developers the edge over competing products that don't use components. Users benefit, too, from the consistency across applications that are built using the same components. Besides that, if any component is misbehaving, all that needs to be done is to remove that component and replace it with a new one that behaves itself. The risk users take in working with applications built on components is much less than the risk of using integrated applications that don't rely on components.

Java offers significant productivity increases over C and C++, and it's not a very difficult jump to move to Java. Many developers are using visual builders, such as Delphi and Visual Basic. Many Java tools now have Visual Basic–like editing and creation of Java controls, so developers can switch between visual building and manual coding as needed, yielding maximum productivity.

Java is cross-platform, but ActiveX is tied to particular tools owned by Microsoft—such as Visual Basic or Visual C++—and particular platforms, most notably 16- and 32-bit Windows. Java components appeal to users on the Internet with its wide range of platforms, but ActiveX appeals to the Windows-only community. The ActiveX Packager brings Java to the desktop, letting developers use the strengths of both.

With Java, developers can create components in the fastest possible time, and the ActiveX Packager opens the market for developers to market components in the ActiveX world and the cross-platform world. ActiveX developers can use the thousands of Internet-ready Java objects already in existence as well as the many ActiveX and OCX objects targeted at the Windows community.

Java and the ActiveX Packager increase programmer productivity and make applications reach the market faster. The ActiveX Packager brings Java to the Windows-only environment, taking advantage of the similarities in the component architectures.

What to Expect from This Book

Several sections in this book cover key technologies. The first section is a foundation builder. Here you learn about distributed objects, Java (an introduction) and some of JavaBean's main concepts, such as RMI, IDL, JDBC, and CORBA. This section is for those readers who need to make sure they get a basic understanding of Java and distributed objects before diving into more complex topics, such as how to build a Bean or an ActiveX control.

In the next part, we talk about JavaBeans. We explain what a Bean is and discuss persistence, events, properties, introspection, and all the jargon related to Beans. These are new concepts, so we try to make sure they're described in detail and in an easy-to-understand manner. Finally, we show you how to create a Bean from scratch. We will be using a few Beans in all our examples and eventually show you how to put them together to form an application. The Beans we build will show you object-oriented technology in its true form, but keep in mind that these Beans are being developed to explain JavaBeans fundamentals and illustrate object-oriented technology. Therefore, these Beans might be more basic than what's used in a real-life application.

In the next part of the book, we focus on ActiveX. Here we give you an overview of ActiveX, OLE, COM, and DCOM and describe how they all tie together. Remember that ActiveX, unlike JavaBeans, is a set of technologies. Later, we give you an introduction to *Visual Basic* (VB) and show you step by step how to create an ActiveX control by using VB.

Finally, in the fourth part of the book, we show you how to bridge ActiveX and JavaBeans. We explain how to use the JavaBeans Migration Assistant to convert existing Windows ActiveX components into Beans. We also have something special in this book by one of the *Virtual Reality Modeling Language* (VRML) gurus from Moscow. He shows us how to combine VRML with JavaBeans. You might not be able to find much information about these technologies in other sources, so the contents of this chapter are very valuable.

The last part of the book is a reference section, full of useful information you will find handy. Although this book focuses on JavaBeans, you will find yourself immersed in many other cutting-edge technologies that are affecting the software industry.

Who Should Read This Book?

This book does require some familiarity with object-oriented technology. It would definitely be a benefit if you already know Java, but we have included a chapter on Java and object-oriented technology to be as complete as possible. However, please don't consider the book as an alternative source for learning about Java or other object-oriented technologies, such as C++. Nor is this book a substitute for the JavaBeans API specifications from JavaSoft (`http://splash.javasoft.com/beans`). This book should be used with all the documentation available from JavaSoft to master the Java-Beans technology. Similarly, Microsoft has tons of information on

ActiveX that would be very helpful to master the technology. We couldn't cover everything about the technology, so you should check out Microsoft's site (**http://www.microsoft.com/activex**) for recent detailed documents.

Most of the topics discussed in this book are covered in a shorter, simpler version than what you find in the product documentation so that you can become familiar with the hottest NET components. Keep in mind that most of these components have entire books written about them, so you should see this book as a guideline for deciphering many of the buzzwords you see on the Internet.

This book is for you if you fit into one (or more) of the following categories:

- An intranet /Internet /extranet application developer who wants to create mission-critical cross-platform applications
- A user learning Java who wants to know about JavaBeans, which is the only component architecture of Java
- A software developer who wants an overview of distributed NET components
- A Windows programmer who wants to leap from using OLE/COM to ActiveX
- A student who wants to keep up with cutting-edge component technology

Icons Used in This Book

Two icons have been used to get your attention throughout the text:

NOTE *This icon is used to point out material you might want to remember.*

TIP *This icon is used to give you suggestions on how to perform certain tasks.*

ACKNOWLEDGMENTS

This book wouldn't have been possible if it wasn't for the brilliant team with whom I worked. I want to take this opportunity to thank each one of the team members from the bottom of my heart. If I forget to name someone in my acknowledgements, please forgive me and accept my heartfelt thanks.

First, I want to thank my publishers for believing in me and giving me an opportunity to write. I can never thank my editors, John Wyzalek and Michael Sprague, for their support, inspiration, and belief in me.

Next, I would like to thank my coauthor, Reaz, for being the wonderful, charismatic person he is. He's always been there with me and for me. I can't thank him enough for cheering me up when I felt low and stressed out. I look forward to sharing many more such endeavors with him in the future.

My special thanks to Naushad Kapasi, whose enthusiasm and dedication in helping me write this book can't adequately be expressed in words. If there was a problem I couldn't solve, all I had to do was tell him to look into it. I knew I could rely on him to give me all the correct answers.

I extend my heartfelt thanks to John Small. He is one of the most technically sound and enthusiastic people I have ever met. I wish him all the very best life has to offer.

Thanks to all the contributing authors for helping us write parts of this book. I really appreciate their patience when Reaz and I kept asking them to make small changes to their work. Never once did they complain. I feel fortunate to have worked with such talented people. Together, we form a winning team.

I extend my thanks to Carol Wong from Symantec for sending me a free copy of Symantec Visual Café Pro. It helped to play around with some other application frameworks besides the BeanBox.

I can never thank my colleagues enough, especially Faisal Hoque, Sathish Reddy, Harsha Kumar, Ephrem Bartolomeos, Govind Rao, and TharakaRam Krishnamurthy, for being so encouraging and supportive. Thanks for the moral support you gave me when I needed it most and had no one to turn to.

I extend my heartfelt thanks and best wishes to Dimitry Khabenko for helping me out in time of need. I really do appreciate his making time for me when time is such a luxury.

I thank all those people who joined the team but could not stay to see the success. Eric Ries and Cliff High, thanks for being there. Maybe sometime down the line, we will work together.

My special thanks to Zia Khan for his invaluable feedback as a technical editor and advisor. I am still cleaning out my mailbox from the hordes of information he sent me during the project.

I can never express my appreciation towards my wife, Reshma, for standing by me through thick and thin. I feel absolutely incomplete without her, and I want to let her know how much I appreciate her support. I wouldn't be here if it wasn't for her.

—TARUN SHARMA

First, I would like to thank Jeff Willams, who approached me with this project. Although the project didn't work out with Jeff, I have to admit that without his approach, I probably wouldn't have thought about writing this book.

Next, I want to thank my editors at McGraw-Hill, John Wyzalek and Michael Sprague. John has been a great support throughout the whole project, and I appreciate everything he has done. Thanks to Michael for taking care of the project where John left off.

When I started this project, I didn't realize how the project would expand each day and how the table of contents would keep growing. I had to find some of the well-recognized Internet specialists to help write some of the chapters. I thank all the contributing authors who put hours into their chapters. I especially want to thank John Small, who was like an angel on this project. His sincere help had a positive effect.

Thanks to those who gave us the source code and software on the CD-ROM. I specially want to thank IBM Canada's Sheila Richardson and Terry McElroy for their generous help in getting us the IBM Visual Age software. I truly appreciate their support. Thanks to Zia Khan for editing the book for technical accuracy.

I also want to thank my colleagues at Netscape Corporation for their support and encouragement, with special thanks to Lori Landesman, Eric Korck, David Huntley, Diana Gingrich, Marty Cagan, Mark Lavi, and Shiva Ramamoorthy.

I want to thank my family and friends, too, especially my brother Faisal and sister-in-law, Chris Hoque. The list of things they have done for me would go on and on.

Most important, I want to thank my coauthor, Tarun Sharma. I truly believe there are some unique, nice people on this earth. Tarun and his wife, Reshma, are the true examples. Thanks for being there for me, guys!

Last, but not least, thanks to the Allah who has given me the energy and opportunity to do this project. I take a lot of things for granted, such as not remembering my creator, so I want to make sure the message is clear that I am truly thankful to him or her for always looking out for me!

—REAZ HOQUE

## PART 1

Getting Started

1

Understanding Distributed Objects

In this chapter, we provide a broad overview of distributed object computing. The Internet has fueled a convergence of distributed computing and *Object-Oriented Programming* (OOP) that has resulted in the component revolution. Old software practices can't scale to the Internet's size, so an enormous number of competing technologies have emerged to fill the gap. Our goal is to make some sense out of these technologies and help you understand what distributed objects are all about and how different standards and products compare.

First, we look at distributed computing, distributed objects, and components. Why is there a need for these technologies in the first place, and what problems do they solve? Next, we look at some specific solutions. We focus on *Common Object Request Broker Architecture* (CORBA), ActiveX, and *Remote Method Invocation* (RMI), paying particular attention to where Java fits into all of them. By the end, you'll have a better understanding of what distributed objects are all about and will be able to evaluate the different technologies on the market. You should see this chapter as a "gateway" to the many technologies we discuss later in the book in greater detail.

This chapter will cover the following topics:

- Distributed computing
- Distributed objects
- Components
- Distributed Java objects
- The current state of affairs
- Design patterns
- Component patterns
- Enterprise/architectural patterns
- Future trends

What Is Distributed Computing?

Distributed computing is all about crossing boundaries at the enterprise, application, and object levels. It solves many of the fundamental problems we face in computing today. As software has evolved, the enterprise has become increasingly heterogeneous. With distributed computing, we can cope with systems from multiple vendors, different languages, and different computing platforms.

Crossing Boundaries

Traditional distributed computing is primarily concerned with crossing the network boundaries. Systems are almost entirely proprietary, so the issues of language and operating system boundaries are largely ignored.

Crossing network boundaries is not transparent. A great deal of code has to be integrated into an application to communicate over a network. Products that include 4GL languages are used to develop client software that can talk over the network transparently to the developer; this is what is known as a *fat client*. The primary problem with fat clients is that they require more management because the systems' brains are decentralized and require greater amounts of system resources.

Distributed computing also means crossing boundaries in a standard way (see Figure 1-1). Currently, some languages can interoperate, as can

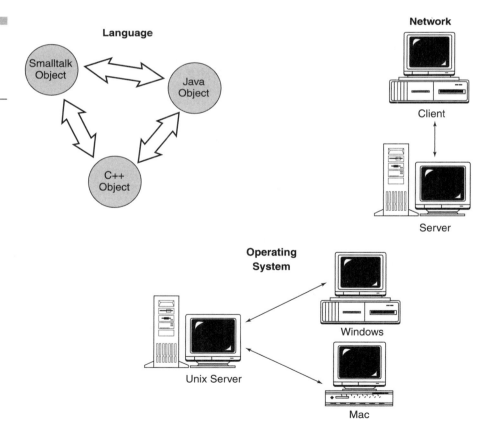

Figure 1-1.
The three barriers: network, operating system, and language.

some operating systems and some networks. However, they all do this in nonstandard ways. The result is that the heterogeneous collection of systems that make up the enterprise are precariously patched together. If you lose your system's architects, you can count on a long, costly period of bringing new people up to speed.

Many applications must be able to cross network boundaries. How easily an application can be programmed to cross these boundaries affects its cost and development time. The majority of development environments produce applications that run on only a single machine at any given time. The application can use the address space of only the machine it's running on. To cross network boundaries, you have to provide separate code that manages the communication over the network. The specification of messages sent over the network, also called the *protocol*, must also be worked out, which means a lot of design and coding. An effective distributed objects system eliminates the need to write networking code and protocols, effectively expanding the address space to the entire network.

Although many companies standardize with one particular platform for their client machines, the diverse needs of an enterprise system often require several different operating systems. With a large investment in a legacy system, a company can migrate to one platform—but it may not be feasible to replace its database systems with the new operating system. This leads to a heterogeneous system in which operating systems must be able to communicate with each other. Some departments might prefer Macs, but others need applications that run only under Windows. Traditionally, to maintain consistency, two applications would have to be developed—one for the Mac and another for Windows—requiring up to twice the amount of time and money.

There are two issues with language boundaries: The first is deciding whether to reuse existing code, and the second is choosing the right tool for the job. Many companies have invested a great deal of time and money into writing code in a particular language, such as C or C++. Unless code written in different languages can work together, this means scrapping the existing code and replacing it with code written in the new language. Not only is this costly, it's also more prone to error because the existing code probably has been thoroughly tested, having been used many times before.

Some languages are better suited to some tasks than others. If you're doing mathematics, Fortran or C might be the best tool for the job, but if you're doing *graphical user interface* (GUI) development, you might want to use Visual Basic or Smalltalk. If you don't have the technology that allows you to cross language boundaries, you will have to make sacrifices in runtime speed or development time.

What Are Distributed Objects?

Distributed objects are a way to make distributed computing a reality. In a traditional system, the client needs to have a great deal of knowledge about the server to talk to it. This tight coupling raises some problems, however. If the server implementation is changed, every single one of its clients must be changed. Since most systems undergo a lot of change in their lifetimes, this becomes costly from a programming and network-management standpoint.

Distributed object technologies allow for looser coupling and change the interaction between the client and the server so that it's all based on *contracts*. As long as an object maintains its contract, or *interface*, it doesn't matter how its implementation changes. This change in interaction is also referred to as a separation of interface and implementation. To put it in more concrete terms, an object on the server makes its method calls public; as long as they don't change, the client won't have to be reprogrammed, even if the server object is modified to carry out the method calls differently.

OOP technologies have increasingly moved toward looser coupling for subsystems, objects, and lower-level event areas such as event handling. One of the original dreams of OOP was to avoid the "spaghetti code" that the procedural approach often seemed to produce. *Spaghetti code* is code that has interactions and interdependencies throughout, meaning that no single part can be isolated from the rest. A programmer needs to know the details of the whole system to work on one small part of it. Looser coupling is a move toward code, modules, and subsystems that have minimal dependencies on each other. This is achieved by creating each subsystem with a clearly defined interface. Other systems must go through this interface to access any of its functions.

Large, complex applications can then be broken up into well-defined subsystems. Developers working on one subsystem don't need to know the implementation details of other subsystems; they need to know only what their public interface is. This subsystem method simplifies code development, and with proper design, the dependencies among subsystems can be reduced. If part of the application needs to be changed, it won't affect the entire system.

Object Orientation

What defines something as being object-oriented? There are three essential components to object-oriented programming: Encapsulation, polymorphism, and inheritance (see Chapter 2, "Object-Oriented Programming Concepts," for more detail).

■ **Encapsulation:** *Encapsulation* is hiding nonessential details. It simplifies the act of using the object, giving it greater appeal for reuse. Also, it's far easier to use the object because you don't have to learn all of its technical details.

■ **Polymorphism:** *Polymorphism* literally means "many forms." It's the simple act of sending the same message to two different objects and causing them to behave differently. If you tell both a computer program and a person to run, you are bound to get different results. This might seem painfully obvious, but before OOP, polymorphism wasn't a feature of most computer languages.

■ **Inheritance:** *Inheritance* allows the program to place objects into real-world categories, which helps the programmer organize a structure.

The underlying goal behind all object-oriented concepts is to model the real world. By doing so, the developer's job is elevated from solving programming problems to solving human problems. Instead of focusing on function calls, parameters, and variables, object-oriented programming lets us talk about the services that objects provide.

Encapsulation is the most important of the three concepts. Imagine if you had to know exactly how an elevator worked before you could use it. That wouldn't be a huge problem if you use only one elevator every day; you would first have to learn how its electrical and mechanical systems worked, and you would be fine. But what would happen if the building upgraded its elevators to a new system? Everyone who used the elevator would have to learn all the implementation details again. If you used a lot of elevators each day, this would cost you a great deal of time and money.

So what do elevators have to do with OOP? In the real world, all we need to know about an elevator is how to use the up, down, and floor selection buttons, or its *public interface*. That makes life much easier. Traditional programming, however, doesn't focus on hiding the implementation details from the user behind a simple interface. Programmers need to know the guts of the system so that the code will perform a particular service.

Like the elevator scenario, this isn't a problem when there's just one person using the system; the number of systems the person uses is small, and the systems never change. However, experience has shown us that most software development requires multiple programmers and that applications become complex very quickly and are anything but stagnant. New versions and upgrades are constantly needed. The low-level details of a system should exist only on a need-to-know basis. Most users of a system or application want to know only what services it provides and how to get it to perform them.

The Three Rs: Reduce, Reuse, Recycle

Although current systems can cross many of these boundaries, the purpose of distributed objects is to reduce, reuse, and recycle. Ideally, with distributed objects, you can reduce your system's complexity, the amount of time required to program and manage it, and the load on your network and server. Through inheritance and encapsulation, individual objects, as well as collections of objects such as frameworks and components, can be reused.

The original dream of OOP focused on reusing objects, but so far this has largely failed to materialize. Most recent efforts have looked toward collections of objects in the form of frameworks and components to provide reuse. (We take an in-depth look at components and frameworks later in this chapter and throughout the book.) For the sake of time- and cost-efficiency, legacy systems and data should be recycled and integrated cleanly into newer systems. The following sections describe some ways that distributed object technologies help reduce, reuse, and recycle.

REDUCE

- **Programming time:** Avoiding network programming can save quite a bit of time. Object technology also promotes code reuse, which can save even more time. Programmers don't have to know the details of each subsystem, so it's easier to divide work up into manageable, easy-to-learn chunks.

- **Complexity:** With greater abstraction and looser coupling, it's easier to simplify a complex system. When a project requires a team of programmers, it's far easier if they need to know only partial details of the whole system.

▪ **Network and server load:** In the network-centered era of the Internet, the traditional client-server model fails miserably. The two-tiered approach of the lone server with many clients doesn't scale well without major investments in hardware. Distributed objects can more easily spread the load across multiple machines.

REUSE   Reuse is possible at several different levels; the lowest one is object reuse. As we mentioned, OOP programming hasn't delivered as much as was hoped in this area. Often, objects are simply too fine-grained to provide valuable reuse. However, if you design your system well, you can often target particular areas for reuse. Don't expect every object to be reusable; but certain types, such as utility objects (database access, currency, special collections, and so forth), are often prime candidates for reuse. You have to analyze your objects and decide which ones are worth abstracting and which aren't.

Component and application framework-level reuse is much more promising. These larger-grained collections of objects generally provide a much higher-level interface than individual objects do. Components and application frameworks are also marketable entities. They are designed to be self-describing and self-contained, so they invite reuse.

RECYCLE   With most companies having large investments in older systems, applications, and code libraries, OOP technologies must be able to recycle these technologies and integrate well with them in order to be successful. The principle of encapsulation is particularly important here. Legacy systems can have an object "wrapper" applied to them that en-

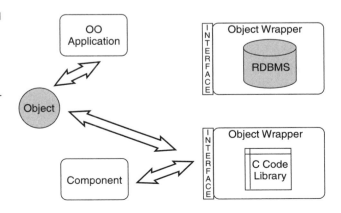

Figure 1-2.

Object-wrapping legacy systems to promote easy interoperability.

capsulates their functions behind an OOP interface (see Figure 1-2). The implementation details are then hidden, making a heterogeneous system look homogeneous. An old procedural system or relational database can be wrapped to make it look like an object with a clearly defined interface, which simplifies the legacy system and reduces programming and maintenance time.

Distributed Computing Today

The greatest barrier to implementing distributed computing today is a combination of cost-effectiveness and inertia. Distributed objects require a businesswide change in focus that can initially cost a lot of money and require a massive change in the status quo. Large businesses must manage risk, and the changes in thinking required by distributed computing are a major risk. This risk is compounded by the cost of migrating systems (that have worked just fine for 10 years) to a distributed object system. A company must balance the long-term benefits of distributed objects with the immediate costs.

In the following sections, we take a look at how the network, *Operating System* (OS), and language barriers are being crossed today and some of the shortcomings of those methods. The problems with our current methodologies are discussed to show why we need distributed object technologies and how they solve many of those problems.

NETWORK BARRIERS Network barriers are primarily crossed through *Remote Procedure Call* (RPC) mechanisms and direct network programming. The majority of Internet-aware applications are programmed by using *sockets*, a low-level network communications interface. Although distributed object architectures might use sockets for communication, the details are hidden, so the programmer needs to concentrate only on the application. This elevates the level of programming and saves time by allowing the programmer to focus on the application logic rather than all the low-level network communications.

RPC is worth mentioning because of its widespread use. RPC is a successful form of distributed computing because you can seamlessly make function calls across a network without worrying about low-level communications. The difference is that you can make only single calls to functions; you can't create an object that has state. Some distributed object systems are written on top of RPC, adding object abilities, but at the cost of efficiency.

OPERATING SYSTEM BARRIERS   To cross the operating systems barrier, interpreted scripting languages are often used. Since the languages aren't compiled to a specific binary format, they can be reused and run in source code format on multiple machines. Some examples of cross-platform scripting languages are TCL, Perl, and Python. In particular, Perl supports an enormous variety of platforms, from DOS to Cray.

Lack of speed is the drawback of interpreted languages. Also, not all of them are designed with the lowest common denominator in mind, so certain features might be available on some of the platforms, but not all.

Another approach to crossing the operating system barrier is to provide a layer on top of the OS that allows you to run binaries compiled for a different OS. Binary compatibility layers exist for many operating systems, such as OS/2, Linux, and other varieties of Unix (to allow you to run Windows applications). If you've ever run an application on top of one of these layers, you know that they're often slower (although the OS/2 compatibility layer is sometimes faster than Windows itself), and not all applications will run on top of the layer. This approach is often convenient, but it's a lot of work on the developer's part. Each binary compatibility layer is bound to have its share of quirks and bugs.

LANGUAGE BARRIERS   To overcome the language barrier and allow code written in one language to integrate seamlessly with code written in another, many languages supply bindings to popular languages, such as C and C++. These bindings are usually nonstandard and far from seamless, even if the two languages come from the same vendor. When the languages come from different vendors, the problems are even worse.

Another approach, although less widely used, is to have a compiler that can compile code to different binary standards. In that way, you can develop an application in your language of choice and then compile several versions of it for different operating systems. In *theory*, this approach allows developers to write the code once, but they still have to deal with different binary distributions.

Drawbacks of Current Practices

Let's examine the drawbacks to current practices of crossing barriers.

NETWORK PROGRAMMING   The primary drawback to the network programming approach is the time and cost involved in writing the code.

Writing socket code and protocols takes a great deal of planning and doesn't lend itself well to incremental development. The resulting system is often inflexible because of its tight coupling. Both the client and the server need extensive knowledge of the protocol. If new features are added or the implementation changes, the protocol might have to be reworked, which means many code changes for both the client and the server.

Because of the system's complexity, new programmers on the team often have difficulty getting up to speed. The subsystems aren't encapsulated well, and the tight coupling means that for the application to work, the new programmer needs to know many of the communications' low-level details. RPC solves some of these problems since writing your own network protocols isn't necessary—but its procedural approach tends to work against encapsulation and reuse of code.

INTERPRETED LANGUAGES   Using interpreted languages is an effective way to cross the OS barrier as long as all your target platforms have interpreters. The problem with this approach is that it causes a "speed hit," often hundreds of times slower than compiled languages. This drawback makes interpreted languages unsuitable for most mid-sized to large applications. They are better suited to small applications and automation tools that complement larger applications.

BINARY COMPATIBILITY LAYERS   As we mentioned, binary compatibility layers are rarely seamless. Not all applications run properly on top of the layer. Additionally, for any given operating system, you probably have only a few binary compatibility layers (usually just Windows). You have to rely on your vendor to update this layer when the target OS is modified.

LANGUAGE BINDINGS   Language bindings are usually specific to each development environment you use, so you must learn each binding and how it works. Like binary compatibility layers, language bindings often have their share of quirks and bugs. If you're trying to work with a large existing body of code in a different language, don't expect everything to work properly on the first try, and *do* expect to program a lot of workarounds. If you change your development environment, you will probably have to scrap much of your work.

SUMMARY OF DRAWBACKS   Current practices for crossing network, OS, and language boundaries have many shortcomings (see Table 1-1). These approaches aren't suited to the Internet's large-scale, open environment.

Table 1-1.

Current Practices
in Distributed
Computing and
Their Drawbacks.

Barrier	Current Practices	Drawbacks
Network	Socket communications	Costly to develop and modify
	Custom/proprietary protocols	Nonstandard
	Remote procedure calls (RPCs)	Procedural, not object-oriented
Operating system	Scripting languages	Slow (usually too slow for large-scale application development)
	Binary compatibility layers	Nonstandard and often buggy
Programming language	Language bindings	Often slower, nonstandard, and buggy
	Development environment that compiles to multiple target platforms	Still requires multiple binary distributions

Distributed computing needs to be based on widely accepted standards,
and the issues of low-level communication and interoperability should be
isolated from the system's developers.

Overview of Distributed Object Systems

Distributed objects are objects that can cross boundaries. In the age of the
Internet, the most fundamental boundary is the network. To be considered a distributed object system, the location of the object must be encapsulated from the user of the object.

Microsoft's *Distributed Component Object Model* (DCOM), CORBA, and
RMI all allow objects to be invoked across network boundaries (see Table
1-2). Java RMI allows you to cross operating system boundaries, too; however, CORBA stands above the rest by also crossing the boundary of computing languages.

The World Wide Web is similar to a distributed object system. The documents are objects stored on a huge network composed of many hardware
configurations and operating systems. The details of how a particular machine stores a document are encapsulated behind a simple *Uniform Resource Locator* (URL) request. The Web server takes the request and retrieves the file in any manner it wants—from the hard drive, a CD-ROM,
or a database—but you shouldn't have to know the details to use the resource. Imagine if you had to know how each operating system and Web

server stored and retrieved its documents to use them. The Web certainly wouldn't work well if these details weren't encapsulated so they're isolated from the user.

The Web manages to cross all the boundaries: Network, OS, and language. It crosses language boundaries by having an agreed-upon language: *hypertext markup language* (HTML). Your documents can be stored in any format you want; you just have to convert them to HTML before you send them. HTML crosses the network boundary through *Hypertext Transport Protocol* (HTTP). The OS boundary is crossed because HTML documents are simply plain-text ASCII documents existing on almost every OS.

Knowing which boundaries are crossed by competing distributed object architectures can help you evaluate which one is right for you. A word of caution, though: Crossing boundaries isn't the only criterion that's important. Issues such as scalability, speed, maturity, and product support have to be addressed, too. Some of these technologies—ActiveX, for example, can cross operating systems and other boundaries. However, they aren't widely used in that manner. Outside factors, such as the owner of the standard, can greatly affect which boundaries they cross, regardless of whether it's theoretically possible.

In the next section, we take an in-depth look at CORBA. It's one of the best examples of distributed object technologies because it's built to cross all the boundaries we've talked about, and it strives to reduce, reuse, and recycle. RMI and ActiveX, however, could turn out to be CORBA's main competitors. RMI is a contender because it's available with *Java Developers' Kit* (JDK 1.1) and uses Java technology to cross the OS boundary. However, ActiveX is most likely the biggest competitor of CORBA for two reasons: First, ActiveX has Microsoft behind it; second, Microsoft has enabled a high level of interoperability between Java and ActiveX because it sees Java as just another language used to write ActiveX controls. As with any Microsoft product, ActiveX is primarily designed to run on one platform—Windows.

Table 1-2.

How well technologies cross barriers.

	Network	OS	Language
ActiveX	✓		✓
RMI	✓	✓	
CORBA	✓	✓	✓

The OMG and CORBA

To address the issues of distributed computing, the *Object Management Group* (OMG) was set up in 1989. The OMG is now a consortium of over 600 companies (with the notable exception of Microsoft) dedicated to standardizing distributed object computing. Despite its large size and bureaucratic nature, it has managed to successfully develop the CORBA standard.

CORBA Architecture

The *Object Request Broker* (ORB) is responsible for handling requests for object services over the network. Through *Interface Definition Language* (IDL), a developer can use a wide variety of languages such as C++, Smalltalk, and Java, to develop network-aware objects.

With the emerging popularity of *Internet Inter-ORB Protocol* (IIOP), a standard protocol for communication between ORBs, operating systems aren't a barrier, either. If you want to have objects on multiple operating systems, you just need to find a ORB vendor that supports your OS. A CORBA object, then, is an object that can exist anywhere on the network, can be written in a variety of languages, and can be housed on several different operating systems. All of these abilities are performed transparently to the object's user.

The CORBA architecture consists of four layers as shown in Figure 1-3.

■ **Object Request Broker layer:** The ORB is the core of CORBA; it basically handles requests for objects.

■ **CORBA Common Object Services layer:** Also referred to as *CORBAServices*, this layer supplies the means to manipulate and use objects. Some examples are naming services to locate objects, event services to handle a variety of push, pull, and multicast events, and object persistence to freeze objects for storage on disk or into a stream.

■ **CORBA Common Facilities layer:** Also called *CORBAFacilities*, this layer is composed of two sublayers: The horizontal frameworks and the vertical frameworks.

The **horizontal frameworks** cover common needs that are less fundamental than the CORBAServices. E-mail, systems manage-

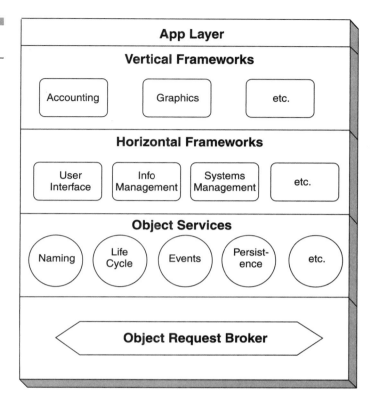

Figure 1-3.
CORBA layers.

ment, and task management are a few examples. In contrast to the vertical facilities, the horizontal facilities can be applied to a wide range of applications.

The **vertical frameworks** are targeted for specific types of applications and industries, such as electronic commerce, oil and gas exploration, and accounting.

■ **Application layer:** The vertical frameworks are still more generic than the final layer, which is not shown in Figure 1-4. There are no CORBA standards for the applications that use these frameworks and services. Obviously, that's left up to the developer.

By using parts of the CORBA architecture, developers can make sure applications have high interoperability. All applications use some of the CORBAServices; they are considered fundamental. Some use the horizontal frameworks, which are useful to most applications. Those applications targeted at more specific needs and industries can use the vertical frameworks to get more standardization with other applications in their domain.

Figure 1-4.
Object Request
Broker layer.

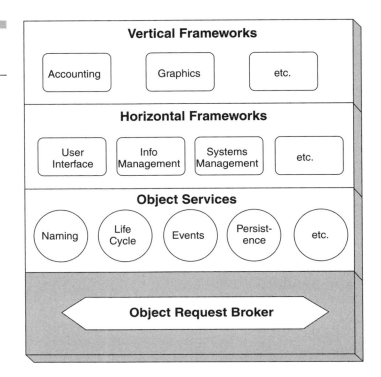

THE ORB An ORB acts as middleware between an object that needs the services of another object on a different machine. Instead of writing socket client and server code, you simply let the ORB take care of the networking. The ORB is the backbone of the CORBA architecture. It's often called an *object bus* because its job is to route object requests and transport them across the network.

Figure 1-5 is a simplification of the ORB architecture. In reality, there is no clear distinction between the client and the server. A particular object can be a server object and a client object at the same time. CORBA is fundamentally a peer-to-peer, not client-server architecture. Any given request clearly has one client and one server, but the requested object on the server might be a client to another object on a different server.

IDL So how does CORBA manage to get all these objects on different platforms using different languages to talk to each other? The answer is the *Interface Definition Language* (IDL). Using IDL, you declare your object's public interface. IDL syntax and semantics are much like C++, so features such as multiple inheritance are allowed. As you might imagine,

Figure 1-5.
CORBA ORB.

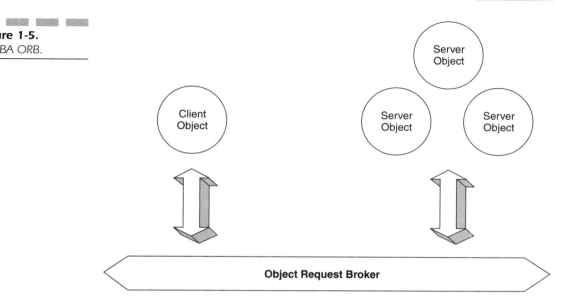

IDL has its own set of data types. Each language must have a mapping to these data types and object definitions.

Language mappings currently exist for C, C++, Smalltalk, Java, and others. All the implementation is left up to that particular language. You write your objects in the language of your choice and then declare their public interface by using IDL.

IDL takes care of the communication from the client object to the ORB on the client machine and then to the server ORB and the server object. CORBA implementations come with an IDL compiler that takes your objects and their IDL interfaces and produces *client stubs* and *server skeletons* (see Figure 1-6). The stubs on the client side translate method calls to ORB calls, which is made at a protocol level, such as IIOP, to be sent over the network to the server ORB. The server ORB receives the request and translates it into a call to the skeleton code. The skeleton code is a wrapper around your server object, so it translates this request into a method call on the target object.

IIOP ORBs must have a way to communicate with each other over the network. A request from a client object is handled by an ORB on the client machine and then sent to an ORB on the server machine, which handles the call to the server object. CORBA doesn't specify one particular protocol that must be used for this communication; anything from TCP/IP to IPX/SPX can be used.

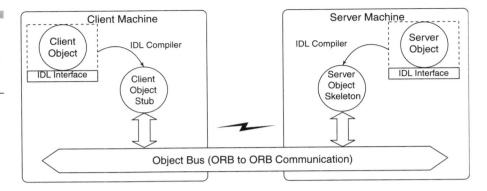

Figure 1-6.
The IDL compiler automatically creates client stubs and server skeletons.

However, with Internet use increasing, it looks like IIOP might become the standard. As we discuss later, this TCP/IP-based protocol could even give HTTP a run for its money. Netscape recently announced that it plans on widely supporting IIOP for object communications. Almost all ORBs on the market use the IIOP protocol.

CORBA Object Services

The CORBAServices supply the essential functionality for objects to work with each other (see Figure 1-7). The ORB provides the bus that bridges networks, but this channel doesn't help very much if you can't find what you're looking for and then communicate in the same language.

CORBAServices answers the basic questions—How can I locate an object? How do I create and destroy new objects? How can I get an object to do what I tell it to do?—and many more. These three fundamental questions address Naming, Life Cycle, and Event Services, which are essentially predefined, horizontally applicable CORBA objects.

NAMING SERVICE   With the ORB, we can now cross network boundaries and have objects on multiple machines anywhere on the network. That's wonderful, but how do you find a particular object that you want to use? The Naming Service allows you to specify an object by name.

LIFE CYCLE SERVICE   This philosophical service answers the existential question "What is life?" It deals with creating and destroying objects. In a single-machine architecture, memory is automatically freed up when the application quits. In a networked environment, when an appli-

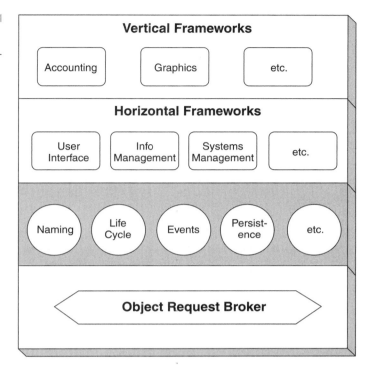

Figure 1-7.
CORBAServices layer.

cation quits, it must have some way of telling all the objects on the network it's using that they are no longer needed.

EVENT SERVICE   Once you've located the object you need and then created it, you need to be able to interact with it. The Event Service allows an object to register itself as a listener for a particular event. When an event, such as a mouse click or a key press occurs, listening objects are notified. The object can then deal with the event in whatever manner it decides is appropriate. This creates a loosely coupled communication channel between different objects. With the help of the ORB, this channel can cross networks.

An object can have two possible roles: A producer or a consumer of events (see Figure 1-8). The method of communicating the event also has two forms: Push and pull. In the push method, the producer of the event notifies the consumers by pushing the event information down the Event Service communications channel to the consumers. The opposite happens for the pull method. Here, the consumers query the event channel as often as they think is appropriate to find out whether the event they are interested in has yet occurred. The push method is sometimes called a *callback*, and the pull method is often called *polling for an event*.

Object Request Broker

CORBA Common Facilities

CORBAServices are aimed at functions fundamental to a good OOP system. The CORBA Common Facilities, or CORBAFacilities, provide a wide range of services that aren't as essential, but are still needed by many applications and industries. The CORBAFacilities are really application frameworks broken up into the two groups mentioned previously: Horizontal frameworks and vertical frameworks.

HORIZONTAL FRAMEWORKS The horizontal frameworks extend CORBA's functionality without modifying its core parts (see Figure 1-9). They supply facilities to manage your objects and user interfaces. The OMG decided to create specifications for these facilities to avoid the problem of each ORB vendor developing its own, noninteroperable systems.

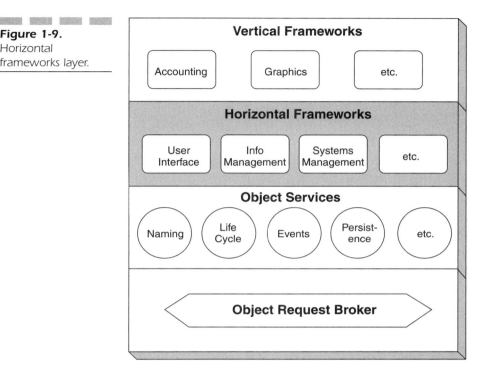

Figure 1-9.
Horizontal
frameworks layer.

- The *User Interface* facility provides the mechanisms for working with compound documents. Similar in function to OpenDoc, it handles allocating visual real estate (screen space, in other words) to components.

- The *Information Management* facility provides document storage and data interchange functions for compound documents, which need to be able to communicate with each other in a standard way.

- The *Task Management* facility covers a wide range of topics, including workflow, automation scripting, and agents.

- The *System Management* facility handles scheduling, logging, security, and workload monitoring; it also extends the Event Service.

VERTICAL FRAMEWORKS   Vertical frameworks are less widely applicable than horizontal frameworks. They are designed to allow standardization of objects aimed at specific industries, business functions, competing standards, and other more obscure areas. This is also the level where many standard business objects are implemented (see Figure 1-10).

Figure 1-10.
Vertical frameworks
layer.

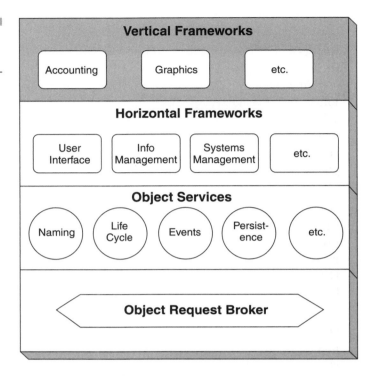

In contrast with the horizontal frameworks, the vertical frameworks are aimed at more specialized areas. Rather than just providing an architecture for commonly used facilities, the OMG made allowances for including software standards to serve particular business needs and industry sectors. Frameworks for fields such as computer manufacturing and accounting are being developed so that business objects with built-in business logic for these areas can be plugged into standard frameworks. The goal is to provide an architecture that allows high-level, specifically targeted frameworks to be included in the CORBA standards. In this way, different vendors and companies can work together to develop CORBA standards that fit their specialized needs.

Commercial ORBs

The first ORBs came out in 1992. Since then, the CORBA specification has advanced by learning from these early implementations. As you might have noticed, ORBs didn't catch on widely in the early days—but the current breed of ORBs have a lot of potential. We're at a turning point right now; the product vendors are struggling to keep up with the latest Internet trends and are just starting to use IIOP and to include Java support in their products.

Some of the CORBA ORBs currently on the market are described in the following sections. As of this writing, none of them support the CORBA 2.0 standard completely. They all vary in their level of support and proprietary extensions. This information is changing rapidly as companies scramble to stake their claim in the emerging distributed object world, so your best bet is to check each of their Web sites for more details.

NEO (HTTP://WWW.SUN.COM) Solaris NEO is the basis of Sun's distributed object technology. NEO is a CORBA 2.0 ORB that supports the IIOP protocol. It currently runs only on Sparc Solaris, but Intel Solaris support is expected soon. *Java Objects Everywhere* (JOE) is an IIOP-compliant ORB written entirely in Java that is shipped with NEO. JOE is meant to be primarily a client-side ORB that can be downloaded by Web browsers.

ORBIX (HTTP://WWW.IONA.COM) Iona's strong involvement in the OMG has made its ORB one of the best on the market. Orbix is available on a wide variety of platforms and uses IIOP as its default protocol. Like Sun, Iona has a scaled-down ORB written entirely in Java that's designed to be downloaded with applets. Named OrbixWeb, it performs much the same function as JOE does.

SOM (HTTP://WWW.IBM.COM) IBM's SOM provides a language-independent distributed object infrastructure. SOMObjects is their CORBA 2.0 ORB implementation. SOM has traditionally been the basis for OpenDoc, IBM's compound document model; however, with release 3.0 of SOM, IBM seems to have abandoned support for OpenDoc. SOMObjects supports IIOP and many CORBAServices. It doesn't currently support the OMG's preliminary Java IDL mapping.

VISIBROKER (HTTP://WWW.VISIGENIC.COM) Visigenic is making waves by partnering with Netscape to provide a distributed object infrastructure for its Web browsers and servers. A runtime version of their Java ORB will be included in every version of Netscape Navigator 4.0. VisiBroker for Java has the added benefit of not requiring the developer to write any IDL—its IDL compiler takes your Java source and creates the IDL files for you.

Evaluating ORBs

Choice is wonderful, but sometimes it makes your job more difficult. Products are constantly being upgraded, and you're bound to run into problems getting past the marketing hype. The most important thing to find is what part of the CORBA 2.0 specification the products don't support right now. Their marketing literature will tell you all about the features they do support and plan on supporting "very soon now." You'll have to decide whether "very soon now" is soon enough. Here are some questions to ask ORB vendors:

- Which of the OMG language mappings do you support?
- Which CORBAServices do you support?
- Do you have any proprietary extensions?
- Does your ORB have IIOP support?
- Do you have an all-Java client ORB?

What Are Components?

As objects started to mature and enter the mainstream, the dream of OOP —reduce, reuse, and recycle—didn't fully materialize. In particular, the ideal of reuse through inheritance seemed to be minimal in real-world applications. The problem is that objects are often too specialized to make reuse valuable. Developers started to realize that larger parts with simple, well-defined interfaces were better suited to reuse.

This realization led to several revolutions in the OOP industry: Design patterns, frameworks, business objects, components, and many more ideas that focused on larger scale reuse. Components, in particular, lead the way with the popularity of *Visual Basic Controls* (VBXs) and the later *OLE Custom Controls* (OCXs).

Business Objects and Components

Business objects and components are similar because both are *large-grained objects* or collections of objects. A large-grained object is composed of regular objects, but hides all its details behind a public interface (see Figure 1-11).

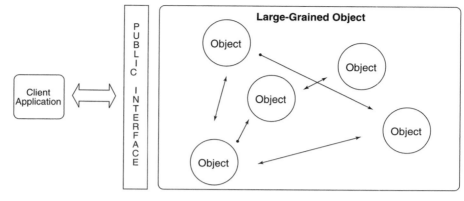

Figure 1-11.
Large-grained objects hide smaller objects and their interactions behind a public interface.

A *component* is a large-grained object with a higher-level interface than the sum of its parts would provide. That's the key distinguishing feature between a component and a code library. Also, a component should be a self-contained entity that can potentially be marketed on its own. It's similar to a code library because it's not a complete application; instead, it's meant to be plugged into an application and used. The most common example of a component is a GUI widget, such as a button, a slider, or a file selection box.

Business objects are a subset of components that have built-in business logic. They are modeled after the real world to provide specific business functions. Business objects might be, for example, designated as **Customer**, **OrderHandler**, or **Product**.

The business object market isn't as mature as the component market (referring mainly in this case to visual components, such as GUI widgets), mostly because of a lack of a standard communications infrastructure. Until CORBA ORBs or another distributed object bus fully catches on, business objects aren't feasible.

To aggregate a collection of large-grained business objects (possibly from multiple vendors) into a useful application, the objects must be able to communicate with each other. Frameworks for visual GUI components have been around for years, but business object frameworks are just starting to emerge. Although the concepts are very similar, business objects have lagged behind because of their abstract nature. You can't *see* a business object the same way you can see a button or a scrollbar.

FRAMEWORKS   While we are on the topic of groups of objects, it's worth mentioning *frameworks*, which are also collections of objects (see

Figure 1-12.
Components versus
frameworks.

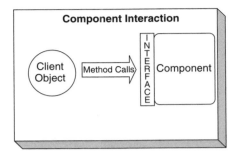

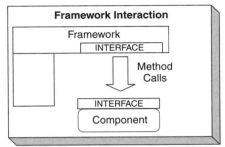

Figure 1-12.
Components versus
frameworks.

Figure 1-12). However, a framework is used in exactly the opposite way that a component is used. A component is plugged into an application, but an application is plugged into a framework. In coding terms, that means your application makes calls to a component, and a framework makes calls to your object or application. For this procedure to work properly, your application must conform to the interface specified by the framework. Another notable difference between components and frameworks is that although both are generally groups of objects, to gain the benefits of the three Rs, components are usually small groups of objects, and application frameworks might be large groups of objects or even groups of components.

For example, JavaSoft's AppletViewer (or the Applet player in Netscape) is a framework. You plug your applet in, and the framework makes calls to it such as **init()**, **start()**, **stop()**, and **destroy()**, in order to run it. *Servlets* (server-side applets) are another example of applications that run within a framework. In contrast, GUI widgets are components that are plugged into your applet; you call them rather than vice versa.

OOP AND COP   We are now witnessing a shift by many developers from OOP to *Component-Oriented Programming* (COP). COP augments OOP by adding the concept of a component, which is just a group of objects hidden behind a well-defined interface. If a client program wants to access the services of one of the component's objects, it must go through the component's interface. The objects in the component are free to communicate among each other freely, which completely decouples the client from the components' implementation, reducing the dependencies among objects in an application. Isolating groups of objects and reducing individual object dependencies make it far easier to make changes. If a method needs to be added or removed, only the code in that component needs to be modified. A component is effectively a unit of reuse.

ActiveX

ActiveX is a banner that flies over several different Microsoft technologies for enabling distributed objects, components, and compound documents. ActiveX is not just *Object Linking and Embedding* (OLE) renamed; it encompasses a wider range of technologies that all came about from OLE. The first version of OLE offered simple cut-and-paste capabilities. When OLE2 came out, Microsoft introduced its underlying communications layer as a separate entity called *Component Object Model* (COM). With this infrastructure, developers could create components called OLE controls, or OCXs. OLE controls are useful only on a single machine, so they are not distributed objects.

When Microsoft announced their belated plans for the Internet in 1995, they introduced the next generation of OLE/COM: ActiveX. With the 4.0 release of Windows NT, they have upgraded COM to DCOM, which is the underlying communications infrastructure for ActiveX. They also plan to include DCOM in the next release of Windows 95. This is an important move in the world of distributed objects because it creates a ubiquitous infrastructure for distributed object computing.

There's a lot of confusion in the marketplace over exactly what ActiveX is. Basically, it's a general name for all of Microsoft's distributed object infrastructure, so it includes COM, DCOM, OLE, and OCXs. OLE controls are now called *ActiveX controls*, and Microsoft's compound documents are called *ActiveX documents*. You learn more about ActiveX in Chapter 13, "Understanding ActiveX."

Component Models

If we have all these components, how do we get them to work together to form an application? The answer is *component models*. You plug your components into a componenet module in order to run them and make sure they will interoperate. To run properly, they must conform to the component model's interface. Although conforming to one particular interface limits your creativity and what you can and can't do, it ensures that all the components can interoperate and use each other in a standard way.

Component models must offer several different services for components to interoperate effectively. These services include metadata facilities, graphical editing, automation and scripting, and event handling, described in the following list:

■ For components to be used dynamically, a client must be able to find out information about the component on the fly. This information is called *metadata*, or data about the component itself, and the process of a component finding out about itself is called *introspection*.

■ Most components are visual entities. They occupy a specific amount of visual real estate onscreen and can be interacted with visually. It makes sense, then, to build components visually. Placing and editing components by the drag-and-drop method is essential for making development easy.

■ Scripting languages are used to dynamically manipulate components. For example, you might want to determine the position of a component at runtime rather than compile time. A component framework needs to provide facilities for this kind of scripting and automation.

■ Components aren't very useful unless you can interact with them. Event handling allows a component to respond to mouse clicks and keyboard events.

The two component models we examine most closely in this book are JavaBeans and ActiveX controls. With Netscape and IBM fully supporting JavaBeans as their component models, it looks like the component war will be much the same as the browser war. The same goes for the distributed object war between CORBA and DCOM. Luckily, the "Microsoft versus the rest of the industry" battle might not affect component developers much. Beans can interoperate quite well with ActiveX controls.

JAVABEANS JavaBeans supply the critical link between the cross-platform potential of the Java language and the need for interoperability at a component level. With its inclusion in the JDK 1.1, JavaBeans promises to be a major contender in the component arena. So what is a JavaBean? A *Bean* is a visual component that adheres to the JavaBean interfaces for its interaction with other components. Because Beans can interoperate with ActiveX, OpenDoc, and Netscape LiveConnect, they are not only cross-platform (because they're written in Java), they are also cross-application. JavaBeans cross barriers very effectively.

JavaBeans have all the functionality one would expect from a good component model. Beans are self-describing through the introspection and reflection classes. The `BeanInfo` class is another way to find out information on a Bean at runtime. JDK 1.1 has completely reworked the event handling of JDK 1.02 to provide a more loosely coupled mechanism.

Hooks for visual editing ability is a fundamental part of the JavaBeans architecture. A Bean can be customized by editing its property sheet. Automation, however, is left up the application or environment that uses the components. In the case of Netscape, JavaBeans can be manipulated through JavaScript and LiveConnect. You learn more about JavaBeans in Chapter 4, "JavaBeans Fundamentals."

ACTIVEX CONTROLS DCOM is the other important component standard. OLE and COM gradually changed in response to the needs of the Internet and became ActiveX and DCOM. An ActiveX object is really just a DCOM object.

ActiveX allows you to leverage off existing applications and components that you have written or that have been developed by third-party vendors. It's not difficult to migrate an OCX to ActiveX. There are already many complex ActiveX controls available. As early as summer 1996, Microsoft was demonstrating a PowerPoint slide viewer within a Web browser. Visual C++ and Visual Basic developers don't have to worry about JavaBeans putting them out of a job.

Compound Documents

One of the areas in which components are most important is in word processing and other, nontextual, documents. Without the ability to embed spreadsheets, drawings, and other documents within an existing document, you're stuck working in several different programs and having to export the contents of one document into a format that the other document can handle. This structure of documents within a document is called a *compound document*.

The compound document is really a collection of components that can come from different applications made by different vendors. An important part of compound documents is their visual nature. A document (or component) embedded within another document is allocated a certain amount of visual space. Users must also be able to edit the embedded document in place; they shouldn't have to launch another application with its own separate window.

The document must also provide a behind-the-scenes way to store the embedded document and supply a communications channel between the container document and the embedded document. Most of this communication is done at runtime. The container has to be able to query the component to find out what services it supports and how to display itself.

OPENDOC   OpenDoc is a compound document framework that was developed like CORBA. In 1993, an industry consortium called CI Labs (Component Integration Labs) was started by industry leaders, such as Apple, IBM, and Sun, to address the needs of compound document standards.

Like the OMG, CI Labs is composed of most of the industry (who have an interest in components), with the exception of Microsoft. To be more accurate, CI Labs *was* composed of most of these industry leaders. At the time of this writing, CI Labs had been disbanded. The standards and technologies they developed, including LiveObjects component standard and the LiveObjects Component Test Suite, will be dispersed among its member organizations. It hasn't been determined yet which companies will take over developing and promoting the various standards and technologies.

THE COMPONENT SHAKEDOWN   With the emerging popularity of ActiveX and JavaBeans, the future of OpenDoc is questionable. The disbanding of CI Labs has left OpenDoc the responsibility of IBM. IBM stated that it plans on going with JavaBeans as its component model. Because many organizations are heavily invested in OpenDoc, IBM released the OpenDoc binaries and source code as freeware. They also stated that they will no longer officially support OpenDoc. Proponents of OpenDoc have approached Sun to propose OpenDoc as the overlying architecture for JavaBeans. Sun's official position is that it will leave the JavaBeans-OpenDoc integration up to other companies. It seems that only a tight integration with JavaBeans can save OpenDoc.

ACTIVEX DOCUMENTS   Like their OLE predecessors, ActiveX documents allow you to embed a document within a document. Your Word document, for example, can contain an Excel spreadsheet and a PowerPoint slide. A key feature is that you can edit the document *in place*. Double-clicking on your embedded spreadsheet doesn't mean you have to launch a new application with a separate window. The current window's menu and toolbars simply change to reflect the new set of tools that you need to edit the spreadsheet.

NETSCAPE PLUG-INS   Netscape plug-ins generally aren't considered to be a major compound document framework because of their newness and lack of many of the features of most compound document frameworks; however, they are currently one of the most widespread forms of compound documents on the Web. As such, they're useful as a comparison to more developed models. By looking at the evolution of the Netscape plug-in framework, you can get a better idea of what exactly a compound document framework needs in order to work well.

Plug-ins started as a simple method of displaying a different document within an HTML document, although they couldn't communicate with each other or with the HTML on the page they were contained in. They were simply allocated some real estate on a Web page, received mouse and keyboard commands, and were allowed to execute within this visual space. With LiveConnect, Netscape has created a more useful compound document framework.

Plug-ins now have many of the features of the other compound document frameworks, such as automation scripting, communication with other plug-ins, and interaction with HTML pages and forms. The glue that makes LiveConnect work is the JavaScript programming language. Although this sounds exciting, the technology is anything but stable, and features such as drag-and-drop and copy-and-paste aren't used. Plug-ins are binary objects that are not cross-platform, and most don't support more than a couple of platforms. In the future, we expect most plug-ins to be replaced entirely by JavaBeans. Until recently, plug-ins were the only solution available for displaying content other than HTML in a browser window.

Distributed Java Objects

First came Java applets, downloadable, platform-independent programs that could run within Web browsers. Java applets are a form of mobile code, but aren't distributed objects by themselves, because separate applets can't communicate with each other and interoperate. Before JDK 1.1, the only method of communication back to the server was through URLs or sockets, neither of which allowed for a simple, clean method of transparently using objects back on the server. The need for a full-fledged distributed object infrastructure was apparent.

Everyone from CORBA vendors to JavaSoft to Microsoft have jumped on the Java bandwagon. Almost all new ORBs supporting Java, Microsoft, and JavaSoft have developed two-way bridges between ActiveX and Beans, and a variety of different distributed object implementations, such as RMI, have emerged.

Applets

The applet framework allows code to be loaded and run dynamically in a secure environment. By themselves, applets are not components because they lack features such as interoperability, transparent applet-to-server communication, and a self-describing mechanism. The applet framework does provide a way to get basic applet info, such as the author and copyright, but it doesn't have the facilities for the introspection necessary for dynamic interoperability with other applets.

Applets are basically standalone downloadable applications, not components. JavaBeans fill the need for a Java-based component model. By combining JavaBeans and a distributed objects infrastructure, such as RMI or CORBA, applets can be built from components that are interoperable across the Internet. Applets are the first step toward a Web of objects that can all communicate with each other and interoperate. You learn more about applets in Chapter 2, "Object-Oriented Programming Concepts."

Java Development with CORBA

As we mentioned, almost all of the ORB vendors are working on Java support, which is divided into two main types: Language support, in the form of a Java-to-IDL mapping, and ORB-level support, by supplying an ORB written entirely in Java.

Language support is fundamental because it allows you to create CORBA objects with Java. The second, ORB-level support, ensures that if you have a Java-based client, it can communicate back to your server objects. The Java client simply downloads the ORB classes and runs them dynamically. The drawback to this approach is the time required to download the classes. Fortunately, Java-aware clients, such as Netscape and Internet Explorer, cache the classes so the download delay occurs only once.

The approach most ORB vendors have taken with Java is to have two ORBs. The main ORB on the server side is a binary compiled on a specific platform. The second ORB, for the client side, is written entirely in Java so it can be downloaded and run on the fly. Any ORB can act as a client or a server, but in general, the client-server model stands. One particular ORB is designated as the main object server, and the others are clients. The server ORB has the greatest load, so a native binary is the best way to make sure it meets speed and load requirements. In this way, vendors can provide a fast, scalable architecture, yet still have cross-platform support for clients. Until Java gets faster and proves its scalability and robustness, we will undoubtedly see most vendors supplying a native ORB as well as a Java ORB.

RMI

RMI is a distributed object system that allows programmers to transparently cross Java Virtual Machines. RMI is not CORBA-compliant, but it offers similar functions. When JavaSoft released RMI, many people were puzzled because Sun was already working on JOE, a CORBA-compliant, Java-aware ORB. RMI is designed to solve a different set of problems. Despite a great deal of overlap between CORBA and RMI, the latter is perfect if you need a lightweight, all-Java solution.

Note that the RMI wire format, or communications protocol, is proprietary and not based on IIOP, which is the most serious drawback to RMI. It allows Java objects to talk only to other Java objects that have been compiled using RMI. However, it provides a simple means for your application to cross Java Virtual Machines by embedding distributed object capabilities directly into the core Java language. JavaSoft recently announced that it plans on adding IIOP support to RMI. Because of the protocol's nature, only a subset of the RMI capabilities will be available if you choose to use IIOP. JavaSoft will be working with the OMG to extend IIOP so it can support more of the functions that RMI offers.

The name *remote method invocation* is a little misleading. RMI is more than just a remote procedure/method call mechanism. Objects have a life cycle, so they are created, then the methods are called, and finally they are automatically destroyed by *Garbage Collection* (GC), the automatic freeing up of memory (destroying of objects) by the language when objects are no longer needed. Languages like C++ leave destroying objects up to the programmer. This method gives the programmer more control, but greatly increases the chance of bugs in a program. Distributed GC, or GC across different virtual machines, is a feature found in RMI but not in CORBA.

Java IDL

Just to make things even more complicated, JavaSoft has come out with Java IDL. Java IDL is an ORB that, unlike RMI, uses the OMG's mapping of IDL to Java. This feature is beneficial because your Java objects can be reused on different ORBs. Java IDL currently uses a proprietary protocol called the Door ORB, but JavaSoft plans to add IIOP as a protocol option. JavaSoft will also bundle Java IDL and the ORB runtime classes with a future version of the JDK.

To sum up the confusion, JavaSoft and Sun offer three Java-distributed object solutions. JOE is a full CORBA-compliant ORB written in Java that uses IIOP for its communications. It is meant to be used along with NEO, the server ORB, which is available only for Solaris. At almost the same time, RMI came along and was eventually bundled with JDK 1.1. RMI is not CORBA compliant and uses its own proprietary communications protocol. It's designed for a homogeneous Java environment that doesn't need all the features of a full CORBA system. Currently in alpha development, Java IDL is an ORB that uses the OMG's Java-to-IDL mapping and has its own wire protocol. JavaSoft plans on using CORBA's IIOP protocol in the future and will bundle Java IDL with the JDK.

Until JavaSoft's plans for Java IDL are clearer, we advise you to stick with either RMI or JOE (or one of the other Java ORBs). CORBA, and therefore JOE, are designed for heterogeneous systems and will give your application an open migration path. RMI is cheap and lightweight and assumes your environment is all Java.

JavaSpaces

Distributed objects often need a way to share data while on the network. Often these needs are as simple as shared access to a variable. *Tuple Spaces* are a simple storage mechanism that allow you read and write a simple key-value pair (a *Tuple*) to a network storage location. The purpose of these spaces is to provide a simple distributed persistence system and make it easier to program distributed algorithms (see Figure 1-13).

Can't this be done by using an *Object-Oriented Database Management System* (OODBMS) or, in CORBA, by designating a particular object as a shared data-storage object? Both methods would work just fine, but if all you need are simple key-value pairs, then an OODBMS is overkill. Writing a CORBA object is a good solution, but the implementation won't necessarily be standard. A standard Tuple Space could be added to the CORBAServices to solve this problem.

JavaSoft's answer to these needs is JavaSpaces, which allow an object to read and write an Entry (Tuple) to and from a JavaSpace. An object can also ask a JavaSpace to notify it whenever a particular kind of Entry is made. An Entry consists of a key, which is just a string to denote its

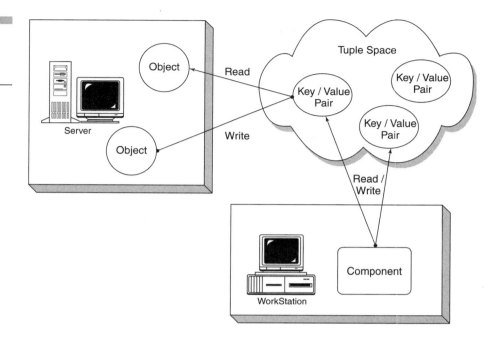

Figure 1-13.
JavaSpaces for distributed object persistence.

name, and a value, which is any Java object. This method is a simple way for cooperating distributed objects to share data and perform duties asynchronously. The following list explains some of the goals of JavaSpaces:

- Provide a mechanism for simplifying the development of distributed object systems.
- Keep the client-side classes 100 percent pure Java and as small as possible.
- Leave the actual server implementation open; it could be a dedicated JavaSpace server, an OODBMS with a JavaSpace interface, or a traditional RDBMS.
- Later, supply a method for replicating entire JavaSpaces.

JavaSoft is currently working on distributed events and transactions. JavaSpaces also rely on RMI and object serialization for communication and object storage. Security is handled by an access control list.

The Current State of Affairs

Let's look at what the industry is up to in distributed object technology.

Netscape's Plans

Netscape's *Open Network Environment* (ONE) is its answer to Microsoft's DCOM and ActiveX. In addition to RMI, Netscape 4.0 also has a runtime version of Visigenic's CORBA ORB for Java. This move has the potential to open up the whole area of distributed objects. Before this, the only option for making client software CORBA-aware was to install an ORB on each client machine, which isn't a viable option for public Web sites, or have the client download the ORB bytecode, which could take quite a while over a slow connection. The ORB code is cached for the next time, but first impressions count. For an intranet-based system, this download time might not hamper things, but if your software attracts many first-time users, they might not stick around through the initial download.

JDK 1.1

The greatest impact JDK 1.1 will have in the area of distributed objects is the introduction of RMI and Beans. RMI offers a free alternative to CORBA , and Beans are a competitor to ActiveX components. With more and more operating systems including a *Java Virtual Machine* (JVM), combined with wide support for JDK 1.1 in Web browsers, we will have an infrastructure in which JDK 1.1 is ubiquitous on both the client and server. Although proprietary libraries and those containing native code threaten the homogeneity of this infrastructure, as long as the core of Java is widely supported, the possibilities for software developers will be incredible. In particular, Microsoft's plans for Java will have a huge impact on the Java infrastructure and development ideals. You learn more about JDK 1.1 in Chapter 4.

RMI versus CORBA

The debate on RMI versus CORBA has been raging since RMI was first introduced. Proponents of CORBA tend not to welcome a single-language, proprietary system, and the RMI camp points out that despite both being distributed object infrastructures, the two technologies have many differences. The end result is that you should choose the right tool for the job. CORBA is ideal for larger, heterogeneous systems, particularly if you want to leverage off existing object libraries and legacy systems. If your needs are diverse, you can even develop your objects in different languages.

RMI, on the other hand, is perfect if you're developing an application from scratch and plan on using only Java. You don't need to program any IDL, so you can save a great deal of time that you might otherwise have spent learning the technology and programming. Because RMI isn't an open standard and has less industry support, the migration path of an application developed with RMI might not be as good. CORBA is rapidly expanding to include many horizontal and vertical services. Being a core part of the Java *Application Program Interface* (API), RMI isn't likely to expand and offer the same range of services.

Beans versus ActiveX

The component market is growing rapidly, and it will be interesting to watch how the different component standards, such as Beans, ActiveX, and OpenDoc, shape up. The Beans versus ActiveX debate becomes less important now that Microsoft has introduced technology making it possible for Beans to appear as ActiveX objects to other ActiveX objects and vice versa. The real issue, then, is that Beans are not platform-specific, but ActiveX objects currently are. This is changing, though, as Microsoft is planning initiatives to allow ActiveX objects to be compatible with a wider variety of hardware and operating systems. Microsoft is also considering turning over some of its horizontal component APIs over to a standards body. You learn more about JavaBeans versus ActiveX in Chapter 13, "Understanding ActiveX."

What About Agents?

Agents are another buzzword to go along with *objects* and *distributed computing*. Dozens of products coming to market all claim to use agent technology. Definitions of agents range from a simple Web browser (a user agent) to extremely intelligent, mobile units of code that travel from machine to machine completely autonomously. A simple, broad definition of an *agent* is an application or piece of code that does something on someone's behalf. The current wave of agents on the market are neither intelligent nor mobile. The majority of them are simple asynchronous clients that gather information for a user, usually done as a background process or while the user is offline.

A more exciting area of agent technology is *mobile agents*, self-contained units of code that can move from machine to machine. As opposed to the client-server model, where requests are made by the client to the server across the network, these agents are actually sent across the network and run on the remote machine. Once on the remote machine, they are executed within safe "sandbox" security and can either gather information and propagate it or do some work on the server, such as updating its data or reconfiguring it.

A series of database queries is a good example of the differences between the ORB-based approach and the agent-based approach. Suppose you want to query a remote database many times and then analyze the results according to a rule set. Using the CORBA distributed object model, you would instantiate a remote object on the database server and make multiple method calls to that object. As you receive the data on the client end, you would compile the results and analyze them according to your rule set. This approach is very network-intensive, because you're constantly making method calls and receiving potentially large amounts of data each time you make a query (see Figure 1-14).

The agent approach would be to put the brains inside the agent and send the agent over to the database server (see Figure 1-15). The agent would then make the queries to the database on the machine itself, reducing the amount of network communication. After all, the client wants only the analysis of the data, not the data itself. This requirement offloads the intelligence to the agent rather than the client software (the agent is really a client, but it's a mobile client). This sounds wonderful, but its applications are limited. If you have a 100Mb Ethernet network and your data sets aren't huge, reducing the amount of network communication might not matter much. However, the Internet opens up a whole new set of applica-

Figure 1-14.
ORB-based approach.

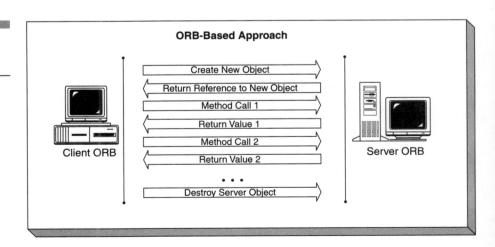

Figure 1-15.
Agent-based
approach.

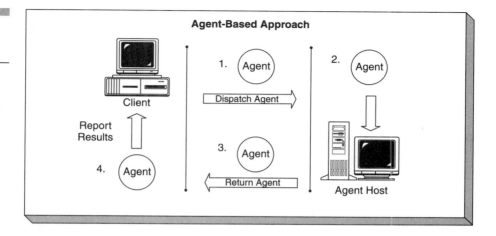

tions for agents. Clients are often communicating over slow modem lines, and there's no guarantee of network bandwidth from point to point.

Agents aren't so much competitors to distributed objects as simply another form of them. Their functionality complements the peer-to-peer and client-server models.

Comparison of Various Methods

Now that we've surveyed different distributed computing infrastructures, how do you decide which one fits your needs? As usual, there's no simple answer. Assuming your distributed computing infrastructure is based on object technology and you're looking for a mainstream approach, the top three candidates are ActiveX, RMI, and CORBA. At the risk of overgeneralizing, the following sections offer a few guidelines (see Figure 1.16).

ACTIVEX Any product that Microsoft pushes hard is bound to be used often and by many people. If you have invested heavily in Microsoft products and are developing for a closed system like an intranet, then ActiveX might be ideal. Its lack of a sandbox security model isn't as much of a problem for intranet-based systems. For security reasons, we don't recommend it for public consumption, although the ability to easily adapt current Windows applications into ActiveX controls might overshadow this drawback. With its OLE background and tight integration with common Microsoft developer products such as Visual C++ and Visual Basic, you shouldn't run into many problems finding programmers.

Figure 1-16.
Which boundaries
the different tech-
nologies cross.

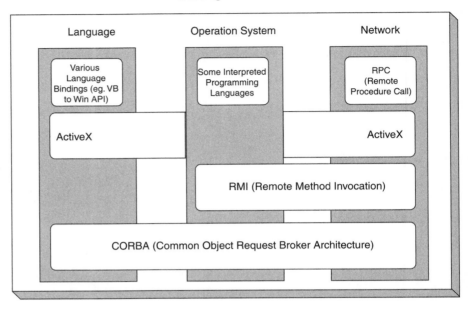

Figure 1-16.
Which boundaries
the different tech-
nologies cross.

RMI The simplicity of RMI has its appeal. Without the need for IDL, developers need to program only Java. Essentially, RMI is a lightweight version of CORBA, which is perfect for projects that don't require multiple language support or all the features CORBA offers. The single-language model also permits several functions that CORBA currently doesn't, such as passing objects by value and automatic distributed garbage collection.

CORBA CORBA is bound to cost more than the other choices initially, but it offers a superior architecture to ActiveX and a far better migration path than RMI. It isn't proprietary, as RMI and ActiveX are (although this might be changing for ActiveX); it offers a wider range of services; and it crosses more boundaries.

Design Patterns

Design patterns are a hot new area of software engineering. Its roots are in Christopher Alexander's work on urban planning and building architecture. He recognized the usefulness of recording common architecture patterns in a standard template format. Software engineers picked up on his work as a way to record OOP design patterns and common system architectures.

Catalogues of patterns fill the need raised by the question "Hasn't someone already done this before?" Odds are many people have gone through the same analysis and design decisions that you face. How many *Online Transaction Processing* (OLTP) systems, online shopping malls, and even simple business-employee tables have been designed before? Yet each time, we sit down and redesign what has been done before.

Basically, a design pattern is just a solution to a problem in a particular context that's recorded in a standard way. OOP promotes code reuse, and design patterns promote design reuse. In addition to promoting reuse, they are a way of recording and passing on experience. A design pattern isn't always the most obvious solution to a problem. The best solution, discovered through trial and error, isn't always the first one a developer thinks of. By using design patterns, the experience of a developer who has worked with a particular design before can be used as a teaching tool for other developers.

Design patterns are always given reference names. We do this in everyday development, but it isn't formalized. For example, *client-middleware-database architecture* and *three-tier architecture* refer to the same things. The latter term is more succinct than the former and gives us a useful label for discussing this architecture with others, so the names of design patterns give us vocabulary for discussing design issues. If the members of a development team have a common vocabulary, they are in a better position to discuss the pros and cons of different approaches.

By themselves, design patterns are useful teaching tools, but in collections, they form the basis for a common vocabulary and understanding. Collections of design patterns grouped together logically are called *catalogues*. A catalogue of design patterns with interaction between the patterns, then, becomes a *pattern language* (see Figure 1-17). By interactions, we mean that the patterns refer to other patterns to explain their purpose, just as a dictionary defines words by using other words. With all the developers on a team or all the members of a discussion group speaking the same pattern language, communication of ideas is greatly enhanced.

Design Patterns and Distributed Objects

Design patterns are an excellent way to understand distributed object computing. The rise of design patterns in software engineering has somewhat

Figure 1-17.
Catalogues of design
patterns become a
common language
for developers.

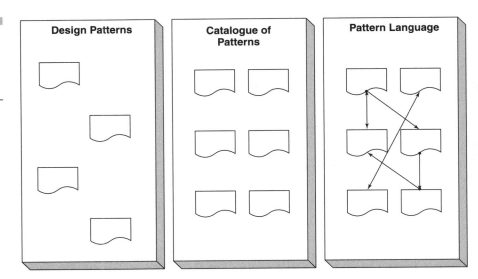

paralleled the increase in interest in distributed objects. Distributed object computing deals with large, complex systems that need to be described simply. The OOP part of distributed objects tries to model the real world and get developers to focus on solutions to problems at a higher level, instead of implementation and "plumbing" details. Design patterns and pattern languages fit these needs very well.

In the following pages, we take a look at the technologies discussed in this chapter and present them again in a pattern language; this method gives you a catalogue of problems and solutions that will help make sense of the rapidly expanding and changing area of distributed objects and components. The patterns presented here are a higher level than traditional design patterns. We have focused on matching some of the different technologies discussed with a problem that they solve well in a particular context. This focus will give you a better idea of how Java, RMI, CORBA, ActiveX, and so forth, might fit your needs.

Design patterns are expressed in a standard template notation. Each pattern has a *Name*, a *Problem*, a *Context*, a set of *Forces*, a *Solution*, a list of key *Benefits* and *Consequences*, and an *Example*. This is a scaled-down version of some of the other popular pattern languages, but it fits our needs of explaining without going into too much specific implementation detail. So here is a blank design pattern template; keep in mind that its purpose is to present a solution to a problem, given its context:

Name: **Short descriptive name of the solution**

PROBLEM   Description of the problem.

CONTEXT   Details of the problem. What is the scale of the solution: enterprise, system, application, or object level? Is it Internet or intranet based?

FORCES
- A bulleted list of the key forces that shaped the decision toward the proposed solution.
- Tight budget is one example.
- Short timeline is another.
- Bandwidth restrictions are a force that shapes many Internet solutions.

SOLUTION   A discussion of how the problem was solved and how the forces were handled. This could be a particular technology (such as Java or ActiveX), a system architecture, an object framework, or a methodology.

BENEFITS   A list of the key benefits, such as increased manageability, better system load balance, and so forth.

CONSEQUENCES
- A list of the key consequences.
- No solution is perfect, so the consequences are a warning about side-effects.

EXAMPLE   Here you can include sample code, a diagram, a case study, or examples of the pattern to better explain the problem and solution.

The applet provides a simple example of a design pattern. Applets were developed as a solution to a particular problem in the context of the Web. The problem was that the Web opened up the world as one huge network, but HTML forms and CGI programs weren't powerful enough for the needs of most applications. Because of the Web's public nature, cross-platform support and security are major concerns. Also, the solution had to encompass multiple platforms, or it wouldn't be adequate to replace HTML and CGI. There are no guarantees on network bandwidth, so the solution had to take this factor into account.

Before we go on to the example, it is worth noting that the preceding paragraph (if it included a description and diagram of how applets work) says the same thing as the design pattern we are about to present. So what is the point of describing such a simple idea in a structured design pattern? The benefit of design patterns such as these becomes more evident when you lay a number of them side by side and use them together. As opposed to unstructured paragraph descriptions, it's far easier to compare different solutions and understand how they solve a particular problem.

Design patterns give you a high-level, structured view of solutions to common problems and an understanding of the big picture. They also make sure the same information is presented each time, which makes it easier to compare different problems and solutions. That being said, here's a simple design pattern for applets (see Figure 1-18).

Name: **Downloadable, Secure Executable Application**

PROBLEM   To allow a client to be able to download and run an application safely and dynamically.

CONTEXT   Internet based; must be able to run within a Web browser.

FORCES
▓ The Internet comprises a wide variety of operating systems.

▓ Limited bandwidth.

▓ The application will be untrusted by users, so it shouldn't have full access to their machines.

▓ Users shouldn't have to do any installation for each new application they run.

SOLUTION   A Java applet that can be downloaded from a Web page and run in a Web browser that has the Java Virtual Machine built into it. This solution crosses the OS barrier. Applets are designed to be small and run in their own secure "sandbox." The applet framework within a Web browser dynamically loads and runs the applet without any need for installation.

BENEFITS
▓ Cross-platform support.

- Small application size.
- Good security—applets run within their own sandbox.
- Any changes to the application don't require reconfiguration on the client end.

CONSEQUENCES
- Because the application is not trusted, it's limited in what it can do.
- Applications can't be too complex because many users could be communicating over slow modem lines.

EXAMPLE   Some design patterns from the previous discussions on distributed object technologies are offered in the following sections. They don't represent the only possible uses for the technologies, but they should give you an idea of which solution is right for the given problem and set of forces. Since we're talking about very similar technologies, often the problem is the same, but the context and forces are different, requiring a different solution.

Component Patterns

Name: Leveraging Off OLE

PROBLEM   Development of interoperable software components.

CONTEXT   Intranet based; company has a significant investment in Microsoft software.

Figure 1-18.
Downloadable, secure executable application.

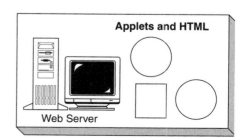

FORCES

- Rewriting existing code is expensive and could introduce bugs.
- The company might already have libraries of OCXs.
- Tight integration with Windows applications might be necessary.

SOLUTION   Components can be developed as ActiveX controls. Existing OCXs can be converted to ActiveX more easily than they can be rewritten for a different component model. ActiveX controls can interact easily with the host environment and its applications.

BENEFITS

- Company can leverage off existing OLE/COM code.
- Components have full access to client machines.
- Development can be done with familiar tools and languages.

CONSEQUENCES

- If non-Windows clients are added to the intranet, they might not be able to use the components.

EXAMPLE   The leverage off OLE is shown in Figure 1-19.

Name: **Portable Intranet Parts**

PROBLEM   Development of interoperable software components.

CONTEXT   Intranet based; the components can be used in applications as well as within applets and must be cross-platform.

FORCES

- The components must work on a variety of client platforms.
- Client machines might not have much computing power, so the components must be small.

SOLUTION   Develop the components using JavaBeans technology. This will make the components usable on any OS that has the JDK 1.1 on it. Beans can also interoperate with ActiveX controls and are a better option, unless a company has a large investment in Windows-based products (see "Leveraging Off OLE" pattern).

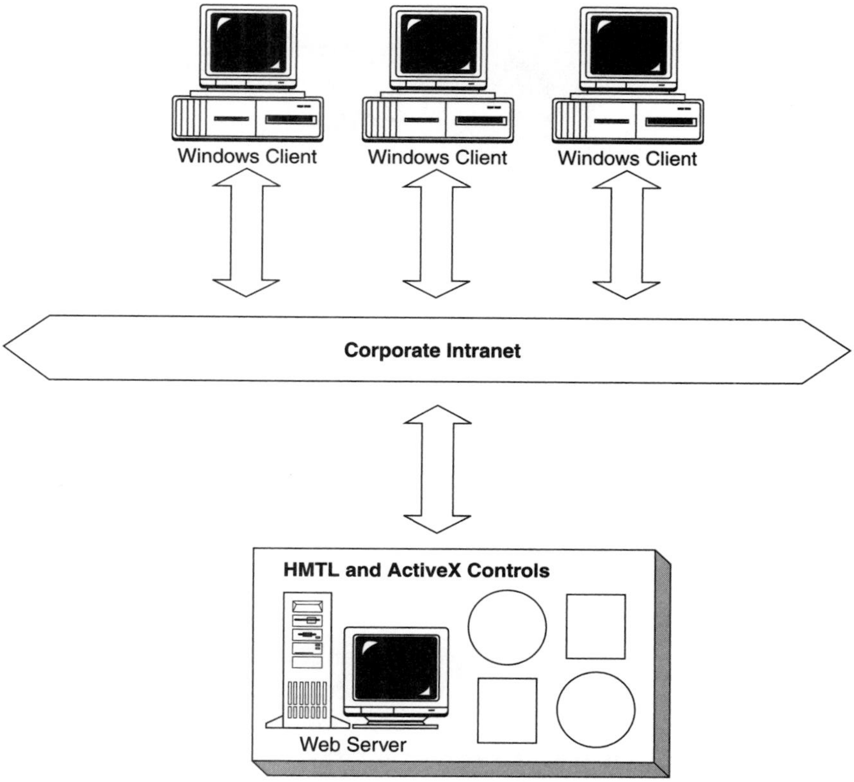

Figure 1-19.
Leverage off OLE.

BENEFITS

■ Write once, run anywhere.

■ Can be integrated with RMI (see "Crossing JVMs" pattern).

CONSEQUENCES

■ Current components might have to be rewritten in Java.

EXAMPLE   Portable intranet parts are shown in Figure 1-20.

Name: Marketable Microsoft Components

PROBLEM   Development of interoperable software components.

CONTEXT   Internet based; target market uses Microsoft operating systems and applications.

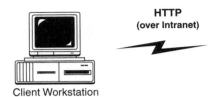
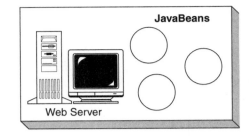

Figure 1-20.
Portable intranet
parts.

FORCES
- Components must be marketable to the public for a wide variety of uses.
- Tight integration with Windows OS and applications.
- Client machines might have little computing power.
- Clients might be downloading components over slow network connections.
- Security.

SOLUTION   Components can be developed as ActiveX controls. Existing OCXs can be converted to ActiveX more easily than they can be rewritten for a different component model. ActiveX controls can interact easily with the host environment and its applications. Security is provided through digital signing. This pattern differs from the Leveraging Off OLE pattern because it's Internet based and the focus is on creating resellable components. The range of uses for the components can't be fully known in advance.

BENEFITS
- Company can leverage off existing OLE/COM code.
- Components have full access to client machines.
- Components can run within Microsoft Internet Explorer.

CONSEQUENCES
- Components can't be transported to other platforms, so the market is limited.

EXAMPLE   Marketable Microsoft components are shown in Figure 1-21.

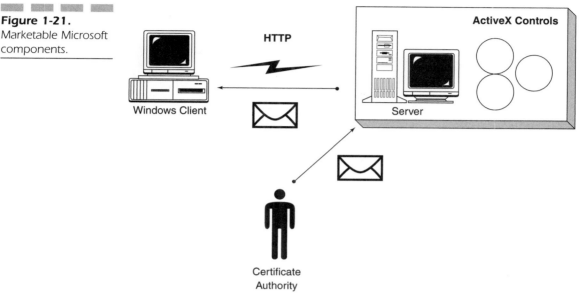

Figure 1-21.
Marketable Microsoft
components.

Name: Cross-Platform Marketable Components

PROBLEM To develop software components for the widest possible market.

CONTEXT Internet; the components can be used in applications as well as within applets.

FORCES

▨ The components must work on a variety of client platforms.

▨ Security.

▨ Client machines might not have much computing power, so the components must be small.

SOLUTION Develop the components using JavaBeans technology. This will make the components usable on any OS that has the JDK 1.1 on it. Beans can also interoperate with ActiveX controls. The Beans approach will ensure that the components can be sold to the widest possible market.

BENEFITS

- Allows components to be marketed to a wider audience than other methods do (see "Marketable Microsoft Parts" pattern).
- Write once, run anywhere.
- Can be integrated with RMI (see "Crossing JVMs" pattern).
- Leverages off Java security.

CONSEQUENCES

- Current components might have to be rewritten in Java.

EXAMPLE   Cross-platform marketable components are shown in Figure 1-22.

Enterprise/Architectural Patterns

Name: Crossing JVMs

PROBLEM   To allow Java objects to interoperate seamlessly across multiple Java Virtual Machines.

CONTEXT   Application; can be Internet or intranet based. Homogeneous Java environment. Starting application from scratch or integrating into existing Java code.

FORCES

- Need a cheap, simple solution.
- Might want to use applets that run in a Web browser.
- Bandwidth could be an issue.

Figure 1-22.
Cross-platform marketable components.

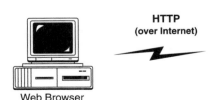

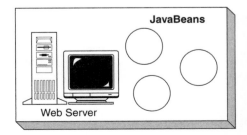

HTTP
(over Internet)

Web Browser

JavaBeans

Web Server

SOLUTION Use the RMI classes in JDK 1.1 and modify any existing Java objects so they can be implemented as remote objects. A browser that has JDK 1.1 support, such as Netscape 4.0, is used for any applets that are implemented with RMI. For intranet-based applications, compare to the "Homogenizing the Enterprise" pattern.

BENEFITS
- Seamless remote object capability.
- Ease of use.
- No investment in large-scale commercial ORBs.

CONSEQUENCES
- RMI objects can't be transported to a CORBA-based system.
- Future development must be done completely in RMI.

EXAMPLE Crossing JVMs is shown in Figure 1-23.

Name: **Homogenizing the Enterprise**

PROBLEM To integrate the heterogeneous collection of systems that make up the enterprise.

Figure 1-23.
Crossing JVMs.

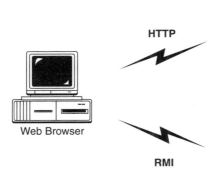
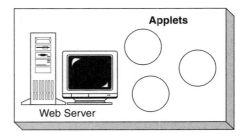
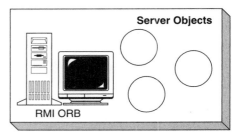

CONTEXT   Enterprise; can be intranet based. There are usually large legacy systems and code libraries in a variety of languages. An interative approach is preferred to minimize risk. The current approach of patching all the systems together is too costly and error prone in the long run.

FORCES
- Multiple programming languages must be supported.
- Flexibility and the system's migration path are extremely important.
- Ongoing product support is necessary.
- It's too costly to scrap many of the legacy systems and code libraries.
- Risk management must be considered.

SOLUTION   CORBA technologies are introduced gradually into the enterprise. Smaller systems can be written from scratch in the language of choice, and larger legacy systems are wrapped one by one into CORBA objects, starting with a few low-risk projects. The first few will be the proof of how well the concept works, and any additional risks or pitfalls can be recorded. Integration of these initial systems gives the developers a better idea of timelines and costs for integrating the entire enterprise.

BENEFITS
- The heterogeneous system now looks homogeneous.
- Allows leveraging off existing systems and code.
- The precarious patch-as-we-go methodology is abandoned.

CONSEQUENCES
- Large investment of time and money.

EXAMPLE   Homogenizing the enterprise is shown in Figure 1-24.

Name: ORBlet

PROBLEM   To make CORBA available to Java applets.

CONTEXT   Internet.

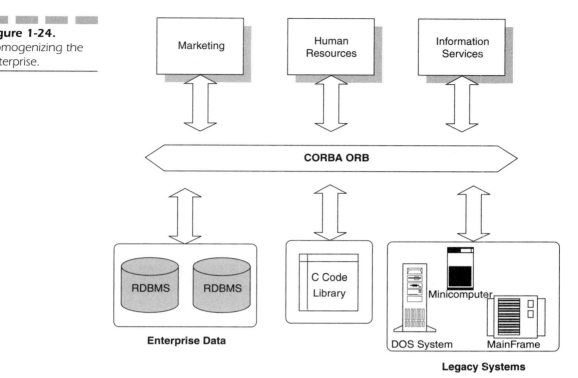

Figure 1-24.
Homogenizing the enterprise.

FORCES
- Bandwidth restrictions.
- Limited computing power on client end.
- Multiple client platforms.

SOLUTION   The ORBlet is a downloadable CORBA ORB written entirely in Java. The Web browser downloads the ORB code along with the applet, which creates an ORB bus across the Internet, from the applet to the server. The server also needs to have an ORB running on it, but not necessarily a Java ORB. Both ORBs must be able to speak the same protocol (such as IIOP). Can be used with the "Homogenizing the Enterprise" pattern.

BENEFITS
- Ubiquitous distributed object infrastructure.
- Client doesn't need to install ORB software first.
- Changes to ORB software don't involve any additional client reconfiguration.

CONSEQUENCES

▓ Intial running of the applet can be very slow because of ORB size; caching makes subsequent executions faster.

EXAMPLE   This method is currently being used by a wide variety of ORB vendors, such as Sun (JOE) and Iona (OrbixWeb).

Name: **Migrating the Microsoft Enterprise**

PROBLEM   To allow a client to download and run an application within its Web browser.

CONTEXT   Enterprise; can be intranet based. Both the client and application are located on a closed network, so security is not an issue. The clients that run the software are all Windows based.

FORCES

▓ Clients need easy access to enterprise data.

▓ Tight integration with existing Windows applications.

▓ The company already has a significant investment in Microsoft software.

▓ The company might already have libraries of OCXs.

▓ Security and trust relationships are not an issue.

▓ Bandwidth isn't usually an issue, but server load could be.

SOLUTION   Applications are written by using the ActiveX family of technologies and are given access to enterprise data sources over the network. This ensures a solution that works well with existing Windows applications. The components can be developed through the "Leveraging Off of OLE" pattern.

BENEFITS

▓ Company can leverage off existing OLE/COM code.

▓ Applications have full access to client machines.

▓ Development can be done with familiar tools and languages.

CONSEQUENCES

▓ If non-Windows clients are added to the enterprise, they might not have access to the software.

EXAMPLE   Migrating the Microsoft enterprise is shown in Figure 1-25.

What's Next?

Each year has had its share of people who have prophesied that it would be the year of the ORB. This year is no exception. In many ways, distributed object technologies were a solution looking for a problem. It's not that they weren't designed specifically to solve many of the problems in developing software that runs on networks, but no problem was big enough to justify large-scale, widespread investment in distributed object technology.

The Internet has now provided the problem to fit the distributed object solution. The sheer size of the Internet, both in terms of network vastness and the number of users and servers, combined with the amount of money to be made on the Internet and with Internet technologies, has resulted in

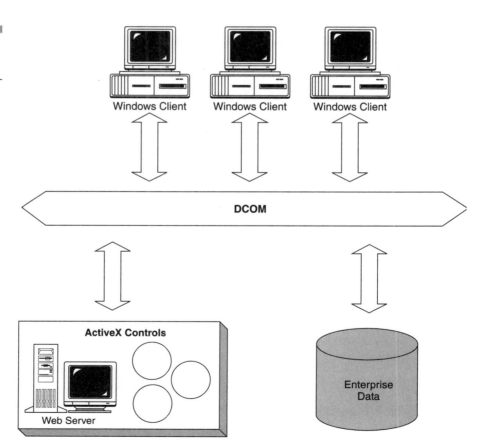

Figure 1-25.
Migrating the
Microsoft enterprise.

a distributed object explosion. With ORBs being built into many of the new Web servers and every Netscape client including an ORB, we don't think it's going too far out on a limb to say that 1998 will be the year of the ORB.

Next Generation of ORBs

The next generation of CORBA ORBs will have improved scalability, greater support for Java, and a higher level of CORBA compliance. Each ORB vendor tends to add its own additional proprietary functionality. However, the OMG is quick to pick up on the best of these improvements and add them to the CORBA specification. ORBs have not proven themselves yet in the scalability department, but we expect this to change rapidly in the next few years. Integrating ORBs with Netscape Navigator has made them more commonplace, which will undoubtedly cause a revolution in the area of distributed objects. With this increased market interest, the quality of CORBA implementations is bound to increase. ORBs will continue to run faster and support a wider variety of horizontal and vertical CORBA services.

The Future of RMI

RMI has barely come out, but many people are wondering if it will be around long. With the enormous popularity of CORBA, why bother with a proprietary, single-language distributed object architecture with fewer features? Many people have questioned whether JavaSoft will continue to support RMI in the future. The answer from JavaSoft is that RMI is a core part of Java and will remain so. They point out that for many, if not most, applications only one language is needed. RMI has the added benefit of being able to send objects across the network and run them directly in an application. No extra layer of abstraction is needed at the language level, such as with CORBA's IDL, so development is simplified. RMI looks like it will be around as long as Java is, and it could turn out to be CORBA's major competitor.

Large-Scale Business Objects

We're witnessing a revolution in component software. The next step will be large-scale business objects. In theory, the enterprise can be built by buying business objects and gluing them together through scripting languages and an object bus, such as CORBA. Your enterprise will be composed of business objects, such as `Employee`, `Invoice`, `Client`, `Order`, and so forth, that you glue together and provide a user interface for. The large-grained business objects have all the business logic built into them, so you just need to customize them when necessary and create rules for their interactions.

Digital Signing

Digital signing is quickly becoming a big business. As we discussed, it still leaves a lot of questions unanswered. By itself, it doesn't provide adequate security for downloading and executing untrusted applications over the Internet. Digital signing is better suited to Internet commerce and authentication of business transactions. Traditionally, this has been the role of signatures. You sign a check or a business contract, not a piece of code. However, it complements the sandbox security model very well by adding an extra layer of authentication.

HTTP and IIOP

Many believe the Web's future protocol will be IIOP, not a new and improved version of HTTP. Included in this list is Tim Berners-Lee, the inventor of the Web. HTTP is a lighter-weight protocol than IIOP, but the Web's future isn't limited to text and images, so a more powerful, flexible protocol is needed. Whether this happens is still up in the air. The installed base of HTTP browsers and servers is huge; however, the impact might not be significant. New Web servers on the market will likely support both HTTP and IIOP. When a browser connects to the server, it first sends the protocol it supports, such as HTTP/1.1. Because the browser initiates the conversation, the server can then decide which protocol to use. This maintains backward compatibility while offering a whole new range of services.

Do We Need Other Languages?

Does the Internet need only one programming language? (The RMI versus CORBA debate in particular brings up this issue.) Our answer is an unequivocal no. Software developers often get into a niche where they develop similar types of software and participate in circles that have the same interests. This niche could be GUI-based software, database systems, or applications for specific industries. This specialization often leads to one specific view on software development. Languages such as Smalltalk and ADA are popular in some circles, but huge industry sectors wouldn't even consider using these languages for development. "Doesn't everyone use either C++ or Visual Basic?" they seem to be saying. With the diversity of the Internet, however, no single programming language can be the answer, which puts CORBA in a better position than any of its competitors. CORBA allows you to develop in a wide variety of languages and use existing code libraries in different languages.

CONCLUSION

A Nobel prize winner once pointed out that of all the barriers to technological progress, perhaps the greatest is the software problem—or more specifically, the human problem associated with software development. Until we can develop large-scale, mission-critical systems that don't tend to crash, and can be completed in a timely manner, progress in almost all areas of technological development is slowed. Distributed object computing doesn't offer instant solutions for project management, but it does allow large-scale networked software to be broken up into separate isolated systems. The separate systems of objects and components can be more easily managed and tested. As distributed object systems become more commonplace, there is hope that software development will become more manageable and applications will be of higher quality.

2

Object-Oriented Programming Concepts

Over the years, certain programming languages have proved most convenient for creating different types of applications, performing simulations, or conducting research. Before we explain the advantages of the Java platform in today's world, let us take a brief look at the programming developments that led to its creation.

FORTRAN was created for scientists and engineers as a bare-bones language that can quickly perform complicated numeric calculations. At the opposite end of the programming spectrum is Lisp, an interpreted language that's a favorite for use in artifical intelligence research because of its coding flexibility, abstraction capabilities, and similarity to certain thinking and reasoning processes. C has been used and reused in every field for building complex applications, doing simulations, and conducting research. C quickly became the language of choice for many programmers because of its speed, utility, and ease of use.

Within the past decade, with the emergence of C++ (created by Bjarne Stroustrup in the early 1980s at AT&T Bell Labs), *Object-Oriented Programming* (OOP) has become the programming style of choice for application development and many other related tasks. C++ was developed as an addition to C, transforming C from a procedure-oriented to an object-oriented language. The great strengths that C++ holds over ordinary C were immediately obvious. Suddenly, it was possible to build applications faster and with less effort. Abundant C libraries were available for immediate use in C++, and the library of reusable C++ code grew. Prewritten, nonapplication-specific code could be quickly integrated into new applications, making it easy for programmers to collaborate on projects and work more efficiently in general.

Imagine you're one of 20 programmers working together to develop a specific application. Usually, the easiest way to contribute is by producing your code as a self-contained object, one that can be accessed, changed only in specific ways, and made to perform a certain set of predefined functions. Everyone else can just use that object's functions without having to worry about how it was made or whether they are going to destroy your code while they're putting everything together. This method makes all code reusable and speeds application development time—a great advantage of C++. Imagine, however, trying to use C++ in a networked environment; both co-workers and the applications you're creating are no longer system-specific in operation. Your applications need to be Internet-capable, and this is where Java comes in.

With the onset of the World Wide Web, an entirely new model of programming has developed. Your environment is totally networked. In the old days, applications were platform-specific; different systems were created for PCs, UNIX machines, and Macs. This specialization worked because your company was most likely set up globally with the same operating system; everyone working together had the same platform. At the customer end, you knew what sort of system your customer had.

Well, things have changed. Now, your old team of co-workers might be developing from their computers anywhere in the world, and your customer is online. Your teammate could be working on a PC in Alaska while you have your trusty UNIX machine in San Francisco. How are you both going to write code that can work together? What environment will that code work for? How are you going to develop networked applications that your customers will use? The answer is, of course, program in Java.

Java is built to be platform-independent, network-enabled, secure, and highly portable. It's designed to allow the same Java code to run on a PC, a UNIX machine, or any other computer. Java's backbone is an intermediate virtual machine for which all Java code is written and compiled; this machine is the key to Java's versatility. It can reside on any operating system that has the correct interpreter, so Java actually becomes architecture-neutral and operating-system-neutral.

This chapter and the next chapter are really just an overview and introduction to object-oriented programming and Java. However, they should serve you well as you begin to get into more complicated technical subjects later in the book. This chapter covers all the basics of object-oriented programming.

This chapter will cover the following topics:

- *Object-Oriented Programming* (OOP) concepts
- Objects and classes
- Encapsulation
- Message passing
- Inheritance
- Polymorphism

Object-Oriented Programming (OOP)

This section of the chapter is for programmers from a structured procedural programming background (such as C, Pascal, or FORTRAN) who have heard only the hype surrounding Java and object-oriented programming languages and for others who might not know anything about OOP. This section covers the fundamental concepts of OOP and gives you a stable foundation for approaching Java and object-oriented languages. Without a simple understanding of OOP, it's difficult to write and understand Java programs because *all* code written in Java is an object or is inherited from an object—two fundamental OOP concepts. We discuss these concepts in more detail later in the chapter.

What's the difference between a structured procedural-based programming technique and an object-oriented programming technique? Traditional procedural-based programming consists of developing data structures and then using these structures to perform specific tasks within programs. When you program procedurally, you first determine how you will manipulate the data, and then you craft structures that allow you to transform the data more easily. In OOP, the process is quite different: You initially develop the objects or data structures, and then you determine the programs that will manipulate these objects.

Why deal with objects in the first place? Defining and handling objects is how we as humans understand our world and our interactions with the world. We look at countless varieties of trees, animals, and people and then imagine infinite variations or instances of these objects. When we see a table, we all recognize it as a table even if we have never seen that particular table before. We do this because this instance of the table "behaves" like a table and might have elements you can describe that define the table's "state:" It has legs (three or more) and perhaps something is located on top of the table. If we recognize the world as consisting of "categorized objects," why and how should we program in an object-oriented fashion?

Why OOP?

Object-oriented programming allows us to deal with "object" abstractions in a programming environment. We tend to look at the world in a generally hierarchical, logically categorizable, and connected sense. We can see how larger structures consist of smaller organizations that perform particular tasks to accomplish goals. When we discuss OOP, we're describing a flexible, consistent structure that makes programming "things" much easier. OOP makes programming easier because at its fundamental level, it's built to be changeable, reusable, compartmentalized, and distributable. OOP increases productivity in the compile, test, and run cycles because the language's structure lets multiple programmers work on the same code without explicitly knowing how their code or perform in a complete program. This is beneficial because it tends to move the application-coding process to a much earlier phase in software development. Projects that start conceptually can be compartmentalized and then coded by individual programmers.

OOP affords enhanced reliability. We can think of a program's components as self-contained smaller programs. It's much easier to debug smaller programs that "plug" into a larger framework than to determine problems or change single behaviors in large amounts of procedural code. OOP contributes to improved maintenance of large programs because less control is given to the "top-level" manipulations of the entire program (like traditional programming) and more responsibility is given to "localized packages" within the program. Less control from the top also permits reduced global interaction, which is always beneficial in determining program interaction and development. A good example of top-level control is changing a control feature in a global function, which in turn changes the entire program and all its functions inclusively.

OOP is built for an efficient, quick-moving industry. OOP programs are built to be reusable, augmentable, and extendable. Classes in OOP structures are built with definable interfaces that allow programmers to reuse code as "black box" abstractions rather than "sift" through older code and remove blocks or lines to be integrated into new code. OOP pushes the details of objects out of sight so programmers can deal with behavior and interfaces at a much more abstract level.

In the following section, we offer a conceptual introduction to OOP and industry terminology. We briefly touch on the fundamentals of classes, objects, encapsulation, message passing, inheritance, and polymorphism. These terms are the core for discussing and understanding object-oriented programming. To make the concepts in this section easier to understand, we compare them to real-world situations. All the examples in this chapter describe the "object orientedness" of a symphony orchestra and its potential implementation in an object-oriented programming environment. We start with the basics and build on our knowledge as we progress.

OOP Concepts

CLASSES   *Classes* in OOP are convenient ways of bundling methods and variables together. Everything you write in Java is inside a class. Classes, which contain methods (*functions* to C programmers) and variables, are templates for making objects. In the template, the programmer defines the behavior and state of the objects to be constructed from these templates. Classes are convenient ways to generalize, observe, categorize, itemize, and distinguish "elements" within the program. A program can have any number of classes interacting within it.

Imagine we're devising a program to describe an entire symphony orchestra. We can think about the orchestra as a series of many smaller, separate elements that are easier to handle and understand. For example, in a symphony orchestra, we would need a `violin` class, which might have a method called `playNote` and a variable called `currentNote`. The method describes the behavior of the class; *behavior* is "something the object can do." The variables in the class define the current state (or potential states) of the objects made from the class.

Working with this concept, we would also need a **Drum** class in the symphony orchestra. Instead of having a **playNote** method, the **Drum** class might have a **playBeat** method and could contain a variable such as **howHard** (to beat the drum). You can see that different classes would have separate characteristics; they can sometimes have the same characteristics, but they would be implemented differently by the individual class objects.

A **Flute** class might have the same methods and variables as the **Violin** class, such as **playNote** and **currentNote**, but the implementation of these "sounds" by the objects would be quite different. This distinction is important to remember when dealing with abstractions because the classes should be responsible for the actual implementation. In this example of the "sound," we should be able to handle these objects within a program without worrying about what each object is actually doing internally.

A class can have any number of methods and variables, but for efficient OOP design, the programmer should keep classes small and understandable. If a class becomes too large, it should probably be divided into smaller subclasses.

OBJECTS   Objects are derivatives of the class' template. When you create an object from a class, you're actually creating an *instance* of the class. We can think about this in terms of the **Violin** class mentioned previously: When we finally implement the **Violin** class, we're actually making an object. We can understand this more clearly by knowing that an orchestra might have up to 50 violinists, each of which would be instances (objects) of the **Violin** class. Objects should have at least three distinguishing features—identity, state, and behavior—as described in the following list:

- **Identity:** All objects have an identity, which refers to the object's name. For example, if we create an instance of the **Violin** class, we would give it a name, as shown here:

  ```
  Violin firstChair = new Violin();
  ```

  You can see in this example that we now have an object called **firstChair** (which is from the **Violin** class). This example, written in English, would be "Create a new instance of the Violin class and call that object firstChair." Following this logic, we can create multiple instances of the **Violin** class:

```
Violin secondChair = new Violin();
```

■ **State:** All objects have *state*, meaning "what the object is currently doing." In the **Violin** class, for example, we have the variable **currentNote**; this is the state of the object. The object might be playing an A# or nothing at all. The **Violin** class could also have the variable **nameOfViolinist**, which would contain the performer's name. Note that the **nameOfViolinist** variable doesn't refer to the object's identity; it would be a variable within the **Violin** class.

■ **Behavior:** All objects have *behavior*, which depends on what types of messages they can accept. *Messages* are ways in which objects communicate with other objects. In the orchestra example, the **Violin** class accepts the message **playNote**. This message is an instruction to the object. When we give the object the **playNote** message, we're not concerned with how that object will play the note; we just want the object to make a sound. We can explain the OOP concept by using another example: If your uncle plays the accordion, and you have no idea how to play that instrument or even how it works, you could still instruct your uncle to play a middle C note, and he would play it. You have no idea what process your uncle went through to produce that sound, but you wouldn't need to because he still played the note. This is exactly how OOP works. Objects are responsible for carrying out and managing their own behaviors.

ENCAPSULATION Encapsulation, a fundamental part of OOP, is needed to guarantee successful programming and should always be implemented within all classes. *Encapsulation* is another way to describe *data hiding*. We have defined an object as a "bundled package" of methods and variables, so we can imagine that, in a program, multiple objects are created and interact with one another to perform a task. Programs and objects interact with data only through the object's methods; this is the key to OOP's reusability, consistency, and reliability.

In the orchestra example, we have a **Violin** class with the method **playNote** and the variable **currentNote**. This is somewhat misleading because the **Violin** class would need other methods and variables to work in an orchestra, but we will explain that later. The variables within the **Violin** class should be encapsulated so that other objects don't have direct access to them. We can do this by thinking of the **Violin** class as a black box. We might not know what variables are inside this black box; we just want to know how to interact with the object on an abstract level. We can determine, therefore, that we would actually need a method to change the note, instead of interacting with the variable directly. The object should be smart enough to get the work done.

To change the **currentNote** variable, we could provide a **setNote** method. We would also need a method, such as **getNote**, to determine what note is actually playing. The **getNote** method would just return the value of the **currentNote** variable.

By creating methods like **getNote** and **setNote**, we make the object responsible for interacting with other objects. You don't want another object to have direct access to the variable **currentNote**; doing so is potentially dangerous for programs in terms of reusability. If another object wants to know what the **currentNote** variable is, it should ask the **Violin** class provide the current note by using the **getNote** method. Or, if another object wants to change the **currentNote** variable of the **Violin** class, it would communicate by using the **setNote** method.

The fundamental idea of encapsulation is to make the object responsible for itself and for handling its internal state. Other objects shouldn't be able to reach into the **Violin** class and change the **currentNote** variable. Other objects must ask the **Violin** class to change the **currentNote** variable by using a method like **setNote**.

MESSAGE PASSING   *Message passing*, the fundamental key to object interaction in a program, is basically a way for objects to communicate and interact with one another. Messages and abstraction allow objects to interact in ways that seem quite logical.

In the previous example describing object encapsulation, we discussed the **Violin** class with the methods **playNote**, **setNote**, and **getNote**. We can imagine that a symphony conductor might want to call an object of the **Violin** class and tell it to play a specific note. The **Conductor** class doesn't need to know how the **Violin** class will play a note or the technical aspects of playing that note; it just wants to tell the **Violin** class's object to play a note, which it can do by calling that object's **playNote** method:

```
Violin firstChair = new Violin();
firstChair.playNote();
```

This code can be read as follows: "Create a new instance of the Violin class and name that object firstChair; then tell the firstChair object to play a note."

Methods in the **Violin** class can also be overloaded. For example, the **Violin** class might actually have two methods called **playNote()**:

```
playNote();
playNote(note);
```

In the first case of the method `playNote()`, we would assume the `Violin` object would play the `currentNote` (a variable inside the object). If the method `playNote(note)` is called with an additional parameter called `note`, we would assume the `Violin` object would set the internal variable `currentNote` to the value `note` that was passed before playing that note.

Overloading methods is very common in OOP and Java programming, and it's an easy way to understand real-world abstractions. The key to overloading methods is that each method declaration that's overloaded should be unique in terms of the parameters passed to the method. The parameter can be unique in its type and/or the number of parameters passed to the method, as shown in this example:

```
playNote();
playNote(note);
playNote(piece);
```

These are three variations of the `playNote` method. The first two are obviously different from one another, but `playNote(note)` and `playNote(piece)` are similar because only one parameter is passed to the method. The difference is that in the `playNote(note)` method, a single note would be passed to the `Violin` object. In the `playNote(piece)` method, an entire piece of music would be sent to the `Violin` object to be played. For these methods to work, we have to define two new classes —`note` and `piece`.

INHERITANCE *Inheritance* is a powerful concept of OOP, allowing the program to place objects into real-world categories and helping the programmer organize a structure. Conceptually, all objects in Java use inheritance. All objects are inherited from the "cosmic base class: Object" (which is discussed later). Inherited objects can be managed and recoded much more easily than in traditional programming because the objects are packaged into real-world categories with particular behaviors and states.

When an object inherits a *superclass* object (also known as the *base class* or *parent class*), it also inherits the methods and variables from that superclass. For example, we could have a class `SymphonyEmployee`, and within `SymphonyEmployee`, we can keep track of the employee variables `name` and `dateHired`.

We can then derive new objects that inherit the superclass `SymphonyEmployee`, such as `StageHand`, `Musician`, and `Conductor`. Each of the subsequent employees has names and dates hired (the `name` and `dateHired` variables, which are inherited), but each new class can also have specific characteristics. For example, `Musician` would need the variable **instrumentPlayed**, which wouldn't be included in **StageHand** and **Conductor**. The simplest way to think about inheritance is to think about *is-a* relationships. **Musician** *is-a* **SymphonyEmployee**, **StageHand** *is-a* **SymphonyEmployee**, and **Conductor** *is-a* **SymphonyEmployee**.

POLYMORPHISM   *Polymorphism* is another way of saying that "objects know how to do the right thing." Objects are "smart" enough to determine in their hierarchical inheritance structure which method should be used during message passing. For example, many objects can have the same method name, such as **playNote**. The **playNote** method can be used in the **Violin** class as well as in the **Flute** class. We used a similar example in the previous section on message passing, with the **Violin** class having many variations of the method **playNote**, which can be called with different parameters.

Polymorphism becomes particularly important when an object is inherited from a superclass. For example, the **Violin** class could be inherited from the **StringSection** class, and the **StringSection** class could also have a **playNote** method. If we're dealing with a **Violin** class (containing the method **playNote**), which *is-an* instrument that inherits **playNote** from the **StringSection** class, how does Java know which method the **Violin** object should use? If the **playNote** method was called by a **Violin** object, it would choose the **playNote** method implemented within the **Violin** class.

How does this work? The key to polymorphism is a concept called *late binding* (or *dynamic binding*). The compiler doesn't generate the code to call a method at compile time (called *static binding*, for C programmers), but instead determines the methods every time the object is defined. Java can accomplish this feat by first checking whether the subclass has a method with that name and the same matching parameters. If the match is true, Java will use this method. Otherwise, Java will check with the superclass (parent) for a method with that name and the same parameters. This procedure continues up the hierarchical inheritance chain until Java finds a method with the same name and parameters.

Java is different from other object-oriented languages, such as C++, which allows overloading of both methods and operators. Generally, in Java we can overload only methods, although some Java objects come with built-in operator overloading, such as the + operator. As programmers implementing polymorphism, we need to deal only with overloading methods.

CONCLUSION

Object-oriented programming is constructed to deal with abstractions, concepts, and categories in much the same way we humans think about the world. OOP is an effective way to reuse basic elements of code, to increase productivity when writing code, and to enhance reliability of code. You should now have a basic understanding of the following fundamental OOP concepts: Classes, objects, encapsulation, message passing, inheritance, and polymorphism. These terms are used throughout the book to describe how OOP code is written and implemented.

Object-oriented programming is the way to go, as you have seen in this chapter. We have introduced some useful background on OOP so that you can move on to other technologies.

Introduction to Java

In Chapter 2, we were introduced to object-oriented programming. In this chapter, we concentrate purely on Java. We start by having a look at the history of Java and how it came to embody so much of our current programming mentality through a careful look at how Java really works. We then get into the fundamentals of the language —syntax, structure, and so forth—and apply them to writing some real interactive applets. To make our tour of Java complete, we look at the direction in which Java is heading and where to look to learn more about the current state of Java.

This chapter will cover the following topics:

- A brief history of Java
- A definition of Java
- Java versus JavaBeans
- Behind the scenes with Java—the runtime system
- Java applications and applets
- Latest trends
- Java tools
- Noted books on Java
- Core Java resources
- Noted Web sites using Java
- Additional Java resources

A Brief History of Java

Before we begin with the more technical descriptions of Java as an environment and as a programming language, we will take a look at the history of Java. This gives us an important perspective when we're programming in Java. From this perspective, we can better understand why Java has been built with certain characteristics and functions. This section gives you a brief overview of the development of Java, from a computer language used in cable TV switchboxes to the powerful programming language we know today.

Java began in 1991 at Sun Microsystems. A six-member team, code named "Green," was formed within Sun—their only task being to "create something cool." James Gosling, leader of the team and a Sun Fellow, wanted to develop a computer language that would allow appliances, such as VCRs or cable TV switchboxes, to talk to each other.

The Green Team researched a wide variety of electronic devices and found that each one had a different *Central Processing Unit* (CPU). This severely limited the possibilities available to each device because manufacturers were tied to the devices' hardware and wiring constraints. In addition, most of these devices used chips with a limited amount of programming space. The team set to work trying to devise a way around these restrictions. Finally, they hit on a possible answer—the team conjectured (correctly!) that with a new style of software programming language, it might be possible to free manufacturers from the limits of their hardware. The Green Team's only task then was to dream up the language.

The Green Team's software solution was a programming language called Oak (evidently named for a tree growing outside James Gosling's window at Sun). The language was based on C++, with some rather important fundamental differences. The team wanted to keep the spirit of C++, both in syntax and object orientation, but they also worked hard to find solutions to problem elements of C++. They wanted it to be easy for C++ programmers to work in Oak, and they wanted to free them from certain constraints they saw in C++.

Oak was designed to be portable, generating intermediate code for a "hypothetical" or "virtual" machine. This is different from C++, which must be compiled for each machine it's used on directly. The virtual machine can be used on any platform that has the right kind of interpreter. Also, Oak was designed to deal with memory allocation, garbage collection, and pointers in a new way.

The idea of an intermediate hypothetical machine isn't completely new. Niklaus Wirth, designer of Pascal, made use of this concept. With the onset of PCs, the *University of California at San Diego* (UCSD) developed Pascal and p-code commercially with much the same idea. They're still in use today. However, these programming environments were based on Pascal's procedure-oriented programming instead of the object-oriented programming of C++.

In 1992, the first product using Oak was introduced. Called "*7," it was a hand-held device that combined a remote control with a small visual interface. The Green Team's goal with this product was to design a piece of technology that would be easy and fun to use. The visual interface they created featured an animated character as its guide. This character, "Duke," was created by Joe Palrang, and is now the official mascot for the Java environment.

With this introduction to Oak, Sun turned the Green Team into a company called First Person, which spent most of 1993 and 1994 searching for buyers of their new technology—with no success. The potential of the technology wasn't fully understood. It took the birth of Mosaic and the *World Wide Web* (WWW) to realize the power of the technologies the Green Team had developed.

In the middle of 1994, the Green Team had a breakthrough idea. As Gosling has said in an interview with *SunWorld*, "[we realized that] we could build a real cool browser . . . so we built it." Well, we all know this project turned into more than just a "cool browser." The browser Gosling was referring to, *webrunner*, was presented at Sunworld in May of 1995. The browser itself supported what are now known as *applets*, and at Sunworld, the first applet made its debut, with Duke waving to his parents over the Internet. That was the birth of the Java we know today.

In January 1996, Netscape released Netscape 2.0, a Java-enabled browser (by this time Oak's name had been changed to Java). With this endorsement, Java exploded onto the computer scene.

What Is Java?

It's important to realize that Java is more than just a programming language; it's an entire set of specifications for an entire platform. In fact, the full name of Java is actually the Java Programming Language Platform, but the name is always shortened to just Java. In this section, we briefly describe some of Java's features that make it so powerful in today's computing environment.

We have found that the actual description of what Java does and what it's good for is best summed up by the developers of Java themselves, so in this section we have provided summaries and discussions of some of the main goals the developers had in creating Java. To get more information on the Java environment, you can visit the Sun Systems home page online (`http://java.sun.com:80/doc/language_environment`). There you can find the complete white paper specifications for Java, written by the developers. In this section, you learn about the following Java characteristics:

- Object-oriented
- Robust
- Distributed
- Secure
- Architecture neutral
- Portable
- Multithreaded

Object-Oriented

As mentioned, Java's foundation is C++. Java was designed to encompass a primary syntax and usage that would closely mimic that of C++. The developers of Java wanted to make the transition for C++ programmers as easy as possible. In addition, Java adopts the basic object-oriented ideas that make C++ such a powerful language. In their words, "The object-oriented facilities of Java are essentially those of C++." However, although C++ is actually a transformation of C into an object-oriented language, Java is truly object-oriented from the ground up. Everything in Java is an object, from strings to audio files (except for a few basic data types such as numbers).

Robust

When the Java developers used C++ as their model, they worked hard to quantify what they didn't like in C++ so they could address these issues in Java. They found some of the biggest problems in C++ to be pointer arithmetic mistakes and memory allocations. Java deals with all these concerns, making the language extremely robust. First, the Java model, in the words of the white paper, "eliminates the possibility of overwriting memory or corrupting data." It does this by taking care of memory allocation and pointers itself. Also, Java takes care of potential problems by instituting a strict code-checking and verification system that from the beginning spots situations that look error-prone, so that at runtime your code is error free.

Distributed

Unlike C++, Java was built to be distributed, taking full advantage of a networked computing environment. The networking capabilities built into Java are extremely powerful. There are routines for copying with *File Transfer Protocol* (FTP) and HTTP issues, and distant URLs can be manipulated as easily as local files. These communication tools for linking distributed objects across networks are crucial for our current age of Internet programming and application development.

Secure

With networked and distributed environments comes the problem of security. Imagine downloading Java applets with no security check for viruses or other aspects of tampering; the WWW would be a scary place indeed! Java has several features to keep it secure, including automatic memory allocation and code verification. We will discuss security issues in more detail—first, when we discuss the Java runtime system, and second, when we introduce applets.

Architecture Neutral

One of the Java's most important features, which you will hear about throughout this book, is that it's built to be architecture neutral. Once your code is written, the Java compiler itself actually generates intermediate bytecode that's architecture independent. The bytecode is created for the Java Virtual Machine. This machine doesn't actually exist; it's a set of specifications that can be used to create interpreters to read and execute the Java code on any machine. In this way, every system can understand and use the same original piece of Java code.

Portable

To enhance Java's architecture-neutral aspect, the developers got rid of any machine-dependent specifications to make the Java platform completely portable. Binary data, number types, and strings are all clearly specified as cross-platform. This was an important concern for the Java developers because they didn't want to give one machine an unfair advantage for creating a Java runtime system. That would lessen the cross-platform capabilities they were trying to establish.

Multithreading

Java has unique multithreading capabilities that make simple and advanced threading quite straightforward. A program that can multithread can perform more than one task at the same time. A chat room is a prime example of a program that's easily written with threads. With threads, each time a new member logs on, a new thread is added, taking on the task of giving the member the latest information as well as relaying what he or she has to say. Java's threading capabilities include prioritization of threads, communication between threads, and the suspension of threads.

By now, you should have a pretty good idea of Java's basic capabilities. We hope you're as excited as we are to start using some of these features, but before we go any deeper into Java, we want to make a brief digression to address an issue that might need some clarification. Recently, there has been a lot of talk about something called JavaBeans. What are these JavaBeans? Are they different from Java or Java applets?

Behind the Scenes with Java: The Runtime System

In this section, we're going to take a quick look at how Java actually works, not from the programming point of view, but from a computer designer's point of view. We're going to take an in-depth look at how the Java system is built to process and execute the Java code and why it was built that way.

To give you a good understanding of what's really happening behind the scenes when you compile and run your Java code, we're going to explore step-by-step the transformations your code undergoes, from the program you wrote on your computer to the final execution of the code. We look at the runtime system itself and examine the relationship of the Java Virtual Machine to the runtime system. In addition, we describe in detail what the Java Virtual Machine actually is, what it does, and why it exists. Finally, we take a look at Just-In-Time Compilers, learn how they work, and learn why they're the fastest solution for executing Java code available on the market today.

Imagine you have just finished writing your Java code. Do you know what has to happen to your code before it can be executed? It still has a long, long way to go. There are four main stages the code must still pass through so that it can be correctly executed:

1. Compilation for the Java Virtual Machine
2. Class loader
3. Code verification
4. Code execution

Figure 3-1 illustrates how these stages relate to one another as part of the runtime system. Notice that the stages can be split into two categories—compilation and interpretation.

Figure 3-1.
Diagram of the Java
runtime system.

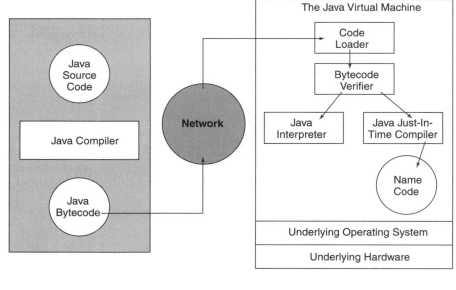

COMPILATION   INTERPRETATION

Compilation

The Java compiler is basically like any normal compiler, such as a C compiler. It's in charge of transforming the higher level code we use to program into code that can be read by a machine (*assembler code*). At the same time, some important characteristics of the Java compiler need to be examined. To take a look at them, let's compare the Java compilation process and the C compilation process.

For starters, the Java code is compiled, not for a specific machine as it would be in C, but for the Java Virtual Machine, a machine that literally doesn't exist. The compiled code is actually an intermediate bytecode written for the specifications of the Java Virtual Machine. This code can be transferred easily from system to system, making the platform-neutral capabilities that have become the hallmark of the Java language a reality. This is only the beginning of the compilation features that were brought together to make sure Java would be cross-network and cross-operating-system safe.

Java doesn't give the programmer any control of the memory layout for a particular program or system. If we, as programmers, had such control, we could easily give the wrong memory addresses or overwrite important information. When the intermediate bytecode is run by the interpreter, a memory layout is created only at runtime. An index is made to reference methods at this time, and the first time any method is called, it's looked up. After a method is looked up once, only the index number need be used from then on. In this way, the benefits of the symbolic referencing are preserved. This is done primarily for security, and to make sure any classes being used as superclasses (from which other classes inherit) will have their information stored in the right place, even if they have since been updated.

The compiled Java code, also called the *intermediate Java bytecode*, is composed of opcodes and operands. Opcodes are a set of specific commands that the virtual machine understands, and operands are the data needed for the opcodes. These pieces of information are basically in a stream that the computer must deal with. Each command is an 8-bit number, and each address is a 32-bit number. You might be wondering how the interpreter can locate and handle a specific command or address in this stream of information; this is covered in the next section.

Interpretation

We have encountered the role of the interpreter briefly in our discussions about the portability of the Java language. An interpreter can take on any number of forms, but its main duty is executing Java code for a particular machine. It's the job of the interpreter to run the platform-independent intermediate code that the Java compiler has created for the standard Java Virtual Machine. There are three steps in the interpretation process—the code must be loaded, the code must be verified, and the code is then executed.

Loading the Code

The appropriately named Code Loader in the interpreter has the job of loading the Java code. This step involves bringing together and organizing all the information needed to execute a particular piece of Java code. This information includes any classes you use or inherit from within your Java program.

The classes are laid out in a specially calculated way to maximize the protection of imported classes while allowing for flexibility between local ones. Each imported class is given its own namespace. In this way, without a specific call to a class located outside an imported class, this imported class can't interfere with any other class. This effectively protects imported classes from one another and the current local environment. Conversely, the local classes all share one common namespace and are free to share information with one another.

It's only after all the classes have been imported that the memory layout for the code is determined. This method enhances the security of the Java platform and solves the inheritance problems we mentioned in the section on compilation.

Verifying the Code

Before the loaded code can be executed, Java has yet another safety mechanism in place to check for potentially hazardous situations. The interpreter contains a bytecode verifier that looks through the entire piece of code, checking for any possibly dangerous situations, such as the following:

- Forged pointers
- Access restriction violations
- Not accessing objects as they are
- Stack overflows or underflows
- Calls to methods with inappropriate arguments
- Illegal data conversion

Verifying the code is important for the following reasons. First, it adds one more security measure for making sure a malicious piece of code isn't run. For instance, if you were about to load a dangerous applet, it would be stopped by the bytecode verifier before it could be loaded. Second, it's part of the Java platform added by the Java development team to help the debugging process. Because all the problems previously listed are known problems, having the interpreter verify their existence effectively cuts down on the time spent debugging. The Java executable code is then that much closer to being error-free, which helps in terms of fewer crashes at runtime and overall faster execution.

Executing the Code

The code is finally ready to be executed once it has been tested by the code verifier. There are many ways to execute the code, but in the end they all must lead to the conversion of the current verified code into a set of operations that the particular machine waiting to perform the code can understand.

One way the code could be executed is to convert all of it, in one big chunk, into native code (platform-specific) at runtime. Then, when the conversion is complete, the compiled code can run straight through without interruption. That's basically how C and C++ programs are executed. In C, however, you compile the code ahead of time for a specific machine; in this case, you would actually have to wait for the compilation at runtime. Another way to execute the Java code is in a style more similar to Lisp and other interpreted languages. In this case, the interpreter can actually read the code line by line and interpret it as the code is being run.

What's done now is a combination of these two methods. The second method of reading the code a segment at a time is used, but instead of just interpreting the code, a *Just-In-Time* (JIT) compiler actually converts the verified code to the machine code of the current system, as in the first method we described. JIT compilers combine the strengths of the two methods while working around their weaknesses. They have proved to be much faster than any other method of execution, for almost every task. We will talk more about JIT compilers after we cover the Java Virtual Machine.

It should be clear now that there's a lot going on behind the scenes with Java to ensure the environment's portability. From the compilation of your initial code into intermediate bytecode written for the Java Virtual Machine, through the loading of the code, the verification of the code, and finally the execution, the runtime environment must deal with many issues of security and platform independence. We have only touched briefly on the Java Virtual Machine so far, focusing more on the actual process of compilation and execution, so let's get a better handle on what the Java Virtual Machine is all about.

Java Virtual Machine

We have mentioned the JVM, but so far we haven't clearly defined what it is. This section takes a more in-depth look at the JVM and how it works.

Essentially, the JVM is a technique used to make Java code platform-independent. JVM specifications were designed to give as much freedom as possible to the builders of Java interpreters so that every platform could eventually support an interpreter that could execute any Java code. For this reason, the JVM exists merely as a set of requirements or rules. Basically, the developers of Java are leaving a set of instructions that tell how code can be used and accessed. Any Java interpreter that knows these requirements knows it has an intermediate bytecode with certain characteristics. The Java compiler creates these characteristics, and then as long as the interpreter has been built with these specifications in mind, it should be able to interpret and execute the intermediate bytecode correctly.

If this discussion is getting a bit too abstract, you can also think of the JVM as an imaginary CPU, one that can be placed on top of any existing computer. Every computer has a CPU, and each CPU is unique, with its own specifications and rules. The JVM is no exception. Rather than copying an existing CPU and its instruction set, such as Intel's x86 that drives PCs or Sun's Sparc Chips, the Java team created their own Java instruction set. Platform neutrality was once again the driving force behind this decision because the Java team didn't want to favor one existing chip over any other.

The JVM consists of a set of components, as follows:

- An instruction set
- A register set
- A stack
- A garbage-collection heap
- A method area

As long as these components maintain the functionality outlined by the Java development team, it doesn't matter how the JVM is implemented. The JVM could be built to compile the intermediate byte code to native code or implemented as an actual chip to quickly deal with the intermediate bytecode; the options are open. In fact, Sun is developing a chip that will transform the Java Virtual Machine into a real machine. Let's take a look at the specifications for each of the machine's components.

Instruction Set

Java has its own specific set of opcodes and operands used to describe the code when it reaches the intermediate bytecode level. The set is built specifically for Java to deal with its particular needs, such as multithreading. Each bytecode is either an *opcode*, which is an 8-bit number describing a specific method, or an *operand*, which varies in length starting from 8 bits, and is data needed for the opcodes. The opcodes and operands are aligned to 8 bits, to control the code's compactness, instead of to 32 bits or 62 bits as is typical. The JVM uses the *big endian* encoding scheme, which means that the larger order bits are stored in lower memory spaces.

The instruction set was built to be small and compact, so it can be easily transferred from platform to platform. The decision to incorporate an intermediate stage for the code composed of this instruction set for the JVM (instead of trying to port the code raw or compile it specifically for each machine) was made as part of the Java developers' compromise between portability and speed.

Register Set

A *register* is used to hold information about the system's current state. Because registers vary so greatly from system to system, the Java developers didn't want to interfere with the performance of individual local systems already in place. For this reason, the Java platform has only the simplest register system with the following four variables:

- The program counter, or the **pc**
- The pointer to the top of the operand stack, or the **optop**
- The pointer to the next execution environment, or the **frame**
- The pointer to the first local variable in the current environment, or the **vars**

Stack

The JVM is a stack-based machine. When the JVM deals with the intermediate bytecodes, a stack frame is created for each method in a class. The frame is used for storing the following:

- Local variables
- Information about the execution environment
- Operands

Garbage Collecting

The JVM has a unique garbage-collecting mechanism. It takes the control of garbage collection out of the hands of the programmer and takes on the responsibility itself. In most implementations of the Java interpreter, garbage collection is done as a background thread, which gives good performance while relieving the programmer of concerns about recycling the memory.

Method Area

The bytecode of Java methods is stored in the Method Area. Its specifications are purposely quite vague; in fact, no specifications at all are given by the Java development team for the layout of this memory area. This increases the overall portability of the Java platform by not tying Java to one type of memory configuration. It also aids in the overall security of the Java platform because if a programmer doesn't know ahead of time where the memory locations will be, it's much more difficult to interfere with them.

Exploring the Java Virtual Machine

This was our first look at the JVM's inner workings. You should have a better idea of why it's so crucial to the complete Java platform and how it has been designed to maintain Java's portability, security, architecture neutrality, and networking capabilities. We have listed many resources at the end of this chapter to give you more information if you want to explore these topics further. They include suggestions for finding more information about the JVM, a list of current related products, and a guide to other writings. There are also descriptions of the latest up-and-coming Java technologies and URLs of important related online information.

Now that we have a good idea of how the Java Virtual Machine is set up from an abstract viewpoint, we're going to explore some actual implementations of the JVM. We will visit the Microsoft Virtual Machine and Just-In-Time compilers to get a better grasp of how the abstract rules and requirements the Java team devised are used and improved to create the technology we're using today.

The wonderful idea behind the JVM is that it's not set in stone. In fact, developers can work around the Java development team's basic structure, adding onto the system and taking it one step further. For this reason, the reach and capabilities of the JVM continue to grow daily. New tools for executing Java applications are being developed more rapidly, and new possibilities are opening up in every direction, from the use of JavaBean components to the seamless integration of ActiveX and Beans. One recent release of the Virtual Machine—the Microsoft Virtual Machine—is especially notable for its integration of a variety of new features, its speed, and its reliability. We will take a brief look at why this particular machine is so special, what features it has to offer, and how it's influencing Java's future.

Microsoft Virtual Machine

In the beginning of April 1997, Microsoft unveiled the prerelease of their latest version of the Java Virtual Machine, called the Microsoft Virtual Machine (version 4.0). This version is currently marked for inclusion in Internet Explorer 4.0. The machine is worth examining because it introduces some interesting new features that could greatly enhance Java's production capability. These features include the integration of ActiveX and JavaBeans components and technologies, a new and improved *Abstract Window Toolkit* (AWT), and enhanced programming capabilities for international applications.

Probably the most critical addition to the Microsoft Virtual Machine is the incorporation of JavaBeans and ActiveX-related controls. As we mentioned, JavaBeans can greatly enhance the application production scheme. On top of this, if it can be used with ActiveX via bridges, JavaBeans becomes an even more powerful tool. A JavaBeans programmer can quickly and easily create not only network-based cross-platform solutions, but also cross-application environment solutions.

You should learn more about the Microsoft Virtual Machine, especially if you're working in a Windows environment. There are many other features, some of which we have just touched on, that make an exciting backdrop from which to create Java applications. Some other features include increased speed, JDK 1.1 support, a new security model, and advanced debugging support. If you want to know where to look for more information on this technology, see the "Java Tools" section at the end of this chapter.

Before turning to Java programming and your first applets, we'd like to discuss using Just-In-Time compilers to enhance Java's runtime performance. When we discussed the final execution of Java code earlier in this chapter, we mentioned this compiler briefly; in the following section, we describe the process in more depth.

Just-In-Time Compilers

Probably the biggest concern about the Java platform is that it's just not as fast as C++. Yes, there's a certain amount of compromise you make to balance portability, security, and speed. However, with the introduction of JIT compilers, the overall runtime performance of Java code has been improved dramatically. In particular, the Just-In-Time compiler by Symantec (`http://cafe.symantec/`) has proved much faster than all the rest. It has recently been integrated into Sun's Java Development Kit as a step towards ensuring the fastest Java platform possible.

The JIT compiler is a part of the Java runtime system, or the interpreter. It's essentially an implementation of the interpreter's execution portion, as specified for the Java platform. The JIT is actually a hybrid of two somewhat more standard execution alternatives.

One possible method of code execution is to take all the intermediate Java bytecode, convert it to native code, and then run the entire native code program with no waits or stops. This is basically how C++ is run, except that you can compile the code ahead of time in C++. Here, the user would actually have to wait for the code to be compiled at runtime. So, the eventual native code would be extremely fast, but the wait isn't worth it. Another alternative for code execution is interpreting the code line by line, on the fly—the method originally favored for delivering the Java code. However, the interpretation process doesn't run very quickly on any machine.

The JIT compiler combines these two alternatives by taking the intermediate bytecode produced for the JVM and converting it to the native code of a specific machine. The twist is that it does this at runtime, "just in time" for the next piece of code to be executed. In this way, it provides the speed of the native code with the speed of the on-the-fly compilation. In addition, it greatly speeds up execution when there are many repetitive commands. In an interpreted environment, these commands would have to be interpreted separately each time, but with the JIT compiler, once the command is compiled, it can be immediately executed as native code again and again.

Summary of the Java Runtime Review

In the preceding sections, we have taken you through the stages in the life of Java code as it goes through the necessary paces before it can be executed on a specific machine. Also, we introduced the process of Java code being converted and ported in an intermediate bytecode format designed specifically for the JVM. We then looked at the role of the interpreter that must execute the Java code. We noted the three stages the Java code undergoes to be executed: Loading of the code, verification of the code, and execution of the code. To better explain the runtime process, we gave a more detailed picture of the JVM and its inner workings, as well as explaining more about the rise of JIT compilers. All this information should be helpful as we now turn our attention toward learning about Java as a programming language and writing your first applets.

Java Basics: Applications and Applets

Our behind-the-scenes investigation of the Java environment has come to an end. Now it's time for the exciting task of learning to program in Java and creating Java applications and Java applets. In this section, we're going to take a whirlwind tour of the Java language, programming in Java, and the differences between Java applications and applets. At the end, we will be creating some interactive applets of our own.

First, we will become familiar with the Java programming process. We will compare it to writing code in C/C++ and also begin to delve into the differences and similarities between Java and C++ in syntax, overall language structure, object-oriented aspects, and development procedures. We will then begin a short overview of the Java programming language, learning about the variables, arrays, classes, packages, and so forth that we need to be able to write our first programs. Along the way, we will introduce Java syntax and some lines of code to illustrate and emphasize the important points of what we're learning. With this knowledge, we will then focus on applets and programming for the Internet. We will discuss the difference between applets and applications, and learn about applet security and why it's important in today's programming environment.

All this information is, of course, just a prelude to the moment we've all been waiting for—writing interactive applets. We will end this section with some fun applets for you to experiment with. They will get you started on your way to becoming an interactive programming wizard.

Getting Started in the Java Environment

If you're used to programming in C or C++, you should have no problems getting used to the Java programming environment. Just as in C/C++, there are many options available for producing your Java code. One, you might choose to do your programming in a commercial development environment. There are many on the market from which to select; we suggest checking out Microsoft J++ and Symantec Visual Café to start. Another alternative is to program in an editor and compile your code from the command line. In UNIX, for example, you can write your programs in emacs and compile in an xterm window, or you can run and compile your code from the DOS window on a PC. The latter method is the one we suggest as we begin to explore some sample code. To work from the command line this way, you need a Java compiler installed in your system. A good place to find one is the Sun Java site. There you can download the latest version of the Java Development Kit and learn how to install it correctly.

We're now ready to begin our exploration of the Java language. As we proceed, you will undoubtedly notice many similarities between Java and C++. You will learn about Java data types, variables, strings, arrays, conditional statements, and control loops, learn how classes and packages help in organization, and finally put everything together to begin creating some simple programs. Along the way there will be lots of examples to illustrate the concepts.

Variables

Java is an example of a *strongly typed language*, which means that every variable declared in a program must be clearly defined as a declared type, or the code can't (and won't) be compiled. Variables can take on many forms, from instances of classes, as we will see later, to simpler forms. Basically, they fall into two categories—reference types, which we will learn about later, and primitive types.

There are eight primitive data types in Java: The six number types (four integers and two floating points), one character type, and one Boolean type. As we learn about each type, we will also learn how to declare and define a variable of that type and learn about the scope of operations available to each type.

- **Number types:** Number types are used in Java to allocate memory for the numbers used in any program. There are six types split into two categories—integers and floating points. The most common number types are int and double.

- **Integers:** In general, integer numbers are declared to be of type int. Byte and short types are often too small for the job at hand, and long is usually just too large (see Table 3-1).

- **Floating point:** Most floating-point numbers are declared as double because the float declaration is a little small (see Table 3-2).

Table 3-1.

Integer Types and
Their Memory
Allocations

Type	Bytes
byte	1
short	2
int	4
long	8

Table 3-2.

Floating-Point
Types and Their
Memory
Allocations.

Type	Bytes
float	4
double	8

- **Character type:** The char type is used to denote characters in the Unicode encoding scheme. Unicode is designed to encompass most of the characters used in all written languages throughout the world. To do this, it was designed as a 2-byte code, allowing for 65,536 characters. This is different from the ASCII/ANSI code, which is 1-byte code able to track 255 characters.

- **Boolean type:** The Boolean type in Java is unique from the Boolean type recently added in C++. It has two values, **true** and **false**. It's used for logical testing with relational operators, but you can never convert Boolean values to numbers as you can in C/C++.

Declarations and Initializations

Declaring and initializing variables in Java is quite similar to C and C++. First, mention the type of the variable and then give the variable a name. Traditionally, names in Java are lowercase for the first word in the name and capitalized for any subsequent word. No underscores are used to delineate words. For example, in C a variable could be named **my_variable_name**, but in Java this same variable would be called **myVariableName**. Let's get some practice initializing some variables by declaring some that could be used to describe a family.

```
int numberOfChildren; //int is the most common size for an
                      //integer
```

```
byte numberOfDogs;
int numberOfChildren, numberOfDogs; /*you can declare
    multiple variables on the same line, both of these
    are declared int*/
```

You should notice a few extra elements other than the simple variable declarations present in the preceding code. The semicolon is used to delineate a complete expression, just as in C. The double front slash (//) indicates the beginning of a comment, most often used when you have only one line of commentary. The words enclosed between front slashes and asterisks are comments as well. This type of commentary is most often used for multiple lines or blocks of code, or if you know a comment is going to grow with time. A note of warning: Remember, with this commentary, it's not possible to embed comments within comments. If you try to do this, you will find that the compiler ends the comment where the embedded comment ends.

Now that we have declared our variables, we must learn how to initialize them. To do this, you create a statement with the variable name on the left followed by an equals sign and the value on the right. This value could be quite simple or very complex. It can be a number, an expression, the value returned by a method, and so forth. Let's initialize some variables:

```
int numberOfDogs;        //declaring the variable
numberOfDogs = 1;        //then initializing-our family has
                         //one dog
```

You can also declare and initialize variables on the same line, as shown:

```
int numberOfDogs = 1 ;   //declaring & initializing the
                         //variable
char firstLetter = 'A'; //notice the single quotes
```

Now that we know how to declare and initialize basic variable types, let's find out what operations exist for manipulating them.

Operators — Arithmetic

Java uses the normal arithmetic operators for addition, subtraction, multiplication, and division: +, -, *, and /. In addition, it has a remainder function, or **mod** function, denoted as %, which returns the remainder of a specified division. Let's look at some examples in Listing 3-1.

```
int i, j;
float foo;

i = 9 + 2;     //Add, i is evaluated to 11
j = 9 - 2;     //Subtract, j is evaluated to 7
i = j * 2      //Multiply, 7 * 2, evaluate to 14
j = i / 2      //Divide, 14 / 2, evaluate to 7
j += 9;        //Shortcut, Add 9 to j, evaluate to 16.
j -= 9;        //Shortcut, Subtract 9 from j, evaluate to 9.
j = 9 % 2      //Modulus, evaluate to 1

foo = 9.0 / 2.0      //Divide, evaluate to 4.5
foo = 9.0 % 2.5      //Modulus, evaluate to 1.5

foo = 9.0 % 2        /* Modulus, evaluate to 1.0 (float).
                     The 2 is temporarily converted to a
                     floating point for the duration of the
                     calculation.*/
```

Operators—Conversions and Casting

Once a variable has been declared, its type can't be changed. However, the type can be changed temporarily, for use in a calculation, for example. There are two ways in which this is done: You can "cast" the variable yourself, or the compiler can do it for you. In general, it's best to let the compiler take care of these issues, such as multiplying an integer by a float to return an integer. A simple example of this is the last mathematical statement given in Listing 3-1. In this case, the compiler casts the integer to a float for the duration of the calculation and returns a float. To cast a variable yourself, you could do the following:

```
int j = 3;
float foo;
foo = 1.0 * (float) j;     //j is converted to 3.0, foo=3.0
float foobar = 7.7;
int k = (int) foobar / j; //k is 2
```

In this example, **foobar** is temporarily converted to an int (the value is 7). The calculation is then carried out, producing an int result, which would be 2. In general, casting variables yourself is a bad idea. The compiler is smart enough to carry out the necessary casting operations.

Operators — Increment/Decrement

Java supports increment and decrement operators, just like C/C++. Let's take a look at how this works:

```
int numberOfChildren = 2;
int i = 5;
numberOfChildren++;//numberOfChildren is now 3.
i--;              //i is now 4.
```

These operators exist in both *prefix* and *postfix* form. The prefix form is shown above and the postfix form is `--i` or `++i`, just as in C.

Operators — Math

In addition to the basic arithmetic operators, Java has many built-in mathematical methods available for immediate use. They are located in the `Math` class that we will explore in more detail shortly. For now, let's learn about some of the methods and how they're used.

You might have noticed how the math methods are called by using the `Math` class. We will learn much more about this later, but as a brief introduction, this is the way in which programmers tell the Java compiler where the methods are located. For instance, for the absolute value, we

Listing 3-2.
Sample math methods.

```
int answer;
float result, random;

answer = Math.abs(-3);     //answer = the absolute value of
                           //(-3), 3.
answer = Math.max(8,4);    //answer = the maximum of 8 & 4,
                           //8.
answer = Math.pow(6,4);    //answer = 6 to the 4th power,
                           //1296.

result = Math.log(6);      //result = the natural log of 6,
                           //1.79176
result = Math.sqrt(5.0);   //result = the square root of 5.0,
                           //2.23607
result = Math.sin(3.0);    //result = the sin of 3 radians,
                           //0.14112

random = Math.random();    /*random = a random number between
                              0.0 & 1.0,like 0.546753*/
```

want to use the method defined in the Java **Math** class, so we call it by saying **Math.abs(number)**.

PARENTHESES AND HIERARCHY In general, the hierarchy and precedence of operations in Java is the same as that of C and C++. Parentheses can be used to delineate or change the existing hierarchy. Here are some examples:

```
int i, j, k;
i = 9 * 7 + 6;              //i = 69;
j = 9 * (7 + 6);            //j = 117;
k = (6 + 4)- (3 * (7 - 2)); //k = -5;
```

RELATIONAL AND BOOLEAN OPERATORS It's often necessary to be able to test whether a given statement is **true** or **false**. Java has several operators for testing these relationships between numbers. When used, these operators return a Boolean value, which is either **true** or **false**. Here are some examples to get a better idea of how we can use these operators:

```
(2 == 5)          //returns false, 2 is not equal to 5.
(6 != 7)          //returns true, 6 is not equal to 7.
(7 > 6)               //returns true, 7 is greater than 6.
((7 + 9) < (7 + 10)) //returns true, 16 is smaller than 17.
((-6) >= (-5))        /*returns false,-6 is not greater
                        than or equal to -5.*/
(0 <= 0)          //returns true, 0 is smaller than
                  //or equal to 0.
```

You should notice that we have **(2 == 5)**, not **(2 = 5)**. The second expression isn't allowed as a relational expression. This is useful to keep in mind because the compiler accepts only the double equals sign as a Boolean operator.

COMBINING BOOLEAN OPERATORS It's also possible to combine multiple Boolean operators in the same expression. This can often be useful if you want to perform a task when either A or B is **true** or when A and B are both **true**. You will notice that they're basically the same as in C and C++.

That's all we're going to say for now about declaring and using numbers. We're going to shift our focus from these, the most basic types of variables we can declare, to start learning about some more complex variable types —strings and arrays. Both of them will be needed as we write our first Java programs. You should notice there are some fundamental differences between strings and arrays in Java and their counterparts in C/C++.

Listing 3-3.
Some sample
Boolean expressions.

```
!(9 == 9)
/*returns false, the ! negates the value inside the
     parentheses, which is true, 9 does equal 9.*/

((7 <= (6*2)) && ((-2+3) == 1)))
/*returns true, the || is the 'or' symbol. It indicates if
     both of the expressions is true, return true,
     otherwise return false.*/

((0 < 0.1) || (9 < 68))
/*returns true, the && is the 'and' symbol. It indicates if
     one of the expressions is true, return true,
     otherwise return false.*/
```

Strings

In Java, *strings* are not just arrays of characters, as they are in C. They are actually instances of the Java **string** class. If you're coming from a C background, it might help you to think of a string variable as a **char*** pointer. Strings are denoted by placing double quotes around a sequence of characters, as follows:

```
String nothingThere = " "; //creates an empty string.
String nameOfMyDog = "Mutt"; //creates a string "Mutt".
```

To join two strings together, you use the + sign:

```
String nameOfMyDog = "Mutt";
String nameOfYourDog = "Rover";
String sentence = nameOfMyDog + " and " + nameOfYourDog +
     " like to play together.";
```

The string sentence would then read: "Mutt and Rover like to play together." Notice how you can join string variables with new strings that are in double quotes. Notice also that we had to add spaces inside " **and** " to end up with the correct spacing for our sentence. The + sign joins the strings exactly as they are given without adding any extra spaces.

What if we need to find the length of a string? In C, we would look for the first null character in the array, but strings in Java aren't arrays of characters. In Java, the length is given by the **length** method. To find the length of **nameOfMyDog**, we would do the following:

```
int n = nameOfMyDog.length();    //n is equal to 4
```

Java counts string lengths with the first character in the string at position 0. If we want to find a substring of **nameOfYourDog**, we would want to use the **substring** method. Here's how we would find the first four letters in the string:

```
String s = nameOfYourDog.substring(0,4);//this returns
                                        //"Rover"
```

This might seem a bit confusing because counting from 0 to 4 at first glance would seem to produce 5 character slots, not 4. However, in Java the **substring** function counts from 0 inclusive to 4 exclusive, so it really is counting only from 0 to 3, returning 4 characters.

To check whether two strings are equal, you can use the **equals** method, which returns **true** if the strings are equal and **false** if they are not:

```
nameOfMyDog.equals("Mutt");//this returns true.
```

A note of warning: You should not use **==** when comparing strings. Instead of comparing whether the strings themselves are true, it looks to find whether the strings are stored within the same memory space.

Another method used to compare strings with one another is the **compareTo** method:

```
nameOfMyDog.compareTo("Mutt");
```

These basic string methods provide a good foundation for the programs we will soon be writing. Now, let's briefly look at the array class and then really get into the thick of it with an introduction to classes and packages in Java.

Array

Arrays in Java are examples of first-class objects. They are created somewhat differently than the strings and variable types we have explored up to this point. The first difference is that they must be defined by using the **new** operator, as follows:

```
int[] januarySales = new int[31];
```

This statement creates an array that can hold 31 integers. For instance, if you wanted to know how many copies of your latest software package you sold every day in January, you could keep track of that information in this array. The array entries are numbered from 0 to 30, not from 1 to 31.

We're now ready to learn how to place data in our array. Let's pretend we sold 60 copies on January 1. To fill the first slot with the number 60, do the following:

```
int[] januarySales = new int[31];
januarySales[0] = 60;
```

This could be a somewhat tedious way to fill up our array, especially if most days we sold the same number of copies, and only a few had interesting information. A short way to fill an array would be by using a **for** loop, just as in C. This is looking ahead a little bit because we haven't really discussed control structures, but let's fill up our array with the number 60:

```
for (int j = 0; j < 31; j++)
januarySales[j] = 60;
```

Maybe you had an especially good day on January 10, and you sold 100 copies of your software package. Let's add that to the array:

```
januarySales[9] = 100;
```

The entries in arrays can be used just like any other variables for calculations, reference, and so on. To access the information stored in the array—for instance, to find out how many packages you sold on January 10th—do the following:

```
int janTen = januarySales[9]; //janTen will equal 100.
```

There's also an even quicker way to initialize arrays given in Java. Let's look at this one briefly:

```
String[] dogNames = {"Mutt", "Rover", "Peanut", "Spot"};
```

In this case, you don't need to call **new**, as in the previous example, while declaring your array.

Once you create an array, you can't change its size, as you would in C or C++. If you need to do this, you must use vectors, which we will discuss later. However, you can change the values of each array entry and assign arrays to other arrays. If you assign one array to another one, both arrays actually refer to the same set of values; they are pointers, so any change made to one will change the other one as well. You can also easily copy just one part of an array to another array, which can be extremely useful. This is done by using the **arraycopy** method.

In general, you should have noticed that arrays in Java are most like pointers to arrays in C and C++. If you keep this in mind, it should be easy to make the transition. Now, let's take a look at the conditional statements and control loops that can bring some action to our variables.

Syntax: Conditional Statements and Loops

The syntax used to control flow in Java is basically identical to that of C and C++. You probably already noticed that when we got ahead of ourselves and introduced the **for** loop while showing you how to place values within an array. Because the syntax between the two languages is so similar, we will briefly present the Java commands and look at some examples of each command at work.

Before we learn about specific loops and conditional statements, let's find out how to define a block in Java. We need to understand what blocks are to predict the scope of variables in our programs and the overall flow of our programs. A *block* is defined by surrounding any number of statements within a pair of curly brackets: { }. The scope of the variables is defined within the blocks we create, with the stipulation that if a block is within another block and both exist at the same time, the same variable can't be defined within both of these blocks simultaneously.

SYNTAX With this brief introduction to blocks—which again are essentially the same as in C and C++—let's learn about the syntax Java uses to control the flow of our programs. Take a look at some sample statements a teacher might find useful, describing the assignment of letter grades when we know the number grades out of 100. First let's declare some variables:

```
int numberGrade;//declaring the variables
char letterGrade;
String remark;
```

Now let's assign our first letter grades, as shown in the following sections.

IF We know that everyone in our class with a number grade 90 or above should receive a letter grade of *A*:

```
if (numberGrade >= 90)
    letterGrade = 'A';
```

What if we want to add a comment for those A students? To add more than one statement to be completed within the scope of the **if** statement, we add curly brackets around the multiple statements, as follows:

```
if (numberGrade >= 90) {
   letterGrade = 'A';
   remark = "Excellent work";
}
```

What if not all the grades are above 90? We need a more general case to encompass more grading possibilities. To create a case for those other grades, we can use the else statement.

ELSE For now, we will just offer a remark for all the students who aren't receiving an *A*. We will get more specific about the other grades in a moment.

```
if (numberGrade >= 90) {
   letterGrade = 'A';
   remark = "Excellent work";
}
else
   remark = "Room for improvement";
```

Of course, there's a big difference among the grades left over. *B* work should be awarded differently from failing the course. We will use the **else...if** statement to cover this more general conditional case of including all the possible grades.

ELSE IF That should give you a good basis as we start using conditional statements in our programs. Now let's turn to the basic control loops the Java language offers.

Listing 3-4.
Sample **else...if** statement.

```
if (numberGrade >= 90) {
   letterGrade = 'A';
   remark = "Excellent work";
}
else if ((numberGrade >= 80)) {
   letterGrade = 'B';
   remark = "Good job";
}
else if ((numberGrade >= 70)) {
   letterGrade = 'C';
   remark = "Room for improvement";
}
else
   letterGrade = 'F';
   remark = "Please see me immediately";
```

LOOPS Imagine you're a teacher and you want to write a program that loops through all the number grades in the class and calculates which students currently have *A*'s and which need to improve their grades. We will learn how to use the two basic Java control loops for this purpose, with every student receiving either an **A** for his or her work or an *I* for incomplete.

WHILE There are six students in the class, and we're going to create three arrays—one of letter grades, one of number grades, and one of comments, as follows:

```
int[] numberGrade = {95, 45, 78, 97, 88, 72};
int[] letterGrade = new char[6];
String[] remark = new String[6];
```

We already know the number grades, so we have placed those in the array. We want to write a **while** loop that allows us to fill in the last two arrays we have just made.

FOR It's possible to write the same functionality into a **for** loop, also:

```
for (j=0; j<6, j++) {
  if (numberGrade[j] >= 90) {
    letterGrade[j] = 'A';
    remark[j] = "Excellent work";
  }
  else {
    letterGrade[j] = 'I';
    remark[j] = "Room for improvement";
  }
}
```

In fact, the **for** loop can just be thought of as a shorthand way of writing a specific type of **while** loop. We won't spend any more time on these control structures because they're quite similar to C/C++, as we're

Listing 3-5.
Example of a **while** loop.

```
int j=0;
while (j < 6) {
  if (numberGrade[j] >= 90) {
    letterGrade[j] = 'A';
    remark[j] = "Excellent work";
  }
  else {
    letterGrade[j] = 'I';
    remark[j] = "Room for improvement";
    }
  j++;
}
```

sure you've noticed. Instead, let's turn our attention to learning about classes and packages in Java, and then finally to our first Java programs.

Classes

Classes are templates for user-defined objects in an object-oriented language. Java, as you will see, is truly object-oriented from the ground up; within it, you will learn to be quite flexible with classes and their relationship to object-oriented programming and object design. To begin exploring Java classes, let's look more closely at some different parts within one class structure.

We will walk through the following class step-by-step to begin to understand what's actually happening in even the simplest Java program:

```
public class Simple {
  public static void main (String argv[]) {
    String myDog = "Mutt";
    System.out.print("My dog is called " + myDog);
  }
}
```

Let's take the simple class and define a variable **myDog** and assign a value of **"Mutt"**. You will remember from earlier in this section how to assign variables. We will add onto this a statement that prints the value of the variables to standard output:

```
String myDog = "Mutt";
System.out.print("My dog is called " + myDog);
```

In this code, we first assign the string variable **myDog** to the value **"Mutt"**. The next line then uses **System.out.print()**; to tell the Java program to take the contents between the parentheses and print it to the standard output.

To have our Java program actually print the preceding statement, we need to define a **main** inside a class definition. This is very similar to programming in C, in which the body of the program would be defined within the **main()** definition. In Java, this is done as in the following:

```
public static void main (String argv[]) {
  String myDog = "Mutt";
  System.out.print("My dog is called " + myDog);
}
```

We will look at this in more detail in the next section when we write and compare applets and applications. For now, we will briefly describe what the following piece of code is doing.

You should see a series of keywords: **public static void**, which are located directly in front of the **main()** definition. These keywords define the behavior of the definition. The keyword **public** describes how accessible the **main()** method should be. The keyword **static** describes the **main()** method as a class method and not an instance method. Finally, the keyword **void** indicates what the **main()** method will return; in this case, the method returns no value.

Now that we have worked our way from the inside out, we're ready to describe the class defintion. The class definition defines some properties about the class. The first thing to recognize is the name of the class:

```
public class Simple {
}
```

The name of the class is **Simple**. This is important to note because it's also the name of the Java source file: **Simple.java**. Once compiled, the file will conveniently be called **Simple.class**.

The class definition also has keywords that describe the class' properties —**public** and **class**. The **public** keyword decribes how accessible the class will be, and the **class** keyword indicates that a class is being defined.

This program is very elementary. To compile and run it, you first need to type the entire contents of the program into a file:

```
public class Simple {
   public static void main (String argv[]) {
    String myDog = "Mutt";
    System.out.print("My dog is called " + myDog);
   }
}
```

Save this file with the name **Simple.java** and compile it using the Java compiler with the command:

```
javac Simple.java
```

Once the program has been compiled, you will notice that you now have two files: **Simple.java** and **Simple.class**. You can execute the program by using this command:

```
java Simple
```

This command tells the Java Virtual Machine to load the object `Simple`, which loads the `Simple.class` file and executes the contents, returning this:

```
My dog is called Mutt
```

If you're interested in understanding more about classes, especially in relation to object-oriented programming, don't worry because we will come back to this topic in the OOP section of the chapter. For now, we will give you a brief overview of packages in Java and then begin to explain your first real Java programs. So if the description we have given on running your code isn't in-depth enough depth, we will provide more details shortly.

Packages

The classes in Java language are grouped into packages, which make up the Java API. This collection of packages is a constantly growing resource upon which to base your Java programming needs. All your code will be built at least partially from these packages.

Only one package in Java is implicit in all Java programs—the java.lang package. The rest, whether written by you, or as part of the Java API, must be referred to explicitly in your code by using the **import** statement with the java.awt package as follows:

```
import java.awt.*;     //imports all the classes in the awt
                       //package
import java.awt.graphics; /*this imports only the graphics
                            class within the awt package.*/
```

Let's take a moment to learn about all the packages currently in the Java API:

- **package java.applet:** The java.applet package is a relatively small package containing the `Applet` class from which all applets are derived. Applets have a set of behaviors that include `init()`, `start()`, `stop()`, and `destroy()`. These methods control applet execution and initialization.

- **package java.awt:** The java.awt package, or Advanced Windowing Toolkit, provides classes for developing GUIs. The classes can be divided into four categories:

1. Graphics

2. Components

3. Layout managers

4. Image manipulation

The graphics class provides classes for graphical widgets (buttons, menus, checkboxes, and so on) and drawing elements (lines, text, and so forth). These classes access other graphics classes, such as `Color` and `Font`, that give more precise visual control. All these graphics objects are put into components such as frames and panels. They are arranged visually by using the layout managers that are in charge of controlling how the objects are placed within a container.

Recent additions to the AWT class include extending the functionality of a `Clipboard` class in the java.awt.datatransfer package, as well as image manipulation filters in the java.awt.image package.

- **package java.beans:** JavaBeans extends Java's "Write Once, Run Anywhere" capability to reusable component development. In fact, JavaBeans takes interoperability a major step forward—your code runs in every application environment as well as on any operating system.

- **package java.io:** This package contains classes of objects defined for basic *Input / Output* (I/O). Included here are input/output streams for strings, files and buffered data.

- **package java.lang:** This is the most essential package in the language. It contains classes that supply objects corresponding to primitive data types, such boolean, int, or float. A `Boolean` object (notice how the object name is capitalized) is much different from its `boolean` (lowercase) counterpart. Although this package could be thought of as the foundation of Java, the objects in this package have a set of behaviors and attributes just like any other class in the other packages, as we will see shortly. Also included in this package are classes for threads and strings as well as classes for mathematical functions and constants.

- **package java.math:** The math package contains functions such as square root, sine, random, log—all your basic functions and many more. Two new classes have recently been added, which are `BigInteger` and `BigDecimal`. `BigInteger` numbers provide operations for modular arithmetic, GCD calculation, primality testing, prime generation, and single-bit manipulation. `BigDecimal` numbers are ideal for monetary calculations; they supply operations for basic arithmetic, scale manipulation, comparison, format conversion, and hashing.

- **package java.net:** This package is the Java mechanism for network access and control. Included are classes for sockets and URLs.

- **package java.rmi:** RMI allows you to create distributed Java-to-Java applications, in which the methods of remote Java objects can be invoked from other Java virtual machines, possibly even on different hosts.

- **package java.security:** This is a new package that contains both low-level and high-level functionality. The security package allows for digital signatures, message digests, and key and certificate management.

- **package java.sql:** *Java Data Base Connectivity* (JDBC) is a standard SQL database access interface, providing uniform access to a wide range of relational databases.

- **package java.util:** Just as the name implies, this is a class of utilities including classes for dates, stacks, and vectors. **JAR** is a new class in the java.util.zip package that allows class files, sounds, and images to be archived for easier distribution. This greatly enhances the speed of transmission time for network requests.

We need to keep all these packages in mind as we begin to write our first applets and applications. Let's take a more in-depth look at how applets work, learn about security issues involving applets, see why applets and applications are different, and finally write some complete Java programs.

Applets

A Java applet is a program that can be included in a Java-enabled Web browser, such as Netscape, Microsoft Internet Explorer, or Mosaic. The process of loading and viewing applets is simple in networked environments, which is one of the reasons why they're so popular. To load the applets you will be creating into Web pages, you need to have two files: The class file of the Java applet and an HTML file that communicates the location of the applet (on the network) to the browser and any additional relevant information on the applet.

Applets run because of four methods in the **Applet** class:

- **init():** Java calls the **init()** method when the applet is loaded for the first time. This method is used for setting up initializations within an applet and for processing **<PARAM>** tags that can send applet parameters from the HTML document that loaded the applet.

- Functionality:
- Called by the browser when the applet is loaded into the system
- Always called before the **start()** method is called
- The default implementation by **Applet** does nothing
- Subclass of **Applet** should override **init()** if it needs to initialize variables, create threads, load images, and so on
- **start():** Java calls this method automatically after the **init()** method. The **start()** method is used to keep track of the focus of the applet. A user visits a page with an applet and sees it running, then leaves the page to visit another site; after returning to the page with the applet, the **start()** method is called again. This method can be called more than once within an applet (unlike the **init()** method).

Functionality:

- Called by the browser to start **applet** execution
- Called after the **init()** method and each time the applet is revisited in a Web page
- The default implementation by **Applet** does nothing
- Subclass of **Applet** should override if it has operations that must be performed each time the Web page containing it is visited (for example, to resume animation)
- **stop():** The **stop()** method is called automatically in your applet when the user either moves to another HTML page or when the applet loses visual focus (for example, if the user scrolls away from an applet, which is then no longer visible within the HTML page).
- Functionality:
- Called by the browser to stop execution—that is, if the Web page is being replaced or the current applet is about to be destroyed
- The default implementation by **Applet** does nothing
- Subclass of **Applet** should override if it has operations that must be performed each time the Web page containing it is no longer visible (for instance, if we want to stop an animation)
- **destroy():** Java calls the **destroy()** method for applets when the user quits the browser. The programmer of applets doesn't need to worry about freeing up the used memory of a Java applet. Remember, Java has a built-in garbage collection system.

■ Functionality:

■ Called by the browser when it's getting rid of an applet to reclaim the resources the applet is tying up

■ The default implementation by `Applet` does nothing

■ Subclass of `Applet` should override if it has operations that must be performed before the applet is destroyed (for example, to kill threads)

WHY IS JAVA SECURITY SUCH A BIG DEAL   As we enter a new paradigm of computing, one that's much more interconnected and networked, completely new issues arise for writing software. Java applets and applications are built within this new paradigm and are specially designed to move relatively "freely" within a networked environment. Applets in particular are built to be downloaded from a remote site and then executed on your local machine.

But what about security? Is it safe to download any applet? Without security, you would never know whether the applet you're downloading is hostile or friendly.

The applets you run on your machine are purposely limited in the scope of what they can and can't do. In the Java programming language, applets can't run any local executable program. For example, a Java applet couldn't tell the Notepad application to launch, and for our benefit, couldn't run the Format program in C:\DOS. Applets are also restricted in their scope of communication; they are allowed to "talk" back only to the host from which they originated.

Of course, the level of security varies. In some browser implementations of Java, local applets are allowed to read and write to the local computer's file system, but other browsers have much stricter "rules" of interaction. For instance, Netscape doesn't allow Java applets to read files, write files, get file information, delete files, or run another application at any time. No applets downloaded from the Internet are able to load libraries or define native method calls. Imagine if the applet could make native method calls; then it could potentially have direct control over the entire computer!

The Java security mechanism is a system composed of several interlocking layers that each in turn check whether an applet is safe and can be trusted. The security is implemented both at the language level and during the compilation process. We discussed this process while we were learning how the Java Virtual Machine functioned earlier in this chapter. Briefly, if the compilation process has been somehow reconfigured, Java checks and verifies the program's intermediate bytecode. Simple tests are done at this level to make sure the code doesn't forge pointers or violate access restrictions. Tests are also performed to check whether the code accesses APIs and classes as they are, whether calls to methods are done with the same number of arguments of the proper type, and whether there will be any stack overflows. After this testing process, the code must also be checked and approved by the Class Loader. The final level of detection takes place on the local system and the network. The interfaces must be secured before any applet is allowed to run.

Security in Java is designed to be robust. As an important component of the Java environment, it has been built into the language from the ground up. A lot of research has been carried out to carefully design and implement the security features in the Java Virtual Machine and the Java APIs. At the same time, the language isn't bullet-proof. To contend with this, all discovered bugs are immediately reported to Sun where they can be evaluated and fixed, if necessary. A good reference to keep in mind for the latest in Java and browser security is the Princeton Secure Internet Programming Web site at `http://www.cs.princeton.edu/sip/News.html`. This group has documented bugs in Java since November 1995.

The Java security we have discussed so far is really just the beginning of the Java security we will see in the future. Perhaps the biggest advance in recent security features was the first release of the Java Security API in JDK version 1.1. This API begins to address some of the bigger security issues Sun needs to come to terms with. It includes functionality for digital signatures, message digests, abstract interfaces for key management, and certificate management, as well as features for access control. This first release of the Java security API also provides tools that can sign JAR files, which means that any applets downloaded by the appletviewer in signed JAR format (by someone you trust) can be assured as friendly and given the same rights and privileges as local applications on the same machine.

The features in the JDK 1.1 should be seen as a groundwork. They will be enhanced in later releases that will have more comprehensive and sophisticated security mechanisms. These mechanisms will include a more complex method of dealing with signed JAR files, integrating greater diversity in establishing and incorporating levels of trust into the system. Specific APIs will also be developed to support X.509 v3 certificates, as well as other certificate formats. In addition, control of access will be improved to allow more functionality in this area.

Now that we know a little about how applets work and how the Java team has offered a security system that allows applets to freely travel across the Internet, let's turn to making our first applets. First, we will write an applet and an application, comparing the two to give you a better understanding of the differences in these two Java programs, and then we will explore some fun interactive applets that you can use as you begin to write your own.

Applets Versus Applications

At this point, you might be wondering what makes applets so different from other Java applications. There are a few important differences between applets and standalone programs (applications). First, Java applications are built to run independently without an Internet browser. In fact, one of the first applications written entirely in Java was a browser itself—the HotJava browser built by Sun. HotJava was the first browser that allowed interactive applets to run over the Internet. Since then, many more robust applications, ranging from intranet software to telephony systems, have been written entirely in Java. They include Applix's Anyware Office, the Corel Office for Java by the Corel Corporation, and Dynamo by the Art Technology Group. Applets, on the other hand, are built solely to run and function in a networked environment within Internet browsers.

To give you a better idea of some of the basic differences between applets and applications, we're now going to look at some simple programs. Actually, these are our first complete programs in Java! We will walk through two similar examples of code; one is an applet that loads in a browser and displays inside a Java-enabled browser the following text:

```
Hello World! from inside a Java applet...
```

The other is a Java application that displays the following text at the command line:

```
Hello World! from inside a Java application...
```

We will describe the basic elements of each program and describe the features that make them unique as they operate in their separate environments.

SAMPLE APPLET   The following code in Listing 3-6 can be used as the starting point for developing an applet. It's available on the CD-ROM that accompanies this book in the file called **HelloApplet.java** and then compile with the javac compiler. The javac compiler will then produce a file called **HelloApplet.class** (assuming everything was compiled properly).

Listing 3-6.
The HelloApplet
applet.

```
import java.awt.*;
import java.applet.*;

public class HelloApplet extends Applet
{
   public void paint(Graphics g)}
Font ourFont = new Font("Helvetica", Font.BOLD, 24);
{
   g.setFont(ourFont);
   g.drawString("Hello World! ", 30,40);
   g.drawString("from inside a Java applet...", 60,40);
   }
   }
```

For the applet to run within an Internet browser, it's also necessary to write some HTML code that tells the browser to load the applet we have just made. Use the file called **hello.html** on the CD-ROM. The source for the HTML code looks like Listing 3-7.

To view the applet, make sure that both the **hello.html** and the **HelloApplet.class** files are in the same directory. This is necessary because the **HelloApplet.class** is being referenced in the HTML code through a relative URL. This occurs when we call **CODE="HelloApplet.class"**. We have just given the name of the file directly, so it must reside in the same directory as the HTML that calls it.

At this point, we're ready to test our applet. Open the local file **hello.html** in a Java-enabled browser, and you should see this text:

```
Hello World! from inside a Java applet...
```

This is our first official Java applet!

Let's now look at how to make an application that has a similar function to the applet we just created.

SAMPLE APPLICATION   We're going to jump right into our application and give you the code immediately:

```
public class HelloApplication
{
 public static void main(String[] args)
 {
      System.out.println("Hello World! ");
    System.out.println("from inside a Java application...");
   }
}
```

Place this in a file called **HelloApplication.java** and then proceed as follows. At the command line, type **javac HelloApplication.java**. This command compiles the Java file and creates **HelloApplication.class**. To run the application, type **java HelloApplication**, and the following should appear at the command line:

```
Hello World! from inside a Java application...
```

You should have noticed there are quite a few differences between the applet and this application. In fact, except for a few similarities in syntax, they seem to have little else in common. We realize a lot of this code might be foreign to you, but for now we'll just focus on a few aspects of the program that define applets as opposed to applications.

WHAT MAKES AN APPLET AN APPLET   Here are some clues:

▪ Must be defined as a subclass of the **Applet** class

Every applet is a subclass of the **Applet** class and must be defined as such. In the preceding example, our subclass was named **HelloApplet**. This definition procedure is important not only for helping to define a program as an applet, but also because the applets we create usually inherit a wide range of functionalities from the **Applet** class.

▪ Must implement one of the following methods: **init()**, **start()**, **paint()**

You might have been wondering how the applet begins. What sign is there that tells the browser what part of the applet to execute first? Well, every applet uses one of three methods to begin execu-

Listing 3-7.
Helloapplet
HTML code.

```
<HTML>
  <HEAD>
   <TITLE> A Simple Applet </TITLE>
  </HEAD>
  <BODY>
   Here is an applet inside of the browser:
   <P>
   <APPLET CODE="HelloApplet.class" WIDTH=150 HEIGHT=25>
   </APPLET>
  </BODY>
</HTML>
```

tion: `init()`, `start()`, or `paint()`. They're used instead of the `main()` method that applications use.

▓ Used with HTML and the `<APPLET>` tag

Applets are designed for the WWW. They are included inside HTML pages simply by placing the `<APPLET>` tag in the location you want in your Web page. You can specify the height and width of your applet so that when the browser encounters this request it will leave enough room to load your applet correctly.

WHAT MAKES AN APPLICATION AN APPLICATION   Here are some more clues:

▓ Must define a class

Every Java application must have at its core a class definition because in Java, everything must exist within a class, whether they're variables or methods. There's no such thing as a global variable or function.

▓ Must have a `main()` method

Just as the `init()`, `start()`, or `paint()` methods are used to indicate the starting point of every applet, the `main()` method serves this function in applications. It works by giving the name of the class you want to execute to the Java interpreter. The interpreter then finds and begins the `main()` method in that class. The `main()` method is in control of the overall flow, resources, and methods of the entire application.

Interactive Applets

In this section, we will walk you through three applets for creating a Java Seer program. What is a Java Seer? Basically, an oracular applet that tells your fortune. Why a Java Seer? You never know when an applet like that might come in handy, and the skills you pick up creating these applets can be transferred directly to all applets.

The first applet will describe how to use the AWT widgets to make and take advantage of simple user interfaces within applets. The second applet will build on the knowledge we gained from the first applet and introduce methods that generate responses to user questions. The third applet will transform the previous applets by introducing graphics and the `paint()` method.

MAGIC1 JAVA SEER APPLET   This first applet is quite simple and will explain how to create a simple user interface. The following code can be typed into an editor and saved as **Magic1.java**, or you can use the file on the CD-ROM (see Figure 3-2). This file can then be compiled with the javac compiler by using this command:

```
javac Magic1.java
```

Following Listing 3-8 is the HTML code that can be loaded into a Java-enabled browser; the applet will then load and run.

Let's look more closely at what's happening in the code in the previous example. We can look at the applet as a series of parts. Magic1 applet is the entire code for the applet. Inside the code are individual sections and methods. We will walk though the separate methods in the class. An outline of the code structure follows:

> **Magic1 Applet**
>> API Packages
>> **Class Magic1**
>>> **Button 1 clicked method**
>>> Initialization
>>> Event Handling
>>> Declared Controls

API PACKAGES   The first section of the code describes the packages and methods we will be using in the applet. You can see that we're importing references to all the classes in the java.awt, java.applet, and java.lang packages. By importing these packages, we can use any one the classes defined in these methods through the following code:

```
import java.awt.*;
import java.applet.*;
import java.lang.*;
```

CLASS MAGIC1   Our applet is defined as a class by the following line of code:

```
public class Magic1 extends Applet { }
```

You will notice that **Magic1** extends **Applet**; this means that Magic1 is inheriting all its base methods from the **Applet** class. All our code is defined within the **Magic1** class.

Figure 3-2.
Screenshot of the
Magic1 applet.

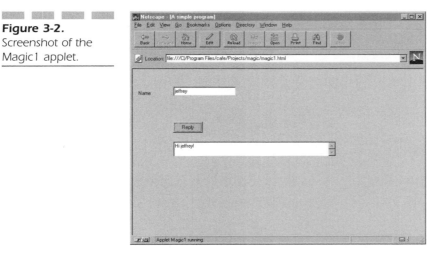

Listing 3-8.
Magic1 applet.

```java
import java.awt.*;
import java.applet.*;
import java.lang.*;

public class Magic1 extends Applet {

void button1_Clicked(Event event) {
textArea1.show();
String name = textField1.getText();
textArea1.setText("");
textArea1.insertText("Hi " + name + "!", 0);
}

public void init() {
setLayout(null);
resize(486,203);
textField1 = new java.awt.TextField();
textField1.reshape(82,26,145,24);
add(textField1);
label1 = new java.awt.Label("Name");
label1.reshape(3,32,45,19);
add(label1);
button1 = new java.awt.Button("Reply");
button1.reshape(82,109,68,26);
add(button1);
textArea1 = new java.awt.TextArea();
textArea1.hide();
textArea1.reshape(82,155,374,38);
add(textArea1);
}
```

Continues

Listing 3-8.
Continued.

```
public boolean handleEvent(Event event) {
if (event.target == button1 && event.id ==
     Event.ACTION_EVENT) {
button1_Clicked(event);
}
return super.handleEvent(event);
}


java.awt.TextField textField1;
java.awt.Label label1;
java.awt.Button button1;
java.awt.TextArea textArea1;


}
```

BUTTON 1 CLICKED METHOD   This method is called whenever the button on the applet is clicked. Within this method, four tasks are being performed. After the button is clicked, the **textArea1** is displayed. When the applet is first created, you will notice that the **textArea1** is hidden. A new string is then created that contains the contents of whatever is in the **textField1**. This is done by using the **getText()** method of the java.awt.**TextField** class. The text in the **textArea1** is then cleared by replacing any current text in the **TextArea** with " ". Last, new text is then printed into the **textArea1**. This text consists of "**Hi**" and the name that's currently in the **textField1**.

```
void button1_Clicked(Event event) {
textArea1.show();
String name = textField1.getText();
textArea1.setText("");
textArea1.insertText("Hi " + name + "!", 0);
}
```

INITIALIZATION   This method is the **init()** method of applets, which we discussed earlier. The **init()** method is called by the browser to determine how the applet should be set up and viewed. The **setLayout()** method sets the layout manager for this container, and in this case the manager is null. The applet is then resized to 486 pixels × 203 pixels. You will then see four roughly similar parts of code that each make separate AWT widget controls.

We will make a textField, then a label, then a button, and finally a textArea. Each of these widgets has three lines of code. First, a **TextField** is created; the **TextField** is then resized to start at coordinate (82,26) and extend 145 pixels in the X direction and 24 pixels in the Y direction. A label is then created. A *label* is a piece of text that can be used for visual purposes. A button is then made, and finally, a **TextArea** is made and then hidden after it's created.

EVENT HANDLING   The next method allows the applet to handle and manage events that take place through the applet user interface. We're concerned about one potential user event for this first applet. We just want to know when the button is clicked:

```
public boolean handleEvent(Event event) {
if (event.target == button1 && event.id ==
Event.ACTION_EVENT) {
button1_Clicked(event);
}
return super.handleEvent(event);
}
```

DECLARED CONTROLS   The declared controls for this applet begin to describe the variables in the class itself. In this applet, we're declaring only the following:

```
java.awt.TextField textField1;
java.awt.Label label1;
java.awt.Button button1;
java.awt.TextArea textArea1;
```

HTML FOR THE MAGIC1 JAVA SEER APPLET   The following HTML code is available on the CD-ROM as **magic1.html**. The code in Listing 3-10 can also be copied and pasted into a text editor and saved as **magic1.html**. Once this file is loaded in a Java-enabled browser, the preceding class will load and run.

MAGIC2 JAVA SEER APPLET   The second applet we will examine builds on the knowledge we gained from the first applet and introduces an AWT location for users to enter a question. The Java Seer program then randomly selects from a few preselected responses and answers your question. You will notice an additional button that clears the name and question fields.

The following code can be typed into an editor and saved as **Magic2.java**, or you can use **Magic2.java** on the CD-ROM (see Figure 3-3). This file then can be compiled with the javac compiler by using this command:

```
javac Magic2.java
```

Following this code in Listing 3-11 is the HTML code that can be loaded into a Java-enabled browser; the applet will then load and run.

Listing 3-9.
Magic1 **init()**
method.

```
public void init() {
setLayout(null);
resize(486,203);
textField1 = new java.awt.TextField();
textField1.reshape(82,26,145,24);
add(textField1);
label1 = new java.awt.Label("Name");
label1.reshape(3,32,45,19);
add(label1);
button1 = new java.awt.Button("Reply");
button1.reshape(82,109,68,26);
add(button1);
textArea1 = new java.awt.TextArea();
textArea1.hide();
textArea1.reshape(82,155,374,38);
add(textArea1);
}
```

Listing 3-10.
Magic1 HTML code.

```
<HTML>
<HEAD>
<TITLE> A simple Java Seer program </TITLE>
</HEAD>
<BODY>
Here is the first applet:<P>

<APPLET CODE="Magic1.class" WIDTH=486 HEIGHT=203></APPLET>

</BODY>
</HTML>
```

Figure 3-3.
Screenshot of the
Magic2 applet.

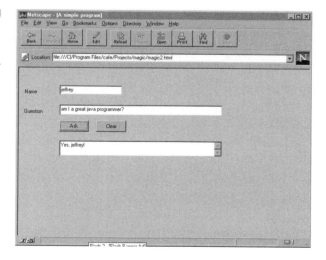

Listing 3-11.
Magic2 applet.

```java
import java.awt.*;
import java.applet.*;
import java.lang.*;

public class Magic2 extends Applet {

void button1_Clicked(Event event) {
String name = textField1.getText();
String response = chooseResponse(); //get a random response
textArea1.show(); // show the textarea
textArea1.setText(""); // erase text in the answer area
textArea1.insertText(response + " " + name + "!", 0);
}

void button2_Clicked(Event event) {
   textArea1.setText("");
textArea1.hide();
textField1.setText("");
textField2.setText("");
}

    String chooseResponse() {
      int number = (int)(Math.random()*8);
      String responses[] = {"Of course,",
        "No way,",
        "Looks good,",
        "Need more time, ask again later,",
        "No doubt,",
        "Yes,",
        "No,",
        "I can't answer that,"
        };
    return (responses[number]);
  }

public void init() {
setLayout(null);
resize(486,203);
textField1 = new java.awt.TextField();
textField1.reshape(82,26,145,24);
add(textField1);
textField2 = new java.awt.TextField();
textField2.reshape(82,71,374,27);
add(textField2);
label1 = new java.awt.Label("Name");
label1.reshape(3,32,45,19);
add(label1);
label2 = new java.awt.Label("Question");
label2.reshape(2,79,56,18);
add(label2);
button1 = new java.awt.Button("Ask");
```

Continues

Listing 3-11.
Continued.

```
button1.reshape(82,109,68,26);
add(button1);
button2 = new java.awt.Button("Clear");
button2.reshape(167,109,68,26);
add(button2);
textArea1 = new java.awt.TextArea();
textArea1.hide();
textArea1.reshape(82,155,374,38);
add(textArea1);
}

public boolean handleEvent(Event event) {
if (event.target == button1 && event.id ==
    Event.ACTION_EVENT) {
button1_Clicked(event);
}
if (event.target == button2 && event.id ==
    Event.ACTION_EVENT) {
button2_Clicked(event);
}
return super.handleEvent(event);
}

java.awt.TextField textField1;
java.awt.TextField textField2;
java.awt.Label label1;
java.awt.Label label2;
java.awt.Button button1;
java.awt.Button button2;
java.awt.TextArea textArea1;

}
```

Magic2 Applet

API Packages

Class Magic1

Button 1 clicked method

Button 2 clicked method

Choose Response method

Initialization

Event Handling

Declared Controls

We will explain the three methods shown in bold type for this applet. The remainder of the applet is built much like the first applet.

BUTTON 1 CLICKED METHOD The following method is similar to the button click method from our first applet except for the line that assigns the **String** variable response from the **chooseResponse()** method. The method still hides and shows the **textArea** and will display the response from the **chooseResponse()** method plus the name inserted into the name **textField1**:

```
void button1_Clicked(Event event) {
String name = textField1.getText();
String response = chooseResponse(); //get a random response
textArea1.show(); // show the textarea
textArea1.setText(""); // erase text in the answer area
textArea1.insertText(response + " " + name + "!", 0);
}
```

BUTTON 2 CLICKED METHOD The following method is implemented when the second button (the Clear button) is clicked in the applet. This applet is responsible for four tasks: Clear the text in the **textArea1**, hide the **textArea1**, clear the text in **textField1**, and clear the text in **textField2**.

```
void button2_Clicked(Event event) {
   textArea1.setText("");
textArea1.hide();
textField1.setText("");
textField2.setText("");
}
```

Listing 3-12.
Magic2 oracular
responses.

```
String chooseResponse() {
  int number = (int)(Math.random()*8);
  String responses[] = {"Of course,",
    "No way,",
    "Looks good,",
    "Need more time, ask again later,",
    "No doubt,",
    "Yes,",
    "No,",
    "I can't answer that,"
    };
  return (responses[number]);
}
```

CHOOSE RESPONSE METHOD The `chooseResponse()` method selects a random integer between 0 and 7. The method then initializes a string array that's filled with a variety of responses. A response is then returned to the calling applet with the value of the random integer in the position of the array.

HTML FOR THE MAGIC2 JAVA SEER APPLET This HTML code in Listing 3-13 is the same as the HTML code from our first applet, except the applet loaded through this page is called Magic2. It's available as `magic2.html` on the CD-ROM.

MAGIC3 JAVA SEER APPLET The last applet we will walk through creates a Java Seer applet that introduces you to using graphic tools, such as loading images over the network, and painting text with a `paint()` method. The structure for responses, entering a question and a name, are the same as the Magic2 applet (see Figure 3-4).

Listing 3-13.
Magic2 HTML code.

```
<HTML>
<HEAD>
<TITLE> A simple Java Seer program </TITLE>
</HEAD>
<BODY>
Here is the second applet:<P>

<APPLET CODE="Magic2.class" WIDTH=486 HEIGHT=203></APPLET>

</BODY>
</HTML>
```

Figure 3-4.
Screenshot of the
Magic3 applet.

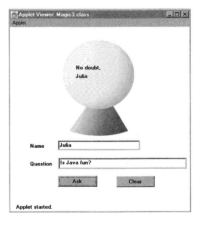

Listing 3-14.
Magic3 applet.

```java
import java.awt.*;
import java.applet.*;
import java.net.*;
import java.lang.*;

public class Magic3 extends Applet {
void ask_Clicked(Event event) {
    repaint();
}

void clear_Clicked(Event event) {
textField2.setText("");
textField1.setText("");
repaint();
}

  String chooseResponse() {
    int number = (int)(Math.random()*8);
    String responses[] = {"Of course,",
      "No way,",
      "Looks good,",
      "Ask again later,",
      "No doubt,",
      "Yes,",
      "No,",
      "I can't answer that,"
      };
    return (responses[number]);
  }

public void init() {
setLayout(null);
resize(409,412);
ask = new java.awt.Button("Ask");
ask.reshape(109,349,89,26);
add(ask);
textField1 = new java.awt.TextField();
textField1.reshape(109,266,187,23);
add(textField1);
textField2 = new java.awt.TextField();
textField2.reshape(110,307,292,26);
add(textField2);
name = new java.awt.Label("Name");
name.reshape(32,271,70,15);
add(name);
question = new java.awt.Label("Question");
question.reshape(32,313,70,15);
add(question);
clear = new java.awt.Button("Clear");
clear.reshape(242,350,87,26);
add(clear);
```

Conrinues

Listing 3-14.
Continued.

```
try {
    String s1 =
"http://www.americasguide.com/research/ball.gif";
    URL ball = new URL(s1);
    image1 = Toolkit.getDefaultToolkit().getImage(ball);
       }
     catch(MalformedURLException e) {
     System.out.println("Error in URL " + e);
     }
}

public void paint(Graphics g) {
  g.drawImage(image1,60,0, this);
  if (textField1.getText().compareTo("") != 0) {
  g.drawString(chooseResponse(),150,100);
  g.drawString(textField1.getText(), 150,120);
  }
  else {
   g.drawString("Enter name & Question", 135, 100);
  }
}

  public boolean handleEvent(Event event) {
if (event.target == clear && event.id ==
Event.ACTION_EVENT) {
clear_Clicked(event);
}
if (event.target == ask && event.id == Event.ACTION_EVENT)
    {
ask_Clicked(event);
}
 return super.handleEvent(event);
   }

java.awt.Button ask;
java.awt.TextField textField1;
java.awt.TextField textField2;
java.awt.Label name;
java.awt.Label question;
java.awt.Button clear;
   private Image image1;
}
```

Here's the outline of the preceding code with the similarities to our first applet in normal text and the differences in bold type.

Magic3 Applet

API Packages

Class Magic1

> **Button 1 (ask) clicked method**
> **Button 2 (clear) clicked method**
> Choose Response method
> **Initialization**
> **Paint Method**
> Event Handling
> **Declared Controls**

BUTTON 1 (ASK) AND BUTTON 2 (CLEAR) METHODS The two buttons in this Magic3 Java Seer class perform a different task from the buttons in applets 1 and 2. You will notice that both methods have this line:

```
repaint();
```

The **repaint()** method in both of these button click methods calls the **paint()** method that we describe later. The **repaint()** method updates any activity in the graphics context.

INITIALIZATION You will also notice a few new things in the **init()** method of the Magic3 Java Seer applet. In particular, you will see this code:

```
try {
    String s1 =
"http://www.americasguide.com/research/ball.gif";
    URL ball = new URL(s1);
    image1 = Toolkit.getDefaultToolkit().getImage(ball);
    }
    catch(MalformedURLException e) {
      System.out.println("Error in URL " + e);
    }
```

In this code, you should notice a block that includes **try{}** and **catch() {}**. This code is called *catching exceptions*. When you catch an exception in Java, it's checked at runtime at actual execution to make sure the applet can run the section of code between **try{}**; if the applet has a problem completing the code in the **try{}** statement, the applet jumps to the exception statement and then completes the information in that area.

The **init()** method is also setting up a string that contains a URL. This string is then converted to a URL, and a larger scheme for loading the images is determined.

PAINT() METHOD The **paint()** method of the applet is responsible for adding graphics to the applet. The applet loads an image as a URL and refreshes the graphic screen. To put graphic images or graphic text into a window, you have to override the **paint()** method from the **Component** class. The **paint()** method has one parameter, **Graphics** (in our case, **g**). The **Graphics** object is responsible for keeping track of the variables and the state of the **Component**. You will notice that to draw graphics text (painting text) or to place an image in our context, we need to use the methods of the **Graphics** object:

```
public void paint(Graphics g) {
   g.drawImage(image1,60,0, this);
   if (textField1.getText().compareTo("") != 0) {
   g.drawString(chooseResponse(),150,100);
   g.drawString(textField1.getText(), 150,120);
   }
   else {
    g.drawString("Enter name & Question", 135, 100);
   }
}
```

We have one image: **image1**. It's a declared variable for the applet. To have it display graphically on the screen, we need to use the **drawImage()** method of the **Graphics** object:

```
boolean drawImage(Image img, int x, int y, ImageObserver
     observer)
```

We use **drawImage()** in the following method:

```
g.drawImage(image1, 60, 0, this);
```

We call this method with four parameters: The image we would like to draw, the x-coordinate (of the upper-left corner), the y-coordinate of the upper-left corner, and the object to be notified of the rendering process (**ImageObserver observer**—in this case, the **Graphics** object **g**).

Text can be graphically drawn in the **Graphics** object by using this method:

```
void drawString(String str, int x, int y)
```

We use the **drawString()** method in the following method:

```
g.drawString(textField1.getText(), 150,120);
```

DECLARED CONTROLS You will also notice that an image is defined as one of the variables in the following class, as well as the buttons, labels, and text areas defined in the previous Java Seer applets:

```
private Image image1;
```

HTML FOR THE MAGIC3 JAVA SEER APPLET   The HTML code shown in List-ing 3-15 is the same as the previous HTML code except that the applet loaded through this page is called Magic3. It's **Magic3.html** on the CD-ROM. Note that the following applet and HTML code should be loaded with the appletviewer supplied with the Java Development Toolkit. We have discussed the security options of Java in detail, so we note that if this applet is called in a browser, it will result in a security violation by loading a foreign URL. If you load this applet in the appletviewer, the im-age for the external URL loads properly.

The three applets we have shown should give you a brief introduction to simple programming with Java in a browser environment. We have shown how to use the AWT to place interfaces and to get and change the content of windows. We have shown how to make a simple method in the applets that computes a response and how to display the result in a **textArea** wid-get and within a graphic context. Now that we're pros at writing applets, let's take a more abstract look at Java's object-oriented aspects.

Java Versus JavaBeans

Simply put, JavaBeans is a platform-neutral component architecture for Java and its developers. Of course, you have to understand what a com-ponent architecture is before you understand what this statement really means, so let's take a look at component architecture and component mod-els before we go any further.

Recently, component models have emerged as a great way to quickly and easily construct applications by creating a simple structure for com-bining, reusing, and transforming software components. A component model is an architecture and set of *Application Programming Interfaces*

Listing 3-15.
Magic3 HTML code.

```
<HTML>
<HEAD>
<TITLE> A simple Java Seer program </TITLE>
</HEAD>
<BODY>
Here is the third applet:<P>

<APPLET CODE="Magic3.class" WIDTH=409 HEIGHT=412></APPLET>

</BODY>
</HTML>
```

(APIs) that allow programmers to actually take components written by anyone and combine them using tools within a visual interface to create new applications and components. This entire process is dynamic. Products such as Microsoft's Visual Basic and Borland's Delphi have been used in application development for years and serve as good examples of component-assembly development models.

At its core, the component assembly model consists of two major elements and six different services or capabilities. The two elements are *components* and *containers*. Components can be anything from a simple GUI widget to a complex application. For example, the component could be visual, like a button; audio-based, like a musical score; or even an entire database-driven application. Containers exist to hold these components together; they supply the context and environment for component interaction.

The six major services of a component model ensure that the components can dynamically communicate, interact, and build with one another within a container. For these functions to exist, the components must be able to show their interfaces to other components, save and show their particular individual properties, and take part in event handling. In addition, the container and component must have a mechanism for storing the state of components, and there must be a visual interface with application-building tools for manipulating the components. Finally, some form of packaging for the components is necessary so that they can be easily distributed and reused.

JavaBeans is a complete component model. The components in the JavaBean model are called the *Beans*, which can be used, reused, and manipulated in a wide variety of ways. They can be applets, but they don't have to be. They can also be applications, GUI widgets, audio scores, and so forth. How can you tell a Bean from a normal piece of Java code? Beans must by definition have the following distinguishing characteristics:

- **Introspection:** This enables the building tools used in the application builder container to look at the Bean and analyze how it works.

- **Customization:** This enables developers to use application-building tools to change the Bean's events. These changes are wide in scope, from the Bean's visual appearance to its behavioral aspects, from audio output to overall functionality. Customization also allows Beans to communicate with one another and connect to each other, allowing further customization of each Bean's internal and external functionality.

- **Properties:** Each Bean must have a way to expose its current state or properties to its environment. Properties can be, for example, the color of a button for a GUI widget, the last note played in an audio file, or the current user name for a particular application. Making these properties accessible to the Bean's outside environment allows establishing standard mechanisms, which can then find out information about the Bean and modify it, if necessary.

- **Persistence:** This characteristic is important if a Bean is customized in the application builder. There must be a way to store the newly-customized features safely so they can be used in the newly-built application and remain easily accessible for future use. Each component's state must be stored within the container's context, or application builder, and also within the context of its relationship to the other components in the application.

To make JavaBeans a true component model, not only must the Beans have the preceding characteristics, but the model must also encompass the following services:

- **Visual application builder tools**: Every component model must have a set of visual tools used to build new applications and work with the components. JavaBeans is no exception. Currently, many application builder tools are available for JavaBean developers, including Visual Café by Symantec, Java Workshop by SunSoft, Jbuilder by Borland, and Visual Age by IBM. If you're interested in finding out more about these tools and many others, you will find a summary of URLs and references at the end of this section.

- **Packaging:** Beans must be easily distributable and redistributable. To make this possible, they must be packaged so that all the resources from which they're made can be sent and retrieved in a compact, unified form. For this purpose, the JavaBeans model includes the *Java ARchive* (JAR) file format. The JAR format is similar to the *Tape Archival* (TAR) format used in UNIX. It packages the Bean's class file with the resources needed, such as images, sounds, files, and so on. This set of resources becomes one unified object that can then be easily disseminated.

JavaBeans isn't merely a standard component model. It builds on the strengths of the Java platform to create a new paradigm in component architecture. These are some of the features of JavaBeans that are inherited from Java:

- **Network-awareness**: JavaBeans is built to be network-aware. It builds on Java's strengths to deliver security, TCP/IP support, and easy downloading.

- **Bridges:** JavaBeans is built to work with proprietary platforms as well as specifically JavaBean-ready containers. The JavaBean code is designed to run on every operating system and in any application environment. Bridges connect Beans to ActiveX so that components with the JavaBeans API can be ported to Microsoft Internet Explorer, Visual Basic, Word, and many other applications. The most recent release of the JavaBeans bridge for ActiveX is available for download at the Sun Java development site (**http://beans/**).

- **Platform:** JavaBeans builds on Java's existing portable platform strengths. With the Java libraries, language, and virtual machine currently available in Web browsers, and soon within the operating systems themselves, Java will truly work on all operating systems. JavaBeans uses Java as a base, allowing JavaBeans to become platform-neutral too. In addition, with bridges being built to ActiveX, Beans will take on both cross-application and cross-platform capabilities.

The JavaBeans architecture expands the functionality of the Java platform to a new level. It allows for more dynamic programming interaction, greater coding flexibility, and the reuse of Java components to quickly create platform-neutral applications.

We hope this brief detour has clarified the distinction between JavaBeans, Java, and applets. There's more about this topic later in the book, but for now, let's turn our focus to the Java platform for a look at the runtime system.

Latest Trends

We will now describe in more detail current Java resources and the different directions in which Java is heading. We begin by taking a look at the latest trends in Java development. We know what exciting opportunities Java has; all around us, the uses for Java are turning into reality. From e-commerce to telephony, the world of Java is expanding to fill an entirely new space in our networked landscape. Let's take a moment to glance at the following trends: Java Management, E-Commerce, Java Media, and telephony.

Java Management

`http://java.sun.com:80/products/JavaManagement/index.html`

Now there's a way to easily develop system, network, and service management applications. The Java development team has come up with the Java Management API to provide interface guidelines, classes, and specifications to make it easier for developers to create complex management applications for varied networks quickly and easily. The following is a partial list of the API contents:

- Java Managment API User Interface Style Guide: This is a paper that supplies guidelines for developing Web interfaces using Java. It's used to create a standard for interfaces to follow.
- *Admin View Module* (AVM): This module provides graphical building blocks to make it easier to create user interfaces in distributed management applications. It's an extension of the Java AWT.
- Managed Data Interfaces: This set of interfaces allows connections between a Java management application and a relational database. They support mapping classes and instances to a relational database.
- Applet Integration Interfaces: These interfaces make it possible for developers to integrate Java applets into the Java Management API.

E-Commerce

`http://java.sun.com:80/products/commerce/index.html`

Commerce on the Internet has become increasingly possible with more implementation of secure payment methods. JavaSoft has been creating the Java E-Commerce tools that will take Internet payment to another level.

Imagine not only that commerce is safe and secure online, but that every application created for commerce has the built-in possibility of communicating and receiving information with or from any other application. That's the idea behind the new JavaSoft programmer tools for commerce. These tools allow all applications written with them to interact with other authorized Java applications.

The complete commerce package produced by JavaSoft is called the Electronic Commerce Framework. The first application built with this framework is called the Java Wallet, which can be used for online shopping and electronic payments. Some features of the framework include the following:

- **Cassettes:** Signed JAR files with controlled entry points. Used to handle specific commerce tasks over the network. Similar to an applet.
- **Gates:** Authentication methods.
- **Permits:** Returned by the gates.
- **Ticket:** Non-reusable token for authorizing a piece of code to perform a specific task.

Java Media

`http://java.sun.com:80/products/java-media/jmf/index.html`

The Web is becoming a hotbed of multimedia activity. The Java Media Framework is designed to provide a platform-independent means of building diverse media players. The framework supports such media as Quick-Time, AVI, WAV, and MIDI. Here are brief introductions to some of the major sections in the Media Framework:

- Media sources: Java media players can be designed to present many different types of sources. Each player is built to play only one type of source, ranging from files to live broadcasts. In general, there two main types of media sources—reliable and streaming. In the reliable source, the client is guaranteed to receive all the information from that source. In a streaming source, the client will have to deal with gaps in data occuring during transmission.
- Media players: These are software that can process a certain type of data. It also has time functions. It implements methods defined by the following interfaces:

    Clock: Controls basic timing and synchronization

    Controller: Preloads data and gets system resources

    Duration: Calculates duration of media

    Player: Supports user controls

▥ Media events: This protocol makes sure that if an asynchronous call on the player is made, the system will be listening for such an occurrence. The system also listens for error reports. Two types of objects post events: The gain controls and the controllers. Controller events can be placed in three separate categories:

Change notifications

Transition events

Error events

Telephony

`http://java.sun.com:80/products/javatel/index.html`

The basic idea behind the *Java Telephony API* (JTAPI) is that it will allow any size of telecommunications and telephony vendors to bring their technologies together with the technology of the Internet. The JTAPI was built to encompass more than just telephony capabilities. It can also be used for creating such applications as digital phone systems or video-conferencing.

The Telephony API is split into a core package with many different support packages working alongside. The core provides the needed functionality for basic tasks in the telephony model. These functions include establishing a connection, taking care of different devices, dealing with phone numbers, and assigning a hardware-based provider subsystem.

The additional packages in the JTAPI provide services such as the following:

▥ Advanced call control

▥ Integration with the Java Media API

▥ Privacy for data communications

▥ Time-based and synchronous network communications

JavaSoft has plans to integrate the JTAPI with the Media API we just discussed. This integration should remove much of the overlap that currently exists in the two systems in terms of audio and video operations.

These trends are by no means the only ones Java is following right now. To check out all the information on what's hot in Java, visit Sun's Java product site. The URL of their products page is:

`http://java.sun.com:80/products/index.html`.

Java Tools

Java tools are literally being introduced daily. We will describe some environments for developing Java, from programming simple Java applets to database connectivity and robust Java applications. These tools can be divided into several categories: *Interactive Development Environments* (IDEs), authoring and animation tools, development tools, and database connectivity tools. We suggest you take advantage of the offers these software companies have to test out their products for yourself. For the most part, these tools can be downloaded and used on a trial basis; in other cases, they're available as crippled packages (for example, the save function is disabled).

Interactive Development Environments

Depending on your programming proficiency and development intent, the products on the market vary widely. Some environments allow the creation of graphical user interfaces, contain debugging features, have object and class management, and include program control and evaluation. We will list a few of these robust packages as complete IDEs:

- **Visual Café Pro:** `http://cafe.symantec.com`

  Visual Café Pro allows you to connect the Web pages you create to databases. It has built-in tools that allow you to see the data structures graphically and uses wizards to create dialog boxes and applications with dynamic connections to data tables. It also allows drag-and-drop programming for building simple Web applets or robust Internet applications. Visual Café works intuitively, generating Java code from the objects you create in a visual environment.

- **Passport IntRprise:** `http://www.passport4gl.com`

  Passport is designed to make large-scale, complex applications easy to build and maintain. The Passport environment also includes an object-oriented 4GL, a Visual SQL Editor, a Visual Object Editor, a Visual Logic Editor, Rapid Application Development tools, and an EAR Editor.

- **Java Workshop:** `http://www.sun.com/sunsoft`

  Java Workshop is built to allow you to create applets while writing very little code or none at all. The workshop environment is also designed to help develop standalone Java applications. It supports standards-based APIs, such as RMI and JDBC, for creating more robust Java Enterprise applications.

Development Tools

These tools are not all-inclusive like the IDE tools mentioned, but offer superb development environments for creating full-scale applications as well as simple applets:

■ **Visual Café:** `http://cafe.symantec.com`

Visual Café is very similar to Visual Café Pro without the database connectivity options. It offers a drag-and-drop environment with visual layout options for defining buttons, form fields, and panels while generating the Java code behind the behaviors you define.

■ **Visual J++:** `http://www.microsoft.com/`

Visual J++ is a GUI product development environment for writing and maintaining Java and ActiveX code. J++ allows easy creation of applets and contains an advanced class viewer for understanding Java objects. J++ 1.1 includes database support for common database products.

■ **Apptivity:** `http://www.apptivity.com`

Apptivity is a visual development tool and server for creating multitier, high-performance Java applications. It provides distributed database connectivity and data-aware controls for building applications that can connect to popular databases, such as Informix, Microsoft, Oracle, Sybase, and IBM DB2.

Authoring and Animation Tools

Java authoring and animation tools are a different breed altogether from the IDE tools. These tools are primarily targeted at beginning or intermediate Java programmers. They commonly have programming wizards that help you develop customized applets from a given structure.

■ **AppletAce:** `http://www.macromedia.com/software/powerapplets`

AppletAce is a standalone Java program that allows you to visually configure and test Macromedia's Java PowerApplets. PowerApplets that are currently configurable and customizable include Animator for easy creation of animated logos, Banners for customizing colors, text, and scrolling options, Bullets for developing unique horizontal bars and new bullets, Charts for creating charts from data, Imagemaps for graphics, and Icons for Web buttons and clickable graphics objects.

■ **Liquid Motion Pro:** `http://www.dimensionx.com`

Recently acquired by Microsoft, Dimension X's Liquid Motion Pro allows easy creation of Java-based multimedia authoring and publishing. Liquid Motion is a drag-and-drop environment for creating animation with motion and sound without writing any Java code or programming anything at all.

■ **Coda:** `http://www.randomnoise.com`

Coda is a Web site builder written entirely in Java. Coda's unique environment offers developers a graphics canvas for precisely positioning, staging, and configuring text, graphics, and other media objects. The graphics canvas is a bonus for allowing true WYSIWYG, down to the very pixel.

Noted Books on Java

When you're programming, it's often useful to have some books at your side. Here's a collection of some of the books we recommend checking out at your local bookstore:

■ *On To Java* by Patrick Henry Winston and Sundar Narasimhan.

Patrick Winston is one of the founding fathers of artificial intelligence. Winston writes precisely and concisely for an audience already familiar with programming structures. Winston is also the author of *On to C* and *On to C++*.

■ Addison Wesley collection

The Java Programming Language by Ken Arnold and James Gosling

The Java Language Specification by James Gosling, Bill Joy, and Guy Steele

Java Application Programming Interface Volume 1: Core Packages

Java Application Programming Interface Volume 2: Window Toolkit and Applets by James Gosling, Frank Yellin, and The Java Team

A good reference set.

■ McGraw-Hill

The Java Developer's Tool Kit by Kevin Leininger

Java: The Complete Developer's Kit by Jason Manger

These books can help you "Java-cize" your site. They help you get up-to-date on current Java development tools and how these tools can be used on the WWW.

- O'Reilly series

Exploring Java by Pat Niemeyer

Java in a Nutshell: A Desktop Quick Reference for Java Programmers by David Flanagan

Java Threads by Scott Oaks and Henry Wong

Java Language Reference Manual by Mark Grand

Java Network Programming by Elliotte Rusty Harold

Java AWT Reference by John Zukowski

Java Virtual Machine by John Meyer and Troy Downing

A complete series to deal with all your Java programming questions. From Java threads to the Java Virtual Machine, this series definitely has all the bases covered.

- SunSoft Press collection

Java By Example by Jerry Jackson and Alan McClellan

Instant Java by John Pew

Core Java by Gary Cornell and Cay S. Horstmann

Graphic Java by David Geary and Alan McClellan

This group of books is especially strong for its realistic appraisal of the Java language's strengths and weaknesses. The later books in particular are extremely useful when it's time to delve into the more detailed aspects of Java programming. They have clear sample code, fine writing, and information that you need.

Core Java Resources

Java is truly a product of the Internet. All the information you could need about the language is online and readily available. Here are some core resource pages:

Sun

Sun's main Java page:

`http://www.javasoft.com`

Sun's FAQ page:

`http://www.javasoft.com/faq2.html`

JDK page for Solaris, Win95, Windows NT, and MacOS:

`http://www.javasoft.com/products/jdk/1.1/`

Microsoft

Microsoft's Java resource page:

`http://www.microsoft.com/java`

Microsoft's Java Strategy:

`http://www.microsoft.com/java/jstratwp.htm`

Java and ActiveX:

`http://www.microsoft.com/activeplatform/actx-gen/ajava.asp`

Gamelan:

`http://www.gamelan.com`

Noted Web Sites Using Java

This section has an eclectic collection of sites to take a peek at. The only thing they all have in common is Java.

America's Guide Senior Infoserver (AGSI)

`http://www.americasguide.com`

AGSI is a senior-related information site driven entirely by Java. It includes a Java search engine, a Webcrawler, and a back-office suite.

Castanet

`http://www.marimba.com`

Castanet is a server and client software that uses push technologies. It works under the channels concepts with a tuner to get information over the Internet.

Deep Blue

`http://www.chess.ibm.com`

Check out the site where Deep Blue made history as the first computer ever to beat the world chess champion Garry Kasparov. You can view all the famous chess matches with IBM's special Java Chess applet.

Dynamo

`http://www.atg.com`

Dynamo is produced by the Art and Technology group. It consists of the Dynamo server, the Dynamo ad station, the Dynamo profile station, the Dynamo retail station, and the Dynamo Developer's Kit. Dynamo is written entirely in Java and is geared toward managing large business Web sites.

Self-Test Online

`http://www.selftestonline.com`

This site uses Java networking technology to test people online with examinations such as a typing test, a hearing test, and a series of job and interest tests.

Java Resources

For daily information on Java, visit these sites. They have the links, the up-to-the-minute information, and the tips you need to be a Java expert.
A very complete Java site with applets, links, and resources:

`http://www.apl.jhu.edu/~hall/java/`

The Cup O'Joe Java Shop:

`http://www.cupojoe.com`

Digital Cats' Java Resource Center (available in English or Japanese):

`http://www.javacats.com`

JARs:

`http://www.jars.com`

Java Repository:

`http://java.wiwi.uni-frankfurt.de`

JavaWorld Magazine + (online version):

`http://www.javaworld.com`

Javology Magazine:

`http://www.javology.com`

Team Java:

`http://www.teamjava.com`

Yahoo's Java section:

`http://www.yahoo.com`

CONCLUSION

This chapter has given you a whirlwind tour of the Java programming language and environment. From the beginning, when we introduced Java, to the latest trends and technologies transforming Java daily, we have covered a tremendous amount of material.

At this point, you should be familiar with many different aspects of the Java programming environment. In this chapter, we first looked at Java in relation to other programming languages. We discovered why and how Java is so important in today's networked environment. We then took a look at the history of Java. This gave us a clearer perspective of why Java is the way it is today and how it took shape from the beginning seeds of an idea from the Green Team at Sun. Next, we took a quick look at Java-Beans. You will find this information to be important in the rest of the book as we devote more time to this exciting topic.

After the basic background on Java and JavaBeans, we began to explore in more depth how Java really works. We traced the route of Java code after it's written, as it's used to execute a program. We examined in detail the Java Virtual Machine and the rise of Just-in-Time compilers. We then learned the basics of the Java programming language and created some of our own applets. We looked at basic Java data types, objects, loops, and syntax—everything needed to make those cool applets, and then we jumped in and made our own. You walked through the process of creating three different interactive applets, all different versions of what we call the Seer Applet. This process should be a big help as you turn to making your own applets. Finally, we gave you up-to-date information on Java resources.

JavaBeans

4

JavaBeans
Fundamentals

JavaBeans was announced in the summer of 1996. Ever since its inception, JavaBeans has caused a lot of speculation and hype—speculation, because not every great new technology succeeds, and hype, because every effort possible was being put into JavaBeans to make it successful. Although Java is an object-oriented language that provides support for platform independence, multithreading, and networking, it initially lacked a few important elements. JavaBeans complemented Java by filling in for those missing elements, including support for visual assembly of software components, object persistence, and distributed computing. JavaBeans not only added the missing functionality, but also made Java programs more portable and interoperable with many component models, including Microsoft's ActiveX, Netscape's LiveConnect, and IBM's OpenDoc.

This chapter will cover the following topics:

- Definition of JavaBeans
- Software components
- Goal of the JavaBeans API
- Difference between a Bean and a class library
- Properties, events, and methods of Beans
- Design time versus runtime considerations
- Security issues
- Distributed processing with Beans
- Visibility of Beans
- Multithreading in Beans
- Internationalization

What Is a JavaBean?

A *JavaBean* is a reusable software component that can be manipulated visually in a builder tool. What's so different about Beans compared to other *Application Program Interfaces* (APIs), such as the Microsoft Foundation Classes? Beans are live objects that can be manipulated from an application builder. In other visual development tools, components dragged and dropped onto the work area have events for the code that must still be written. The application builders lay out the skeleton so the programmers can fill in the code, and then the code is compiled and linked to form an executable application.

With JavaBeans, however, the component is a live object in the sense that the component is being executed while you build the application. The objects respond to other objects within the application as you build it. Therefore, what you're developing is not only the application's layout, but also the application's behavior. A Bean can be manipulated as a live object from within application builders; you develop the final application without having to write a single line of code.

Software Components

If we delve into history a bit, we find that many great inventions resulted from a scientist trying to solve a real-world problem. Software components have been developed because of a need for programmers to be able to reuse their code. For years, programmers have rewritten code to solve a problem; when they need to solve the same problem again in a slightly different situation, they often have to rewrite that code again. Programmers don't want to rewrite code but sometimes they are forced to; the operating environment has changed, and the code that worked earlier no longer operates in the new environment. Sometimes, the original code wasn't generic enough to handle varied situations, and programmers often can't utilize previous work in each new development effort.

To ensure reusability of code, the concept of programming first shifted from procedural programming to modular programming; then data abstraction was introduced, and finally object-oriented programming was developed. Object-oriented programming provided the most reusability of code because it allowed programmers to derive from previously built classes, thus extending the functionality of the existing code. Even though object-oriented programming cut down development costs and frustration levels among programmers, it wasn't the best model. Programmers had to depend heavily on the documentation of these classes to use them, so programming efforts weren't eliminated altogether.

Although people had begun to realize the benefits of object-oriented programming, *Graphical User Interfaces* (GUI) and event-driven programming were becoming more popular and companies like Microsoft, Borland, and Symantec started making *Integrated Development Environments* (IDEs) for programmers. An IDE has all the basic tools a programmer needs (compiler, editor, debugger, and so forth) integrated into one environment. Resource workshops allowed programmers to drag and drop objects such as buttons and edit boxes on a work area and associate code with them. With this new tool, visual programming was born, and products like Microsoft Visual Basic, Microsoft Visual C++, and Borland's Turbo C++ caused a revolution in programming. Developers could now build reusable software components that could be visually dragged and dropped onto a work area; they could associate code with events, set properties, and invoke methods.

The software component architecture consists of *software components* and *builder tools*. Software components are reusable, self-sufficient building blocks that can communicate with other software components; builder tools are typically IDEs that enable software components to be laid out visually and help develop event-driven applications.

For example, a Web page authoring tool could be used as a builder tool, with which Java applets (or JavaBeans) could be dragged and dropped to make an interactive page; another potential builder tool would be a document editor that includes some Beans as part of a compound document.

Software component architecture allows developers to build applications by assembling preexisting software components, enabling the developers to concentrate on business logic without writing the same components over and over again. This method is analogous to building a car by putting together components like the steering wheel, the tires, and the engine without really needing to know how to build the valves or the cables that go into making the engine. If people building cars had to know the process of making rubber so they could create a tire, they couldn't focus on the ultimate goal of engine performance.

Visual Basic was one of the premier IDEs that popularized using software components to build applications. Visual Basic developers could drag and drop typical components, such as buttons, edit boxes, and images, and create applications. Software components have three major attributes:

- **Properties:** Properties are the attributes of a component. For example, the number of rows and columns, the height, and the width are attributes of a table component. In a real-world component such as a speaker, volume, bass, and treble could be the attributes. These properties can be manipulated at design time or runtime in an IDE by using property sheets. The component architecture usually has a method for revealing its properties to the application builder. These properties can be changed at runtime through code. For example, a speaker's volume could be increased or decreased by adjusting the knob component. Developers can save the component's properties when saving the application; this feature is known as *persistence*.

- **Events:** Components can cause events to trigger certain actions. For example, pressing an on/off button on an audio system triggers the system; the action of pressing the button is an *event*. In typical IDEs, developers have to write code to send messages to the objects being affected by a particular event. For example, if turning the volume knob is done by using a mouse, the developer would trap this event and invoke methods from the speaker object, asking it to increase the volume. Many IDEs have code windows that pop up when the developer specifies an event to be trapped by a particular component.

▦ **Methods:** The methods of a component are functions that can be called from within the application, requesting the component to carry out a particular task and internally set its state. For example, turning the volume knob could invoke a method called `setVolume` in the speaker object, which would then decide to satisfy or deny the request. In addition to performing the task, the speaker object would set its internal state (maybe a number indicating the current volume level) and call methods of other objects that are affected by the event.

There's a major difference between JavaBeans and the software component technology used by other visual application builders. Most IDEs allow developers to lay out the components on the work area and associate code with events that a component can track. Once the developers have written the code, they compile it to build the application. What they see in the final application might look slightly different from its design-time version.

With JavaBeans, developers don't necessarily have to write code to build an application; it's simply a matter of dragging a particular component's events and connecting to another component's event listeners. For example, in Visual C++, when developers want to increase the speaker's volume when the knob turns, they select the `mouseClick` event on the knob and call the method `speakers.setVolume(newVolume)`. Next, they compile the code and link it to get the new function. However, if developers tried to do the same thing with JavaBeans, all they would have to do is connect the knob's `mouseClick` event to the event listener on the speaker and have it change the `Volume` property to the new value. They wouldn't have to write a single line of code, do any compiling, or link the application again to accomplish that.

Although other technologies require programmers to do most of the work, JavaBeans and the core reflection APIs allow the IDE to do most of the work. Besides, since all the components on the application framework are being executed as the developers are manipulating them, what developers see is the application's final version; there are no surprises.

Goal of the JavaBeans API

The JavaBeans API is specifically designed to define a software component model for Java so that third-party software vendors can develop components that are easily integrated into a complex business application. If you were writing an application that required both word processing and spreadsheet functions, for example, you could go to a software store and pick up a word processing Bean, a spreadsheet Bean, and maybe some edit box and button Beans; then you would simply drag and drop them onto your application in an application builder tool, connect them, customize them to suit your business requirement, and save the application. You could easily develop applications without writing a single line of code.

These are the goals for JavaBeans API specifications as outlined by Sun:

- Support for a range of component granularity

  Simple JavaBeans will be available that can be put together as part of a composite application. There could also be more complicated Beans that behave like applications; they could be part of compound documents such as Web pages. Sun expects most Beans to be small- to medium-sized components. The simple ones should be easy to implement and provide a reasonable amount of default behavior.

- Portability

  One of the main goals of JavaBeans architecture is to provide platform-independent component structure. Most software component architectures currently on the market are platform-specific (for example, Microsoft's VBX and OCX technology works only with Windows, and widgets work with X-Windows). A pure JavaBean developed under UNIX should behave the same regardless of the operating system. However, if a JavaBean is embedded in a platform-specific container, then the JavaBean's APIs should be integrated into the native component architecture. This portability will supply bridges to ActiveX, CI Labs' OpenDoc, and Netscape's LiveConnect. JavaBeans should be capable of working in a wide range of different environments where they can handle and run events and respond to method invocations.

- Uniform, high-quality API

  Platforms that don't support the entire JavaBeans API must provide harmless and reasonable defaults, which would allow component developers to program to a consistent set of APIs without having to check whether a feature is supported on every specific platform. In other words, component developers shouldn't have to provide default behavior for every unsupported feature on specific platforms.

■ Simplicity

The easiest way to reduce the risk of having many unsupported features in the API is by keeping the API simple and compact. A simple API is easier to learn and use.

Most of these goals have been met, and Sun is making efforts to meet the rest of them.

The Difference Between a Bean and a Class Library

JavaBeans are basically Java classes that have their interfaces defined according to the JavaBeans API specifications. These classes can be used programmatically as well as through application builders. What, then, is the difference between regular classes and Beans? Technically, all Beans are regular classes, and all classes are potential Beans. However, there are a few differences. Regular Java objects might not support the following features, but all Beans must support them:

■ **Introspection:** Beans can be examined by using the `Introspector` class, which uses the core reflection API to discover classes, interfaces, and methods and their parameters at runtime. Introspection allows a builder tool to analyze a Bean by using a `BeanInfo` object at runtime, manipulate its properties, and invoke methods.

■ **Customization:** Customization lets a builder tool customize a Bean's appearance and behavior.

■ **Events:** Events allow the Beans in an application to communicate and connect. They let a Bean broadcast information to other related classes when a Bean's state changes.

■ **Properties:** Developers can use properties to customize a Bean's appearance and behavior.

■ **Persistence:** A Bean's state can be saved and restored by using persistence. When developers create applications with a builder tool, they can customize a Bean's appearance, which can be saved at any time. When the application is restarted, the Bean's saved appearance is loaded.

Even though all Java classes can potentially be recognized as Beans, it's best to implement only those modules intended to be visually manipulated within builder tools as Beans. Some functionality, however, is still best provided through a programming (textual) interface rather than a visual manipulation interface. For example, a database object could be a class library, but the query object could be a Bean. The SQL statement to be executed could be a property, and the execute process could be a method in such a Bean.

Features of Beans: Properties, Events, and Methods

As in other component architectures, the three most important features of JavaBeans are their properties, events, and methods.

Properties

Properties, an inherent part of JavaBeans, are used to control the appearance and behavior of a Bean. They are basically named attributes associated with a Bean that can be read or written by calling *read accessor methods* (getters) or *write accessor methods* (setters). Typically, these attributes are a Bean's private data members. They are also used to represent the current state of a Bean. You should never be able to access these attribute members directly. They must always be accessed—that is, read from or written to—by using accessor methods. Properties show up in the following ways:

- Properties can be exposed in scripting environments as though they were fields of an object. For example, you can set the `Volume` property of a speaker Bean in a JavaScript environment as `speaker.Volume=FULL_BLAST`. Even though it appears as though you're directly writing to the private data member `Volume` of the speaker Bean, internally it must be a setter method that sets the value. So even though you write `speaker.Volume=FULL_BLAST`, there is still a method call into the target object (speaker) to set the property, and the target object has full programming control over rejecting or accepting such a request.

- Properties can be accessed through programming code when other components call their getter and setter methods.

- Properties can be presented and manipulated from a property sheet in a builder tool.
- Bean properties can be persistent and stored away as part of the Bean's persistent state.

Properties need not be simple data fields; they could be computed fields, too. For example, setting the **audioSystem** Bean's **musicTypeSelection** property to **JAZZ** might internally change the value of other properties, such as **Bass** and **Treble**, to new values.

JavaBeans support simple properties as well as indexed properties. *Simple properties* are single-valued; for example, the **Volume** property of a speaker Bean can hold only one value of type **int**. Boolean properties are special types of simple properties that can have only one of two states —true or false. **VolumeFullBlast** in a speaker Bean is an example of a Boolean property. *Indexed properties* are accessed like arrays. The index type currently supported is integers. Indexed properties are used to access arrays, vectors, or list-type properties.

Simple and indexed properties don't support event-driven notification between Beans. JavaBeans supports two types of semantics—bound properties and constrained properties. Often, other Beans need to be informed about a change in the state of a property. For example, setting the **musicTypeSelection** property in an **audioSystem** Bean might require the **graphicsEqualizer** Beans to repaint their display settings. A *bound property* notifies a target object when its value changes; these target objects can react to the change when notified but can't prevent the property from being changed. In the preceding example, **musicTypeSelection** is a bound property. However, if a Bean has a *constrained property*, the controlling Bean (notified Bean) can prevent the controlled Bean (the Bean whose property is being changed) from changing its property. For example, if the **Bass** property of the speaker Bean is constrained, the **audioSystem** Bean could actually prevent the **Bass** value from being changed outside a given range, depending upon the current **musicTypeSelection** property setting.

Events

The success of JavaBeans lies mainly in the ability of Beans to connect to other objects through events. Events allow a Bean to notify other objects of a change in its state and react to a change in the state of other objects.

Event-based systems are *asynchronous*; they react to events raised by external systems and don't wait for things to happen in sequence. For example, if you designed a form in a typical C program, it would be a series of output and input statements. You input data as the program asks for it and then you validate each value. In an event-driven system, you display all the form elements and then leave it up to the users to enter the data in whatever order they like. You validate each value after the user has entered it, depending on which form element notifies you of change in its state (or value). Similarly, other events, such as timers, are triggered without a user's intervention.

JDK 1.1 uses the *delegation event model*. *Delegation* is the act of empowering others to accomplish a task for you. In the Java delegation event model, event sources are empowered to act for listener classes by calling a listener's method when an event occurs. Listeners have to be registered with classes that generate events. Whenever an event that has been registered occurs, the object that generated the event calls the appropriate method of the listener.

Java has two types of events: Low-level and semantic. A *low-level event* represents user interactions with a visual component onscreen that corresponds to some input device. A mouse click or a key press are low-level events. *Semantic events* are higher level events that represent a user's interaction with a window component—a click on a scrollbar, for example. Even though at a low level it's a mouse click event, at a semantic level the user intends to see parts of the window currently cut off by using the scrollbar.

Methods

Methods are interfaces that request Beans to perform a particular function, so `setVolume` would actually be a method of the speaker Bean, requesting it to increase or lower the volume. Most of the methods in a Java-Bean must follow certain design signatures to make sure the application builder tools understand the method's function. For example, the `setVolume` and `getVolume` methods of the speaker Bean tell the application builder tool that the speaker has a property called `Volume`, which can have certain integer values. Similarly, other methods, such as `isVolumeFullBlast`, can return a true or false value, depending on whether the speaker is operating at maximum. Other methods that direct a Bean to do something can only be called through programming code. At the same time, a Bean can have other methods that the Bean developer decides not to give access to or designates for internal processing only. Such methods aren't accessible to other Beans or application builder tools.

Design Time Versus Runtime Considerations

JavaBeans can run in many different environments, in any container, and on any platform. They are manipulated from a builder tool in a running state as live objects. When a Bean runs within a builder tool, the environment is known as the *design environment*. Within the design environment, a Bean must display its properties, methods, and events to users so they can manipulate the Bean's appearance and behavior and connect it to other objects on the application canvas.

However, once the application is built and saved, there's little need for customization, so there's not much need for design information and introspection. The design time information and customization code could potentially be a large part of the Bean. If Bean developers decide to incorporate a setup wizard for customizing the Bean when it's loaded, it could potentially eclipse the runtime code in the Bean. Therefore, JavaBeans API specifications make sure there's a clear split between a Bean's design time aspects and runtime aspects, so it's possible to use a Bean in an application without needing to download all the design time code. Bean developers can put their design time interfaces (introspection and customization) in a class other than the runtime interfaces (event handlers, properties, and other methods).

Security Issues

Security is a major concern among most users. It wasn't such an issue until some disturbing news hit the headlines: in one instance ActiveX components were written to manipulate Quicken files to transfer money to a hacker's account; in another case, malicious Java code, acting as a trusted applet, was written to damage a user's hard disk. The thought of components downloading on the client's local hard disk and installing themselves as a result of merely viewing a Web page made many people uncomfortable. With the power of executable files residing and executing from the client hard disk came the responsibility of protecting the user's machine from accidental or intentional harm. The two main component technologies that allow components to be downloaded onto the client machine from the Web are JavaBeans and ActiveX. Both these technologies have different methods of avoiding harm to the client. JavaBeans run within a controlled environment provided by the Java Virtual Machine, known as the SandBox, and ActiveX controls use digital certificates.

Before an ActiveX control developed by a particular vendor is downloaded to your machine for the first time, a confirmation is requested, providing the certificate number and some information about the company that developed the control. Microsoft goes by the philosophy that if you trust the company that gave the certificate, then you trust the company that developed the control, and you trust every control they develop. However, no security manager actually verifies what the ActiveX control is trying to do, so ActiveX controls potentially have more security loopholes than JavaBeans do.

The JavaBeans SandBox security system is made up of several elements:

- The Java Virtual Machine that interprets and executes the byte code generated by the Java compiler.

- The Byte Code verifier that actually verifies the bytes downloaded to the client; they don't perform any illegal operations that will corrupt the Java Virtual Machine itself.

- The Class Loader, which verifies that the classes being loaded are authentic.

- The Security Manager that controls the resources the class tries to access. By default, all applets loaded on a client machine are untrusted and have very little access to the client resources. They don't have access to the file system, the client network, or printers, and have access only to that part of the memory in which the Java Virtual Machine is executing. However, trusted Java applets and Beans have more access to resources. The philosophy of trusted applets is the same as that of ActiveX controls.

JavaBeans developers are expected to develop Beans so that they can be run as part of untrusted applets, using the following guidelines:

- **Introspection:** Bean developers should assume they have unlimited access to the high-level introspection APIs and low-level reflection APIs at design time, but have limited access to them at runtime.

- **Persistence:** Bean developers should assume that their Beans can be serialized and deserialized in design time and runtime environments, but they shouldn't assume they can control where the serialized data is read from and written to in the runtime environment.

■ **GUI Merging:** Untrusted applets won't be permitted to perform any kind of GUI merging with their parent applications. For example, if the browser is the application's container, the application menu bar won't be merged with the browser menu bar. However, Beans nested within the application itself will be able to merge their menu bars.

Thus JavaBeans can be trusted and provide more security to the client machine than ActiveX controls can.

Distributed Processing with Beans

Not every machine can do everything well. Some systems, such as the Apple Macintosh and Microsoft Windows '95, handle front ends well, and other systems, such as UNIX and Windows NT, handle back-end jobs (such as databases and other server programs) well. It makes sense to distribute jobs to the machines and operating systems best suited to do them. In the past decade, use of the client-server architecture has become more widespread. Now, with the popularity of the Internet, clients and servers are spread across the world.

Even though JavaBeans are designed to work well in a nondistributed environment, the architecture can be scaled to cater to the distributed World Wide Web environment. A good system is often logically divided between local processing and remote processing. Local processing benefits from good communication within a local machine, and remote accesses suffer from slower data transfer because of network traffic and communication failures. Most of the software written for such environments has a minimal number of remote interactions and includes built-in caching algorithms and batch updates. JavaBeans APIs are targeted for use in a virtual machine with alternative mechanisms for Bean developers to connect back to network servers.

These are the three primary network access mechanisms, shown in Figure 4-1, available to JavaBeans developers:

■ **Java RMI:** *Remote Method Invocation* (RMI) introduces a distributed programming environment for Java clients to invoke services of remote Java servers within distributed Java applications. RMI offers a pure solution to the problem of heterogeneous distributed computation. The distributed system interfaces can be designed in Java, and clients and servers can be developed that implement the interfaces. Java RMI calls are automatically and transparently delivered from the client to the server.

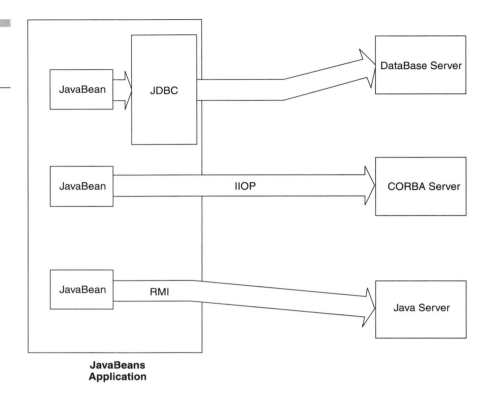

Figure 4-1.
JavaBeans primary
network access
mechanisms.

**JavaBeans
Application**

■ **Java IDL:** The Java *Interface Definition Language* (IDL) system
implements the CORBA-distributed object model. All the system
interfaces must be defined in the CORBA IDL. Then Java stubs
are generated from the IDL interfaces, allowing JavaBean clients
to call into IDL servers. Since CORBA IDL is a multilanguage,
multivendor, distributed computing environment, JavaBean clients
can access Java as well as non-Java IDL servers.

■ **JDBC:** JavaBean components can access SQL databases through
Java *DataBase Connectivity* (JDBC) APIs. The database can be on
the same machine as the client or on remote database servers.

Visibility of Beans

Some JavaBeans might have no GUI representation. For example, one
component of the audio system could be a timer Bean that shuts down the

system when no one touches it for a specified period of time, or after a CD has stopped playing. These Beans are the same as visible Beans, except they have design time appearance, not runtime appearance. They can call methods, prompt events, save persistent states, and so on. Because they have a design time appearance, they can be manipulated and customized in application builders. Some Beans might have a runtime appearance depending on where they're run. For example, an access control JavaBean could have a server presence to configure it, but not a client presence.

Multithreading in Beans

JavaBeans can run in a multithreaded environment. With this multi-threading feature, many Beans could be simultaneously firing events, calling methods, and setting properties of a particular Bean. JavaBeans developers must take care that the Bean behaves as expected in a multi-threaded application.

Internationalization

Even before the Internet became popular, product developers had to take localization into consideration. *Internationalization* is simply support in a software component for displaying dates, time, currencies, help messages, and so forth in local languages. Even in English, there's a difference between European English and U.S. English. Most JavaBeans programmers are expected to write code in terms of locale-independent programming names. However, some parts of the JavaBean displays must handle multilanguage issues, such as whether properties can be edited through property editors and status bar messages. A JavaBean might have a property called `Color` that should read `Colour` if the Bean is being used in England. The help messages that show up on the application's status bar should be in the local language, too. There are other issues in writing locale-independent code; differences in the length of strings, for example, shouldn't disrupt the display. To support the internationalization of JavaBeans, some internationalization classes have been added to JDK 1.1. Bean developers who expect their Beans to be used internationally must use these internationalization classes to make their classes accessible around the globe.

CONCLUSION

Application development with components is a great way to develop software, especially business applications, without writing a single line of code. JavaBeans gives developers a chance to concentrate completely on business logic. In this chapter, we looked at some of the basics of software components and introduced the basic JavaBeans concepts. We discussed properties, methods, events, security, and some implementation issues, such as distributed processing, multithreading and internationalization. As we move along, we will dive into each of these topics and try to understand them in more detail.

JavaBeans Properties

This chapter explains properties, an integral part of Java-Beans. *Properties* are attributes of a Bean that control its appearance and behavior. In the chapters that follow, we use some basic Beans and add to them to illustrate all the key ideas and concepts.

We'll begin by creating these basic Beans; then we move on to explain some JavaBeans properties concepts and extend our Beans to include properties that can be manipulated through property sheets.

This chapter will cover the following topics:

- Our basic Beans
- Properties

Our Basic Beans

To begin our example, we will use the following three Beans: **CarBean**, **TrafficLightBean**, and **RoadPatrolBean**. These Beans are very simple (so simple that you might not consider them to be Beans). We will extend these Beans over the next few chapters to make them full-fledged Beans.

CarBean

The **CarBean** simulates the working of a simple car. The **CarBean** extends from the Canvas component and implements the Serializable and the imageObserver interface. The **CarBean** has the following methods: **constructor**, **paint()**, and **imageUpdate()**. It stores the images to be displayed in the **m_CarImages** variable that's of the type Image.

The **constructor** function sets the Bean's dimensions with the **setSize()** method. It then loads the images into the **m_CarImages** variable by using the Toolkit's **getImage()** method.

The **paint()** method overrides the Canvas' **paint()** method. The **Graphics** object's **drawImage()** method is used to display the image.

The **imageUpdate()** method of a component, such as Canvas, is called when more information about an image (that had been previously requested using an asynchronous interface such as **drawImage**) becomes available. The **imageUpdate()** method of a component incrementally draws an image on the component as more of the image's bits are available. The **ALLBITS** flag in the **infoflags** argument to **imageUpdate()** indicates that a static image is now complete and can be drawn in its final form.

The **CarBean** is a very simple Bean; in the following sections, we will enhance this Bean's functionality.

Listing 5-1.
The basic **CarBean**.

```java
package Cars;

import java.awt.*;
import java.io.*;
import java.Beans.*;
import java.awt.image.*;


/**
 * The CarBean simulates the working of a Car.
 * Depending on its speed the CarBean could load
    appropriate images.
 *
 */
public class CarBean extends     Canvas
                        implements Serializable,
                                    ImageObserver
{
    // constructor
    public CarBean ()
    {
        super ();

        setSize (IMG_WIDTH, IMG_HEIGHT);
          if (m_CarImages == null)
            {
            m_CarImages = new Image [NUM_IMAGES];

            Toolkit tk = getToolkit ();
            m_CarImages[0] = tk.getImage
                ("c:/McGrawHill/Bean/Cars/Car.gif");
            m_CarImages[1] = tk.getImage
                ("c:/McGrawHill/Bean/Cars/MovingCar.gif");
        }
    }

    public void paint (Graphics g)
    {
        boolean bRet;
            bRet = g.drawImage (m_CarImages[0], 0, 0,
                this);
    }

    public boolean imageUpdate (Image img, int infoFlag,
        int x, int y, int width, int height)
    {
        if ( (infoFlag & ALLBITS) != 0)
        {
            repaint ();
```

Continues

Listing 5-1.
Continued.

```
                return false;
        }

        return true;
    }

    private static Image[]    m_CarImages = null;

    private final static int NUM_IMAGES = 2;
    private final static int IMG_HEIGHT = 60;
    private final static int IMG_WIDTH = 205;
}
```

RoadPatrolBean

The **RoadPatrolBean** depicts a road patrol officer. Its implementation is almost the same as the **CarBean**. The **RoadPatrolBean** extends from the Canvas component and implements the Serializable and the imageObserver interface. This Bean has the following methods: **constructor**, **paint()**, and **imageUpdate()**. It stores the image to be displayed in the **m_CopImage** variable of type Image.

The **constructor** function sets the Bean's dimensions by using the **setSize()** method. It then loads the image into the **m_CopImage** variable with the Toolkit's **getImage()** method.

The **paint()** method overrides the Canvas' **paint()** method. The **drawImage()** method of the **Graphics** object is used to display the Road Patrol image.

The **imageUpdate()** method is the same as the one explained for the **CarBean** in the previous section.

This Bean, too, is very simple, so in the following sections, we enhance its functionality.

Properties

Properties are the attributes that control the appearance and behavior of a JavaBean. Typically, these attributes are foreground/background colors, dimensions, and other visual aspects of a Bean. These properties may be primitive data types such as integers and floats or objects such as color and strings. To be able to manipulate the values, we need to see accessor methods in depth.

```java
package Cars;

import java.awt.*;
import java.io.*;
import java.Beans.*;
import java.util.*;
import java.awt.image.*;

/**
 * The RoadPatrolBean simulates the working of a Road
      Patrol.
 *
 */
public class RoadPatrolBean     extends      Canvas
                                    implements
                                        Serializable,
                                            ImageObserver
{
    // constructor
    public RoadPatrolBean ()
    {
        setSize (IMG_WIDTH, IMG_HEIGHT);

        if (m_CopImage == null)
      {
            Toolkit tk = getToolkit ();
            m_CopImage = tk.getImage
                ("c:/McGrawHill/Bean/Cars/Cop.gif");
      }
    }


    public void paint (Graphics g)
    {
            g.drawImage (m_CopImage, 0, 0, this);
    }

    public boolean imageUpdate (Image img, int infoFlag,
        int x, int y, int width, int height)
    {
        if ( (infoFlag & ALLBITS) != 0)
        {
            repaint ();
            return false;
        }

        return true;
    }

                      private static Image m_CopImage = null;
    private final static int IMG_HEIGHT = 136;
    private final static int IMG_WIDTH  = 111;
}
```

Accessor Methods

There are two types of accessor methods—*getters* and *setters*. A Bean should always define getter methods for its properties. Setter methods are optional and provide a means for modifying the Bean's property.

A read-only property supplies only getter methods, but a read-write property provides getter and setter methods. Getter and setter methods should follow naming conventions, as explained in the next section.

Single-Valued Properties

A single-valued property is the most common type. The value of this property is stored as the Bean's private data members, and getter/setter methods are provided to modify its value. The getter and setter accessor methods should conform to the following naming conventions: **get<*PropertyName*>()** and **set<*PropertyName*>()**; **<*PropertyName*>** is the actual name of the property.

This is a single-valued property syntax:

```
<PropertyType> get<PropertyName> ()
void set<PropertyName> ( <PropertyType>  value)
```

The **CarBean** and **RoadPatrolBean** are simple Beans, but even simple Beans need some properties, so let's add some properties to them.

We defined the **CarBean** as having two properties: The current speed (**Speed**) and the maximum speed (**MaxSpeed**). These two property values are maintained in the **m_iSpeed** and the **m_iMaxSpeed** integer variables. The **getSpeed()** and **setSpeed()** methods are accessor methods for the **Speed** property, and **getMaxSpeed()** and **setMaxSpeed()** are the accessor methods for the **MaxSpeed** property.

The **paint()** method is modified so that it displays the appropriate car image, depending on the current speed. The **Graphics** object's **drawImage()** method is used to display the image.

We would like the **RoadPatrolBean** to enforce a maximum speed on other Beans. For this reason, we define a **MaxSpeed** property for the **RoadPatrolBean**. Its property value is maintained in the **m_iMaxSpeed** integer variable. The **getMaxSpeed()** and **setMaxSpeed()** are the accessor methods for the **MaxSpeed** property.

TrafficLightBean

Now we define a third Bean: the **TrafficLightBean**, which simulates the working of a road traffic light. It has three states—red, orange, and green. At regular user-set intervals, it changes its state. The **TrafficLightBean** uses the help of the **MyTimer** class to be notified at the end of each interval.

Listing 5-3.
The **CarBean** extended with the **MaxSpeed** and **Speed** properties.

```java
package Cars;

import java.awt.*;
import java.io.*;
import java.Beans.*;
import java.awt.image.*;


/**
 * The CarBean has a maximum and a current speed as its
     basic properties.
 * This Bean is specified a maximum speed at which it
     could go up to. It has
 * a current speed, which could be from zero to the
     maximum speed specified.
 *
 * Depending on its current speed the CarBean loads
     appropriate images.
 *
 * @see                    RoadPatrolBean
 * @see                    TrafficLightBean
 */
public class CarBean extends     Canvas
                        implements Serializable,
                                    ImageObserver
{
    // constructor
    public CarBean ()
    {
        super ();

        setSize (IMG_WIDTH, IMG_HEIGHT);
          if (m_CarImages == null)
      {
            m_CarImages = new Image [NUM_IMAGES];

            Toolkit tk = getToolkit ();
            m_CarImages[0] = tk.getImage
                ("c:/McGrawHill/Bean/cars/Car.gif");
            m_CarImages[1] = tk.getImage
                ("c:/McGrawHill/Bean/cars/MovingCar.gif");
      }
    }
```

Continues

Listing 5-3.
Continued.

```java
public void paint (Graphics g)
{
    boolean bRet;
    if (m_iSpeed == 0)
    {
        bRet = g.drawImage (m_CarImages[0], 0, 0,
            this);
    }
    else
    {
        bRet = g.drawImage (m_CarImages[1], 0, 0,
            this);
    }
}

public boolean imageUpdate (Image img, int infoFlag,
    int x, int y, int width, int height)
{
    if ( (infoFlag & ALLBITS) != 0)
    {
        repaint ();
        return false;
    }

    return true;
}


// Moving property ***********************************
/**
 * Returns a boolean whether the car is moving or not
 * @see #setMoving
 */
public boolean isMoving ()
{
        if (m_iSpeed == 0)
                return false;

        return true;
}

/**
 * The dummy set method for the Moving property
 * @see #isMoving
 */
public void setMoving (boolean b)
{

}
```

Listing 5-3.
Continued.

```
    // Speed (current) property ****************************
    /**
     * Returns the current speed
     * @see #setSpeed
     */
    public int getSpeed ()
    {
        return m_iSpeed;
    }


    /**
     * Sets the current speed
     * @see #getSpeed
     */
    public void setSpeed (int iNewSpeed)
    {
            m_iSpeed = iNewSpeed;
        repaint ();
    }



    // Maximum Speed property *****************************
    /**
     * Returns the maximum speed.
     * @see #setMaxSpeed
     */
    public int getMaxSpeed ()
    {
        return m_iMaxSpeed;
    }


    /**
     * Sets the maximum speed.
     * @see #getMaxSpeed
     */
    public void setMaxSpeed (int iNewSpeed)
    {
        m_iMaxSpeed = iNewSpeed;
        repaint ();
    }

    private int    m_iSpeed      = 55; // mph
    private int    m_iMaxSpeed   = 55; // mph

    private static Image[]    m_CarImages = null;

    private final static int NUM_IMAGES = 2;
    private final static int IMG_HEIGHT = 60;
    private final static int IMG_WIDTH = 205;
}
```

Listing 5-4.
The
RoadPatrolBean
extended with the
MaxSpeed property.

```java
package Cars;

import java.awt.*;
import java.io.*;
import java.beans.*;
import java.util.*;
import java.awt.image.*;

/**
 * The RoadPatrolBean has a maximum speed as is its basic
     property.
 *
 * @see            CarBean
 * @see            TrafficLightBean
 */
public class RoadPatrolBean    extends       Canvas
                               implements    Serializable,
                                             ImageObserver
{
    // constructor
    public RoadPatrolBean ()
    {
        setSize (IMG_WIDTH, IMG_HEIGHT);

        if (m_CopImage == null)
        {
            Toolkit tk = getToolkit ();
            m_CopImage = tk.getImage
                    ("c:/McGrawHill/Bean/cars/Cop.gif");
        }
    }


    public void paint (Graphics g)
    {
        g.drawImage (m_CopImage, 0, 0, this);
    }

    public boolean imageUpdate (Image img, int infoFlag,
        int x, int y, int width, int height)
    {
        if ( (infoFlag & ALLBITS) != 0)
        {
            repaint ();
            return false;
        }

        return true;
    }
```

Listing 5-4.
Continued.

```
// Maximum speed Property ******************************
/**
 * Returns the maximum speed
 * @see #setMaxSpeed
 */
public int getMaxSpeed ()
{
    return m_iMaxSpeed;
}


/**
 * Sets the maximum speed
 * @see #getMaxSpeed
 */
public void setMaxSpeed (int iNewMaxSpeed)
{
    m_iMaxSpeed = iNewMaxSpeed;
    repaint ();
}


// private data members ******************************
private int    m_iMaxSpeed        = 60;

private static Image m_CopImage = null;

private final static int IMG_HEIGHT = 136;
private final static int IMG_WIDTH  = 111;
}
```

MyTimer

The **MyTimer** class extends the **Thread** object. The **constructor** function of the **MyTimer** class takes two parameters. The first parameter is an object that implements the CallBackInterface, which contains a **wakeup()** method with no parameters.

The object passed into the first variable is stored in one of its data members: **m_cb**. The second parameter is an integer variable (**m_iTimeInterval**) specifying the time interval after which it notifies the object passed through the first parameter. It notifies the object by calling the **wakeup()** method. The **run()** method has an infinite **WHILE** loop in which it sleeps for the specified time interval and then executes the CallBackInterface's **wakeup()** method.

The **TrafficLightBean** extends from the Canvas component and implements Serializable, imageObserver, and the Cars.CallBackInterface

Listing 5-5.
The CallBackInterface
for the **MyTimer**
class.

```
package Cars;

/**
 * The CallBackInterface provides an interface that is
     implemented
 * by the object using the MyTimer class.
 *
 * MyTimer calls the implemented wakeup method after the
     specified
 * time interval.
 *
 * @see            MyTimer
 * @see            TrafficLightBean
 */
public interface CallBackInterface
{
    public void wakeup ();
}
```

Listing 5-6.
A **Timer** class
for use in the
TrafficLightBean.

```
package Cars;

/**
 * The MyTimer class is a timer class that notifies an
     object
 * after every time interval.
 *
 * The object needs to implement the
     Cars.CallBackInterface.
 *
 *
 * @see            CallBackInterface
 * @see            TrafficLightBean
 */
public class MyTimer extends Thread
{
    public MyTimer (Cars.CallBackInterface cb, int
        iTimeInterval)
    {
        m_cb = cb;
        m_iTimeInterval = iTimeInterval;
    }

    /**
     * The setTime method is used to specify the time
           interval
     */
    public void setTime (int iTimeInterval)
```

Listing 5-6.
Continued.

```
{
    m_iTimeInterval = iTimeInterval;
}

public void run ()
{
    while (true)
    {
        try
        {
            sleep (m_iTimeInterval);
            m_cb.wakeup ();
        }
        catch (java.lang.InterruptedException e)
        {
            System.out.println (e);
        }

    }
}
private CallBackInterface    m_cb;
private int                     m_iTimeInterval;
}
```

interface. This Bean has the following methods: **constructor, paint()**, and **imageUpdate()**. The **wakeup()** method provides the implementation of the CallBackInterface and also has some private helper methods. It stores the images to be displayed in the **m_LightImages** variable of type Image. Its **m_timer** data member is defined as type **MyTimer**.

The **state** property of this Bean is stored in the **m_cInitialState** variable of type Color. The **getState()** and **setState()** are accessor methods of this property. The private data member **m_cState** is used to store the current state of the **TrafficLightBean**. The red, orange, and green time interval properties are stored in following variables: **m_iRedTimeInterval**, **m_iOrangeTimeInterval**, and **m_iGreenTimeInterval**. Accessor methods are provided to get and set these properties.

The **constructor** method sets the Bean's dimensions by using the **setSize()** method. It then loads the images into the **m_LightImages** variable using the Toolkit's **getImage()** method. It sets its initial state to red. It constructs a new **MyTimer** object and executes its **start()** method. The **start()** method is implemented by the **Thread** class from which the **MyTimer** class extends.

The **paint()** method overrides the Canvas' **paint()** method. Depending on the current state, it displays the appropriate traffic light image. The **Graphics** object's **drawImage()** method is used to display the image. The **imageUpdate()** method is explained in the previous section on the **CarBean**.

The `wakeup()` method calls the private method `nextState()` to change its state and then executes the `repaint()` method, which forces the `paint()` method to be called. The `getColorFromState()` private method converts the state represented as an integer to type Color. The `getStateFromColor()` private method converts the state represented as a color to type Integer.

Listing 5-7.
The TrafficLightBean.

```
package Cars;

import java.awt.*;
import java.io.*;
import java.beans.*;
import java.awt.image.*;


/**
 * The TrafficLightBean class has three states: red,
       orange, and green. It changes
 * its state after specified time intervals. It uses the
       MyTimer class to notify
 * it at specified time intervals.
 *
 * Depending on its state the TrafficLightBean loads
       appropriate images.
 *
 * @see            MyTimer
 * @see            CarBean
 */
public class TrafficLightBean extends        Canvas
                              implements      Serializable,
                                              Cars.CallBack-
                                              Interface,
                                              mageObserver

{
    // constructor
    public TrafficLightBean ()
    {
        setSize (IMG_WIDTH, IMG_HEIGHT);
        if (m_LightImages == null)
        {
            m_LightImages = new Image [NUM_IMAGES];

            Toolkit tk = getToolkit ();
            m_LightImages[0] = tk.getImage
            ("c:/McGrawHill/Bean/cars/RedSignal.gif");
```

Listing 5-7.
Continued.

```
            m_LightImages[1] = tk.getImage
            ("c:/McGrawHill/Bean/cars/OrangeSignal.gif");
            m_LightImages[2] = tk.getImage
            ("c:/McGrawHill/Bean/cars/GreenSignal.gif");
    }

    // set initial state
    m_cState = Color.red;

    //start timer
    m_timer = new Cars.MyTimer
        (this, m_iRedTimeInterval);
    m_timer.start ();
}

public void paint (Graphics g)
{
    if (m_cState == Color.red)
        g.drawImage (m_LightImages[0], 0, 0, this);
    else if (m_cState == Color.orange)
        g.drawImage (m_LightImages[1], 0, 0, this);
    else
        g.drawImage (m_LightImages[2], 0, 0, this);
}


public boolean imageUpdate (Image img, int infoFlag,
    int x, int y, int width, int height)
{
    if ( (infoFlag & ALLBITS) != 0)
    {
        repaint ();
        return false;
    }

    return true;
}


// State Property **************************************
/**
  * Return the state of the Traffic Light. This is a
        bound property.
  * @see #setState
  */
public String getState ()
{
    switch (getStateFromColor (m_cInitialState))
    {
    case RED:
        return "Stop";
```

Continues

Listing 5-7.
Continued.

```java
        case ORANGE:
            return "Caution";
        case GREEN:
            return "Go";
        }
        return null;
}


/**
 * Sets the state of the Traffic Light. This is a
     bound property.
 * @see #getState
 */
public void setState (String sNewState)
{
    int iNewState = 0;
    if (sNewState.equals ("Stop") )
    {
        iNewState = RED;
    }
    else if (sNewState.equals ("Caution") )
    {
        iNewState = ORANGE;
    }
    else if (sNewState.equals ("Go") )
    {
        iNewState = GREEN;
    }

    m_cState = m_cInitialState = getColorFromState
            (iNewState);
    repaint ();
}



// RedTimeInterval Property ***************************
/**
 * Returns the red time interval.
 * @see #setRedTimeInterval
 */
public int getRedTimeInterval ()
{
    return m_iRedTimeInterval;
}

/**
 * Sets the red time interval.
 * @see #getRedTimeInterval
 */
public void setRedTimeInterval (int iRedTimeInterval)
{
```

Listing 5-7.
Continued.

```
        m_iRedTimeInterval = iRedTimeInterval;
}


// OrangeTimeInterval Property ************************
/**
 * Returns the orange time interval.
 * @see #setOrangeTimeInterval
 */
public int getOrangeTimeInterval ()
{
    return m_iOrangeTimeInterval;
}

/**
 * Sets the orange time interval.
 * @see #getOrangeTimeInterval
 */
public void setOrangeTimeInterval
    (int iOrangeTimeInterval)
{
    m_iOrangeTimeInterval = iOrangeTimeInterval;
}


// GreenTimeInterval Property ************************
/**
 * Returns the green time interval.
 * @see #setGreenTimeInterval
 */
public int getGreenTimeInterval ()
{
    return m_iGreenTimeInterval;
}

/**
 * Sets the green time interval.
 * @see #getGreenTimeInterval
 */
public void setGreenTimeInterval (int
    iGreenTimeInterval)
{
    m_iGreenTimeInterval = iGreenTimeInterval;
}

// implementation of CallBackInterface ***************
/**
 * The wakeup method is an implementation of the
 *    CallBackInterface
 */
public void wakeup ()
```

Continues

Listing 5-7.
Continued.

```java
{
    Color cOldState = nextState ();
    repaint ();
}

// private methods ***********************************
private Color getColorFromState (int iState)
{
    switch (iState)
    {
        case this.RED:
            return Color.red;
        case this.ORANGE:
            return Color.orange;
        case this.GREEN:
            return Color.green;
        default:
            return null;
    }
}

private int getStateFromColor (Color c)
{
    if (c == Color.red)
        return RED;
    else if (c == Color.orange)
        return ORANGE;
    else if (c == Color.green)
        return GREEN;
    else
        return 0;
}

private synchronized Color nextState ()
{
    Color cOldState = m_cState;
    if (m_cState == Color.red)
    {
        m_cState = Color.green;
        m_timer.setTime (m_iGreenTimeInterval);
    }
    else if (m_cState == Color.green)
    {
        m_cState = Color.orange;
        m_timer.setTime (m_iOrangeTimeInterval);
    }
    else if (m_cState == Color.orange)
    {
        m_cState = Color.red;
        m_timer.setTime (m_iRedTimeInterval);
    }
    else
```

Listing 5-7.
Continued.

```
     {
          m_cState = Color.red;
          m_timer.setTime (m_iRedTimeInterval);
     }
     return cOldState;
}

// private data members ******************************
private Color m_cState                = Color.red;
private Color m_cInitialState         = Color.red;

private int    m_iRedTimeInterval     = 1400;
private int    m_iOrangeTimeInterval  = 500;
private int    m_iGreenTimeInterval   = 2000;

private MyTimer m_timer;

// constants *****************************************
private static final   int RED         = 1; // red
private static final   int ORANGE      = 2; // orange
private static final   int GREEN       = 3; // green

private static Image[] m_LightImages = null;

private final static int NUM_IMAGES = 3;
private final static int IMG_HEIGHT = 112;
private final static int IMG_WIDTH = 60;

}
```

Boolean Properties

A *Boolean property* is a type of single-valued property; it has two states—
true and *false*. Instead of using **get<*PropertyName*>()** to access a single-
valued property, JavaBeans specifies the **is<*PropertyName*>()** naming convention as a getter accessor method for Boolean Properties. The naming
convention for the setter method is the same as for the single-valued properties. Note that both the getter and setter methods need to be defined for
a Boolean property; for the single-valued property, the setter methods don't
need to be defined.

An example of a Boolean property is the **CarBean**'s **Moving** property. This
property has the following getter and setter methods. The **setMoving()**
method is a dummy function; it's just there so JavaBean recognizes **Moving**
as a property:

```
Public boolean isMoving ();
Public void setMoving (boolean b);
```

Indexed Properties

JavaBeans also has properties that can contain multiple values, which could be zero or more. A particular value in the collection can be referenced by an index, so these properties are referred to as *indexed properties*.

The getter and setter methods have the same naming conventions as the single-valued property. In addition, getter and setter methods can be provided to access and modify individual elements in the collection. These getter and setter accessor methods have a syntax similar to the single-valued property accessor methods, except that they take an additional integer argument.

Here is the single-valued property syntax:

```
<PropertyType>[] get<PropertyName> ()
void set<PropertyName> ( <PropertyType> [] values)
```

This is the multivalued property syntax:

```
<PropertyType> get<PropertyName> (int index)
void set<PropertyName> ( int index, <PropertyType> value)
```

If the Bean supports the single-valued form of accessor methods, the internal data members must implement the collection as an array, which exposes the internal implementation. Therefore, use these accessor methods only if they're absolutely necessary. The multivalued form of accessor methods doesn't have this drawback and encapsulates the implementation of the indexed property.

NOTE *Note that the current 1.0 release of JavaBeans restricts the type of the index to an integer. The BDK 1.0 BeanBox doesn't support indexed properties.*

Assume that the **TrafficLightBean**'s time intervals were stored not as three different properties, but as an indexed property. The data member would have to be defined as an integer array of index three. The variable would be declared as follows:

```
int[] m_iTimeIntervalArray = {1400 , 500, 2000};
```

The getter and setter methods would look like this:

```
public int getTimeInterval (int index);
public void setTimeInterval (int index, int iTimeInterval);
```

Bound and Constrained Properties

The single-valued and indexed properties merely define a property. What we would like to do is notify other Beans if there's a change in a property. JavaBeans has two ways to notify interested listener Beans.

A Bean can supply a means for other Beans to be registered as listeners. The listeners are somewhat "tied" to that property because they're notified of every change in it. This property is, therefore, called a *bound property*.

A Bean can also provide a mechanism for registered listeners to approve of a change in one of its properties. If all the registered listeners approve of the change, then—and only then—can the source Bean change the property's value. Because this property is rather limited as to when it can change its value—depending on approval by other Beans—it's called a *constrained property*.

Bound Properties

Here are some guidelines for implementing a bound property:

1. Identify the bound properties in the source Bean.

2. The source Bean should have a way to register and deregister listeners and to notify listeners of a change in that property, and it should manage the list of listeners.

3. The target Bean should implement the PropertyChangeListener interface. The target Bean can take any necessary action to respond to that property's change event.

REGISTER AND DEREGISTER LISTENERS The source Bean can register and deregister Beans that implement the PropertyChange-Listener interface, which is inherited from the java.util.EventListener interface. The PropertyChangeListener defines only one method—`propertyChange()`—which is called by the Bean whose bound property has changed. The Bean with the bound property calls the `propertyChange()` method of the listener Bean by firing the `PropertyChange` event. The `propertyChange()` method takes a `PropertyChangeEvent` object as an argument.

NOTIFY LISTENERS   The source Bean notifies the listener Bean of a property change by firing a **PropertyChange** event, as mentioned. The **PropertyChangeEvent** object contains the name of the changed property, its old value, and its new value. The old and new values must be of type Object.

GRANULARITY OF THE NOTIFICATION MECHANISM   The granularity of the notification mechanism depends on the Bean, not on the property. What this means is that a listener can register to listen to notification messages from a Bean. This Bean can send all registered listeners a notification for one or more of its property changes. It's up to the listener Beans to filter out the property change notification messages they're interested in and take the appropriate action.

PROPERTYCHANGESUPPORTCLASS   **PropertyChangeSupport** is a utility class supplied by JavaBeans. This class provides three methods: **addPropertyChangeListener()**, **removePropertyChangeListener()**, and the **firePropertyChange()**. The first two methods are used to register and deregister listeners and take the PropertyChangeListener as a parameter. Using the framework, the target Bean can register as a listener to the bound property visually. The framework then calls the **addPropertyChangeListener()** and **removePropertyChangeListener()** methods to register or deregister the target Bean.

The **firePropertyChange()** method is used to fire the **PropertyChange** event to notify listeners of a property change. This method takes three parameters: The name of the property, its old value, and its new value. The old and new values must be of type Object. This method basically creates the **PropertyChangeEvent** object from its parameters.

Let's specify **State** as a bound property in the **TrafficLightBean**. One of the possible listeners would be the **CarBean**. Therefore, the **CarBean** registers itself as a listener to the **State** bound property of the **TrafficLightBean**. On a change of state, the **TrafficLightBean** notifies all of its listeners. The **CarBean** changes its speed based on the **State** property of the **TrafficLightBean**.

For the **TrafficLightBean** to support bound properties, it supplies the **addPropertyChangeListener()** and the **removePropertyChangeListener()** to register and deregister listeners. To maintain the list of listeners, **PropertyChangeSupport** is used. The data member **m_change** is defined as a member of the **PropertyChangeSupport** class. The **constructor** method of **PropertyChangeSupport** takes in a parameter of type Object, which is basically the source Bean reference. The **addPropertyChangeListener()** only calls the **ProperyChangeSupport**'s **addPropertyChangeListener()** method, and **the** **removePropertyChangeListener()** only calls the **ProperyChangeSupport**'s **removePropertyChangeListener()** method.

The **wakeup()** method changes the state of the **TrafficLightBean**. In this method, the listeners are notified of the change in **state** by calling the **PropertyChangeSupport**'s **firePropertyChange()** method.

Listing 5-8.
The
Traffic-LightBean
extended with the
firePropertyChange()
method.

```
package Cars;

import java.awt.*;
import java.io.*;
import java.beans.*;
import java.awt.image.*;


/**
 * The TrafficLightBean class has three states: red,
     orange, and green. It changes
 * its state after specified time intervals. It uses the
     MyTimer class to notify
 * it at specified time intervals.
 *
 * Depending on its state the TrafficLightBean loads
     appropriate images.
 *
 * Its state is a bound property. It notifes registered
     listeners of its change
 * in state.
 *
 * @see           MyTimer
 * @see           CarBean
*/
public class TrafficLightBean extends        Canvas
                               implements    Serializable,
                                             Cars.CallBack-
                                             Interface,
                                             ImageObserver

{
    // constructor
    public TrafficLightBean ()
    {
        setSize (IMG_WIDTH, IMG_HEIGHT);
        if (m_LightImages == null)
        {
            m_LightImages = new Image [NUM_IMAGES];
```
                                                    Continues

Listing 5-8.
Continued.

```
            Toolkit tk = getToolkit ();
            m_LightImages[0] = tk.getImage
              ("c:/McGrawHill/Bean/Cars/RedSignal.gif");
            m_LightImages[1] = tk.getImage
              ("c:/McGrawHill/Bean/Cars/OrangeSignal.gif");
            m_LightImages[2] = tk.getImage
              ("c:/McGrawHill/Bean/Cars/GreenSignal.gif");
        }

        // set initial state
        m_cState = Color.red;

        //start timer
        m_timer = new Cars.MyTimer
              (this, m_iRedTimeInterval);
        m_timer.start ();
    }

    public void paint (Graphics g)
    {
        if (m_cState == Color.red)
            g.drawImage (m_LightImages[0], 0, 0, this);
        else if (m_cState == Color.orange)
            g.drawImage (m_LightImages[1], 0, 0, this);
        else
            g.drawImage (m_LightImages[2], 0, 0, this);
    }


    public boolean imageUpdate (Image img, int infoFlag,
int x, int y, int width, int height)
    {
        if ( (infoFlag & ALLBITS) != 0)
        {
            repaint ();
            return false;
        }

        return true;
    }



    // State Property ************************************
    /**
     * Return the state of the Traffic Light. This is a
         bound property.
     * @see #setState
     */
    public String getState ()
    {
        switch (getStateFromColor (m_cInitialState))
```

Listing 5-8.
Continued.

```
    {
    case RED:
        return "Stop";
    case ORANGE:
        return "Caution";
    case GREEN:
        return "Go";
    }
    return null;
}

/**
 * Sets the state of the Traffic Light. This is a
 *     bound property.
 * @see #getState
 */
public void setState (String sNewState)
{
    int iNewState = 0;
    if (sNewState.equals ("Stop") )
    {
        iNewState = RED;
    }
    else if (sNewState.equals ("Caution") )
    {
        iNewState = ORANGE;
    }
    else if (sNewState.equals ("Go") )
    {
        iNewState = GREEN;
    }

    m_cState = m_cInitialState = getColorFromState
        (iNewState);
    repaint ();
}


// RedTimeInterval Property ****************************
/**
 * Returns the red time interval.
 * @see #setRedTimeInterval
 */
public int getRedTimeInterval ()
{
    return m_iRedTimeInterval;
}

/**
 * Sets the red time interval.
```

Continues

Listing 5-8.
Continued.

```java
 * @see #getRedTimeInterval
 */
public void setRedTimeInterval (int iRedTimeInterval)
{
    System.out.println("Called "+iRedTimeInterval);
    m_iRedTimeInterval = iRedTimeInterval;
}


// OrangeTimeInterval Property ************************
/**
 * Returns the orange time interval.
 * @see #setOrangeTimeInterval
 */
public int getOrangeTimeInterval ()
{
    return m_iOrangeTimeInterval;
}

/**
 * Sets the orange time interval.
 * @see #getOrangeTimeInterval
 */
public void setOrangeTimeInterval (int
    iOrangeTimeInterval)
{
    m_iOrangeTimeInterval = iOrangeTimeInterval;
}


// GreenTimeInterval Property ************************
/**
 * Returns the green time interval.
 * @see #setGreenTimeInterval
 */
public int getGreenTimeInterval ()
{
    return m_iGreenTimeInterval;
}

/**
 * Sets the green time interval.
 * @see #getGreenTimeInterval
 */
public void setGreenTimeInterval (int
    iGreenTimeInterval)
{
    m_iGreenTimeInterval = iGreenTimeInterval;
}

// implementation of CallBackInterface ***************
/**
```

Listing 5-8.
Continued.

```
     * The wakeup method is an implementation of the
          CallBackInterface
     */
    public void wakeup ()
    {
        Color cOldState = nextState ();
        if (m_cState == Color.red)
        {
            m_change.firePropertyChange ("State",
                "Caution", "Stop");
        }
        else if (m_cState == Color.orange)
        {
            m_change.firePropertyChange ("State", "Go",
                "Caution");
        }
        else if (m_cState == Color.green)
        {
            m_change.firePropertyChange ("State", "Stop",
                "Go");
        }

        repaint ();
    }


    // methods to add and remove listeners
        ****************
    /**
     * The addPropertyChangeListener method is used to add
          bound property listeners
     * @see #removePropertyChangeListener
     */
    public void addPropertyChangeListener
        (PropertyChangeListener pcl)
    {
        m_change.addPropertyChangeListener (pcl);
    }


    /**
     * The removePropertyChangeListener method is used to
          remove bound property listeners
     * @see #addPropertyChangeListener
     */
    public void removePropertyChangeListener
        (PropertyChangeListener pcl)
    {
        m_change.removePropertyChangeListener (pcl);
    }
```

Continues

```java
// private methods ************************************
private Color getColorFromState (int iState)
{
    switch (iState)
    {
        case this.RED:
            return Color.red;
        case this.ORANGE:
            return Color.orange;
        case this.GREEN:
            return Color.green;
        default:
            return null;
    }
}

private int getStateFromColor (Color c)
{
    if (c == Color.red)
        return RED;
    else if (c == Color.orange)
        return ORANGE;
    else if (c == Color.green)
        return GREEN;
    else
        return 0;
}

private synchronized Color nextState ()
{
    Color cOldState = m_cState;
    if (m_cState == Color.red)
    {
        m_cState = Color.green;
        m_timer.setTime (m_iGreenTimeInterval);
    }
    else if (m_cState == Color.green)
    {
        m_cState = Color.orange;
        m_timer.setTime (m_iOrangeTimeInterval);
    }
    else if (m_cState == Color.orange)
    {
        m_cState = Color.red;
        m_timer.setTime (m_iRedTimeInterval);
    }
    else
    {
        m_cState = Color.red;
        m_timer.setTime (m_iRedTimeInterval);
    }
    return cOldState;
```

Listing 5-8.
Continued.

```
        }

        // private data members ******************************
        private Color m_cState              = Color.red;
        private Color m_cInitialState       = Color.red;

        private int    m_iRedTimeInterval    = 1400;
        private int    m_iOrangeTimeInterval = 500;
        private int    m_iGreenTimeInterval  = 2000;

        transient private MyTimer m_timer;
        private PropertyChangeSupport m_change
                                            = new Property-
                                              ChangeSupport
                                              (this);

        // constants ********************************************
        private static final   int RED       = 1; // red
        private static final   int ORANGE    = 2; // orange
        private static final   int GREEN     = 3; // green

        private static Image[] m_LightImages = null;

        private final static int NUM_IMAGES = 3;
        private final static int IMG_HEIGHT = 112;
        private final static int IMG_WIDTH = 60;

    }
```

The **CarBean** needs to implement the PropertyChangeListener interface.
If it doesn't, the BeanBox takes care of that, generating the hookup
adapter class that would implement the interface. The **CarBean** provides
the **propertyChange()** method to implement the PropertyChangeListener interface. This function takes the **PropertyChangeEvent** object as
a parameter. The **PropertyChangeEvent** object has methods to get information about the property name, old value, and new value. The
CarBean's **propertyChange()** method depends on the new value supplied
by the **TrafficLightBean** to change its speed.

Constrained Properties

Constrained properties offer a way for other Beans to control a property's change in value. Before a value of a constrained property can be
changed, the new value must be approved by all its vetoable listeners.

```java
package Cars;

import java.awt.*;
import java.io.*;
import java.Beans.*;
import java.awt.image.*;


/**
 * The CarBean has a maximum and a current speed as is its
     basic properties.
 * This Bean is specified a maximum speed that it could go
     up to. It has
 * a current speed, which could be from zero to the
     maximum speed specified.
 *
 * Depending on its current speed, the CarBean loads
     appropriate images.
 *
 * It implements the PropertyChangeListener interface. It
     can register
 * with the TrafficLight Bean to get notifications for the
     TrafficLight
 * changes.
 *
 * The maxiumum speed is a vetoable property. The
     RoadPatrolBean could be
 * a listener to this vetoable property.
 *
 * @see RoadPatrolBean
 * @see TrafficLightBean
 */
public class CarBean extends     Canvas
                        implements Serializable,
                                    PropertyChangeListener,
                                    ImageObserver
{
    // constructor
    public CarBean ()
    {
        super ();

        setSize (IMG_WIDTH, IMG_HEIGHT);
    if (m_CarImages == null)
    {
            m_CarImages = new Image [NUM_IMAGES];

            Toolkit tk = getToolkit ();
            m_CarImages[0] = tk.getImage
                ("c:/McGrawHill/Bean/Cars/Car.gif");
            m_CarImages[1] = tk.getImage
```

Listing 5-9.
Continued.

```
                              ("c:/McGrawHill/Bean/Cars/MovingCar.gif");
            }
    }

    public void paint (Graphics g)
    {
        boolean bRet;
        if (m_iSpeed == 0)
        {
            bRet = g.drawImage (m_CarImages[0], 0, 0,
                this);
        }
        else
        {
            bRet = g.drawImage (m_CarImages[1], 0, 0,
                this);
        }
    }

    public boolean imageUpdate (Image img, int infoFlag,
        int x, int y, int width, int height)
    {
        if ( (infoFlag & ALLBITS) != 0)
        {
            repaint ();
            return false;
        }

        return true;
    }


// moving property ***********************************
/**
 * Returns a boolean whether the car is moving or not
 * @see #setMoving
 */
public boolean isMoving ()
{
if (m_iSpeed == 0)
return false;

return true;
}

/**
 * The dummy set method for the Moving property
 * @see #isMoving
 */
public void setMoving (boolean b)
```

Continues

```
{

}


    // Speed (current) property ****************************
/**
 * Returns the current speed
 * @see #setSpeed
*/
    public int getSpeed ()
    {
        return m_iSpeed;
    }

/**
 * Sets the current speed
 * @see #getSpeed
*/
    public void setSpeed (int iNewSpeed)
    {
if (m_bCop == true)
{
m_iSpeed = 0;
}
else
{
m_iSpeed = iNewSpeed;
}

        repaint ();
    }


    // Maximum Speed property *****************************
/**
 * Returns the maximum speed. This is a constrained
    property.
 * @see #setMaxSpeed
*/
    public int getMaxSpeed ()
    {
        return m_iMaxSpeed;
    }

/**
 * Sets the maximum speed. This is a constrained property.
 * @see #getMaxSpeed
*/
    public void setMaxSpeed (int iNewSpeed)
    {
int iOldSpeed = m_iMaxSpeed;
```

```
            try
            {
                m_vetoChange.fireVetoableChange ("MaxSpeed",
                                            new Integer
                                            (iOldSpeed),
                                            new Integer
                                            (iNewSpeed) );
            }
            catch (PropertyVetoException e)
            {
                System.out.println ("New Speed = " + iNewSpeed
                    + " vetoed !!!");
                return;
            }

            m_iMaxSpeed = iNewSpeed;
            repaint ();
        }


// propertyChange ***********************************
/**
 * The propertyChange method is an implementation for the
    PropertyChange interface
*/
    public void propertyChange (PropertyChangeEvent event)
    {
// Handle only State events coming from other Beans.
if (event.getPropertyName().equals ("State"))
{
if (event.getNewValue ().equals ("Stop"))
setSpeed (0);
else if (event.getNewValue ().equals ("Caution"))
setSpeed (getMaxSpeed () / 2);
else if (event.getNewValue ().equals ("Go"))
setSpeed (getMaxSpeed ());

System.out.println ("Property: " + event.getPropertyName ()
    +
" Old: " + event.getOldValue () +
" New: " + event.getNewValue () +
" Speed: " + getSpeed ());
repaint ();
}
    }


// methods to add and remove listeners ****************
/**
 * The addVetoableChangeListener method is used to add
    vetoable property listeners.
```

Continues

Listing 5-9.
Continued.

```
 * @see #removeVetoableChangeListener
 */
    public void addVetoableChangeListener
        (VetoableChangeListener pcl)
    {
        m_vetoChange.addVetoableChangeListener (pcl);
    }

/**
 * The removeVetoableChangeListener method is used to
   remove vetoable property listeners.
 * @see #addVetoableChangeListener
 */
    public void removeVetoableChangeListener
        (VetoableChangeListener pcl)
    {
        m_vetoChange.removeVetoableChangeListener (pcl);
    }

    private int    m_iSpeed      = 55; // mph
    private int    m_iMaxSpeed   = 55; // mph

    private boolean m_bCop = false;
    private static Image[]   m_CarImages = null;

    private VetoableChangeSupport m_vetoChange
                                = new VetoableChange-
                                  Support (this);

    private final static int NUM_IMAGES = 2;
    private final static int IMG_HEIGHT = 60;
    private final static int IMG_WIDTH = 205;
}
```

The listeners need to implement the VetoableChangeListener interface, and they have the right to veto the change in the other Bean's constrained property.

REGISTER AND DEREGISTER LISTENERS The source Bean can register and deregister Beans that implement the VetoableChangeListener interface, which is inherited from the java.util.EventListener interface.

NOTIFY LISTENERS The source Bean notifies the listener Bean of a property change by firing a **PropertyChange** event. The **PropertyChangeEvent** object contains the name of the changed property, its old value, and its new value. The old and new values must be of type Object.

VETOABLECHANGESUPPORT CLASS **VetoableChangeSupport** is a utility class provided by JavaBeans. This class supplies three methods: **addVetoableChangeListener()**, **removeVetoableChangeListener()**, and **firePropertyChange()**. The first two methods are used to register and deregister listeners and take the VetoableChangeListener as a parameter. Using the framework, the target Bean can visually register as a listener to the bound property. The framework then calls the **addVetoableChangeListener()** and **removeVetoableChangeListener()** methods to register or deregister the target Bean.

The **firePropertyChange()** method is used to fire the **PropertyChange** event to approve the listeners of a property change. This method takes three parameters: The name of the property, its old value, and its new value. The old and new values must be of type Object. This method basically creates the **PropertyChangeEvent** object from its parameters. This method should catch the **PropertyVetoException**. If a **PropertyVetoException** is raised, then the property value can't be changed, else the property value can be changed to its new value.

The listener Bean needs to implement the VetoableChangeListener interface, which defines the method **vetoableChange()**. This method takes a **PropertyChangeEvent** as a parameter and throws a **PropertyVetoException**. The listener can examine the new and the old values of a constrained property of the **PropertyChangeEvent**, which is a parameter of the **vetoableChange()** method. The **PropertyChangeEvent** provides the following methods: **getNewValue()**, **getOldValue()**, and **getPropertyName()**. In the **vetoableChange()** method, the listener can approve the new value by simply returning from the function, or the listener can disapprove the new value by sending a **PropertyVetoException**.

MaxSpeed can be a constrained property of the **CarBean**. One of the possible vetoable listeners would be the **RoadPatrolBean**. Therefore, the **RoadPatrolBean** registers itself as a vetoable listener to the car's **MaxSpeed** property. When the car needs to change its maximum speed, it notifies all its vetoable listeners. The **CarBean** can change its maximum speed, depending on approval or disapproval from its listener Beans.

For the **CarBean** to support the constrained properties, it provides the **addVetoableChangeListener()** and the **removeVetoableChangeListener()** methods to register and deregister listeners. (Refer to Listing 5-9.) To maintain the list of listeners, **VetoableChangeSupport** is used. The data member **m_vetoChange** is defined as a member of the **VetoableChangeSupport** class. The **constructor** method takes in a parameter of type Object, which is basically the source Bean reference. The **addVetoableChangeListener()** only calls the **VetoableChangeSupport**'s **addVetoableChangeListener()**

method, and the `removeVetoableChangeListener()` only calls the `VetoableChangeSupport`'s `removeVetoableChangeListener()` method.

The `setMaxSpeed()` method changes the maximum speed of the `CarBean`. In this method, the listeners are asked for approval by calling the `VetoableChangeSupport`'s `fireVetoableChange()` method. The method is called in a `try` block; if any vetoable listeners disapprove of this maximum speed change, they return a `PropertyVetoException`. Therefore, if `PropertyVetoException` is sent by any of its listeners, the maximum value can't be changed to the new value. If all the vetoable listeners approve of the change in `MaxSpeed`, then the speed is changed, and the `repaint()` method is called to display the right image based on the new `MaxSpeed`.

The `RoadPatrolBean` needs to implement the VetoableChangeListener interface. The `RoadPatrolBean` provides the `vetoableChange()` method to do this. This method takes the `PropertyChangeEvent` object as a parameter. The `PropertyChangeEvent` object supplies methods to get information about the property name, old value, and new value. The `RoadPatrolBean`'s `vetoableChange()` method approves or disapproves of the `CarBean`'s new maximum speed, depending on its maximum allowable speed. The `RoadPatrolBean` can disapprove the maximum speed by returning a `PropertyVetoException`.

Listing 5-10.
The
RoadPatrolBean
extended to handle
vetoable change
fired by the
CarBean.

```
package Cars;

import java.awt.*;
import java.io.*;
import java.Beans.*;
import java.util.*;
import java.awt.image.*;

/**
 * The RoadPatrolBean has a maximum speed as is its basic
     property.
 *
 * It implements the VetoableChangeListener so that it can
     veto the
 * maximum speed change in other Beans if that speed is
     greater than
 * its maximum speed.
 *
 * @see          CarBean
```

Listing 5-10.
Continued.

```
 * @see              TrafficLightBean
 */
public class RoadPatrolBean    extends      Canvas
                               implements   Serializable,
                                            Vetoable-
                                            ChangeListener,
                                            ImageObserver
{
    // constructor
    public RoadPatrolBean ()
    {
        setSize (IMG_WIDTH, IMG_HEIGHT);

        if (m_CopImage == null)
        {
            Toolkit tk = getToolkit ();
            m_CopImage = tk.getImage
                ("c:/McGrawHill/Bean/Cars/Cop.gif");
        }
    }


    public void paint (Graphics g)
    {
        g.drawImage (m_CopImage, 0, 0, this);
    }

    public boolean imageUpdate (Image img, int infoFlag,
        int x, int y, int width, int height)
    {
        if ( (infoFlag & ALLBITS) != 0)
        {
            repaint ();
            return false;
        }

        return true;
    }


    // Maximum speed Property *****************************
    /**
     * Returns the maximum speed
     * @see #setMaxSpeed
     */
    public int getMaxSpeed ()
    {
        return m_iMaxSpeed;
    }
```

Continues

Listing 5-10.

Continued.

```
/**
 * Sets the maximum speed
 * @see #getMaxSpeed
 */
public void setMaxSpeed (int iNewMaxSpeed)
{
    m_iMaxSpeed = iNewMaxSpeed;
    repaint ();
}


// vetoable change event handler ***********************
/**
 * The vetoableChange method is an implementation for
     the VetoableChangeInterface
 * @exception     java.Beans.PropertyVetoException
 *                     if the RoadPatrolBean disapproves
                          of the new maximum speed value
 *                     it throws a PropertyVetoException
 */
public void vetoableChange (PropertyChangeEvent event)
        throws PropertyVetoException
{
    Integer I = (Integer) event.getNewValue();

    if (I.intValue () > m_iMaxSpeed)
    {
        throw new PropertyVetoException ("New Value
            greater than " + m_iMaxSpeed, event);
    }

    System.out.println ("Property: " +
                        event.getPropertyName () +
                        " Old: " + event.getOldValue
                        () +
                        " New: " + event.getNewValue
                        () +
                        " Speed: " + getMaxSpeed ());
}


// private data members *****************************
private int    m_iMaxSpeed          = 60;

private static Image m_CopImage = null;

private final static int IMG_HEIGHT = 136;
private final static int IMG_WIDTH  = 111;
}
```

CONCLUSION

In this chapter we introduced the concept of properties and how they can be manipulated to manage Beans' appearance and behavior. We classified the properties into single-valued and indexed properties. We also saw how other Beans could be notified of a change in a property's value as well as give other Beans the option of keeping the new value from being set. We saw the different design signatures required to implement and register Beans. Even though we haven't seen events until now, we can go ahead and write a functional Bean and manipulate its properties visually.

6

JavaBeans Events

In this chapter, we introduce the delegation events model, then move on to an explanation of events in JavaBeans. We explain events with the help of some simple example Beans and show how these Beans communicate with each other by notifying other Beans of changes to their states and user-triggered events.

This chapter will cover the following topics:

- The JDK 1.1 delegation events model
- Listener interfaces and event adapters
- A simple example
- Low-level events
- Semantic events
- User-defined `ActionEvent` in action
- AWT enhancements
- Emerging frameworks
- JDK 1.1 Abstract Windowing Toolkit (AWT) enhancements
- An event-generating Bean
- Hookup adapters

The JDK 1.1 Delegation Events Model

These are the primary goals Sun wanted to achieve when designing the new delegation model:

- The model should be simple and easy to learn.
- The application code and the *Graphical User Interface* (GUI) code should be loosely coupled—that is, there should be a clean distinction between the two logical modules.
- Error checking at compile time should be strong, to create robust event-handling code.
- The model should be flexible enough to use components in a wide variety of applications.
- The model should allow runtime introspection of the events a component generates and observes.
- The new model should keep its compatibility with the old model.

Delegation means empowering someone else to act on your behalf, and it's the foundation for the new delegation model JDK 1.1 is based on. As we mentioned, two entities share a relationship: The *event source* (event generator) and the *event listener* (event handler). An event source is an object that can detect events; the event listener is an object that can react to an event when notified. An event source can notify many listeners about an event that has occurred. For example, pressing the power off button on an audio system could notify the tuner and the speakers to switch themselves off. Similarly, a single listener class could be used to instantiate many listener objects that could monitor different event sources.

To create this relationship, an event listener has to be registered with an event source. Registration is nothing but a request by the event listener to be notified of all events it's designed to handle. After the listener object is registered, any occurrence of the specified events automatically calls the appropriate method in the listener object. Before we delve into code and see how this new model works, let's get acquainted with some new terms in the following sections.

Listener Interfaces and Event Adapters

Event listeners are used as targets for performing actions when an event occurs. Any class that wants to receive event notifications implements the required listeners and registers itself with the event source generator by calling the add listener function.

A class that handles window events, for example, needs to implement the WindowListener interface, and then register this implemented interface with the event source. Whenever the event source generates the window event, it will notify all registered listeners. The following table shows a list of event listeners and their classes:

Listener Interface	Event Source Class
ActionListener	`Button`, `List`, `MenuItem`
AdjustmentListener	`ScrollBar`
ComponentListener	`Component`
ContainerListener	`Container`
FocusListener	`Component`
ItemListener	`Choice`, `CheckBox`, `CheckBoxMenuItem`, `List`
KeyListener	`Component`

Listener Interface	Event Source Class
MouseListener	`Component`
MouseMotionListener	`Component`
TextListener	`TextArea`, `TextField`
WindowListener	`Dialog`, `Frame`, `Window`

If you were designing your own class that generates events, you would have to create an interface for this class and define every possible event that could be generated. If you were developing a `Switch` class and a `Fan` class, for example, `Switch` would be an event source, and `Fan` would be the event consumer. You would have to define an interface that consisted of the events shown in Listing 6-1.

If you wanted the `Fan` class to listen to events being generated by the `Switch` class, you would have to implement the SwitchEventListener interface and then register it with the `Switch` object. Then, whenever the switch was turned on, the fan would be notified. (See Listing 6-2.)

Implementing a listener interface requires you to override every method specified in the interface, even if it means overriding them with empty methods.

Adapter classes are event listener interfaces implemented as classes, with every method in the interface implemented as null methods. You can extend these adapter classes and override the methods you want to handle. Event adapters are used to call methods of target classes that don't implement their own listener interfaces. Application frameworks such as the BeanBox generate and compile adapter classes at runtime to connect Beans.

Listing 6-1.
A sample interface
for the SwitchEvent.

```
import SwitchEvent;

public interface SwitchEventListener{
    public void switchOn(SwitchEvent switchEvent);
    public void switchOff(SwitchEvent switchEvent);
    public void switchIncreaseSpeed(SwitchEvent
        switchEvent);
    public void switchDecreaseSpeed(SwitchEvent
        switchEvent);
    public void switchError(SwitchEvent switchEvent);
}// End of interface SwitchEventListener
```

Listing 6-2.
A sample event
handler for the
SwitchEvent.

```
import SwitchEvent.java

public class FanHandler implements SwitchEventListener{
    public void switchOn(SwitchEvent switchEvent){
        StartRotating();
    }
    public void switchOff(SwitchEvent switchEvent){
        StopRotating();
    }
    public void switchIncreaseSpeed(SwitchEvent
        switchEvent){
        IncreaseSpeed();
    }
    public void switchDecreaseSpeed(SwitchEvent
        switchEvent){
        DecreaseSpeed();
    }
    public void switchError(SwitchEvent switchEvent){
    }
}
```

Listing 6-3.
An adapter class
for the
SwitchEventListener.

```
import SwitchEvent.java

class SwitchEventAdapter implements SwitchEventListener{
    public void switchOn(SwitchEvent switchEvent){
    }
    public void switchOff(SwitchEvent switchEvent){
    }
    public void switchDecreaseSpeed(SwitchEvent
        switchEvent){
    }
    public void switchIncreaseSpeed(SwitchEvent
        switchEvent){
    }
    public void switchError(SwitchEvent switchEvent){
    }
}
```

Listing 6-3 is an example of the SwitchEventAdapter. It has every method in the SwitchEventListener implemented as null methods. If your fan could only be turned on and off, but the speed couldn't be controlled, you could extend the SwitchEventAdapter and override only the `switchOn()` and `switchOff()` methods.

NOTE *Adapters are listener interfaces implemented on classes with all inter-faces implemented as null methods.*

A Simple Example

Let's take a simple example (see Listing 6-4) and see how event notification actually works.

Listing 6-4.
An example of AWT event handling using the delegation event model.

```java
import java.awt.*;
import java.awt.event.*;

public class EventTest{
    public static void main(String[] args){
        EventSourceHandler source =
                new EventSourceHandler();
    }
}

class EventSourceHandler{
    public EventSourceHandler(){
        Frame dummyFrame = new Frame();
        dummyFrame.setSize(200,200);
        dummyFrame.setTitle("Event Test");
        dummyFrame.setVisible(true);

        //Create Listeners that will process the mouse
            events
        MouseProcListen mouseProcListen = new
            MouseProcListen();
        MouseProcAdapt mouseProcAdapt = new
            MouseProcAdapt();

        //Register listeners so they can be notified of
            mouse events on this object
        dummyFrame.addMouseListener(mouseProcListen);
        dummyFrame.addMouseListener(mouseProcAdapt);
    }
}

class MouseProcListen implements MouseListener{
    public void mouseClicked(java.awt.event.MouseEvent
        arg0) {
        System.out.println("MouseListener: Event
            mouseClicked occured");
    }

    public void mousePressed(java.awt.event.MouseEvent
        arg0) {
    }

    public void mouseReleased(java.awt.event.MouseEvent
        arg0) {
```

Listing 6-4.
Continued.

```
        }

        public void mouseEntered(java.awt.event.MouseEvent
            arg0) {
        }

        public void mouseExited(java.awt.event.MouseEvent arg0)
    {
        }
    }


class MouseProcAdapt extends MouseAdapter{
    public void mouseClicked(java.awt.event.MouseEvent
        arg0) {
        System.out.println("MouseAdapter: Event
            mouseClicked occured");
    }
    public void mouseReleased(java.awt.event.MouseEvent
        arg0) {
        System.out.println("MouseAdapter: Event
            mouseRelease occured");
    }
}
```

In Listing 6-4, these are the most important lines of code:

```
MouseProcListen mouseProcListen  = new MouseProcListen();
MouseProcAdapt mouseProcAdapt = new MouseProcAdapt();
```

The EventSourceHandler wants to be notified of all mouse events occurring in the **dummyFrame** object. In the new delegation model, the EventSourceHandler would have to empower other objects to handle the mouse events on its behalf. It does so by implementing two objects—**mouseProcListen** and **mouseProcAdapt**—to handle these notifications and take appropriate action. In the first case, the listener object is created by implementing the MouseListener interface, which requires all the methods defined in the interface to be overwritten. These methods can be overwritten by skeleton code, too, if you're not really interested in handling those events. The **MouseAdapter** class is a convenience class that by default overrides all the methods in the MouseListener interface with skeleton code. Therefore, if you want to ignore most of the events sent to the listener, you can extend the **MouseAdapter** class and override only those methods you want to implement.

The following code fragment establishes the relationship between the event generator and the event listener. Whenever a mouse event occurs in the **Frame** object named **dummyFrame**, the listener objects are automatically notified:

```
dummyFrame.addMouseListener(mouseProcListen);
dummyFrame.addMouseListener(mouseProcAdapt);
```

If the user clicks the mouse within the frame, that triggers the **mouseClicked** event. Because two listeners are registered with mouse events in the **Frame**, both of them are notified. The event is passed on to the **mouseProcListen** and **mouseProcAdapt** objects. Here, the event handler matching the **mouseClicked** event is called. Because two listeners are waiting for this event, you will see two onscreen messages indicating that the **mouseClicked** event was fired. When the mouse is released, the handler matching the **mouseReleased** event is called, and you can see the corresponding message onscreen. In JDK 1.1, these events are asynchronous, and the order in which the event handlers are called isn't guaranteed.

From this discussion, the benefits of the delegation events model are quite apparent. Code has to be written for only those events that must be tracked. You can choose to ignore or filter out the other events, in which case the Java runtime environment won't even send those events to your application. This has a direct impact on performance as compared to JDK 1.0, in which every event, regardless of whether you wanted to know about it, was sent to the application. Also, note that the application logic is now in the **Listener** class. Compare this to the JDK 1.0 **model**, where you would have written your application logic in the **EventGenerator** class. You would be forced to derive the **EventGenerator** class from the **Frame** object and then override the **handleEvent()** method. Therefore, the JDK 1.0 abstraction of the **EventGenerator** class would be something like "An EventGenerator object is a frame" compared to our abstraction in JDK 1.1, which reads "An EventGenerator object has a frame." The JDK 1.1 abstraction is closer to the object-oriented model than is JDK 1.0.

Low-Level Events

Java has two types of events—*low-level* and *semantic*. Low-level events are directly associated with the user interacting with some visual component on the screen. JDK 1.1 has eight low-level events: **ComponentEvent**, **ContainerEvent**, **FocusEvent**, **WindowEvent**, **PaintEvent**, **InputEvent**, **KeyEvent**, and **MouseEvent**. Low-level events, like all events, are derived from the base class **java.util.EventObject**. Figure 6-1 shows the hierarchy of low-level events.

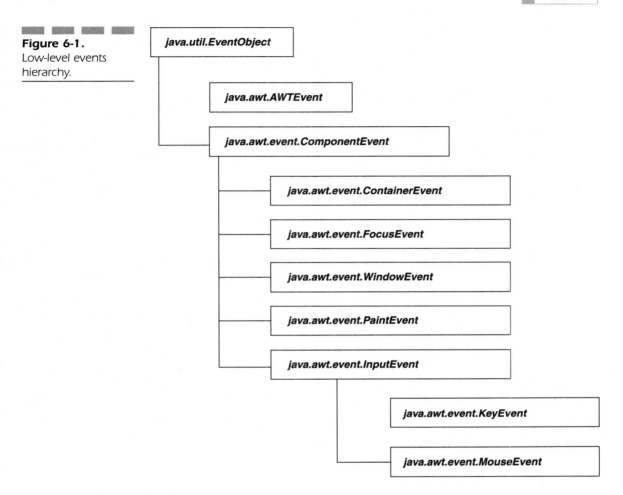

Figure 6-1.
Low-level events
hierarchy.

The base class is `java.util.EventObject`. Because all low-level events are associated with visual components onscreen, the next class in the low-level events hierarchy is obviously the `java.awt.AWTEvent` class. The `ComponentEvent` class is next in the hierarchy; it's the root event class for all component-level events. These events are for notification purposes only. The AWT subsystem automatically handles component moves and resizes internally so that the GUI layout works properly, regardless of whether a program is receiving these events. `ContainerEvent`, `FocusEvent`, `WindowEvent`, and `PaintEvent` are derived from the `ComponentEvent` class.

`ContainerEvent` is used for notification purposes only. AWT automatically adds or removes `Container` objects internally. `FocusEvent` occurs whenever the component loses or gains focus, either through programming or by the user tabbing through components or using the mouse. This event can be permanent or temporary. If the user tabs into an edit box, the focus event would be permanent, but if the user drags a scrollbar on the window containing the focused component, it loses focus only for the time when the user is dragging the scroll bar. In such cases, the focus event is temporary.

WindowEvent occurs whenever the user's activity affects a window, such as minimizing, maximizing, opening, closing, or otherwise changing the window.

PaintEvent is triggered every time a user's action invalidates a portion of the component; for example, the user might move a window so that it partially covers a component on the screen. When the user moves the window again to reveal the hidden part, a paint event is triggered, asking the component to redraw itself. However, unlike the other events that can have listeners registered to take action on the event, **PaintEvent** has no listeners. Developers must override the paint/update method to make sure the component is rendered properly.

Finally, **java.awt.event.InputEvent** is derived from the **ComponentEvent** class. This class forms the basis of the **KeyEvent** and **MouseEvent** classes. The **KeyEvent** class, as the name suggests, represents the events that happen when the user presses a key. Many events are potentially generated when a key is pressed; for example, a key press is typically followed by the release of the key. In this case, the current component (the one that has the focus) receives two events—one for key press and one for key release. Developers must take care of handling only one of these events. Similarly, **MouseEvent** is generated when the user interacts with the current component by using a mouse, whether it's clicking a mouse button or simply moving the mouse.

Semantic Events

Semantic events are higher-level events that encapsulate the user's intentions, instead of just sending out a message that the user has performed some physical action on a component. An **ActionEvent** can be a combination of many low-level events. In other words, when users press a button, their intention is to execute some action related to the button. When users press the Quit button, they obviously want to quit the application. When users drag the scrollbar downward, they want to page through the current document so they can see the part that's not currently onscreen. Semantic events are broken down into four events, all derived from `java.awt.AWTEvent`: `ActionEvent`, `AdjustmentEvent`, `ItemEvent`, and `TextEvent`. Figure 6-2 shows the hierarchy of the semantic events supported by JDK 1.1.

The hierarchy, as always, starts with `java.util.EventObject`, followed by `java.awt.AWTEvent`. Semantic events are results of low-level events associated with the components. The `ActionEvent` is generated by buttons, lists, and menu items. We can always implement the `ActionEvent` for any user-defined objects derived from `java.awt.Component` by extending those base classes, if the abstraction so demands. Later in this chapter, we show you how to extend the `Frame` class to generate an `ActionEvent`. The `AdjustmentEvent` is generated when some adjustment to the visual component needs to be made. For example, scrollBars generate this event when the user drags the scrollbar or clicks the arrow buttons to move the elevator button. Developers can then trap this event to display the correct location of the elevator button, depending on how far the user has paged through the current document. You can also develop custom components, such as a track bar (a bar that shows the progress of the current task), that generate the `AdjustmentEvent` and allow developers using your component to update the track bar display. `ItemEvent` is linked with items that can be selected, such as `Choice`, `CheckBox`, `CheckBoxMenuItem`, and `List`. Finally, `TextEvent` is generated when the user changes the contents in a `TextArea` or `TextField`.

Figure 6-2.
Semantic events
hierarchy.

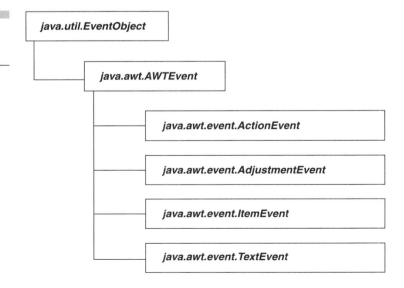

So, the distinction between the low-level events and semantic events is the level of abstraction given to developers using components. Remember, every semantic event also generates a low-level event, but a good abstraction of an object allows developers to view objects at a higher level, allowing them to think in terms of the application rather than keystrokes and mouse movements.

We discussed properties in the previous chapter. The **PropertyChangeEvent** is derived directly from **java.util.EventObject**. It's used by a component or a Bean to notify other interested components or Beans that it has changed its property value or is about to change its value, allowing them to update themselves or prevent the original component from changing its value.

User-Defined **ActionEvent** in Action

Objects like buttons, lists, and menu items already generate an **ActionEvent**. However, if we were to write our own class and wanted this new object to generate an **ActionEvent**, we would have to write code to let other objects register themselves with the object (see Listing 6-5). Let's extend our **EventTest** class now so it can handle **ActionEvents**, too. Since our **EventSourceGenerator** class has a frame, we could add **MouseListeners** to handle mouse events. However, the **Frame** class doesn't generate **ActionEvent**, so let's extend it to do that. We would have to implement **addActionListener()**, **removeActionListener()**, and **processActionEvent()** to allow other objects to register with this newly extended **Frame** object. We would also need to generate the **ActionEvent** when a user clicks on the frame. Therefore, as we pointed out, most **ActionEvent** handling can also be done at a lower level by handling the **mouseClicked** event. It depends on the abstraction that your object demands. We would need to extend the **MouseAdapter** class to override the **mouseClicked** event to generate the **ActionEvent**.

Let's examine the source code. Because we need the frame to be able to generate the **ActionEvent**, let's extend the frame class. **MyFrame** needs to keep track of all the listeners interested in the **ActionEvent**. The easiest way is to keep adding new listeners to a **Vector**.

Because we want to generate an **ActionEvent** when the **mouseClicked** event occurs, we have to add a mouse listener to this class. Remember that the adapter class is a convenience class in which all the listener methods are overridden with empty methods so that you override only

```
import java.awt.*;
import java.awt.event.*;
import java.util.Vector;

public class ActionEventTest{
    public static void main(String[] args){
        EventSourceGenerator source = new
            EventSourceGenerator();
    }
}

class MyFrame extends Frame{
    private Vector myActionListeners = new Vector();

    MyFrame()
    {
        MyFrameMouseProcAdapt myFrameMouseProcAdapt = new
            MyFrameMouseProcAdapt(this);
        addMouseListener(myFrameMouseProcAdapt);
    }
    public synchronized void addActionListener
        (ActionListener l)
    {
        myActionListeners.addElement(l);
    }

    public synchronized void removeActionListener
        (ActionListener l)
    {
        myActionListeners.removeElement(l);
    }

    protected void processActionEvent(ActionEvent e)
    {
        Vector listener;

        synchronized (this)
        {
            listener = (Vector) myActionListeners.clone();
        }

        for (int i=0; i<myActionListeners.size();i++)
        {
            ActionListener l;
            l = (ActionListener)listener.elementAt(i);
            l.actionPerformed(e);
        }
    }
}

class MyFrameMouseProcAdapt extends MouseAdapter{
```

Continues

Listing 6-5.
Continued.

```java
    private MyFrame myFrame;

    MyFrameMouseProcAdapt(MyFrame f)
    {
        myFrame = f;
    }

    public void mouseClicked(java.awt.event.MouseEvent
        arg0) {
                ActionEvent actionEvent = new
                    ActionEvent(myFrame,0,null);
                myFrame.processActionEvent(actionEvent);
    }
}


class EventSourceGenerator{
    public EventSourceGenerator(){
        MyFrame dummyFrame = new MyFrame();
        dummyFrame.setSize(200,200);
        dummyFrame.setTitle("Event Test");
        dummyFrame.setVisible(true);

        //Create listeners that will process the mouse
            events
        MouseProcListen mouseProcListen = new
            MouseProcListen();
        MouseProcAdapt mouseProcAdapt = new
            MouseProcAdapt();
        ActionListen actionListen = new ActionListen();

        //Register listeners so they can be notified of
            mouse events on this object
        dummyFrame.addMouseListener(mouseProcListen);
        dummyFrame.addMouseListener(mouseProcAdapt);
        dummyFrame.addActionListener(actionListen);
    }
}

class MouseProcListen implements MouseListener{
    public void mouseClicked(java.awt.event.MouseEvent
        arg0) {
        System.out.println("MouseListener: Event
            mouseClicked occured");
    }

    public void mousePressed(java.awt.event.MouseEvent
        arg0) {
    }

    public void mouseReleased(java.awt.event.MouseEvent
        arg0) {
    }
```

Listing 6-5.
Continued.

```
        public void mouseEntered(java.awt.event.MouseEvent
            arg0) {
        }

        public void mouseExited(java.awt.event.MouseEvent arg0)
    {
        }
    }

class ActionListen implements ActionListener{
    public void actionPerformed(ActionEvent e){
        System.out.println("ActionListener: Reached here");
    }
}

class MouseProcAdapt extends MouseAdapter{
    public void mouseClicked(java.awt.event.MouseEvent
        arg0) {
        System.out.println("MouseAdapter: Event
            mouseClicked occured");
    }
    public void mouseReleased(java.awt.event.MouseEvent
        arg0) {
        System.out.println("MouseAdapter: Event
            mouseRelease occured");
    }
}
```

those methods you want to handle. The **MyFrameMouseProcAdapt** class extends the **MouseAdapter** class and overrides the **mouseClicked** event. In this method, we create an **ActionEvent** object that requires three parameters:

- The object generating the event. In our case, this is the **MyFrame** object.

- The event ID. Because a user can take many kinds of actions, this ID helps identify the action type. In our case, the only event we will generate happens when the **mouseClicked** event occurs, so there's no need to have an ID associated with this object, and we pass a **0** to this parameter.

- The command associated with a particular action. For example, when selecting a particular menu item, you might want a method *X* of an object *Y* to be executed. You can specify this command while creating the **ActionEvent**, and a developer can later extract this information by using the **getActionCommand()** method and executing it. In our case, we have set it to null.

After the **ActionEvent** object is created, we call the **processActionEvent()** method of the **MyFrame** class.

We want to allow other objects to listen to the **ActionEvent** generated by **MyFrame**, so we must supply a method called **addActionListener()** that takes an **ActionListener** object as a parameter. We add this **ActionListener** to the **Vector** maintained by **MyFrame**.

Because we let other objects listen to the **ActionEvent**, we must also give them a way to stop listening when they're done. For this, we provide a method called **removeActionListener()** that takes an **ActionListener** as a parameter. All we do in this method is remove the **ActionListener** specified in the parameter from the **Vector**.

Note that both these methods are synchronized so that their execution is mutually exclusive, and while one **ActionListener** is being added, no **ActionListener** can be removed.

Finally, we supply a method called **processActionEvent()** that takes an **ActionEvent** as a parameter. First, we clone the **Vector** of **ActionListeners** in a synchronized block to make sure the list of listeners doesn't change until all the listeners currently registered are informed. We invoke the **actionPerformed()** method of every **ActionListener** in the cloned **Vector**, passing the **ActionEvent** object as a parameter.

Now we have a **Frame** that can generate an **ActionEvent**. As in the previous EventTest example, we need to implement the ActionListener interface. In this simple example, all we're doing is printing out a message to illustrate that the method is indeed being called. Then we need to add two familiar statements to the **EventSourceGenerator**:

```
ActionListen actionListen = new ActionListen();
dummyFrame.addActionListener(actionListen);
```

These two statements register the **EventSourceGenerator** with the **MyFrame** object. When the user clicks within the frame, besides the **mouseClicked** events being handled, you will also see a message from the **ActionEvent** handler.

AWT Enhancements

Nearly every JavaBean you see will incorporate some kind of visual display. A JavaBean must make use of the AWT for visual effects, even if it's only at design time.

In this section, we examine AWT enhancements. A thorough understanding of the much-improved AWT is a prerequisite to working with and developing JavaBeans because a majority of the Beans you create and use will no doubt be visible. Because all the AWT's widgets are elementary JavaBeans themselves, being familiar with the events they deliver will greatly enhance your understanding and use of them. You will also learn the design pattern of all JavaBean events—that is, delegation. We'll also survey important AWT add-ons, including Microsoft's *Application Foundation Classes* (AFC) and JavaSoft's newly announced *Java Foundation Classes* (JFC). Lotus' Infobus will add a new *Dynamic Data Exchange* (DDE) capability to these emerging frameworks.

JDK 1.1 AWT Enhancements

The AWT of JDK 1.0.*x* is somewhat lacking when it comes to GUI development beyond relatively simple applets. The components of AWT 1.0.*x* cover only the bare essentials. The newer AWT 1.1.*x* has a completely reworked event-handling mechanism based on delegation, yet maintains backward compatibility with 1.0.*x*. To simplify using this event delegation, the Java language has undergone revisions to allow for inner classes, which facilitate elegant implementation of event handlers. The older inheritance-based event model has been slightly revised and is still available for deriving new components. The event queue is now accessible to the applications programmer so that events can be posted programmatically instead of remaining under the exclusive control of the GUI manager. The newer event model is essential to the architectural requirements of the JavaBeans API. All AWT components now qualify as simple JavaBeans.

Additional AWT 1.1 niceties include cursor availability on a per component basis—the `setCursor()` method has been moved to the `Component` class. Scrolling is faster and easier to implement with the newly introduced `ScrollingPane` component. Pop-up menus, conspicuously absent in AWT 1.0.*x*, are also included, along with menu shortcuts. Mouseless operation is now integrated into the GUI paradigm. `Component`s provide support for their own printing and more flexible font support for internationalization. The newer AWT also allows implementation of lightweight *User-Interface* (UI) widgets derived directly from the `Component` and `Container` classes instead of the `Canvas` and `Panel` classes. Lightweight components can be irregular in shape and transparent since they are not being tied to peer components associated with the hosting platform. A new Clipboard API with extensible data formats is available now and will allow drag-and-drop operations in an upcoming release of the JDK.

Shortcomings of the 1.0.*x* Event Model

The 1.0.*x* event model is centered around the **handleEvent()** method of the container holding the GUI component triggering that event. Under the 1.0.*x* scheme, the **handleEvent()** method hands off the event to convenience methods for handling mouse, key, focus, and action events. The mouse events are typically handled by the following methods:

```
mouseEnter()
mouseExit()
mouseMove()
mouseDown()
mouseDrag()
mouseUp()
```

The key events can be handled by the following two methods:

```
keyDown()
keyUp()
```

The focus events are conveniently handled by the following:

```
gotFocus()
lostFocus()
```

All action events are passed on to this method for filtering:

```
action()
```

An action event is fired if the user double-clicks on a list item, clicks a button or menu item, or presses Enter in a text field.

All these methods are members of the **Component** class, so they are inherited by the **Container** class. To use these methods, new classes must be derived from the **Container** component to override them, typically a derivative of the **Frame** or **Dialog** class. (Both the **Frame** and **Dialog** classes are descendants of **Container**, which in turn is derived from **Component**.) The logic for handling any window interaction requires deriving a new class, usually overriding the **handleEvent()**, **action()**, and perhaps other convenience methods. Because the convenience methods don't provide comprehensive coverage of all possible events, the **handleEvent()** method must almost always be overridden. A lengthy **Switch** statement is often required in the overriding **handleEvent()** and **action()** methods to crack the event and implement its handler.

Perhaps with simple applets, this approach is satisfactory, but it doesn't scale well to more complex applications. Besides requiring a significant number of derived classes, this approach violates the object-oriented principle of encapsulation. The logic of the program ends up being embedded within the derived GUI components instead of being encapsulated within the data model it operates on, thus causing a maintenance nightmare. Furthermore, because the overridden methods are in the direct line of event propagation, all events must trickle through user code regardless of whether they're ever used. Subtle bugs can be easily introduced back into the event stream by improper event handling that might go undetected until unrelated features are added later.

Generic Event Model of JDK 1.1.*x*

Even in JDK 1.0.*x*, the java.util package included the **Observable** class and **Observer** interface, which together define an elementary event model. Within this model, any object implementing the Observer interface can register its interest in or dependence on an **Observable** object by calling its **addObserver()** method. When the **Observable** object notes a state change it deems worthy of broadcasting, it calls its **notifyObservers()** method, which in turn calls the **update()** method of each dependent observer. This design pattern takes the first step toward decoupling the observable from its observers. The decoupling is accomplished by sending messages (objects) to observers over a notify channel established at run-time, instead of the hard-coded approach of directly calling methods of specific observers determined at compile time.

A *design pattern* is a logical scheme of interaction between cooperating objects abstracted from its specific implementation. For example, the **Observable-Observer** design pattern could be implemented entirely within the **Object** class itself. Suppose **Object** had methods called **addObserver()** and **deleteObserver()** and also **notifyObservers()** and **update()**. In this case, any object could observe any other object, and the **Observable-Observer** design pattern would have been replicated faithfully in its functional essence. The design pattern describes the process in principle rather than a specific implementation of the design logic.

Unfortunately, the **Observable** class provides only one broadcast channel so that all dependents are notified for every event whether they're interested in it or not. Furthermore, the dependent object must implement code to infer what event actually happened. Because there's only one incoming update channel on the observer side, it must embody code for every different type of **Observable** object it might be observing to make this determination. The red warning light should already be flashing in your mind indicating yet another violation of the *Object-Oriented Programming* (OOP) principle of encapsulation.

Encapsulation dictates that the agent triggering the event knows the semantic interpretation of the event and doesn't leave it up to each observer to decide. On the other end, the observer should implement a specific event handler directly, without having to consider the originator to determine what event actually occurred. With such an ideal scenario, the observer could be written before the observable was even designed! That's equivalent to saying the observer is reusable because it doesn't need to be modified for each new type of observable that might come along. Likewise, the **Observable**, knowing the events it triggers, should be able to be written without knowledge of the object types implementing the appropriate event handlers.

The new generic event model of JDK 1.1.*x* is more pliable than the **Observable-Observer** scheme provided for in the java.util package and the inheritance scheme used in the AWT of 1.0.*x*. It's based on delegation rather than inheritance. The handling of an event can be delegated to any class implementing the event listener interface it requires. The methods of this interface correspond to the different types of events that can be published. Typically, these events are related to some aspect of the publishing entity. For example, a window could publish window events to a window listener interface with the methods of this interface representing different window events. Remember, this event model isn't restricted to the AWT. Perhaps there's only one event the interface must handle, in which case there would be only one method member. This design pattern always exhibits (at least) the following three features:

```
interface AspectListener extends java.util.EventListener
Publisher.addAspectListener(AspectListener)
Publisher.removeAspectListener(AspectListener)
```

There must always be a listener interface, ultimately extended from java.util.EventListener. The EventListener interface is a tagging interface and declares no members. Through introspection, it can be determined whether this interface is part of an overall event design pattern. The publishing class must be declared with methods for registering and unregistering event listeners. The names of these methods must follow the naming convention **addXXXListener** and **removeXXXListener** so that introspection can identify their participation in the event design pattern. Notice that both methods take exactly one parameter—**XXXListener**—which is mandatory. If all requirements are met, it's assumed that an event delegation pattern for *XXX* has been implemented. In our case, the events have something to do with *Aspect*. The specific events of *Aspect* are named as methods of the AspectListener interface. It's common, though not required, for these methods to all have one parameter, the **EventObject**:

AspectEvent extends java.util.EventObject.

The **EventObject** argument typically contains additional information on the event. The **EventObject** class maintains a temporary reference to the event's source. The **EventObject** also implements the Serializable interface, allowing events to be streamed for either persistence purposes or transmission to a remote location by a socket stream. The following example in Listing 6-6 shows an event publisher and two listeners.

Listing 6-6.
Generic event
delegation model.

```
class AspectEvent extends java.util.EventObject
{
   AspectEvent(Object source)
     { super(source); }
}

interface AspectListener extends java.util.EventListener
{
   public void event1(AspectEvent ae);
   public void event2(AspectEvent ae);
}

class AspectAdapter implements AspectListener
{
   public void event1(AspectEvent ae) {}
   public void event2(AspectEvent ae) {}
}

public class Aspect
{
   AspectListener al = null;

   void addAspectListener(AspectListener al)
     { this.al = AspectEventMulticaster.add(this.al,al); }
```

Continues

Listing 6-6.
Continued.

```java
    void removeAspectListener(AspectListener al)
      { this.al = AspectEventMulticaster.remove(this.al,al);
          }

  void publishEvent1()
  {
    if (al != null)
      al.event1(new AspectEvent(this));
  }

  void publishEvent2()
  {
    if (al != null)
      al.event2(new AspectEvent(this));
  }

  public static void main(String[] args)
  {
    Aspect a = new Aspect();

    a.addAspectListener(
      new AspectAdapter() {
        public void event1(AspectEvent ae)
          { System.out.println("Alpha heard event 1"); }
      }
    );

    AspectListener beta;

    a.addAspectListener(
      beta = new AspectListener() {
        public void event1(AspectEvent ae)
          { System.out.println("Beta  heard event 1"); }
        public void event2(AspectEvent ae)
          { System.out.println("Beta  heard event 2"); }
      }
    );

    a.publishEvent1();
    a.publishEvent2();

    a.removeAspectListener(beta);
    System.out.println("Beta has been removed");

    a.publishEvent1();
    a.publishEvent2();

    System.exit(0);
  }
}

class AspectEventMulticaster
```

Listing 6-6.
Continued.

```
    implements AspectListener
{
  private AspectListener a, b;

  private AspectEventMulticaster
    (AspectListener a, AspectListener b)
  {
    this.a = a;
    this.b = b;
  }

  private AspectListener remove(AspectListener al)
  {
    if (a == al) return b;
    if (b == al) return a;
    AspectListener a2 = remove(a,al);
    AspectListener b2 = remove(b,al);
    if (a2 == a && b2 == b)
      return this;
    return add(a2,b2);
  }

  static AspectListener add
    (AspectListener a, AspectListener b)
  {
    if (a == null) return b;
    if (b == null) return a;
    return new AspectEventMulticaster(a,b);
  }

  static AspectListener remove
    (AspectListener a, AspectListener b)
  {
    if (a == b || a == null)
      return null;
    if (a instanceof AspectEventMulticaster)
      return ((AspectEventMulticaster)a).remove(b);
    return a;
  }

  public void event1(AspectEvent ae)
  {
    a.event1(ae);
    b.event1(ae);
  }

  public void event2(AspectEvent ae)
  {
    a.event2(ae);
    b.event2(ae);
  }
}
```

The **AspectEvent** constructor passes on its source parameter to the **EventObject** constructor. Because the purpose of this example is to demonstrate the essence of the event delegation design pattern, no additional information is held within **AspectEvent**, which would only obscure the design pattern. **AspectEvent** is optional because the methods of the AspectListener aren't required to have arguments. Because all the AWT 1.1.*x* have arguments, they are shown here. The AspectListener interface is required, however, and must have at least one event handler method. The AspectListener is ultimately going to have to be implemented before it can be used, so the **AspectAdapter** class is supplied for convenience. If a listener interface declares half a dozen methods and you want to handle only one of them, it's much easier to derive the method from the adapter. The method you want to handle can be more easily overridden than repeatedly re-implementing the interface and having to stub off the extras.

The **Aspect** class is the publisher of aspect events 1 and 2. As required by the delegation design pattern, this class implements the **addAspectListener()** and **removeAspectListener()** methods. It should be possible for more than one listener at a time to be registered to receive aspect events. Perhaps a **Vector** of AspectListeners should be maintained internally by the **Aspect** class, but that would entail a costly overhead when only one listener is listening for the majority of the time. The **AspectEventMulticaster** class is used instead. Notice that the **AspectEventMulticaster** implements AspectListener. Internally, it holds two references to AspectListeners. These references could refer to additional multicasters, if more than two listeners are registered. Because the multicaster is an AspectListener, the code of the **AspectClass** can treat it as such. Regardless of how many listeners are registered, they can all be treated as a single listener transparently. If you examine the **AspectEventMulticaster** class, you can see how the links are maintained and how the events are propagated to all leaf nodes.

Notice how the **Aspect** class' **publishEvent1()** and **publishEvent2()** methods invoke the corresponding methods of the listener interface—**event1()** and **event2()**, respectively. Any listeners registered are notified of the events.

The **main()** method demonstrates the registration of listeners and the publishing of events. An anonymous inner class is declared and created in one step with the following code:

```
new AspectAdapter() {
     public void event1(AspectEvent ae)
        { System.out.println("Alpha heard event 1"); }
   }
```

The actual object created is derived from **AspectAdapter()** overloading only the **event1()** method. Anonymous inner classes can't declare constructors. However, arguments could have been passed to the base class **AspectAdapter** constructor if required. The second listener (that is, beta) uses another form of anonymous construction that implements the AspectListener interface instead of the AspectAdapter. As a result, every method of the AspectListener interface must be defined, which isn't too burdensome in this case. The beta object actually extends **Object** and implements AspectListener.

The output from this example is shown here (inner classes are covered in more detail in a later section):

```
Alpha heard event 1
Beta heard event 1
Beta heard event 2
Beta has been removed
Alpha heard event 1
```

Actually, there's a far more important reason for using the multicaster in the AWT event model. The term **multicaster** can also mean "multiple casts to different branches of a listener hierarchy." The **AspectEventMulticaster** class in the previous example mimics the operation of the real **AWTEventMulticaster** class, which not only allows registering multiple listeners but also multiple types of listeners. These listener interfaces (WindowListener, MouseListener, ComponentListener, and so on) are all derived from the AWTEventListener interface. Because the **AWTEventMulticaster** implements all these derived interfaces, it can be used throughout the AWT components to register multiple listeners.

AWT Event Model of JDK 1.1.*x*

All AWT event objects are now rooted in the **java.awt.AWTEvent** class, which extends the **java.util.EventObject** class. AWT event objects roughly correspond to event categories and contain information pertinent to all the events in a category. All AWT event listeners extend the java.util.EventListener interface. Recall that EventListener is simply a tagging interface, declaring no methods. The methods of any listener interface correspond to the specific events in its category. In other words, the listening interface is a collection of all the events (methods) in that category. The interface's methods represent the handlers of those events.

The events listener example from the previous chapter can be used to verify Table 6-1. All methods of these interfaces take one parameter, the same event object for all methods. For example, the WindowListener interface has seven methods to handle window events—opened, closing, closed, iconified, deiconified, activated, and deactivated. Each of these

Table 6-1.

AWT Event Listener Interfaces and Event Sources.

Interface	Methods (Handlers)	Event Object (Details)	Sources (Add/Remove)
ActionListener	actionPerformed	ActionEvent	Button, TextField, List, MenuItem
AdjustmentListener	adjustmentValue-Changed	AdjustmentEvent	Scrollbar, ScrollPane
ComponentListener	componentResized componentMoved componentShown componentHidden	ComponentEvent	Component
ContainerListener	componentAdded componentRemoved	ContainerEvent	Container
FocusListener	focusGained focusLost	FocusEvent	Component
ItemListener	itemStateChanged	ItemEvent	Choice, List, CheckboxMenu-Item, Checkbox
KeyListener	keyTyped keyPressed keyReleased	KeyEvent	Component
MouseListener	mouseClicked mousePressed mouseReleased mouseEntered mouseExited	MouseEvent	Component
MouseMotionListener	mousedMoved mouseDragged	MouseEvent	Component
TextListener	textValueChanged	TextEvent	TextComponent
WindowListener	windowOpened windowClosing windowClosed windowIconified windowDeiconified windowActivated windowDeactived	WindowEvent	Window

methods takes one argument: **WindowEvent**. **Window** objects are the source of all window events. Because **Frame** and **Dialog** are descendents of **Window**, they can register WindowListeners and publish window events.

Suppose you're interested in handling a window event, such as **windowClosing**. When the user clicks the Destroy button on a **Frame**, the **windowClosing** event is published to all registered WindowListeners. The example in Listing 6-7 shows how the main window of an application can cause the Java Virtual Machine (JVM) to exit.

MainFrame has a class (static) variable called **exitOnDispose**. If set to true, the **dispose** method of a **MainFrame** object will call **System.exit(0)** to exit the Java Virtual Machine. Obviously, an applet doesn't want to call **System.exit(0)**, so **exitOnDispose** is initialized to false. Only in **main()** is it set to true, indicating that the frame is the main window of an

Listing 6-7.
Handling window
closing events.

```
import java.awt.*;
import java.awt.event.*;
import java.util.*;

public class MainFrame extends Frame
{
   static boolean exitOnDispose = false;

   public void dispose()
   {
      super.dispose();
      if (exitOnDispose)
        System.exit(0);
   }

   public MainFrame()
   {
      addWindowListener(
        new WindowAdapter()     {
            public void windowClosing(WindowEvent e)
              { dispose(); }
         }
      );
   }

   public static void main(String[] args)
   {
      exitOnDispose = true;
      MainFrame mf = new MainFrame();
      mf.setVisible(true);
   }
}
```

application, instead of an applet. Whether the frame is in an applet or application, when the user clicks the Destroy button, the window should be disposed of along with all its resources. Therefore, a window event listener must be registered with the window to handle **windowClosing** events. This is done in the **MainFrame()** constructor with a call to **addWindowListener()**, which registers our **windowClosing()** handler. As mentioned earlier, **Frame** is derived from **Window**, which declares the **addWindowListener()** method.

Listener adapters are available for all the listener interfaces shown in Table 6-2 that have more than one method (that is, event handler). An *adapter* is a class implementing the listener interface. The methods do nothing except return. You can verify this by examining the source code for **java.awt.event.WindowAdapter**. The **windowClosing** event is the only one of interest, so it's the only one that needs to be overridden in **MainFrame**.

```
new WindowAdapter()     {
            public void windowClosing(WindowEvent e)
              { dispose(); }
        }
```

The construction used to extend **WindowAdapter** is known as an *anonymous inner class*. (Inner classes are covered in more detail in the following section.) The preceding code snippet returns a **WindowAdapter** object (**WindowListener**) with the **windowClosing()** method calling the **dispose()** method of the **MainFrame** object it's associated with (that is, within).

The listener interfaces shown in Table 6-2 that have only one method don't have adapters. These single events are also semantic events. The AWT considers semantic events to be high-level events that might consist of one or more low-level events—the remaining events in the table. The semantic events were deliberately written as single event listeners and are expected to be the most heavily used. There's no difference, however, in the AWT's handling of semantic versus low-level events.

INNER CLASSES   A thorough understanding of inner classes is necessary to take advantage of the new event delegation model, although inner classes are useful elsewhere, too. In the original Java 1.0 language specification, only top-level classes were allowed. There was no provision for nesting class definitions. Furthermore, the language was strictly based on classes, with the atomic unit of compilation being the class. However, with the advent of the event delegation mechanism, there was a pressing need to synthesize method pointers or standalone procedures. Inner classes offer an ingenious solution while not breaking the JVM nor the language's class structure and simplicity. Inner classes can be defined close to where they're used, as members of an enclosing class, locally within a block of statements, or anonymously within an expression, as has been shown previously.

The anonymous inner class is a syntactic convenience for sidestepping the need of explicitly extending the adapter or implementing the listener interface. Note that an anonymous inner class can't declare a constructor. The previous example could be modified, as shown in Listing 6-8, to demonstrate an inner class being declared within a block of statements.

The exact name given by the compiler to the **Dispose** class is **MainFrame1Dispose** so the JVM can find the class without revision to its design. Of course, the **Dispose** class can't be used outside the scope it's declared within. In the case of the anonymous **Dispose**, the class name given by the compiler was **MainFrame$1**. The **Dispose** class could also be moved outside the constructor, appearing instead as a member of the **MainFrame** class.

If the inner class was declared as a member of the class, it would have a name that could be referenced elsewhere outside the enclosing class. In this case, the class name generated by the compiler would have been **MainFrame$Dispose**. The numbering has to do with the order in which it appears as an anonymous or local defined class. In either case, it's not important because it's inaccessible outside the block. The point is simply that inner classes, although changing the language specification, didn't break the JVM. If **Dispose** were declared as a public member of **MainFrame**, then you could refer to it as **MainFrame.Dispose**, just as though it were any other class. (The dollar signs and numbers are used for the class files because periods would indicate a subpackaging.)

Notice that the inner classes of this example had access to all the other members of the **MainFrame** class. This is understandable because **Dispose** is declared within **MainFrame**. But an inner class is more than just within the scope of the enclosing class. In a sense, it's part of the implementation

Listing 6-8.
Local inner class.

```
...
public MainFrame()
{
  class Dispose extends WindowAdapter
  {
    public void windowClosing(WindowEvent e)
      { dispose(); }
  }
  addWindowListener(new Dispose());
}
```

of the enclosing class, being loosely derived from the enclosing class with the added privilege of having access to its private members. After all, it can access all the members of the enclosing class just as though it were a member of the enclosing class. However, the inner class doesn't inherit those enclosing class members, as far as users of the inner class are concerned. An inner class inherits the enclosing class privately. Because multiple inner class objects can be associated with an enclosing class object, perhaps it's better to think of inner classes as internal extensions of the enclosing class. In fact, an inner class object maintains a pointer to its enclosing context— the outer class object it's associated with when it's created. Another way to visualize this is to say that an inner class object is a friend to its enclosing class object, and friends have access to private members. This link to the enclosing object is final—the inner class object can be created only within an irrevocably enclosing object context. This is how the `windowClosing()` method could call `dispose()` of the `MainFrame` object in Listing 6-7.

Figure 6-3 shows the resulting screen display when executing the application in Listing 6-9. At the bottom of the frame is a status line that reports the last item selected from either the list box on the left or the choice box on the right.

Figure 6-3.
Screen display of
Listing 6-9.

Listing 6-9.
StatusLineDemo.java.

```java
import java.awt.*;
import java.awt.event.*;

public class StatusLineDemo extends Frame
{

  static class StatusLine extends Label
  {
    class ItemAdapter implements ItemListener
    {
      public void itemStateChanged(ItemEvent e)
      {
        Object[] i = e.getItemSelectable()
                .getSelectedObjects();
        if (i.length > 0)
          setText((String)i[0]);
        else
          setText("");
```

Listing 6-9.
Continued.

```
      }
    }
    StatusLine() {}
    ItemListener itemAdapter()
      { return new ItemAdapter(); }
  }

  static boolean exitOnDispose = false;

  public void dispose()
  {
    super.dispose();
    if (exitOnDispose)
      System.exit(0);
  }

  public StatusLineDemo()
  {
    super("StatusLineDemo");
    addWindowListener(
      new WindowAdapter()
        {
          public void windowClosing(WindowEvent e)
            { dispose(); }
        }
    );
    StatusLine sl = new StatusLineDemo.StatusLine();
    add("South",sl);
    List l = new List();
    l.addItem("One");
    l.addItem("Two");
    l.addItem("Three");
    l.addItemListener(sl.new ItemAdapter());
    Choice c = new Choice();
    c.addItem("One");
    c.addItem("Two");
    c.addItem("Three");
    c.addItemListener(sl.itemAdapter());
    Panel p = new Panel();
    p.add(l);
    p.add(c);
    add("Center",p);
    pack();
  }

  public static void main(String[] arg)
  {
    exitOnDispose = true;
    StatusLineDemo sld = new StatusLineDemo();
    sld.setVisible(true);
  }
}
```

Both inner classes and nested top-level classes are used in Listing 6-9. An inner class object is linked to its enclosing object, but a nested top-level class object doesn't have this contextual relationship. Notice that the **StatusLine** class in Listing 6-9 is a static member class of the **StatusLineDemo** class. The **StatusLine** class, being a static member, can't have an internal link to a particular **StatusLineDemo** object, so it's a top-level class nested within the scope of the **StatusLineDemo** class. However, the **ItemAdapter** class is an inner class of the **StatusLine** class, so every **ItemAdapter** object is related to its enclosing **StatusLine** object. There might be more than one **ItemAdapter** object for a **StatusLine** object. (Note that local and anonymous classes in static methods must be nested top-level classes rather than inner classes.)

The context of a top-level class object is defined by its implicit **this** reference. An inner class not only has the context of its **this** reference, but also the context of its enclosing object. Therefore, the **ItemAdapter** has an implicit **this** reference and an implicit **StatusLine.this** reference. Just as you could use **this** explicitly to resolve ambiguity, you can also use **StatusLine.this** explicitly, if needed. Notice that the **itemStateChanged()** method calls the **setText()** method of its **StatusLine** parent context. This could have been explicitly stated as **StatusLine.setText((String)i[0])** to resolve ambiguity, if there were any confusion about which **setText()** was intended.

The **StatusLine** class is essentially a label that provides event handlers for **itemStateChanged** events, using those events to set the label's text. The **StatusLineDemo** constructor creates a **StatusLine** and then attaches listeners from that **StatusLine** object to a **List** object and a **Choice** object. Notice how the **StatusLine** object is created:

```
StatusLine sl = new StatusLineDemo.StatusLine();
```

Because the **StatusLine** class is within the scope of **StatusLineDemo**, it's unnecessary to fully qualify the class name of **StatusLine** with the **StatusLineDemo** prefix. However, you can do so when it's required to specify a nested class. Remember, **StatusLine** is a nested top-level class, so it can be created apart from a **StatusLineDemo** object context. This isn't true, however, for an inner class object, which can't exist outside the context of its enclosing object. Since **ItemAdapter** is an inner class of **StatusLine**, it must be created within a StatusLine object context. This is demonstrated by the qualifier **new** operator:

```
l.addItemListener(sl.new ItemAdapter());
```

The **ItemAdapter** is created in the context of the previously created **StatusLine** object, now referenced by **sl**. The ItemListener created for the

`Choice` object is returned from the `itemAdapter()` method of `StatusLine`. In this method, the `new` operator is implicitly `StatusLine.new`, but the prefix isn't mandatory because the enclosing context is understood, as shown:

```
ItemListener itemAdapter()
     { return new ItemAdapter(); }
```

Note that the StatusLineDemo example in Listing 6-9 demonstrates the use of Table 6-1. The table indicates that a `List` object can fire two different semantic events: an `ActionEvent` or `ItemEvent`. According to the documentation, the `ActionEvent` for a `List` indicates that an item has been double-clicked, which isn't what we wanted. The `ItemEvent`, however, indicates an item in the `List` has been either selected or deselected, which is the event we want to handle. The same is true for the `Choice` object. Of course, `List` and `Choice` are derived from `Component`, but `Component`'s low-level events aren't of interest.

It's also possible to extend an inner class; the only concern is that all inner class constructors are called in the context of an enclosing class object. No special provisions are necessary if the extending class is also an inner class of the same enclosing class (see Listing 6-10). However, if the extending class is a top-level class (nested or otherwise), then a enclosing class object is required to qualify the call to `super()` of the extended inner class. At first glance, qualifying the call to `super()` might seem strange, as though we were calling the enclosing class constructor or one of its methods called `super()`. This isn't the case, however. Recall the context qualifier for the `new` operator. You can think of `super()` as being context qualified. The code in Listing 6-10 accomplishes nothing itself other than to compile without errors, demonstrating the proper use of context qualifiers.

Local variables and parameters can now be declared as final in 1.1.x. Any local variable or parameter referenced by a local or anonymous nested class must be declared final. Listing 6-11 shows why this restriction is necessary. The `FinalLocal` class has a method called `foo()` in which `Bar`, a nested class, is declared. The `foo()` method returns a `Bar` object that uses the local variable to construct a string. The problem arises if the local variable isn't final. What would be the string value returned by `Bar.toString()`: 1 or 2? Obviously, the local variable's value is destroyed upon exit from `foo()`, so its value must be held somewhere. After compiling `Bar`, the problem of holding (synchronizing) a changeable reference becomes insurmountable, so local variables and parameters referenced by a nested class must be final. `Bar` is an inner class in this case, but even if the `foo()` method were static and `Bar` were therefore a nested top-level class, it would make no difference. The ambiguity wouldn't have been eliminated.

Listing 6-10.
Extending inner
classes.

```java
public class Enclosing
{

  class Inner1 {}

  class Inner2 extends Inner1 {}

  static class NestedTopLevel extends Inner1
  {
    NestedTopLevel(Enclosing e)
      { e.super(); }
  }

  public static void main(String[] args)
  {
    Enclosing e = new Enclosing();
    Inner1 i1 = e.new Inner1();
    Inner2 i2 = e.new Inner2();
    NestedTopLevel ntl = new NestedTopLevel(e);
    TopLevel tl = new TopLevel(e);
  }
}

class TopLevel extends Enclosing.Inner1
{
  public TopLevel(Enclosing e)
    { e.super(); }
}
```

Listing 6-11.
Final local variables.

```java
public class FinalLocal
{

  public Object foo()
  {
    final int x = 1;
    class Bar
    {
      public String toString()
        { return Integer.toString(x); }
    }
    // x = 2;
    return new Bar();
  }

  public static void main(String[] arg)
  {
    FinalLocal lf = new FinalLocal();
    System.out.println(lf.foo());
  }
}
```

There is a workaround solution, however. Listing 6-12 shows how **Bar** can be made to reflect the last value held by the local array. The final reference to a mutable array satisfies the need to be synchronized on an immutable reference.

Without nested top-level and inner classes, the new event delegation model would be difficult to use. Nested classes allow for other elegant implementations, too.

INHERITANCE-BASED EVENT HANDLING The event delegation model was designed to remove non-GUI code from extended components and quite often negates the requirement for those extensions in the first place. However, sometimes a new GUI component is required. In that case, inheritance-based event handling might be appropriate. Often, low-level event processing is required to implement the derived component's behavior and this should naturally be encapsulated within. With inner classes, however, a strong case can be made for not overriding the event-processing methods of the inherited AWT component. Other methods of the derived component can just as easily attach listeners to themselves instead. If this isn't adequate, inheritance-based event handling might be the only solution left.

All GUI events are passed to the **processEvent()** method of **Component**. The **processEvent()** method is the equivalent of **handleEvent()** in JDK 1.0.*x*. If the component is a **Window**, the **processEvent()** method of **Window**

Listing 6-12.
Final local variable workaround.

```
public class FinalLocal2
{

  public Object foo()
  {
    final int[] x = { 1 };
    class Bar
    {
      public String toString()
        { return Integer.toString(x[0]); }
    }
    x[0] = 2;
    return new Bar();
  }

  public static void main(String[] arg)
  {
    FinalLocal2 lf = new FinalLocal2();
    System.out.println(lf.foo());   // output:   2
  }
}
```

calls `processWindowEvent()`, if the event is an instance of `WindowEvent`. Otherwise, it calls `Container`'s `processEvent()`, which will call `processContainerEvent()` if the event is a `ContainerEvent`. Finally, if it's neither a `WindowEvent` nor a `ContainerEvent`, the `processEvent()` method of `Component` will be called and fan out with a call to one of the following, depending on the category of the event:

```
processComponentEvent(),
processFocusEvent(),
processKeyEvent(),
processMouseEvent(),
processMouseMotionEvent()
```

You should override the appropriate `processEvent()` method to implement your component. It's crucial for your overridden method to call the superclass' method to ensure proper operation.

To improve GUI performance, the listener model was conceived so that unnecessary events wouldn't waste processing time by being needlessly delivered. If a listener type isn't registered with a component, those events aren't delivered. Therefore, if no WindowListeners are registered with a window component, the `processWindowEvent()` will never be called by default. You override the default by calling the `enableEvents()` method with the mask for the event type you're interested in receiving, so to allow window events, you would call the following:

```
enableEvents(java.awt.AWTEvent.WINDOW_EVENT_MASK);
```

Listing 6-13 shows a rework of the example given in Listing 6-7, using inheritance rather than listeners.

Notice that the `processWindowEvent()` method passes all events but the window closing event to its superclass. If this call to `super.processWindowEvent()` weren't made, events such as `WindowActivate` would be lost.

CONSUMING EVENTS   Form layout tools of modern RAD IDEs must work with live components at design time to improve developer productivity. When a button is clicked at design time, it shouldn't fire the underlying handler. The button would have to be clicked if the design tool wanted to allow the designer to drag the button around the form. This action shouldn't be interpreted as "pushing" the button. Therefore, the input must be consumed by the design tool. Both the `KeyEvent` and `MouseEvent` classes extend their common `InputEvent` base class. Input events can be consumed at design time by the `consume()` method of `InputEvent`, thus preventing its eventual propagation to the component's

Listing 6-13.
Inheritance-based
window closing.

```java
import java.awt.*;
import java.awt.event.*;
import java.util.*;

public class MainFrame extends Frame
{
  static boolean exitOnDispose = false;

  public void dispose()
  {
    super.dispose();
    if (exitOnDispose)
      System.exit(0);
  }

  protected void processWindowEvent(WindowEvent e)
  {
    if (e.getID() == WindowEvent.WINDOW_CLOSING)
      dispose();
    else
      super.processWindowEvent(e);
  }

  public MainFrame()
  {
    enableEvents(AWTEvent.WINDOW_EVENT_MASK);
  }

  public static void main(String[] args)
  {
    exitOnDispose = true;
    MainFrame mf = new MainFrame();
    mf.setVisible(true);
  }
}
```

peer. However, the event will still propagate to other listeners. The other listeners can call **isConsumed()** if they want to determine their appropriate behavior.

EVENT QUEUE   The 1.1 event model opens up the GUI event queue to the developer. However, it's useful only in driving user interface program logic and not the GUI itself. For example, you could stuff the **WINDOW_ICONIFIED** event in the queue, and any window listeners implementing handlers for **WINDOW_ICONIFIED** would respond. However, the GUI manager isn't going to iconify the window for you. Perhaps there's some value in sampling events for live layout tools, but the GUI event queue isn't a good medium to couple program logic through. You should implement your own generic event mechanism to do this. The `java.awt.EventQueue` class has methods for posting, peeking, and fetching events. The following expression returns the system event queue:

```
java.awt.Toolkit.getDefaultToolkit().getSystemEventQueue();
```

The `getSystemEventQueue()` method is protected by a SecurityManager check that prevents applets from having direct access to the system queue.

OLD AND NEW EVENT MODEL COMPATIBILITY   It's best to write new code using only the new event model. Realistically, however, there might be a need to reuse existing GUI classes. A component is recognized by the AWT as being either a 1.0.*x* event model "target" or a 1.1 event mode "source," but not both. If you have worked with the older `java.awt.Event` class, you will remember that the target field referred to the component triggering the event. Because all events were delivered to the container holding the components, the target referred to a component within it. Calling the component originating the event the *target* was an unfortunate choice of terms. Of course, with the new model, listeners are now registered with the component from which an event directly emanates.

If a component has a listener of any kind registered or an event type of any kind explicitly allowed by calling `enableEvents()`, the component is recognized by the AWT as a new 1.1 event model source component. All other components are treated as 1.0.*x* components, with events being delivered through the `handleEvent()` method. Should an old-style component have a listener registered, the `handleEvent()` mechanism is turned off, breaking any code depending on event delivery through the `handleEvent()`, `actionEvent()`, or convenience methods.

With the old model, all events are delivered to the container holding the component that originated the event. If the event isn't handled, it's passed to the parent container, and so on. In the new model, events emanate from the components and don't propagate up the containment hierarchy. If a component is of the old style, the event still propagates up the containment hierarchy, regardless of whether the parent containers are of the new type. Likewise, if the component is of the new type, the event won't propagate up the containment hierarchy, regardless of the type of the parent containers. In other words, events starting off as the old style remain that way throughout their life cycle, and likewise for the new.

ScrollPane

Working with scrollbars is a tedious, implementation-intensive exercise. Fortunately, a **ScrollPane** component has been added to AWT 1.1, which not only reduces the required implementation effort, but also improves scrolling performance. Only one child component can be managed by the **ScrollPane** component. This child often ends up being a panel containing other components. Vertical and horizontal scrollbars can be specified on an as-needed, always, or never basis. The never basis is useful if the application wants to implement its own scrollbars and to simply use the **ScrollPane** as a panning device.

Listing 6-14 shows how a grid of labels can be panned by a **ScrollPane** container. A label's text is simply the Cartesian coordinates of the grid cell it occupies. Figure 6-4 shows the screen display of the **Scroller** example.

Listing 6-14.
Scroller example.

```java
import java.awt.*;
import java.awt.event.*;

public class Scroller extends Frame
{
  class LabelGrid extends Panel
  {
    LabelGrid(int x, int y)
    {
      setLayout(new GridLayout(y,x));
      for (int i = 1; i <= y; i++)
        for (int j = 1; j <= x; j++)
          add(new Label(i + "," + j));
    }
  }

  static boolean exitOnDispose = false;

  public void dispose()
  {
    super.dispose();
    if (exitOnDispose)
      System.exit(0);
  }

  public Scroller()
  {
    super("Scroller Example");
    addWindowListener(new WindowAdapter() {
```

Continues

Listing 6-14.
Continued.

```
    public void windowClosing(WindowEvent e)
       { dispose(); } } );

  ScrollPane scroller =
    new ScrollPane(ScrollPane.SCROLLBARS_AS_NEEDED);
  scroller.add(new LabelGrid(10,20));

  Adjustable vadjust = scroller.getVAdjustable();
  Adjustable hadjust = scroller.getHAdjustable();
  hadjust.setUnitIncrement(10);
  vadjust.setUnitIncrement(10);

  scroller.setSize(235, 245);

  add("Center", scroller);
  pack();

}

public static void main(String args[])
{
  Scroller test = new Scroller();
  test.exitOnDispose = true;
  test.show();
}
}
```

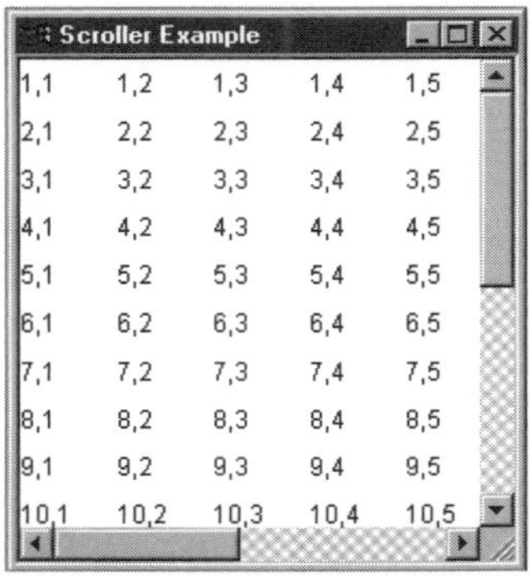

Figure 6-4.
Screen display of
Listing 6-14.

Table 6-1 is slightly inaccurate because **ScrollPane** doesn't register AdjustableListeners directly. The objects returned by **getVAdjustable()** and **getHAdjustable()** have the **addAdjustableListener()** method instead for their respective scrollbars. **ScrollPane** will play a central role in developing input forms for data-intensive applications and data-aware Java-Bean table components.

Pop-up Menus, Menu Shortcuts, and Mouseless Operation

Pop-up menus, menu shortcuts, and other focus transversal keystrokes are essential to the GUI power user. Pop-up menus are sometimes re- ferred to as *context menus* or *object menus*. The idea is for any selected item on the desktop to have a context-sensitive menu readily available to the user. The AWT 1.0.*x* supports only pull-down menus, those that are attached to a menu bar or menu item. The AWT 1.0.*x* doesn't support menu shortcuts, either.

The `PopupMenu` class of AWT 1.1 makes creating and invoking reusable menus easy. Figure 6-5 shows a frame with two text input fields. Each has the same pop-up menu that simply sets the field text to the text of the se- lected menu item.

`PopupMenu` is a subclass of `Menu`, with the important addition of the `show()` method:

```
public void show(Component origin, int x, int y);
```

Calling `show()` causes the menu to pop up over the origin component with an (x,y) offset. The `show()` method is modal. For the pop-up menu to work, it must be added to a `Container` component holding the origin component. This parent container is the menu's umbilical cord to the GUI event stream. The parent container can be any container in the ori- gin component's containment hierarchy. In this way, a menu can be reused for multiple widgets. The `java.awt.Component` class now has the `add()` and `remove()` methods for attaching the pop-up menu to the con- tainment hierarchy. Note that a pop-up menu can be owned by only one component (container) at a time. However, it's possible to use the `show()` method to display the menu for more than one widget in the container owning the menu.

```
Component.add(PopupMenu popup)
Component.remove(MenuComponent popup)
```

Figure 6-5.
Two TextFields with pop-up menus.

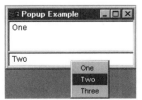

Listing 6-15 shows the source code for the **Popup** example shown in Figure 6-5. The **PopupMenuExtended** class makes using pop-ups even easier by encapsulating the handling of pop-up triggers and the routing of menu item selections to their designated handlers. Remember that the pop-up menu can be owned by only one component at a time. This container component can be anywhere in the containment hierarchy of the widgets that will be using the pop-up. In the **main()** method, the frame is assembled first, followed by the construction and initialization of the pop-up menu. The menu is then added to the frame, its only owner. The pop-up is then attached to the two **TextFieldExtended** widgets for which it will be acting as the pop-up. Notice that the **TextFieldExtended** class implements ActionListener setting the field text to that of the action command. The questions now are how does the action event arrive at the text field, and what is the text of the command that gets pasted?

Listing 6-15.
Pop-up example.

```java
import java.awt.*;
import java.awt.event.*;
import java.util.*;

public class PopupMenuExtended extends PopupMenu
   implements ActionListener, MouseListener
{
   private Hashtable actions = new Hashtable();
   private Component context = null;

   public MenuItem add(MenuItem mi)
   {
      super.add(mi).addActionListener(this);
      return mi;
   }

   public void add(String label)
      { add(new MenuItem(label)); }

   public void attach(Component c, ActionListener[] a)
   {
      c.addMouseListener(this);
      actions.put(c,a);
   }

   public void detach(Component c)
   {
      if (actions.containsKey(c))  {
         c.removeMouseListener(this);
         actions.remove(c);
      }
   }
```

Listing 6-15.
Continued.

```java
public void actionPerformed(ActionEvent e)
{
  MenuItem c = (MenuItem) e.getSource();
  int size = getItemCount();
  for (int i = 0; i < size; i++)  {
    MenuItem mi = getItem(i);
    if (mi == c)  {
      ActionListener[] a
        = (ActionListener[])actions.get(context);
      if (i >= a.length)
        a[0].actionPerformed(e);
      else
        a[i].actionPerformed(e);
      break;
    }
  }
}

private void show(MouseEvent e)
{
  if (e.isPopupTrigger())  {
    Component c = e.getComponent();
    if (actions.containsKey(c))  {
      e.consume();
      context = c;
      show(c, e.getX(), e.getY());
    }
  }
}

public void mouseClicked(MouseEvent e) { show(e); }
public void mousePressed(MouseEvent e) { show(e); }
public void mouseReleased(MouseEvent e) { show(e); }
public void mouseEntered(MouseEvent e) {}
public void mouseExited(MouseEvent e) {}

public static void main(String[] args)
{
  Frame f = new Frame("Popup Example");
  f.addWindowListener(
    new WindowAdapter() {
      public void windowClosing(WindowEvent e)
        { e.getWindow().dispose(); System.exit(0); }
    }
  );
  PopupMenuExtended p = new PopupMenuExtended();
  p.add("One");
  p.add("Two");
  p.add("Three");
  f.add(p);
```

Continues

Listing 6-15.
Continued.

```
class TextFieldExtended extends TextField
   implements ActionListener
{
   public void actionPerformed(ActionEvent e)
      { setText(e.getActionCommand()); }
}

TextFieldExtended t;
f.add("Center", t = new TextFieldExtended());
p.attach(t,new ActionListener[] { t });
f.add("South", t = new TextFieldExtended());
p.attach(t,new ActionListener[] { t });
f.setSize(200,100);
f.setVisible(true);
   }
}
```

Notice when attaching the **TextFieldExtended** object to the pop-up that an ActionListener array is supplied as the second parameter:

```
p.attach(t,new ActionListener[] { t });
```

The **new ActionListener[] { t }** expression is an anonymous array construct. The array has no name, similar to an anonymous nested class having no name. Anonymous array constructs are new to Java 1.1 and, as you can see, are convenient for implementing concise expressions. The ActionListener array specifies a mapping between the menu items in the pop-up menu and their corresponding **actionPerformed()** handlers. There's either a one-to-one mapping—one listener per menu item—or one listener used for all menu items. The **attach()** method reveals that a hashtable dictionary of attached widgets and their associated action listeners is used to maintain this map.

The **PopupMenuExtended** class implements the MouseListener interface so that it can listen to the mouse events emanating from each of its attached widgets. The **attach()** method adds the **PopupMenuExtended** object as a mouse listener to each widget it's attached to. Notice that several of the mouse event handlers call **show()**, which determines whether the event is a trigger request for a pop-up menu. It's necessary to sample the click, press, and release mouse events to see whether the **isPopupTrigger()** method of the **MouseEvent** returns true. This is necessary because native platforms having different looks and behaviors signal a pop-up menu differently, some with a rapid mouse down-and-up motion and others with a click. The **isPopupTrigger()** method makes platform determinations clear, but it's still unknown which event signals the pop-up.

Before showing the pop-up, the **show()** method consumes the mouse event and sets the **Component** context. Recall that consuming an event prevents the event from being passed to the **Component**'s peer for handling but not from other registered listeners. Consuming the **PopupMenuEvent** over a **TextField** prevents the native peer's Edit menu from appearing after our pop-up menu. Setting the context allows the subsequent dispatch of any action events fired from pop-up menu items on to their intended handlers.

The **PopupMenuExtended** object is its own action listener for every item added to the menu. Both of the **add()** methods inherited from **java.awt.PopupMenu** are overridden to accomplish this. After the pop-up is displayed and the selection made, the resulting action event is filtered through the **actionPerformed()** method of the **PopupMenuExtended** object. Because the previous call to the **show()** method set the widget context, the action event can be passed on to the proper action listeners associated with that widget. The **actionPerformed()** method looks up the action listener(s) of the context widget and dispatches the action event for the menu item selected, delivering it to the handler designated for the widget. In our case, menu item's text is used to set the contents of the text field. Although **PopupMenu** is easy to use, we think you'll find using **PopupMenuExtended** even easier, having encapsulated the mouse pop-up trigger and the handler mapping within one convenient object. The **PopupMenuExtended** class will be used in later examples.

Menu shortcuts are straightforward. The following code snippet creates two menu items with shortcuts. The AWT and platform determine the presentation of shortcut feedback through the menu item:

```
Menu menu = new Menu("File");
menu.add(new MenuItem("Save...",new MenuShortcut('S')));
menu.add(new MenuItem("Save As...",new
MenuShortcut('S',true)));
```

This code was used to produce the display shown in Figure 6-6.

The focus traversal API is also straightforward. The following method has been added to the **java.awt.Component** class and its peer:

```
public boolean isFocusTraversable()
```

Figure 6-6.
Menu shortcuts.

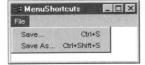

If a component can accept keyboard focus, the method returns true. The peer class needs to have the same method because different platforms have different traversal rules. If the method returns false, the AWT's focus manager bypasses the component when traversal is instigated by tabbing. Suppose you want to derive your own component from **Canvas** (a lightweight, for example). **Canvas.isFocusTraversable()** returns false by default, so you're obliged to override **isFocusTraversable()** if your new component needs to get focus. Don't forget to catch the **MouseDown** event on the new component and use **requestFocus()** also. When your new component gets focus, it needs to offer some type of visual feedback indicating that it has focus so users won't get lost.

Lightweight Components

The AWT 1.1 now supports *lightweight components*, those derived directly from the **java.awt.Component** and **java.awt.Container** classes. This feature allows components to bypass having native opaque windows associated with them, so lightweights don't tie up as many system resources. They can also be transparent or irregular in shape, but their bounding box will remain rectangular until the arrival of the Java2D API. Lightweights are 100 percent implemented in common Java code, so they maintain a consistent look and behavior across platforms. Any existing subclasses of **Canvas** and **Panel** can be converted to lightweights by simply changing their superclasses to **Component** and **Container**, respectively. The lightweight user interface framework will be used in an upcoming version of the AWT to implement pure Java common-code versions of the basic AWT controls. This will provide a foundation for a common, cross-platform look and behavior, and allow the user to "hot plug" different looks and behaviors.

Painting lightweight components is usually double-buffered because their direct rendering tends to cause screen flickering. Figure 6-7 shows the screen display of an oval label. The source is shown in Listing 6-16. The **OvalLabel** constructor uses the new **java.awt.SystemColor** class to map the label's color to those defined by the host system. The

Figure 6-7.
Lightweight label.

Listing 6-16.
Lightweight label.

```java
import java.awt.*;
import java.awt.event.*;

public class OvalLabel extends Component {

  private String label;
  private Image buf;
  private static int margin = 20;

  public OvalLabel(String label)
  {
    this.label = label;
    setBackground(SystemColor.control);
    setForeground(SystemColor.controlText);
  }

  public void update(Graphics g)
    { paint(g); }

  public void invalidate()
  {
      super.invalidate();
      buf = null;
  }

  public void paint(Graphics g)
  {
    if (buf == null)  {
      Dimension d = getSize();
      buf = createImage(d.width,d.height);
      Graphics bg = buf.getGraphics();
      bg.setClip(0,0,d.width,d.height);
      bg.setColor(getBackground());
      Font f = getFont();
      if (f != null)  {
        FontMetrics fm = getFontMetrics(getFont());
        int w = fm.stringWidth(label) + margin;
        int h = fm.getHeight() + margin;
        bg.fillOval(d.width/2-w/2,d.height/2-h/2,w,h);
        bg.setColor(getForeground());
        bg.drawString(label,d.width/2 - w/2 + margin/2,
            d.height/2 + fm.getMaxDescent());
      }
      bg.dispose();
    }
    g.drawImage(buf, 0, 0, null);
  }

  public Dimension getPreferredSize()
  {
    Font f = getFont();
```

Contnues

Listing 6-16.
Continued.

```
   if (f != null) {
     FontMetrics fm = getFontMetrics(getFont());
     return new Dimension
       (fm.stringWidth(label) + margin, fm.getHeight() +
            margin);
   }
   return new Dimension(100, 100);
 }

 public Dimension getMinimumSize()
   { return getPreferredSize(); }

 public static void main(String[] args)
 {
   Frame f = new Frame("Oval Label");
   f.addWindowListener(
     new WindowAdapter()
     {
        public void windowClosing(WindowEvent e)
          { System.exit(0); }
     }
   );
   f.add("Center",new OvalLabel("Hello World!"));
   f.setSize(150,100);
   f.setVisible(true);
 }
}
```

SystemColor class is new to AWT 1.1. The update() method is overridden, calling the paint() method directly to prevent erasing the component's background before painting. The buffered image in held in the buf variable. It's discarded when the component is invalidated. The paint() method re-renders the oval label only when buf is null. The rendering is done to the image in memory, not directly to the screen. This memory image is then drawn onscreen during paint() requests. Admittedly, the OvalLabel is rather elementary, but it demonstrates what it takes to build lightweight components. Visual JavaBeans are almost always lightweight components or containers.

Clipboard and Drag-and-Drop

Modern GUI environments allow users to transfer data between applications. The transfer paradigm is typically formed when a Clipboard object negotiates the transfer. Currently, the AWT allows Clipboard operations only through native widgets that support it, such as TextField and

TextArea. However, the AWT now includes a data transfer API on which higher level protocols, like Clipboard and Drag-and-Drop, can be based. A Clipboard API is included in AWT 1.1, with Drag-and-Drop to follow in a later release.

The data transfer API is implemented in the java.awt.datatransfer package. It's centered on the Transferable interface. For an object to be transferable, it must implement the Transferable interface. The **java.awt.datatransfer.StringSelection** class provides a transferable wrapper for strings. Figure 6-8 shows the Clipboard being used to transfer a list selection to a button label. Neither the **List** nor **Button** classes have native Clipboard abilities. Listing 6-17 shows how the Clipboard transfer was accomplished.

Figure 6-8.
Clipboard operations.

Listing 6-17.
Enabling Clipboard operations.

```java
import java.awt.datatransfer.*;
import java.awt.event.*;
import java.awt.*;
import java.io.*;

public class ClipboardDemo
{

   final static Clipboard clipboard =
     Toolkit.getDefaultToolkit().getSystemClipboard();

   static void copy(String text)
   {
     if (text != null)  {
       StringSelection ss = new StringSelection(text);
       clipboard.setContents(ss,ss);
     }
   }

   static String paste(Object requestor)
   {
     Transferable content = clipboard.getContents
          (requestor);
     if (content != null &&
       content.isDataFlavorSupported(DataFlavor.
```

Continues

Listing 6-17.
Continued.

```
                          stringFlavor))   {
         try   {
           return (String)
             content.getTransferData(DataFlavor.stringFlavor);
         }
         catch (UnsupportedFlavorException ufe) {}
         catch (IOException ioe) {}
      }
      return "";
   }

   public static void main(String[] args)
   {
      Frame f = new Frame("Clipboard Demo");
      f.addWindowListener
      (
         new WindowAdapter()
         {
           public void windowClosing(WindowEvent e)
              { e.getWindow().dispose(); System.exit(0); }
         }
      );
      final List l = new List();
      l.addItem("List Item One");
      l.addItem("List Item Two");
      l.addItem("List Item Three");
      f.add("Center", l);
      final Button b = new Button("Button Label");
      f.add("South",b);
      f.setSize(200,150);
      f.setVisible(true);
      PopupMenuExtended editMenu = new PopupMenuExtended();
      editMenu.add("Copy");
      editMenu.add("Paste");
      f.add(editMenu);
      editMenu.attach(l,
         new ActionListener[]
         {
           new ActionListener()
           {
             public void actionPerformed(ActionEvent e)
               { copy(l.getSelectedItem()); }
           },
           new ActionListener()
           {
             public void actionPerformed(ActionEvent e)
               { l.addItem(paste(l)); }
           }
         });
      editMenu.attach(b,
         new ActionListener[]
         {
           new ActionListener()
```

Listing 6-17.
Continued.

```
    {
        public void actionPerformed(ActionEvent e)
        { copy(b.getLabel()); }
    },
    new ActionListener()
    {
        public void actionPerformed(ActionEvent e)
        { b.setLabel(paste(b)); }
    }
});
    }
}
```

The system Clipboard can be accessed through the Toolkit. To copy text (or any other data) to the Clipboard, it must be wrapped in an object implementing the Transferable interface. Therefore, the **StringSelection** class is used to wrap the text (see the **copy()** method). Setting the contents of the Clipboard notifies any previous Clipboard owner that its ownership rights have been revoked—it no longer has to ensure the validity of the contents it posted there. Ownership is granted to the new owner, as specified in the call to **setContents()**:

```
public synchronized void setContents(Transferable contents,
ClipboardOwner owner);
```

The Clipboard owner should try to preserve the contents it posts to the Clipboard until its **lostOwnership()** method is called. The Clipboard-Owner interface consists of one method:

```
public abstract void lostOwnership(Clipboard clipboard,
Transferable contents);
```

The **getTransferData()** method of the transferable contents object should throw the **IOException** if its data is no longer available or otherwise invalid when it's requested by a Paste operation. The **StringSelection** class implements both the ClipboardOwner and Transferable interfaces. The Clipboard ownership feature isn't used in this example because **StringSelection** does nothing when its lostOwnership() method is called. (It isn't necessary for the contents and owner to be one and the same object, as shown in this example.) Because a **StringSelection** is simply a string constant with a Transferable wrapper, it can be posted and forgotten—there will never be a need to throw an **IOException** or respond in some way to lost ownership.

The contents of the Clipboard are returned by the **getContents()** method:

```
public synchronized Transferable getContents(Object
       requestor);
```

The **Transferable** object returned must be able to list the different data formats (also called *flavors*) in which it can serve up its data so that interested recipients can negotiate their favorite type to perform the transfer. The requestor isn't presently used, but you can use your own internal Clipboard, so it might prove useful in an overridden version of **getContents()**.

The AWT currently supports two data formats: **stringFlavor** and **plainTextFlavor**. The **StringSelection** class supports both and can respond by returning either a String or InputStream through **getTransferData()** for **DataFlavor.stringFlavor** or **DataFlavor.plainTextFlavor**, respectively. In this example, the **paste()** method requests the **stringFlavor** because it's the easiest type to work with for the task at hand. Consult the **StringSelection.java** source code if you want to implement your own transferable wrapper or data format.

The **main()** method of the **ClipboardDemo** class builds a list and a button. The **PopupMenuExtended** class from an earlier example is reused to provide the pop-up Edit menu. All glue code is in the ActionListener handlers associated with the list and button, mapping the menu selections to the proper Copy and Paste operations. Review the **PopupMenu** example if this portion of the code is unclear.

Emerging Frameworks

Application frameworks allow high-quality applications to be delivered rapidly. An *application framework* is a collection of related, cooperating classes that become the application's foundation. These reusable classes, the result of many years of coding effort, supply the common functional elements of an application and thereby minimize redundant design, implementation, and testing requirements. Developers can then spend their time more productively on the essence of an application rather than waste time on its window dressing. It's nearly impossible to build a successful commercial application without the competitive edge that an application framework brings to a project. To minimize download times in a distribution-heterogeneous environment, the application framework classes must be incorporated into browsers, negating the need to download its classes. The emerging frameworks discussed in the following sections should become widely available and prove to be promising candidates upon which to base your future applications.

AFC

The *Application Foundation Classes* (AFC) is a comprehensive collection of commercial-quality Java classes. Because the classes are written in common Java code, they are platform independent. A prerelease version of the AFC GUI libraries is now included in Microsoft's SDK 2.0 (Software Development Kit for Java 1.1), which is available for download from `http://www.microsoft.com/java/`. The GUI classes (over 30 in all) include toolbars, tree controls, and tabbed dialog boxes. All the components are fully customizable and extensible. Configurable features include textures, wide-styled pens, multiple fonts, and resource loading. AFC is build around the AWT, unlike other class libraries, so developers can maximally reuse their existing AWT code and expertise.

The AFC Enterprise libraries will provide support for a full range of distributed computing services. Data access components will support JDBC, ODBC, and ADO access models and will include a wide array of data-aware controls that will become a part of the AFC GUI libraries. Directory services will allow accessing and manipulating remote directories through *Lightweight Directory Access Protocol* (LDAP). Support for transaction services is available now with *Microsoft Transaction Server* (MTS). Object interoperability classes will be based on DCOM. The Enterprise libraries should by available in their entirety by the fourth quarter of 1997 and included in the Microsoft Virtual Machine for Java incorporated into Internet Explorer 4.0.

IFC and JFC

The *Internet Foundation Classes* (IFC) was the first widely available AWT enhancement library to overcome the shortcomings of AWT 1.0.2. It provided an event delegation mechanism similar in function to what's now available in AWT 1.1. It also supplied a rich assortment of lightweight components, including a sophisticated drag-and-drop ability. An IFC "application" additionally gave one or more applets the ability to talk to each other. IFC was ahead of its time. Until browsers incorporate the newer Java Virtual Machine based on 1.1, other solutions have been hard-pressed to deliver the performance or features of IFC-enabled applets.

Due in part to competition from the upstart AFC libraries, JavaSoft, Netscape, and IBM have announced a single, unified application framework API for Java named *Java Foundation Classes* (JFC). JFC will become part of the core Java standard when it's released sometime around the end of 1997. All of IFC's major features will be incorporated into JFC, including lightweight user interface components and a streamlined application framework that's single-threaded. Netscape will shipped IFC 1.1 as its last version of IFC in May 1997. This version is available for download from **http://developer.netscape.com/library/ifc/index.html**.

Infobus

Adopting the Infobus technology will bring a dynamic data exchange ability to Java's core APIs later this year. The Infobus architecture allows cooperating components to communicate through a standard data flow interface. Data and its consistency can be discovered at runtime. Components that make up an Infobus application can be classified as data producers, data consumers, and data controllers. Unlike the bound properties of JavaBeans, the consistency of the data to be exchanged need not be known at design time. Unlike the AWT's Clipboard API, the Infobus allows components to communicate programmatically across the bus without requiring user interaction. The reach of the bus can conceiveably extend beyond the boundary of the JVM by using RMI/CORBA-enabling components that export and import the flow of data.

AWT Wrap-Up

Programs compiled under 1.0.x should run unchanged on runtime systems based on 1.1.x, as long as the programs don't depend on bugs in earlier releases for their proper operation. Programs compiled under 1.1.x appear to run on earlier implementations if they don't make use of 1.1.x features. This backward compatibility hasn't been rigorously tested, however. Many method names have been changed in the newer AWT to make the API more consistent. A *sed (stream editor)* script is provided for UNIX users to automate updating the names in older code. The compiler also has a depreciation option to flag obsolete names that will eventually be unsupported in later releases.

The AWT of JDK 1.1.x demonstrates a vast improvement in quality and performance with even more features soon to come. Later versions of the AWT will have all components supporting the "hot plug" look and behavior, so either a native look and behavior or a common look and behavior across all platforms can be chosen for viewing. More sophisticated components, such as TreeView and Table, are on the way, too. Such components are available now from third-party vendors (such as AFC and IFC), but a common, richer set in the AWT API will be beneficial to all. A new Java 2D API will layer into the AWT, yielding advanced graphics-rendering capabilities, such as rotational and scaling transforms, image compositioning, advanced text handling, and more. The AWT is rapidly becoming a mature GUI environment.

An Event-Generating Bean

Now that we know how the delegation model works, let's see it in action by developing a Bean that generates events. We will build upon the same **RoadPatrolBean** we used to illustrate a vetoable property in Chapter 5. We will extend the **RoadPatrolBean** to generate one event: A **copEvent**. There's more than one way to abstract the **RoadPatrolBean**, so instead of having this Bean generate only one event and encapsulate the reason for it to be generated, we could have made it generate two events, the **PullOver** event and the **LetGo** event. The **copEvent** is instantiated from a class called **CopEventObject**. Let's examine this class in some detail.

Listing 6-18.
CopEventObject
class.

```
package Cars;

import java.util.*;

public class CopEventObject extends EventObject
{
    public CopEventObject (Object o, int iReason)
    {
        super (o);
        m_timeOfEvent = System.currentTimeMillis ();
        m_iReason = iReason;
    }

    public long getTimeOfEvent ()
    {
        return m_timeOfEvent;
    }

    public int getReason ()
    {
        return m_iReason;
    }
```

Continues

Listing 6-18.
Continued.

```
// reason
public static final int PULLOVER = 1;
public static final int RESUME   = 2;

private long m_timeOfEvent;
private int  m_iReason = PULLOVER;

}
```

The `CopEventObject` class has two private data members: The time the event occurred and the reason for the event. By default, the reason for the event to be generated is pulling over. This abstraction is basically meant for other Beans that can be pulled over, like a car Bean or a truck Bean. However, you might want this to signify other things, too. The class has two static constants defined, **PULLOVER** and **RESUME**. It's good practice to use static constants to document the value being used, so that if the object's internal representation ever changes, other applications that use this object still remain valid. The constructor explicitly executes the parent classes' constructor and then sets the reason and the time the event occurred. It has two read accessors. The `getReason()` method allows the listeners to introspect why this event occurred and take action accordingly. The `getTimeOfEvent()` method returns the time the event occurred. You might have noticed that there are only read accessor methods—no write accessors—in this event object; that's because event objects should be immutable. By allowing the event object's data to change, you potentially let the programmer unintentionally change the event. If this event is passed to many other objects, there's a chance of having some inconsistent behavior that might affect the application flow. The only time the object's data should be set is when the object is created. Not only does making the event object immutable make it secure from tampering, it also eliminates the need for synchronizing the read and write accessor methods. Because the data can only be read from and not written to, the code generated doesn't need to explicitly put a lock on the data, thus optimizing the code.

Next, we need to define an interface for this `copEvent`. If you need to develop an object that listens for `copEvents`, you would need to implement this interface. The interface for this `copEvent`, shown in Listing 6-19, is very simple.

NOTE *Events are immutable; hence, they have read access methods, but no write accessors. The values are set once during construction of the event object.*

Listing 6-19.
The listener interface for *CopEvents*.

```
package Cars;

import java.util.*;

public interface CopListener extends EventListener
{
    public void handleCopevent (Cars.CopEventObject ce);
}
```

To generate **copEvents**, the **RoadPatrolBean** must implement two methods: **addCopListener()** and **removeCopListener()**. The **RoadPatrolBean** maintains a **Vector** of CopListeners. Every time a new Bean registers itself with the **RoadPatrolBean**, the **addCopListener()** method is called; every time a Bean unregisters itself, the **removeCopListener()** method is called. There are two other methods of importance to us, the **pullOver()** and the **letGo()** methods. When the **pullOver()** method is called, the **RoadPatrolBean** creates a **CopEventObject** with a **PULLOVER** reason. It then clones the **Vector** of CopListeners. For each **CopListener** object in the **Vector**, it calls its **handleCopEvent()** method, passing the **copEvent** to it. Depending on how these listeners have implemented **handleCopEvent()**, they will take different actions. Similarly, the **letGo()** method initiates a **CopEventObject** with a **LETGO** reason and notifies all registered listeners.

Hookup Adapters

The difference between Beans and regular Java classes is that Java classes are used through programming code; Beans are used in Bean IDEs. They need to communicate with other Beans, and no code changes need to be made to get them to plug and play. The IDEs need to generate code to create simple adapters between classes.

The **RoadPatrolBean**, for example, couldn't generate the **PullOver** event or the **LetGo** event on its own (unless it used some randomize functions or the **CarBean** crossed the speed limit). We would need some sort of a button to interface with the **RoadPatrolBean**; when the button is pressed and it generates a **MOUSE_CLICKED** event, a call to the **pullOver()** method should be made. This should happen even though the **ourButton** Bean and the **RoadPatrolBean** were written independently with no prior knowledge of each other's existence. Therefore, to link these two classes, the Bean IDE—

Listing 6-20.
RoadPatrolBean
generating
CopEvents.

```
package Cars;

import java.awt.*;
import java.io.*;
import java.beans.*;
import java.util.*;
import java.awt.image.*;

public class RoadPatrolBean      extends        Canvas
                                 implements     Serializable,
                                                etoableChange-
                                                Listener,
                                                ImageObserver
{
    // constructor
    public RoadPatrolBean ()
    {
        setSize (IMG_WIDTH, IMG_HEIGHT);
        if (m_CopImages == null)
        {
            m_CopImages = new Image [NUM_IMAGES];

            Toolkit tk = getToolkit ();
            m_CopImages[0] = tk.getImage
                ("c:/McGrawHill/Bean/Cars/Cop.gif");
            m_CopImages[1] = tk.getImage
                ("c:/McGrawHill/Bean/Cars/PulloverCop.gif");
        }

    }


    public void paint (Graphics g)
    {
        g.drawImage (m_CopImages[0], 0, 0, this);
    }

    public boolean imageUpdate (Image img, int infoFlag,
int x, int y, int width, int height)
    {
        if ( (infoFlag & ALLBITS) != 0)
        {
            repaint ();
            return false;
        }

        return true;
    }

    // InitialState Property *****************************
    public int getMaxSpeed ()
    {
```

```java
                return m_iMaxSpeed;
    }

    public void setMaxSpeed (int iNewMaxSpeed)
    {
        m_iMaxSpeed = iNewMaxSpeed;
        repaint ();
    }

    // vetoable change event handler *********************
    public void vetoableChange (PropertyChangeEvent event)
            throws PropertyVetoException
    {
        Integer I = (Integer) event.getNewValue();

        if (I.intValue () > m_iMaxSpeed)
        {
            throw new PropertyVetoException ("New Value
                greater than " + m_iMaxSpeed, event);
        }

        System.out.println ("Property: " + Z
            event.getPropertyName () +
                        " Old: " +
                        event.getOldValue () +
                        " New: " +
                        event.getNewValue () +
                        " Speed: " + getMaxSpeed
                        ());
    }


    // methods to add and remove Cop Listeners
************
    public synchronized void addCopListener (CopListener l)
    {
        m_CopListeners.addElement (l);
    }
    public synchronized void removeCopListener
        (CopListener l)
    {
        m_CopListeners.removeElement (l);
    }

    public void pullOver ()
    {
        Vector v;
        Cars.CopEventObject ceo = new Cars.CopEventObject
            (this, Cars.CopEventObject.PULLOVER);

        synchronized (this)
```

Continues

Listing 6-20.
Continued.

```
        {
            v = (Vector) m_CopListeners.clone ();
        }

        for (int i=0; i < v.size (); i++)
        {
            Cars.CopListener cl = (Cars.CopListener)
                v.elementAt (i);
            cl.handleCopevent (ceo);
        }
    }

    public void letGo ()
    {
        Vector v;
        Cars.CopEventObject ceo = new Cars.CopEventObject
            (this, Cars.CopEventObject.RESUME);

        synchronized (this)
        {
            v = (Vector) m_CopListeners.clone ();
        }

        for (int i=0; i < v.size (); i++)
        {
            Cars.CopListener cl = (Cars.CopListener)
                v.elementAt (i);
            cl.handleCopevent (ceo);
        }
    }

    // private data members ******************************
    private int    m_iMaxSpeed        = 60;

    private Vector m_CopListeners    = new Vector ();
    private static Image[] m_CopImages = null;

    private final static int NUM_IMAGES = 2;
    private final static int IMG_HEIGHT = 136;
    private final static int IMG_WIDTH = 111;
}
```

in our case, the BeanBox—generates an event hookup adapter. The event hookup class implements the MouseListener interface and executes the **pullOver()** method from the **mouseClicked()** method. The source code for the generated file is given in Listing 6-21.

The BeanBox then compiles this event hookup class and passes it to the **addMouseListener()** method as a listener. After this listener is added

Listing 6-21.
Automatically
generated event
hookup file.

```
package tmp.sun.beanbox;
import Cars.RoadPatrolBean;
import java.awt.event.MouseListener;

public class ___Hookup_143ab072e9 implements
java.awt.event.MouseListener, java.io.Serializable {

    public void setTarget(Cars.RoadPatrolBean t) {
        target = t;
    }

    public void mouseClicked(java.awt.event.MouseEvent
        arg0) {
        target.pullOver();
    }

    public void mousePressed(java.awt.event.MouseEvent
        arg0) {
    }

    public void mouseReleased(java.awt.event.MouseEvent
        arg0) {
    }

    public void mouseEntered(java.awt.event.MouseEvent
        arg0) {
    }

    public void mouseExited(java.awt.event.MouseEvent arg0)
{
    }

    private Cars.RoadPatrolBean target;
}
```

to the **ourButton** Bean, the **PULLOVER** event is generated every time the
button is pressed.

CONCLUSION

In this chapter, we discussed the JDK 1.1 delegation model and saw its
advantages over JDK 1.0. We also saw some examples to illustrate events
handling and learned several new terms in this chapter. We learned about
listeners and adapters and saw how the BeanBox generates hookup files
to get independent Beans to communicate with each other. When creating

Beans, take into consideration the types of events they can generate, and then abstract the event class accordingly. Try to keep it simple and logical.

We discussed AWT enhancements in depth. An understanding of the AWT's event delegation mechanism is mandatory for writing your own JavaBean components because JavaBeans must adhere to these design patterns.

Persistence and Connectivity

Forms designed with JavaBeans will have to persist from one design session to the next, and applications will undoubtedly have to connect to data or remote objects. For JavaBeans to ultimately have meaning and usefulness, then, they must have some concept of a visual, persistent, connected context, which we explore in this chapter. The JavaBeans you design or buy need to focus on helping you deal more productively with this context.

JavaBeans must be persistent to be saved along with the *Graphical User Interface* (GUI) forms in which they're embedded. Visual development consists primarily of laying out JavaBeans on a form and then wiring them up to perform useful functions. These forms need to be saved between design sessions—the reason for the requirement for JavaBean persistence. We also cover advanced aspects of object serialization, Java's primary persistence mechanism, so that your Beans can take advantage of versioning and other serialization options. Object serialization also plays an important role in facilitating *Remote Method Invocation* (RMI).

Most applications today need to connect to distributed data sources across a network. Important transport technologies that are built on top of Java's networking *Application Programming Interface* (API) include RMI, the *Interface Definition Language* (IDL) of CORBA, and *Java Data-Base Connectivity* (JDBC) APIs. This chapter covers everything you need to know to get started on using these vital technologies in the JavaBeans you develop or use. Most commercial Beans you see will incorporate some aspect of these APIs.

This chapter will cover the following topics:

- Object serialization
- RMI
- IDL
- JDBC

Object Serialization

What exactly is object serialization? It certainly involves taking an object and storing its primitive field values onto a stream. But what about any internal references to other objects? If all other objects referenced (either directly or indirectly) aren't also stored, the root object can't be faithfully restored to its exact former state. Therefore, object serialization often means flattening a neighborhood of associated objects into a sequential (serial) stream of bytes.

Why is object serialization so important? Once in a serialized form, this object mesh can be saved to a standard file or *Binary Large Object* (BLOB) field of a database to cause lightweight persistence. Visual development environments will surely make heavy use of object serialization not only to save forms, but also to allow cut-and-paste operations of selected Java-Bean components in layout tools. Perhaps a serialized object will need to be communicated to a remote location through a socket stream running on top of a serial communications line. Java has always been a code-mobile system. It's only natural that object mobility and remoteability would follow by popular demand. In remote method invocations, a remote method call wouldn't be possible if its parameters couldn't be transported to the remote site.

The good news is that Java's object serialization API makes serialization as easy as implementing the Serializable interface. The best part is that the Serializable interface has no methods! It's simply a tagging interface so that an **ObjectOutputStream** can determine through introspection whether an object is allowed to be serialized. The reflections API can be used to determine the fields of an object and their respective types. Once the fields are known, serialization is reduced to simply writing these values to and from a stream. Granted, negotiating an object mesh requires a somewhat sophisticated algorithm. Fortunately, the algorithm and its implementation have been encapsulated in the **ObjectOutputStream** and **ObjectInputStream** classes.

Many of the core API classes implement the Serializable interface, so serialization of those objects and their derivatives requires just opening an object stream and writing the object. The following code snippet shows how to save an AWT **Button** object to a file (both the **ObjectOutputStream** and **ObjectInputStream** classes are found in the java.io package):

```
FileOutputStream fos = new FileOutputStream("Button.ser");
ObjectOutputStream out = new ObjectOutputStream(fos);
out.writeObject(new Button("Persistent"));
```

Perhaps you want to send the **Button** object to a remote location, as shown here:

```
ObjectOutputStream out = new
ObjectOutputStream(socket.getOutputStream());
out.writeObject(new Button("Persistent"));
```

The following code shows how to retrieve the **Button** object:

```
FileInputStream fis = new FileInputStream("Button.ser");
ObjectInputStream in = new ObjectInputStream(fis);
Button b = (Button) in.readObject();
```

The following code shows how to receive the **Button** object at the re-mote location:

```
ObjectInputStream in = new ObjectInputStream
    (socket.getInputStream());
    Button b = (Button) in.readObject();
```

It should be noted that neither static nor transient fields are serialized. All other fields, including private fields, are serialized.

Custom Serialization

No doubt an application will sometimes need to modify how objects are serialized. Suppose a private field must be serialized but not without be-ing encrypted first. The object serialization API supplies hooks so that this procedure can be readily accomplished.

SERIALIZABLE INTERFACE   Classes implementing the Serializable interface have the option of declaring either a **writeObject()** method or a **readObject()** method or both. Listing 7-1 shows one way to customize serialization with these optional methods. Notice that the **Employee** class implements the Serializable interface, so **Employee** objects are serializ-able. **Employee** has two fields: **commonKnowledge** and **confidential**. The **confidential** field must not be sent in the clear, so it's marked as tran-sient. Therefore, the standard serialization process will skip over the **confidential** field. However, we want the **confidential** field to be seri-alized in an encrypted form.

The **writeObject()** method of the **ObjectOutputStream** class first looks to see whether the object being serialized implements a **writeObject()** method. If it does, that method is called instead of calling the **ObjectOutputStream**'s **defaultWriteObject()** method. Because **Employee** does implement **writeObject()**, it's called instead of relying on the default serialization. It turns out that our **Employee writeObject()** method turns right around and calls **defaultWriteObject()** anyway, which serializes only the **commonKnowledge** field, skipping the **confidential** field because it's transient. (If **defaultWriteObject()** is called from some-where other than inside the writeObject method, the **NotActiveException** is returned.) The **ObjectOutputStream** class also declares methods for

```java
import java.io.*;

public class Employee implements Serializable
{
  public String commonKnowledge = "";
  protected transient String confidential = "";

  public Employee
    (String commonKnowledge, String confidential)
  {
    this.commonKnowledge = commonKnowledge;
    this.confidential = confidential;
  }

  private void writeObject(ObjectOutputStream stream)
    throws IOException
  {
    stream.defaultWriteObject();
    stream.writeUTF(encrypt(confidential));
  }

  private void readObject(ObjectInputStream stream)
    throws IOException
  {
    try { stream.defaultReadObject(); }
    catch (Throwable t) {}
    confidential = decrypt(stream.readUTF());
  }

  protected static String encrypt(String msg)
    { return msg; }

  protected static String decrypt(String msg)
    { return msg; }

  public static class Manager extends Employee
  {
    private transient String secret = "";
    private transient String topSecret = "";

    public Manager
      (String commonKnowledge, String confidential,
       String secret, String topSecret)
    {
      super(commonKnowledge,confidential);
      this.secret = secret;
      this.topSecret = topSecret;
    }

    private void writeObject(ObjectOutputStream stream)
      throws IOException
```

Continues

Listing 7-1.
Continued.

```
  {
    stream.writeUTF(encrypt(secret));
  }

  private void readObject(ObjectInputStream stream)
    throws IOException
  {
    stream.registerValidation(new ManagerValidate(),1);
    secret = decrypt(stream.readUTF());
  }

  private class ManagerValidate
    implements ObjectInputValidation
  {
    public void validateObject()
      throws InvalidObjectException
    {
      topSecret = "n/a";
      System.out.println("Manager Validated");
    }
  }

  public String toString()
  {
    return "Manager\n{\n  commonKnowledge = " +
        commonKnowledge
      + "\n  confidential = " + confidential
      + "\n  secret = " + secret
      + "\n  topSecret = " + topSecret
      + "\n}";
  }
}

public static void main(String[] args)
{
  try {
    ByteArrayOutputStream baos = new
        ByteArrayOutputStream();
    ObjectOutputStream out = new
        ObjectOutputStream(baos);
    Manager m = new Manager(
      "likes Java", "vacation time accrued",
      "under contract", "being considered for promotion"
    );
    System.out.println(m);
    out.writeObject(m);
    out.flush();
    ByteArrayInputStream bais =
      new ByteArrayInputStream(baos.toByteArray());
    ObjectInputStream in = new ObjectInputStream(bais);
    m = (Manager) in.readObject();
    System.out.println(m);
```

Listing 7-1.
Continued.

```
        } catch (Throwable t) { System.out.println(t); }
        System.exit(0);
    }
}
```

serializing all types of data. In this example, the `confidential` field is first encrypted and then written to the object stream by calling the `writeUTF()` method. Looking ahead to the `readObject()` method of `Employee`, we see that the process is reversed by calling the `readUTF()` method of the `ObjectInputStream`. Of course, the contents must be decrypted before re-assigning it back to the `confidential` field. The `encrypt()` and `decrypt()` methods currently do nothing except return the string passed in, but this is where any encryption and decryption should take place.

The `readObject()` of the `ObjectInputStream` class looks to see whether the object being serialized implements a `readObject()` method. If it does, it's called instead of calling the `defaultReadObject()` method. Of course the `Employee` class does implement the `readObject()` method, so it's called. Again, the `readObject()` turns right around and calls the `defaultReadObject()` to extract the `commonKnowledge` field before proceeding to the special handling of the `confidential` field.

Whenever an object needs to implement a special serialization technique or perhaps add information to the object stream, the `writeObject()` and `readObject()` methods can be optionally declared by the serializable object. There's no requirement that both, or neither, must appear. For example, you might want to use the `writeObject()` method to monitor the serialization process, in which case there would be no corresponding `readObject()` method.

In the case of a derived object, at each level of the hierarchy the `ObjectOutputStream` checks whether that level implements the `writeObject()` method. Each level's `writeObject()`, if it appears, is responsible only for that level's declared fields. Therefore, it's possible to selectively take over portions of the serialization process. In our example, the `Manager` class extends the `Employee` class. `Manager` is a nested top-level class (see the inner class section of AWT enhancements to understand the distinction between nested top-level and inner classes). The `Manager` class introduces two additional fields (`secret` and `topSecret`) besides the two inherited from `Employee`. Both of these fields are marked transient, so if the `Manager` class didn't implement the `writeObject()` and `readObject()` methods, there would be no way for these fields to appear in the object stream. As it turns out, the `topSecret` field isn't to leave the building (that is, not to appear in the object stream), so the `writeObject()` and `readObject()` methods skip it. The only remaining field—`secret`—is transient, so there's really no need for `writeObject()` to call the `defaultWriteObject()` method, which has nothing to serialize at this level. Likewise, there's no reason for `readObject()` to call the `defaultReadObject()` method. The `secret` field is encrypted and decrypted as the `Employee`'s `confidential` field is. It's important to see that the `Manager`'s `writeObject()` and `readObject()` methods deal only with the declared fields of `Manager` and not the fields inherited from `Employee`. Therefore, there's no reason for them to call their superclass versions. They will be called by the `ObjectOutputStream` and `ObjectInputStream`, respectively.

A validation hook is used to set the `topSecret` field of the reconstituted `Manager` object to `n/a` (not available) because this field doesn't appear in the object stream. The call to the `registerValidation()` method must appear only within a `readObject()` method, or else the `NotActiveException` exception will be returned. The validation object must implement the ObjectInputValidation interface. This interface declares the `validateObject()` method, which is called after the entire object and its associated neighborhood is completely reconstituted. The second parameter to `registerValidation()` is a priority that indicates the order in which validation objects will be called. For example, if `Employee`'s `readObject()` method registered a validation object, it would most likely be a higher priority than `Manager`'s because it would seem logical that base class fix-up should be accomplished before proceeding to derived class fix-up, but the order is completely up to the developer. The `ManagerValidate` class is an inner class of `Manager`. Therefore, a `ManagerValidate` object appears only in the context of a `Manager` object. This is a perfect example of the usefulness of inner classes outside the realm of implementing AWT event handlers. Actually, the `topSecret` field could have been initialized in the `readObject()` method itself. The approach taken here was simply to demonstrate the validation mechanism. The validation mechanism proves indispensable in complex object neighborhoods that require fix-ups after being reconstituted. The mechanism will play an important role inside IDEs that reconstitute JavaBeans forms that often require fix-ups.

In the `main()` method, the object stream is kept in memory this time in a byte array stream. The `Manager` object is created and displayed on `System.out`. It's then serialized, reconstituted, and displayed again. The output is shown here:

```
Manager
{
  commonKnowledge = likes Java
```

```
        confidential = vacation time accrued
        secret = under contract
        topSecret = being considered for promotion
}
Manager Validated
Manager
{
        commonKnowledge = likes Java
        confidential = vacation time accrued
        secret = under contract
        topSecret = n/a
}
```

EXTERNALIZABLE INTERFACE It's possible to bypass the serialization algorithm of the `ObjectOutputStream` and `ObjectInputStream` classes entirely on an object-by-object basis. Instead of implementing the Serializable interface, the class wanting to handle its own serialization should implement the Externalizable interface instead. The Externalizable interface declares two methods:

```
public void writeExternal(ObjectOutput stream)   throws
        IOException;
public void readExternal(ObjectInput stream)   throws
        IOException;
```

Any object implementing the Externalizable interface has accepted complete responsibility for the serialization process. There's no class-level parsing whatsoever—it's an all-or-nothing affair. A rework of the previous is shown in Listing 7-2. The validate hook had to be given up—remember, you're entirely on your own for any object implementing the Externalizable interface. Notice also that the `writeExternal()` and `readExternal()` methods are responsible for serializing their super types, unlike `writeObject()` and `readObject()` that only dealt with their own declared fields.

OBJECT STREAM CUSTOMIZATION For demanding applications, it's possible to extend the `ObjectOutputStream` and `ObjectInputStream` classes. The `ObjectOutputStream` provides hooks so that we can annotate classes in the stream and replace objects, serializing substitutes in their place:

```
ObjectOutputStream:
    annotateClass
    replaceObject
```

Listing 7-2.
Externalized
serialization.

```java
import java.io.*;

public class Employee implements Externalizable
{
  public String commonKnowledge = "";
  protected transient String confidential = "";

  public Employee() {}

  public Employee
    (String commonKnowledge, String confidential)
  {
    this.commonKnowledge = commonKnowledge;
    this.confidential = confidential;
  }

  public void writeExternal(ObjectOutput stream)
    throws IOException
  {
    stream.writeUTF(commonKnowledge);
    stream.writeUTF(encrypt(confidential));
  }

  public void readExternal(ObjectInput stream)
    throws IOException
  {
    commonKnowledge = stream.readUTF();
    confidential = decrypt(stream.readUTF());
  }

  protected static String encrypt(String msg)
    { return msg; }

  protected static String decrypt(String msg)
    { return msg; }

  public static class Manager extends Employee
  {
    private transient String secret = "";
    private transient String topSecret = "";

    public Manager() {}

    public Manager
      (String commonKnowledge, String confidential,
       String secret, String topSecret)
    {
      super(commonKnowledge,confidential);
      this.secret = secret;
      this.topSecret = topSecret;
    }
```

Listing 7-2.
Continued.

```java
    public void writeExternal(ObjectOutput stream)
      throws IOException
    {
      super.writeExternal(stream);
      stream.writeUTF(encrypt(secret));
    }

    public void readExternal(ObjectInput stream)
      throws IOException
    {
      super.readExternal(stream);
      secret = decrypt(stream.readUTF());
      topSecret = "n/a";
    }

    public String toString()
    {
      return "Manager\n{\n   commonKnowledge = " +
          commonKnowledge
        + "\n   confidential = " + confidential
        + "\n   secret = " + secret
        + "\n   topSecret = " + topSecret
        + "\n}";
    }
  }

  public static void main(String[] args)
  {
    try {
      ByteArrayOutputStream baos = new
          ByteArrayOutputStream();
      ObjectOutputStream out = new
          ObjectOutputStream(baos);
      Manager m = new Manager(
        "likes Java", "vacation time accrued",
        "under contract", "being considered for
            promotion"
      );
      System.out.println(m);
      out.writeObject(m);
      out.flush();
      ByteArrayInputStream bais =
        new ByteArrayInputStream(baos.toByteArray());
      ObjectInputStream in = new ObjectInputStream(bais);
      m = (Manager) in.readObject();
      System.out.println(m);
    } catch (Throwable t) { System.out.println(t); }
    System.exit(0);
  }
}
```

Correspondingly, the **ObjectInputStream** can resolve an annotated class and revert back from a substituted object:

```
ObjectInputStream
    resolveClass
    resolveObject
```

Basically, **resolveClass** is the inverse function of **annotateClass**. Likewise, **resolveObject** is the inverse of **replaceObject**. There are many ways these hooks can be used. For example, **annotateClass** is used by RMI to tag marshaled parameters with the URL of their class bytecodes. On the receiving side, **resolveClass** can fetch the class bytecode, if necessary. It's even conceivable to serialize static fields with these hooks. The replace and resolve object hooks could be used for writing and reading backward-compatible files, even those so drastically different that object stream versioning can't cope with the problem. Another use could be in monitoring (logging) object transmissions.

In Listing 7-3, the **ObjectOutputStream** and **ObjectInputStream** are extended for the sole purpose of monitoring the serialization process. Notice in the **ObjectOutputStreamMonitor** constructor that **enableReplaceObject()** must be called with its parameter set to true to turn on the **replaceObject()** method. The **annotateClass()** method simply reports that the class specification has just been serialized and placed onto the stream. This is a perfect place to serialize the URL of the class code, as mentioned earlier. The example stuffs class comments here. The **replaceObject()** reports that a person is about to be serialized (how dreadful). The **replaceObject()** is the place to return an impostor, if desired.

Listing 7-3.
Object Stream
Monitoring

```
import java.io.*;

public class ObjectStreamMonitor
{

   static class ObjectOutputStreamMonitor extends
       ObjectOutputStream
   {

     public ObjectOutputStreamMonitor(OutputStream out)
       throws IOException
     {
       super(out);
       enableReplaceObject(true);
     }
```

Listing 7-3.
Continued.

```
    protected void annotateClass(Class cl) throws
        IOException
    {
      System.out.println("Already serialized class: "+cl);
      writeUTF("Class Comments");
    }

    protected Object replaceObject(Object obj) throws
        IOException
    {
      System.out.println("Serializing object: "+obj);
      return obj;
    }
  }

  static class ObjectInputStreamMonitor extends
      ObjectInputStream
  {

    public ObjectInputStreamMonitor(InputStream in)
      throws StreamCorruptedException, IOException
    {
      super(in);
      enableResolveObject(true);
    }

    protected Class resolveClass(ObjectStreamClass v)
      throws IOException, ClassNotFoundException
    {
      System.out.println("Deserializing: " + v.getName()
        + "\n serial version UID: " +
            v.getSerialVersionUID());
      return super.resolveClass(v);
    }

    protected Object resolveObject(Object obj)
      throws IOException
    {
      System.out.println("Deserializing object: "+obj);
      return obj;
    }
  }

  public static class Person implements Serializable
  {
    String myName = null;
    Person friend1 = null;
    Person friend2 = null;

    public Person() {}
```

Continues

Listing 7-3.
Continued.

```java
    public Person(String myName)
      { this.myName = myName; }

    public void friends(Person friend1, Person friend2)
    {
      this.friend1 = friend1;
      this.friend2 = friend2;
    }

    public String toString()
      { return myName; }
  }

  public static void main(String[] args)
  {
    try {
      Person john = new Person("John");
      Person stella = new Person("Stella");
      Person patty = new Person("Patty");
      Person wayne = new Person("Wayne");
      john.friends(stella,wayne);
      stella.friends(john,patty);
      patty.friends(stella,wayne);
      wayne.friends(patty,john);
      ByteArrayOutputStream baos = new
          ByteArrayOutputStream();
      ObjectOutputStreamMonitor out =
        new ObjectOutputStreamMonitor(baos);
      out.writeObject(john);
      out.flush();
      ByteArrayInputStream bais =
        new ByteArrayInputStream(baos.toByteArray());
      ObjectInputStreamMonitor in =
        new ObjectInputStreamMonitor(bais);
      john = (Person) in.readObject();
    } catch (Throwable t) { System.out.println(t); }
    System.exit(0);
  }
}
```

The `ObjectInputStreamMonitor` class monitors the deserialization process. Notice how the `enableResolveObject()` must be called in the constructor to enable the `resolveObject()` method. The `resolveClass()` method reports the class being deserialized. Classes are serialized by means of a `ObjectStreamClass` descriptor. This descriptor includes the fully-qualified name of the class and its serialization UID. This ID uniquely identifies the original version of this class that the current class is capable of writing and reading. Notice that the class comments put in the stream during serialization are completely ignored. The stream is written so that everything is blocked in records, which means optional data can be automatically skipped! If a URL is present, it's here that the class could be loaded. The `resolveObject()` method reports the object just completing deserialization. If there had been a substitution previously, here is the place to revert back to the original type or subtype.

The `main()` method creates four persons and establishes friendships. When a person gets serialized, so do all of his or her friends and their friends, and so on and so on, until we have a transitive closure. The transitive law states that if A is related to B and B is related to C, then A is related to C by transitivity. In other words, any friend of yours is a friend of mine. Here is the output of Listing 7-3:

```
Serializing object: John
Already serialized class: class ObjectStreamMonitor$Person
Serializing object: Stella
Serializing object: Patty
Serializing object: Wayne
Deserializing: ObjectStreamMonitor$Person
serial version UID: 741017918808968728
Deserializing object: Wayne
Deserializing object: Patty
Deserializing object: Stella
Deserializing object: John
```

It's important to point out how intelligent the serialization algorithm is. Notice that the `Person` class is serialized only once, as is each of the four persons. The `ObjectOutputStream` is clever enough to realize whether a person has already been serialized and not repeat the process. The friendship ring is known in mathematical terms as a *cyclic graph*. The serialization process doesn't loop forever around this cycle. Likewise, deserialization doesn't re-create duplicate friends from each person's perspective. Instead, it correctly creates each person uniquely with all references between persons being properly reestablished. What's important to know is that if you replace an object, every reference to it will be replaced.

Versioning

It's not uncommon for class declarations to be modified over the life cycle of an application. When serialization is involved, the need to maintain compatibility between versions often arises. The serialization mechanism can manage versioning automatically and transparently if the evolved class follows the compatibility guidelines outlined in this section. There's no need to write class-specific code to handle the variances. It's common for commercial JavaBean developers to release upgrades; because most Beans will participate in some type of RAD form persistence, commercial Bean developers must understand and observe requirements for serialization compatibility.

To remain backward-compatible, the evolved class must maintain the original class' contract; in other words, the evolved class must preserve the interface of the original class and its behavior. The interface refers to the methods, and the behavior refers to the side-effects produced by invoking those methods. The evolved class can certainly add methods without destroying compatibility. This arrangement allows versioning without the original class' anticipation. The evolved class has to be the accommodating partner, so it must be designed keeping in mind that it can be deserialized from an original class object in a worst-case scenario.

The evolved class can also add fields. During deserialization, if the added field is absent from the stream, the original class knows no difference, and the evolved class simply sets the field to its default value. If the added field is present, then the original class ignores it, skipping to the next item on the stream. The serialization mechanism skips unknown objects automatically. If the evolved class deletes a field, the original class might not be able to fulfill its contract—that is, the behavior behind the interface might be corrupted. Primitive types might not be modified because their stream representations aren't interchangeable. Changing the field access modifiers (public, package, protected, and private) has no effect on serialization. However, changing a nonstatic field to static or a nontransient field to transient destroys compatibility because it's equivalent to deleting a field. The reverse is okay because it's the equivalent of adding a field.

Classes can be added within the evolved class hierarchy because it's the equivalent of adding methods or fields. Classes inside the hierarchy can't have their derivation order rearranged because the hierarchy ordering is explicit in the stream. Removing classes could delete fields and methods and thus destroy compatibility. When these "ghost" objects appear in the stream, their primitive values are discarded, but the internally referenced objects are reconstituted and held in a holding pen because other objects in the neighborhood can still reference them. Remember, only one copy is stored on the stream. If it happens to be within a deleted class object, the reference fix-ups can't be made throughout the rest of the neighborhood.

The `writeObject()` and `readObject()` methods can be added and removed at will throughout the hierarchy of the evolved class, as long as these methods uniformly call their default `WriteObject()` and default `ReadObject()` counterparts in uniform order. These calls are typically the first order of business. Obviously, optional data might be lost to the original class. It should be noted that object validation could be disrupted by the absence of a `readObject()` method that calls `registerValidation()`.

Converting between Serializable and Externalizable destroys compatibility. Remember, Externalizable uses a user-defined serialization mechanism. Either way, the serialization mechanism can't cope with this change because implementation information embedded in the stream is inconsistent with the class. Removing either Serialization or Externalizable also destroys compatibility because it's equivalent to deleting fields. It's okay for internally referenced objects that were formerly not serializable to become so. In the original class, such fields are equivalent to being transient, which has the same effect as adding fields.

The evolved class must include the serial version UID of the original class it's compatible with, which can be determined by using the serialver utility. Suppose we wanted to revise the `Button` class to display an icon as well as a text label. (We would never do this in practice because the AWT is sacred and should never be modified.) To determine the UID, the command would be the following:

```
serialver java.awt.Button
```

This command would return the following:

```
static final long serialVersionUID = -8774683716313001058L;
```

To use the interactive version, you must invoke serialver with the `-show` option:

```
serialver -show
```

The `serialVersionUID` constant must appear as a member of our evolved `Button` class declaration. The `serialVersionUID` is a computed hashcode. Details of the hash algorithm can be found in the JDK documentation. If the compatibility guidelines were followed, our `Button` class could serialize itself into a stream from which the original class could deserialize it. Likewise, it could deserialize an original `Button` object with a default value being substituted for the missing icon. The original `Button` class wouldn't have had to anticipate a later version to ensure serialization compatibility.

Remote Method Invocation

RMI allows methods of remote objects to be invoked just as though they were locally executing in the same *Java Virtual Machine* (JVM). Without the RMI abstraction, an application would have to develop specific protocols for communicating through socket streams to remote applications. RMI makes this process practically transparent to the developer. Instead, the same object model is used with remote objects as is used with local objects. RMI uses object serialization to marshal parameters and the network transport to communicate between objects.

Regular objects can use RMI to give them remote capabilities. Unlike CORBA, you don't have to write any special IDL code; however, like CORBA, stubs and skeletons for client and server objects are generated for you. In many ways, the RMI architecture is a scaled-down version of the CORBA architecture (see Figure 7-1).

The remote reference layer handles the semantics of the invocation. It acts as a layer of abstraction between the network plumbing and the object stubs and skeletons. The transport layer is responsible for managing connections and keeping track of remote objects that reside in its address space. The transport layer isn't currently based on an open standard, such as IIOP, but it's a published protocol, so a bridge between RMI's proprietary transport protocol and IIOP is feasible. Without IIOP support, RMI limits you to interoperation only with other RMI objects.

Figure 7-1.
RMI architecture.

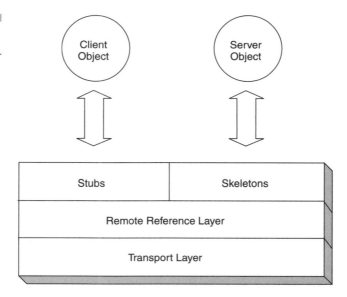

The first step in making a object remotely accessible is to declare its behavior in a remote interface, as shown in Listing 7-4. Our object is a message that can be set and read remotely. This interface must extend the java.rmi.Remote interface. Furthermore, all methods must explicitly declare the possible throwing of **java.rmi.RemoteException**. The **detail** field of **RemoteException**, if not null, is the actual exception that caused the **RemoteException** to be returned.

The second step is to implement this object as it will be instantiated on the remote server. Listing 7-5 shows the implementation of the message. Notice that the **MessageImpl** class extends the **java.rmi.server.UnicastRemoteObject** class. The **UnicastRemoteObject** class implements the functionality necessary to export an object and make sure remote references are valid only as long as the singleton server object is alive. The implementation of **Message** is quite elementary. Note that the default message is **Hello World!**—so what else is new?

Listing 7-4.
Remotely accessible behavior.

```
package MessageRMI;

public interface Message extends java.rmi.Remote
{
   public String getmsg() throws java.rmi.RemoteException;
   public void setmsg(String arg) throws java.rmi.RemoteEx-
ception;
}
```

Listing 7-5.
Remote object.

```
package MessageRMI;

public class MessageImpl
   extends java.rmi.server.UnicastRemoteObject
   implements Message
{
   private String msg = "Hello World!";

   public String getmsg() throws java.rmi.RemoteException
     { return msg; }

   public void setmsg(String arg) throws
        java.rmi.RemoteException
     { msg = arg; }

   public MessageImpl() throws java.rmi.RemoteException
     {}
}
```

With the `MessageImpl` declared, it's time to run the RMI compiler:

```
rmic MessageRMI.MessageImpl
```

The preceding `rmic` (RMI compiler) command produces the stub and skeleton classes:

```
MessageImpl_Skel.class
MessageImpl_Stub.class
```

The skeleton class is used on the server side to unmarshal parameters and actually invoke the method on the remote object executing on the server. The stub class is used on the client side to marshal the parameters and make the remote call.

Now the server application can be written. The code for the message server is shown in Listing 7-6. The security manager is set, and then the remote object is created and bound to an exported name. In this example, the exported `Message` is known as `Dave's MessageBoard` to distinguish it from other `Message` objects that might be running elsewhere on the network.

With the server in place, it's time to implement the client that will access the remote message. Listing 7-7 shows the implementation of the client. After setting the security manager, the remote local proxy is fetched with the static `lookup()` method of the `java.rmi.Naming class`. The remote object is given a URL:

```
rmi://localhost/Dave's MessageBoard
```

This URL specifies the RMI protocol. The host is local, and the service is Dave's MessageBoard. To test this remote application, we had two processes, each running a Java Virtual Machine, on the computer. The `localhost` refers to a TCP/IP loop back to the same machine. Because the server ap-

Listing 7-6.
Remote server.

```java
package MessageRMI;

public class MessageServer
{
  public static void main(String[] args)
  {
    System.setSecurityManager(new
        java.rmi.RMISecurityManager());
    try {
      Message m = new MessageImpl();
      java.rmi.Naming.rebind("Dave's MessageBoard",m);
    } catch (Throwable t) { System.out.println(t); }
  }
}
```

plication registered Dave's MessageBoard as a service, the client is able to connect. Calling the **getmsg()** method of the Message interface, the **"Hello World!"** string is returned and printed on the system output print stream.

After all files are compiled, we're ready to bring the application online. Three separate processes are used to conduct the test:

```
rmiregistry
java MessageServer
java MessageClient
```

First, the RMI registry must be booted with the **rmiregistry** command. If you're using on UNIX, you can run these jobs in the background. In Windows, you can run three separate DOS windows. After the Registry is up, start the server with the **java MessageServer** command. Last, start the client, and in a moment you will see **Hello World!**.

RMI makes distributed computing a snap if the remote application is also written in Java.

Interface Definition Language

The IDL of CORBA is a language-neutral remote object interface specification language. *Language-neutral* means that a remote object could be written in COBOL, FORTRAN, Java, or any language for which there's IDL mapping. The Java IDL API will soon become part of the core Java

Listing 7-7.
Client.

```
package MessageRMI;

public class MessageClient
{
  public static void main(String[] args)
  {
    System.setSecurityManager(new
        java.rmi.RMISecurityManager());
    try {
      Message m = (Message)
        java.rmi.Naming.lookup("rmi://localhost/
            Dave's MessageBoard");
      System.out.println(m.getmsg());
    }
    catch (Throwable t)  {
      System.out.println(t);
    }
  }
}
```

APIs. In this section, we rework the RMI example, using IDL and CORBA instead. Please compare the steps in this section with those in the previous RMI section.

CORBA is a set of standards set forth by the *Object Management Group* (OMG; `http://www.omg.org`) that specifies how objects can be wrapped in language-neutral wrappers and plugged into an object bus. Objects exported to the object bus can be called by any other object plugged into the bus. The importance of this is that any two cooperating objects need not be implemented in the same language, nor do they necessarily need to be executing on the same platform. The *Object Request Broker* (ORB) that manages the object bus makes these issues transparent to any object being plugged in. The *Internet Inter-Orb Protocol* (IIOP) of CORBA 2.0 specifies how two ORBs from different vendors can communicate with each other. Therefore, IIOP allows disparate object bus universes to be snapped together like Legos.

The first job is to specify the remote message object interface in language-neutral terms. Listing 7-8 shows the IDL specification of this interface. Attributes implicitly have accessor methods—**set** and **get**. Each target language environment will have an IDL-to-implementation language generator.

The idlgen tool generates Java code:

```
idlgen -fno-cpp -fno-cpp -fclient -fserver -j ..
     Message.idl
```

The **-fno-cpp** instructs the idlgen not to invoke the C++ processor on the IDL file, and the **-fclient** instructs idlgen to generate the client stub code. Because the server object will also be written in Java, for this example, the **-fserver switch** is also specified. Notice in the IDL specification for messages that we have a MessageIDL module and a Message interface. In the IDL-to-Java mapping, modules are mapped to package names. The **-j ..** instructs idlgen to place the generated code in the parent of the current directory. It so happens that **Message.idl** resides in the MessageIDL subdirectory so the generated code ends up right back in the same directory as the IDL file. The idlgen command generates the following files:

Listing 7-8.
IDL message spec.

```
module MessageIDL  {
  interface Message  {
    attribute string msg;
  };
};
```

```
MessageOperations.java
MessageRef.java
MessageStub.java
MessageHolder.java
MessageSkeleton.java
MessageServant.java
```

To implement the remote object, we implement the **MessageServant**, which in turn extends the MessageOperations interface. An easy way to remember this is that the servant usually does all the work. Listing 7-9 shows the implementation of **MessageImpl**. Notice that each method must explicitly declare the possible throwing of the **sunw.corba.SystemException** exception. Again, the implementation is elementary.

Now we turn to implementing the server application, as shown in Listing 7-10. The **sunw.door.Orb** class extends the **sunw.corba.Orb** class that specifies a common portable ORB core API for interfacing with different

Listing 7-9.
Remote object
implementation.

```
package MessageIDL;

public class MessageImpl implements MessageServant
{
    private String msg = "Hello World!";

    public String getmsg() throws sunw.corba.SystemException
        { return msg; }

    public void setmsg(String arg) throws
            sunw.corba.SystemException
        { msg = arg; }
}
```

Listing 7-10.
Remote object server.

```
package MessageIDL;

public class MessageServer
{
    public static void main(String[] args)
    {
        sunw.door.Orb.initialize(4000);
        sunw.door.Orb.logConnections(true);
        MessageRef mr = MessageSkeleton.createRef(new
                MessageImpl());
        try  { sunw.door.Orb.publish("Dave's MessageBoard",mr);
    }
        catch (Throwable t)  { System.out.println(t); }
    }
}
```

ORBs. The door transport is a Java-to-Java transport connecting two portable ORB core engines, so it acts like an ORB, but only for plugging in Java objects. In this sense, it's nothing but RMI in disguise. It's intended for testing the portable ORB API. Also supported on Sun Solaris is Sun's NEO transport for talking to NEO ORB servers (Interestingly, NEO doesn't stand for anything). A NEO ORB is a real full-fledged ORB. The portable ORB core also supports an IIOP transport for talking to any vendor's CORBA 2.0-compliant ORB, so in reality, the portable ORB core API isn't an ORB at all. It doesn't need to be because once the IIOP transport allows it, any vendor's ORB can be plugged in. You can think of the portable ORB core API as a specification for transport drivers to implement to allow their ORBs to be interchangeable with any other vendor's ORB. This is similar to how ODBC allows any relational database manager to be used interchangeably.

Initialize the `sunw.door.Orb` connection with logging turned on so that we can monitor objects plugging into the ORB object bus. The `createRef()` static method of the `MessageSkeleton` class wraps the remote `MessageImpl` object in a remote reference that can then be published (exported) to the object bus.

Listing 7-11 shows the implementation of the client application. The static `createRef()` method of the `MessageStub` class is used this time to get a handle to the remote message object. The handle must be attached to a remote object—or, in CORBA terms, the reference must be resolved to the actual remote object. The URL of the remote object is passed as a parameter to the `resolve()` method.

This time the protocol is IDL and the subprotocol (transport) is `sunw.door`. Because this distributed application is being tested on a single

Listing 7-11.
Message client.

```
package MessageIDL;

public class MessageClient
{
   public static void main(String[] args)
   {
     MessageRef mr = MessageStub.createRef();
     try {
       sunw.corba.Orb.resolve
         ("idl:sunw.door://localhost:4000/Dave's
             MessageBoard",mr);
       System.out.println(mr.getmsg());
     }
     catch (Throwable t)   { System.out.println(t); }
   }
}
```

CPU, we connect to the local host on the arbitrary port numbered 4000. Recall from the previous listing that the door "ORB" was initialized on port 4000 of the local host and that the remote message object was again established as the service named Dave's MessageBoard. If resolving the reference to the remote object succeeds, the `getmsg()` method is called, resulting in the `Hello World!` output appearing on the system output print stream.

All that's left to do is to start the server and then the client in separate process spaces:

```
java MessageServer
java MessageClient
```

Currently, the most popular Java ORB is the VisiBroker by Visigenics (`http://www.visigenic.com`). It has been adopted as the ORB of choice by many of the major corporations, including Netscape. VisiBroker will be included in the next version of Netscape Communicator. VisiBroker has its own IDL2Java generator with slightly different classes and naming. However, the steps for exporting and importing a CORBA object are basically the same as the ones explained here. When the IIOP transport arrives, you can simply use the portable ORB core API to connect to VisiBroker because it's a fully compliant CORBA 2.0 ORB supporting IIOP. Visigenics offers a free trial VisiBroker download from their site.

Caffeine is a joint product from Netscape and Visigenics that provides an RMI-like interface on top of VisiBroker for Java. A Java2IIOP code generator generates IIOP-compliant stubs and skeletons from RMI interfaces. Now you can have your CORBA cake with Java, without the aftertaste of IDL!

Java Database Connectivity

JDBC API provides a vendor-independent interface to relational database managers. JDBC is a takeoff of ODBC, developed originally by Microsoft. Your first task is installing the JDBC driver supplied by your RDBMS vendor. Because JDBC is relatively new, there might not be a JDBC driver available yet. Intersolv publishes a JDBC-ODBC bridge on its Web site so you can talk through an ODBC driver to its RDBMS. The bridge supports Windows 95, Windows NT, and SPARC/Solaris 2.4 and 2.5, so you can use this bridge to talk to Access. Intersolv also has JDBC drivers for Windows 95 and Windows NT that talk to Informix 7.2, Oracle 7, and Sybase System 10 (visit `http://www.intersolv.com/products/demo-dd-jdbc.htm`).

In this section, we've used InterServer, which allows remote TCP/IP connections to the Borland Interbase RDBMS. InterClient is a JDBC driver that talks through InterServer to Interbase. Both InterServer and InterClient are available for download from `http://www.borland.com` and installation is relatively easy. (The local Interbase engine came with Delphi; perhaps you obtain one from a C++ developer.)

Next, you must create a database with your RDBMS software. In the following example, the database is named Birthdays and is stored in D:/InterClient/BIRTHDAYS.GDB.

Listing 7-12 shows how to connect to the Birthdays database, create the Birthdays table, insert records, and perform some simple queries. At the beginning of the **Birthdays** class are several static strings that can be reconfigured for your database and JDBC driver. The InterClient JDBC driver is implemented in the **borland.interclient.Driver** class. The example uses the SYSDBA login with **masterkey** as the password.

Listing 7-12.
JDBC.

```java
import java.util.*;
import java.text.*;
import java.io.*;
import java.sql.*;

public class Birthdays
{
   static String jdbcDriver = "borland.interclient.Driver";
   static String dbUser = "SYSDBA";
   static String dbPassword = "masterkey";
   static String dbURL =
 "jdbc:interbase://localhost/D:/InterClient/BIRTHDAYS.GDB";
   static int DATE = Types.TIMESTAMP;

   public static void main(String[] args)
   {
      // load JDBC sql.Driver
      try {
         Class.forName(jdbcDriver);
      } catch (Throwable t) { System.err.println(t); }

      // Connect to Database
      Properties dbProps;
      dbProps = new Properties();
      dbProps.put("user",dbUser);
      dbProps.put("password",dbPassword);
      Connection connection = null;
      try {
         connection =
```

```
    DriverManager.getConnection(dbURL,dbProps);
    try {

      // Create table
      Statement stmt = connection.createStatement();
      try {
        try {
          stmt.execute("CREATE TABLE BIRTHDAYS "
            + "( LAST_NAME CHAR(20) NOT NULL,
                  FIRST_NAME CHAR(15), "
            + "DOB DATE, PRIMARY KEY(LAST_NAME))");
        } catch (Throwable t) { System.out.println(t); }

        // Insert Records
        try {
          stmt.executeUpdate("INSERT INTO BIRTHDAYS "
            + "( LAST_NAME, FIRST_NAME, DOB ) "
            + "VALUES ( \"Elias\", \"Wayne\",
                  \"9-Aug-1966\" )");
          stmt.executeUpdate("INSERT INTO BIRTHDAYS "
            + "( LAST_NAME, FIRST_NAME, DOB ) "
            + "VALUES ( \"Thieman\", \"Tom\",
                  \"19-Apr-1912\" )");
          stmt.executeUpdate("INSERT INTO BIRTHDAYS "
            + "( LAST_NAME, FIRST_NAME, DOB ) "
            + "VALUES ( \"Walker\", \"Rene\",
                  \"7-Jul-1993\" )");
          stmt.executeUpdate("INSERT INTO BIRTHDAYS "
            + "( LAST_NAME, FIRST_NAME, DOB ) "
            + "VALUES ( \"McLean\", \"Erin\",
                  \"17-Oct-1974\" )");
        } catch (Throwable t) { System.out.println(t); }

      } finally { stmt.close(); }

    } finally { connection.close(); }

    // Reconnect to Database
    connection =
DriverManager.getConnection(dbURL,dbProps);
    try {

      // Query with dynamic sql statement
      String sql = "SELECT * FROM BIRTHDAYS WHERE
          LAST_NAME = ?";
      PreparedStatement pstmt =
          connection.prepareStatement(sql);
      try {
        pstmt.setString(1,"Walker");
        DisplayResultSet(System.out,pstmt.
            executeQuery());
```

Continues

Listing 7-12.
Continued.

```
            pstmt.setString(1,"Elias");
            DisplayResultSet(System.out,pstmt.
                executeQuery());
        } finally { pstmt.close(); }

        // Query with static sql statement
        sql = "SELECT * FROM BIRTHDAYS";
        Statement stmt = connection.createStatement();
        try {

DisplayResultSet(System.out,stmt.executeQuery(sql));
        } finally { stmt.close(); }

    } finally  { connection.close(); }

  } catch (Throwable t) { System.err.println(t); }
}

  public static void DisplayResultSet(OutputStream out,
     ResultSet rs)
  {
    try {
     ResultSetMetaData md = rs.getMetaData();
     String columnNames = "";
     int columnCount = md.getColumnCount();
     for (int i = 1; i <= columnCount; i++)  {
         String columnName = md.getColumnName(i);
         while (columnName.length()
             < md.getColumnDisplaySize(i))
           columnName = columnName + " ";
         columnNames = columnNames + "   " + columnName;
     }
     System.out.println("\n"+columnNames);
     System.out.println
       ("———————————");
     String values;
     DateFormat df =
SimpleDateFormat.getDateInstance(DateFormat.FULL);
     while (rs.next())  {
        values = "";
        for (int i = 1; i <= columnCount; i++)
          if (md.getColumnType(i) == DATE)
            values = values + "   " +
                 df.format(rs.getDate(i));
          else
            values = values + "   " + rs.getString(i);
        System.out.println(values);
     }
   } catch (Throwable t) { System.err.println(t); }
  }
}
```

JDBC specifies databases as URLs. The dbURL in our example uses the jdbc protocol and interbase subprotocol. (The vendor driver checks whether the subprotocol is supported.) Again, the host is local and the database is specified as a filename, as required by the Interbase engine. The **DATE** field is simply a mapping that we used later in the **DisplayResultSet()** method to indicate the mapping between Interbase's DATE type and the JDBC types specified in the **java.sql.Types** class.

The first order of business is to load the JDBC driver. The driver can be loaded several ways besides using the ClassLoader approach show here. Loading the driver class causes it to be automatically registered with the JDBC DriverManager. An alternative is to simply create an instance of the driver with the **new** operator. The driver could also be specified as a system property:

```
java -Dsql.drivers=borland.interclient.Driver
```

The **-D** switch instructs the Java runtime to define the **sql.drivers** property.

The next step is to actually make a connection to the database. The DriveManager's **getConnection()** method has several variations. We chose to demonstrate the URL and properties approach. The URL specifies the RDBMS, and the properties supply the user login and password.

Once the connection is established, a generic statement is created, which in turn is used to create the Birthdays table. Standard SQL-92 is being used. (A driver must be SQL-92 entry-level-compliant to be considered 100 percent JDBC compliant.) Notice that the **execute()** method is used when no result set will be returned as a result of executing the SQL. The generic statement represents a static SQL statement, so it can be reused to perform row inserts. This time, however, the **executeUpdate()** method is used to insert rows in the table. Use **executeUpdate()** with SQL **INSERT**, **UPDATE**, or **DELETE** commands. When the insertion is complete, the statement is closed along with the connection. It's important to always close your statements and connections because it's unpredictable when the Java garbage collection will, if ever, get around to finalizing these objects.

Next, a connection is reestablished to the database and both prepared and static statement queries are used to access data. The prepared statement is compiled by the database engine at the time of its creation, if this is a supported feature of the database. Notice that parameters are specified with a **?** and are numbered starting at 1, not 0. In the case of the prepared statement, the **last_name** is set to **Walker**, and the query is executed by calling the **executeQuery()** method, passing the **ResultSet** to the example's **DisplayResultSet()** method.

Examining the **DisplayResultSet()** method, we see that every **ResultSet** object has **ResultSetMetaData**. The *metadata* is data about the data; it includes the number of columns in a result set row and their names, as well as a lot of other information. The metadata is used here to build the column heading string for display purposes.

The **ResultSet** object is basically an SQL cursor wrapper. Its **next()** method advances the cursor to the next row and fetches the data from the database transparently. **ResultSet** has methods defined for all the different SQL types returning the Java-mapped objects. For example, we use the **getString()** method to return an SQL **CHAR** field and the **getDate()** method to return an SQL **DATE** field. The columns can be specified by their index or field name. Because **DisplayResultSet** is a semigeneric implementation to display a result set, the example uses the numeric index. Notice that the metadata reveals the data type of any particular field.

Returning back to where we left off in the **main()** method, the **prepareStatement** is reused with **Elias** as the value of **last_name** this time. Presumably, the query has already been optimized by precompiling, so the result should be relatively fast. The **close()** method must be called to release the compiled statement back to the server.

Finally, a static statement is once again used to display the entire contents of the Birthdays table. The output of this example is shown in Figure 7-2.

The **CallableStatement**, used to execute stored procedures, wasn't shown, but this quick survey has given you a high-level overview of the feature-rich JDBC API.

Figure 7-2.
Output of Listing 7-12.

LAST_NAME	FIRST_NAME	DOB
Walker	Rene	Tuesday, July 06, 1993
LAST_NAME	FIRST_NAME	DOB
Elias	Wayne	Monday, August 08, 1966
LAST_NAME	FIRST_NAME	DOB
Elias	Wayne	Monday, August 08, 1966
Thieman	Tom	Thursday, April 18, 1912
Walker	Rene	Tuesday, July 06, 1993
McLean	Erin	Wednesday, October 16, 1974

CONCLUSION

Bean designers will need to consider object serialization's provisions for versioning so that Bean upgrades perform flawlessly. No doubt business object Beans will need to communicate remotely either to other objects through RMI or CORBA or to data stored in a relational database manager through the JDBC API.

8

JavaBeans and Core Reflection APIs

The reflection API allows *introspection*, a process whereby classes and objects currently in the Java Virtual Machine can be examined at runtime. Every aspect of a class, its constructors, methods, and fields, can be examined. For example, a constructor from a class unknown at the time of implementation can nevertheless be retrieved and invoked at runtime. Likewise, an object's methods can be invoked without foreknowledge of their names or parametric signatures. Even the fields of an arbitrary object can be uncovered and accessed. Classes and objects can literally describe their own APIs (protocols).

The reflection API was introduced to the core Java APIs beginning with Java 1.1 and is implemented as a new sub-package of java.lang named java.lang.reflect. Introspection is used extensively by the JavaBeans, object serialization, and *Remote Method Invocation* (RMI) APIs, thereby playing a central, underlying role in a dynamic and distributed Java environment. The reflection API is crucial to the implementation of class browsers, object inspectors, advanced debuggers, and *Rapid Application Development* (RAD) tools. With the introduction of introspection, the reflection API reinvents Java, making it into a full-fledged self-declarative language on par with Smalltalk. You can think of introspection as a mechanism by which the symbol tables, typically used by compilers (such as C/C++), are made available to your Java application, allowing that application to "discover" class protocols programmatically.

JavaBean components present reflected information in a standardized format that's understandable by *Integrated Development Environments* (IDEs) that support the JavaBean specification. This allows RAD tools to inspect and modify JavaBean components at design time. In one sense, the JavaBean specification is the next level of abstraction built on top of the reflection API. By the time you read this, the second version of the JavaBeans specification will have been released, code-named "Glasgow."

This specification allows a Bean to reverse-introspect its container, whether it's an IDE or another JavaBean. Because IDEs will increasingly be coded in pure Java (for example, SuperMojo and Java WorkShop 2.0), this container will probably be another JavaBean that's part of the IDE itself. Soon Beans will be able to introspect data "published" by other Beans in an upcoming API known as InfoBus. All this wouldn't be possible without the reflections API, so this chapter gives you a solid, complete grounding in the reflections technology.

This chapter will cover the following topics:

- Metaclasses
- Members
- **Array** class

Metaclasses

Metaclasses make introspection possible. A *Metaclass* is a class that describes a class. There's only one Metaclass class in Java, namely the **Class** class, so for every class, there's an instance of the **Class** class to represent it. The Java Virtual Machine creates a **Class** object for every class and interface that has been loaded. This **Class** object provides access to **Metamember** objects, which represent each member of the underlying class or interface. The **Metamember** classes consist of the **Constructor**, **Method**, and **Field** classes. Although the **Class** class is implemented in the java.lang package, the **Constructor**, **Method**, and **Field** classes are implemented in the java.lang.reflect subpackage.

A **Metaclass** object and its associated **Metamember** objects describe everything the Java compiler could ever possibly know about the API of a class. There's even a **Class** object for the **Class** class and **Class** objects for the **Constructor**, **Method**, and **Field** classes! Therefore, the **Metaclass** mechanism provides a completely parsed view of any class, interface, or object to the applications programmer. This might all sound a little confusing at first, but once you see it in operation your questions should be quickly answered.

Quick Tour

Let's take a quick tour of Java's **Metaclass** mechanism by working through an example using the **Constructor**, **Method**, and **Field** objects. Suppose we have a class **Foo**, as shown in Listing 8-1.

Foo has a integer field named **x**. It also has two constructors, one the default and the other taking the initializing parameter for **x**. Last, **Foo** has a method named **setX()** that sets the value of **x**. Given any **Foo** object, we can determine its class programmatically by invoking the **getClass()** method inherited from **java.lang.Object**, as shown here:

```
Foo aFoo = new Foo();
Class metaFoo = aFoo.getClass();
```

Listing 8-1.
Foo.

```
public class Foo
{
    public int x;               // field
    public Foo()                // default constructor
        { x = 0; }
    public Foo(int x)           // another constructor
        { this.x = x; }
    public void setX(int x)     // method
        { this.x = x; }
}
```

Class objects can be generated only by the *Java Virtual Machine* (JVM). There's a `Class` object available for every class or interface loaded into the JVM. Once we know an object's class, we can examine metadata about it—constructors, methods, and fields, as shown here:

```
Constructor[] constructors = metaFoo.getConstructors();
Method[] methods = metaFoo.getMethods();
Field[] fields = metaFoo.getFields();
```

This `Metaclass` mechanism is polymorphic because for any object, `Foo` or otherwise, these descriptor objects can be retrieved generically. Therefore, any object or its class is completely self-describing at runtime—even those classes that haven't been implemented or even designed. Suppose an object of type `Foo` isn't available? No problem. The `Class` class defines a static method for retrieving any `Class` object:

```
public final class Class extends Object {
...
public static Class forName(String className);
```

So we could just as easily have coded the following:

```
Class metaFoo = Class.forName("Foo");
```

A `Constructor` object retrieved from the `Class` object for `Foo` can be used to create new objects of type `Foo`. Let's say we want to construct a new `Foo` initialized to `1`. The code snippet of Listing 8-2 shows how this might be done.

First, the `Class` object for `Foo` is retrieved from the JVM, and then the array describing the formal parameters of the desired constructor is initialized, specifying one primitive integer type parameter. In other words, we want the `Foo` constructor that takes one integer argument. Likewise, the array containing the actual parameters—that is, a single integer—is initialized.

Now we're ready to call up the constructor. This time, because the constructor's parametric signature is known, the `getConstructor()` method

Listing 8-2.
Construct a **Foo**.

```
Class metaFoo = Class.forName("Foo");
Class[] paramTypes = { int.class };
Object[] actualParams = { new Integer(1) };
Constructor constructor =
    metaFoo.getConstructor(paramTypes);
Foo foo1 = (Foo) constructor.newInstance(actualParams);
System.out.println(foo1.x);
```

is called instead of the `getConstructors()` method shown previously. With the constructor in hand, a new instance of `Foo` is created by using an actual parameter having a value of `1`. This is done by calling the `Constructor` object's `newInstance()` method with the `actualParams` array. The `newInstance()` method unwraps the `Integer` object, linking it with the `int` parameter of the constructor. This value is then printed to the system's output print stream.

Here the `setX()` method is invoked on the `Foo` object. Continuing from the previous code snippet, we have the following:

```
Method setX = metaFoo.getMethod("setX",paramTypes);
actualParams[0] = new Integer(2);
setX.invoke(foo1,actualParams);
System.out.println(foo1.x);   // foo1.x == 2
```

Because the name of the `Foo` method is known, along with its parametric signature, the `getMethod()` method is called instead of the `getMethods()` method shown earlier. Notice that the `Method` class itself has a method that invokes the underlying method on a `Foo` object in this case.

Because the `x` field of `Foo` is public, it can be modified directly instead of invoking the `setX()` method. Continuing on from the previous code snippet, the field descriptor for `Foo`'s `x` field is retrieved:

```
Field x = metaFoo.getField("x");
x.setInt(foo1,3);
System.out.println(foo1.x);   // foo1.x == 3
```

Again, the name of the field is known, so the `getField()` method is called instead of the `getFields()` method. (For each Java primitive type, there is a get/set pair of accessors that are also provided.) The `x` value is set to `3` in this example and then printed on the system's output stream. This exercise is by no means exhaustive in demonstrating the power of the reflection API, but it's meant to show that applications and applets can indeed work with constructors, methods, and fields discovered programmatically at runtime.

As you might have deduced by now, Java's `Class` class is the foundation of Java's `Metaclass` mechanism. Without a `Metaclass` facility, introspection wouldn't be possible. With languages such as C or C++, the `Metaclass` data is embodied in the symbol tables created by the compiler at compile time, but they aren't available to the applications programmer at runtime. Without some form of introspection, modern visual RAD IDEs wouldn't be possible. As you might know ,there are now several RAD IDEs available for C++, but only because the IDE itself has gone to great lengths internally to provide `Metaclass` data to the RAD at design time. However, this design time `Metaclass` data still isn't available at runtime. Beginning with Java 1.1, we now have a complete `Metaclass` mechanism at our disposal at runtime. This feature introduces many exciting possibilities, like implementing RAD IDEs in pure Java itself without great difficulty or resorting to native methods. Once again, these are the key classes facilitating introspection in Java:

```
java.lang.Class
java.lang.reflect.Constructor
java.lang.reflect.Method
java.lang.reflect.Field
```

The `Constructor`, `Method`, and `Field` descriptor objects retrieved from a `Class` object completely describe the protocol for objects of that class. These descriptors allow the programmer to invoke the different constructors and methods, and access or modify fields.

Also included in the reflection API are the two additional classes:

```
java.lang.reflect.Modifier
java.lang.reflect.Array.
```

The `Modifier` class has static methods that provide for decoding the access modifier flags returned by the other classes, and the `Array` class allows programmatic array creation, access, and modification, regardless of the component type or number of dimensions. These classes are covered in more detail a little later on. Let's turn our attention now to the heart of the reflection API.

PseudoClass

With the overall scheme of the reflection API in view, we're now equipped to go back and examine the `Class` class in detail. The `Class` class is the foundation of Java's reflection API; however, it's packaged in java.lang, and the rest of the reflection API is found among the classes defined in the java.lang.reflect subpackage. This is because the `Class` class existed before the reflection API was added in version 1.1. Although the `java.lang.Class` class has no declared fields, it's nevertheless useful to visualize it as having a pseudo class structure with fields to better understand and internalize the functionality of the `Metaclass` system. Actually, the JVM maintains this information in its own internal data structures. The real `java.lang.Class` API returns the essence of this information with native method calls to the JVM. The **PseudoClass** shown in Listing 8-3 is simply a gimmick to bring to the surface what might be a reasonable facsimile of the structure used to represent the data held within the JVM. You won't find **PseudoClass** in any of the core packages; it's our invention for illustrating Java's **Metaclass** system by externalizing the data held within the JVM.

The **superclass** field points to the base class of this class—in other words, the class that this class extends. Please note that interface hierarchies are linked to their superinterfaces (if any) through the **implementedInterfaces** array, even though an interface is said to extend a superinterface. Therefore, the superclass link is for classes only, not interfaces! In the **PseudoClass** object for **Object**, the **superclass** "field" is null. Remember, **PseudoClass** exists in essence somewhere within the JVM. In the case of the previous **Foo** class, the superclass chain is as follows:

```
metaFoo.superclass ->
  metaObject.superclass ->
    null
```

The **superclass** field of **Foo**'s **PseudoClass** points (links) to **Object**'s **PseudoClass** object. Therefore, you can think of the overall, composite **Metaclass** of **Foo** as a conglomerate of the individual **PseudoClass** objects for each class in **Foo**'s hierarchy linked by the superclass chain. Each **PseudoClass** describes (reflects) metadata about its respective class level —constructors, methods, and fields declared (introduced) at that class level. Therefore, the declared fields of a derived class consist of the aggregate of all **declaredField** arrays found along the superclass chain. Because interfaces are allowed to have final fields, these too would be included, having been garnered from the **implementedInterfaces** link.

Listing 8-3.
PseudoClass.

```
final class PseudoClass
{
  Class superclass;            // null for Object
  String fullyQualifiedName;
  Constructor[] declaredConstructors;
  Method[] declaredMethods;
  Field[] declaredFields;
  Class[] implementedInterfaces;
  Class arrayComponentType;    // null if not array
  int accessModifiers;         // public, static, etc.
  Class declaringClass;        // outer class
  Class[] declaredClasses;     // inner classes/interfaces
}
```

The fully qualified name of the class is held within the **fullyQualifiedName** string field of **PseudoClass**. Actually it's returned by the native method **getName()** of the **Class** object with the JVM somehow fabricating it.

The **declaredConstructors** array includes all the constructors declared by this class—public, protected, default (package), and private. By *default* we don't mean the default constructor, but the default scope constructor that might or might not have arguments. If this class doesn't declare any constructors, this array has a length of zero. Remember, none of the array variables in the **PseudoClass** are ever null. If there are no members to represent, the respective array simply has a length of zero.

The **declaredMethods** array includes all the methods declared by this class regardless of their scope—public, protected, and so on. If there are no methods declared, this array has a length of zero, but the reference is never null.

The **declaredFields** array contains all the fields declared by this class, regardless of their scope. If no fields are declared by this class, the array has a length of zero.

If this object represents a class, the **implementedInterfaces** array includes all the interfaces (that is, **Class** objects representing those interfaces) explicitly implemented by this class. The order of the interface objects in the array corresponds to the order in which they are named in the **implements** clause of the underlying class declaration. However, if this object represents an interface rather than a class, the **implementedInterfaces** array includes all the interfaces extended by the underlying interface (in the order in which they're named) in the **extends** clause of the underlying interface declaration. If the class implements (or the interface extends) no interfaces, the **implementedInterfaces** array has a length of zero.

If this object represents an array, the **arrayComponentType** variable holds the **Class** of the array's component type. If this object doesn't represent an array, then **arrayComponentType** is null. For arrays, the **declaredConstructors**, **declaredMethods**, and **declaredFields** arrays all have a length of zero. Please note that the length of the **declaredFields** array in no way reflects the length of the underlying array!

The **accessModifiers** variable is a set of flags bits representing the scope of this class—public, default, protected, or private—and modifying concepts, such as abstract, static, final, transient, volatile, native, and/or synchronized.

The **declaringClass** variable is used by inner classes to specify their enclosing class. Reflective information on inner classes isn't currently operational in JDK 1.1.

The `declaredClasses` array includes all inner classes and inner interfaces declared within this class. It's not currently operational in JDK 1.1.

`Class` Class

Instead of the `PseudoClass` class presented previously, the real `java.lang.Class` class has the private native methods that supply the same information, as shown in Listing 8-4, but with a slightly different twist. There's no public constructor for this class; only the Java VM is allowed to instantiate a `Class` object.

The `getConstructors0()` method returns an array of either the declared constructors of this class or the public constructors of all inherited classes. The `which` parameter determines which one with either `Member.DECLARED` or `Member.PUBLIC`. (The Member interface is discussed later.) If the call is made specifying `Member.DECLARED`, the equivalent of the `declaredConstructors` array of `PseduoClass` is returned. If the call specifies `Member.PUBLIC`, only the public constructors of each `declaredConstructors` array, along the entire superclass chain, are returned in a `Constructor[]` array.

The `getMethods0()` method behaves similarly. Either the equivalent of the `declaredMethods` array is returned if `Member.DECLARED` is specified, or only the public methods from each `declaredMethods` array along the entire superclass chain are returned.

The `getFields0()` method returns an array of either the declared fields of this class (interface) or the public fields of all inherited public fields.

For any of these returned arrays, the length will be zero if no member is qualified for membership in the requested result array, so there's never a need to test for null; use the length instead.

Listing 8-4.
Class private methods.

```
public final class Class extends Object
{
  ...
  private native Constructor[] getConstructors0(int which);
  private native Method[] getMethods0(int which);
  private native Field[] getFields0(int which);
  private native Constructor getConstructor0
    (Class[] parameterTypes, int which);
  private native Method getMethod0
    (String name, Class[] parameterTypes, int which);
  private native Field getField0(String name, int which);
}
```

You might be looking for a particular constructor, method, or field. To request a specific constructor, call **getConstructor0()** with a **Class[]** array containing the **Class** objects of its parameters in the order in which they appear in the constructor's declaration. You must indicate whether it's a **DECLARED** or **PUBLIC** member. Requesting a method is similar to requesting a constructor except you must also specify the method's name in the call to **getMethod0()**. A request for a **DECLARED** method indicates a method declared explicitly at this class level, but a request for a **PUBLIC** method indicates a public method declared at any level along the superclass chain. In the case of a field, you must supply its name along with the **Member.DECLARED/PUBLIC** specification in the call to the **getField0()** method.

The public API of the **Class** class simply rewraps these private methods to provide its reflective metadata. For example, **getField(String)** calls **getField0(String,Member.PUBLIC)** and **getDeclaredField(String)** calls **getField0(String, Member.DECLARED)**. If *Declared* appears in the method name, you're requesting a declared member of this class, whether it's public, default, protected, or private. In other words, the member requested must be explicitly declared within this class versus being inherited. The counterpart methods (without *Declared* in the name) return only public members, regardless of the class within the hierarchy in which they were declared. If you specifically need to retrieve a nonpublic member from a base class, you must follow the superclass chain until you reaching its declaring class, fetching it at that level with a **getDeclaredXXX()** method, in which *XXX* stands for **Constructor**, **Method**, or **Field**.

Now we examine the reflective portion of the **Class** class that presents the equivalence of **PseudoClass** data. Possible exceptions will be considered while we're at it.

The **getSuperclass()** method returns the base class object and the **getName()** method returns the fully-qualified class name. Notice the call to **getConstructors0(Member.PUBLIC)** in **getConstructors()**. As mentioned previously, the **getConstructors()** method returns only the public constructors of the classes in the hierarchy—that is, along the superclass chain. The rest of the methods shown operate as expected, following the public versus declared patterns already discussed.

But what are these calls to **checkMemberAccess()** doing here? It's the Java security model coming into play. The SecurityManager decides whether the application or applet is allowed to request public or declared members. Listing 8-6 shows the code for the **checkMemberAccess()** method of **Class**.

As demonstrated previously, the **forName()** static method returns the **Class** object for the specifically named class directly from the Java VM.

Listing 8-5.
Class reflective
methods.

```
public final class Class extends Object
{
  ...
  public native Class  getSuperclass();
  public native String getName();

  public Constructor[] getConstructors()
    throws SecurityException
  {
    checkMemberAccess(Member.PUBLIC);
    return getConstructors0(Member.PUBLIC);
  }
  public Constructor[] getDeclaredConstructors()
    throws SecurityException
  {
    checkMemberAccess(Member.DECLARED);
    return getConstructors0(Member.DECLARED);
  }
  public Constructor getConstructor(Class[] parameterTypes)
    throws NoSuchMethodException, SecurityException
  {
    checkMemberAccess(Member.PUBLIC);
    return getConstructor0(parameterTypes, Member.PUBLIC);
  }
  public Constructor getDeclaredConstructor(Class[]
      parameterTypes)
    throws NoSuchMethodException, SecurityException
  {
    checkMemberAccess(Member.DECLARED);
    return getConstructor0(parameterTypes,
        Member.DECLARED);
  }

  public Method[] getMethods() throws SecurityException
  {
    checkMemberAccess(Member.PUBLIC);
    return getMethods0(Member.PUBLIC);
  }
  public Method[] getDeclaredMethods() throws
      SecurityException
  {
    checkMemberAccess(Member.DECLARED);
    return getMethods0(Member.DECLARED);
  }
  public Method getMethod(String name, Class[]
      parameterTypes)
    throws NoSuchMethodException, SecurityException
  {
    checkMemberAccess(Member.PUBLIC);
    return getMethod0(name, parameterTypes, Member.PUBLIC);
  }
```

Continues

Listing 8-5.
Continued.

```
public Method getDeclaredMethod
   (String name, Class[] parameterTypes)
   throws NoSuchMethodException, SecurityException
{
   checkMemberAccess(Member.DECLARED);
   return getMethod0(name, parameterTypes,
      Member.DECLARED);
}

public Field[] getFields() throws SecurityException
{
   checkMemberAccess(Member.PUBLIC);
   return getFields0(Member.PUBLIC);
}
public Field[] getDeclaredFields() throws
   SecurityException
{
   checkMemberAccess(Member.DECLARED);
   return getFields0(Member.DECLARED);
}
public Field getField(String name)
   throws NoSuchFieldException, SecurityException
{
   checkMemberAccess(Member.PUBLIC);
   return getField0(name, Member.PUBLIC);
}
public Field getDeclaredField(String name)
   throws NoSuchFieldException, SecurityException
{
   checkMemberAccess(Member.DECLARED);
   return getField0(name, Member.DECLARED);
}

public native Class[] getInterfaces();

public native Class getComponentType();

public native int getModifiers();

public Class getDeclaringClass()
   { return null; }   /* not implemented */

public Class[] getClasses()
   { return new Class[0]; }   /* not implemented */

public Class[] getDeclaredClasses()
   throws SecurityException
{
   checkMemberAccess(Member.DECLARED);
   return new Class[0];   /* not implemented */
}
}
```

Listing 8-6.
Reflective security.

```
private void checkMemberAccess(int which)
{
  SecurityManager s = System.getSecurityManager();
  if (s != null) {
    s.checkMemberAccess(this, which);
  }
}
```

If the class isn't currently in the VM and can't be loaded, then the **ClassNotFoundException** is thrown. This method is useful for loading classes at runtime. If the specific class is known at implementation time, it's more efficient to use class literal expressions, which are covered later.

The **isInterface()** method returns true if this **Class** object represents an interface. Likewise, **isArray()** returns true if this **Class** object represents an array. These methods are for convenience. Without them, we would be forced to code something like the following:

```
Member.isInterface(Class.forName("Foo").
    getModifiers()));
```

or

```
if (Class.forName("Foo").getComponentType() != null)
  // isArray;
```

The **newInstance()** method is also a convenience method for invoking the default constructor—the constructor taking no arguments. If this class object represents an abstract class or interface, the **InstantiationException** is thrown. If the class is inaccessible, such as a private class or a nonpublic class from another package, the **IllegalAccess-Exception** is thrown. This method was available before the arrival of the reflection API and was the only way to create an object in Java, apart from the **new** operator. An alternate way to invoke the default constructor is through the **Constructor** object for the default constructor that's covered later.

The **isInstance()** method is the dynamic equivalent of the Java language **instanceof** operator. So this statement

```
if (Class.forName("Foo").isInstance(f1))
```

is equivalent to:

```
if (f1 instanceof Foo)
```

```
public final class Class extends Object
{
   ...
   public static native Class forName(String className)
     throws ClassNotFoundException;
   public native boolean isInterface();
   public native boolean isArray();
   public native Object newInstance()
     throws InstantiationException, IllegalAccessException;
   public native boolean isInstance(Object obj);
   public native boolean isPrimitive();
   public native boolean isAssignableFrom(Class cls);
}
```

If **f1** were any subclass of the class **Foo**, **isInstance()** would return **true** as expected. If **Foo** were an interface, and if **f1** or any of its inherited classes implemented the **Foo** interface, this method would also return **true**.

If the **Class** object represents an array, the **isInstance()** method returns **true** if the argument is an array with components of the same type. It will also return **true** if the argument is an array with a component type that can be converted to the **componentType()** of the array class by an identity or widening conversion. (Data conversions are covered in a later section.) If the conversion fails, the **ClassCastException** is thrown. For example, a **Foo** object being derived from **Object** can be converted with a widening reference conversion to an **Object** object so **isInstance()** will return **true** in the following case:

```
Object[] d = new Object[1];
Foo[] f = new Foo[10];
if (d.getClass().isInstance(f))
   System.out.println("Foo can be cast to Object via a
        widening conversion");
```

The **isPrimitive()** method determines whether this **Class** object represents a primitive Java type. (See the section on class literals.)

The **isAssignableFrom()** method returns **true** whenever an object of the argument class can be converted with an identity conversion or widening reference conversion to an object of the class represented by the **Class** object. In other words, if this statement

```
d.getClass().isInstance(f)
```

is true, then this statement

```
d.getClass().isAssignableFrom(f.getClass())
```

is true, if **f** and **d** are not Java primitive types. For primitive types, **f** and **d** must be identical for the method to return **true**. Therefore, the only qualifying widening conversions are reference and not primitive widening conversions. Note that the **isAssignableFrom()** method throws a **NullPointerException** if its **argument** parameter is null.

PRIMITIVE TYPES It should be pointed out that there are nine **Class** objects for the eight primitive Java types and void. Wrapper classes are now available for all eight types and void, also. These wrapper classes have the same names as the primitive types they represent. For example, **Boolean** wraps the value of the primitive type boolean, so every primitive has an object version of itself so that primitive types can be specified anywhere an object argument is required. Table 8-1 shows the primitive types in the left column and the classes that are their object counterparts in the right column.

These wrapper classes all declare the **TYPE** field, which holds the **Class** object corresponding to its primitive type counterpart. The expressions shown in Table 8-2 represent the eight primitive type **Metaclasses** and the **Metaclass** for void.

These wrapper classes play an additional indispensable role in passing actual arguments to methods, such as the following:

```
Constructor.newInstance(Object[] initargs)
Method.invoke(Object obj, Object[] args)
```

Table 8-1.

Object Wrappers for Primitive Types.

Primitive Type	Wrapper Class
Boolean	**Boolean**
char	**Character**
byte	**Byte**
short	**Short**
int	**Integer**
long	**Long**
float	**Float**
double	**Double**

Table 8-2.

Primitive Type Class Expressions.

```
Boolean.TYPE

Character.TYPE

Byte.TYPE

Short.TYPE

Integer.TYPE

Long.TYPE

Float.TYPE

Double.TYPE

Void.TYPE
```

CLASS LITERALS   Class literals offer a convenient way to access the `Class` object of any type known at implementation time. This is the class literal for the `Object` class:

```
Object.class
```

This is equivalent to the `Class` object returned from the `Class.forName()` method:

```
Object.class == Class.forName("java.lang.Object")
```

A class literal takes the form of the type name followed by a period and the token `class`. The type could just as easily have been an interface, array, or Java primitive type. The following are all valid class literals:

```
Enumeration.class
Object[][].class
Boolean.class     // same as Class.forName("Boolean")
boolean.class     // same as Boolean.TYPE
void.class
```

Syntactically, `class` appears to be a field of the class, interface, array, primitive type, or void in much the same way that `length` appears to be a field of an array object. A class literal evaluates an object of type Class, the `Class` object for the named type (or for void). Note that a class literal never contains an expression, only a type name. The overhead expenditure of a class literal is on the order of a field access rather than a method call, as is the case with the `forName()` method.

The class literal form is often more convenient and more efficient than `Class.forName()`, especially when dealing with inner classes. A class literal for reference types doesn't raise any checked exceptions, but it can raise **NoClassDefFoundError**.

The nine wrapper classes for primitive types and void each have the following field that's initialized to the **Class** object of its respective primitive type:

```
public static final Class TYPE;
```

These **TYPE** fields are equivalent to the class literal of their respective primitive types or void.

Please don't confuse the **Class** object for a primitive type with its corresponding wrapper **Class** object. For example, don't confuse these statements

```
boolean.class == Boolean.TYPE
   // Class object for boolean
```

with these statements:

```
Boolean.class == Class.forName("Boolean")
   // Class object for Boolean
```

The class literal syntax is convenient to use with methods that require **Class** objects as arguments. Note that the compiler is responsible for taking into account the import statements and ambient package when resolving the type name of a class literal (see Table 8-3).

Table 8-3.

Equivalent Primitive Type Class Expressions.

Class Literal	Wrapper TYPE Field
boolean.class	Boolean.TYPE
char.class	Character.TYPE
byte.class	Byte.TYPE
short.class	Short.TYPE
int.class	Integer.TYPE
long.class	Long.TYPE
float.class	Float.TYPE
double.class	Double.TYPE
void.class	Void.TYPE

```
private static String getName(Class clazz)
{
   if (clazz.isArray())
     return getName(clazz.getComponentType())
        + "[]";
   return clazz.getName();
}
```

As a side note, because `getName()` returns a convoluted class name for arrays, we often use our own `getName()` recursive function, shown in Listing 8-8, to get a more user-friendly form.

If `clazz` represents an array, `getName()` is recursively called with the array component type. The nesting stops and the recursion ends if the class doesn't represent an array—if, for example, we've arrived at the base component type of a multidimensional array. Therefore, the following statement

```
getName(Object[][].class)
```

returns the string

```
"java.lang.Object[][]"
```

instead of something strange, like this:

```
"[[Ljava.lang.Object"
```

HIERARCHIES   The `Class` class can be used to list the pedigree of a class—that is, the classes it extends and the interfaces it implements. Such information is essential when implementing a class hierarchy browser, for example. In the following example, an enumeration of the class hierarchy is assembled. Note that Java supports only single inheritance, so there's only one trail of superclass links to follow. The elements of this enumeration are `Class` objects representing each class in the hierarchy, starting with the `Class` object for the `Object` class and progressing downward along the derivation hierarchy until arriving back at the `c` class, the class whose lineage we're seeking.

The first `classLineage()` method (Listing 8-9) calls itself recursively, looking for the end of the `getSuperclass()` chain. Because the `getSuperclass()` method returns `null` for the `Object` class, the recursion exits and the nesting of `classLineage()` method is stopped. As the recursion stack is popped, at each level of the nesting the respective `Class` object of the hierarchy is inserted into the lineage vector. The order in the lineage vector, therefore, progresses from the `Class` object for `Object`

Listing 8-9.
Parsing class
hierarchy.

```
static void classLineage(Vector lineage, Class c)
{
   if (c != null)  {
     classLineage(lineage,c.getSuperclass());
     lineage.addElement(c);
   }
}

static Enumeration classLineage(Class c)
{
   Vector lineage = new Vector();
   classLineage(lineage,c);
   return lineage.elements();
}

static Enumeration classLineage(String className)
{
   try {
     return classLineage(Class.forName(className));
   } catch (ClassNotFoundException e) { return null; }
}
```

down the hierarchy to the most derived class. The progression is downward across the hierarchy as the recursion is unwinding upward through its previous nesting.

The second `classLineage()` method simply initializes the lineage vector, calls the first method, and then returns the lineage vector's enumeration of elements, which are the `Class` objects representing each class in the hierarchy.

The third `classLineage()` method is a variation of the second, except that a class name string can be substituted for the `Class` object itself.

The `listHierarchy()` method (Listing 8-10) shows how the class hierarchy can be listed on a print stream. Again, recursion is used to achieve the indentation of the listing. If there are more elements remaining in the hierarchy enumeration, the current element (class) is printed out first. Notice that `Class` has a method called `getName()`, which returns the name of the class. Then the `listHierarchy()` method calls itself on the next derived class of the hierarchy, but with the indentation increased by two spaces. This gives the nice "tree" layout effect to the listing. When there are no more elements in the hierarchy to list, the recursions exit and the method call stack is popped.

To print the hierarchy of java.awt.Frame on the system's output stream, we first retrieve the enumerated hierarchy for java.awt.Frame and then proceed to list it on System.out:

```
static void listHierarchy
   (PrintStream out, Enumeration hierarchy, String indent)
{
  if (hierarchy.hasMoreElements())  {
    out.println(indent+((Class)hierarchy.nextElement()).
     getName());
    listHierarchy(out,hierarchy,indent+" ");
  }
}
```

```
Enumeration hierarchy
   = classLineage("java.awt.Frame");
listHierarchy(System.out,hierarchy,"");
```

The output looks like this:

```
java.lang.Object
   java.awt.Component
      java.awt.Container
         java.awt.Window
            java.awt.Frame
```

Listing interfaces is a little more complicated. Although a class can only inherit singularly, it can implement multiple different interfaces. These interfaces can extend other interfaces in turn, and a base class can do the same. This time we're going to list the complete hierarchy, including interfaces, but in the opposite order from the most derived class or interface back ultimately to **Object**.

Again, recursion is used to build a vector of vectors (see Listing 8-11). The first element of the vector is always a **Class** object representing a class or interface. The remaining elements of the vector are themselves vectors of the same makeup. Therefore, a class will have the **Class** object representing that class as the first element of its vector; likewise, an interface will have the **Class** object representing that interface as the first element of its vector. The next elements of the vector will be the vectors representing the interfaces that this class implements or this interface extends. In the case of a class, the process is repeated for the superclass, adding the vector representing the superclass after any vectors representing interfaces. Recursion will also be used to display the ancestry (see Listing 8-12).

The vector **v** contains the entire ancestry, starting with the remaining most derived class or interface. On the initial call, **descendant** is **null**. The first class or interface is extracted from the enumeration. Because **descendant** is **null**, an **implements** or **extends** clause isn't displayed. The

Listing 8-11.
Parse class and interface hierarchy.

```
static Vector ancestry(Class c)
{
  if (c != null)  {
    Vector v = new Vector();
    v.addElement(c);   // class or interface
    Class[] i = c.getInterfaces();
    for (int j = 0; j < i.length; j++)
      v.addElement(ancestry(i[j]));
    Vector a = ancestry(c.getSuperclass());
    if (a != null)
      v.addElement(a);
    return v;
  }
  return null;
}
```

Listing 8-12.
List class and interface hierarchy.

```
static void listAncestry
   (PrintStream out, Class descendant,
    Vector v, String indent)
{
  Enumeration e = v.elements();
  if (e.hasMoreElements())  {
    Class c = (Class) e.nextElement();
    String clause = "";
    if (descendant != null)
      if (descendant.isInterface() || !c.isInterface())
        clause = "extends ";
      else
        clause = "implements ";
    out.println(indent + clause + c.getName());
    if (e.hasMoreElements())  {
      while (e.hasMoreElements())
        listAncestry(out,c,(Vector)e.nextElement(),
          "   "+indent);
    }
  }
}
```

fully qualified name of the class or interface is printed on the stream with the proper indentation. If there are any more elements in the vector, they are superinterfaces followed by superclasses. The recursion begins by **listAncestry()**, calling itself for each of these superclasses or superinterfaces. This time, **descendant** is passed the derived class so that the superclass or superinterface can determine the proper clause to print. Only a class is said to implement an interface. An interface extends an interface; likewise, a class extends a class. As before, the indentation is increased by two spaces at each level of the hierarchy.

Displaying the ancestry is straightforward. First, the ancestry vector of vectors is built with a call to **ancestry()**. Notice the use of the class literal form, this time for java.awt.Frame:

```
Vector v = ancestry(java.awt.Frame.class);
listAncestry(System.out,null,v,"");
```

Then the **listAncestry()** method is called, with **descendant** being **null** and **indentation** being the empty string, so that the most derived class—java.awt.Frame—appears flush left with no **derivation** clause. The output looks like this:

```
java.awt.Frame
  implements java.awt.MenuContainer
  extends java.awt.Window
    extends java.awt.Container
      extends java.awt.Component
        implements java.awt.image.ImageObserver
        implements java.awt.MenuContainer
        implements java.io.Serializable
        extends java.lang.Object
```

With the coverage of **java.lang.Class** complete, it's time to turn our attention to the member descriptor classes, but not before we discuss the overall considerations of security and data conversions.

Security

Access to the reflection API is controlled by the SecurityManager on a class-by-class basis. The **SecurityManager** class has a new method named **checkMemberAccess** that decides whether access should be granted to a reflective member object: A **Constructor**, **Method**, or **Field** object. Any code can interrogate a reflective member object about its declaring class, name, access modifiers, and so forth. However, Java language control remains in effect, enforcing encapsulation and, therefore, preventing a nonvisible underlying member from being operated upon. For example, a private field can't be accessed outside its declaring class with the **Field.get()** or **Field.set()** method. There are two levels of security: The first is access to the reflective member determined by the SecurityManager, and the second is Java's language access control.

Data Conversions

The **Method.invoke()**, **Field.get()**, and **Array.get()** methods all return objects. It's obvious that the underlying method return type, the field type, and the array component type aren't always going to be objects. When they are primitive values, a wrapping conversion must be performed to create an object that will hold that primitive value so it can be returned in a generic fashion.

Both **Constructor.newInstance()** and **Method.invoke()** take **Object[]** arguments specifying the actual parameters to pass to the underlying constructor and method, respectively. Obviously, the formal parameters of the underlying constructor and method aren't always going to be objects themselves, so a simple unfolding of these actual argument arrays isn't enough. Some kind of argument conversion must take place. Only identity and widening conversions are acceptable.

The **Field.set()** and **Array.set()** methods take object arguments. If the underlying field type or array component type is a primitive type, an unwrapping conversion and possibly a widening conversion must be performed automatically. If the type is some object derived from **Object**, a widening reference conversion must be performed automatically.

These data conversions are explained in the following section.

WRAPPING The **Method.invoke()**, **Field.get()**, and **Array.get()** methods all return objects. In the case of **Method.invoke()**, the object represents the value returned by the underlying method. For **Field.get()**, it's the underlying field value that's returned, and **Array.get()** returns the indicated indexed component. If the value to be returned by **Method.invoke()**, **Field.get()**, or **Array.get()** is a primitive type, it must first be wrapped in an appropriate wrapper object. This wrapping is performed automatically by these methods and is known as a *wrapping conversion*. Table 8-4 shows the primitive type in the left column and the class of the object it's automatically wrapped in on the right.

UNWRAPPING The **Constructor.newInstance()**, **Method.invoke()**, **Field.set()**, and **Array.set()** methods all take argument arrays of **Object**. In the case of **Constructor.newInstance()** and **Method.invoke()**, whenever the underlying formal parameter is a primitive type, the actual argument object is unwrapped automatically. For **Field.set()** and **Array.set()**, if the underlying field or component is a primitive type, the actual argument object is also unwrapped automatically.

Table 8-4.

Wrapper Classes for Primitive Types.

Primitive	Wrapper
Boolean	`Boolean`
char	`Character`
byte	`Byte`
short	`Short`
int	`Integer`
long	`Long`
float	`Float`
double	`Double`

INDENTITY   When one reference is assigned to another reference, or a primitive value to another value, a conversion always takes place, at least conceptually. When the types are the same, it's nevertheless called a *conversion*, specifically the *indentity conversion*. This concept allows for consistent handling of all assignments, thus allowing for the explicit redundant type cast as a legal construct in the language.

NARROWING   A *narrowing* primitive conversion occurs when significant digits are truncated, such as when converting an integer to a byte. In effect, the conversion lops off important bits. However, with a narrowing reference, there's no truncation; rather, there's not enough information available to assign, thus leaving open the possibility of some of the target fields being left undefined. For example, if an `Object` instance were assigned to a derived class, fields not declared in `Object` would be left undefined. A narrowing conversion is sometimes called an *illegal down cast* because the cast is down the derived hierarchy that isn't there.

WIDENING   A *widening* primitive conversion causes no loss of significant digits; no bits are truncated. Instead, sign extension takes place. Table 8-5 is a list of allowed widening primitive conversions. The column on the left represents the type being converted to any one of the types listed in the right-hand column.

   A widening reference conversion is another story. Every field of the target object is guaranteed to be present in the source object. After all, the source must be ultimately derived from the target! Perhaps not all source fields participate in the assignment, but certainly none of the target fields

Table 8-5.

Primitive Type Widening Conversions.

Source	Target
byte	short, int, long, float, double
short	int, long, float, double
char	int, long, float, double
int	long, float, double
long	float, double
float	double

are left undefined. If class **S** is a subclass of **T**, **S** is converted to **T** by a widening reference conversion.

If the target of a widening reference conversion is an interface, the source object must somehow implement that interface. In other words, the interface has to be represented by an implemented interface of some object in the hierarchy of the source object. The target interface might be a super-interface of one of those implemented interfaces. If class **S** implements interface **I**, **S** is converted to **I** by a widening reference conversion. If **I'** is a subinterface of **I**, **I'** is converted to **I** by a widening reference conversion.

The `Constructor.newInstance()`, `Method.invoke()`, `Field.set()`, and `Array.set()` methods all take actual argument arrays of `Object`. Unwrapped values destined for primitive formal arguments are permitted to undergo widening primitive conversions in their assignment to the formal parameters. It's also acceptable for reference arguments to undergo widening reference conversions in their assignment to their formal parameters.

Members

The Metamembers classes describe the `Constructor`, `Method`, and `Field` members of a class. These descriptors are returned by the methods found in the `Class` class, as explained earlier. Within a program, these descriptors can be used to construct new instances, invoke methods, and access field values. Each descriptor implements the java.lang.reflect.Member interface. The `java.lang.reflect.Modifier` class is a helper class that provides static methods for decoding the access modifiers of these members as well as the modifiers of the declaring class.

Member Interface

The java.lang.reflect.Member interface is implemented by all three member descriptor classes: `Constructor`, `Method`, and `Field`. Its methods provide the common format all members must furnish for introspective purposes (see Listing 8-13).

The `PUBLIC` and `DECLARED` constants were shown earlier and are used internally by `Class` class methods, such as `getConstructors()`. The `getDeclaringClass()` method returns the `Class` object representing the underlying class to which this member belongs. The `getName()` method returns the simple name of the member—that is, the constructor, method, or field name. The `getModifiers()` method returns the modifier flags, which are covered in the following section.

Modifier Class

The `Modifier` class (Listing 8-14) has all static members that can be used to decode the modifier flags of classes, constructors, methods, and fields. Its protocol is straightforward and shown in Listing 8-14. These methods take as an argument the modifier flags represented by an integer value. They all return a boolean `true` if the particular flag in question is set. The modifier flag constants themselves are not shown. If the decoder methods are used, there's little need to use the individual flags directly.

Constructor Class

The `Constructor` class (Listing 8-15) not only implements the Member interface but also provides information such as the formal parameters of the underlying constructor and any declared exceptions. It also supplies a

Listing 8-13.
The java.lang.
reflect.Member
interface.

```
public interface Member
{
   public static final int PUBLIC = 0;
   public static final int DECLARED = 1;

   public Class getDeclaringClass();
   public String getName();
   public int getModifiers();
}
```

Listing 8-14.

java.lang.reflect.
Modifier.

```
public class Modifier {

   public static boolean  isInterface(int)

   /*  Listed in canonical order */

   public static boolean  isPublic(int)
   public static boolean  isProtected(int)
   public static boolean  isPrivate(int)

   public static boolean  isAbstract(int)
   public static boolean  isStatic(int)
   public static boolean  isFinal(int)
   public static boolean  isTransient(int)
   public static boolean  isVolatile(int)
   public static boolean  isNative(int)
   public static boolean  isSynchronized(int)
}
```

Listing 8-15.

java.lang.reflect.
Constructor.

```
public final class Constructor implements Member
{
   public Class getDeclaringClass();
   public String getName();
   public native int getModifiers();
   public Class[] getParameterTypes();
   public Class[] getExceptionTypes();
   public boolean equals(Object obj);
   public int hashCode();
   public String toString();
   public native Object newInstance(Object[] initargs)
      throws InstantiationException, IllegalAccessException,
        IllegalArgumentException, InvocationTargetException;
}
```

mechanism by which the underlying constructor can be executed. There's no public constructor for this class; only the Java VM is allowed to instantiate a **Constructor** object. You can get **Constructor** references with the **getConstructors()**, **getDeclaredConstructors()**, **getConstructor()**, and **getDeclaredConstructor()** methods of the **Class** object representing the class targeted for introspection.

The **getParameterTypes()** method returns an array of the **Class** objects representing the formal parameters in their declaration order. If the underlying constructor is the default constructor, the **Class** array returned has a length of zero. The **getExceptionsTypes()** method returns an array of **Class** objects representing the exceptions in the order they appear in the declaration of the underlying constructor. Again, the returned array has a length of zero if there are none. Two **Constructors** are equal if they are declared by the same class and have the same formal parametric signature—that is, the same type and order. The **hashcode** is simply the hash code of the name of the declaring class. The string representation of a **Constructor** reads essentially the same as the source code declaration of the underlying constructor prototype, except that the access modifiers appear in canonical order, as prescribed by the Java language reference, and the parameter names are fully qualified with package prefixes.

The **newInstance()** method allows you to invoke the underlying **Constructor**. The actual parameters are automatically unwrapped whenever their corresponding formal parameters are primitive types. All parameters can undergo widening conversions, if necessary. If the underlying class is abstract, the **InstantiationException** is thrown. Of course, the underlying constructor must be in visible scope or else the Java language access control forces the **IllegalAccessException** to be thrown. If the actual parameters don't agree with the signature of the formal parameters—for example, they have the wrong number or are incompatible— the **IllegalArgumentException** is thrown. If the underlying constructor throws an exception, it's wrapped in an **InvocationTargetException** and rethrown. If successful, the newly-created object is returned.

Method Class

The Method class (Listing 8-16) is used generically to represent any class or interface method. It completely describes the method and allows it to be invoked on any object that's an instance of its declaring class. There's no public constructor for this class; only the Java VM is allowed to instantiate a **Method** object. You can get **Method** references with the **getMethods()**, **getDeclaredMethods()**, **getMethod()**, and **getDeclaredMethod()** methods of the **Class** object representing the class targeted for introspection.

Because **Method** implements the Member interface, its **getDeclaringClass()**, **getName()** and **getModifiers()** methods have already explained previously.

The **getReturnType()** method returns the type returned by the underlying method. Suppose the underlying method returns a boolean. In that case, **boolean.class** (or **Boolean.TYPE**) is returned from **getReturnType()**. If a Boolean is returned instead, **getReturnType()**

would return **Boolean.class**. (If this seems confusing, please review the previous section on class literals.) Remember that **void** is represented by **void.class** (or **Void.TYPE**).

The **getParameterTypes()** method returns an array containing the types of the formal parameters in the order in which they were declared by the underlying method. If the underlying method takes no parameters, the returned array has a length of zero.

Explicitly declared exceptions are returned by the **getExceptionTypes()** method. If there are none, the returned array has a length of zero.

Two **Method** descriptors are equal if they are declared by the same class and have the same name and the same parameter types.

The **hashcode** is computed by exclusive-ORing the hashcodes of the underlying method's name and its declaring class name.

The string externalization of a **Method** reads essentially the same as the source code declaration of the underlying method prototype, except that the access modifiers appear in canonical order. This order is prescribed by the Java language specification and both the return type and parameter names are fully qualified—that is, prefixed with the package name. The method name is also fully qualified, with the package class name prefixed.

The **invoke()** method invokes the underlying method on the specified object with the specified parameters. Of course, values of primitive types must be wrapped in objects within the **args** array. These values are automatically unwrapped and linked with their respective formal parameters. Both primitive and reference parameters can participate in widening conversions, as necessary, during this process. Any linking mismatch between

Listing 8-16.
java.lang.reflect.
Method.

```
public final   class Method implements Member
{
   public Class getDeclaringClass();
   public String getName();
   public native int getModifiers();
   public Class getReturnType();
   public Class[] getParameterTypes();
   public Class[] getExceptionTypes();
   public boolean equals(Object obj);
   public int hashCode();
   public String toString();
   public native Object invoke(Object obj, Object[] args)
      throws IllegalAccessException,
               IllegalArgumentException,
         InvocationTargetException;
}
```

actual and formal parameters causes the `IllegalArgumentException` to be thrown.

The argument linking process proceeds as follows: First, the number of arguments is checked. Then actual parameters destined for primitive formal parameters are unwrapped to their bare primitive values. Next, both primitive values and reference parameters are linked to their corresponding formal parameters by either identity or widening conversions. If all has gone well to this point, invoking the underlying method can begin.

If the underlying method is static, the `invoke()` method's `object` parameter is ignored because an instance isn't required to access a class member. If the `object` parameter is `null` and the underlying method is an instance method, the `NullPointerException` is thrown. If the `object` parameter doesn't implement the underlying method—that is, if it's not an instance of the declaring class—the `IllegalArgumentException` is thrown. Remember that Java's language access control must be enforced, so if the underlying method isn't visibly in scope at the point of invocation, the `IllegalAccessException` is thrown. Static methods are invoked exactly as are the methods on the declaring class. Instance methods are dynamically dispatched, so they invoke any more derived overriding methods, if present. If the invoked method throws an exception, it's wrapped in an `InvocationTargetException` and rethrown by `invoke()`. If the return type of the underlying method is a primitive type, the actual return value is automatically wrapped in an object. For example, a boolean primitive value is returned within a `Boolean` object. If the return type of the underlying method is void, `invoke()` returns `null`.

The example shown in Listing 8-17 lists the events delivered by a class. To qualify, the class must have a method named `addXXXListener` taking one parameter named `XXXListener`, which must be an interface. The `delivered()` method in Listing 8-17 loads the `Class` object for the named class. All the methods of the underlying class are then searched for any matching the `addXXXListener` pattern and having one parameter named `XXXListener` that must be an interface. If the method satisfies the requirements, the `interface` parameter is added to the enumeration of events delivered.

The listing of an event delivery includes the name of the class triggering events that are delivered to an interface. The fully qualified name of the interface follows on the next line, with subsequent lines listing the interface's method names. The names of these methods represent the events that can be delivered. The `Events.class` example can be run from the command line and optionally takes a list of class arguments to inspect for event-firing capability. When no command line arguments are given, the

```java
import java.lang.reflect.*;
import java.util.*;
import java.io.*;

public class Events
{
  public static Enumeration delivered(String className)
  {
    Vector listeners = new Vector();
    Class clazz;
    try {
      clazz = Class.forName(className);
    } catch (Throwable t) { return listeners.elements(); }
    Method[] methods = clazz.getDeclaredMethods();
    for (int i = 0; i < methods.length; i++)  {
      Method method = methods[i];
      Class[] parameters = method.getParameterTypes();
      String methodName = method.getName();
      if (methodName.endsWith("Listener") &&
        methodName.startsWith("add")  &&
        parameters.length == 1)  {
        Class parameter = parameters[0];
        if (parameter.isInterface() &&
          parameter.getName().endsWith(methodName.
              substring(3)))
            listeners.addElement(parameter);
      }
    }
    return listeners.elements();
  }

  public static void listListeners
    (PrintStream out, String className)
  {
    Enumeration listeners = delivered(className);
    if (listeners.hasMoreElements())
      out.println(className + " delivers: ");
    while (listeners.hasMoreElements())  {
      Class listener = (Class) listeners.nextElement();
      out.println("  "+listener.getName());
      Method[] methods = listener.getMethods();
      for (int i = 0; i < methods.length; i++)
        out.println("      " + methods[i].getName());
    }
  }

  public static void main(String[] args)
  {
    if (args.length > 0)
      for (int i = 0; i < args.length; i++)
        listListeners(System.out,args[i]);
```

Continues

Listing 8-17.
Continued.

```
      else
         listListeners(System.out,"java.awt.Component");
   }
}
```

event triggering capabilities of a `java.awt.Component` object is reported. Although this example is short, you might find it helpful in exploring the AWT's widget classes to see what events they could be firing. Other variations of this example could be listing all the classes that implement a particularly named method or perhaps all the methods with a particular parametric signature, regardless of their name.

The real power lurking in a **Method** object, however, is its ability to invoke the underlying method on an object. The next example demonstrates the ProtocolAdapter design pattern. It goes beyond the concept of event listeners that you learn about in the next several chapters. *Event listeners* are interfaces that allow for event delegation. In fact, the idea of Java's event delegation design pattern came from protocol adapters in other object-oriented programming languages. After the design pattern of a generic protocol adapter is understood, event listeners are just a simple variation.

Implementing an event listener interface allows an object to listen for those events. The methods of the interface have prescribed names and parametric signatures. The type and order of a method's formal parameters (including its return type) constitute a method's complete signature. The protocol adapter allows methods matching in signature alone to be invoked. There's no requirement that the method must have a particular name or that the listening object must implement a particular interface. The name *ProtocolAdapter* comes from the idea that if an object has a method whose signature is good to go, then there's really no need to worry about the method name, its declaring class, or what interface it implements. Instead of redesigning the hierarchy, the event is simply fed through a protocol adapter on the fly.

In the example shown in Listing 8-18, the ProtocolAdapter maintains two private variables: The receiver object and the selector of the method to be invoked on the receiver. The **invoke()** method simply takes the **args** array and invokes the selected method on the receiving object, passing the **args** array to the method. Neither the name of the method nor the pedigree of the receiver is checked; only the signature of the method needs to match. The static **invoke()** method takes an array of ProtocolAdapters and invokes each one that has an appropriate signature for the actual

Listing 8-18.
Protocol adapter.

```java
import java.awt.*;
import java.awt.event.*;
import java.lang.reflect.*;

public class ProtocolAdapter
{
  private Object receiver;
  private Method selector;
  public ProtocolAdapter
    (Object receiver, Method selector)
  {
    this.receiver = receiver;
    this.selector = selector;
  }

  public Object invoke(Object[] args)
    throws IllegalAccessException,
        IllegalArgumentException,
      InvocationTargetException
    { return selector.invoke(receiver,args); }

  public static void invoke
    (ProtocolAdapter[] candidates, Object[] args)
    throws IllegalAccessException, A
        IllegalArgumentException,
      InvocationTargetException
  {
    Class[] types = getParameterTypes(args);
    for (int i = 0; i < candidates.length; i++)
      if (candidates[i].signaturesMatch(types))
        candidates[i].invoke(args);
  }

  public boolean signaturesMatch(Class[] types)
  {
    Class[] selectorTypes =
      selector.getParameterTypes();
    if (types.length != selectorTypes.length)
      return false;
    for (int i = 0; i < types.length; i++)
      if (!selectorTypes[i].equals(types[i]))
        return false;
    return true;
  }

  public static Class[] getParameterTypes(Object[] args)
  {
    Class[] classes = new Class[args.length];
    for (int i = 0; i < args.length; i++)
      classes[i] = args[i].getClass();
    return classes;
```

Continues

```java
    }

    public static void main(String[] args)
    {
      Frame f = new Frame();
      f.addWindowListener(
        new WindowAdapter()
          {
            public void windowClosing(WindowEvent e)
            {
              e.getWindow().dispose();
              System.exit(0);
            }
          }
      );
      Label l = new Label();
      TextArea ta = new TextArea();
      f.add("North",l);
      f.add("Center",ta);
      Class[] signature = { String.class };
      try  {
        ProtocolAdapter[] targets = {
          new ProtocolAdapter
            (f,Frame.class.getMethod("setTitle",signature)),
          new ProtocolAdapter
            (l,Label.class.getMethod("setText",signature)),
          new ProtocolAdapter
            (ta,TextArea.class.getMethod("setText",
                signature))
        };
        Object[] actualParams = { "Hello ProtocolAdapters"
            };
        invoke(targets,actualParams);
      } catch(Throwable t) {}
      f.pack();
      f.setVisible(true);
    }
}
```

arguments being passed, ignoring those that don't. It calls the **signaturesMatch()** method to determine which adapter should be invoked. The signature of the actual arguments is deduced with a call to the **getParameterTypes()** method.

The **main()** method demonstrates the use of the **ProtocolAdapter** class. First a **Frame** is constructed. When the user clicks the **Frame**'s Destroy button on the border's upper-right corner, the user expects the window to close. The AWT's GUI manager delivers the **windowClosing** event to all registered listeners, so **addWindowListener()** is called with a **WindowAdapter** that disposes of the window after receiving the **windowClosing** event. The **WindowAdapter** class implements the WindowListener interface. Only the **windowClosing** event is overridden because that's the only event of interest. Because this is a demo application, **System.exit()** is also called to end the application. The strange-looking construct that begins with **new WindowAdapter()** is called an *anonymous inner class* that conveniently allows us to extend the **WindowAdapter** class and create it all in one expression.

Blank **Label** and **TextArea** components are then added to the **Frame**, keeping in mind that the default layout is the **BorderLayout**. The **Label** is placed in the north sector and the **TextArea** is placed in the center. Of course, we could have created both components with the initializer string **"Hello ProtocolAdapters"**, but instead the **ProtocolAdapter** will be used to set the **Frame** title and **Label** and **TextArea** text all at the same time. Therefore, the **ProtocolAdapter** array named **targets** is initialized with the adapters for all three. Remember, the adapter must be initialized with the receiver and method selector. Notice the use of the class literals and the call to the **Class** method **getMethods()**. Each indicated method is retrieved and assigned along with the receiver object to its respective ProtocolAdapter. The actual parameter—**"Hello ProtocolAdapters"**—is initialized, and all adapters having a signature of one String formal parameter are invoked. Therefore, all three methods are invoked and the text is set in the title of the **Frame** with the **Frame.setTitle()** method, as the text for the Label is set with the **Label.setText()** method and the contents of the **TextArea** with the **TextArea.setText()** method. Finally, the **Frame** is packed and shown. ProtocolAdapters are particularly useful for eleventh-hour glue code, saving the programmer from redesigning interface hierarchies.

Field Class

The **Field** class (Listing 8-19) supplies information about the underlying field's type and access to its value by using get/set method pairs. Because **Field** implements the Member interface, it can also supply information on the field's declaring class, name, and access modifiers. There's no public constructor for this class; only the Java VM is allowed to instantiate a **Field** object. You can get **Field** references with the **getFields()**, **getDeclaredFields()**, **getField()**, and **getDeclaredField()** methods of the **Class** object representing the class targeted for introspection.

Two **Field** objects are considered the same (equal) only if the two fields are declared by the same class, having the same name and type. The

hashcode of a **Field** object is computed by exclusive-ORing the hash codes of the name of the field and the name of its declaring class. The string externalization of a **Field** reads essentially the same as the source code declaration of the underlying field's prototype, except that its access modifiers appear in canonical order, as prescribed by the Java language reference. Also, both the type and field names are fully qualified, with their package name and package class name prefixed, respectively.

The **get()** method ignores the object argument if the underlying field is a static member, because an instance of the class isn't necessary to access a class member. If the field is an nonstatic member (an instance member) and the argument is **null**, **get()** throws the **NullPointerException**. If the field type is a primitive Java type, it's first wrapped in one of the eight wrapper classes and then returned. For example, a boolean primitive value is returned within a **Boolean** object. To retrieve the primitive type directly, use the **getBoolean()** rather than the **get()** method. Specific **getXXX()** methods are provided for all eight primitive Java types (not shown). If the underlying field is restricted by the Java language access control—for example, if the field is private—the **get()** method throws the **IllegalAccessException**. If the instance passed to **get()** as an argument doesn't define the specified field, the **IllegalArgumentException** is thrown.

Listing 8-19.
java.lang.reflect.Field.

```
public final  class Field implements Member
{
   public Class getDeclaringClass();
   public String getName();
   public native int getModifiers();
   public Class getType();
   public boolean equals(Object obj);
   public int hashCode();
   public String toString();
   public native Object get(Object obj)
      throws IllegalArgumentException,
          IllegalAccessException;
   public native boolean getBoolean(Object obj)
      throws IllegalArgumentException,
          IllegalAccessException;
   public native void set(Object obj, Object value)
      throws IllegalArgumentException,
          IllegalAccessException;
   public native void setInt(Object obj, int i)
      throws IllegalArgumentException,
          IllegalAccessException;
}
```

The **set()** method ignores the **object** argument if the underlying field is a static member because an instance of the class isn't necessary to access a class member. If the field is a nonstatic member (an instance member) and the **object** argument is **null**, **set()** throws the **NullPointerException**. If the field type is a primitive Java type, the value argument is automatically unwrapped. If the new value can't be converted to the underlying field type by an identity or widening conversion, an **IllegalArgumentException** is thrown. An identity conversion is simply assigning a type to its same type. A example of a widening primitive conversion is converting from a byte to long, so that no significant digits are lost. In the case of objects, a widening reference conversion is one in which a more derived class instance is assigned to a baser (extended from) class instance. Information is truncated, leaving no fields undefined after the assignment. Notice with a widening conversion that truncating information is desirable in the case of objects, but unacceptable in the case of primitive types.

To set the value of a primitive type directly—for example, integer—you have the option of using **setInt()** instead. Specific **setXXX()** methods are provided for all eight primitive Java types (not shown). If the underlying field is restricted by the Java language access control—for example, the field is protected and the **set() Field** method is called from outside the hierarchy and package—the **set()** method throws the **IllegalAccessException**. If the **object** argument supposedly containing the actual field is not an instance of the field's declaring class—that is, it doesn't actually define the specified field—the **IllegalArgumentException** is thrown.

The example shown in Listing 8-20 implements an elementary generic object serializer. Only the public fields, declared and inherited, are serialized and then only if they aren't transient. If the fields are primitive Java types, they are converted to strings, which are then streamed. If the fields are object references, then the public fields of these objects are serialized in turn.

There are several drawbacks to this system; namely, the values of non-public fields are lost. Furthermore, objects must have a declared default constructor to be qualified for serialization with this scheme. Also, no provision has been made to prevent infinite looping of the algorithm if circular object references occur. Even without a circular reference path, a leaf object can be referenced from two diverging branches that reconverge at this leaf, resulting in a second copy of the object being streamed out. After reconstruction, the object will appear twice (the original and its clone), with one branch referencing each and the overall structure of the reconstituted neighborhood of objects failing to reconverge, as was the case with the original. Therefore, the original graph structure of objects

Listing 8.20
Elementary Object
Serialization

```
import java.io.*;
import java.util.*;
import java.lang.reflect.*;
import java.awt.*;

public class ObjectSerializer
{

  public static void main(String[] args)
  {
    class Dim3 extends Dimension
    {
      public int depth;
      public Dim3() {}
      public Dim3(int width, int height, int depth)
      {
        super(width,height);
        this.depth = depth;
      }
      public String toString()
      {
        return getClass().getName()+
          "[width=" + width + ",height=" + height
          + ",depth=" + depth + "]";
      }
    }

    ByteArrayOutputStream out
      = new ByteArrayOutputStream();
    DataOutputStream dos = new DataOutputStream(out);
    Dim3  d3 = new Dim3(1,2,3);
    writeObject(dos,d3);
    ByteArrayInputStream in
      = new ByteArrayInputStream(out.toByteArray());
    d3 = (Dim3) readObject(new DataInputStream(in));
    System.out.println(d3);
  }

  public static void writeObject
    (DataOutput out, Object obj)
  {
    try {
      out.writeBytes(obj.getClass().getName()+"\n");
      Enumeration f = getFields(obj);
      while (f.hasMoreElements())
        writeField(out,(Field)f.nextElement(),obj);
    } catch (Throwable t) {}
  }

  private static Enumeration getFields(Object obj)
  {
    Class c = obj.getClass();
```

Listing 8-20.
Continued.

```
    Field[] f = c.getFields();
    Vector v = new Vector(f.length);
    for (int i = 0; i < f.length; i++)
      if (!Modifier.isTransient(f[i].getModifiers()))
        v.addElement(f[i]);
    return v.elements();
  }

  private static void writeField
    (DataOutput out, Field f, Object obj)
  {
    if (f.getType().isPrimitive())
      try {
        out.writeBytes(f.get(obj).toString()+"\n");
      } catch (Throwable t) {}
    else
      writeObject(out,obj);
  }

  public static Object readObject(DataInput in)
  {
    Object obj = null;
    try {
      obj = Class.forName(in.readLine()).newInstance();
      Enumeration f = getFields(obj);
      while (f.hasMoreElements())
        readField(in,(Field)f.nextElement(),obj);
    } catch (Throwable t) { System.out.println(t); }
    return obj;
  }

  private static void readField
    (DataInput in, Field f, Object obj)
  {
    try {
      Class c = f.getType();
      if (c.isPrimitive())
        f.set(obj,getWrapper(c,in));
      else
        f.set(obj,readObject(in));
    } catch (Throwable t) {}
  }

  private static Object getWrapper
    (Class c, DataInput in)
  {
    String value = "";
    try { value = in.readLine(); }
    catch (Throwable t) {}
    if (c == Boolean.TYPE)
      return new Boolean(value);
    if (c == Character.TYPE)
```

Continues

Listing 8-20.
Continued.

```
      return new Character(value.charAt(0));
   if (c == Byte.TYPE)
      return new Byte(value);
   if (c == Short.TYPE)
      return new Short(value);
   if (c == Integer.TYPE)
      return new Integer(value);
   if (c == Long.TYPE)
      return new Long(value);
   if (c == Float.TYPE)
      return new Float(value);
   if (c == Double.TYPE)
      return new Double(value);
   return null;
  }
}
```

isn't preserved by this algorithm. The object serialization API covered in the next chapter overcomes these and other drawbacks. The point here is to demonstrate the plausibility of a generic serialization facility given—indeed, requiring—a self-describing language capability as seen in the reflection API.

Our ObjectSerializer has only static methods. The **Dim3** class is an example of a inner class. (Class declarations can now be nested beginning with version 1.1 of Java.) The purpose of **Dim3** is to add a third dimension to the two-dimensional **java.awt.Dimension** class and thereby demonstrate the ability of the serializer to handle declared and inherited fields.

In the **main()** method, after the initialization of the output stream and **Dim3** instance, a call to **writeObject()** is made. The **writeObject()** method takes any object and serializes its public, nontransient fields, declared or inherited, and streams them out into its stream argument, after which **main()** initializes an input stream containing the contents of the previously serialized object. The **main()** method then proceeds to recreate this object from the input stream with a call to **readObject()**. The reconstituted **Dim3** object is then displayed on the standard System.out print stream:

```
ObjectSerializer$1$Dim3[width=1,height=2,depth=3]
```

The naming convention of inner classes is covered in the documentation that comes with the JDK. You can loosely translate it as "Dim3 is a class within the first static method of the declaring class **ObjectSerializer**."

The **writeObject()** method first writes out the object's fully qualified class name on a line by itself. It then calls the **ObjectSerializer.getFields()** method to retrieve a listing of all the public fields, declared and inherited, that are nontransient. Notice the use of the **Modifier** class to decode the transient flag in the **getFields()** method. The **writeField()** method is then called for each qualifying field to serialize it. If the field's type is primitive, its value is converted to a string and streamed out, again on its own line. If the field is a reference to another object, the process repeats with a call to **writeObject()** for the referenced object. If we were to examine the contents of the serialized stream, it would look like this:

```
ObjectSerializer$1$Dim3
1
2
3
```

The **readObject()** method is used to re-create the object from its serialized form. Reversing the process, **readObject()** first extracts the class name from the stream and fetches the **Class** object for that class from the Java VM. Given the **Class** object for **Dim3**, **newInstance()** is called to create a **Dim3** object by using its default constructor. (Please note that more elaborate serialization schemes might use something other than the default constructor.) Given a **Dim3** object, we can once again call our **getFields()** method to retrieve the field descriptors for all of **Dim3**'s publicly declared and inherited nontransient fields. Once we have the enumeration of the fields, their values are extracted from the stream one by one with the **readField()** method. If the field is a primitive Java type, we extract its value from the stream into a wrapper class (see **getWrapper**). This wrapping of the primitive value is necessary to pass it as a generic argument in the call to the **Field.set()** method, which automatically unwraps the value and reassigns it to its respective field.

Notice that the **readObject()** method is not hard-coded for **Dim3**, but rather for objects in general. The algorithm is generic, thanks to the Reflection polymorphic **Metaclass** mechanism embodied in the protocol of the **Class** class.

We didn't serialize the transient fields because *transient* indicates that the underlying field isn't meant to persist. The Java language access control precludes us from saving anything other than public fields. Obviously, the real object serialization API doesn't have the burden of this language security restriction. The JDK documentation mentions that in later releases there will be a relaxation of these language access restrictions for debuggers, inspectors, and so forth, written into the specification.

Array Class

All members of the **Array** class (Listing 8-21) are static, so **Array** can't be instantiated. You can use the **Array** class to create arrays and to get or set values within arrays. To determine whether an object is an array, retrieve the **Class** object and call the **isArray()** method:

```
foo.getClass().isArray().
```

Likewise, to determine the component type of an array you could code something like this:

```
anArray.getClass().getComponentType().
```

First, it must be determined whether an object is an array. If it is, the component type can also be easily determined. Both pieces of information can be obtained with methods of the **Class** object representing the array.

Listing 8.21
java.lang.reflect.Array

```
public final class Array
{
    public static Object newInstance
        (Class componentType, int length)
            throws NegativeArraySizeException;
    public static Object newInstance
        (Class componentType, int[] dimensions)
            throws IllegalArgumentException,
                NegativeArraySizeException;
    public static native int getLength(Object array)
        throws IllegalArgumentException;
    public static native Object get
        (Object array, int index)
            throws IllegalArgumentException,
                ArrayIndexOutOfBoundsException;
    public static native void set
        (Object array, int index, Object value)
            throws IllegalArgumentException,
                ArrayIndexOutOfBoundsException;
}
```

Given an array and its component type, the static methods of the **Array** class can then be used to access and modify the array's components.

The following two statements are equivalent:

```
String[] strings = new String[10];
String[] strings = Array.newInstance(String.class,10)
```

The **newInstance()** method throws the **NullPointerException** if the **componentType** argument is **null**. If the length is negative, the **NegativeArraySizeException** is thrown. There's an overloaded version of the **newInstance()** method for multidimensional arrays. Again, the following two snippets are equivalent:

```
int[][][] xyz = new int[10][10][10];
int[] dim = { 10, 10, 10 };
int[][][] xyz = Array.newInstance(int.class,dim);
```

Typically, an implementation of Java supports a maximum of 255 dimensions. If any dimension exceeds the allowed upper bound or if the dimension argument has no dimensions (an array length of zero, for example), the **IllegalArgumentException** is thrown. The **getLength()** method returns the length of the array. If the **array** argument isn't an array, the **IllegalArgumentException** is thrown.

The **get()** method returns the value of the indexed component from the array, wrapping it if it's a primitive Java type. If the index is negative or greater than or equal to the array's length, the **ArrayIndexOutOfBoundsException** is thrown. When dealing with an array with more than one dimension, you have to call the **get()** method several times to get to the value of a particular component, as shown:

```
int[][] xy = { { 1, 2 }, { 3, 4 }, { 5, 6 } };
System.out.println(Array.get(Array.get(xy,1),1));    // 4
```

The first **get()** method returns a one-dimensional array, requiring a second call to **get()** to get to the final component.

The **set()** method assigns a reference or value to the array at the indicated indexed location, depending on whether the component type is an object reference or primitive type, respectively. If the component type of the array is a primitive Java type, the value passed as an object argument to **set()** is automatically unwrapped. If the unwrapped value can't be converted by an identity or widening conversion to the component type, the **IllegalArgumentException** is thrown. To set the value of a component in an array having more the one dimension requires one or more calls to **get()** and finally one call to **set()**:

```
int[][] xy = { { 1, 2 }, { 3, 4 }, { 5, 6 } };
Array.set(Array.get(xy,1),1,new Integer(-4));
System.out.println(Array.get(Array.get(xy,1),1));    // -4
```

Not shown are the eight get/set pairs for assigning primitive types directly.

CONCLUSION

Using the reflection API, an application can programmatically construct new instances of any class or array, so it's now possible to delay the decision of what to construct until runtime! Introspection conducted with the reflection API also allows discovering and invoking methods at runtime. Similarly, it's also possible to access and modify fields of any object or class. Elements of an array can be accessed similarly. For example, a generically-implemented object inspector can dissect an object of any class, polymorphically. This goes far beyond the polymorphism of virtual functions in which the polymorphic root class must be known at implementation time. In effect, Java's **Metaclass** system rooted in the **Class** class serves as the polymorphic root of a self-describing language.

Readily available from a **Class** object are instances of three new classes —**Constructor**, **Method**, and **Field**—that completely describe the protocol (API) of the underlying class. Because an object's **Class** object is accessible at runtime, a complete description of the object's protocol is also accessible. Therefore, you can discover the protocol of a JavaBean programmatically—that is, at design time—within a RAD IDE. Similarly, a generic, automated object serialization facility is feasible, given any object's self-describing ability. Object serialization in turn gives rise to the RMI's requirement for marshaling objects across a socket stream. Without the reflection API, Java would be little more than a code mobile system instead of a robust, self-declaring, remoteable language. Without the reflection API, visual development with JavaBeans wouldn't be possible.

9

Custom
Component Editors
for JavaBeans

JavaBeans can be used through program code, but that defeats their purpose. Most of the time, JavaBeans are manipulated through property editors. However, these property editors, by default, can handle only basic classes, such as numbers, strings, color, fonts, images, and possibly sound. They can't handle abstraction. Also, you can't usually predict which IDE your Bean will be used in. Bean developers, therefore, need a way to supply editors for properties that certain IDEs (integrated development environments) can't handle. Custom editors can be written that can be recognized and used for Beans you develop.

In this chapter, we see how to create custom property editors by extending the **PropertyEditorSupport** class, implementing the PropertyEditor interface, and directing the Property Editors to use our customized property editors by extending the **BeanInfo** class.

This chapter will cover the following topics:

- Custom property editors
- Customizing the `TrafficLightBean`
- The PropertyEditor interface

What Is a Custom Property Editor?

A *custom property editor* interacts with the IDE to display or edit a Bean property. The property editor retrieves a value from the instance of a Bean and displays it. After the value is changed, it's transmitted back to the Bean by calling the associated `set()` method.

All JavaBeans frameworks are required to implement the PropertyEditor interface. JavaBeans supplies a class called `PropertyEditorSupport` that provides a default implementation of PropertyEditor. You can extend this class and redefine those methods you want to implement, instead of implementing all the methods of PropertyEditor. We will use this approach to customize our `TrafficLightBean`'s initial state property.

The PropertyEditor interface is a standard way to accept values for your Bean's properties. You might want to change the way a property sheet behaves for many reasons, although often it is to validate the data being added (for example, for a `TrafficLightBean`, any color other than green, red, or orange is invalid). You might want to display an image representing the property you're changing and generate custom editor components; you could, for example, show all three states in another window and let the user choose from them.

Validating Data

It is essential to validate the data being handed over to your Bean. If the values are being set through code, you can throw exceptions and force the developers using your classes to handle them. However, in a JavaBean that's manipulated from within an IDE, you would have to leave it up to the IDE to trap such exceptions and return a generic message. If the error is trapped in the PropertyEditor interface, you can control the messages and make them more informative.

Besides preventing the user from entering invalid values, JavaBeans tend to be smaller because the validation and exception-handling code lies within the property editors, not in the application where your JavaBean is being used. Even though Beans should have error-handling capabilities, most of the code you see while configuring the Bean or gluing it to other Beans appears only in the property editors. This configuration code doesn't need to be in the final application where your Bean is being used, making your Bean's size much smaller.

Displaying Images in Property Sheets

One of the goals of JavaBeans development is to make application development for the nonprogrammer as easy as possible. It's been said that a picture is worth a thousand words, so representing a property's value in terms of an image is usually an effective technique. For example, you could accept a color choice from users, instead of getting them to visualize or memorize all the possible values for red-green-blue combinations or the names of colors. You could let them select their colors from a palette and display the selected color value as a filled rectangle.

You might also want to use an icon to display the concept of a class's property. For example, if you had a speaker Bean, you could have an icon representing the volume next to the edit box where you accept valid values for the speaker Bean's volume.

Displaying a List Box of Valid Values

If the values for a property are a small fixed set of possible alternatives, you can display the values in a list. For example, for our **TrafficLightBean**, the only possible values are **Stop**, **Caution**, and **Go**. One of the benefits of having such a list is that there's really no need for any sort of validation because the user can't enter values that aren't on the list.

Generating a Custom Editor

If you want to make the user interface for setting the value more user-friendly, you can generate a custom editor. For example, to set the volume of a speaker, you can actually show a volume knob that the user can rotate clockwise (by clicking on it) to increase the volume and counter-clockwise to decrease it.

The PropertyEditor Interface

The interface for the PropertyEditor is shown in Listing 9-1.

The PropertyEditor interface has methods for exchanging objects between a framework and a property editor, setting and getting values for properties as text, displaying properties in a custom *graphical user interface* (GUI) and registering/deregistering `PropertyChangeListener` listeners.

The `setValue()` method is used to set the value of the property that's being viewed or edited from the property editor; this method should be the only way for an editor to set the value of a property in a Bean. The `getValue()` method is used by the IDE to retrieve the object's current value. The `paintValue()` method is used to paint a graphical representation of the Bean's property within a given rectangle in the property editor. The IDE calls the `isPaintable()` method to determine whether a custom editor has implemented the `paintValue()` method. The `getJavaInitializationString()` method is used to get the Java code required to initialize a variable with the current property value. The `getAsText()` method returns the value of the property in its textual form, and the `setAsText()` method is its counterpart. It allows users to enter the value for the property as text. Developers have to implement this method, parse the string supplied as input, and create an object from it. If the property has a finite set of values to display and accept from, the `getTags()` method can be used.

The IDE uses an array of strings that represent the values for the property and populates a `Choice`, `List`, or `PopupMenu` component in the Bean's

Listing 9-1.
The PropertyEditor
interface.

```
package java.beans

public interface PropertyEditor{
Object getValue();
void setValue(Object value);
String getAsText();
void setAsText(String) throws java.lang.
    IllegalArgumentException;
void addPropertyChangeListener(PropertyChangeListener
    listener);
void removePropertyChangeListener(PropertyChangeListener
    listener);
String[] getTags();
Component getCustomEditor();
boolean supportsCustomEditor();
String getJavaInitializationString();
boolean isPaintable();
void paintValue(Graphics graphics, Rectangle rect);
}
```

property sheet. The **getCustomEditor()** method is used to create a custom user interface for editing the Bean's property. This method returns a component, like **Canvas** or **Panel**, that the IDE can place in a new window or merge into an existing panel. The **supportsCustomEditor()** method should return true if the PropertyEditor returns a component when **getCustomEditor()** is called.

The **addPropertyChangeListener()** method is used to add listener objects that need to be notified when the property's value changes. The primary listener is the IDE, which needs to know when the value of the Bean property in the PropertyEditor changes so that it can call the Bean's corresponding write accessor method with the changed value. The **removePropertyChangeListener()** method is used to remove the listener, primarily the IDE.

Customizing the TrafficLightBean

As our **TrafficLightBean** stands right now, nothing can stop someone from entering any value for its initial state. The easiest way to prevent this is to give the user a drop-down list box for the initial state property. To do this, we need to tell the PropertyEditor that the default method of accepting input from the user has been overridden. Listing 9-2 shows how we do this by extending the **BeanInfo** class and specifying the custom property editors through calls to the **setPropertyEditorClass()** method.

The **TrafficLightStateEditor** is the custom property editor for the state property. It extends the **PropertyEditorSupport** class and overrides its **getTags()** method. The **PropertyEditorSupport** class is a basic implementation of the PropertyEditor interface that mostly supports String values. It supplies basic implementations of the **getValue()**, **setValue()**, **getAsText()**, and **setAsText()** methods. The **addPropertyChangeListener()** and **removePropertyListener()** methods are implemented to inform the IDE of changes to the property's values.

The **TrafficLightStateEditor** (Listing 9-3) overrides the **getTags()** method simply by returning an array of strings, each corresponding to a valid value of the state property, such as **Stop**, **Caution** and **Go**.

Now the property sheet uses this custom editor and displays the states in a drop-down list box, as shown in Figure 9-1.

Now that we can control the input to the state property, let us also control the input to the **RedTimeInterval** property. To do so, we will write a custom editor to accept the input for the **RedTimeInterval** property from a scrollbar.

Listing 9-2.
The **BeanInfo**
class for the
TrafficLightBean
to set a custom
property editor
for the initial state
property.

```
package Cars;

import java.beans.*;

/**
 * The TrafficLightBeanBeanInfo is the BeanInfo class for
    the TrafficLightBean.
 *
 * This BeanInfo class is used to expose only some of the
    properties of the
 * TrafficLightBean. It also defines a customized property
    editor for the
 * TrafficLightBean's state property.
 *
 * @see             TrafficLightBean
 * @see             TrafficLightStateEditor
 */
public class TrafficLightBeanBeanInfo extends
    SimpleBeanInfo
{

    public BeanDescriptor getBeanDescriptor()
    {
        BeanDescriptor desc = new BeanDescriptor
            (TrafficLightBean.class);
        desc.setDisplayName("Customized Traffic Light
            Bean");

        desc.setShortDescription("This bean illustrates a
            custom editor");
        return desc;
    }

    // Property Descriptors
    public PropertyDescriptor[] getPropertyDescriptors ()
    {
        PropertyDescriptor[] props = null;

        try
        {
            PropertyDescriptor p;
            p = new PropertyDescriptor ("State",
                TrafficLightBean.class);
            p.setPropertyEditorClass
                (TrafficLightStateEditor.class);

            PropertyDescriptor pr;
            pr = new PropertyDescriptor
                ("RedTimeInterval",
                TrafficLightBean.class);
```

Listing 9-2.
Continued.

```
                            PropertyDescriptor po;
                            po = new PropertyDescriptor
                                    ("OrangeTimeInterval",
                                     TrafficLightBean.class);

                            PropertyDescriptor pg;
                            pg = new PropertyDescriptor
                                    ("GreenTimeInterval",
                                     TrafficLightBean.class);

                            props = new PropertyDescriptor [4];
                            props [0] = p;
                            props [1] = pr;
                            props [2] = po;
                            props [3] = pg;
                    }
                    catch (IntrospectionException e)
                    {
                            System.out.println (e);
                    }
                    return props;
            }
    }
```

Listing 9-3.
The custom property
editor for the state
property of the
TrafficLightBean.

```
package Cars;

import java.beans.*;

/**
 * The TrafficLightStateEditor defines a customized
     property editor for the
 * TrafficLightBean's state property.
 *
 * @see              TrafficLightBean
 * @see              TrafficLightBeanBeanInfo
*/

public class TrafficLightStateEditor
    extends PropertyEditorSupport
{
    public String[] getTags ()
    {
        String result[] = {"Go", "Caution", "Stop"};
        return result;
    }
}
```

Figure 9-1.
The states listed in the custom editor.

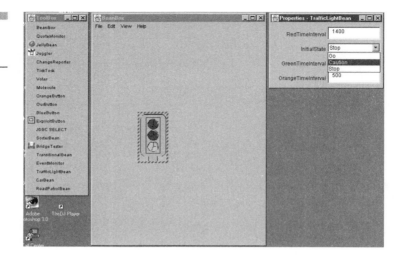

First, we need to specify the custom property editor for the **RedTimeInterval** property through a call to the **setPropertyEditorClass()** method. (Refer to Listing 9-4.) You will find the code for the editor itself in Listing 9-5.

We start by extending the **Panel** class and then implementing the PropertyEditor interface. Also, because we want to accept the input from the scrollbar (which generates the adjustment event when it's manipulated), we have to implement the AdjustmentListener interface.

TrafficLightTimerEditor has three private data members: A **Scrollbar** (**timerBar**), an **Integer** (**redTimerInterval**), and a **PropertyChangeSupport** (**propertyChangeSupport**) for bound properties. The Integer data member holds the value for the **RedTimerInterval** property.

In the constructor function, we create a scrollbar and add it to the panel. We also register the AdjustmentListener that we implemented to handle adjustment events in the scrollbar. The AdjustmentListener gets the new value of the scrollbar, multiplies it by 100 (because we set the **RedTimeInterval** property in milliseconds—we don't want users to repeatedly press the scrollbar if they want, for example, to set the interval to 5000 milliseconds), updates the scrollbar position, and calls **setValue()**. The **setValue()** method sets the value of the **redTimeInterval** data member, and then fires a **propertyChange** event. Because we're interested only in the new value, the old value is set to null, and the new value is set to the value calculated from the displacement of the scrollbar. The **isPaintable()** method returns true to indicate that we do want to display a value in the property sheet, and the method **paintValue()** actually does the painting.

```
package Cars;

import java.beans.*;

/**
 * The TrafficLightBeanBeanInfo is the BeanInfo class for
     the TrafficLightBean.
 *
 * This BeanInfo class is used to expose only some of the
     properties of the
 * TrafficLightBean. It also defines a customized property
     editor for the
 * TrafficLightBean's state property.
 *
 * @see            TrafficLightBean
 * @see            TrafficLightStateEditor
 */
public class TrafficLightBeanBeanInfo extends
     SimpleBeanInfo
{

    public BeanDescriptor getBeanDescriptor()
    {
        BeanDescriptor desc = new BeanDescriptor
            (TrafficLightBean.class);
        desc.setDisplayName("TrafficLightBean");

        desc.setShortDescription("This bean illustrates a
            custom editor");
        return desc;
    }

    // Property Descriptors
    public PropertyDescriptor[] getPropertyDescriptors ()
    {
        PropertyDescriptor[] props = null;

        try
        {
            PropertyDescriptor p;
            p = new PropertyDescriptor ("State",
                TrafficLightBean.class);
            p.setPropertyEditorClass
                (TrafficLightStateEditor.class);

            PropertyDescriptor pr;
            pr = new PropertyDescriptor
```

Continues

▋▋▋ ▋▋▋ ▋▋▋ ▋▋▋

Listing 9-4.
Continued.

```
                        ("RedTimeInterval",
                        TrafficLightBean.class);
                pr.setPropertyEditorClass
                        (TrafficLightTimerEditor.class);

                PropertyDescriptor po;
                po = new PropertyDescriptor
                        ("OrangeTimeInterval",
                        TrafficLightBean.class);

                PropertyDescriptor pg;
                pg = new PropertyDescriptor
                        ("GreenTimeInterval",
                        TrafficLightBean.class);

                props = new PropertyDescriptor [4];
                props [0] = p;
                props [1] = pr;
                props [2] = po;
                props [3] = pg;
        }
        catch (IntrospectionException e)
        {
                System.out.println (e);
        }
        return props;
    }
}
```

▋▋▋ ▋▋▋ ▋▋▋ ▋▋▋

Listing 9-5.
The custom property
editor for the
RedTimeInterval
property of the
TrafficLightBean.

```
package Cars;

import java.awt.*;
import java.beans.*;
import java.awt.event.*;


public class TrafficLightTimerEditor extends Panel
        implements PropertyEditor,
        AdjustmentListener{
        private Scrollbar timerBar;
        private Integer redTimerInterval;

        private PropertyChangeSupport propertyChangeSupport =
                        new PropertyChangeSupport(this);

        public TrafficLightTimerEditor()
        {
```

Listing 9-5.
Continued.

```
        timerBar = new Scrollbar(Scrollbar.HORIZONTAL, 0,
            50, 0, 300);
        timerBar.addAdjustmentListener(this);
        add(timerBar);
    }

    public void adjustmentValueChanged(AdjustmentEvent e){
        Integer i = new Integer(e.getValue()*100);
        System.out.println(i.toString());
        timerBar.setValue(e.getValue());
        setValue(i);
    }

    public void setValue(Object object){
        redTimerInterval = (Integer) object;
        propertyChangeSupport.firePropertyChange
        ("redInterval",null,redTimerInterval);

    }

    public Object getValue(){
        return redTimerInterval;
    }


    public boolean isPaintable(){
        return true;
    }

    public void paintValue(Graphics g, Rectangle r){
        g.drawRect(r.x, r.y, r.width, r.height);
        g.drawString(redTimerInterval.toString(), r.x+2,
            r.y+r.height/2);
    }

    public Component getCustomEditor()
    {
        return this;
    }

    public boolean supportsCustomEditor()
    {
        return true;
    }

    public void addPropertyChangeListener
        (PropertyChangeListener listener){
        propertyChangeSupport.addPropertyChangeListener
            (listener);
    }
```

Continues

Listing 9-5.
Continued.

```
public void removePropertyChangeListener
       (PropertyChangeListener listener){
    propertyChangeSupport.removePropertyChange-
              Listener(listener);
}

public void setAsText(String s)throws
     java.lang.IllegalArgumentException{

}

public String getAsText(){
    return null;
}

public String[] getTags(){
    return null;
}

public String getJavaInitializationString(){
    return null;
}
}
```

Figure 9-2.
The custom property
editor for the
RedTimeInterval
property.

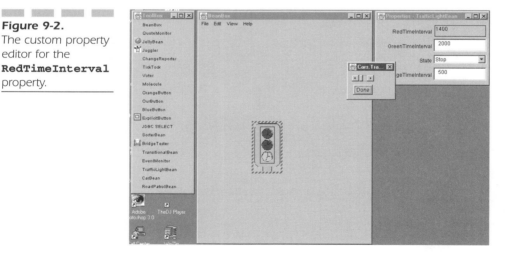

It's a simple function that displays the value of **redTimeInterval** within a box in the property sheet.

Now our custom property editor for the **RedTimeInterval** property looks like the one shown in Figure 9-2.

CONCLUSION

As a JavaBean developer, you must design and develop custom editors for JavaBeans. In this chapter, we have seen how to provide custom editors for properties. With this information as a starting point, use your imagination to make the property editors as user-friendly as possible. Remove the code from the Bean that's needed at design time and put it in the custom editors so that your Beans stay small. Your aim as a Beans developer should be to keep editors small, simple, and functional. Always keep the user in mind, because often your user is someone who knows how to drag-and-drop objects, but isn't a Java wizard.

10

Packaging Beans

As we have seen in the previous chapters, a Bean is a set of class files associated with resource files such as images, sounds, and so forth. It's important to package the Beans after creating and testing them so that others can use them. In this chapter, we learn about the specifications for and advantages of JAR files, the jar utility used to create these files, and the javakey utility used to digitally certify applets for authentication purposes. Finally, we will create some JAR files and digitally sign them.

This chapter will cover the following topics:

- Goals of packaging Beans
- Overview of JAR files
- The manifest file
- The jar utility
- Digital signatures
- The javakey utility
- JAR files and digital signatures
- The signature file

Goals of Packaging Beans

The JavaBeans specification defines the format and conventions needed to package JavaBeans so that an application framework can use them. Once created, tested, and packaged, they can be used in building applications. The JAR file specifications don't apply to project files or applications that have been built by using Beans, so packaging the applications and the Beans used to create them is left up to the applications' implementers.

Overview of JAR Files

With the new JAR technology, we can store Beans and their associated resources, such as images, sounds, and serialized objects. A JAR file is based on the popular ZIP archive file format. Vendors can develop and put several Beans in a JAR file for shipping. The Beans in the JAR file can share all the resources in the JAR file. Besides these features, application builders such as the BeanBox look specifically for Beans in JAR files.

Because a JAR file can consist of more than one Bean, there has to be a way to supply additional information about the Beans in the file. This information is provided in the form of *manifest files*. The classes in a JAR file can be digitally signed by the applet author to authenticate their origin. Therefore, Beans running within signed applets have more privileges than those running within unsigned applets. They can be allowed to manipulate files and network host connections. Class-signing information is also given in the manifest files. A list of all the Beans in the JAR file, as well as information about a particular Bean, can be easily extracted from JAR files.

A JAR file has several entries defining one or more JavaBeans in the package. All the class entries in the JAR file follow the **<name>:<value>** format. The **<value>** is the standard slash-separated package structure. For example, a class entry for **MyButton** would look like this:

```
Name: myCompany/visibleBeans/myButton/myButton.class
```

Each JavaBean can include entries that define the following:

■ The classes required by the Bean (these classes aren't necessarily all JavaBeans).

■ A serialized prototype of a Bean used to initialize the Bean.

■ Optional help files in HTML format to provide documentation for the JavaBean.

If the JavaBean is expected to be used across the world in different languages, the JavaBean might need internationalization information to localize itself.

NOTE *A JAR file must have at least one of the first two components listed previously. If the JavaBean is localized, there might be multiple versions of the help files, one per locale. These entries must have names in the **<name>:<value>** format; the **<value>** would be of the form **<locale>/.../<name>.html***

The JAR file can also include optional resource files, such as images, sounds, or videos, if they're needed by the packaged JavaBeans. A single JAR file can have any number of resource files, and all those resources can be shared by any JavaBean packaged in the same JAR file.

JavaBeans Naming Conventions

A JavaBean's name is a String composed of names separated by a period. Bean names are unique in their domain. The Bean's name is the same as the class representing it, or its serialized object. To avoid name collisions, Bean developers should follow the standard Java naming convention for classes: The top-level package name is the name of the company developing the JavaBeans.

Advantages of Using JAR Files

The JAR file format is based on the industry standard ZIP file format. These are some of the advantages of using JAR files:

- JAR files are platform-independent.
- JAR files, written in Java, are open standard and can be fully extended.
- JAR files are backward-compatible with existing applet code.
- JAR files help logically organize JavaBeans and their related components.

Since multiple applets and their resources (sounds and images) are stored in one JAR file, all the required components are downloaded to the browser in a single *HyperText Transport Protocol* (HTTP) request, much faster than downloading individual files.

JAR files are compressed, which reduces the time needed to download Beans and their elements. Also, individual files in the JAR file can be digitally signed by the applet author to authenticate their origin.

Including JAR Files in HTML Pages

To improve performance, JAR files can be included in HTML pages. The **archive** parameter is an extension to the **<applet>** tag that allows applets to be loaded from the JAR file. Including the following tag would load the **Calendar** class from the **Utilities.jar** JAR file:

```
<applet code=Calendar.class
   archive = "jars/Utilities.jar"
   width = 150
    height = 300>
</applet>
```

The **code** parameter specifies the name of the applet to execute, but the resources used by the applet would be loaded from the Utilities.jar file in the preceding example. After the archive file is downloaded and separated into its components, all references to other classes and objects, such as images or sounds, are then looked up in the archive. If the objects aren't in the archive, they are searched for on the server from which the applet was downloaded. Multiple JAR files can be specified in the **archive** parameter, as shown in this example:

```
<applet code=Calendar.class
   archive = "jars/Utilities.jar, jars/DateManipulate.jar"
   width = 150
   height = 300>
</applet>
```

In this case, each JAR file would be downloaded, and references to the objects in each of these JAR files would be looked up before going out to search on the server.

Identifying JavaBeans in a JAR File

If there are many classes and serialized objects in the JAR file, but each one isn't necessarily a Bean, how do application builders pick out which ones are Beans? Even though every class and serialized object in the JAR file isn't necessarily a Bean, it potentially could be. If developers specifically want to differentiate Beans from regular classes, they must include a manifest file in the JAR file. The manifest files specifically pinpoint actual Beans from the list of potential Beans in the JAR file. If a manifest file isn't included in the JAR file, then every file is regarded as a potential Bean.

TIP *JDK1.1 supplies an Application Program Interface (API) to query the contents of a JAR file.*

The Manifest File

The manifest file stores metainformation about the archive's contents. It's an ASCII file that stores information about the files in a JAR file. There can be exactly one manifest file in the archive, with the pathname META-INF/MANIFEST.MF. The information in the manifest file is represented as *name:value* pairs. Groups of name:value pairs are known as *sections*, which are separated from other sections by empty lines.

The manifest file consists of a list of files in the archive. Not all files in the archive need to be listed in the manifest file, but all signed files and those classes that represent Beans must be listed. The manifest file itself must not be listed. Here is an example of a manifest file with an explanation of each directive:

```
#
# Manifest version number (mandatory)
#
Manifest-Version: 1.0

#
# one section for each file in the archive (at least those
    that are signed or are Beans)
#
Name: myCompany/visibleBeans/myButton/myButton.class

#
# Indicate whether this class file is a Bean
#
Java-Bean: True

#
# Digest algorithms used for encryption/signing; a list of
    each algorithm used
#
Digest-Algorithms: MD5

#
# base64 representation of MD5 digest; one line for each
    algorithm used
#
MD5-Digest: (base64 representation of MD5 digest)

Name: myCompany/visibleBeans/myButton/buttonPainter.class
Digest-Algorithm: MD5 SHA
MD5-Digest: (base64 representation of MD5 digest)
SHA-Digest: (base64 representation of SHA digest)
```

NOTE   *Generating base64 representations of the mentioned algorithms is beyond the scope of this book. However, it's not important to know the algorithms for creating JAR files because the jar utility, explained in the following section, automatically creates base64 representations of MD5 and SHA hashes for you.*

The Jar Utility

The jar utility, used to create JAR files, is a general-purpose archiving and compression tool based on ZIP and the ZLIB compression format. However, it was designed primarily to facilitate packaging Java applets or applications into a single archive. This is the command line used to invoke the jar utility:

```
jar <options> <jarfilename> <list of files to compress>
```

Following is the list of options used with the jar utility:

- **-c**: Creates a new or empty archive on the standard output.
- **-t**: Lists the table of contents from standard output.
- **-x <list of files>**: Extracts all files, or just the named files, from standard input. If a file is omitted, then all files are extracted; otherwise, only the specified file or files are extracted.
- **-f**: The second argument specifies a JAR file to process. In the case of creation, **-f** refers to the name of the JAR file to be created (instead of on **stdout**). When used with the **-t** or **-x** options, **-f** identifies the JAR file to be listed or extracted.
- **-v**: Generates verbose output on **stderr**.

If any of the files in the list being archived is a directory, then that directory is processed recursively. Here's a typical use:

```
jar cf myButton.jar myButton.class
myButtonImplementation.class depressed_state.gif
raised_state.gif
```

In the preceding example, the class files **myButton.class** and **myButtonImplementation.class** and the images **depressed_state.gif** and **raised_state.gif** in the current directory are placed in a file named **myButton.jar**. A manifest file is automatically generated by the jar utility and is always the first entry in the JAR file. By default, it's named **META-INF/MANIFEST.MF**.

If you have a preexisting manifest file that you want the jar utility to use for the new JAR archive, you can specify it by using the **-m** option, as shown in this example:

```
jar cmf myManifestFile myButton.jar myButton.class
    myButtonImplementation.class depressed_state.gif
    raised_state.gif
```

When files are added to a JAR archive, the file and its MD5 and SHA hashes are stored. The hashes are entered into the manifest file. It's easy to view and process the contents of the manifest file because it's an ASCII file.

Digital Signatures

You can generate digital signatures for archive files. A signature verifies that a file came from a specified entity known as the *signer*. To generate a signature for a particular file, the signer must have a public/private key pair associated with it and one or more certificates authenticating its public key. The javakey utility is used to build and manage a persistent database of entities and their keys and certificates, as well as indicate whether each entity is considered trusted. Trusted applets enjoy a few more privileges than regular applets.

The Javakey Utility

Javakey, a command tool packaged with JDK, is required to generate digital signatures for archive files. Javakey manages two types of entities—identities and signers.

Identities are entities, such as people, companies, or organizations, that have a public key associated with them. These identities can have one or more certificates authenticating their public keys. A *certificate* is a digitally signed statement from an entity saying that the public key of some other entity has a particular value. If you trust the entity that signed a certificate, you trust that the association in the certificate between the specified public key and another particular entity is authentic. Javakey currently handles X.509 certificates.

Signers are entities that have private keys, which can be used for signing files, in addition to corresponding public keys. A signer must have a public and private key pair associated with it, and at least one certificate authenticating its public key, before it can sign files.

Database Usernames for Identities and Signers

All javakey entities have a username local to the database managed by javakey. A username is created by using **-c** (create an entity) or **-cs** (create a signer). All javakey commands issued later must use this same username to refer to the entity.

Associating Trust with Javakey Entities

You can use javakey to declare certain entities as trusted on your system. All applets in JAR files that are signed by a trusted entity using javakey run with the same full rights as local applications. These applets aren't limited according to the original Java security model. To trust the applet, the database managed by javakey must hold a copy of the certificate for the public key of the entity that signed the applet. The javakey database stores the entity username, certificates, and trust level. You can specify the trust level of an entity while creating it or modify it at a later time.

To create a trusted signer named **duke**, you can issue the following command:

```
javakey -cs duke true
```

To create an untrusted signer named **bob**, you can issue either of the following commands:

```
javakey -cs bob false
javakey -cs bob
```

By default, an entity is always untrusted, but you can subsequently change trust levels. For example, to make **duke** an untrusted entity, you would use this command:

```
javakey -t duke false
```

To make **bob** a trusted entity, use this command:

```
javakey -t bob true
```

Javakey allows you to inspect the state of the entire database or a single specified entity. You can see the state of the entire entity database by using the following command:

```
javakey -ld
```

To see the state of a single entity, use the following command:

```
javakey -li duke
```

Database Location

The database maintained by javakey is stored in a file named **identitydb.obj**. This file can contain private keys, so it should be kept in a secure location. By default, this database is created in the JDK installation directory. You can move this file to another location, specified by setting the value of the **identity.database** property in the master security properties file called **java.security**. For example, you could specify the location of the file by using the following directive:

```
identity.database=/etc/identitydb.obj
```

The java.security file is located in *<JDK installation directory>*/**lib/security**.

Generating a Certificate

To create a certificate, you must create a directive file supplying the following information:

- Information about the issuer (the signer of the certificate)
- Information about the subject (the entity being authenticated by the certificate)
- Information about the certificate itself
- The name of the algorithm used to generate the signature (DSA by default)
- The name of the file in which to store a copy of the certificate

After creating the certificate directive file, you can issue the following command to generate the certificate:

```
javakey -gc <certificate directive filename>
```

Javakey uses information supplied in the database file and the information stored in the database, such as the public key of the entity whose key is to be certified and the private key of the issuer.

Here is an example of a certificate directive file with explanations of each directive:

```
#
# Information about the issuer (mandatory)
# Database username. This is the name of the signer issuing
```

```
            the certificate.
#
issuer.name=rhoque

#
# The certificate to use for the signing (required if
      issuer.name is not equal to subject.name)
# Since the issuer can have more than one certificate,
      this specifies which of the certificates is to be used
      to sign the certificate file to authenticate the
      subject's public key. This value should be a number
      generated by javakey when importing or creating the
      issuer's certificate. You can get these numbers by
      using the -ld or -li javakey option.
#
issuer.cert=1

#
# Information about the subject (mandatory)
# Database username. This is the name of the entity whose
      public key is being authenticated by the issuer of the
      certificate.
#
subject.name=tsharma

#
# These components refer to the subject's common name,
      organizational unit, organization, and country.
subject.real.name=Tarun Sharma
subject.org.unit=Marketspace
subject.org=System Icon, Inc.
subject.country=USA
#
# Information about the certificate
#The information specifies that the certificate is valid
      from the start date and time to the end date and time.
# The dates can be specified in any format recognized by
      the java.util.Date method accepting String as an
      argument.
#
start.date=15 Apr 1997
end.date=14 Apr 1998

#
# The serial number is a unique number for a given issuer
      to distinguish this certificate from other certificates
      signed by the issuer.
#
serial number=1001

#
# Signature algorithm (default is Digital Signature
      Algorithm, DSA)
```

```
# A non-DSA algorithm can be used if (1) the specified
    name is a standard algorithm name, (2) there is a
    statically installed provider supplying the
    implementation of the algorithm, and (3) the signer's
    keys are suitable for the specified algorithm.
#
signature.algorithm=MD5/RSA

#
# Name of the file to which to save a copy of the certifi-
cate (optional)
#
out.file=cert.cer
```

Certificates and Files

You can display, import, and export certificates that are stored as files. To display a certificate stored as a file, use the following command:

```
javakey -dc certfile.cer
```

This command displays the following information about the certificate stored in the file `certfile.cer`:

- The certificate type
- Information about the subject
- Information about the public key
- The algorithm and its parameters
- The unparsed key bits
- The certificate validity dates
- Information about the issuer
- Information about the signature algorithm used
- The certificate serial number in hexadecimal

Use the following command to import a certificate from a file:

```
javakey -ic duke certfile.cer
```

You can use the following command to export a certificate to a file:

```
javakey -ec duke 1 certfile.cer
```

This command would export duke's certificate number 1 to a file named `certfile.cer`. This certificate number is the number assigned by javakey when creating or importing the certificate. You can see the certificate numbers by using the **-ld** or **-li** javakey option.

Javakey Options

- **-c id [true|false]**: Creates a new identity with database username identity. The optional true or false designation specifies whether the identity is trusted. The default is false.

- **-cs signer [true|false]**: Creates a new signer with database username signer. The optional true or false designation specifies whether the signer is trusted. The default is false.

- **-t [id|signer] [true|false]**: Sets the trust level for the specified identity or signer.

- **-l**: Lists the usernames of all entities in the database managed by javakey.

- **-ld**: Lists and provides detailed information about all entities in the database managed by javakey.

- **-li [id|signer]**: Provides detailed information about the specified identity or signer.

- **-r [id|signer]**: Removes the specified identity or signer from the database.

- **-ik id keyfile**: Imports the public key in the file **keyfile**, associating it with the specified identity. The key must be in X.509 format.

- **-ikp signer pubfile privfile**: Imports the key pair (the public key in the file **pubfile** and the private key in the file **privfile**), associating them with the specified signer. The keys must be in X.509 format.

- **-ic [id|signer] certfile**: Imports the public key certificate in the file **certfile**, associating it with the specified entity (identity or signer).

- **-ii [id|signer]**: Sets information for the specified identity or signer.

- **-gk signer algorithm keysize [pubfile] [privfile]**: Generates a key pair (a public key and associated private key) for the specified signer by using the specified algorithm, generating keys of length keysize bits. If a file **pubfile** is specified, the public key will be written to that file. If a file **privfile** is also specified, the private key will be written to that file. Do the latter with great care; private keys must remain private, or your security system is compromised.

- **-g signer algorithm keysize [pubfile] [privfile]**: Shortcut for the **-gk** command to generate a key pair for the specified signer.

- **-gc <certificate directive file>**: Generates a certificate according to information supplied in the **<certificate directive file>**.

- **-dc certfile**: Displays the certificate stored in the file **certfile**.

- **-ec [id|signer] <certificate number> <certificate output file>**: Exports the certificate numbered **<certificate number>** from the specified entity to the **<certificate output file>**.

- **-ek [id|signer] pubfile [privfile]**: Exports the public key for the specified identity or signer, and (optionally) the private key for a signer.

- **-gs <signature directive file> jarfile**: Signs the specified JAR file according to information supplied in the signature directive file.

JAR Files and Digital Signatures

Javakey can be used to sign and verify JAR files. Java licensees are expected to honor the signature generated with javakey, which can sign the JAR files by using the DSA or, in some cases, the MD5/RSA algorithm.

Digital Signature Algorithm (DSA) is the algorithm used *by Digital Signature Standard* (DSS), a government standard developed by the *National Institute of Standards & Technology* (NIST) and the NSA. *Rivest-Shamir-Adleman* (RSA) is the name of a popular algorithm used for encryption and signing. JDK 1.1 provides an implementation for DSA but not for RSA, because the inventors of the RSA hold a patent on that algorithm.

Key pairs can also be used to encrypt files when they're used with a matching encryption algorithm. A DSA key pair can be used for signing only, but an RSA key pair can be used for signing or encryption.

If the signer's public and private keys are DSA keys, javakey signs the JAR file using DSA. If the signer's keys are RSA keys, javakey tries to sign the JAR file using the MD5/RSA algorithm. However, for javakey to sign the JAR file using any other algorithm, there must be a statically installed provider supplying an implementation for the MD5/RSA algorithm.

For both the DSA and MD5/RSA algorithms, the signer must have a public key and a private key. The private key is used for signing, and the certificate of the public key is included in the signature file.

The Signature File

Signing a JAR file involves generating a signature for a given signer and including that signature in the JAR file. A signed JAR file includes at least one signature file in addition to the manifest file. There is one signature file per signer. Signing a JAR file requires the signer to be part of the database managed by javakey and to have an associated key pair and at least one certificate. To generate a signature, a signature directive file is necessary. Each directive file contains a signer profile.

Here is an example of a sample signature directive file with explanations of each directive:

```
#
# JAR signing directive file used by javakey to sign a JAR
    file
#

#
# Database name of the signer to use (mandatory)
#
signer=tsharma

#
# Certificate number to use for this signer (mandatory).
    This value should be the value generated by javakey
    when creating or importing the certificate.
#
cert=1

#
# Certificate chain depth of a chain of certificates to
    include. Not supported at the time this chapter was
    written, so the value is zero.
#
chain=0

#
```

```
# Name to give to the generated signature file and
      associated signature block.
# The name must be at most eight characters long.
# The generated signature file and associated signature
      block will have this filename with an extension of
      .SF and .DSA, respectively.
#
signature.file=TARUNSGN

#
# Name to give the signed JAR file (optional)
#
out.file=signedJar.jar
```

Once the JAR file and the directive file have been created, the following javakey command can be used to sign the JAR file:

```
javakey -gs <name of directive file> <name of JAR file>
```

The output of this command is a signed JAR file, whose name is the one indicated by the **out.file** property, if any, specified in the directive file. If the **out.file** property is not filled out, the signed filename is the same as that of the initial JAR file, but with the suffix .SIG. The .SF and .DSA files are added to the JAR file in a META-INF directory. If the signature directive file in the preceding example is used, the files added will be **META-INF/TARUNSGN.SF** and **META-INF/TARUNSGN.DSA**.

CONCLUSION

JAR files are a standard, convenient way to package Beans and regular applets. We recommend that you use JAR files even when you're packaging regular applets. They help organize the classes and the resources they use. In the next chapter, we will actually use some Beans from JAR files and get acquainted with an application builder: The BeanBox.

11

The BeanBox

Throughout our discussions in this book, we have been throwing around the terms *application framework*, *builder tools*, *containers*, and so on. All these terms mean basically the same thing: A platform that can hold all the Beans together and allow them to communicate with each other through events and event handlers. Containers can be very sophisticated and varied. They can be a complete integrated development environment, like Symantec's Visual Café, or they can simply be an HTML editor that can contain Beans and make the application available over the Web. BeanBox is one such container distributed with the BDK for Bean developers to test out their Beans. It can build Bean-based applications, but it isn't robust enough yet to handle large-scale application development. The BeanBox is free, so you have unrestricted access to its use. It lets you focus on the basics of JavaBeans without needing to learn the specifics of any particular commercial framework.

This chapter will cover the following topics:

- Defining a BeanBox framework
- Starting BeanBox
- Getting an overview of the BeanBox user interface
- Creating a simple application with BeanBox
- Putting our Beans together
- Learning about RAD IDEs

What Is the BeanBox Framework?

The *JavaBeans Developer's Kit* (BDK) 1.0 has a simple framework, shown in Figure 11-1. This framework includes a container called BeanBox, a collection of Beans organized in a ToolBox, and a property editor called Property Sheet. All these components give you visual aids for installing and customizing Beans.

The BeanBox is a simple test container used to try out the BDK sample Beans and your own newly-created Beans. If a Bean you have created runs properly in the BeanBox, you can be confident it will work properly with other commercial tools. The BeanBox is considered a reference builder tool environment.

The BeanBox isn't intended to be a fully functional development tool for creating applications with Beans; instead, it's intended to provide a simple example of how Beans can be manipulated visually. It's not de-

Figure 11-1.
The BDK 1.0 BeanBox framework includes a BeanBox container (in the center), the Beans ToolBox (to the left), and a BeanBox property editor.

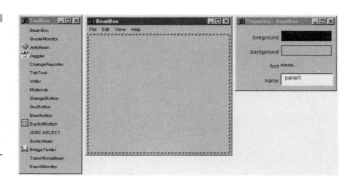

signed to be convenient for building *Graphical User Interface* (GUI) applications or to have the look and behavior you might find in other tools. Even so, the BeanBox is an indispensable tool for Bean development because it gives you a simple test environment for trying out Beans.

In Figure 11-1, some Beans have icons associated with them. These Beans use a Bean information class (**BeanInfo**) to specify which icon to display in visual development environments. Other Beans are listed in the ToolBox by name only.

Starting BeanBox

Before you can run BeanBox, you need to have two major components installed on your computer:

■ Java Developer's Kit (JDK) 1.1.2 or later
■ JavaBeans Developer's Kit (BDK) 1.0

Both kits are provided with this book's CD-ROM and can also be found on the Internet at JavaSoft's Web site: **http://java.sun.com:80/products/**. The BDK is available for Solaris 2.5, Windows 95, and Windows NT 4.0 platforms. However, the BDK is "pure Java" and should run on any JDK 1.1–enabled system.

To install JDK 1.1, follow the instructions supplied with the kit. Be sure to check your system environment settings after installation to reflect the latest update. Your **CLASSPATH** variable must point to the new location of the Java classes supplied with JDK 1.1. To check the **CLASSPATH** variable on Windows system, start a DOS session and type **SET** at the prompt. Press Enter and find the **CLASSPATH** variable in a list of system variables. If you're using a UNIX system, type **echo $CLASSPATH** and check its value. For more information on setting environment variables, please check your operating system's documentation.

Also, you need to have the JDK bin directory on your system path. To check this, examine the value of the **PATH** environment variable. This environment variable is used by most Intel operating systems to search for executable files.

When you install BDK, go to the BeanBox folder and type **run.bat** (for Windows) or **run.sh** (for UNIX). This program file is a simple script file (a batch file in DOS and a shell script in UNIX) that sets the **CLASSPATH** environment variable and starts the BeanBox application. You will see an initializing message on the screen and then three frames very similar to Figure 11-1.

In the following sections, we take some existing Beans distributed with the BDK and put them together, showing how Beans are "glued" together to form fully functional applications. We also take the Beans built during the previous chapters to form an application that demonstrates various concepts. All the applications we're building should be used just for understanding and clarifying concepts; they don't solve any real-life problems. However, if you do work with some real Beans that solve real-life problems, you can use the same concepts explained in this chapter to come up with a complete business application, without writing a single line of code.

Complete Overview of the BeanBox User Interface

File Menu

Use the File menu to load Beans, save Beans, serialize components, load JAR files, clear the current working frame, and print the current working frame.

When the BeanBox starts, it loads all the JAR files that it finds in the jars directory. The BeanBox uses the manifest file in each JAR file to identify any existing Bean classes and adds those Beans to its ToolBox palette.

To add your Bean to the BeanBox, you must wrap it in a JAR file that has a manifest file describing the Bean (explained in Chapter 10, "Packaging Beans").

Once you have a suitable JAR file, simply add it to the jars directory and restart the BeanBox, or load the JAR file directly by choosing the LoadJar . . . item from the File menu. To temporarily store applications developed with BeanBox, use the File menu's Save . . . and Load . . . items.

Edit Menu

The Edit menu has options to cut, copy, and paste components; create component reports; configure your Beans with the Customizer; and select events for the components.

Choose the Report . . . item if you want to see all the properties, methods, and events that the Beans Introspector has found on a selected Bean.

This menu choice generates a summary report to standard output of the introspection information for the selected Bean.

For those Beans that have a customized item, you can choose the Customize . . . item from the Edit menu. This choice opens a dialog window with the Bean's Customizer. Two of the sample Beans have a Customizer. **ExplicitButton** has a simple Customizer that just lets you set the button's label. The **JDBC SELECT** Bean has a much more interesting Customizer that tries to connect through JDBC to a local database to help you create a SQL query.

Events Menu

The Events menu has a submenu for all the different kinds of events that the currently selected Bean fires. These events are grouped and named according to their EventListener interfaces.

View Menu

With the View menu, you can disable or enable the design mode and hide or show invisible Beans.

When you choose Disable Design Mode from the View Menu, the ToolBox and Bean Property Sheet windows are hidden.

Help Menu

You can use the Help menu to get information about the current release of the BeanBox you're using and to link to an HTML file with information on how to work with BeanBox.

Creating a Simple Application Using BeanBox

The easiest way to understand how BeanBox works is to use it. You can construct simple Beans applications without writing any Java code. As a first example, let's build a simple Juggling Dukes application in which two Dukes start or stop juggling, depending on which one is activated.

First, we need to instantiate our two little fellows into the BeanBox. Beans can be instantiated by simply clicking on them in the ToolBox and placing them on the Canvas in the BeanBox. Point the mouse cursor at the icon with the Juggler label in the ToolBox window and click the mouse. Notice that the cursor changed its shape, indicating that the **Juggler** Bean has been selected. Now simply move your cursor to the BeanBox window and click the mouse again to place the first **Juggler** onto the working frame (the Beanbox's Canvas). The **Juggler** will appear and start juggling beans immediately. The thin frame surrounding the **Juggler** indicates that it's currently selected. You can move or resize the Bean by clicking on this frame and dragging it with the mouse.

After you repeat the same sequence for the second **Juggler**, your screen should look like the one shown in Figure 11-2.

Now both **Jugglers** are juggling their beans together. We want to make one of the **Jugglers** stop when the other is selected. To do that, we will use some of the available events. BeanBox allows you to connect an event from the currently selected Bean to a target event that's handling a method in any other Bean. Select your first **Juggler**, and then click the Edit option on the menu bar. From the Edit menu, choose Events, then Mouse, and finally mouseClicked, as shown on Figure 11-3.

Figure 11-2.
The BeanBox container after we placed two **Jugglers**.

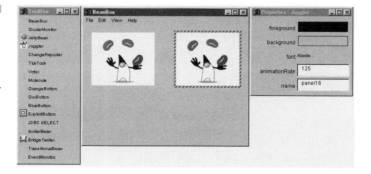

Figure 11-3.
Choosing the **mouseClicked** event for the **Juggler** Bean.

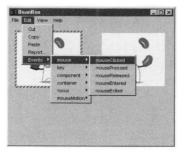

Notice a tail following your mouse cursor and originating in `Juggler` 1. This tail shows that you're about to link the selected event with its target. Point the mouse to `Juggler` 2 and click. The EventTargetDialog window should appear now, listing all the possible events you can process with the `Juggler` Bean. Select the `stopJuggling` event and click OK (see Figure 11-4).

The BeanBox then generates and compiles an adapter class for processing this event. You can check the action immediately by clicking inside the `Juggler` 1 frame. `Juggler` 2 will stop jugging the beans and freeze. Now repeat the same procedure for `Juggler` 2.

After selecting both `Jugglers`, neither one is moving. We need to add some more functions to make the selected juggler start juggling beans again. To do this, select `Juggler` 1 and select the `mouseClicked` event for him. It's OK that we have already used that event; you can add extra functions without overwriting the initial event processing. Select as a target for the event the same `Juggler` who will produce the event. Now select `startJuggling` in the EventTargetDialog window. Do the same with the second `Juggler`.

To change the animation rate at which the `Juggler` juggles his beans, all you have to do is increase or decrease the number in the Property Sheet for that `Juggler`. To do that, select the `Juggler` Bean in the BeanBox framework and update the `animationRate` property, as shown in Figure 11-5.

Now let's check a couple of other Beans and their functions. Place two more Beans onto the BeanBox working frame: `Molecule` and `TickTock`, as shown in Figure 11-6.

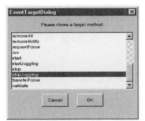

Figure 11-4.
The EventTarget-
Dialog window for
the **Juggler** Bean.

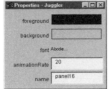

Figure 11-5.
Changing the
animationRate
property for the
Juggler.

Our aim is to rotate the **Molecule** in both the X and Y dimensions at a specified pace. The **TickTock** Bean has an event, shown in Figure 11-7, that occurs when the Bean's property changes.

Select the **propertyChange** event, and point the mouse cursor to the **Molecule** Bean. In the EventTargetDialog window, select rotateOnX or rotateOnY, depending on how you want your **Molecule** Bean to be rotated (see Figure 11-8).

Figure 11-6.
The BeanBox working frame after we added two more Beans: **Molecule** and **TickTock**.

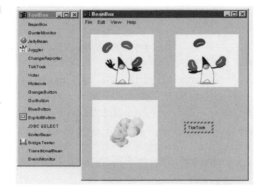

Figure 11-7.
Selecting the **propertyChange** event for the **TickTock** Bean.

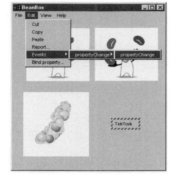

Figure 11-8.
The **rotateOnX** method for the targeted **Molecule** Bean.

By changing the property interval of the **TickTock** Bean, we can regulate the rotation speed.

Putting Our Beans Together

Now that we know how to put together some of the Beans that come with the BDK, let's try and put together the Beans we built in the previous chapters.

Instantiate the **CarBean** in the BeanBox. As soon as you select the **CarBean** and place it on the BeanBox Canvas, you should see a moving car. The moving car image is the same as a stopped car, except there's some smoke behind the car (see Figure 11-9). The Property Sheet for the **CarBean** has two properties related to the car: The current speed and the maximum speed. The maximum speed is the speed at which the car travels when there's no event to reduce its speed or stop it. The current speed changes depending on the events the car is handling. The **maxSpeed** property of the **CarBean** is a *Vetoable property*; therefore, if another Bean wants to stop this property from changing, it can do so. The traffic cop could actually prevent the **CarBean** from speeding.

Next, instantiate the **TrafficLightBean** in the BeanBox (see Figure 11-10). You should be able to see the traffic light changing its state at regular intervals as soon as you place it on the Canvas. The state of the **TrafficLightBean** changes at specified intervals in the Property Sheet; you can change these intervals in terms of milliseconds. The *interval* is the time the **TrafficLightBean** remains in the selected state. If you set the **RedTimeInterval** property of the Bean to 2000, for example, the **TrafficLightBean** remains in the Stop state for 2000 milliseconds. It fires a **propertyChange** event on every state change. Therefore, the state of the **TrafficLightBean** is a *Bound property*. It notifies other Beans that are

Figure 11-9.
The **CarBean**
in the BeanBox.

interested when the state changes. In our case, we want the **CarBean** to react to these states. We want the **CarBean** to start moving when the signal is green, reduce speed when the signal is orange, and come to a halt when the signal turns red.

Now instantiate the **RoadPatrolBean** in the BeanBox (see Figure 11-11). The **RoadPatrolBean** can generate **Cop** events, which are *user-defined events* to his Cop listeners. For example, you can make the **RoadPatrolBean** pull over the **CarBean**. When it does so, the **CarBean** won't move, no matter what the traffic signal is, until the **RoadPatrolBean** lets the **CarBean** go.

**Figure 11-10.
TrafficLightBean**
in place.

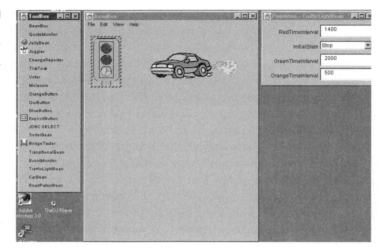

**Figure 11-11.
RoadPatrolBean**
in place.

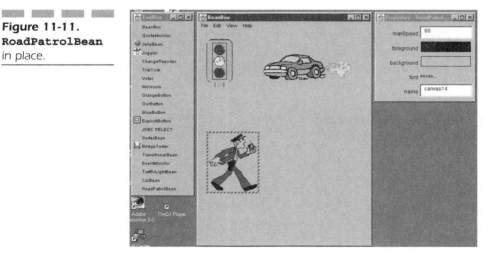

Now, let's relate the Beans so that they can handle events and communicate with each other. First, we need to make the **CarBean** react to the **TrafficSignalBean**. The **TrafficSignalBean** can inform interested Beans of a change in its state, so we have to register the **CarBean** as a listener to the **TrafficSignalBean**'s **propertyChange** event. To do this, select the **TrafficLightBean** by clicking on its image on the Canvas. From the Edit menu, choose the propertyChange submenu and then the **propertyChange** event, as shown in Figure 11-12.

The BeanBox positions a line under your mouse cursor that you can use to connect to the **CarBean**. Drag the line to the **CarBean** and click the mouse button over its image (see Figure 11-13).

The BeanBox responds with an EventTargetDialog window. Select the **propertyChange** target method, as shown in Figure 11-14.

As soon as you make this link, the BeanBox generates and compiles an adapter class. If you're interested, you can have a look at the source code the BeanBox generates and compiles. You will find it in the bdk/Beanbox/tmp/sun/beanbox directory with a name such as **__Hookup_143956e3d3.java**. This name is generated by the Beanbox, so it might differ when you try out the example.

If you look at the source code of this generated file, you can see that all the BeanBox does is implement the interface for the source event. It sets the target Bean to the Bean you specified in the EventTargetDialog for the **setTarget** method. It implements the source event you specified in the Edit | Events menu and makes a call to the target object's event target method.

Figure 11-12.
Making the
CarBean react to
TrafficSignalBean.

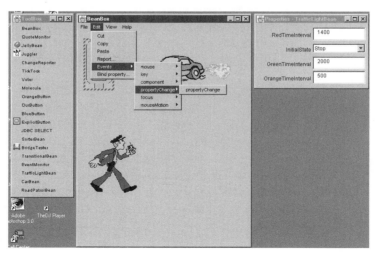

Figure 11-13.
Connecting to the
CarBean.

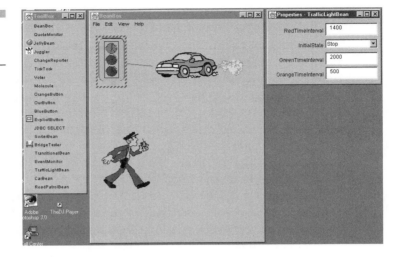

Figure 11-14.
The EventTarget-
Dialog window for
the **CarBean**.

The adapter file generated by the BeanBox is basically a mediator that tells the BeanBox which target method to invoke when a source event is fired.

Now that we have made the **CarBean** react to the changing states of the **TrafficLightBean**, you should be able to see action immediately. Notice that as the **TrafficLightBean** is changing states, the **CarBean** changes images to illustrate the behavior. At the same time, you should see messages that display the **CarBean**'s current speed and the signal it's receiving.

Next, we want to prevent the **CarBean** from speeding. If you select the **CarBean** now and set its maximum speed to 100 mph, that's the speed at which the **CarBean** will travel. However, you might want to prevent the **CarBean** from going over the speed limit of 60 mph. You can enforce that by making the **RoadPatrolBean** check the value of the **CarBean**'s **maxSpeed** property and prevent it from increasing to over 60 mph. To set this behavior in our example, select the **CarBean**. From the Edit menu, choose the Events submenu, then the vetoableChange submenu, and finally the **vetoableChange** event. Drag the line from the **CarBean** to the **RoadPatrolBean** and click the mouse button. The BeanBox responds with an EventTargetDialog window. Select the **vetoableChange** target method. Now if you try to change the **maxSpeed** property of the **CarBean**, it won't change to a value greater than the **RoadPatrolBean**'s **maxSpeed** property.

Now that we have prevented the **CarBean** from breaking the speed limit, let's give the **RoadPatrolBean** the right to pull the **CarBean** over if it breaks some other law. To do this, the **CarBean** must listen to events generated by the **RoadPatrolBean**. These events are user-defined, so they're different from an AWT event, such as **mouseClicked**. The **RoadPatrolBean** generates **Cop** events that specify which action the car will take. The action could be to pull over or let go.

To establish this relationship between the **CarBean** and the **RoadPatrolBean**, select the **RoadPatrolBean**. From the Edit menu, choose the Events submenu, then the Cop submenu, and finally the **handleCopevent** event. Drag the line from the **RoadPatrolBean** to the **CarBean** and click the mouse button. The BeanBox responds with an EventTargetDialog window. Select the **handleMyCopevent** target method. Now when the **RoadPatrolBean** generates the **Cop** event, depending on the message sent to the **CarBean**, the **CarBean** will either come to a halt or start moving again. How do we get the **RoadPatrolBean** to generate the **Cop** event? For that, we need to put two other existing Beans on the Canvas. Select the **OurButton** Bean to generate events that would trigger the **Cop** events.

Select and drop the **OurButton** Bean from the ToolBox onto the Canvas. Select the Property Sheet and change the button's label to **Pull Over**. Instantiate another **OurButton** Bean and change its label to **Let Go**. Select the Pull Over button. From the Edit menu, choose the Events submenu, then the Mouse submenu, and then the **mouseClicked** event. Drag the generated line to the **RoadPatrolBean** and click the mouse button. From the EventTargetDialog window, select the **pullover** target method. Perform the same steps for the Let Go button, except select the **letGo** target method. Now when you click the Pull Over button, the **RoadPatrolBean** will generate a **Cop** event that forces the **CarBean** to stop; when you click the Let Go button, the **RoadPatrolBean** will generate a **Cop** event that lets the **CarBean** start moving again (see Figure 11-15).

Figure 11-15.
Stopping the
CarBean with
user-defined events.

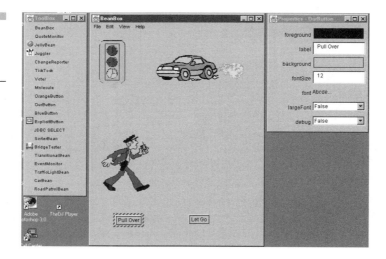

As you have seen, we developed a complete traffic-monitoring system without writing a single line of code. All we did was drag-and-drop some components and link them up.

RAD IDEs

Components are the technology that will take *Rapid Application Development* (RAD) to the next level. The idea behind RAD is to provide a development environment that requires as little coding as possible. Components are key to this technology because they're visual in nature and highly interoperable, their behavior can be detected at runtime, and they are built for reuse. RAD tools have two main features to help you avoid coding—wizards and visual builders.

Wizards guide you through the development by asking questions and getting information. In the background, the wizard builds the application to your specifications. This format is useful for getting a quick start on a simple application, but is far too rigid for serious development. Also, most wizards lack complete explanations of all the choices they have to offer on each screen.

Visual builders have been used successfully for years. *Visual Basic* (VB) became enormously popular because it allowed the programmer to develop Windows applications far faster than coding by hand allowed. First-generation RAD tools such as VB provide drag-and-drop programming for creating GUI programs. Despite Microsoft's repackaging (for example, functions are now called *methods*), it's not object-oriented, and the visual programming stops as soon as you have placed your GUI components on-screen. The rest of the development must be coded by hand.

The next generation of RAD tools has added true object-oriented capabilities and allows developers to create much more of the application in the visual environment.

Java Studio and WorkShop

Java Studio from Sun combines HTML and Java authoring into a powerful desktop productivity tool for Web designers, content creators, and working professionals. *What You See Is What You Publish* (WYSIWYP) translates to "Java For the Rest of Us." Nonprogrammers who must regularly lend their expertise to constructing complex, compelling Internet sites will have over 75 components to choose from in constructing their pages. These components will include GUI, multimedia, and data-aware tables, charts, and graphs. HTML version 3.2 tags are supported along with direct table editing, client-side image maps, and text flow-around images. Perhaps the Java maxim will have to be changed to "Write once, run anywhere, by anyone." Since Corel and Novell have already announced the co-packaging of Java Studio with their upcoming products, soon millions of desktops will be ready to consume the JavaBeans you develop. Java WorkShop 2.0, also from Sun, is the only true multiplatform development environment for Java on the market today. This RAD tool allows developers to create JavaBeans components, applets, and applications incorporating JDK 1.1. The second edition of *Inside Java WorkShop* will cover features new to 2.0.

Open JBuilder

Open JBuilder combines a Java-optimized tool set with RAD concepts pioneered in Borland's Delphi environment. The Visual Component Designer is used to design an applet or application. Simply drag-and-drop components from the component palette onto a form, set its properties, add Java code to handle its events, compile, and presto—instant Java! Like Delphi, JBuilder is a two-way tool, so you can conveniently switch back and forth between visual design and pure Java code, all without any cryptic comments or other do-not-disturb code placeholders.

Visual Age for Java

IBM's Visual Age for Java successfully brings the power of its advanced Parts Workbench technology to Java. Since Smalltalk was the major inspiration for Java's internal design, it's only fitting for a Java IDE to complete the port with this Smalltalk-based approach to development. From the moment you install Visual Age for Java, you realize you're working in a high-quality, world-class environment. I had my first Java "Hello World" program up and running in 10 seconds flat! A Scrapbook window allows you to highlight snippets of code and execute them. The "Hello World" program was literally one line: `System.out.println("Hello World")`. The Scrapbook supplies a compilation context for Java code. The IDE is centered around a Workbench that seamlessly integrates project, package, and class browsers with a syntax-highlighting editor into one continuum —not to mention debugging. IDEs don't come cleaner than this! Also integrated into the environment is a repository and support for team development. The Visual Composition Editor allows you to drag-and-drop components and then interconnect them visually. This two-pronged overall approach to development encourages separating an underlying data module from its various user interface views. This is a superb tool for large-scale corporate development.

CONCLUSION

This chapter has explored some practical issues of Bean development. You learned about available frameworks for designing Beans, then installed the Java Developer's Kit and the JavaBeans Developer's Kit (which you must watch carefully to avoid unnecessary troubleshooting after installation). From there, you took the plunge into visual Bean manipulation with the BeanBox Test Container, using some basic examples.

As you have probably realized by now, JavaBeans can make application development easy if you abstract your components well. Java can make this abstraction easier through interfaces and a clear event-handling delegation model. JavaBeans still needs to mature as a technology, but it's right on track. There is a lot of scope for application frameworks, but nothing that can't be achieved. Soon, application developers will be dragging-and-dropping components on a Canvas and then customizing them.

12

Creating an Application with JavaBeans

In this chapter, we will develop a complex JavaBeans application. Many of the Beans features are illustrated, such as complex event throwing and catching, custom property editors, serialization, and **BeanInfo** classes. We will build a simple Bean from scratch, test it out in the *JavaBeans Developer's Kit* (BDK), and create a complex client-server application using prebuilt Beans and AWT *Graphical User Interface* (GUI) components.

This chapter will cover the following topics:

- A HockeyPool JavaBeans example
- HockeyPool requirements
- HockeyPool design
- Application building
- Client application

A HockeyPool JavaBeans Example

The application we're building is a distributed hockey pool. A hockey pool is a game in which people try to predict which *National Hockey League* (NHL) players will have the most points—the sum of all goals scored and assists made—at the end of the regular or playoff season. The application consists of a client and a server. The client application handles an individual user's request to join the pool, picks players, and shows the updated pool status—who's been picked, whose turn it is, and so forth. The server application receives requests to join the pool and to pick players, and broadcasts the pool updates to each of the clients. Note that this client-server application could easily be adapted to any other distributed multiplayer timed game.

The JavaBeans Developer's Kit provides an environment for connecting Bean properties, events, methods, and testing whether the Beans specifications have been followed. It doesn't supply an environment for building a Bean from scratch or for building robust applications with the AWT. JavaSoft's intention is for third-party tools and other development environments to provide these functions. We will use the BDK to test a simple **Timer** Bean and a third-party development environment for developing the HockeyPool application.

Vision

The first thing we'll look at is the application requirements: a description of the problem and the application. Next comes designing the application solution, when we define the required components and the tools we will use. Finally, we'll go step-by-step through creating the components and the application. We'll delve into one component—the `Timer` Bean—in great detail to demonstrate how to create a standalone component. To create the `Timer` Bean, we'll follow these steps:

■ Build the `Timer` Bean in your favorite text editor or Java compiler.

■ Package the Bean into a JAR file (a Java ARchive file).

■ Import the Bean into the BDK to test the Beans specifications—
Bean info, property editor, and event support.

Then we'll use a visual builder tool to integrate the `Timer` Bean with other GUI components to create a robust application. Using the visual builder, we will do the following:

■ Create a new workspace.

■ Add components to the workspace.

■ Connect component properties, events, and methods.

■ Add nonvisual classes and methods.

■ Test the application.

Outputs

The application consists of several files. Let's take a quick look at what the files are and a short description of them (see Table 12-1).

HockeyPool Requirements

Twice a year, at the start of the regular season and the start of the play-offs, hockey fans around the world get together in groups of a dozen or so for a few hours on a Sunday afternoon or Monday night to pick hockey players (and drink beverages). The prize is the envy of their friends and cold cash. It's often difficult to get all the poolsters together in one room at the same time, so hockey pools are ideal for the Web and Java-based delivery.

Poolsters are the people who participate in the hockey pool. They subscribe to the pool, and then choose players. The poolsters pick in a particular order; then the order reverses itself. This means that in a 10-

Table 12-1.

*Files and File
Descriptions.*

VisibleTimer.java	The **VisibleTimer** Bean
MaximumTimeEditor.java	The property editor for the timer's maximum time
VisibleTimerBeanInfo.java	Bean info file for the **VisibleTimer**
timer.mk	Makefile for building the timer
timer.jar	Java archive file containing the timer
ServerState.java	State of hockey pool; broadcast to all clients
MessageServer.java	Server application; waits for client requests
MessageHandler.java	Server thread for each pool participant
RankedListHandler.java	Utility class for ranking players
BeansDemo.java	The client application class

poolster pool, the order goes 1 through 10, then 10 through 1. We have a shortcut: The starting order is the order in which poolsters downloaded the applet and subscribed to the pool. We limit our pool to 10 poolsters. Some pools are very complicated, with mandatory defensemen, penalty minutes, goalie stats, and so forth. Although this information is very interesting to die-hard fans, it doesn't help demonstrate Beans.

A player can be chosen by only one poolster. The goal of a hockey pool is to pick the players who will have the highest sum of their points, in either the regular season or the playoffs. Pool picking is timed. Usually each poolster is allowed a maximum of two minutes to make a pick. Toward the end of the pool, the picks can take an excruciatingly long time, so a time limit is crucial; that's why a simple timer is incorporated into our application.

Poolsters usually rank the players in the order that they will score points. The hockey pool application supplies a list of available players that the poolster can rank. We time the choosing so that when the time has expired, the top-ranked player is automatically picked for the poolster.

The hockey pool application has three phases. The first phase is sign-up. Interested poolsters start the HockeyPool application and express interest in joining. After the required number of poolsters is registered, the pool-picking phase starts. After all the players have picked the requisite numbers of players, each poolster's picks are stored for later access, perhaps by a hockey pool statistics program or for manual entry.

HockeyPool Design

The HockeyPool Client is a multithreaded application, with a GUI interface consisting of three phases—sign-up, pick, and picking complete. The client application has a moderately complicated GUI with several components:

- The poolster's name
- The last selected player
- The time left for the poolster to pick
- A list of players currently selected by a selected poolster
- An option list to select which poolster's players to look at
- A list of available and ranked players
- A button to select the top-ranked available player
- Buttons to move an available player up or down in ranking
- A button to delete an available player
- A button and text box to add a player to the poolster's available players
- A menu list containg options for joining a pool, saving and loading ranked players, saving selected players, and exiting the application
- A dialog box for users to enter their names and server addresses when joining a pool
- A dialog box for the filename used to save and load ranked or selected players
- A dialog box indicating that a particular player can't be ranked because he's already ranked or picked
- A dialog box indicating that the picking phase has started
- A dialog box indicating that the picking phase is finished

During the picking complete phase, users are asked whether they would like to store their picks in a file.

HockeyPool Server is a multithreaded application, too. It performs these functions:

- Receive registrations during the sign-up process
- Receive pick requests from each client
- Distribute the state of the pool to each client

Timer Component

The **Timer** Bean is a standalone component that can be integrated into any application requiring a visual timer. It has the following properties:

- Counts down the time in seconds.
- Displays the current time.
- Emits an event when the timer strikes 0.
- Has a configurable maximum time; only a few time intervals (15, 30, 45, 60, and 90 seconds) are provided.
- Can be reset to the maximum time.
- Can be enabled or disabled.

Timer Design

For our **VisibleTimer**, we will create a **Timer** class and a property editor for the maximum time. The property editor allows only the specified maximum time intervals to be selected from a development environment's property sheet editor. Because there's a property editor, a **BeanInfo** class must be created; it specifies any property editors or customizers for a particular Bean.

Because the timer is visual, we will use a java.awt.Canvas for the GUI. To implement the time tracking in the Bean, we use threads. Threads can be defined and managed through the Runnable interface, which provides a **run()** method declaration that must be implemented by our class. Table 12-2 shows the properties or attributes of our **Timer**.

The font, background color, and foreground color will be inherited from the **Canvas**. AWT components don't have bound properties—they don't emit a "propery changed" event when a property is changed. We will force our **Canvas**-based **Timer** to emit "property changed" events by overriding the appropriate set methods.

The behavior of our timer is implemented with methods and events. Table 12-3 describes the timer methods. (We don't need to describe the set and get methods for properties at this point.)

Our timer will emit "property change" events sent whenever an editable property in a development environment is changed. The only bound property will be the **maximumTime** event—the "0 seconds left" event. Rather than create our own event type, we will treat "0 seconds left" as a property change. The property change utility package has easy methods for adding listeners to the property listener list and for firing the property change to each event in the list.

Table 12-2.

Timer Properties and Descriptions.

maximumTime	Time to count down from when reset or starting for the first time, in seconds
currentTime	Current time of timer, in seconds
timerEnabled	Indicates whether the timer is enabled
send0SecondsEvent	Indicates if the timer should emit an event when it reaches 0 seconds
timerThread	Thread responsible for counting seconds
send0SecondsEventList	List of listeners to 0 second event
propertyListenerList	List of listeners for property changes

Table 12-3.

VisibleTimer Methods.

resetTimeLeft	Reset the time left to the maximum time
run	Run the thread
paint	Display the time left on the screen.

NOTE   *Creating a new event type would be more difficult due to strongly typed versus weakly typed events. The Java event model is a strongly typed event model—that is, each event listener must be made explicitly aware of what events it's listening for. GUI applications often handle many different types of events, such as property changes and action events. In the* **Timer** *Bean, we simplify this problem by making the property change event handler routine determine the source of the property change and handle it appropriately.*

If we were to create our own event, we would need to do the following:

- Create a new event type: The event is a new class, **TimeExpire**, which is a subclass of the **EventObject**. This class has two constructors: One that takes a message and one that doesn't. The **java.beans.PropertyChangeEvent** and **java.awt.event.Action-Event** are two examples.

- Create the event type listener interface: This interface must contain a method declaration that will be called whenever the event occurs. The java.beans.propertyChangeListener and java.awt.event.ActionListener interfaces are two examples.

■ Handle the strongly typed event: The component that is a sink for the event must implement the event type listener interface and must add itself as a listener for the event type.

NOTE   *We would need to create a new interface, create a new class, and embed handler functions in our containing component for each and every custom event. This would dramatically increase the code size if we have tens or hundreds of custom events.*

Timer Code

As Jerry Maguire would say, show me the code! So, let's take a look at the `VisibleTimer.java`.

Listing 12-1.
VisibleTimer.java

```
package VisibleTimer;

import java.beans.*;
import java.awt.*;
/**
* VisibleTimer, a class to implement a visible timer that
      has bound properties,
* emits an event when zero seconds is reached.
*
*/
public class VisibleTimer extends java.awt.Canvas
      implements Runnable {
    private          int timeLeft = 30;
    private          int maximumTime = 30;
    private          boolean send0SecondsEvent = true;
    private     transient    Thread timerThread = null;
    private          boolean timerEnabled = false;
    private          PropertyChangeSupport
        send0SecondsEventList = new
        PropertyChangeSupport(this);
    private          PropertyChangeSupport
        propertyListenerList = new
        PropertyChangeSupport(this);

    /** Constructor, we do the screen initialization */
    public VisibleTimer()
    {
        super();
```

```
        setFont(new Font("TimesRoman", Font.PLAIN, 14));
        setBackground(Color.lightGray);
        setSize(100,100);
        startTiming();

    }


    /** Add property change listeners for the 0 seconds
        event and the property change events */
    public void addFireAt0SecondsListener(java.beans.
        PropertyChangeListener a0SecondListener) {
        send0SecondsEventList.addPropertyChangeListener
            (a0SecondListener);
        return;
    }
    public void addPropertyChangeListener
        (PropertyChangeListener newListener) {

propertyListenerList.addPropertyChangeListener(newListener);
        return;
    }
    protected void finalize()
    {
        stopTiming();
        timerThread = null;
    }

    /* Set of accessor functions, also known as getters */
    public boolean getFireAt0Seconds(){
        return send0SecondsEvent;
    }
    public int getFontSize() {
        return getFont().getSize();
    }
    public synchronized int getMaximumTime(){
        return maximumTime;
    }
    public synchronized int getTimeLeft(){
        return timeLeft;
    }
    public synchronized boolean isTimerEnabled()
    {
        return timerEnabled;
    }

    /* Draw the time left in the paint method */
    public void paint(Graphics g)
    {
        int width = getSize().width;
        int height = getSize().height;
```

Continues

Listing 12-1.
Continued.

```
        g.draw3DRect(0, 0, width - 1, height - 1, false);
        g.setFont(getFont());
        g.drawRect(2, 2, width - 4, height - 4);

        FontMetrics fm = g.getFontMetrics();
        Integer Time = new Integer(timeLeft);
        String timeString = new String( Time.toString());
        g.drawString( timeString,
            (width - fm.stringWidth(timeString)) / 2,
                (height + fm.getMaxAscent() -
                    fm.getMaxDescent()) / 2);
    }

    /* Remove the property listeners */
    public void removeFireAt0SecondsListener
        (PropertyChangeListener l) {
        send0SecondsEventList.
            removePropertyChangeListener(l);
    }
    public void removePropertyChangeListener
        (PropertyChangeListener l) {

propertyListenerList.removePropertyChangeListener(l);
    }
    public void resetTimeLeft()
    {
        setTimeLeft(maximumTime);
    }
    public void run()
    {
        try {
        while(true) {
                /* A classic poll/sleep combo.
                Loop until timer is enabled, then sleep
                    for 1 second
                Could be done by a wait */
                while ( !isTimerEnabled()) {
                    Thread.sleep(100);
                }
                timerThread.sleep(1000);
                setTimeLeft( getTimeLeft() - 1 );
                repaint();
            }
        } catch (InterruptedException e) {
        }
        timerThread = null;
    }

    /* Property change methods, aka setters */
    public void setFireAt0Seconds( boolean newValue )
    {
        boolean oldValue = send0SecondsEvent;
```

Listing 12-1.
Continued.

```java
            send0SecondsEvent = newValue;
            propertyListenerList.firePropertyChange
                ("send0SecondsEvent",
                new Boolean(oldValue), new Boolean(newValue)
                    );
    }
    /**
    * Set the current font
    */
    public void setFont(Font newFont) {
        Font oldFont = getFont();
        super.setFont(newFont);
        propertyListenerList.firePropertyChange("font",
            oldFont, newFont);
    }
    /**
    * Set current font's size.
    */
    public void setFontSize(int newFontSize) {
        Font oldFont = getFont();
        setFont(new Font(oldFont.getName(),
            oldFont.getStyle(), newFontSize));
        propertyListenerList.firePropertyChange("fontSize",
            new Integer(oldFont.getSize()), new
                Integer(newFontSize));
    }
    public void setMaximumTime( int newMaxTime )
    {
        Integer oldMaxTime = new Integer(maximumTime);
        maximumTime = newMaxTime;
        propertyListenerList.firePropertyChange(
            "maximumTime", oldMaxTime, new
            Integer(maximumTime));

    }
    /**
    * Set the time left. If 0 seconds is reached at there
        are listeners, fire
    * the 0 seconds left event
    */
    public synchronized void setTimeLeft(int timeRemaining)
        {
        int oldTime = timeLeft;
        timeLeft = timeRemaining;

        if( timeRemaining == 0 && getFireAt0Seconds() )
        {
            send0SecondsEventList.firePropertyChange
            ("0SecondsLeft", null, null);
        }
```

Continues

Listing 12-1.
Continued.

```
        // fire time change to any interested parties
        propertyListenerList.firePropertyChange("TimeLeft",
            null, null );
        return;


    }
    /** Enable/Disable the timer. If the timer changes
        state, the thread needs to be
    * either suspended or resumed, depending upon the
        original and new state.
    */
    public synchronized void setTimerEnabled(boolean
        isEnabled)
    {
        timerEnabled = isEnabled;


    }
    public synchronized void startTiming() {

        if (timerThread == null) {
            timerThread = new Thread(this);
            timerThread.start();
        }
        timerEnabled = true;
    }
    /**
    * Stop the timer thread.
    */
    public synchronized void stopTiming() {
        timerEnabled = false;
        repaint();
    }
}
```

MaximumTimeEditor

We need to create a maximum time editor property sheet class, named
MaximumTimeEditor. JavaSoft added a **java.bean.PropertyEditorSupport**
class to provide a simple way of creating a property editor. There are two
useful benefits of **PropertyEditorSupport**: A list of propertyChange-
Listeners and a **firePropertyChange()** method that notifies the listeners.

A property editor shouldn't modify the properties directly. Instead, it
should store a copy of the property for modification and notify any listeners when the copy changes. The **setValue(Object value)** method
sends the copy of the property to the property editor. After receiving a

property change notification, the listener calls the `getValue()` method on the property editor, and then calls the Bean's set property function—also known as a *setter*—to set the property value. The `PropertyEditorSupport` will implement this design, and the BeanBox is a valid listener.

The `MaximumTimeEditor` has only a few options, or *pick list*, which is constructed from a set of valid tagged names. The property editor must override the `getTags()` method to return a string array with all the valid property values. `getTags()` returns a list of strings, which are valid entries in the maximum time property box. Bean development environments will call the `getTags()` method of classes listed in the property descriptor list of `BeanInfo` files.

The `MaximumTime` property is an integer, so we also need to create functions to convert the integers to string values. The `getAsText()` and `setAsText(String)` methods convert the property value's textual representation to and from the property's actual type. These methods must read and write from the property's local copy. The `setAsText()` method must also call the `firePropertyChange()` method.

In your favorite text editor or Java *Integrated Development Environment* (IDE), create the `MaximumTimeEditor.java` file in Listing 12-2.

Listing 12-2.
MaximumTime-
Editor.java.

```
package VisibleTimer;

/**
 * MaximumTimeEditor Class provides a getTags method for the
         valid maximum
 * seconds property of the VisibleTimer class
 *
 */
public class MaximumTimeEditor extends
      java.beans.PropertyEditorSupport {
    int tempMaxTime = 0;

    public String getAsText() {
        return String.valueOf(tempMaxTime);

    }
    public String[] getTags() {
        String[] result = {
            "15", "30", "60", "120" };
            return result;
    }
    /**
```

Continues

Listing 12-2.
Continued.

```
 * @return the value of the property.
 */
public Object getValue() {

    return new Integer(tempMaxTime);
}
public void setAsText(String text) throws
    IllegalArgumentException {
    tempMaxTime = Integer.parseInt(text);
    firePropertyChange();
}
/**
 *    Set maximumTime value that is to be edited.
 * Note that this object should not be modified by the
        PropertyEditor,
 * rather the PropertyEditor should create a new object
 * to hold any modified value.
 */
public void setValue(Object value) {

    tempMaxTime = ((Integer)value).intValue();
}
}
```

The `BeanInfo` Class

To describe changes to the default characteristics of our Bean, such as custom property editors, we must create a `BeanInfo` class that allows any arbitrary development environment to import our Bean. The `BeanInfo` file is the cornerstone of the new *design-time mode*. This mode precedes compile-time and runtime modes. In the spirit of making simple things simpler, JavaSoft has provided a `java.beans.SimpleBeanInfo` that makes creating a `BeanInfo` file easy. We don't need to create an event list or custom icons, but they're easy to add. All we must do is change the default property descriptors to add our custom property editor.

The last class for the timer is its `BeanInfo` class. It must be named `<classname>BeanInfo` to correspond to a particular class name, and it's a subclass of the `SimpleBeanInfo` class. We will create a single method, `getPropertyDescriptors()`, to return the list of `PropertyDescriptors` that are valid for the Bean. Each `PropertyDescriptor` contains the property name, the class the property belongs to, and a class to handle the property editing. The Bean development environments will call the `getPropertyDescriptors()` method for the list of property descriptors, then call `getTags()` on each descriptor.

```
package VisibleTimer;

import java.beans.*;
/**
 * VisibleTimerBeanInfo is the bean info for the Visible
      Timer
 * getPropertyDescriptors is used to specify the properties
      that are visible
 * in a BDK, and any property editors associated with them
 *
 */
public class VisibleTimerBeanInfo extends
      java.beans.SimpleBeanInfo {

    public PropertyDescriptor[] getPropertyDescriptors() {
         try {


              // Construct a PropertyDescriptor for a
                    property that has setX and getX
                    accessors.
              // Methods setMaximumTime()  and
                    getMaximumTime() must exist.
              // The property name must start with a lower
                    case character. It will be
              // capitalized for the get and set methods.

              PropertyDescriptor maximumTime = new
                    PropertyDescriptor("maximumTime",
                    VisibleTimer.class);
              maximumTime.setPropertyEditorClass
                    (MaximumTimeEditor.class);


              // Alternatively, another form of
                    PropertyDescriptor takes the method
                    names for
              // the get and set methods of the property.
                    In this case the property name may
              // or may not correspond to an actual property
                    name. This is useful for
              // displaying a text string with spaces in the
                    development environment, or
              // for

              PropertyDescriptor background =
                    new PropertyDescriptor("background color",
                         VisibleTimer.class,
                    "getBackground", "setBackground");
              PropertyDescriptor font =
```

Continues

Listing 12-3.
Continued.

```
                      new PropertyDescriptor("font",
                          VisibleTimer.class);
                  maximumTime.setBound(true);

                  PropertyDescriptor result[] = { maximumTime,
                          background, font,  };
                  return result;
          } catch (Exception ex) {
              System.err.println("VisibleTimerBeanInfo:
                      unexpected exception: " + ex);
              return null;
          }
      }
  }
```

Makefile

The final step in creating a Bean is packaging it into a JAR file. The terms *jar file*, *JAR file*, *JAR*, and *Java Archive* all refer to the same thing. The JAR contains a *manifest*, or list of contents, that includes the class files and any auxiliary files, such as images, movies, sounds, or any other media files. Our JAR will hold the **Timer** class, the timer's **BeanInfo**, and the **MaximumTimeEditor** property editor. In Listing 12-4, we create a makefile that handles compiling .java files as well as packaging the .class into a .jar file.

There are some subtleties in constructing the JAR:

- Manifest Name entities have forward slashes (**/**). This is a clear example of the UNIX background of Sun and JavaSoft.

- Blank lines are required between Name entities in the manifest.

- The files in the JAR must be loaded from the correct relative directory level. Therefore, the **jar** command must be run from the directory directly above any files used. For example, **jar cfm myjar.jar dave\demo\timer.class** will add **timer.class** to the correct relative directory in the JAR.

- A separate manifest file can be used. Keeping the manifest in the makefile keeps all the information about the files in the JAR in one file.

- The BeanBox has a menu option to load JARs manually. For our simple example, adding a JAR to the **bdk\jars** directory doesn't affect the performance of the BeanBox much. For those with many JARs, performance reasons might dicate loading manually.

**Listing 12-4.
timer.mk.**

```
# The makefile for the visible TimerBean.

CLASSFILES= \
    VisibleTimer\VisibleTimer.class \
    VisibleTimer\MaximumTimeEditor.class \
    VisibleTimer\VisibleTimerBeanInfo.class

DATAFILES=

JARFILE= visibletimer.jar

all: $(JARFILE)

# Create a JAR file with a suitable manifest.

$(JARFILE): $(CLASSFILES) $(DATAFILES)
    jar cfm $(JARFILE) <<manifest.tmp VisibleTimer\*.class
Name: VisibleTimer/VisibleTimer.class
Java-Bean: True
<<
    copy $(JARFILE) c:\bdk\jars

SUFFIXES: .java .class

{VisibleTimer}.java{VisibleTimer}.class :
    set CLASSPATH=.
    javac $<

clean:
    -del VisibleTimer\*.class
    -del $(JARFILE)
```

Building the JAR

Now that we have the .java files and the makefile, all we have to do is build the Bean. Make sure your **CLASSPATH** environment variable references the JDK 1.1 class files and your **PATH** environment variable references the JDK 1.1 binary path, as well the BDK directories:

```
PATH=c:\jdk1.1\bin; c:\bdk\bin
CLASSPATH=c:\jdk1.1\lib\classes.zip; c:\bdk\beanbox\classes
```

We must also have the nmake utility installed. It can be found at the Microsoft FTP site, under the Softlib\MSLFILES directory. The URL is **ftp://ftp_microsoft.com/softlib/mslfiles/nmake15.exe**. Then run nmake15 after downloading by typing:

```
C:>nmake15
```

Next, create the **visibletimer.jar** file by typing:

```
C:>nmake -f Timer.mk
```

Testing the Bean

The Bean can now be tested in any Bean development environment. We will use the BDK from JavaSoft. We will also create a simple test application using our Bean. The test application starts and stops the timer and reflects the timer's property changes in a text area.

The BDK uses JARs found in the **jars** directory under the **bdk** directory, usually **c:\bdk\jars**. Notice that the makefile automatically copies the JAR into this directory.

All classes imported into the BDK should have package names. The April 1997 release of the BeanBox uses the tmp.sun.beanbox package for all default packages in handler code. Of course, this means that default packages aren't supported properly. Figure 12-1 shows the BeanBox with our simple test application.

To test the Bean, first run the BeanBox by double-clicking the **run.bat** file in the \bdk\beanbox directory or changing directories to **\bdk\beanbox** and then typing **run.bat.** Three frames of the BeanBox will be displayed. The left frame is the ToolBox, which has a palette of prebuilt parts. The center frame is the graphical area for adding and editing components. The

Figure 12-1.
Test application in
the BeanBox.

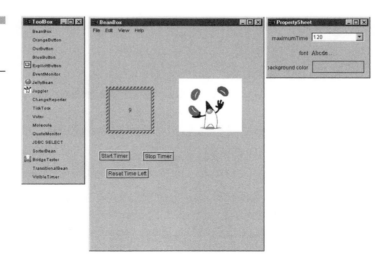

right frame is the Property Sheet that shows the properties of the selected Bean.

Now add the `VisibleTimer` to the BeanBox. To do this, select the `VisibleTimer` from the toolbox, then select the location for it in the Bean-Box.

The next step is to add three `ourButton` controls and the `Juggler` component from the ToolBox to the BeanBox. The first button we're adding is the Stop button, so label the first button control `Stop`.

To activate the Stop button, connect its `actionPerformed` event to the `stopTiming()` method of the `VisibleTimer`. Start by selecting the Stop button, and you'll see a pop-up menu. Choose the Edit | Events | button-Push | actionPerformed menu item. You will now see a red line, which you attach to the `VisibleTimer`. The EventTargetDialog box opens; select the `stopTiming()` method, then click the OK button.

Label the second button control `Start` and connect its `actionPerformed` event to the `startTiming()` method of the `VisibleTimer` in the same manner. For the final button, label it `Reset Time`. Connect its `actionPerformed` event to the `resetTimeLeft()` method of the `VisibleTimer`.

Finally, connect the `fireAt0Seconds` event of the `VisibleTimer` to the `fireAction()` method of the Reset Time button so our timer will never go into negative time.

We will now bind a property in one component to a property in another component. Select the `VisibleTimer` and you'll see a pop-up menu. Choose the Edit | Bind property menu item to open the PropertyName-Dialog box. Select the `maximumTime` property from the list of properties, and click the OK button. You should see the familiar red line. Select the `Juggler` and you'll see the PropertyNameDialog box. Select the `animationRate` property from the list, and click the OK button. We have now bound the `maximumTime` property to the `Juggler`'s animation rate.

Try playing with the Bean: Start the timer, stop the timer, set the maximum time, reset the time. If everything seems to work, save the Bean-Box environment by choosing the File | Save menu item. Enter a valid filename with a .SER extension in the Filename area. The .SER extension denotes a serialized file and is a customary (but not required) extension.

Building the Application

Now we will create a robust client-server multiperson HockeyPool application. We will use IBM's *Visual Age for Java* (VAJ) as the JavaBeans

IDE. At the time of this writing, there are few fully Beans-compliant development environments, but we expect that many will emerge. We'll start with a brief description of how to use Visual Age for Java, then describe the steps for creating the application. We will try to keep the steps development-environment-neutral so that any IDE can be used. (A copy of VAJ is on the CD-ROM that comes with this book.)

Visual Age Commands

VAJ has several major components. We won't go into the details of all its features, just the ones we will be using. VAJ has an incremental compiler, which means that any changes to a method are compiled when saved. Any running executables will be updated with the new compiled code. The key components we will use are the Workbench and the Composition Editor.

The Workbench has a list of all the projects, packages, classes, interfaces, unresolved problems, and methods in the workspace. The Java elements can be edited in the workspace, or the Composition Editor component can be used on a particular package or class.

The Composition Editor has a graphical view for creating components with the usual palette of components, a visual application view, and a property sheet editor.

To build our application, we will be using the Composition Editor and the Workbench. Let's look first at what we will do in the Composition Editor. We add components to the Composition Editor by selecting the component from the palette, and then selecting the location for the component in the composition view. We set properties by double-clicking a component, and then changing the specific property in the popup menu.

We also connect events, methods, and properties. To connect an event from one object to a method on another object, select the source object and then click the right mouse button. You will see an Options pop-up menu. Choose the Connect menu item, and you will see the Connection Options pop-up menu. This menu lists commonly used methods and actions, as well as an "All features" option that displays the All Features dialog box, which lists all the available methods, properties, and events for the class, including any parent classes. Select the available event. A dotted line is displayed. Select the target object of the dotted line to bring up the All Features dialog box. Select the property, method, or event of the target object. The connection is now visible.

Most methods require parameters, and these parameters can be connected visually. The instructions are the same as those in the preceding discussion, except that the target object is a connection between two objects. The target property will be a connection property, and the connection only has properties corresponding to the method arguments on the target object's method.

To set the font for any components added to a frame, simply set the font for the frame. Any components added to it will use the frame's font.

To add objects to the Composition Editor, choose the Options | Add Part menu item in the Composition Editor. Select the object's class by typing in the class name or by browsing the list of classes, then clicking the OK button. Select the location of the object. Canvases and panels can be placed on the frame, but nonvisual Beans must not be placed on any frames, canvases, or menus.

The Workbench also offers considerable functionality. We import .java files by choosing the Workbench's File | Import menu item to open the Import Files dialog box. Enter the project name in the first text box. Click the browse button by the list box, and a File dialog box is displayed. Select the .java files to import, and then click the OK button. The .java files are imported and compiled into the selected project.

Export a VAJ project file to .java or .class files by selecting the project, package, or classes to export. Choose the File | Export menu item to open the Export to Files dialog box. Click the browse button. A File dialog box is displayed. Select the output format—.java or .class. Select the target directory, and click the OK button. The specified project, package, or classes are exported to the selected output format.

For our example, we add methods to classes by selecting. Choose the Selected | Add methods menu item to bring up the Method Properties dialog box. Enter the method interface information, and click the Finished button. This creates the method in the class and opens the method in the Workbench for editing.

HockeyPool Application Roadmap

We will go through building the HockeyPool client-server application step-by-step. We will import required Java files, specifically the nonvisual files and the **visibleTimer**. Then we will populate the client application with components, connect them, and test the client application. The list of components we will produce is given earlier in this chapter. Then we will create the server application, test it by itself, and integrate it with the client application. Figure 12-2 shows the completed client application in the VAJ Composition Editor; Figure 12-3 shows the running client application.

Figure 12-2.
Client in Visual Age
for Java.

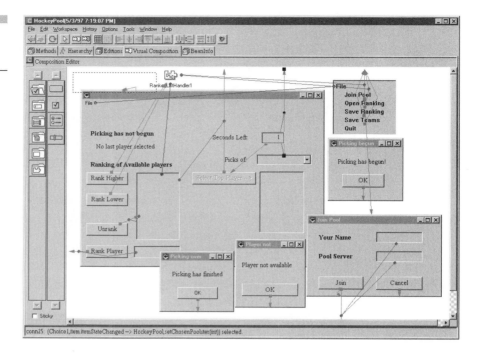

Figure 12-3.
Client application.

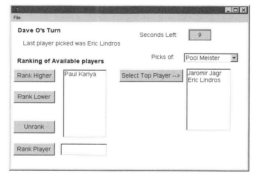

Client Application

In this section, we will create the client application. Start the visual builder—VAJ in our case—and create a new project and applet. Call both the project and the applet "HockeyPool." VAJ prompts you at startup to create a new applet, so select the Create Applet option. Bring up the Visual Builder when prompted. The HockeyPool project with a default package containing the **HockeyPool** class is in the Workbench.

Import the `VisibleTimer.java` files into the HockeyPool project. When that's finished, you will see a new package, the VisibleTimer, in the HockeyPool project in the Workbench. Reduce the applet GUI size. The applet is a panel; since we will be using a frame for menu components, the panel should be minimized.

We can now add some components to the GUI, all in Times Roman, 14 point font. To add a component, select the item in the palette, then click on the location you want. The results are shown in Figure 12-2. Applets are panels and can't have menus, so we need a frame. Add a frame and set the frame's title to `HockeyPool Client`. You will see it listed as `Frame0`. Set the Frame's font to Times Roman, 14 point.

Now create a label for the poolster's name. Set the initial text to `Picking has not begun`. You see it as `Label1`. Then create a label for the last selected player with the initial text `Player picked:`. You see it as `Label2`. Next, create a label for ranking available players with the text `Ranking of Available Players` in bold, which you see as `Label3`.

Create a label for the "time left" string with the initial text `Seconds remaining:`. You see it as `Label4`. Create a label for the "Picks of" string, with the text `Picks of:`; you see it as `Label5`. Create a choice list to select which poolster's players to view, which you see as `Choice1`. Create a list of players currently chosen by a selected poolster; you see it as `List1`. Create a list of available and ranked players, which you see as `List2`.

Create a button, Button1, to select the top-ranked available player, labeled `Select Top Player->`, and the `Enabled` property should be disabled. Create `Button2` and `Button3` to move an available player up or down in ranking, and label them `Rank Higher` and `Rank Lower`. Create a button labeled `Unrank` to delete an available player; you see it as `Button4`. Create a button labeled `Rank Player` and a text field to add a player to the poolster's available players; you see them as `Button5` and `TextField1`. Create a menu bar belonging to `frame0`; you see it as `menu1`. You will now see the frame, a menu bar, and a line connecting the frame to `menu1`.

Change the menu bar's single menu list to contain the text `File`, and then add some menu items to the File menu list. The first menu item added is labeled `Join a pool`, with the `actionCommand` of `Join`; you see it as `MenuItem1`. The next menu item is `Open Ranking`, with the `actionCommand` of `OpenRanking`; you see it as `MenuItem2`. The next menu item is `Save Ranking`, with the `actionCommand` of `SaveRanking`; you see it as `MenuItem3`. Another menu item is `Save Teams`, with the `actionCommand` of `SaveTeams`; you see as `MenuItem4`. The final menu item is `Exit`, with the `actionCommand` of `Exit`; you see it as `MenuItem5`.

Then create a dialog box indicating that a particular player can't be ranked because he's already ranked or picked. The dialog box is titled

Player not available; you see it as **Dialog1**. Create a button labeled **OK**, which you see as **Button6**. Create a label with the text **Player already ranked or selected**, which you see as **Label6**.

Create a dialog box indicating that the picking phase has begun, with the text **Picking has begun!**, and a button labeled **OK**, which you see as **Dialog2**, **Button7**, and **Label7**.

Create a dialog box indicating that the picking phase is finished, with the text **Picking has finished** and the button labeled **OK**; you see them as **Dialog3**, **Button8**, and **Label8**.

Next, create a dialog box for the Join request and two labels with the text **Your Name** and **Pool Server**, which you see as **Label9** and **Label10**. Create two text fields, which you see as **TextField2** and **TextField3**, and two buttons labeled **OK** and **Cancel**, which you see as **Button9** and **Button10**.

Then add the time left for the player to pick. Select the Add Part menu item, then specify **VisibleTimer** as the class name.

Now that all the GUI components are in place, we need to add the non-visual components. These provide the functions that we will link to the GUI components. First, add the **ServerState** componen; this class encapsulates the state of the HockeyPool. The state is broadcast to the client whenever it changes, such as when poolsters join or make picks.

The class has a few methods beyond the property set and the constructors. The method **addPick()** adds a validated player to the current poolster's selection, and **addPoolster()** adds a poolster to the current pool. The **isPlayerAvailable()** method checks whether the player has been selected by a poolster, and **setNextPoolster()** moves the pick to the next poolster in order.

Import the **ServerState.java** file into the HockeyPool project (see Listing 12-5).

Next we import the **RankedListHandler** class. It encapsulates the ranked list in the frame. Any access to the ranked list, such as adding, deleting, or ranking players, or saving/restoring the list from a stream, uses this class.

Now we add the **RankedListHandler** class to the Composition Editor. Use the **add part** command, specify **RankedListHandler** class, and place it in the Composition Editor, which displays **RankedListHandler1**.

Next, import the java.net, java.io, java.util, and java.lang packages into HockeyPool.java. The code we add looks like the following:

```
import java.net.*;
import java.io.*;
import java.util.*;
import java.lang.*;
```

Listing 12-5.
ServerState.java.

```java
import java.io.*;
import java.util.*;
/**
 * ServerState class.  Encapsulates the state of the Hockey
 *     Pool.
 * Numerous properties: list of poolsters, vector of vector
 *     of picks by poolsters, current round
 * current poolster, whether picking has commenced
 */
public class ServerState implements java.io.Serializable {
    private      String lastPlayerSelected = null;
    private      Vector poolsterNames; // Name of entrants
    private      Vector poolsterPicks; // All the picks
            made
    private       boolean pickingPlayers = false; // True if
            picking is occuring
    private       boolean pickingOver = false; // True of
            picking is over
    private       int currentRound = 0; // current round,
            starts at 0
    private       int currentPoolster = 0; // current
            poolster in round, starts at 0
    private final      int maxRounds = 3; // Maximum number
            of rounds
    private final      int maxPoolsters = 2; // Maximum
            number of poolsters
    // The number of picks will be maxRounds *
            maxPoolsters, so 6 players total will be picked
    private final      String[] rankedPlayers = {"Joe
            Sakic", "Jaromir Jagr", "Eric Lindros", "Paul
            Kariya"};

    // Initialize the server state
    public ServerState()
    {
        poolsterNames = new Vector();
        poolsterPicks = new Vector();
    }
    /**
     * Copy constructor.  Needed due to bug in JDK 1.1.1
     *     where thread cannot broadcast state.
     * Seems object to be serialized's reference must be on
     *     the stack
     */
    public ServerState( ServerState origState)
    {
        // Copy the last player selected
        setLastPlayerSelected(
            origState.getLastPlayerSelected());
        // Copy the poolsterNames vector
```

Continues

Listing 12-5.
Continued.

```
      poolsterNames =
            (Vector)origState.getPoolsterNames().clone();

      poolsterPicks = new Vector();

      // Copy each vector in the original ServerState's
            poolsterPicks vector to
      // the new poolsterPicks vector
      Vector tempVector;
      for( int i = 0; i <
origState.getPoolsterPicks().size(); i++)
      {
            tempVector = (Vector)origState.
                  getPoolsterPicks().elementAt(i);
            poolsterPicks.addElement(
(Vector)tempVector.clone());
      }
      currentPoolster = origState.getCurrentPoolster();
      currentRound = origState.getCurrentRound();
      pickingPlayers = origState.isPickingPlayers();
      pickingOver = origState.isPickingOver();
   }
   /**
   * Add a validated pick. This method assumes that the
         playerName is valid
   */
   public synchronized void addPick( String playerName )
   {
      Vector currentPoolsterPicksVector = (Vector)
            (poolsterPicks.elementAt(currentPoolster));
      currentPoolsterPicksVector.addElement( playerName
            );
      setLastPlayerSelected(new String(playerName));
   }
   /**
   * Add a poolster to the pool. If maximum players
         reached, set pickingPlayers
   */
   public synchronized boolean addPoolster( String
      poolsterName )
   {
      // Check to see if in picking state
      if( !pickingPlayers && !pickingOver )
      {
         poolsterNames.addElement(poolsterName);
         poolsterPicks.addElement(new Vector());
         Vector temp = (Vector)(poolsterPicks.
               elementAt(0));
         if( poolsterNames.size() == maxPoolsters )
         {
               pickingPlayers = true;
         }
```

Listing 12-5.
Continued.

```
                return true;
        }
        else
        {
            return false;
        }
    }

    /** The accessor, or getter methods for the state */
    public int getCurrentPoolster()
    {
        return currentPoolster;
    }
    public int getCurrentRound()
    {
        return currentRound;
    }
    public String getLastPlayerSelected()
    {
        return lastPlayerSelected;
    }
    public Vector getPoolsterNames()
    {
        return poolsterNames;
    }
    public Vector getPoolsterPicks()
    {
        return poolsterPicks;
    }
    public String[] getRankedPlayers()
    {
        return rankedPlayers;
    }
    public boolean isPickingOver()
    {
        return pickingOver;
    }
    public boolean isPickingPlayers()
    {
        return pickingPlayers;
    }
    /**
    * Check if playerName is available for selection.
    * Loop through the double-indexed vector of
    *     poolsterPicks
    * Return true if parameter is not in vector
    */
    public synchronized boolean isPlayerAvailable( String
        playerName )
    {
        // Need to check for duplicates in picked players
```

Continues

Listing 12-5.
Continued.

```
        for( int i = 0; i < poolsterPicks.size(); i++ )
        {
            Vector poolsterVector =
                (Vector)poolsterPicks.elementAt(i);
            for( int j = 0; j < poolsterVector.size();
                j++ )
            {
                if(
poolsterVector.elementAt(j).equals(playerName ))
                {
                    return false;
                }
            }
        }
        return true;
    }
    public void setLastPlayerSelected( String player )
    {
        if( player != null )
        {
            lastPlayerSelected = new String(player);
        }
    }
    /**
    * Adjust the currentRound and currentPoolster variables
        to next poolster. If all
    * picks are complete, set the pickingPlayers and
        pickingOver booleans.
    */
    public synchronized void setNextPoolster()
    {
        if(currentRound == maxRounds - 1 &&
            currentPoolster == 0 )
        {
            // We have odd # of rounds, so poolster == 0
                is last pick in odd rounds
            pickingPlayers = false;
            pickingOver = true;
        }
        if( (currentRound % 2) == 0 )
        {
            // On even rounds, we loop forward through
                poolsters
            if( currentPoolster == maxPoolsters - 1) {
                currentRound++; // Last pick of round, so
                    next round
            } else {
                currentPoolster++;
            }
        }
        else
        {
```

Listing 12-5.
Continued.

```
                   // On Odd rounds, we loop back through
                       poolsters
                   if( currentPoolster == 0 )
                   {
                       currentRound++; // last pick of round, so
                           next round
                   }
                   else
                   {
                       currentPoolster-;
                   }
               }
           }
    }
```

Listing 12-6.
RankedListHandler.
java.

```
import java.io.*;
import java.awt.List;
/**
* RankedListHandler. Encapsulates a java.awt.list so that
    it can be serialized.
* The Handler enables the visible awt list component to be
    kept, rather than
* deleted and re-instantiated when it is the list read from
    disk
* Handles adding, moving, deleting items, and reading and
    writing the
* list to a steam.
*/
public class RankedListHandler implements
    java.io.Serializable {
    private     List list = null;

    public RankedListHandler()
    {
        list = null;
    }
    public RankedListHandler(java.awt.List thisList )
    {
        list = thisList;
    }
    public List getList( )
    {
        return list;
    }
    /**
    * Move selected item down 1 place in list
    */
```

Continues

Listing 12-6.
Continued.

```
public void moveItemDown1( )
{
    if( list == null ) {
        return;
    }

    // Get the selected index
    int selectedIndex = list.getSelectedIndex();
    if( selectedIndex == -1 )
    {
        return;
    }

    // Add the selected item 2 after the index,
    // Then delete the selected index.
    list.addItem( list.getSelectedItem(), selectedIndex
        + 2 );
    list.remove(selectedIndex  );
    list.select( selectedIndex + 1);
}
/**
* Move selected item up 1 place in list
*/
public void moveItemUp1( )
{
    if( list == null ) {
        return;
    }
    int selectedIndex = list.getSelectedIndex();
    if( selectedIndex == -1 || selectedIndex == 0 )
    {
        return;
    }

    // Add the selected item before the item before
        the selected item
    list.addItem( list.getSelectedItem(), selectedIndex
        - 1 );
    list.remove(selectedIndex + 1 );
    list.select( selectedIndex - 1);
}
private void readObject(ObjectInputStream stream)
    throws IOException
{
    if( list == null ) {
        list = new List();
    }
    else {
        list.removeAll();
    }
    int count;
    // Read the number of items of the stream
    // Then read each item of the stream and add it to
```

Listing 12-6.
Continued.

```
            the list
      try {
          count = stream.readInt();
          for( int i = 0; i< count; i++ ) {
              list.add((String)stream.readObject());
          }
      }
      catch( Exception e ) {
      //        throw e;
      }

  }
  public void setList( List newList )
  {
      if( list == null ) {
          list = newList;
          return;
      }
  }
  public void setListWithState( List newList, ServerState
      state )
  {
      if( list == null ) {
          list = newList;
          return;
      }
      // need to copy lists
      list.removeAll();
      int count = newList.getItemCount();
      for( int i = 0; i< count; i++ ) {
          if( state.isPlayerAvailable(newList.
              getItem(i)))
          {
              list.add(newList.getItem(i));
          }
      }

  }

  /** Write the list to the stream, Number of items then
      each item in the list */
  private void writeObject(ObjectOutputStream stream)
      throws IOException
  {
      if( list == null ) {
          return;
}
      stream.writeInt(list.getItemCount());
      for( int i = 0; i < list.getItemCount(); i++ ) {
          stream.writeObject( list.getItem(i));
      }
  }
}
```

Change the applet to implement the Runnable interface by adding **implements Runnable** to the applet. The new class declaration should be as follows:

```
public class HockeyPool extends java.applet.Applet
        implements Runnable {
```

Create the instance variables in HockeyPool.java:

```
static   int DEFAULT_PORT = 8000;
private  java.io.ObjectInputStream in = null;
private  java.lang.Thread listener = null;
private  java.io.DataOutputStream out = null;
private  java.net.Socket s = null;
private  ServerState state = null;
private  int chosenPoolster = 0;
private  String myName = null;
```

Now create a **joinPool()** method on the HockeyPool application. It will be called when the Join Pool menu item is selected. It connects to a socket, sends a **JOIN** request, and then spawns a thread to listen for state changes.

Listing 12-7.
The **joinPool()**
method.

```
/**
 * Join a pool. Connect to socket serverURL.
 * If server found, then write a JOIN string followed by
       the name.
 * Start thread upon completion of JOIN request.
 */
public void joinPool( String name, String serverURL) {
    if (this.s == null ) {
        try
        {
            // Create a socket to communicate to the
                  specified host and port
            this.s = new Socket( serverURL, DEFAULT_PORT
                 );
            // Create streams for reading and writing Z
                  objects to
            // and from the socket.

            InputStream tempIn = this.s.getInputStream();
            in = new ObjectInputStream(tempIn);
            out = new DataOutputStream
                 (this.s.getOutputStream());
            out.writeUTF(new String( "JOIN"));
            out.flush();
            out.writeUTF( name);
```

Listing 12-7.
Continued.

```
            out.flush();
            myName = new String( name );
            listener = new Thread(this);
            listener.start();
        } catch ( Exception ex )
        {
            ex.printStackTrace();
        }
    }
    return;
}
```

Next, create an **openRanking()** method. It will be called when the Open
Ranking menu item is selected. It creates the needed streams, reads the
stored **RankedListHandler** (which encapsulates the visible ranked list),
and then calls the existing **RankedListHandler**'s **setListWithState()**
method to swap the retrieved list.

Listing 12-8.
The **openRanking()**
method.

```
/**
 * Open a stored player ranking.
 */
public void openRanking( RankedListHandler currentList ) {
    try {
        FileDialog fd = new FileDialog( new Frame(),
            "Open Ranking", FileDialog.LOAD );
        fd.show();
        String fname = fd.getDirectory() + fd.getFile();
        if( fd.getDirectory() == null || fd.getFile() ==
            null )
        {
            return;
        }

        FileInputStream F = new FileInputStream(fname);
        ObjectInputStream O = new ObjectInputStream(F);
        // Restore the stored RankedListHandler
        RankedListHandler newList =
            (RankedListHandler)O.readObject();
        // Change the currentList to the new list
        currentList.setListWithState(newList.getList(),
            getState());
    } catch (Exception ex)
    {
        ex.printStackTrace();
    }
}
```

Now, create a `saveRanking()` method. It will be called when the Save Ranking menu item is selected. It saves the `RankedListHandler`—and, therefore, the ranked list—to a file.

Now, create a `saveTeams()` method. It will be called when the Save Teams menu item is selected. It saves the current selections in the hockey pool to a file in text format.

The next step is creating a `run()` method. It's called after the thread created in the `joinPool()` method is started. It listens for messages from the server and updates the hockey pool state with the state message received.

Listing 12-9.
The `saveRanking()` method.

```
/**
 * Save player ranking
 */
public void saveRanking( RankedListHandler theList )
{
    try {
        FileDialog fd = new FileDialog( new Frame(), "Save
            Ranking", FileDialog.SAVE );
    fd.show();
        String fname = fd.getDirectory() + fd.getFile();
        if( fd.getDirectory() == null || fd.getFile() ==
            null )
        {
            return;
        }
        FileOutputStream F = new FileOutputStream(fname);
        ObjectOutputStream O = new ObjectOutputStream(F);
        O.writeObject(theList);
        O.flush();
        O.close();
    } catch (Exception ex)
    {
        ex.printStackTrace();
    }
}
```

Listing 12-10.
The `saveTeams()` method.

```
/**
 * Save all teams
 */
public void saveTeams(   )
{
    try {
        FileDialog fd = new FileDialog( new Frame(), "Save
            Teams", FileDialog.SAVE );
        fd.show();
        String fname = fd.getDirectory() + fd.getFile();
        if( fd.getDirectory() == null || fd.getFile() ==
```

```
            null )
            {
                return;
            }
        FileOutputStream F = new FileOutputStream(fname);
        PrintStream O = new PrintStream(F);
        Vector poolsterPicks =
            getState().getPoolsterPicks();
        for( int i = 0; i < poolsterPicks.size(); i++ )
        {
            O.println( ((String)(getState()
            .getPoolsterNames().elementAt(i))) +
            "'s team" );
            Vector poolsterVector = z
                (Vector)poolsterPicks.elementAt(i);
            for( int j = 0; j < poolsterVector.size(); j++ )
            {
                O.println( (String)
                    (poolsterVector.elementAt(j)) );
            }
        }
        O.flush();
        O.close();
    } catch (Exception E)
    {}
}
```

```
/**
 * Run method for the thread created when a pool is joined.
     Listens for state
 * broadcasts from the server and updates the state when
     received.
 */
public void run() {
    try {
        while( true ) {
            Object o = in.readObject();
            setState( (ServerState)o );
        }
    } catch (Exception ex)     {
        ex.printStackTrace();
    } finally {
        listener = null;
        try {
            out.close ();
        } catch (Exception ex) {
            ex.printStackTrace ();
        }
    }
    return;
}
```

Now, create a `rankPlayer()` method. It's called whenever the Rank Player button is clicked. It checks the entered player name against the list of currently ranked players and the currently chosen players to make sure duplicates aren't allowed. Valid player names are added to the ranked list of players.

Next, create a `makeSelection()` method. It's called when the timer expires or the Pick Top Player button is clicked. It sends a pick request to the server. The player selected is the top item in the sourceList or the string "No player selected" if there are no items in the sourceList.

Listing 12-12.
The `rankPlayer()`
method.

```
/**
 * Add a player to the ranking if available, otherwise pop
     up the player
 * not available dialog box
 */
public void rankPlayer(String s) {
    String[] tempString = getList2().getItems();
    for( int i = 0; i< tempString.length; i++ )
    {
        if( tempString[i].equals(s) )
        {
            getDialog1().show();
            return;
        }
    }
    if (!getState().isPlayerAvailable(s))
    {
        getDialog2().show();
    }
    getList2().addItem(s);
    return;
}
```

Listing 12-13.
`makeSelection()`
method.

```
/**
 * Make a player selection. Sends a pick request to the
       server. The player
 * selected is the top item in the sourceList, or the
       string "No player selected"
 * if there are no items in the sourceList.
 */
public void makeSelection( java.awt.List sourceList )
{
    String selectedPlayer;

    if( sourceList.getItemCount() == 0 ) {
        selectedPlayer = "No player selected";
    } else {
```

Listing 12-13.
Continued.

```
            selectedPlayer = sourceList.getItem(0);
        }
        try {
            out.writeUTF("PICK");
            out.flush();
            out.writeUTF(selectedPlayer);
            out.flush();
        } catch (Exception ex)      {
            ex.printStackTrace();
        }
    }
}
```

Now, create the `refreshState()` method. It's called in the `setState()` method. It refreshes the user interfaces with the new pool state. It updates the Last Player Selected label, the Current Pick label, the Poolster List choice, the Ranked Players list, the enabling of the Select Player button, the enabling of the `Timer`, and the Players Selected list.

Next, create a `setChosenPoolster()` method. It sets the `chosenPoolster` to a specified index value, and then refreshes the Selected Player list to show the `chosenPoolster`'s picks.

Create a `setState()` method. It's called in the `run()` method when a state message has been received.

```
public synchronized void setState(ServerState newState)
{
    state = newState;
    refreshState();
}
```

Then create a `getState()` method; it's called to retrieve the pool state:

```
public synchronized ServerState getState()
{
    if( state == null )
    {
        state = new ServerState();
    }
    return state;
}
```

Create an `exit()` method that's called when the Quit menu item is selected:

```
public void exit()
{
    System.exit(0);
    return;
}
```

Listing 12-14.
refreshState()
method.

```java
/**
* Refresh the UI with the new state. The components updated
    include:
* Last player picked, current pick, choice of poolsters,
* list of players available, enabling of Select Player
    button,
* enabling of timer, list of players selected
*/
public synchronized void refreshState() {

    // Update choice of players
    Choice choice = getChoice1();
    choice.removeAll();
    for( int i = 0; i< state.getPoolsterNames().size();
        i++ )
    {
        choice.add((String)((state.getPoolsterNames())
            .elementAt(i)));
    }

    // Set default text for current poolster. It will be
        overridden if picking has ended
    // or the pool is in the midst of picking
    String label3text = "Picking has not commenced";
    // Update Current player selection
    if( state.isPickingOver())
    {
        label3text = "Pool is over";
        getDialog3().show();
    }

    // Retrieve the current poolster by index the
        currentPoolster value into the PoolsterNames
        vector
    String curPoolster =  (String)
        (state.getPoolsterNames()
        .elementAt(state.getCurrentPoolster()));
    if( state.isPickingPlayers())
    {

        label3text = curPoolster + "'s Turn";
        if( state.getCurrentRound() == 0 &&
            state.getCurrentPoolster() == 0 )
        {
            getDialog2().show();
        }
    }
    // The current poolster is now known, so set the
        label.
    getLabel1().setText(label3text);
    // Update selection button
    getButton1().setEnabled(state.isPickingPlayers() &&
curPoolster.equals(myName));
```

Listing 12-14.
Continued.

```
// Start timer if need be
getVisibleTimer1().setEnabled(state
    .isPickingPlayers());
getVisibleTimer1().resetTimeLeft();

// Update last player selected
if( state.getLastPlayerSelected() != null )
{
    getLabel2().setText( "Last player picked was "
        + state.getLastPlayerSelected());
}

if( state.getLastPlayerSelected() != null )
{
    try {
        getList2().remove
            (state.getLastPlayerSelected());
    } catch( IllegalArgumentException ex ) {}
}

setChosenPoolster( getChosenPoolster());

// Update Ranked players list
List list1 = getList2();
if( list1.getItemCount() == 0 &&
    state.getCurrentRound() == 0 ) // If zero, user
    has changed list
{
    list1.removeAll();
    for( int i = 0; i<
state.getRankedPlayers().length; i++ ) {
        list1.add(state.getRankedPlayers()[i]);
    }
}
    return;
}
```

Modify the **main()** method; any references to VAJ components are removed.

Now we will refresh the interface of the HockeyPool class. We changed the HockeyPool interface by adding methods, and the visual builder must be informed of this. Select a blank area on the Composition Editor, right-click, and then select Regenerate Interface.

Now connect all the parts. To specify a method of the HockeyPool applet, simply click a blank area on the Composition Editor as the target of a connection. The Composition Editor then prompts us with a list of all the methods of HockeyPool.

Listing 12-15.
`setChosenPoolster()`
method.

```
/**
 * Set chosen poolster to parameter
 * Redraw player selected list to show chosen poolster's
     picks
 */
public void setChosenPoolster(int poolster)
{
    chosenPoolster = poolster;
    // Update player list
    List list = getList1();
    list.removeAll();
    Vector poolsterVector = (Vector)
        (state.getPoolsterPicks().elementAt(poolster));
    String     player;
    for( int i = 0; i< poolsterVector.size(); i++ ) {
        player = new String((String)
            (poolsterVector.elementAt(i)));
        list.add(player);
    }
}
```

Listing 12-16.
The **main()**
method.

```
/**
 * main entrypoint - starts the part when it is run as an
     application
 * @param args java.lang.String[]
 */
public static void main(java.lang.String[] args) {
    try {
        HockeyPool aHockeyPool = new HockeyPool();

        aHockeyPool.init();
        aHockeyPool.start();
        aHockeyPool.destroy();
    } catch (java.lang.Throwable exception) {
        System.err.println("Exception occurred in main()
     of HockeyPool");
    }
}
```

Make the following connections in the Composition Editor:

■ Join the Hockey Pool applet's **init()** method to the **Frame**'s **show()** method.

■ Join the Pool menu item's **action.ActionPerformed** event to the Join Pool dialog box's **show()** method.

■ Join the Pool dialog box's Cancel button's **action.ActionPerformed** event to the Join Pool dialog box's **hide()** method.

- Join the Pool dialog box's OK button's **action.ActionPerformed** event to the HockeyPool's **joinPool()** method.

- Join the Pool dialog box's TextField2's **Text** property to the **Name** property of the previous connection.

- Join the Pool dialog box's TextField3's **Text** property to the **serverURL** property of the previous connection.

- Join the Pool dialog box's OK button's **action.ActionPerformed** event to the Join Pool dialog box's **hide()** method. Note that multiple connections from an event are evaluated in the order created. This can be overridden by selecting the Reorder Connections option.

- Open the Ranking menu item's **action.ActionPerformed** event to the HockeyPool's **openRanking()** method.

- Join the RankedListHandler component's **this** property to the previous connection's **currentList** property.

- Join the Save the Ranking menu item's **action.ActionPerformed** event to the HockeyPool's **saveRanking()** method.

- Join the **RankedListHandler** component's **this** property to the previous connections's **theList** property.

- Join the Save the Teams menu item's **action.ActionPerformed** event to the HockeyPool's **saveTeams()** method.

- Join the Quit menu item's **action.ActionPerformed** event to the HockeyPool's **exit()** method.

- Join the Rank Player button's **action.ActionPerformed** event to the HockeyPool's **rankPlayer()** method.

- Join the TextField1's **text** property to the previous connection's **this** property.

- Join the Unrank button's **action.ActionPerformed** event to the Ranked list's **remove(int)** method.

- Join the Ranked list's **selectedIndex** property to the previous connection's **Position** property.

- Join the Rank Higher button's **action.ActionPerformed** event to the **RankedListHandler**'s **moveItemUp1()** method.

- Join the Rank Lower button's **action.ActionPerformed** event to the **RankedListHandler**'s **moveItemDown1()** method.

- Join the Ranked list's **this** property to the **RankedListHandler**'s **list** property.

- Join the **VisibleTimer**'s **fireAt0Seconds.propertyChange** event to the Select Top Player's **actionCommand()** method.

- Join the Select Top Player button's **action.ActionPerformed** event to the HockeyPool's **makeSelection()** method.
- Join the Ranked list's **this** property to the previous connection's **sourceList** property.
- Join the Choice list's **item.itemStateChanged** event to the Hockey-Pool's **selectedPoolster** property.
- Join the Choice list's **selectedIndex** property to the previous connection's **poolster** property.
- Join the Picking Over dialog box's OK button's **action.ActionPerformed** event to the Picking Over dialog box's **hide()** method.
- Join the Picking Begun dialog box's OK button's **action.ActionPerformed** event to the Picking Begun dialog box's **hide()** method.
- Join the Player Not Available dialog box's OK button's **action.ActionPerformed** event to the Player Not Available dialog box's **hide()** method.

Now create a **MessageServer** class file. The **MessageServer** listens for socket connections from clients and creates a **MessageHandler** thread for each connected client.

Listing 12-17.
HockeyPool class with previously listed methods removed.

```
import java.applet.*;
import java.awt.*;
import java.io.*;
import java.net.*;
import java.util.*;

/**     HockeyPool Application client. GUI for player
     selection and pool joining.
* Sends and receives messages from a pool server. Refreshes
     GUI with pool
* state.
*/
public class HockeyPool extends java.applet.Applet
     implements java.awt.event.ActionListener,
     java.awt.event.ItemListener,
     java.beans.PropertyChangeListener,
     java.lang.Runnable {
     private      int chosenPoolster = 0;
     static       int DEFAULT_PORT = 8000;
     private      java.io.ObjectInputStream in = null;
     private      java.awt.Button ivjButton1 = null;
     private      java.awt.Button ivjButton10 = null;
```

Listing 12-17.
Continued.

```
private        java.awt.Button ivjButton2 = null;
private        java.awt.Button ivjButton3 = null;
private        java.awt.Button ivjButton4 = null;
private        java.awt.Button ivjButton5 = null;
private        java.awt.Button ivjButton6 = null;
private        java.awt.Button ivjButton7 = null;
private        java.awt.Button ivjButton8 = null;
private        java.awt.Button ivjButton9 = null;
private        java.awt.Choice ivjChoice1 = null;
private        java.awt.Dialog ivjDialog1 = null;
private        java.awt.Dialog ivjDialog2 = null;
private        java.awt.Dialog ivjDialog3 = null;
private        java.awt.Dialog ivjDialog4 = null;
private        java.awt.Frame ivjFrame1 = null;
private        java.awt.MenuBar ivjFrame1MenuBar = null;
private        java.awt.Label ivjLabel1 = null;
private        java.awt.Label ivjLabel10 = null;
private        java.awt.Label ivjLabel2 = null;
private        java.awt.Label ivjLabel3 = null;
private        java.awt.Label ivjLabel4 = null;
private        java.awt.Label ivjLabel5 = null;
private        java.awt.Label ivjLabel6 = null;
private        java.awt.Label ivjLabel7 = null;
private        java.awt.Label ivjLabel8 = null;
private        java.awt.Label ivjLabel9 = null;
private        java.awt.List ivjList1 = null;
private        java.awt.List ivjList2 = null;
private        java.awt.Menu ivjMenu1 = null;
private        java.awt.MenuItem ivjMenuItem1 = null;
private        java.awt.MenuItem ivjMenuItem2 = null;
private        java.awt.MenuItem ivjMenuItem3 = null;
private        java.awt.MenuItem ivjMenuItem4 = null;
private        java.awt.MenuItem ivjMenuItem5 = null;
private        RankedListHandler ivjRankedListHandler1 =
                   null;
private        java.awt.TextField ivjTextField1 = null;
private        java.awt.TextField ivjTextField2 = null;
private        java.awt.TextField ivjTextField3 = null;
private        VisibleTimer.VisibleTimer ivjVisibleTimer1
                   = null;
private        java.lang.Thread listener = null;
private        java.io.DataOutputStream out = null;
private        java.net.Socket s = null;
private        ServerState state = null;
private     String myName = null;

/**
 * Method to handle events for the ActionListener
     interface.
 * @param e java.awt.event.ActionEvent
 */
```

Continues

Listing 12-17.
Continued.

```java
public void actionPerformed
    (java.awt.event.ActionEvent e) {
  if ((e.getSource() == getMenuItem1()) ) {
      conn1(e);
  }
  if ((e.getSource() == getButton10()) ) {
      conn2(e);
  }
  if ((e.getSource() == getButton9()) ) {
      conn3(e);
  }
  if ((e.getSource() == getMenuItem2()) ) {
      conn6(e);
  }
  if ((e.getSource() == getMenuItem3()) ) {
      conn8(e);
  }
  if ((e.getSource() == getMenuItem4()) ) {
      conn10(e);
  }
  if ((e.getSource() == getMenuItem5()) ) {
      conn11(e);
  }
  if ((e.getSource() == getButton5()) ) {
      conn12(e);
  }
  if ((e.getSource() == getButton4()) ) {
      conn14(e);
  }
  if ((e.getSource() == getButton2()) ) {
      conn16(e);
  }
  if ((e.getSource() == getButton3()) ) {
      conn17(e);
  }
  if ((e.getSource() == getButton1()) ) {
      conn20(e);
  }
  if ((e.getSource() == getButton8()) ) {
      conn22(e);
  }
  if ((e.getSource() == getButton7()) ) {
      conn23(e);
  }
  if ((e.getSource() == getButton6()) ) {
      conn24(e);
  }
  if ((e.getSource() == getButton9()) ) {
      conn27(e);
  }
}
/**
```

```
 * conn0:   (HockeyPool.init() -> Frame1.show())
 */
private void conn0() {
    try {
        getFrame1().show();
    } catch (java.lang.Throwable exception) {
    }
}
/**
 * conn1:   (MenuItem1.action.actionPerformed ->
      Dialog4.show())
 * @param e java.awt.event.ActionEvent
 */
private void conn1(java.awt.event.ActionEvent e) {
    try {
        getDialog4().show();
    } catch (java.lang.Throwable exception) {
    }
}
/**
 * conn10:   (MenuItem4.action.actionPerformed ->
      HockeyPool.saveTeams())
 * @param e java.awt.event.ActionEvent
 */
private void conn10(java.awt.event.ActionEvent e) {
    try {
        this.saveTeams();
    } catch (java.lang.Throwable exception) {
    }
}
/**
 * conn11:   (MenuItem5.action.actionPerformed ->
      HockeyPool.exit())
 * @param e java.awt.event.ActionEvent
 */
private void conn11(java.awt.event.ActionEvent e) {
    try {
        this.exit();
    } catch (java.lang.Throwable exception) {
    }
}
/**
 * conn12:   (Button5.action.actionPerformed ->
      HockeyPool.rankPlayer(java.lang.String))
 * @param e java.awt.event.ActionEvent
 */
private void conn12(java.awt.event.ActionEvent e) {
    try {
        this.rankPlayer(getTextField1().getText());
    } catch (java.lang.Throwable exception) {
    }
```

Continues

Listing 12-17.
Continued.

```java
    }
    /**
     * conn14:  (Button4.action.actionPerformed ->
     *     List2.remove(int))
     * @param e java.awt.event.ActionEvent
     */
    private void conn14(java.awt.event.ActionEvent e) {
        try {
            getList2().remove(getList2()
                .getSelectedIndex());
        } catch (java.lang.Throwable exception) {
        }
    }
    /**
     * conn16:  (Button2.action.actionPerformed ->
     *     RankedListHandler1.moveItemUp1())
     * @param e java.awt.event.ActionEvent
     */
    private void conn16(java.awt.event.ActionEvent e) {
        try {
            getRankedListHandler1().moveItemUp1();
        } catch (java.lang.Throwable exception) {
        }
    }
    /**
     * conn17:  (Button3.action.actionPerformed ->
     *     RankedListHandler1.moveItemDown1())
     * @param e java.awt.event.ActionEvent
     */
    private void conn17(java.awt.event.ActionEvent e) {
        try {
            getRankedListHandler1().moveItemDown1();
        } catch (java.lang.Throwable exception) {
        }
    }
    /**
     * conn18SetTarget:  (List2.this <->
     *     RankedListHandler1.list)
     */
    private void conn18SetTarget() {
        /* Set the target from the source */
        try {
            getRankedListHandler1().setList(getList2());

        } catch (java.lang.Throwable exception) {
            /* Exception occurred. */
            ;
        }
    }
    /**
     * conn19:  (VisibleTimer1.fireAt0Seconds.propertyChange
-> Button1.actionCommand)
```

Listing 12-17.
Continued.

```
 * @param evt java.beans.PropertyChangeEvent
 */
private void conn19(java.beans.PropertyChangeEvent evt)
{
    try {

getButton1().setActionCommand(String.valueOf(evt));
    } catch (java.lang.Throwable exception) {
    }
}
/**
 * conn2:   (Button10.action.actionPerformed ->
 *     Dialog4.hide())
 * @param e java.awt.event.ActionEvent
 */
private void conn2(java.awt.event.ActionEvent e) {
    try {
        getDialog4().hide();
    } catch (java.lang.Throwable exception) {
    }
}
/**
 * conn20:   (Button1.action.actionPerformed ->
 *     HockeyPool.makeSelection(java.awt.List))
 * @param e java.awt.event.ActionEvent
 */
private void conn20(java.awt.event.ActionEvent e) {
    try {
        this.makeSelection(getList2());
    } catch (java.lang.Throwable exception) {
    }
}
/**
 * conn22:   (Button8.action.actionPerformed ->
 *     Dialog3.hide())
 * @param e java.awt.event.ActionEvent
 */
private void conn22(java.awt.event.ActionEvent e) {
    try {
        getDialog3().hide();
    } catch (java.lang.Throwable exception) {
    }
}
/**
 * conn23:   (Button7.action.actionPerformed ->
 *     Dialog2.hide())
 * @param e java.awt.event.ActionEvent
 */
private void conn23(java.awt.event.ActionEvent e) {
    try {
        getDialog2().hide();
```

Continues

Listing 12-17.
Continued.

```
                            } catch (java.lang.Throwable exception) {
                            }
                        }
                        /**
                        * conn24:   (Button6.action.actionPerformed ->
                            Dialog1.hide())
                        * @param e java.awt.event.ActionEvent
                        */
                        private void conn24(java.awt.event.ActionEvent e) {
                            try {
                                getDialog1().hide();
                            } catch (java.lang.Throwable exception) {
                            }
                        }
                        /**
                        * conn25:   (Choice1.item.itemStateChanged ->
                            HockeyPool.setChosenPoolster(int))
                        * @param e java.awt.event.ItemEvent
                        */
                        private void conn25(java.awt.event.ItemEvent e) {
                            try {
                                this.setChosenPoolster(getChoice1()
                                    .getSelectedIndex());
                            } catch (java.lang.Throwable exception) {
                            }
                        }
                        /**
                        * conn27:   (Button9.action.actionPerformed ->
                            Dialog4.hide())
                        * @param e java.awt.event.ActionEvent
                        */
                        private void conn27(java.awt.event.ActionEvent e) {
                            try {
                                getDialog4().hide();
                            } catch (java.lang.Throwable exception) {
                            }
                        }
                        /**
                        * conn3:   (Button9.action.actionPerformed ->
                            HockeyPool.joinPool(java.lang.String,
                            java.lang.String))
                        * @param e java.awt.event.ActionEvent
                        */
                        private void conn3(java.awt.event.ActionEvent e) {
                            try {
                                this.joinPool(getTextField2().getText(),
                                    getTextField3().getText());
                            } catch (java.lang.Throwable exception) {
                            }
                        }
                        /**
                        * conn6:   (MenuItem2.action.actionPerformed -> Hockey-
```

Listing 12-17.
Continued.

```
Pool.openRanking(RankedListHandler))
    * @param e java.awt.event.ActionEvent
    */
    private void conn6(java.awt.event.ActionEvent e) {
        try {
            this.openRanking(getRankedListHandler1());
        } catch (java.lang.Throwable exception) {
        }
    }
    /**
    * conn8:    (MenuItem3.action.actionPerformed ->
        HockeyPool.saveRanking(RankedListHandler))
    * @param e java.awt.event.ActionEvent
    */
    private void conn8(java.awt.event.ActionEvent e) {
        try {
            this.saveRanking(getRankedListHandler1());
        } catch (java.lang.Throwable exception) {
        }
    }
    /**
    * Handle the Applet destroy method.
    */
    public void destroy() {
        /* Handle the Applet destroy method. */
        super.destroy();
    }
    public void exit() {
        System.exit(0);
        return;
    }
    /**
    * Gets the applet information.
    * @return java.lang.String
    */
    public java.lang.String getAppletInfo() {
        return "HockeyPool created using the VisualAge for
            Java Version 1.0 Beta 1.";
    }
    /**
    * Return the Button1 property value.
    * @return java.awt.Button
    */
    private java.awt.Button getButton1() {
        if (ivjButton1 == null) {
            try {
                ivjButton1 = new java.awt.Button("Select
                    Top Player ->");
                ivjButton1.setFont(new
                    java.awt.Font("times new roman", 0,
                    14));
```

Continues

Listing 12-17.
Continued.

```java
                    ivjButton1.reshape(251, 154, 145, 29);
                    ivjButton1.setEnabled(false);
            } catch (java.lang.Throwable exception) {
                System.err.println("Exception creating
                    Button1");
            }
    };
    return ivjButton1;
}
/**
 * Return the Button10 property value.
 * @return java.awt.Button
 */
private java.awt.Button getButton10() {
    if (ivjButton10 == null) {
        try {
            ivjButton10 = new
                java.awt.Button("Cancel");
            ivjButton10.setFont(new
                java.awt.Font("times new roman", 0,
                14));
            ivjButton10.reshape(155, 123, 106, 31);
        } catch (java.lang.Throwable exception) {
            System.err.println("Exception creating
                Button10");
        }
    };
    return ivjButton10;
}
/**
 * Return the Button2 property value.
 * @return java.awt.Button
 */
private java.awt.Button getButton2() {
    if (ivjButton2 == null) {
        try {
            ivjButton2 = new java.awt.Button("Rank
                Higher");
            ivjButton2.setFont(new
                java.awt.Font("times new roman", 0,
                14));
            ivjButton2.reshape(10, 155, 94, 29);
        } catch (java.lang.Throwable exception) {
            System.err.println("Exception creating
                Button2");
        }
    };
    return ivjButton2;
}
/**
 * Return the Button3 property value.
 * @return java.awt.Button
```

Listing 12-17.
Continued.

```
*/
private java.awt.Button getButton3() {
    if (ivjButton3 == null) {
        try {
            ivjButton3 = new java.awt.Button("Rank
                Lower");
            ivjButton3.setFont(new
                java.awt.Font("times new roman",
                0, 14));
            ivjButton3.reshape(10, 205, 94, 29);
        } catch (java.lang.Throwable exception) {
            System.err.println("Exception creating
                Button3");
        }
    };
    return ivjButton3;
}
/**
 * Return the Button4 property value.
 * @return java.awt.Button
 */
private java.awt.Button getButton4() {
    if (ivjButton4 == null) {
        try {
            ivjButton4 = new
                java.awt.Button("Unrank");
            ivjButton4.setFont(new
                java.awt.Font("times new roman",
                0, 14));
            ivjButton4.reshape(10, 275, 94, 29);
        } catch (java.lang.Throwable exception) {
            System.err.println("Exception creating
                Button4");
        }
    };
    return ivjButton4;
}
/**
 * Return the Button5 property value.
 * @return java.awt.Button
 */
private java.awt.Button getButton5() {
    if (ivjButton5 == null) {
        try {
            ivjButton5 = new java.awt.Button("Rank
                Player");
            ivjButton5.setFont(new
                java.awt.Font("times new roman",
                0, 14));
            ivjButton5.reshape(10, 327, 94, 29);
        } catch (java.lang.Throwable exception) {
```

Continues

Listing 12-17.
Continued.

```
                            System.err.println("Exception creating
                                Button5");
                }
        };
        return ivjButton5;
}
/**
 * Return the Button6 property value.
 * @return java.awt.Button
 */
private java.awt.Button getButton6() {
    if (ivjButton6 == null) {
        try {
                ivjButton6 = new java.awt.Button("OK");
                ivjButton6.setFont(new
                        java.awt.Font("times new roman", 0,
                        14));
                ivjButton6.reshape(12, 82, 128, 30);
            } catch (java.lang.Throwable exception) {
                System.err.println("Exception creating
                    Button6");
            }
        };
        return ivjButton6;
}
/**
 * Return the Button7 property value.
 * @return java.awt.Button
 */
private java.awt.Button getButton7() {
    if (ivjButton7 == null) {
        try {
                ivjButton7 = new java.awt.Button("OK");
                ivjButton7.setFont(new
                        java.awt.Font("times new roman", 0,
                        14));
                ivjButton7.reshape(29, 63, 96, 31);
            } catch (java.lang.Throwable exception) {
                System.err.println("Exception creating
                    Button7");
            }
        };
        return ivjButton7;
}
/**
 * Return the Button8 property value.
 * @return java.awt.Button
 */
private java.awt.Button getButton8() {
    if (ivjButton8 == null) {
        try {
                ivjButton8 = new java.awt.Button("OK");
```

Listing 12-17.
Continued.

```
                    ivjButton8.reshape(37, 62, 92, 29);
            } catch (java.lang.Throwable exception) {
                System.err.println("Exception creating
                    Button8");
            }
    };
    return ivjButton8;
}
/**
 * Return the Button9 property value.
 * @return java.awt.Button
 */
private java.awt.Button getButton9() {
    if (ivjButton9 == null) {
        try {
            ivjButton9 = new java.awt.Button("Join");
            ivjButton9.setFont(new
                java.awt.Font("times new roman", 0,
                14));
            ivjButton9.reshape(24, 123, 102, 30);
        } catch (java.lang.Throwable exception) {
            System.err.println("Exception creating
                Button9");
        }
    };
    return ivjButton9;
}
/**
 * Return the Choice1 property value.
 * @return java.awt.Choice
 */
private java.awt.Choice getChoice1() {
    if (ivjChoice1 == null) {
        try {
            ivjChoice1 = new java.awt.Choice();
            ivjChoice1.reshape(398, 112, 125, 30);
        } catch (java.lang.Throwable exception) {
            System.err.println("Exception creating
                Choice1");
        }
    };
    return ivjChoice1;
}
public int getChosenPoolster()
{
    return chosenPoolster;
}
/**
 * Return the Dialog1 property value.
 * @return java.awt.Dialog
 */
```

Continues

Listing 12-17.
Continued.

```java
private java.awt.Dialog getDialog1() {
    if (ivjDialog1 == null) {
        try {
            ivjDialog1 = new java.awt.Dialog(new
                java.awt.Frame());
            ivjDialog1.setLayout(null);
            ivjDialog1.reshape(553, 454, 153, 137);
            ivjDialog1.setTitle("Player not
                available");
            getDialog1().add("ivjButton6",
                getButton6());
            getDialog1().add("ivjLabel6",
                getLabel6());
        } catch (java.lang.Throwable exception) {
            System.err.println("Exception creating
                Dialog1");
        }
    };
    return ivjDialog1;
}
/**
 * Return the Dialog2 property value.
 * @return java.awt.Dialog
 */
private java.awt.Dialog getDialog2() {
    if (ivjDialog2 == null) {
        try {
            ivjDialog2 = new java.awt.Dialog(new
                java.awt.Frame());
            ivjDialog2.setLayout(null);
            ivjDialog2.reshape(593, 281, 164, 122);
            ivjDialog2.setTitle("Picking begun");
            getDialog2().add("ivjLabel7",
                getLabel7());
            getDialog2().add("ivjButton7",
                getButton7());
        } catch (java.lang.Throwable exception) {
            System.err.println("Exception creating
                Dialog2");
        }
    };
    return ivjDialog2;
}
/**
 * Return the Dialog3 property value.
 * @return java.awt.Dialog
 */
private java.awt.Dialog getDialog3() {
    if (ivjDialog3 == null) {
        try {
            ivjDialog3 = new java.awt.Dialog(new
                java.awt.Frame());
```

Listing 12-17.
Continued.

```java
                              ivjDialog3.setLayout(null);
                              ivjDialog3.reshape(352, 483, 162, 119);
                              ivjDialog3.setTitle("Picking over");
                              getDialog3().add("ivjLabel8",
                                      getLabel8());
                              getDialog3().add("ivjButton8",
                                      getButton8());
                      } catch (java.lang.Throwable exception) {
                              System.err.println("Exception creating
                                      Dialog3");
                      }
              };
              return ivjDialog3;
      }
      /**
       * Return the Dialog4 property value.
       * @return java.awt.Dialog
       */
      private java.awt.Dialog getDialog4() {
              if (ivjDialog4 == null) {
                      try {
                              ivjDialog4 = new java.awt.Dialog(new
                                      java.awt.Frame());
                              ivjDialog4.setLayout(null);
                              ivjDialog4.reshape(30, 439, 301, 167);
                              ivjDialog4.setTitle("Join Pool");
                              getDialog4().add("ivjButton9",
                                      getButton9());
                              getDialog4().add("ivjButton10",
                                      getButton10());
                              getDialog4().add("ivjLabel9",
                                      getLabel9());
                              getDialog4().add("ivjLabel10",
                                      getLabel10());
                              getDialog4().add("ivjTextField2",
                                      getTextField2());
                              getDialog4().add("ivjTextField3",
                                      getTextField3());
                      } catch (java.lang.Throwable exception) {
                              System.err.println("Exception creating
                                      Dialog4");
                      }
              };
              return ivjDialog4;
      }
      /**
       * Return the Frame1 property value.
       * @return java.awt.Frame
       */
      private java.awt.Frame getFrame1() {
              if (ivjFrame1 == null) {
```

Continues

Listing 12-17.
Continued.

```
                        try {
                            ivjFrame1 = new java.awt.Frame();
                            ivjFrame1.setMenuBar(getFrame1MenuBar());
                            ivjFrame1.setFont(new java.awt.Font("times
                                new roman", 0, 14));
                            ivjFrame1.setLayout(null);
                            ivjFrame1.reshape(31, 54, 548, 392);
                            getFrame1().add("ivjButton1",
                                getButton1());
                            getFrame1().add("ivjLabel1", getLabel1());
                            getFrame1().add("ivjLabel2", getLabel2());
                            getFrame1().add("ivjLabel3", getLabel3());
                            getFrame1().add("ivjLabel4", getLabel4());
                            getFrame1().add("ivjLabel5", getLabel5());
                            getFrame1().add("ivjChoice1",
                                getChoice1());
                            getFrame1().add("ivjList1", getList1());
                            getFrame1().add("ivjList2", getList2());
                            getFrame1().add("ivjButton2",
                                getButton2());
                            getFrame1().add("ivjButton3",
                                getButton3());
                            getFrame1().add("ivjButton4",
                                getButton4());
                            getFrame1().add("ivjButton5",
                                getButton5());
                            getFrame1().add("ivjTextField1",
                                getTextField1());
                            getFrame1().add("ivjVisibleTimer1",
                                getVisibleTimer1());
                        } catch (java.lang.Throwable exception) {
                            System.err.println("Exception creating
                                Frame1");
                        }
                };
            return ivjFrame1;
}
/**
* Return the Frame1MenuBar property value.
* @return java.awt.MenuBar
*/
private java.awt.MenuBar getFrame1MenuBar() {
    if (ivjFrame1MenuBar == null) {
        try {
            ivjFrame1MenuBar = new java.awt.MenuBar();
            ivjFrame1MenuBar.add(getMenu1());
        } catch (java.lang.Throwable exception) {
            System.err.println("Exception creating
                MenuBar");
        }
    };
    return ivjFrame1MenuBar;
```

Listing 12-17.
Continued.

```
    }
/**
 * Return the Label1 property value.
 * @return java.awt.Label
 */
private java.awt.Label getLabel1() {
    if (ivjLabel1 == null) {
        try {
            ivjLabel1 = new java.awt.Label("Picking
                has not begun");
            ivjLabel1.setFont(new java.awt.Font("times
                new roman", 1, 14));
            ivjLabel1.reshape(19, 47, 162, 30);
        } catch (java.lang.Throwable exception) {
            System.err.println("Exception creating
                Label1");
        }
    };
    return ivjLabel1;
}
/**
 * Return the Label10 property value.
 * @return java.awt.Label
 */
private java.awt.Label getLabel10() {
    if (ivjLabel10 == null) {
        try {
            ivjLabel10 = new java.awt.Label("Pool
                Server");
            ivjLabel10.setFont(new
java.awt.Font("times new roman", 1, 14));
            ivjLabel10.reshape(24, 60, 102, 30);
        } catch (java.lang.Throwable exception) {
            System.err.println("Exception creating
                Label10");
        }
    };
    return ivjLabel10;
}
/**
 * Return the Label2 property value.
 * @return java.awt.Label
 */
private java.awt.Label getLabel2() {
    if (ivjLabel2 == null) {
        try {
            ivjLabel2 = new java.awt.Label("No last
                player selected");
            ivjLabel2.setFont(new java.awt.Font("times
                new roman", 0, 14));
            ivjLabel2.setName("Label2");
```

Continues

Listing 12-17.
Continued.

```java
                    ivjLabel2.reshape(31, 80, 244, 27);
            } catch (java.lang.Throwable exception) {
                System.err.println("Exception creating
                    Label2");
            }
    };
    return ivjLabel2;
}
/**
 * Return the Label3 property value.
 * @return java.awt.Label
 */
private java.awt.Label getLabel3() {
    if (ivjLabel3 == null) {
        try {
            ivjLabel3 = new java.awt.Label("Ranking of
                Available players");
            ivjLabel3.setFont(new java.awt.Font("times
                new roman", 1, 14));
            ivjLabel3.reshape(18, 121, 202, 29);
        } catch (java.lang.Throwable exception) {
            System.err.println("Exception creating
                Label3");
        }
    };
    return ivjLabel3;
}
/**
 * Return the Label4 property value.
 * @return java.awt.Label
 */
private java.awt.Label getLabel4() {
    if (ivjLabel4 == null) {
        try {
            ivjLabel4 = new java.awt.Label("Seconds
                Left:");
            ivjLabel4.setFont(new java.awt.Font("times
                new roman", 0, 14));
            ivjLabel4.reshape(297, 57, 104, 30);
        } catch (java.lang.Throwable exception) {
            System.err.println("Exception creating
                Label4");
        }
    };
    return ivjLabel4;
}
/**
 * Return the Label5 property value.
 * @return java.awt.Label
 */
private java.awt.Label getLabel5() {
    if (ivjLabel5 == null) {
```

Listing 12-17.
Continued.

```
                       try {
                            ivjLabel5 = new java.awt.Label("Picks
                                of:");
                            ivjLabel5.setFont(new java.awt.Font("times
                                new roman", 0, 14));
                            ivjLabel5.reshape(324, 111, 72, 28);
                        } catch (java.lang.Throwable exception) {
                            System.err.println("Exception creating
                                Label5");
                        }
                   };
                   return ivjLabel5;
        }
        /**
         * Return the Label6 property value.
         * @return java.awt.Label
         */
        private java.awt.Label getLabel6() {
            if (ivjLabel6 == null) {
                   try {
                            ivjLabel6 = new java.awt.Label("Player not
                                available");
                            ivjLabel6.setFont(new java.awt.Font("times
                                new roman", 0, 14));
                            ivjLabel6.reshape(14, 20, 128, 35);
                        } catch (java.lang.Throwable exception) {
                            System.err.println("Exception creating
                                Label6");
                        }
                   };
                   return ivjLabel6;
        }
        /**
         * Return the Label7 property value.
         * @return java.awt.Label
         */
        private java.awt.Label getLabel7() {
            if (ivjLabel7 == null) {
                   try {
                            ivjLabel7 = new java.awt.Label("Picking
                                has begun!");
                            ivjLabel7.setFont(new java.awt.Font("times
                                new roman", 0, 14));
                            ivjLabel7.reshape(18, 19, 131, 29);
                        } catch (java.lang.Throwable exception) {
                            System.err.println("Exception creating
                                Label7");
                        }
                   };
                   return ivjLabel7;
        }
```

Continues

Listing 12-17.
Continued.

```java
/**
 * Return the Label8 property value.
 * @return java.awt.Label
 */
private java.awt.Label getLabel8() {
    if (ivjLabel8 == null) {
        try {
            ivjLabel8 = new java.awt.Label("Picking
                has finished");
            ivjLabel8.setFont(new java.awt.Font("times
                new roman", 0, 14));
            ivjLabel8.reshape(24, 17, 125, 30);
        } catch (java.lang.Throwable exception) {
            System.err.println("Exception creating
                Label8");
        }
    };
    return ivjLabel8;
}
/**
 * Return the Label9 property value.
 * @return java.awt.Label
 */
private java.awt.Label getLabel9() {
    if (ivjLabel9 == null) {
        try {
            ivjLabel9 = new java.awt.Label("Your
                Name");
            ivjLabel9.setFont(new java.awt.Font("times
                new roman", 1, 14));
            ivjLabel9.reshape(24, 16, 102, 29);
        } catch (java.lang.Throwable exception) {
            System.err.println("Exception creating
                Label9");
        }
    };
    return ivjLabel9;
}
/**
 * Return the List1 property value.
 * @return java.awt.List
 */
private java.awt.List getList1() {
    if (ivjList1 == null) {
        try {
            ivjList1 = new java.awt.List(0);
            ivjList1.reshape(404, 152, 102, 145);
        } catch (java.lang.Throwable exception) {
            System.err.println("Exception creating
                List1");
        }
    };
```

Listing 12-17.
Continued.

```java
        return ivjList1;
    }
    /**
     * Return the List2 property value.
     * @return java.awt.List
     */
    private java.awt.List getList2() {
        if (ivjList2 == null) {
            try {
                ivjList2 = new java.awt.List(0);
                ivjList2.reshape(123, 155, 99, 159);
            } catch (java.lang.Throwable exception) {
                System.err.println("Exception creating
                    List2");
            }
        };
        return ivjList2;
    }
    /**
     * Return the Menu1 property value.
     * @return java.awt.Menu
     */
    private java.awt.Menu getMenu1() {
        if (ivjMenu1 == null) {
            try {
                ivjMenu1 = new java.awt.Menu("File");
                ivjMenu1.add(getMenuItem1());
                ivjMenu1.add(getMenuItem2());
                ivjMenu1.add(getMenuItem3());
                ivjMenu1.add(getMenuItem4());
                ivjMenu1.add(getMenuItem5());
            } catch (java.lang.Throwable exception) {
                System.err.println("Exception creating
                    Menu1");
            }
        };
        return ivjMenu1;
    }
    /**
     * Return the MenuItem1 property value.
     * @return java.awt.MenuItem
     */
    private java.awt.MenuItem getMenuItem1() {
        if (ivjMenuItem1 == null) {
            try {
                ivjMenuItem1 = new java.awt.MenuItem("Join
                    Pool");
                ivjMenuItem1.setActionCommand("Join
                    Pool");
            } catch (java.lang.Throwable exception) {
                System.err.println("Exception creating
```

Continues

```
                              MenuItem1");
            }
        };
        return ivjMenuItem1;
    }
    /**
     * Return the MenuItem2 property value.
     * @return java.awt.MenuItem
     */
    private java.awt.MenuItem getMenuItem2() {
        if (ivjMenuItem2 == null) {
            try {
                ivjMenuItem2 = new java.awt.MenuItem("Open
                    Ranking");
                ivjMenuItem2.setActionCommand
                    ("OpenRanking");
            } catch (java.lang.Throwable exception) {
                System.err.println("Exception creating
                    MenuItem2");
            }
        };
        return ivjMenuItem2;
    }
    /**
     * Return the MenuItem3 property value.
     * @return java.awt.MenuItem
     */
    private java.awt.MenuItem getMenuItem3() {
        if (ivjMenuItem3 == null) {
            try {
                ivjMenuItem3 = new java.awt.MenuItem("Save
                    Ranking");
                ivjMenuItem3.setActionCommand
                    ("SaveRanking");
            } catch (java.lang.Throwable exception) {
                System.err.println("Exception creating
                    MenuItem3");
            }
        };
        return ivjMenuItem3;
    }
    /**
     * Return the MenuItem4 property value.
     * @return java.awt.MenuItem
     */
    private java.awt.MenuItem getMenuItem4() {
        if (ivjMenuItem4 == null) {
            try {
                ivjMenuItem4 = new java.awt.MenuItem("Save
                    Teams");

ivjMenuItem4.setActionCommand("SaveTeams");
```

Listing 12-17.
Continued.

```
                } catch (java.lang.Throwable exception) {
                    System.err.println("Exception creating
                        MenuItem4");
                }
        };
        return ivjMenuItem4;
    }
    /**
     * Return the MenuItem5 property value.
     * @return java.awt.MenuItem
     */
    private java.awt.MenuItem getMenuItem5() {
        if (ivjMenuItem5 == null) {
            try {
                ivjMenuItem5 = new
                    java.awt.MenuItem("Quit");
                ivjMenuItem5.setActionCommand("Quit");
            } catch (java.lang.Throwable exception) {
                System.err.println("Exception creating
                    MenuItem5");
            }
        };
        return ivjMenuItem5;
    }
    /**
     * Return the RankedListHandler1 property value.
     * @return VisibleTimer.RankedListHandler
     */
    private RankedListHandler getRankedListHandler1() {
        if (ivjRankedListHandler1 == null) {
            try {
                ivjRankedListHandler1 = new
                    RankedListHandler();
            } catch (java.lang.Throwable exception) {
                System.err.println("Exception creating
                    RankedListHandler1");
            }
        };
        return ivjRankedListHandler1;
    }
    public synchronized ServerState getState()
    {
        if( state == null )
        {
            state = new ServerState();
        }
        return state;
    }
    /**
     * Return the TextField1 property value.
     * @return java.awt.TextField
```

Continues

Listing 12-17.
Continued.

```java
    */
    private java.awt.TextField getTextField1() {
        if (ivjTextField1 == null) {
            try {
                ivjTextField1 = new java.awt.TextField(0);
                ivjTextField1.reshape(118, 328, 106, 28);
            } catch (java.lang.Throwable exception) {
                System.err.println("Exception creating
                    TextField1");
            }
        };
        return ivjTextField1;
    }
    /**
     * Return the TextField2 property value.
     * @return java.awt.TextField
     */
    private java.awt.TextField getTextField2() {
        if (ivjTextField2 == null) {
            try {
                ivjTextField2 = new java.awt.TextField(0);
                ivjTextField2.reshape(155, 18, 106, 25);
            } catch (java.lang.Throwable exception) {
                System.err.println("Exception creating
                    TextField2");
            }
        };
        return ivjTextField2;
    }
    /**
     * Return the TextField3 property value.
     * @return java.awt.TextField
     */
    private java.awt.TextField getTextField3() {
        if (ivjTextField3 == null) {
            try {
                ivjTextField3 = new java.awt.TextField(0);
                ivjTextField3.reshape(155, 63, 106, 25);
            } catch (java.lang.Throwable exception) {
                System.err.println("Exception creating
                    TextField3");
            }
        };
        return ivjTextField3;
    }
    /**
     * Return the VisibleTimer1 property value.
     * @return VisibleTimer.VisibleTimer
     */
    private VisibleTimer.VisibleTimer getVisibleTimer1() {
```

Listing 12-17.
Continued.

```
        if (ivjVisibleTimer1 == null) {
            try {
                ivjVisibleTimer1 = new
                    VisibleTimer.VisibleTimer();
                ivjVisibleTimer1.reshape(408, 58, 53, 28);
                ivjVisibleTimer1.setEnabled(false);
            } catch (java.lang.Throwable exception) {
                System.err.println("Exception creating
                    VisibleTimer1");
            }
        };
        return ivjVisibleTimer1;
}
/**
 * Method to handle events for the Applet interface.
 */
public void init() {
    /* Method to handle events for the Applet
        interface. */
    super.init();
    try {
        setFont(new java.awt.Font("times new roman",
            0, 14));
        setLayout(null);
        reshape(13, 13, 191, 48);
        conn0();
        initConnections();
    } catch (java.lang.Throwable exception) {
        System.err.println("Exception occurred in
            init() of HockeyPool");
    }
}
/**
 * Initializes connections
 */
private void initConnections() {
    /* Initialize the connections for the part */
    getMenuItem1().addActionListener(this);
    getButton10().addActionListener(this);
    getButton9().addActionListener(this);
    getMenuItem2().addActionListener(this);
    getMenuItem3().addActionListener(this);
    getMenuItem4().addActionListener(this);
    getMenuItem5().addActionListener(this);
    getButton5().addActionListener(this);
    getButton4().addActionListener(this);
    getButton2().addActionListener(this);
    getButton3().addActionListener(this);
    getVisibleTimer1().addFireAt0SecondsListener(this);
```

Continues

Listing 12-17.
Continued.

```
        getButton1().addActionListener(this);
        getButton8().addActionListener(this);
        getButton7().addActionListener(this);
        getButton6().addActionListener(this);
        getChoice1().addItemListener(this);
        conn18SetTarget();
    }
    /**
     * Method to handle events for the ItemListener
            interface.
     * @param e java.awt.event.ItemEvent
     */
    public void itemStateChanged(java.awt.event.ItemEvent
        e) {
        if ((e.getSource() == getChoice1()) ) {
            conn25(e);
        }
    }
    /**
     * Method to handle events for the
            PropertyChangeListener interface.
     * @param evt java.beans.PropertyChangeEvent
     */
    public void propertyChange
        (java.beans.PropertyChangeEvent evt) {
        if ((evt.getSource() == getVisibleTimer1()) ) {
            conn19(evt);
        }
    }

    public synchronized void setState(ServerState
        newState) {
        state = newState;
        refreshState();

    }
    /**
     * Handle the Applet start method.
     */
    public void start() {
        /* Handle the Applet start method. */
        super.start();
    }
    /**
     * Handle the Applet stop method.
     */
    public void stop() {
        /* Handle the Applet stop method. */
        super.stop();
    }

}
```

Listing 12-18.
MessageServer class.

```java
import java.io.*;
import java.net.*;
/**
* MessageServer. Listens for requests, spawns a
     MessageHandler for each incoming request
*/
public class MessageServer {
    public final static     int DEFAULT_PORT = 8000;
    protected       int port;
    protected       ServerSocket listen_socket;

    /**
    * MessageServer objects listen on a specified port and
        create MessageHandlers for each incoming
    * connection.
    */
    public MessageServer(int port) throws IOException{
        ServerSocket server = new ServerSocket( port );
        while(true) {
            Socket clientSocket = server.accept();
            MessageHandler msgHandler = new
                MessageHandler(clientSocket);
            msgHandler.start();
        }
    }
    public static void main(String[] args) {
        int port = DEFAULT_PORT;
        if (args.length == 1) {
            port = Integer.parseInt(args[0]); // Should
                handle errors
        }
        try {
            // Create a MessageServer for the port
            new MessageServer(port);
        } catch (Exception ex) {
            ex.printStackTrace();
        }
    }
}
```

Now create a **MessageHandler** class file. The **MessageHandler** handles communication between the server and an individual client. It waits for **JOIN** and **PICK** requests, calls the appropriate **serverState()** method based on the request, and sends state changes to each client.

Now run the **MessageServer**. To do this, select the MessageServer executable from the Workbench, then choose the Selected | Run menu item.

You can now run the HockeyPool application by selecting the Hockey-Pool executable in the Workbench and choosing the Selected | Run menu item or by clicking the Test icon in the Hockey Pool Composition Editor.

Listing 12-19.
MessageHandler
class.

```java
import java.io.*;
import java.util.*;
import java.net.*;
/** MessageHandler receives PICK and JOIN requests from a
     client, updates the state
* if needed, and broadcasts the state to all clients.
*/
    class MessageHandler extends Thread {
    protected         Socket client;
    protected         DataInputStream in;
    protected         ObjectOutputStream out;
    protected   static   Vector clients = new Vector();
    protected   static   ServerState state = new
         ServerState();

    public MessageHandler(Socket client_socket) {
        try {
            client = client_socket;
            in = new DataInputStream(client
                 .getInputStream());
            out = new ObjectOutputStream
                 (client.getOutputStream());
        } catch (Exception ex) {
            ex.printStackTrace();
        }
    }
    /**
    * Broadcast the state to each client
    */
    protected synchronized void broadcastState() throws
         IOException
    {
        for (int i = 0; i < clients.size(); i++)
        {
            MessageHandler m =
                 (MessageHandler)clients.elementAt(i);
            ServerState tempState = new
                 ServerState(MessageHandler.state);
            m.out.writeObject(tempState);
            m.out.flush();

        }
    }
    /**
    * Wait for a message, determine message time, and
         update pool.
    * Return true if pool needs to be broadcast, false
         otherwise.
    */
    protected boolean handleMessage( ) throws IOException
    {
        String s = in.readUTF();   // wait for message
```

Listing 12-19.
Continued.

```
          if( s == null )
          {
              System.out.println("No message String in
                  handleMessage");
              return false;
          }
          if( s.equals("JOIN") )
          {
              s = in.readUTF();
              state.addPoolster(s);
          }
          else if( s.equals ("PICK" ))
          {
              s = in.readUTF();

              state.addPick( s );
              state.setNextPoolster();
          } else
          {
              System.out.println("No Valid Message text");
              return false;
          }
          return true;
      }
      /**
       * Add this MessageHandler to the client list, call
            handleMessage to
       * wait for and handle messages, broadcast state if
            needed, and
       * cleanup if any errors
       */
      public void run() {
          try {
              // Add this MessageHandler to the client
                  vector
              synchronized( clients)
              {
                  clients.addElement(this);
              }
              while(true) {
                  // read in a line
                  try {
                      if( handleMessage())
                      {
                          broadcastState();
                      }
                  } catch (IOException ex) {
                      ex.printStackTrace();
                      return;
                  }
              }
```

Continues

Listing 12-19.
Continued.

```
        } catch (Exception ex) {
            ex.printStackTrace();
        } finally {
            synchronized( clients)
            {
                clients.removeElement(this);
                try {
                    client.close();
                } catch (IOException ex2) {
                    ex2.printStackTrace();
                }
            }
        }
    }
}
```

CONCLUSION

We have developed a simple component, the **VisibleTimer** Bean. This chapter has demonstrated how to create a component that complies to the Beans specification for properties, property editors, and **BeanInfo**. Then we showed how BeanBox can test the compliance of a component with the Beans specification. In a stunning completion, we developed a complex client application using the **VisibleTimer** component, AWT components, nonvisible Beans, and serialization, as well as a server application to coordinate clients.

We have seen the power of Beans in developing components from scratch and then using them in any Beans-compliant development environment.

ActiveX

13

Understanding ActiveX

So far we have covered some interesting technologies, such as distributed objects, Java, JavaBeans, and other Java APIs. Now we're introducing something different: ActiveX. This technology has gained quite a bit of recognition since its introduction, so in this chapter, we take a look at why ActiveX is worth knowing about. Keep in mind that ActiveX is a broad technology that's difficult to cover fully in one book. Our intention in this chapter is to give you some basic ideas (mostly client-side) about the technology so that you're well underway to activating your site with ActiveX.

In 1996, when the Internet world was excited about Java, Microsoft had to think of a way to lay its hands on Web technology. Their plan was to come out with a format that many developers were already familiar with, so they simply took their *OLE Control Extension* (OCX) and *Object Linking and Embedding* (OLE) technologies and extended them to what is now called *ActiveX*. It can be used to create interactive, complex, multimedia-savvy Web pages without much programming effort. The best part of ActiveX is that you can use any language to create an ActiveX application known as *ActiveX controls*. This is a big advantage for ActiveX because it gives developers a lot of flexibility.

This chapter will cover the following topics:

- Definition of ActiveX
- How it all started
- Advantages of ActiveX
- Limitations of ActiveX
- Java versus ActiveX
- ActiveX versus JavaBeans
- Components of ActiveX

What Is ActiveX?

ActiveX is a set of technologies that lets you "glue" components or objects together, regardless of the language they were written in. It enhances static Web pages and brings interactive, dynamic, multimedia-enabled information to your desktop (see Figure 13-1). Now you can experience animation, audio, and video through the World Wide Web in much the same way as with traditional software packages. ActiveX offers up-to-date information customization by the user that provides a one-to-one relationship between the customer and producer.

Imagine you're using a corporate intranet in the U.S. and you want to work on a document with a colleague who's in Australia. Wouldn't it be nice to be able to work on the document while you're brainstorming ideas

Figure 13-1.
An ActiveX-enabled page.

with your colleague? ActiveX can easily share your documents from any-where, whether you're working on the Internet, your corporate intranet, or an extranet. This feature is made possible through Microsoft's OLE technology. OLE is a complex family standard that allows storage, registration, and communication between applications.

How It All Started

It all started with Microsoft's first attempt at moving data from one place to another in Windows by using *Dynamic Data Exchange* (DDE). DDE allows you to transfer data with a clipboard, but its data exchange portion is static (DDE also has a macro language, but that's not relevant to this discussion). The data's destination is independent of the source, which means that if you change the source, the destination isn't updated. Another problem is that the application must be able to handle the data before you insert it. For example, if you wanted to place a piece of Visio line art into a text editor, that software would have to know how to handle that type of line art.

To solve some of DDE's limitations, Microsoft came out with OLE; since it is based on DDE's clipboard function, it can create dynamic links. If you change the source, the object in the destination is updated. OLE also lets you place different objects within the same application. For example, you can place a Visio diagram in a text editor, if the text editor supports OLE. Another advantage of OLE over DDE is that you can interact with an object in more than one way. This feature distinguishes OLE from static DDE.

With the first version of OLE, which is part of Windows 3.*x*, the system would slow down because of OLE's memory constraints. OLE 2 managed resources better and solved some of the speed problems. Besides speeding things up, OLE 2 also allows visual editing of an object, the ability to drag-and-drop an object into an application, version management, and more.

So what happens if a machine has both OLE 1 and OLE 2? Can they talk to each other? To make sure that OLE 1 and OLE 2 were compatible, Microsoft came out with a standard known as *Component Object Model* (COM). COM makes 16-bit and 32-bit application-OLE conversations transparent and makes a connection between OLE 1 and OLE 2 applications. How do OLE-enabled applications talk to each other? In the beginning, you had to load both applications to exchange information—not exactly a user-friendly solution. To make data transfer possible, Microsoft came out with a specification called *OCX*. It's a combination of *Dynamic Link Libraries* (DLLs) and objects that gives programmers reusable object-handling routines. This makes it easy for developers to apply these routines without much of the OLE specifications—a helpful feature, because OLE can get really complicated.

What is this DCOM that people have been talking about? *Distributed Component Object Model* (DCOM) is a version of OLE that lets you communicate with other OLE applications over a network. The problem with the previous version of OLE is that it was limited to the user's local machine. Even though you could link an OLE object to another machine, the code had to stay on your machine. DCOM extends that function; it can create OLE links that depend on the code on an external desktop or server. The best part of DCOM is that it uses smart, fast data transfers by combining local and remote processing of the code.

If you create an OCX control for your local machine, you can also use it on the Internet—and that's how OCX, DCOM, OLE, and ActiveX are tied together. When you go to a Web page that contains an ActiveX control, what actually happens? You download an OCX control onto your local machine. The Web page that embedded the OCX control then requests a certain method or property from the control, and you see that activity on the page. ActiveX basically uses the same OCX, DCOM and OLE technology we have been using for years.

Advantages of ActiveX

In today's fast-growing Internet world, viewers like to get hands-on, interactive Web pages. Plain, static pages are not enough to give you the information you need. Web developers need to create pages that offer dynamic content, virtual reality, document sharing, and a one-to-one relationship between the customer and the host site. ActiveX plays a key role in this relationship.

Personalized Web Experience

Do you ever think the information on the Web is so scattered you need to dig around for any information that might interest you? ActiveX can be used to make personalized Web sites, depending on a user's preferences of information, Web page appearance, and so on. This feature can save companies a lot of marketing money because a Web site can be tweaked to a user's profile, and your company can display certain ads of direct interest to that user. As the profile is updated over time, the producer and the customer can establish a one-to-one relationship, making the customer loyal to the company.

Interactive Experience

With interactive Web sites created by using ActiveX, users have the flexibility to make more choices on a page. Customers can get product information, customize a product, perform searches, browse catalogs, and place orders right from their computers. These choices make it possible for a company to reach more customers without additional effort and expense.

Multimedia Effects

As mentioned before, ActiveX brings sound, video, and animation to Web pages. This function can display information more creatively than static text-based Web pages can. A customer buying a car, for example, see a movie clip about the car instead of a static photo in a brochure. It would be even better if you could be in a 3-D virtual world, where you could drive the car, check out the interior, and discover what it would feel like to actually drive the car. ActiveX can be used to do exactly that!

Familiar Technology

Many developers have been creating applications for desktops or networks that perform the same functions as the ActiveX technology. Now they can transfer that knowledge to the Internet by using their previous expertise and tools. In many cases, they can even use the same code they have used for many other purposes. As a result, the learning curve for most developers isn't as steep as it is when learning other new technologies and languages.

Limitations of ActiveX

ActiveX is based on OLE—but OLE objects are compiled and written to run only on Windows. ActiveX controls currently don't work on Macintosh or UNIX operating systems, except through Microsoft's Internet Explorer. This limitation creates a problem for members of the Web community who want to see the World Wide Web from anywhere and from any platform. Also, because of the current nature of OLE, if you want to create platform-independent ActiveX controls (if that's possible in the near future), you will have to create different controls based on the platform. If OLE were changed, that would no longer be true. However, changing OLE could be a problem because many developers have already invested time and effort in creating ActiveX controls with the present OLE specifications.

ActiveX controls tend to be pretty large. They can take 2–3 minutes to download to your system. However, unlike Java applets, controls usually need to be downloaded only once. Still, for someone who has never been to a site with ActiveX controls, this waiting could be tedious. Also, just as with other programs, when you update your control, your visitor has to download it again.

At the time of this writing, only Internet Explorer directly supports ActiveX. Netscape, which enjoys nearly 70 percent of the browser market, doesn't support much of the ActiveX specifications (only ActiveX documents in Navigator 4.0). You can, however, buy a plug-in for $20 from Ncompass Labs Inc. (**www.ncompasslabs.com**) to view ActiveX controls in a Netscape browser.

One of the biggest controversies about ActiveX is security. An ActiveX control can go to the user's hard drive and have access to system files, which creates the possibility of a hacker writing a control that reads and writes directly to that hard drive. The next time the user visits the hacker's site, the control could pass a virus to the hard drive or do some other irreparable harm to the user's system.

To solve this problem, Microsoft has developed a system called *Authenticode* through a company called VeriSign. The way it works is simple. If you're going to develop an ActiveX control, you can get a certificate from a code-signing authority. Once you have that, your visitors see a certificate pop up in their browser when they visit your site (see Figure 13-2). The price for this system is about $400 a year.

Figure 13-2.
An Authenticode confirmation message.

The problem with Authenticode is that it doesn't tell you that the ActiveX control you see in a page is bug- or virus-free; it just tells you who created the control and, if anything goes wrong, who to blame. Moreover, it's not that complicated to get a certificate. A hacker can easily get a certificate under false pretenses and pass on a virus without your knowledge.

Java Versus ActiveX

An important measure of Java's success in the field of distributed objects will be how well it integrates with Microsoft's technologies. This is particularly true in the component field. With the release of J++, Microsoft's Java visual development environment, Java came to DCOM binding, which allows Java to interoperate with ActiveX. Microsoft's strategy is to make Java just another language in which to write ActiveX.

For JavaBeans developers, this strategy solves several problems. Because a Bean can look like an ActiveX control and an ActiveX control can look like a Bean, component developers won't necessarily have to choose between the two component standards.

The operating system barrier still remains, though. An ActiveX component is a binary object, so even if it can look like a Bean to other Beans, it will run only on platforms that accept ActiveX binaries. JavaBeans just require a Java Virtual Machine. The trade-offs of the two technologies need to be weighed by each developer.

So where does that leave ActiveX? First, there's a huge base of Windows code out there. It's easier to change an old OLE control into an ActiveX control than it is to change it into a Bean. Second, if your only target platform is Windows (or whichever platform Microsoft decides to support in the future) and performance is an issue, then you want to go with ActiveX.

ActiveX Versus JavaBeans

Although JavaBeans and ActiveX are similar component technologies, there are quite a few differences between them. The following sections describe how JavaBeans and ActiveX differ.

Security

The JavaBeans security model is based on Java's intrinsic security, which prevents a Bean from performing harmful activities, such as incorrect type casting or illegal memory access. (A Bean is a specialized Java applet; see Chapter Five, "JavaBeans Properites.") Moreover, the Java SecurityManager makes certain that Java programs can't access users' disks, which protects them from harmful code.

Because Java applets can't access a wide variety of resources, Java applets can now be digitally signed with the release of JavaSoft's JDK 1.1. The signed applets let you choose whether you want an applet to have access to your resources or how many resources you want an applet to access. However, this feature doesn't protect users from applets that are poorly written, so intrinsic security is still available to protect users from that problem.

Performance Issues

ActiveX controls can take advantage of the user's local disk, giving the control the ability to take advantage of native APIs, such as OpenGL, DirectX, and so on. This feature gives ActiveX the flexibility to be more multimedia-enabled and more powerful. JavaBeans have all the functionality of any trusted (digitally signed) Java application. An untrusted JavaBeans applet is somewhat limited in its capabilities, just like any standard Java applet. Moreover, at the time of this writing, Java lacked the diverse APIs available to ActiveX, making JavaBeans less attractive.

Platform Issues

As mentioned previously, it's possible to create different ActiveX controls according to the platform, but that means creating multiple controls. This approach obviously isn't standard for the Web, where a Web surfer can have a Mac, a PC, or even a UNIX terminal.

JavaBeans is, for the most part, platform independent. Java has been ported to more than 16 platforms, and JavaBeans follows its path. That's why JavaSoft has marketed JavaBeans as "Write once and run anywhere." This feature makes JavaBeans a better choice for developers coding for multiple platforms.

Other Issues

At the time of this writing, ActiveX provides a wide variety of controls available from both Microsoft and third-party vendors. Some of the controls are free; others, you can buy to plug-and-play in your applications. Although JavaBeans is supported by some of the major Web companies, such as Netscape, IBM, and Borland, very few Beans are actually available for free download or for purchase.

As mentioned, an ActiveX control can be written in any language, giving the developer a wide range of choices. On the other hand, a Bean can be written only in Java. Also, Java doesn't currently have document and container technology as ActiveX does.

Components of ActiveX

Several components of ActiveX need to be examined carefully. These components form the backbone of ActiveX and hold this technology together.

ActiveX Control

One major part of ActiveX technology is the ActiveX control. It's a modular piece of software that can communicate with other programs, enhance interactivity, compute data, and even have its own graphical interface. An ActiveX control is actually a marketing name for former OLE controls (also known as OCX controls), so to perform most of its tasks, it uses OLE to a certain extent. Although every ActiveX control can be an OLE control, not every OLE control is necessarily ActiveX controls. ActiveX controls work the same as Netscape plug-ins, but you don't need to download the control, install it, and then restart the browser to view ActiveX controls. An ActiveX control is downloaded automatically when you load a page that has it embedded. Unlike Java applets, ActiveX controls are "persistent"—once downloaded, they stay on your hard drive. Moreover, ActiveX controls can be programmed to dynamically update themselves based on the user's activity or some other criteria.

ActiveX controls are high-level, reusable components that can be used with other components as "building blocks" within any programming tool that supports ActiveX, such as Internet Explorer 3.0+, Visual Basic, Visual C++ 4.0, or FoxPro. Often, it's easier and more cost-effective to find custom solutions with ActiveX controls. These controls can be used to view movie files, listen to audio files, display animation, compute data, and more. ActiveX controls can communicate with other controls and can be called from a scripting language, such as VBScript or JavaScript. Today, there are over 1000 controls available on the Web that can be downloaded free or at a cost; some are listed in Appendix B, "Some Available ActiveX Controls."

EMBEDDING ACTIVEX CONTROLS ON A PAGE   Unlike Java applets, ActiveX controls are a little complicated to embed in a page. To understand why, let's look at exactly what happens when you access a page containing a control.

When *Internet Explorer* (IE) analyzes the HTML, it hits the **<OBJECT>** tag and processes the **CLSID** argument. This **CLSID** represents a key in the *Registry*, the massive data and information store used to identify objects and applications. When this **CLSID** is processed, IE checks whether the specified **CLSID** exists in the Registry. If it does, it simply uses the information stored there to run the program or object with the specified parameters. If it doesn't find an entry, that means the control hasn't been downloaded and run before. The CAB file we've created for it must be downloaded, extracted, and registered. To do this, IE looks for a **CODEBASE** element in the **<OBJECT>** tag; it indicates the CAB file's download location. After the file is downloaded, the process goes ahead, preparing for instantiation of the object. Why go through all this trouble? This is one of the advantages ActiveX controls have over Java applets. Once a control is downloaded, it doesn't need to be downloaded again unless the **CODEBASE** changes or the user empties his or her cache.

What all this implies is that a **CLSID**, consisting of a long string of letters and numbers, must be placed in the HTML. This string is far too long to memorize; even if you could, there are literally hundreds of ActiveX controls available to developers. Luckily for us, Microsoft has several applications that are specially equipped for inserting ActiveX controls.

Therefore, if you're embedding an ActiveX control by typing it in, it takes a little more work, unless you are using an authoring tool such as the ActiveX Control Pad, which can be found at **http://www.microsoft.com/activeplatform/default.asp**. We strongly recommend that you download this free authoring tool. It makes working with ActiveX controls a lot easier.

Here is a Real Audio (**www.realaudio.com**) control, shown in Figure 13-3, inserted in the HTML page by the ActiveX Control Pad:

```
<OBJECT ID="RealAudio1" WIDTH=401 HEIGHT=137
  CLASSID="CLSID:CFCDAA03-8BE4-11CF-B84B-0020AFBBCCFA">
    <PARAM NAME="_ExtentX" VALUE="10610">
    <PARAM NAME="_ExtentY" VALUE="3625">
    <PARAM NAME="AUTOSTART" VALUE="0">
    <PARAM NAME="NOLABELS" VALUE="0">
</OBJECT>
```

The **<OBJECT>** tag indicates that there's an ActiveX control being inserted in the page. You could put this whole segment in the **<HEAD>** tag or within the **<BODY>** tag of the HTML page.

The **ID** attribute is important when you're trying to call this control from VBScript or JavaScript. This is an important feature in distinguishing among controls when there are many in the HTML page.

The **CLASSID** identifies the control by its unique identification number, just as an OLE object does.

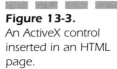

Figure 13-3.
An ActiveX control inserted in an HTML page.

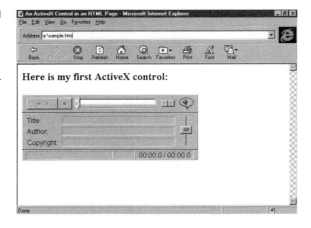

The **WIDTH** and **HEIGHT** define how much space the control will take in the HTML page. This works in much the same way as embedding an image in the page.

The **<PARAM>** attribute indicates the control's property, which you can set while embedding the object in the HTML page or set through VBScript or JavaScript. In the preceding example, **<PARAM NAME="AUTOSTART" VALUE="0">** means the browser shouldn't play a Real Audio file automatically when the page is loaded.

What if users don't have the ActiveX control in their systems? This is where the **<CODEBASE>** tag comes in handy, as shown here:

```
<OBJECT ID="MyControl" WIDTH=401 HEIGHT=137
  ...
<CODEBASE="http://www.domain.com/myControl.OCX">
</OBJECT>
```

This tag tells the browser where to get the component that's not available in the user's system.

CUSTOMIZING A CONTROL   To show you how to customize an ActiveX control, we will use the ActiveX Control Pad that you can download from Microsoft's Web page. When you start the application, you can see that you're ready to insert the control. Choose Insert ActiveX Control from the Edit menu to open a pop-up window that shows all the controls that can be inserted (see Figure 13-4). Now click the OK button after selecting the con-

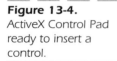

Figure 13-4.
ActiveX Control Pad
ready to insert a
control.

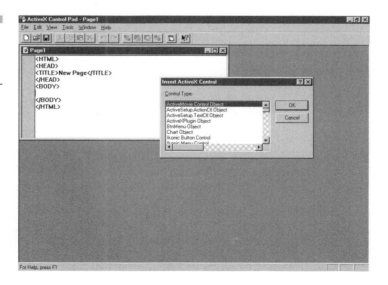

trol. You should see two pop-up windows, shown in Figure 13-5; one window shows the control, and the other shows all the properties that can be modified for the control—that's the key window where you can change the properties. When you save the file and then open it in Microsoft Explorer, you can see that the control now displays the characteristics you selected.

ActiveX Documents

ActiveX documents are another powerful feature of ActiveX technology. This feature not only lets you display spreadsheets, Word files, and other documents over the Internet without converting them into HTML files, but also lets you edit the files in real time. Again, this is an extension of a previous OLE technology known as *OLE Document Objects*. Microsoft modified the Office Binder technology from Microsoft Office to create this new functionality. The best part of ActiveX documents is that you can save the edited version of the document on the server. To make sure that only the current version is saved, OLE plays a big role in ActiveX documents. Now you can share the same document with someone across the world.

The way an ActiveX document works is simple. If an HTML file has a link to a document file (see Listing 13-1), say a Word document, Internet Explorer 3.0+ opens the file inside the browser. The browser also brings up Word's toolbar and menus (see Figure 13-6). This is an old technique known as *in-place editing*. Most OLE 2 clients have this feature from an OLE 2 server. The

Figure 13-5.
An ActiveX control and its property window.

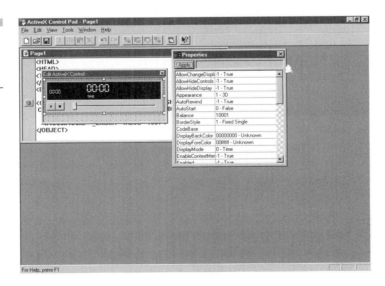

```
<HTML>
<HEAD>
<TITLE>Listing 13-1</TITLE>
</HEAD>
<BODY>
<A href="c:\windows\temp\test.doc">Click Here</a> for the
        Word Document.
</BODY>
</HTML>
```

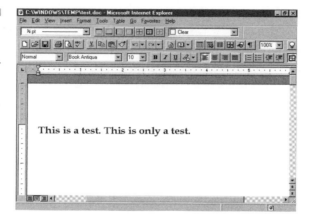

benefit of this technique is that you can save memory because you're actually running one application. Of course, there are some additional processing and memory costs, but it's certainly better than running two applications at the same time.

When you try to make a change to the document, the browser asks whether you want to save the file. If you say yes, it's saved in your local drive. If you want to publish the document to the server, all you have to do is choose **File** and then **Send To** from the menu, then specify the server address where you want to place the file's current version.

ActiveX documents take desktop technology to the Internet by using the browser. Now your browser can adopt changes to let you share a document over the Internet, so you don't have to go back and forth between applications.

ActiveX Scripting

ActiveX scripting is simply having VBScript (formally known as *Visual Basic Scripting Edition*) and JavaScript (Microsoft's version of Java-

Script is known as *JScript*) communicate with ActiveX controls. But why do you need to communicate with ActiveX controls? Let's say you have a form with a button that invokes an ActiveX control to connect to the database. The form has a text box where you can enter your name. After you enter your name, clicking another button lets you upload the data to the ActiveX control. Scripting languages such as JavaScript or VBScript are used in the underlying code for the form. So in this case, scripting languages work as the glue connecting the HTML page and the control. Another advantage of using these two scripting languages is that they can perform tasks on the client side, so you don't have to rely on the server. Obviously, this feature saves the user time and makes interaction between pages easier, especially when you have a slow Internet connection. Besides JavaScript and VBScript, you can easily plug other scripting languages into Microsoft Internet Explorer by simply adding a DLL.

JAVASCRIPT JavaScript is an object-based, cross-platform, event-driven scripting language that can be used on both the client side and server side. Its syntax derives much from Java and C++. Although JavaScript includes the word *Java*, it's not at all like Java. Java is object-oriented, compiled, and difficult to master; JavaScript is interpreted (not compiled, except for server-side JavaScript), easy to learn, and used mostly to perform simple tasks. Moreover, JavaScript is limited to the browser's object model and, unlike Java, isn't an extensive programming language. However, JavaScript can be used to call Java applets, just as ActiveX controls can, and display live content on the Netscape browser (a technology known as *LiveConnect*). Some of the tasks JavaScript can perform are detecting a user's browser, creating pop-up windows, state maintenance, input validation, simple animation, communication between frames, and connecting to a database through a LiveWire server tool.

 TIP *At the time of this writing, JavaScript is fully supported by Microsoft's Internet Explorer and Netscape Navigator browsers, but Navigator is the only browser that supports JavaScript 1.2. In comparison, Microsoft's Internet Explorer 4 (still in beta at the time of this writing) is the only browser to claim full support for the World Wide Web Consortium's official standard for JavaScript.*

JavaScript is embedded in an HTML page, so all the code for client-side JavaScript stays right on the HTML page. To embed a JavaScript segment, you need to use the format shown in Listing 13-2.

Listing 13-2.
Simple JavaScript segment in an HTML page.

```
<HTML>
<HEAD>
<TITLE>Listing 13-2</TITLE>
<Script language="JavaScript>
<!- - Hide the code from JavaScript-incompatible browser

function myFunction(){
     //Code Segment
}

//- done hiding>
</HEAD>
<BODY>
<form>
<input type="button" value="Click Here" name="myButton"
     onClick="myFunction()">
</form>
</BODY>
</HTML>
```

As you can see, the code goes inside the <HEAD> tag; therefore, the code segment is loaded into memory. The function is a typical JavaScript function, much like a C++/Java function. To call the function, use the **onClick** event handler. When a user clicks the form button, the function is invoked.

NOTE   *To learn more about JavaScript, try the following sites:*

- **developer.netscape.com** *(Netscape's DevEdge site)*
- **www.microsoft.com/jscript** *(JScript home page)*
- **http://rhoque.com/book** *(a practical JavaScript programming book)*

Client-side JavaScript calls an ActiveX control's method or property to perform certain tasks (remember that the **<PARAM>** tag of a control indicates some of the properties); that's how the HTML page interacts with ActiveX controls.

NOTE   *When you use the ActiveX Control Pad to make a connection with JavaScript or VBScript by using ActiveX, the tool displays all the possible methods and properties you can call from these string languages.*

VBSCRIPT   VBScript is another powerful cross-platform scripting language of the Web that's actually a subset of the Visual Basic language. It's a high-performance scripting language that can bring interactivity to the Web and create active content on the Web. It works as a link to Java applets and ActiveX controls. If you already have some concept of how to use JavaScript, VBScript will be very easy for you to learn. The same loops, conditional statements, and events apply in VBScript. The only limitation with VBScript is that—at the time of this writing—Internet Explorer is the only browser directly supporting the language. Microsoft plans to use VBScript in environments other than the Internet in the near future.

To embed a script segment, follow the same style as JavaScript. Listing 13-3 gives you an example.

VBScript syntax differs slightly from JavaScript, but both scripting languages are quite similar in structure. Just as with JavaScript, you can put the script segment anywhere in the HTML page. In Internet Explorer, you can call a VBScript segment explicitly within the HTML page, as shown in Listing 13-4.

TIP *To learn more about VBScript, visit* **http://www.microsoft.com/ vbscript**. *You can find full syntax documentation, examples, and more at this site. You can also download a script debugger for Internet Explorer to debug JavaScript and VBScript code. The downloadable file is available from the VBScript site.*

USING VBSCRIPT TO CALL AN ACTIVEX CONTROL   Now let's see how to call an ActiveX control from VBScript. Bill Rollins (**billr@smart.net**) created the example shown in Listing 13-5; it uses Microsoft's Chart control and VBScript (see Figure 13-7). This example demonstrates some options

Listing 13-3.
Simple VBScript segment in an HTML page.

```
<HTML>
<HEAD>
<TITLE>Listing 13-3</TITLE>
<SCRIPT LANGUAGE="VBScript">
<! - -

Function myFunction ()

// Code goes here

End Function

- >
</SCRIPT>
</HEAD>
<BODY>
Simple VBScript Function...
</BODY>
</HTML>
```

Listing 13-4.
Simple VBScript segment in an HTML page.

```
<HTML>
<HEAD>
<TITLE> Listing 13-4</TITLE>
</HEAD>
<BODY>
<form>
<input type="button" Value="Click Here" name="myButton">
<SCRIPT FOR="myButton" EVENT="onClick" LANGUAGE="VBScript">
    //script segment
</SCRIPT>
</FORM>
</BODY>
</HTML>
```

Listing 13-5.
VBScript manipulating an ActiveX control.

```
<!-
Author:     Bill Rollins
Purpose: This HTML example shows how to use Microsoft's
    ActiveX Chart control.
    Properties of the control are changed using
        subprocedures called
    by radio buttons and checkboxes. The AboutBox method
        is called from
    a command button.
Created: 3/16/96
Edited:     3/19/96 - VBScript code edited so there is only
    one procedure for each property.
    3/23/96 - Font sizes changed in title. Added text to
    the Notes section.
            6/01/96 - Change OBJECT tag to match E3 Beta
                    requirements
->


<HTML>
<HEAD>
<TITLE>ActiveX / VBScript Chart Example</TITLE>
</HEAD>

<BODY BGCOLOR=#FFFFCC TEXT=#000000>

<B><FONT SIZE=6>Chart Example</FONT></B><BR>
<FONT SIZE=2>You must be running Microsoft Internet
    Explorer 3.0 and have the <A HREF ="http://
    microsoft.saltmine.com/isapi/activexisv/prmgallery/
    gallery-activex-info.idc?ID=162">Microsoft ActiveX
    Chart control</A> installed to view this
    page.</FONT><BR>
<P>
The chart control enables you to draw charts. The chart's
```

Listing 13-5.
Continued.

```
        types and styles are properties of the control. The
        chart has one method, AboutBox. The chart generates
        no events.

<HR>

<OBJECT
    classid="clsid:FC25B780-75BE-11CF-8B01-444553540000"
    CODEBASE="http://activex.microsoft.com/controls/
        iexplorer/iechart.ocx#Version=4,70,0,1161"
        TYPE="application/x-oleobject"
    id=Chart1
    width=200
    height=200
        align=left
    hspace=0
    vspace=0
>

<param name="_extentX" value="300">
<param name="_extentY" value="150">
<param name="ChartStyle" value="0">
<param name="ChartType" value="4">
<param name="hgridStyle" value="0">
<param name="vgridStyle" value="0">
<param name="colorscheme" value="0">
<param name="rows" value="2">
<param name="columns" value="4">
<param name="data[0][0]" value="30">
<param name="data[0][1]" value="2">
<param name="data[0][2]" value="20">
<param name="data[0][3]" value="40">
<param name="data[1][0]" value="15">
<param name="data[1][1]" value="33">
<param name="data[1][2]" value="21">
<param name="data[1][3]" value="45">
<param name="BackStyle" value="1">


</object>


<SCRIPT LANGUAGE="VBS">
    <!- ' This prevents script from being displayed in
          browsers that don't support the SCRIPT tag.
    ' OPTION EXPLICIT

    ' Calls the AboutBox Method. This displays the Chart
          Object About Box.
    SUB DoChartAboutBox
        Chart1.AboutBox
```

Continues

Listing 13-5.
Continued.

```
    END SUB

    ' Changes the type of chart. WhatType is passed as a
        value (0-5) when one of the Chart Type radio
        buttons is selected.
    SUB DoChartType(WhatType)
        Chart1.ChartType = WhatType
    END SUB


    ' Turns horizontal gridlines on or off depending on
        value of chkHorizontal checkbox.
    SUB DoHorizontalGrid
        if chkHorizontal.Checked = 1 then
            Chart1.HGridStyle = 1
        else
            Chart1.HGridStyle = 0
        end if
    END SUB

' Turns vertical gridlines on or off depending on value of
    chkVertical checkbox
    SUB DoVerticalGrid
        if chkVertical.Checked = 1 then
            Chart1.VGridStyle = 1
        else
            Chart1.VGridStyle = 0
        end if
    END SUB

    ' Sets the background of the chart to Opaque or
        Transparent.
    SUB DoBackground(intBackGround)
        Chart1.BackStyle = intBackGround
    END SUB


->
</SCRIPT>


<TABLE BORDER = 0 XBORDER=5 BGCOLOR="#FFFFCC" WIDTH=300
    ALIGN=LEFT>
<TR><TD colspan=2 BGCOLOR=NAVY ALIGN=CENTER><FONT
    COLOR=FFFFCC>Chart Type</TR>
<TR><TD><INPUT TYPE=RADIO NAME=ChartType
    onClick="DoChartType(0)"> Simple Pie </TD>
<TD><INPUT TYPE=RADIO NAME=ChartType
    onClick="DoChartType(11)"> Simple Column </TD></TR>
<TR><TD><INPUT TYPE=RADIO NAME=ChartType
    onClick="DoChartType(1)"> Pie with Wedge Out </TD>
```

```html
<TD><INPUT TYPE=RADIO NAME=ChartType
    onClick="DoChartType(12)"> Stacked Column </TD></TR>

<TR><TD><INPUT TYPE=RADIO NAME=ChartType
    onClick="DoChartType(2)"> Simple Point </TD>
<TD><INPUT TYPE=RADIO NAME=ChartType
    onClick="DoChartType(13)"> Full Column </TD></TR>

<TR><TD><INPUT TYPE=RADIO NAME=ChartType
    onClick="DoChartType(3)"> Stacked Point </TD>
<TD><INPUT TYPE=RADIO NAME=ChartType
    onClick="DoChartType(14)"> Simple Bar </TD></TR>

<TR><TD><INPUT TYPE=RADIO NAME=ChartType
    onClick="DoChartType(4)"> Full Point </TD>
<TD><INPUT TYPE=RADIO NAME=ChartType
    onClick="DoChartType(15)"> Stacked Bar </TD></TR>

<TR><TD><INPUT TYPE=RADIO NAME=ChartType
    onClick="DoChartType(5)"> Simple Line </TD>
<TD><INPUT TYPE=RADIO NAME=ChartType
    onClick="DoChartType(16)"> Full Bar </TD></TR>

<TR><TD><INPUT TYPE=RADIO NAME=ChartType
    onClick="DoChartType(6)"> Stacked Line </TD>
<TD><INPUT TYPE=RADIO NAME=ChartType
    onClick="DoChartType(17)"> HLC Stock </TD></TR>

<TR><TD><INPUT TYPE=RADIO NAME=ChartType
    onClick="DoChartType(7)"> Full Line </TD>
<TD><INPUT TYPE=RADIO NAME=ChartType
    onClick="DoChartType(18)"> HLC Stock WSJ</TD></TR>

<TR><TD><INPUT TYPE=RADIO NAME=ChartType
    onClick="DoChartType(8)"> Simple Area </TD>
<TD><INPUT TYPE=RADIO NAME=ChartType
    onClick="DoChartType(19)"> OHLC Stock </TD></TR>

<TR><TD><INPUT TYPE=RADIO NAME=ChartType
    onClick="DoChartType(9)"> Stack Area </TD>
<TD><INPUT TYPE=RADIO NAME=ChartType
    onClick="DoChartType(20)"> OHLC Stock WSJ </TD></TR>

<TR><TD><INPUT TYPE=RADIO NAME=ChartType
    onClick="DoChartType(10)"> Full Area </TD></TR>
</TABLE>
```

Continues

Listing 13-5.
Continued.

```
477<TABLE XBORDER=5 WIDTH=125 BGCOLOR="#FFFFCC" ALIGN=LEFT>
<TR><TD BGCOLOR=NAVY ALIGN=CENTER><FONT
     COLOR=FFFFCC>Gridlines</TR>
<TR><TD><INPUT TYPE=CHECKBOX NAME="chkHorizontal"
     onClick="DoHorizontalGrid">Horizontal</TD></TR>
<TR><TD><INPUT TYPE=CHECKBOX NAME="chkVertical"
     onClick="DoVerticalGrid">Vertical</TD></TR>
<TR><TD BGCOLOR=NAVY ALIGN=CENTER><FONT
     COLOR=FFFFCC>Background</TR>
<TR><TD><INPUT TYPE=RADIO NAME=BackStyle
     onClick="DoBackground(1)">Opaque</TD></TR>
<TR><TD><INPUT TYPE=RADIO NAME=BackStyle
     onClick="DoBackground(0)">Transparent</TD></TR>

</TABLE>

<BR CLEAR=ALL>
<BR>

<INPUT TYPE=BUTTON VALUE="About Chart Control"
     NAME="cdmChartAboutBox" onClick="DoChartAboutBox">

<BR CLEAR=ALL>
<BR><BR>

<HR>
<B><FONT SIZE=4>Notes</FONT></B><BR>
The chart's properties on this page are changed by
     selecting the various radio buttons and checkboxes.
     The OnClick event of these intrinsic controls calls
     VBScript procedures that change the chart
     properties.<BR>
<P>
The About Chart Control command button calls the chart's
     AboutBox method.<BR>
<P>
To view the source code for this page, select
     <SAMP>Source</SAMP> from the <SAMP>View</SAMP>
     menu.<BR>
<P>
If you have any questions or comments about this example,
     please send them to <A HREF ="mailto:billr@smart.
     net">billr@smart.net</A>. We would appreciate feedback
     and would like to hear about other developers'
     experiences with these new tools.<BR>
<HR>
</BODY>
<ADDRESS>
<FONT SIZE=2>
&copy; 1996 Rollins & Associates, Inc.<BR>
Page last updated 08/28/96<BR>
Please send comments to <A HREF
```

Listing 13-5.
Continued.

```
         ="mailto:billr@smart.net">billr@smart.net</A><BR>
</FONT>
</ADDRESS>

</HTML>
```

Figure 13-7.
ActiveX and VBScript
example.

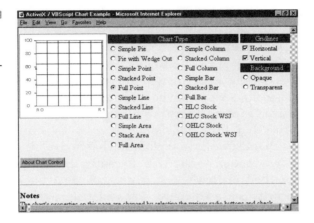

that let you view the style and type (the control's properties) of the chart. The chart has one method: **AboutBox**. Different properties are called from VB-Script when the users make their selections from the radio buttons and checkboxes. Finally, clicking the About Chart Control button invokes the **AboutBox** method.

As you can see, first we had to embed the object and gave it a name: **chart1**. Next, we created three VBScript functions in the page. The first function, **DoChartAboutBox**, does nothing but call the **AboutBox** method, as mentioned. The **DoChartType** function takes the parameter of an integer. When a value is passed to this function, the property of the ChartType control is assigned, and then that specific chart is drawn on the screen.

The **DoHorizontalGrid** function first checks whether the horizontal gridlines option has been checked by the user. If it has, a **1** is assigned to the property **HGridStyle**. Otherwise, a **0** is assigned to the property.

The **DoVerticalGrid** function checks whether the vertical gridlines option is checked. The function assigns a **1** to the **VGridStyle** property if it is; if not, it assigns a **0** to the property.

The **DoBackground** function assigns a background color to the **BackStyle** property. The default background color for the chart is set as Opaque; this function is invoked only if you check the Transparent option.

Note that all the functions are invoked by the event handler **onClick** from HTML form elements on the page.

CONCLUSION

The explosion of the Internet has added a new element to the mix. When Microsoft made the decision to enter the browser market with *Internet Explorer*, it became obvious that IE, like any COM-compliant application, could use OLE controls. Given bandwidth considerations, it was better to abandon certain requirements of the OCX format. Therefore, a buzzword was born: ActiveX. ActiveX controls are essentially the same thing as OLE controls, with reduced requirements (the only requirements are interfaces to register the control and to identify the control's methods and properties). This development allowed Microsoft to leverage a fairly well-established base of developers who were comfortable developing ActiveX controls. ActiveX's interactivity is a major selling point; ActiveX controls have capabilities that Java applets do not.

In this chapter, we have explained what ActiveX is and how it can be used to bring live content to the Web. Recently, this technology has had a huge impact on the Web that will surely expand as ActiveX matures. Regardless of the security concerns, ActiveX has a lot of potential in the market.

14

An Overview of COM and DCOM

The OLE and ActiveX technology we discussed in Chapter 13 is based on the *Compound Object Model* (COM). COM simply takes two pieces of software and connects them in the same machine. *Distributed COM* (DCOM), on the other hand, connects two pieces of software across a network. The problem with traditional software is that it isn't usually integrated—one's data and functions aren't easily available to others. Moreover, software comes with a set of functions that aren't easy to upgrade or remove with better services. There's a need for a new type of distributed, component-based software system, in which two or more pieces of software can be integrated into a single application to offer the best solution, regardless of where this software is located and what language it was created in. To accomplish this, COM and DCOM come into the picture. This chapter gives you a high-level overview of what they are and what they do.

This chapter will cover the following topics:

- Understanding COM
- How COM works
- Benefits of COM
- Distributed COM

Understanding COM

Have you asked yourself, "How do they come out with new computers so fast?" Well, if you thought new components had to be created each time a new PC came out, it would take years to come out with a new computer. Hardware companies obviously reuse the same components and just upgrade others. Unfortunately, the software industry isn't like the hardware industry. Developers still create software from scratch, taking months to ship the product to the market. Imagine if you developed a text editor. Wouldn't it be nice if you could buy a spellchecker component from a company and just plug it into the software you already have (which doesn't have a spellchecker)?

COM technology plays a role in how software can be reused and how different components can be tied together so that you don't have to write every single feature of the software from scratch. Now a company can do nothing but sell components that can be plugged into other software. It can forget about copyright issues or revealing its source code and devote itself totally to supplying the best search engine, spellchecker, merging tool, and so on. Moreover, a company can take advantage of COM's ability to provide easy extensibility beyond regular functions, as well as version control so that components can work perfectly, even though some individual components belong to a previous version. This trend of software reusability and selling specific components is just catching on.

How COM Works

COM works by connecting different objects (known as COM objects) that have different interfaces. These interfaces are actually function calls, also called *methods*, *member functions*, or *requests*. Each interface or method performs a specific action or service. Using its own object technology, COM, like a system service API, establishes the operation through which a client of a service can communicate with multiple providers of that service. After the client and the object establish the connection, COM fades away from the scene. Its only role is to make sure a connection is established so that the client and the object can communicate directly without added overhead (see Figure 14-1). By the way, the methods are related to one another in the same interface. For example, if there's an interface called *lookup*, then there could be methods like `word_lookup()`, `string_lookup()`, `num_lookup()`, and so forth.

NOTE *There are some distinctions between the regular objects you see in C/C++ and COM objects. For example, COM defines a completely standardized mechanism for creating objects and helping clients and objects communicate. Unlike an object-oriented programming environment, these mechanisms are application independent as well as language independent. Therefore, you can use any application environment to communicate between two or more objects and any language to create these objects. This is known as a* binary interoperability standard.

Figure 14-1.
A connection between the client and the object via COM.

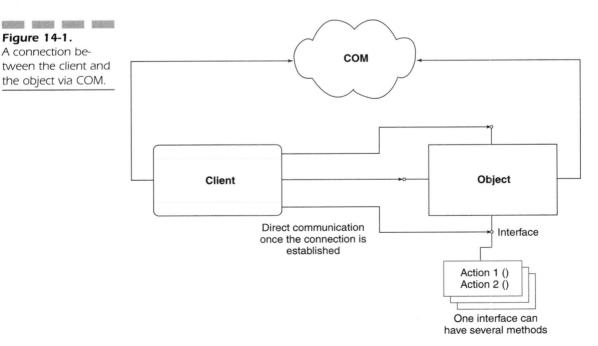

COM

Client

Object

Direct communication once the connection is established

Interface

Action 1 ()
Action 2 ()

One interface can have several methods

To invoke a method, as you can see in Figure 14-1, the client must have a pointer to the interface. As the object provides services through several interfaces, the client must point to the right interface to get the correct service.

Each COM object has its own class. In the same object, one class can provide a service, such as search for words, and another can do something totally different, such as add data or transfer data from one place to another. To run an actual instance of the object, you need to know about the object's class. To do that, you need to use the COM library in the system running COM. This library obviously has access to all the COM object's classes. The client, for example, calls the system library by using a function (not a method) and specifies the class. This action causes the object's class to run. Now the client can call the object's service through the object's methods, just like calling a local function. The client doesn't need to know if the code providing this service might be running on a separate system, in a library, or on a separate operating system. For COM, the services are accessed the same way, regardless of these distinctions, using one standard protocol to communicate between the object and the client.

COM is a true system object model. To support this statement, let's look at the following sections.

Using Globally Unique Identifiers

When you have millions of objects in a distributed environment, it's likely that different object creators have named their objects with the same name as other developers or even the same name as interfaces. This is a potential risk for objects connecting with each other that aren't designed for any kind of communication. To address this problem, COM uses 128-bit integers to identify each object, interface, and class anywhere in the network, across the universe. These integers are unique identifiers known as *Globally Unique Identifiers* (GUIDs); they're the same as the *Universal Unique IDs* (UUIDs) defined by DCE.

Security

For distributed computing, security is a big concern, especially because system object models tend to be too complex for corporate customers and independent software vendors. COM solves this problem with a secure architecture that can be used in an enterprise-wide computing environment.

First, COM checks whether the client actually has permission to run the code associated with a particular object's class. Then COM checks whether the client can load the object and whether access rights are available for the client. Finally, it checks the client's authentication because COM is based on *Remote Procedure Calls* (RPC) security architecture. This is a more sophisticated way of doing a security check than using simple *Operating System* (OS) permissions on code execution and read/write access to data.

Distributed Capabilities

For COM, a network is one computer with a lot of processing power and capabilities, so it doesn't matter if a piece of software is on a separate machine miles away. COM provides a transparent programming (known as *location transparency*) model for small, in-process objects, medium out-of-process objects on the same machine, or huge objects running on the network on another machine. Features such as direct access to object data, properties, or variables are omitted in COM. Therefore, the same service is easier to provide for an in-process object but not necessarily for an out-of-process object.

Code Reusability and Implementation Inheritance

Using inheritance in software development is a useful technique, but it does create a major problem, known as *type-safety* in the specialization interface. When the traditional implementation of inheritance takes place between objects, sometimes the connection can be lost because the traditional implementation (the "contract" or interface) among the objects isn't clearly identified. Therefore, if one object changes its implementation, the behavior of the other object can become undefined. A programmer must update both objects simultaneously to prevent losing the connection. This isn't a problem when the components reside on the same machine or network, but it does create problems in a distributed environment.

COM uses two techniques for code reuse. They are *containment/delegation* and *aggregation*. In the first and most common mechanism, one object (the "inner object") becomes encapsulated to the other object (the "outer object"). The outer object uses the inner object useful for its own implementation as the service provider. In this situation, because the outer object is a client of the inner object, it always uses the inner object's interface as a defined contract. This contract makes sure the inner object won't unexpectedly change its behavior.

COM objects can support multiple interfaces, and an aggregated COM object takes advantage of that feature. In this rare reuse mechanism, where the COM object is a composite object, the outer object exposes an interface from the inner object to the client. This treats the inner object's interface is a part of the outer object. Here it uses a special case to prevent the outer object from implementing an interface that will delegate each function to the same interface in the inner object. This technique is a performance convenience in COM.

Benefits of COM

There are several benefits of using COM:

- COM lets developers build and distribute applications easily and quickly. It offers reusable code as well as scalability from a single processor to a network. Moreover, developers can produce more because they have to learn only one object system for different platforms. With the binary and network standards that COM provides, programmers don't need to write a lot of procedures specialized to communicate among objects.

- With COM's single model for communication between objects, vendors can focus on creating reusable components targeted for specific small segments of the application. This focus lets developers create component-based software without much rewriting and allows the creation of a diverse software market with vendors specializing in certain components.

- Now that software developers are focusing on component-based software, end users have a choice of which objects to plug into their applications and can buy a particular piece from a local software store. Moreover, with COM, users are blessed with thousands of objects on their machines or on the network, already created by software vendors.

- Information system developers can now work on how to combine different components rather than create specific sections of the software. This makes corporations more productive and saves them thousands of dollars on information system managers who can focus on more business-specific tasks.

Distributed COM

The goal of COM was to extend from supporting single systems to a distributed system. This extension would let COM objects reside on any machine in a network and invoke methods of other COM objects on any other machine also connected to the network. A new technology called *Distributed COM* (DCOM) was born. DCOM uses RPCs, which to a client seems as though it's calling an object's method in a local machine, even though the object is actually located across the network. DCOM is available from the Microsoft Web site and can run on Windows NT and Windows 95 (at the time of this writing).

The following sections describe some characteristics of DCOM.

Location Independence

DCOM can hide the location of the software component, whether the component resides locally or somewhere else. No matter where the components are located, the method DCOM uses to connect the client to the component and call its method is identical. No changes are necessary to the source. It's not even necessary to recompile the program. A simple reconfiguration in the system is all that's needed. This characteristic of DCOM makes distributed application development simpler.

Language Neutrality

Because DCOM is an extension of COM, you can use any language, such as C++, Java, Delphi, or COBOL, to create COM objects. This feature makes it easier for businesses to use their expertise to develop applications with the language they're most comfortable with. It also allows rapid prototyping— you can create components with a high-level language, such as Visual Basic, and later reimplement them with some other language, such as C++, to take advantage of DCOM's advanced features, such as threadpooling.

Connection Management

DCOM manages connections to components by maintaining a reference count on each component. It uses a pinging protocol to see whether the client is still active. DCOM counts backwards from three pings. If the client doesn't respond to this protocol, DCOM decreases the count tally. If the count reaches zero, DCOM releases the component. In this way, DCOM offers robust distributed garbage collection. This mechanism is transparent to the application and offers a rich, interactive connection between the client and the server.

Fault Tolerance

DCOM's fault-tolerance technique is robust and easy to implement. For example, if the client detects a component failure, it reconnects to the referring component that originally established the connection. The referral component informs the server that it's no longer active and automatically supplies a new instance of a component running on a different system. The best part about DCOM in this situation is that it can perform tasks such as splitting a component on either the server side or the client side and connect and reconnect to the component in a transparent manner to the client.

Security

DCOM uses security features from Windows that support multiple identification and authentication mechanisms. These security features focus a great deal on the user directory, which stores information such as username, password, public key, and so forth, to validate the user. Most of the other platforms that support DCOM use the same features to offer a complete, secure, distributed architecture.

CONCLUSION

In this chapter, we have given you some more information on COM, which is a critical part of an ActiveX component. We tried to provide just an overview of COM and DCOM in this chapter to reduce complexity. If you want to learn more on COM/DCOM, you should consult the following books:

- *ActiveX from the Ground Up* by John Paul Mueller (ISBN: 0-07-882264-5)
- *Understanding ActiveX and OLE* by David Chappell (ISBN: 1-57231-216-5)

The next chapters cover more detailed information on OLE, the beginnings of how to create an ActiveX control.

15

Visual Basic and OLE

Now that we have discussed what ActiveX is, we will explain how to actually create an ActiveX control, the center of ActiveX's attention. But before we do that, we need to find out what language to use to create a control. Although there are several options, such as *Visual Basic* (VB), Java, and C++, we will use Visual Basic because it's probably the easiest language for creating such controls. This chapter discusses VB in general and is written to give you an idea what this language looks like. If you already know enough about VB, you might want to skip this chapter and go to Chapter 16, "Creating ActiveX Controls with VB5," which walks you through a tutorial on how to actually create a control.

This chapter will cover the following topics:

- An introduction to VB
- OLE programming with VB

An Introduction to VB

Visual Basic is an outgrowth of the family of languages that evolved out of Dartmouth's *Beginner's All-purpose Symbolic Instruction Code* (BASIC). Visual Basic is more than a computer language, however; the great innovation behind VB is its *Integrated Development Environment* (IDE). This environment allows rapid development of processes that are trudgingly slow in other languages. For example, creating a window is pretty much always the same; like many other development processes, it's automated in Visual Basic. The overriding concept behind VB is, to quote Thoreau, "Simplicity, simplicity, simplicity." Although this simplicity comes at the cost of some control over low-level functions, VB is a tremendously powerful development platform.

This is not to say that a nonprogrammer can sit down with Visual Basic and instantly develop sophisticated applications. Like any language, Visual Basic has a learning curve, but it's probably the easiest language for a new programmer to pick up. Given this ease of use, it's no mystery why Microsoft chose it to promote ActiveX.

The new version of Visual Basic, version 5.0, automates the creation of ActiveX controls. Using the same basic model of application construction, VB developers can create ActiveX controls capable of doing almost anything a traditional application can. You can develop ActiveX controls with any language (even Java), but VB is likely to become the main platform for ActiveX control development because of its ease of use.

So we're off. We'll begin with a brief introduction to VB, and then proceed on to the meat of the subject—ActiveX control creation. As with all things in the new development world, control creation begins with objects.

Objects

If you read Chapter 2, "Object-Oriented Programming Concepts," you already learned about object-oriented programming. Object-oriented languages help programmers look at the task in front of them in an intuitive way. To understand what this means, it's helpful to understand what came before. At the dawn of programming, developers work procedurally—that is, everything that happened in the program was placed in one long main procedure. In procedural programming, a word processing program looked like this:

(User starts program)

1. Perform startup, check for files, draw main window.
2. Wait for user input.
3. Process user input, then go back to 2 unless they want to quit; then go to 4.
4. Perform shutdown, prompt for save, free resources.

As the complexity of software increased, the complexity of developing a program increased exponentially. Writing these programs procedurally was difficult; human beings tend to think in discrete terms rather than in a linear, step-by-step fashion. With the advent of C++, an object-oriented version of the language C, the *Object-Oriented* (OO) approach began to take hold. To demonstrate exactly what we mean by OO, let's take a look at that same word processing program written in an object-oriented fashion:

1. Application executes its **Startup** method, creating a **MainWindow** object.
2. When a user entered text, the **MainWindow** would execute a **ProcessInput** method, perhaps referring to the **Application** object to execute its **Save** method.
3. When a user wanted to terminate the program, the **Application** object would execute its **Destroy** method on the **MainWindow** object, as well as executing its **Shutdown** method.

What we're getting at here is a philosophy of programming that allows us to treat problems and solutions as discrete elements, rather than having to eat the entire elephant all at once. The difference might seem insignificant at first, but the impact is tremendous. To use a little more down-to-earth example, think of the things around you as objects having properties and methods. Your light switch has a **State** property that can have two values: **Off** or **On**. When the value of this property changes, it executes either the **Illuminate** or **Darken** method, making the room light or dark. Think of your television as having **Channel** and **Volume** properties. The **Channel** property can have any number of numerical values. Some of these values are meaningless, because no broadcasts are made on that channel. Your **Television** object might have a **Mute** method, which sets the value of the **Volume** property to **0**. Let's introduce one more concept that we'll cover in greater detail later on: events. An event is no more complex than it sounds: It's when something happens. Your **Door** object might have an **Open** event; your **Nose** object might have a **Sneeze** event. As you can see, this way of thinking is very natural and intuitive. By placing code in objects, conceptually, design efficiency was vastly improved.

NOTE *Visual Basic is a massive development environment. To describe every aspect of every code element within VB would be impossible to do in 10 entire books, much less two chapters. Rest assured we will cover the important things, but we'll leave plenty of gems for you to find on your own.*

At the present time, there's no purely object-oriented language. Visual Basic has a distinctively object-oriented nature, nonetheless, and uses several intrinsic objects you should be familiar with.

Modules

In Visual Basic, we compartmentalize, or *encapsulate*, our code. This means that we place code in discrete and logical packages. One of the ways we do this is with code modules, which come in two flavors—class and regular. Regular modules are used as "code buckets," for lack of a better term. Code placed into these modules is available to all other forms, modules, and objects throughout the project. Use code modules when you want to create code elements that will be available to everything throughout the project. For example, we might have an application used to keep track of employee records. We want to have a function that computes the tax bracket according to salary available to the entire project. To do this, first insert a code module into your project by selecting Project | Add Module. With the module selected, press F4. A window appears where you can specify the name of the module—in this case, **Global**. Now press F7, bringing up the code editor for the module; then simply place the code you want to make available in the module. Class modules are used as a template for creating objects. We will discuss classes in detail subsequently.

Form/UserControl Object

The most basic element of a Visual Basic program is the *Form*. Its equivalent in an ActiveX control is the **UserControl** object, with which it shares most of its properties, methods, and events. We will refer to both of these interchangeably from here on as Forms. A **Form** object is a window, like a window that displays Netscape, Control Panel, or any program you use in Windows.

In reality, **Form** or **UserControl** objects are just modules. The difference is that these modules have preset methods, properties, and constants that developers can't modify. Their status as objects gives them all the privileges and duties of a module otherwise.

Command Button

A **CommandButton** is one of the simplest and most familiar controls in Windows. It's a simple, rectangular box with a text label on it (see Figure 15-1). When clicked on, it gives the appearance of being pressed in; when released, it rebounds.

A **Form** with a single **CommandButton** placed on it is shown in Figure 15-1. **CommandButton**s generally serve to give the user a direct way to initiate some action on the part of the program. The **CommandButton** has several properties that are important to understand, described in the following sections.

CAPTION   The **Caption** property of the **CommandButton** in Figure 15-1 is **Command1**. The **Caption** property is used to specify what text will appear on the button.

A **CommandButton**, like all controls, has events. One of the primary events for the **CommandButton** is the **Click** event. This event occurs when the user places his or her mouse over the button and presses one of the mouse buttons. The event procedure looks like this:

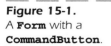

Figure 15-1.
A **Form** with a
CommandButton.

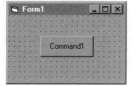

```
Private Sub Command1_Click()

End Sub
```

To make something happen when this event occurs, we place code between the first line and the last line.

TEXTBOX   Another simple but important control is the **TextBox**. The **TextBox** is a rectangular box that can store text entered by the user with the keyboard.

Pictured in Figure 15-2 is a **Form** containing a **TextBox**, which is used within an application to serve as a notepad for users, to store information and to display information. **TextBox**es have several important properties, described in the following sections.

FONT   The **Font** property defines how text will appear in the **TextBox**. When we change the **Font** property, the font selection dialog box shown in Figure 15-3 appears.

There are three lists in the window: Font, Font style, and Size. Font refers to the name of the font; it could be MS Sans Serif, Tahoma, or any other font that's installed on your system. Style refers to the display characteristics of

Figure 15-2.
A **Form** with a
TextBox.

Figure 15-3.
The Font dialog box.

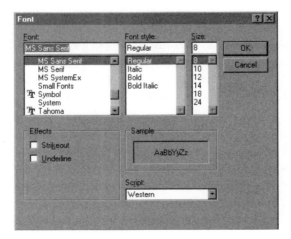

the font: Normal, Bold, Italic, or Bold Italic. The third window, Size, refers to the size in points of the font (a *point* is 1/72 of an inch). Below these main lists are three further options you can specify: StrikeOut, Underline, and Script. Text with the **strikeout** property set to true will appear like this:

~~This is Strikeout text~~

Text with the **Underline** property set to true appears like this:

<u>This is Underlined text</u>

The **Script** property refers to the character set used by Windows. This is a fairly obscure property, and you probably won't need to worry about it.

FORECOLOR   You might wonder why there's no place to specify the color of the text in the Font dialog box. The color of the text is held separate from the **Font** object in the **ForeColor** property. When you change the **ForeColor** property of an object in Visual Basic, you see the dialog box shown in Figure 15-4.

By clicking on a color, you can set the color you want for your text.

TEXT   The **Text** property refers to the contents of the **TextBox**. This value can be set either by the program or by a user entering text into it.

Label

When working with other controls, it can be helpful to place text near them to indicate their purpose. One way to do this is by using the **Label** control, a rectangular box that displays text.

A **Form** containing a **Label** control is shown in Figure 15-5. We have made the form background a different color so that it's easier to see where the **Label** begins and ends. In ordinary usage, a **Label** is the same color as the background so that only the text looks different. **Label**s are used to place text that's not to be changed by the user in an application. The **Label** control's properties are described in the following sections.

Figure 15-4.
The Color Selection
dialog box.

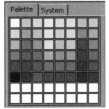

Figure 15-5.
A **Form** with a
Label.

Figure 15-6.
A **Form** with a
transparent **Label**.

BACKSTYLE

The **Backstyle** property has two values: **Opaque** and **Transparent**. The **Label** in Figure 15-5 has its **Backstyle** property set to **Opaque**. The following **Label**, in Figure 15-6, has its **Backstyle** property set to **Transparent**.

As the figure shows, the **BackStyle** property determines whether the background will show through a **Label**, leaving only its caption visible.

CAPTION The **Caption** property defines what text will appear on the **Label**. It's very similar to the **Caption** property of the **CommandButton** object.

FONT The **Font** property defines how text will appear on the **Label**. It's very similar to the **Font** property of the **TextBox** object.

FORECOLOR The **ForeColor** property defines what color the text on the **Label** will be. It's very similar to the **ForeColor** property of the **TextBox** object.

PICTUREBOX Because Windows is a graphical environment, it's often useful to have a holder with which to insert graphics into an application. The **PictureBox** is useful for this purpose.

A **Form** containing a **PictureBox** is shown in Figure 15-7. The image inside is defined by its **Picture** property. **PictureBox**es, can serve like this one, can simply hold a graphic, or they can serve as containers for other objects. This element of a **PictureBox**'s behavior can be useful for creating scrolling viewports or organizing groups of controls. **PictureBox** controls have several important properties, described in the following sections.

Figure 15-7.
A **Form** with a
PictureBox.

AUTOSIZE **AutoSize** is a very useful property. When it's set to true, the **PictureBox** resizes itself so that it's exactly the minimum size needed to hold the image. The **PictureBox** in Figure 15-7 has its AutoSize property set to true.

DRAWWIDTH The **DrawWidth** property determines how wide objects created with graphical methods will be. For instance, if the **DrawWidth** property has a value of **4**, then a line drawn on it with the **Line** method will be four pixels wide.

FILLSTYLE The **FillStyle** property determines how filled objects, like a circle or box, appear. The self-explanatory values for this property are as follows:

- Solid
- Transparent
- Horizontal Line
- Vertical Line
- Upward Diagonal
- Downward Diagonal
- Cross
- Diagonal Cross

FILLCOLOR The **FillColor** property determines what color the "fill" within filled objects will be.

FORECOLOR The **ForeColor** property determines the default color for graphics rendered with graphical methods.

PICTURE The **Picture** control is the picture that appears in the **PictureBox**; it can be a number of graphical file formats. It's important to note that it's not a string or a filename; the following would trigger an error:

```
picPrintBox.Picture = "C:\WINDOWS\TILED.BMP"
```

This property is actually a reference to a **Picture** object in memory. Within the Visual Basic IDE, however, you can specify a filename.

What is filling? I've mentioned it a couple of times. Objects that are solid are *filled*; objects that are outlined are not. Whether and how a graphic is filled depends on the value of the **FillStyle** property at the time the object is drawn. If you want an unfilled object, simply make sure the **FillStyle** property is set to **Transparent** at drawing time.

Variables and Data Types

As you know, the very core of all programming is *variables*, which are used to store information about what's going on in the program. We tend to think of variables as buckets in which you can keep things you need to remember later, like how many times you've gone through a loop, or what text a user entered.

Declaration

When we plan to use a variable in a program, we have to tell the computer so that it can allocate memory before it's used:

```
Dim I As Integer
```

This statement is called a *declaration*. **Dim** means "prepare to use" or "allocate memory for a variable called." The next item (**I**, in this case) is the name we'll use to refer to this variable in the procedure. Finally, we tell VB about the information we expect the variable to hold with its data type. With Visual Basic, if you fail to declare a variable, or declare a variable without specifying a type, VB assumes you meant to declare it as a Variant data type. We'll explain more about this later.

Data Types

Every variable has a certain data type. If the variable itself is a bucket, then the data type would represent the shape of the bucket. The variable's data type defines what kind of information it can hold. The following sections describe several data types used in Visual Basic.

INTEGER A variable of the Integer type can hold any whole number, such as -268 or 112 (as opposed to a real number, such as -268.031 or 112.897), between -32768 and 32767. Integers are good for handling relatively small numbers and for use as counters.

LONG A variable of the Long type can hold any whole number between -2,147,483,648 and 2,147,483,647. Longs are useful for dealing with large numbers and for use as ID numbers for several objects.

SINGLE A variable of the Single type can hold real numbers (numbers with decimal places) between -3.402823E38 and -1.401298E-45—in other words, just about any number you're going to need to worry about. Singles are useful for doing "real" math, such as financial or scientific calculations.

STRING A variable of the String type holds text values. Strings are used, quite simply, to deal with words and numbers that you want to treat as text.

BOOLEAN A variable of the Boolean type holds only two values: True and False. Booleans are used to handle On/Off, True/False, or one-or-the-other situations.

VARIANT A variable of the Variant type can hold anything at all: Integers, Longs, Singles, String, and so forth. Actually, there are a few exceptions, but nothing you need to worry about right now.

You might be asking, "If Variants can hold anything, why not just declare everything as a Variant?" This leads to a discussion of why we need data types in the first place. Let's look at it this way: We have a pickup truck that we're going to use to transport cherries, oranges, and basketballs (bear with me). We need buckets to hold each of them before we can put the buckets in the truck. We can place only one of each item in each bucket. We'll need three different-sized buckets: One for the cherries, one for the oranges, and one for the basketballs. Now, the basketball bucket could hold any one of the three items, but there would be wasted space. To get the most stuff moved per truck trip, we need to have buckets that fit each item as closely as possible. The truck represents your computer's memory. Your computer has a limited amount of memory for storing these variables. The cherry, orange, and basketball represent pieces of information you need to store. Finally, the buckets represent the data types. If we had an infinite amount of memory, we could declare everything as Variant. Because we don't, doing so is very inefficient. The moral of this story?

To maximize the efficiency of your program, declare your variables with a data type that closely fits the type of information you expect it to handle. Declare a variable as a Variant only when no other data type will fit.

Constants

Now that we've talked about things that change, we'll talk about what never changes—constants. *Constants* are used when a static piece of data reappears again and again. For example, in a physics program, we might constantly be referring to the speed of light:

```
E = M * (300,000 km/s)²
```

Here we see a familiar formula. If we wanted to be able to refer to the speed of light, $(300{,}000 \; m/s)^2$, as c, we would declare c as a constant like this:

```
Const C = 300000
```

Note that we didn't have to declare a data type for c. Because c will hold only one value, VB knows exactly how much memory to allot for the constant. Constants should be used as a matter of good programming habits. Look at the following block of code:

```
Profit = 188 * (28.50 - .05 * 28.50)
```

What does it mean? Using constants makes it clear:

```
Profit = UnitsSold * (CostPerUnit - SalesCommision *
CostPerUnit)
```

Although we're creating instructions for computers, we should try to make our code readable and understandable to people, too.

Scope

In addition to having a type, every variable has what is called scope. *Scope* refers to exactly what has access to the variable. There are three essential scopes: **Public**, **Private**, and **Dim**.

PUBLIC Variables declared with the **Public** keyword are available to everything in the world. This might be a little dramatic, but it really is true. A **Public** variable declared within an object model is available to other procedures, other modules, even other applications. The one trick to

`Public` variables is that to access them, you have to specify the module name before the variable name:

```
(within the Form1 module)
Public Test As Single

(within the Form2 module)
MsgBox Form1.Test
```

This requirement does a couple of things. First of all, it results in clearer code; it's always obvious that we're referring to a member of a code module. When we name form modules a little more creatively, this becomes apparent:

```
(within a module called Finance)
Public Principal As Single

(within a module called Amortization)
MsgBox Finance.Principal
```

Second, it allows you to declare the same-named variable across separate modules:

```
(within a module called Finance)
Public Principal As Single

(within a module called Amortization)
Public Principal As Single

(within a module called Form1)
MsgBox Finance.Principal
MsgBox Amortization.Principal
```

`Public` variables might seem really useful, but you must use them with extreme care. Because anyone can access a `Public` variable, anyone can change it. `Public` variables are, therefore, the least reliable and the most likely to cause errors that are difficult to detect.

PRIVATE   Variables that have a scope of `Private` can be accessed only by procedures within the scope in which the variable is declared. The `Private` keyword is used when declaring variables within modules, such as object or code modules. For example, we could declare a variable with a `Private` scope, as follows:

```
Private TestVar As Integer
if we refer to this variable from within another module:
Sub AnotherProc()
    MsgBox TestVar
End Sub
```

However, we would encounter an error, or at best an empty variable. **AnotherProc**, by definition, doesn't have access to another module's internal procedures. It lies within a different scope. **Private** scope is the most desirable; the fewer things that have access to a variable, the better. Of course, some data must exposed to other modules, if not other applications, particularly when creating controls. Rather than declaring variables as **Public**, consider exposing them by using **Property** statements. We'll go over **Property** statements in great detail later on.

DIM   Variables declared with the **Dim** keyword are available to all procedures within the scope of the declaration. If declared within a module, the variable can be accessed by all the procedures within the modules. If the variable is declared at the procedure level, variables are available only within the procedure. We can declare a variable within a module, as follows:

```
Dim Test As Integer
```

The **Test** variable is available to any procedure within the module, but not to procedures outside the module. If we declare a variable within a procedure, the variable is available only to the procedure.

NOTE   *For Visual Basic programmers who worked before version 3.0, the only scope available was* **Dim**. *Version 3.0 introduced the* **Global** *keyword, which has been replaced by the word* **Public**. *Finally, version 4.0 introduced the* **Private** *keyword. This progression of scope means you often hear the word Dim used as a verb by VB developers. When you see the phrase "Dimming a variable," it really means "declaring a variable." To further confuse the issue, you might see the phrase "dimming a variable as* **Public**," *which means "declaring a variable with the* **Public** *keyword."*

User-Defined Data Types and Arrays

When you're dealing with objects, it's useful to be able to treat data as objects. For example, if we're building a program to keep track of a collection of video games, there's a certain way to go about it. First of all, we're going to want to have a variable to keep track of the name of the game. We'll call this variable **Name**:

```
Dim Name As String
```

Simple, right? Even with a game named something like *360*, the data represents a word or a title. There is a problem, however. This variable stores only one name. There is more than one game in this collection, so we'll need to have some way to use this variable as a list. We can do this with arrays. The word *array* sounds scary and technical, but it means nothing more than "list." If you get confused, just throw out the word *array*, and replace it with the word *list*. We have 28 video games, so we need to make an array, or list, 28 items long:

```
Dim Name(1 to 28) as String
```

What we've done here is create a 28-item list, with each item holding text, or String, data. Whenever we want to get an item out of that list, we just refer to the list name with a list number. What that means is that if we want item number 12 from the list, we just do it like this:

```
Video = Name(12)
```

In designing our program, notice that every game we're looking at has several pieces of information we want to keep track of. With these games, we want to store the name of the game, the year it was released, and who manufactured it. One way to do that is like this:

```
Dim Name(1 to 28) as String
Dim ReleaseYear(1 to 28) as String
Dim Manufacturer(1 to 28) as String
```

This is fine, but when we start dealing with the data, it's kind of awkward to have to keep referring to these variables separately when they all refer to the same object. What we really need is a **VideoGame** data type, which consists of three strings: **Name**, **ReleaseYear**, and **Manufacturer**. This data type is called a *User Defined Type* (UDT):

```
Type VideoGame
Name As String
ReleaseYear As String
Manufacturer As String
End Type
```

Notice that we didn't create arrays with each string member of this type. Each video game has only one name, not 28. At this point, all we've done is create a new data type, like Integer or String. We still need to declare an array of this type:

```
Dim MyVideoGame(1 to 28) As VideoGame
```

We now have a variable array, 28 items long, which holds the three pieces of information we need: **Name**, **ReleaseYear**, and **Manufacturer**. Let's say we want to know the **Manufacturer** of the 12th item in our list:

```
Answer = MyVideoGame(12).Manufacturer
```

We refer to individual members of the data type with a dot and the data member.

CONTROL ARRAYS   When we're dealing with several similar controls, we encounter the problem of duplicate code between these controls. For example, we can have ten **TextBox**es on a **Form**. When the control has the focus and the user presses the Enter key, we want the focus to shift to the next **TextBox**, unless it's the last **TextBox** on the **Form**. If that's the case, we want the focus to shift back to the first. To do this, we need to put something like the following in the control's **KeyPress** event (this event defines what happens when the user presses a key):

```
Private Sub txtTextBox_KeyPress(KeyAscii As Integer)
    If KeyAscii = 13 Then 'a keyascii value of thirteen
indicates that the user pressed Enter
            txtNextBox.SetFocus
    End If
End Sub
```

We must place this code within every **TextBox**, replacing the **txtNextBox** with whatever the next **TextBox** is. It's a somewhat inconvenient way to do things, and it gets much worse when we decide to add a new **TextBox** later on. Luckily, VB makes it easier by allowing us to create an array of the **txtTextBox** control and place all the code there. To create a control array, we can simply select the control, and then copy and paste it to the **Form**, or we can change the **Index** property of the first control to **0**, and then change the names of the other controls to **txtTextBox**. When we do so, we receive an additional argument—**Index**—in all the events that tells us which specific control fired the event:

```
Private Sub txtTextBox_KeyPress(Index As Integer,
    KeyAscii As Integer)
    If KeyAscii = 13 Then
        If Index < txtTextBox.Count - 1 Then
            txtTextBox(Index + 1).SetFocus
        Else
            txtTextBox(0).SetFocus
        End If
    End If
End Sub
```

The procedure looks basically the same. First, check to make sure it was the Enter key that the user pressed. If it wasn't, we don't want to do anything in the procedure. Within that test, check to make sure it isn't the last control in the array. The `txtTextBox.Count - 1` phrase gives us the index of the last control in the array. Because our indexes are zero-based, our highest index will be one less than the total number of controls in the array. If this test fails, we're on the last `txtTextBox` in the array, and we need to set the focus back to the first control in the array, `txtTextBox(0)`. This kind of structure is tremendously labor-saving when we have a series of controls that we want to behave in the same way.

COLLECTIONS   Arrays are useful, but sometimes a more powerful, flexible approach is called for. Suppose, for instance, we want to use an array, `ArrayOfStuff`, to store information we'll be recalling often. It's fairly difficult to retrieve information from an array without knowing the index. We can, of course, create another array to store those indexes, but this is wasteful and not very intuitive. We could loop through the array until we find the information, but with anything more than a very small array, we begin to pay a nasty performance penalty. The greater the number of items in the array, the longer it would take to retrieve a piece of information. Furthermore, if we wanted to store different data types within the array, we would have to dimension the array as Variant, which we always want to avoid, if possible. Luckily, VB gives us a fairly easy answer to all these problems—collections.

Collections are like arrays, but easier to work with. A collection is declared like this:

```
Private MyCollection As New Collection
```

We begin with the scope, which is `Private`. `MyCollection` is the name we'll use to refer to the collection. The word *New* means that we'll actually create a space in memory for the collection. Because a collection is actually an object, we need to declare it like an object. Without the `New` keyword, `MyCollection` is an empty object, which makes it worthless unless we use the `Set` keyword to assign it to a nonempty object. `New` allows us to bypass all this and create a Collection from scratch.

Collection objects have the methods and properties dscribed in the following sections.

ADD   The `Add` method takes an item and places it in the collection, assigning it a key. The developer can access the item with this key by using the `Item` method. The `Add` method takes the following arguments:

■ **Item:** This argument represents the item that will be added to the collection.

■ **Key:** This optional argument represents the identifier that will be used later to access the item. Without the **key** argument, items must be identified with their ordinal position in the collection (the ordinal the number 1 to the total number of items in the collection).

COUNT   The **Count** property returns the number of items that have been placed in the collection. It receives no arguments.

ITEM   The **Item** function returns the item specified by the **key** argument passed in the function call. If **key** is a string, then the item corresponding to the **key** argument is returned; if **key** is a number, the item in that position in the collection is returned. If no item corresponds to the **key** argument, an error occurs.

REMOVE   The **Remove** method removes the item that corresponds to the **key** argument. If **key** is a string, the item that corresponds to the **key** argument is removed; if **key** is a number, the item at that position in the collection is removed. If no item corresponds to the **key** argument, an error occurs.

The following procedure in Listing 15-1 illustrates these methods.

When we execute this procedure, we should get the following message boxes:

```
MsgBox iCollection.Count: 2
MsgBox iCollection.Item("Test1"): This is a test
MsgBox iCollection.Item(1): This is a test
MsgBox iCollection.Item(2): This is a test2
```

Note that we get the same result from requesting an item using "Test1" and using the ordinal position, 1. The last two lines are the same. You

Listing 15-1.
A collection example.

```
Sub DoCollections()
    Dim iCollection As New Collection
    iCollection.Add "This is a test", "Test1"
    iCollection.Add "This is a test2"
    MsgBox iCollection.Count
    MsgBox iCollection.Item("Test1")
    MsgBox iCollection.Item(1)
    MsgBox iCollection.Item(2)
    iCollection.Remove (1)
    iCollection.Remove (1)
End Sub
```

might think that would trigger an error because we appear to be removing the same item twice, but that's not the case. Once we remove the first item, the second item shifts and becomes the first item. Therefore, when we tell the collection to discard the first item a second time, it's discarding what was formerly the second item. A little confusing? Think of it this way. The collection is like a stack of dishes. When you remove the top dish, what used to be the second dish is now the first dish. What was the third is now the second, and so on. Therefore, you could remove all the dishes by issuing the same command over and over again: Remove the top dish. That's all that is going on here.

Also, collections can use a special loop to address every one of their members. We'll talk about this in the section on control structures.

SPECIAL COLLECTIONS Visual Basic has some standard collections designed to make developers' lives easier. These collections are described briefly in the following sections.

FORMS COLLECTION The Forms collection consists of all of the forms within a project.

CONTROLS COLLECTION The Controls collection consists of all the controls in the current project, or with a **Form** assignment. Like the following, it consists of all of the controls within another **Form**:

```
Form2.Controls.Count
```

CONTROL ARRAY COLLECTIONS When you create a control array, you also create a control collection. For instance, if you create a control array of three **TextBox**es—**txtTextBox(0)**, **txtTextBox(1)**, and **txtTextBox(2)**—you also have a three-item collection. The implementation is a little different from a traditional collection; there are no **Item**, **Remove**, or Add aspects. The **For...Each** and **Count** elements, however, are just the same:

```
Dim Item As Control
    For Each Item In txtTextBox
        If Item.Text <> "" Then
            MsgBox Item.Text
        End If
    Next Item
```

Notice that we have replaced a Variant object variable with a variable declared as **Control**. In this example, we would loop through each of the

txtTextBox controls in the array; unless the **TextBox** was blank, we would pop up a message box with the contents of the box. This kind of looping becomes especially useful when a control collection changes because of new control instances being loaded.

Procedures and Functions

Now that we understand a little about how data is stored, we can delve into creating actual code. Every program and control has a main procedure. In a regular program, the main procedure will either be the **Sub Form_Load** procedure, which occurs when the startup **Form** is loaded, or **Sub Main**. Within Visual Basic, windows are referred to as **Forms**, where you can put controls and write code. Most of your code will probably reside in event statements for your **Form** or objects on your **Form**.

You can specify code that will occur when something happens on a certain control. For example, suppose you have a button on a **Form** named **cmdButton**. This is the procedure that would occur when the user clicks **cmdButton**:

```
Sub cmdButton_Click()

End Sub
```

We'd like a message box to pop up when the user clicks on the button. The following statement will make the message box say **You clicked me!**:

```
Sub cmdButton_Click()
    MsgBox "You clicked me!"
End Sub
```

This is a fairly straightforward procedure, but with more complex procedures, it can become more difficult. Let's say we want to pop up a message box, change the text in a **TextBox** named **Text1**, change the **Caption** property of a **Label** control called **Label1**, and do a couple of other things:

```
Sub cmdButton_Click()
    MsgBox "You clicked me!"
    Text1.Text = "You clicked him!"
    Label1.Caption = "Yeah!"
    Text1.Width - 500
    Label1.Caption = "You just moved him!"
    Label1.Caption = "Hey, stop that!"
End Sub
```

This is a silly example, but you get the idea. If, for some reason, we wanted to go through this same silly sequence when the user clicked three other buttons, **cmdTwo**, **cmdThree**, and **cmdFour**, we can copy and paste the code, but that's inconvenient. The real problem arises when we decide to modify this procedure. If we want the changes to be reflected across all the buttons, we have to go through each procedure and modify the code again. As you can imagine, that process quickly becomes a nightmare to maintain and debug. What we do instead is create a procedure, shown in Listing 15-2, that we can modify once and then reference in each button.

Whenever we reference this procedure as shown in the following code, and place this line in each additional button, we get the same output:

```
Sub cmdButton_Click()
    SillyProcedure
End Sub
```

If we want to make the message box say **You clicked me with your mouse!** we modify it, once, in the SillyProcedure code listing. We might also want to make the message box say something different for each button. To do this, we modify the SillyProcedure as follows:

```
Sub SillyProcedure(Message As String)
```

We're passing the procedure an argument called **Message**. The next line looks like this:

```
MsgBox Message
```

The rest of the procedure remains the same. To specify the message, we supply the argument in the call to the procedure, as shown in Listing 15-3.

Now, depending on which button you click, you will get a different message.

Suppose we wanted a user to enter a value into a **TextBox**, click a button, and see his or her message with an exclamation mark placed on the

Listing 15-2.
SillyProcedure
example.

```
Sub SillyProcedure()
    MsgBox "You clicked me!"
    Text1.Text = "You clicked him!"
    Label1.Caption = "Yeah!"
    Text1.Width - 500
    Label1.Caption = "You just moved him!"
    Label1.Caption = "Hey, stop that!"
End Sub
```

Listing 15-3.
Command button
code.

```
Sub cmdButton_Click()
    SillyProcedure "You clicked the first!"
End Sub

Sub cmdTwo_Click()
    SillyProcedure "You clicked the second!"
End Sub

Sub cmdThree_Click()
    SillyProcedure "You clicked the third!"
End Sub

Sub cmdFour_Click()
    SillyProcedure "You clicked the fourth!"
End Sub
```

end. What we need is a procedure that can accept the text value as an argument, process the input, and return the argument with the exclamation point appended. A procedure that can return a value is called a *function*. The first line of the function we described would look like this:

```
Function AddAPoint(InitialString As String) As String
```

Notice that we have defined the data type of this function at the end. Because it's returning a value, it must have a data type like any other variable. We define the data type of the argument as a string, too:

```
    AddAPoint = InitialString & "!"
End Function
```

The next two lines involve processing the input and returning control to the procedure that called the function. We use the title of the function, **AddAPoint**, and assign the argument passed to the procedure and an exclamation point to it. This specifies the value that will be returned. The function is used like this:

```
Sub cmdButton_Click()
    Dim Temp As String
    Temp = AddAPoint(Text1.Text)
    MsgBox Temp
End Sub
```

We will use the variable **Temp** to contain the processed input. **Text1.Text** refers to text that a user has typed into **Text1**. On the next line, we invoke the **AddAPoint** function, passing it the value of **Text1.Text** to process and assign the return value to **Temp**. Note that we have enclosed the argument in parentheses; any time an equals sign is involved in a function call, parentheses are necessary. On the last line, we pop up a message box with the value in **Temp**. We broke up these lines for clarity (believe it or not); we really could have done it all in one line like this:

```
MsgBox AddAPoint(Text1.Text)
```

This has been a very simple example, so let's construct a function that's actually useful. This next function determines whether a number is odd:

```
Function IsOdd(TestValue As Integer) As Boolean
    If TestValue Mod 2 = 0 Then
        IsOdd = False
    Else
        IsOdd = True
    End If
End Function
```

The expression **TestValue Mod 2** means "What is the remainder of dividing **TestValue** by two?" This is basic mathematics; all odd numbers have a remainder of something other than zero when divided by two. The first line of the function reads like this in English: "If the remainder of the value of **TestValue** divided by two is zero then . . . ."

This is the definition of an even number, so we make the value of the function **False** (remember, it's a Boolean function). If the first test fails, we set the value of the function to be **True**. To use the function when clicking a button called **Command1**, use the following code:

```
Private Sub Command1_Click()
    If IsOdd(CInt(Text1.Text)) = True Then
        MsgBox "This number is odd."
    Else
        MsgBox "This number is not an odd number."
    End If
End Sub
```

In short, think of procedures as robots; they simply execute a task you give them. Think of functions as a processor; you put something into it, and it transforms what you gave it into something else.

Common Functions and Statements

Conveniently, Visual Basic has several predefined functions and statements you can use. One of the standard statements used by Visual Basic is the **Beep** statement, which triggers a short beep from your PC speaker when used. Here's a really annoying example:

```
For I = 1 to 1000
    Beep
Next I
```

Don't worry about the **For** statement; we'll talk about it later. Right now, it's enough to say that the **Beep** statement in the preceding code will execute 1000 times, which causes a series of annoying beeps to issue from your PC. You should get the point that **Beep** is a common statement that takes no arguments. An example of a statement we've already used several times is the **MsgBox** statement; it takes a number of arguments, some of which aren't always necessary to specify. For instance, we can specify a simple **MsgBox** like the following with only one argument—the message:

```
MsgBox "Howdy!"
```

Further arguments can specify what buttons appear on the **MsgBox** and the caption that appears on its title bar:

```
MsgBox "Abort, Retry, Explode?", vbAbortRetryIgnore,
    "Message Box Test"
```

This statement should cause three buttons—Abort, Retry, and Ignore—to appear on the **MsgBox**. Furthermore, the title bar should now read **Message Box Test**. The **vbAbortRetryIgnore** argument is a constant defined internally by Visual Basic. It's actually equal to **2**, so we could even write a statement like the following and get the same results:

```
MsgBox "Abort, Retry, Explode?", 2, "Message Box Test"
```

You might wonder, "What's the point of having three buttons on the **MsgBox**?" There's no way to know what button they clicked on! As a matter of fact, **MsgBox** also works as a function. A function implies a return value, which in turn implies an equals sign. This means we must now enclose our arguments in parentheses:

```
ReturnValue = MsgBox("Yes or No?", vbYesNo, "Return
    Value Test")
```

In this situation, if the user clicked Yes, the value in **ReturnValue** is **6**. If he or she clicked No, the value is **7**. This gives you an easy way to get quick-and-dirty information from the user, such as:

```
ReturnValue = MsgBox("Do you wish to exit?", vbYesNo,
    "Exiting Program")
If ReturnValue = 6 then
    ExitProgram
Else
    ReturnToProgram
End If
```

In this code, **ExitProgram** and **ReturnToProgram** are procedures we define somewhere else.

Another example of a standard VB function is the **RGB** function. It takes three arguments and returns a value that can be used by objects expecting a specific color format called an **OLE_COLOR**. A **Form** object expects an **OLE_COLOR** for its **BackColor** property:

```
Form1.BackColor = RGB(255, 0, 255)
```

The **RGB** function is actually named after its arguments. **R** stands for *Red*, **G** for *Green*, and **B** for *Blue*. By varying each of these components, the user can specify any color of the spectrum. For a pure, fire-engine red, we would use the following:

```
RGB(255, 0, 0)
```

As you can see, the only argument with a value above zero is **Red**. If we wanted a darker red, we would use this:

```
RGB(127, 0, 0)
```

If we wanted total blackness, we would do it like this:

```
RGB(0, 0, 0)
```

With none of the component colors, Red, Green or Blue, having any value, the color is black. The model we're working from here is called (cryptically enough) the *RGB model*. This is a model of how light behaves. If you were to take a red spotlight and shine it on a space already illuminated by a green spotlight, the result would be a yellow space. That's how light works, and that's how this function works. So, look at our initial function call again:

```
Form1.BackColor = RGB(255, 0, 255)
```

We're mixing equal parts of Red and Blue, so we end up with a nice purple background.

Listing 15-4.
The **ShutDown**
procedure.

```
Sub ShutDown()
    Dim Return As Integer
    Return = MsgBox("Do you wish to shutdown?", vbYesNo,
"Shutdown Program")
    If Return = 6 then
        SaveData
    Else
        Exit Sub
    End If
    MsgBox "This program is shutting down"
End Sub
```

A note on functions and statements: Certain conditions in a procedure or function might arise that mean we don't want to bother finishing the subroutine. VB gives us two straightforward statements—**Exit Sub** and **Exit Function**—to do this. For instance, using the **MsgBox** function, we might query the user about what to do next, as shown in Listing 15-4.

In this procedure, a message box appears, asking users if they want to shut down. If the answer is yes, the program executes a subroutine to save whatever data the user was working on and pops up a second box, telling the user that the program is ending. If the answer is no, the program flow hits the **Exit Sub** procedure and exits the procedure, without the message box. The **Exit Function** statement is implemented in the same way, except that it's used in functions.

Control Structures

After variables, the most essential part of a language must be its *control structures*, which allow a program to interact with changing data. If you've been paying close attention, you'll notice that we've used the word *If* several times already. The **If** statement is the easiest control structure to understand because most of us have to deal with it a daily basis. For example, just about everyone faces this each morning:

```
If (IGoToWork = False) OR (IDoAGoodJob = False)Then
    IWillGetFired
End If
```

This statement reads, in English, "If I don't go to work or I don't do a good job, I'll get fired." Notice that we didn't write this:

```
If (IGoToWork = False) AND (IDoAGoodJob = False) then
```

For this statement to go to the next line where we get fired, both conditions would have to be true. That would imply we can avoid getting fired as long as we just show up. In short, when you use the **OR** keyword between two comparisons, if either comparison is **True**, then the statement is true and continues on to the next line. When you use the **AND** keyword, both conditions must be true to continue on to the next line. We can specify negative comparisons as well:

```
If (IGotoWork = False) AND NOT(ICallInSick = True) Then
    IWillGetFired
End If
```

This reads, in English, "If I don't go to work and I don't call in sick, then I will get fired." You could just as easily say:

```
If (IGotoWork = False) AND (ICallInSick = False) Then
    IWillGetFired
End If
```

This means the same thing. What's important is that it makes sense to you, however you choose to structure it.

GOTO IN VISUAL BASIC   We'll continue talking about control structures in VB by talking about the most maligned, despised, and hated keyword in all of computerdom: **Goto**.

The **Goto** statement causes program flow to immediately and unconditionally move to the target of the **Goto**, like this:

```
    X = Y / 10
    If X < 5 then Goto GreaterThan
LessThan: MsgBox "X is less than 5"
GreaterThan: MsgBox "X is greater than or equal to 5"
```

This simple example hides the horrors that have been wreaked upon developers worldwide by the **Goto** statement. **Goto** statements give rise to *spaghetti code*—code that's indecipherable because of the myriad twists and turns of its composition. It has been replaced by an orderly way of branching and flow control with loops.

The simplest form of loop is the **Do** loop; it always begins and ends with the words *Do* and *Loop*, respectively. All well-formed loops must have a termination condition, a situation that must eventually arise that kills the loop. This condition can be specified in three places: at the **Do** statement, at the **Loop** statement, or within the loop.

```
Do Until X = 5
    X = X + 1
    If X = 5 Then Exit Do
Loop
```

In this example, we have a simple `Do` loop with two termination conditions. The first uses the `Until` keyword, which means exactly what is sounds like. It means "repeat the loop until X equals 5." We could specify the same thing like this:

```
Do While Not X = 5
    X = X + 1
    If X = 5 Then Exit Do
    MsgBox "X = " & X
Loop
```

When you think about it, *Until* really means *While Not*. If I'm not leaving to go to work until 8:00, *While* it's *Not* 8:00, I am not leaving for work. An important difference between how VB understands `Until` and how humans understand it is demonstrated here:

```
Do Until X = 5
    X = X + 2
    If X = 5 then Exit Do
    MsgBox "X = " & X
Loop
```

After the first time through the loop, X = 2; the second, X = 4; and the third, X = 6. The third time through, we've skipped over 5. The loop won't terminate because X is still not 5; indeed, it never will be. When we say "I'm not leaving until 8," what we really mean is that "While it's earlier than 8 (Time < 8), I'm not leaving." The following would correspond to that statement:

```
Do Until X > 8
    X = X + 2
    If X = 8 then Exit Do
    MsgBox "X = " & X
Loop
```

On the third line, we have placed a second termination condition inside the loop. The difference between the two conditions is that if it becomes `True`, we don't finish the loop. In this case, it would mean that there would be no message box telling what X was before the loop terminated. The third termination looks like this:

```
Do
    X = X + 2
    If X = 8 then Exit Do
    MsgBox "X = " & X
Loop Until X > 8
```

The difference? We're guaranteed at least one trip through the loop with this structure. With the first situation, if X had started out greater than 8, we would never have gotten a message box.

Sometimes we know exactly how many times we want to go through a loop. In these situations, we can specify a counter rather than use a termination condition. Rest assured, the termination condition is still there; it's just hidden in the structure of the loop. These "counter loops" are also called **For...Next** loops:

```
Dim I As Integer
    For I = 1 to 10
        MsgBox "I is this: " & I
    Next I
```

Notice the parts of the **For** statement:

- **For**, the keyword indicating we're initiating a **For** loop
- **I**, the counter to be used for the loop
- **1**, the initial value of **I**
- **10**, the terminating value of **I**
- **Next**, the keyword indicating we're done with the loop

Each time the loop hits the **Next** statement, the value of **I** is increased by one. This is the case only by default; if we want **I** to be increased by some other number, we can specify it, as shown in Listing 15-5.

By using the **Step** keyword, each time the loop hits the **Next** statement, we're incremented by 5. Because **10** is the terminating value, the loop

Listing 15-5.
For...Next
examples.

```
Dim I As Integer
    For I = 0 to 10 Step 5
        MsgBox "I is this: " & I
    Next I

Dim I As Integer
    For I = 10 to 0 Step -1
        MsgBox "I is this: " & I
    Next I
```

iterates (repeats) twice (I = 5, then I = 10). **For** loops are a little more forgiving than **Do** loops; if the counter is incremented past the terminating value, the loop terminates anyway. **For** loops also support a terminating event inside the loop, as **Do** loops do:

```
Dim I As Integer
    For I = 1 to 10
        MsgBox "I is this:" & I
        If I = 5 then Exit For
    Next I
```

One final note about **For...Next** loops: There's an ongoing debate about whether deleting the counter from the **Next** statement speeds up the loop, like so:

```
Dim I As Integer
    For I = 1 to 10
        MsgBox "I is this:" & I
        If I = 5 then Exit For
    Next
```

My two cents on this issue: If there's a difference, it's not much. I think the clarity of code you get by not omitting the counter is well worth it.

A special type of **For** loop is used with collections: The **For...Each** loop. The loop iterates once for every item within the collection. This kind of loop is useful for applying a condition to every item in a collection, checking the status of each item, or any process in which every item in a collection is important. It's possible to iterate through a collection like this:

```
Dim I As Integer
Dim Temp As Variant
    For I = 1 To iCollection.Count
        Set Temp = iCollection.Item(I)
        Temp = "This is a test"
    Next I
but the For..Each way is much easier and more elegant:
Dim Temp As Variant
For Each Temp in iCollection
    Temp = "This is a test"
Next Temp
```

We begin by declaring the object variable, in this case **Temp**. The object variable serves as the placeholder for each collection item as it rolls through the loop. We then move on to the **For** statement consisting of three components: The **For...Each** key, the object variable, and the collection name. Once we're in the loop, the **Temp** variable represents the current collection item. We have access to its value or, if it's an object, its public properties and methods. Finally, we enclose the loop code with the **Next** statement, just like a regular **For** loop.

ERROR TRAPPING As hard as we work to avoid **Goto** statements, **Goto** is still useful in several areas. When errors arise in your program (although I'm sure this would never happen), the rest of the code in your procedure doesn't "know" that. You formulated a procedure based on the premise that each line executes error free. To keep this structure intact, you need to have a contingency plan to carry out in the case of error. This contingency plan is called an *error trap*:

```
On Error Goto ErrHandler
    Dim X As Integer
    X = 32768
    Exit Sub
ErrHandler:
    MsgBox "Error number: " & Err.Number & " has
    occurred."
```

In this code, we have **x**, an integer, to which we're trying to assign the value **32768**. As you recall, integer variables can hold up to 32767 only. Assigning that value triggers error number 6, Overflow. This means the data has literally flowed over the space allotted to handle it. If this error occurs in a compiled program without an error trap, the error is fatal. *Fatal* means that the program dies without saving information, without informing the user—altogether pretty nastily. Error trapping is absolutely critical to VB programming. Constructing an error trap is just like constructing an animal trap: You've got to know what you're trying to catch. Although an error trap like the previous example is useful for general error trapping, the more we can figure out in advance about what kind of error is likely to occur, the more effectively we can respond to the error condition:

```
Dim X As Integer
    X = Val(txtTextBox.Text)
```

Here we have **x**, an integer. We're getting the contents of a **TextBox**, **txtTextBox**, and converting it to a number by using the **Val** function. The **Val** function simply takes text and converts it to a number. What type of error is likely to happen? What if the user enters a value like **100000** in the text box? **Val** will return the number **100,000**, which is too large for **x**. Having realized this, we might want to backpedal and make **x** large enough to handle any conceivable value. On the other hand, we might have a good reason for having declared **x** as an integer; perhaps **x** should not exceed **32767**. If that's the case, we can provide a general error trap

Listing 15-6.
Error-handling
example.

```
On Error Goto ErrHandler
    Dim X As Integer
    X = 32768
    Exit Sub
ErrHandler:
    If Err.Number = 6 then
        Exit Sub
    Else
            MsgBox "Error number: " & Err.Number &
" has occurred. " & Err.Description
        Resume Next
    End If
```

for other errors, while custom-building an alternative when error 6 occurs, as shown in Listing 15-6.

Some explanation is in order here. When an error occurs in VB, an **Err** object is created. This object has two major properties, **Number** and **Description**. **Number** refers to the standard VB error number assigned to the condition. In the case of an overflow, **Err.Number** is 6. **Err.Description** provides a brief note on what the error means. In this case, **Err.Description** is simply **Overflow**, although the descriptions are usually one or two sentences. As you can see in this case, if we determine that an overflow occurred, we simply exit the procedure. Otherwise, we pop up a message box explaining the situation. The next line, **Resume Next**, returns program flow to the line immediately following the line that caused the error. One last note on the preceding procedure: Be aware of the **Exit Sub** statement that comes just before the error handler. We place it there so that the error handler is unreachable except by error. Lacking this statement, the error handler would be executed every time the procedure was run.

The other condition under which **Goto** is still useful in VB is when it's used to approximate a **Continue** statement. A **Continue** statement is used within loops to bypass the rest of the loop and skip to the loop's next iteration. **Continue** statements are common in other languages, but conspicuously absent in VB:

```
Do While X < 50
    X = X + 1
    If X = 6 then Goto Continue
    MsgBox "X = " & X
Continue: Loop
```

In this procedure, we want a **MsgBox** to appear every time the loop executes, except when X = 6. When X = 6, we want to skip the message box and continue on to the next trip through the loop. To approximate the

`Continue` statement, we include a line label on the end of the loop; in this case, the `Loop` statement. When X = 6, program flow branches to the line with the `Continue` label, and the loop iterates.

NESTED LOOPS   When we place a logical structure inside another logical structure, this is called *nesting*. To understand what a nested loop is, think about your work schedule. Your day consists of one loop:

```
For Hour = 9 a.m. to 5 p.m.
    DoWork
Next Hour
```

This means "Between the hours of 9 and 5, work" (we're ignoring a lunch hour here). This is one loop we live in. We live in another loop outside this one:

```
For Day = Monday to Friday
    For Hour = 9 a.m. to 5 p.m.
        DoWork
    Next Hour
Next Day
```

Outside this loop, we live in yet another:

```
For Month = January to December
    For Day = Monday to Friday
        For Hour = 9 a.m. to 5 p.m.
            DoWork
        Next Hour
    Next Day
Next Month
```

We could continue on, but you get the point. If we were to stick a counter in the very middle of the loop, this loop could count how many hours we work a year. Of course, we have to define exactly what each of the looping terms means. We could express the equation like this:

```
For WorkHour = 1 to 5080
    DoWork
Next WorkHour
```

But this doesn't allow for changes in the definitions in the outer loops. These nested loops allow us to vary each term according to variables. Let's take a look at a more concrete example in Listing 15-7.

This is a standard procedure we call `TileBitmap`. It's used to get the tiling effect on a graphical control's background. We'll cover it line by line. First, we declare **x** and **y**, which are used to specify X and Y coordinates for

Listing 15-7.
TileBitmap example.

```
Private Sub Form_Click()
    Dim X As Integer
    Dim Y As Integer

    Do While Y < Form1.ScaleHeight
        Do While X < Form1.ScaleWidth
            Form1.PaintPicture picBitmap.Picture, X, Y
            X = X + picBitmap.Width
        Loop
        Y = Y + picBitmap.Height
        X = 0
    Loop
End Sub
```

the picture that will be contained in a `PictureBox` called `picBitmap`. The next line indicates that we terminate the outer loop when the value of `Y` is greater than the height of the form. The next line specifies that the inner loop terminates when `X` is greater than the width of the `Form`. On the next line, we tell `Form1` to display the picture in `picBitmap` at the coordinates of `X` and `Y`. We then increment `X` by the width of the picture and loop again. As we said earlier, if we're past the width of the `Form`, then we continue on to the outer loop, where we increase the Y coordinate by the height of the bitmap and set `X` to zero. We must set `X` to zero so that on the next line we start on the left-hand side again. What we're setting up here is like a painter painting a wall with horizontal stripes. He paints horizontally until he reaches the end of the wall. At that point, he will "increment Y" by going down a row and "set x to zero" by starting over on the left-hand side. He will continue this process until he reaches the bottom of the wall.

In nested loops, what we end up with is a structure that's eerily like code writing itself. Nested loops are a form of recursion, which is always pretty creepy and cool. Keep in mind, however, that in nested loops, the danger of infinite looping is greatly increased. One of the best ways to do this is to treat loops like different levels of reality. You'll notice that in the preceding procedure, the outer loop "knows" about the inner loop; it modifies the value of `X`, even though `X` isn't involved in its loop. But the inner loop doesn't "know" about the outer loop and doesn't affect its values. Think of it like a movie: If there's a fire in a film, we feel tension watching it. We "know" about the conditions in the movie. If, however, there's a fire in a movie theater, the characters in the movie don't feel tension; they don't "know" about the conditions outside their loop. This isn't a rule; there are times when the inner loop does need to affect the conditions outside its loop. When this happens, be extra careful that the terminating condition arises.

Classes

In our discussion of user-defined data types, we created a powerful, compact way of storing information about our games. This solution is useful for simple data storage, but something is still missing. Objects do more than just store information; they *do* stuff. We might want to be able to view a picture of the video game in our program, or have some other action carried out that's specific to the object we're dealing with. We need a way to assign actions, or methods, to our **VideoGame** object. This leads us into a discussion of classes.

As objects are the heart of object-oriented programming in VB, classes are the heart of objects. In the real world, all the members of the class **Dog** have the property **Pedigree** and the method **Bark**. All the members of the **Car** class have the properties **Make** and **Model** and the methods **StartEngine** and **StopEngine**. Keep in mind that an object is not the same as its class: I am a member of the **Human Being** class, but I am not the **Human Being** class itself. Other words that mean the same thing as class are *set* or *group*. A *class* defines the behavior and properties of its members. To create a **VideoGame** class, first add a class module from the Project menu in VB5. Once the module is added, click View and Properties Window in VB5. On this menu, you see the item **Name**, which is what we'll name the Class. Type in **VideoGame**.

Now that we have the module in place, we need to create the **Name**, **ReleaseYear**, and **Manufacturer** properties.

PROPERTIES   Properties are more than just the data members we created with our **VideoGame** type (see Figure 15-8). When a property changes, we can trigger action elsewhere in the program. If a program had a **Color** property, when it changed, we might execute code that would actually change the color of the form. To use properties, we need to create *property statements* to provide this kind of interface to our objects. We can use other variables inside the class module to actually store the values, and our property statements provide a common way to get at those values.

Figure 15-8.
The Class Properties
window.

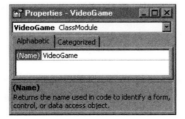

```
Dim iName As String
Dim iReleaseYear As String
Dim iManufacturer As String
```

We have added an **i** in front of each variable to denote that these are *internal* variables.

PROPERTY GET To access the value of a property, we must first create a **Property Get** statement. The first line of a **Property Get** statement looks like this:

```
Property Get Name() As String
```

This should look familiar; it's the same as our declaration of **Name** as a data member earlier. What comes next is a little different, however:

```
    Name = iName
End Property
```

iName is the internal variable we just created. On this line, we're telling this statement to return the value contained in **iName**. On the last line, we simply tell the statement that we're done and to return to the procedure that called it. Within a procedure, using a property looks like this:

```
Dim Game As VideoGame

Answer = Game.Name
```

Of course, we haven't assigned any value to **Name**, so **Answer** ends up being empty.

PROPERTY LET To assign a value, we need to create a **Property Let** statement. This is the statement that's executed when we assign a value to a property:

```
Game.Name = "Discs of Tron"
```

The first line of a **Property Let** statement looks a little different from the **Property Get**:

```
Property Let Name(Str As String)
```

This line indicates that within this statement, whatever value has been assigned to the **Name** property will be referred to as **Str**, and it has a data type of String.

Listing 15-8.
TileBitmap example.

```
Private Sub Form_Click()
    Dim X As Integer
    Dim Y As Integer

    Do While Y < Form1.ScaleHeight
        Do While X < Form1.ScaleWidth
            Form1.PaintPicture picBitmap.Picture, X, Y
            X = X + picBitmap.Width
        Loop
        Y = Y + picBitmap.Height
        X = 0
    Loop
End Sub
```

Remember the **iName** variable we declared earlier? With the following line, we're setting it equal to the value that was passed into the statement:

```
iName = Str
```

In this case, the game's name would be set to the string **Discs of Tron**. Listing 15-8 shows what the other **Property Let** statements would look like.

Sometimes you might actually use an object as a property. Consider our **Car** object; it might be useful to have an **Engine** subobject. The properties would then be broken down into **Car.Engine.Start** and **Car.Engine.Stop**. This sounds strange until you think about some familiar properties in Windows. The **Font** property, for example, has a number of members, such as Name, Size, Bold, and Underline, that are best organized as an object. Indeed, there is a **Font** object in Windows. When working with objects, the **Property Get** statement is almost exactly the same. Because the property is an object, we must use the **Set** keyword:

```
Property Get Font() As StdFont
Set Font = iFont
End Property
```

StdFont is actually the Windows name for the **Font** object. Here, as before, we would have created an internal variable (this time as **StdFont**) to store the information:

```
Dim iFont As StdFont
```

Not too different so far, but to assign a **Font**, we need to use a **Property Set** statement:

```
Property Set Font(Ft As StdFont)
    Set iFont = Ft
End Property
```

Again, we're using the **Set** keyword to assign one object to another. Forgetting to use the **Set** keyword is an easy mistake you will probably make. The error it triggers is Object Variable or With Block Variable not Set. Keep an eye out for this one.

METHODS   We started this whole discussion because we wanted to give our **VideoGame** object a method. An object's method allows it to do something, so we'll give our **VideoGame** object a **DisplayInformation** method to list all its properties at once. To do this, we create a procedure like any other defined in the class module:

```
Public Sub DisplayInformation()
    MsgBox "Name: " & Name
    MsgBox "ReleaseYear: " & ReleaseYear
    MsgBox "Manufacturer: " & Manufacturer
End Sub
```

This simple method pops up three message boxes, displaying the information contained in the class. It's just as easy to create public functions for classes:

```
Public Function Credit(Credits As Integer) As String
    InternalCredits = InternalCredits + Credits
    Credit = "You now have " & InternalCredits & "
    credits."
End Function
```

We have created an imaginary property: **InternalCredits**. Therefore, if the value in the **InternalCredits** property were zero, the following code

```
Sub Form_Click()
    MsgBox Credit(10)
End Sub
```

would yield the following output:

`You now have 10 credits.`

This is very simple stuff. To create a more useful example, suppose we're going to be writing flight simulators. It's helpful to create one single **Physics** class that all the different flight simulators can share. We decide that a useful public function for this module would be one to calculate the drag of an aircraft object that would be elsewhere in the application. It would look something like this:

```
Public Function Drag(Speed As Single, DragCoefficient As
        Single) As Single
    DragCoefficient = DragCoEfficient * Qfactor
    Drag = Speed * DragCoefficient
End Public
```

Be aware that the physics in this statement is utter nonsense. This function takes two arguments: The speed and the drag coefficient of the aircraft. Proceeding into the function, we multiply the **DragCoefficient** times the mythical **Qfactor** (which could be a property, or perhaps a constant). Having been combined with the **Qfactor**, we multiply the **DragCoefficient** by the speed of the aircraft and return the value.

It can also be convenient to have public constants in a class module. This might not seem like an important use of a class module until you consider how many constants are in a field like physics. To create a public constant, simply declare it as public from within the class module:

```
Public Const C=300000
```

C is the speed of light in kilometers per second. Accessing these methods, functions, properties, and constants is just like accessing any object's members.

Game.Cost and **Game.InitialRun** are public constants of the **VideoGame** class. This is how it's implemented inside another class, or even inside another application. To make this class available to another application requires a little bit of tweaking. We'll wrap up the chapter with that.

Listing 15-9.
GameStuff
procedure.

```
Sub GameStuff()
    Dim Game As New VideoGame

    Game.Name = "Spy Hunter"
    Game.ReleaseYear = "1983"
    Game.Manufacturer = "Williams"

    Game.DisplayInformation

    MsgBox Game.Credit(20)

    MsgBox "The amount of money spent on Spy Hunter's
            intial run was $" & Game.Cost &_ Game.InitialRun
```

Listing 15-10.
Collection members
example.

```
Public Property Get ListOfGames(Key As String) As String
    On Error GoTo ErrHandler
    If Key <> "" Then
        ListOfGames = iCollection.Item(Key)
    End If
    Exit Property
ErrHandler:
    If Err.Number = 5 Then
        MsgBox "There is no game in the list by this
            name."
    End If
End Property

Public Sub AddGame(Item As String, Key As String)
    If Item <> "" And Key <> "" Then
        iCollection.Add Item, Key
    Else
        MsgBox "You must specify the name of the game and
            a unique key for it."
    End If
End Sub

Public Property Get Count() As Integer
    Count = iCollection.Count
End Property
```

TIP *There's nothing technically wrong with declaring a collection as public, but we don't advise it. With exposed collections, you have very little control over what goes in or out of it. It essentially becomes an unknown, meaning it's more or less useless. It's much better to implement collections as properties, perhaps with a public method for item addition and removal, such as* `Private iCollection As New Collection`.

We begin by creating an internal collection, `iCollection`, to actually hold the data. This collection will be known as `ListOfGames`. To add a game to the collection, use the following syntax externally:

```
Game.AddGame "Sinistar", "WLLMS1"
```

We've added the name `Sinistar`, using `WLLMS1` as a key. When this code is executed, the `AddGame` procedure is passed `Sinistar` and `WLLMS1` as the `Item` and `Key` arguments, respectively. On the first line of the procedure, we check to make sure the developer hasn't passed empty strings for either of the arguments. To return a game from a `Key` argument we specified earlier, we would use something like this:

```
MsgBox TestControl1.ListOfGames("WLLMS1")
```

This statement would pop up a message box listing the game associated with the key **WLLMS1**, which in this case would be **Sinistar**. You'll notice that we've placed an error handler in the **Property** statement to make sure that if the developer enters a **Key** for which there's no associated collection **Item**, there's no error. If the developer enters the following, he or she would get a message box saying "There is no game in the list by this name":

```
MsgBox TestControl1.ListOfGames("T")
```

The last property we implement is the **Count** property, indicating how many items there are in the list. We simply return the **Count** property of the internal collection in this case.

Another use for keeping collections at arm's length like this is that you can perform management tasks when these procedures occur. It might be useful to know when an item is added to the list. Perhaps we have a graphical interface that would need to be updated whenever an item is added. One way to do this would be with an event, as shown in Listing 15-11.

In our **GameAdded** event, the developer would place whatever code was needed to handle the response. Furthermore, we're incrementing a counter recording how many games have been added by the developer. This number could be different from the **iCollection.Count** property if we decide to add games within the control itself.

We have failed to include a **RemoveGame** statement; we might decide that it's better to have this handled programmatically. In summary, what this extra layer allows you to do is to perform validation, error checking, and any other bookkeeping tasks you might need to do with your collection.

Listing 15-11.
GameAdded event
example.

```
Public Event GameAdded(Item As String, Key As String)
Private GamesAddedByDeveloper As Integer

Public Sub AddGame(Item As String, Key As String)
    If Item <> "" And Key <> "" Then
        iCollection.Add Item, Key
        RaiseEvent GameAdded(Item, Key)
        GamesAddedByDeveloper = GamesAddedByDeveloper + 1
    Else
        MsgBox "You must specify the name of the game and
            a unique key for it."
    End If
End Sub
```

EVENTS After abandoning a linear approach to development, programmers needed a way to respond to system events (such as exiting Windows) and user input. The solution was to remodel this system with what are called *events*. Events are central to object-oriented programming, and understanding them is key to understanding Visual Basic.

Without getting into needless technical detail, Windows constantly "listens" for messages from applications, which it then either handles internally or passes back to the application for processing. To put it simply, every event is either a direct message that Windows handled or is one of several events spawned from a message. In addition to the notification that an event has occurred, an event can pass arguments. Arguments provide information about the event. For example, if a key is pressed on the keyboard, it's useful to know which key was pressed. With mouse events, it might be useful to know where the user clicked on an object or which mouse button the user clicked.

With Visual Basic 5.0, developers can "raise" their own events in a control, which in turn allows users of the application to write their own code in response to the events. It's important to note that not all objects are capable of receiving all events. For example, because of the way it's created within Windows, a **Line** control can't receive mouse events. Mouse events are a central component to Windows programming; let's take a moment to discuss them.

MOUSE EVENTS

- **Click:** This event occurs when a mouse button is pressed and released in rapid succession on an object capable of receiving mouse events. The **Click** event passes no arguments.

- **DblClick:** This event occurs when a mouse button is pressed and released in rapid succession twice on an object capable of receiving mouse events. Exactly how rapidly is a Control Panel setting under Mouse Settings. The **DblClick** event passes no arguments.

- **DragDrop:** This event occurs after a user has pressed his or her mouse button over an object that is capable of being dragged, moved the mouse, and released the button. This event occurs in the object on which the object is dropped, not the object itself. The **DragDrop** event passes three arguments:

  Source: This is the object that was dragged onto the target.

  x: This is the horizontal coordinate on which the user dropped the **Source**.

  y: This is the vertical coordinate on which the user dropped the **Source**.

■ **DragOver:** This event occurs after a user has pressed his or her mouse button over an object that is capable of being dragged and moved the mouse. This event occurs in the object over which the object is dragged. The **DragOver** event passes the following arguments:

Source, X, Y: See **DragDrop**.

State: This argument has three values—**0** for **Enter**, when the user has just dragged the **Source** into the target; **1** for **Leave**, when the user has just dragged it out; and **2** for **Over**, when the user has just dragged the **Source** from one place to another over the target.

■ **MouseDown:** This event occurs when the user presses his or her mouse button on an object capable of receiving mouse events. The **MouseDown** event passes these arguments:

Button: This argument can return one of three values: **1**,which represents the left mouse button; **2**, which represents the right mouse button; and **4**, which represents the middle mouse button, if it's present. If more than one button is pressed simultaneously, the values are added together. If a user presses the left and right button together, the value is **3**.

Shift: This argument returns a value indicating whether the Ctrl, Alt, or Shift keys were pressed when the event occurred. Each of these buttons corresponds to the values **1**, **2**, and **4**, which are added together to form the value. For example, the Ctrl key alone returns a value of **1**, but the Ctrl and Alt keys pressed together return **5** (1 + 4).

X, Y: See **DragDrop**.

■ **MouseMove:** This event occurs when the user moves the mouse over an object capable of receiving mouse events. **MouseMove** passes the same arguments as the **MouseDown** event.

■ **MouseUp:** This event occurs after a user has pressed and then released a mouse button on an object capable of receiving mouse events. **MouseUp** passes the same arguments as the **MouseDown** event.

As you might have already guessed, given the proper timing, all these events can occur consecutively. For example, if I press and release my mouse button as a click, I trigger the **MouseDown** event first, then the **MouseUp** event, and then the **Click** event. The same can be true of a **DblClick** event.

KEYBOARD EVENTS

- **KeyDown:** This event occurs when a key is pressed on the keyboard and an object capable of receiving keyboard events has the focus. The **KeyDown** event passes the following arguments:

  KeyCode: This argument returns a value that represents the physical key being pressed.

  Shift: See **MouseDown**.

- **KeyPress:** This event occurs when a key is pressed on the keyboard and an object capable of receiving keyboard events has the focus. The **KeyPress** event passes the following argument:

  KeyAscii: This argument is different from **KeyCode**; it returns a value that represents the character on the keyboard rather than the physical key.

- **KeyUp:** This event occurs after a key has been pressed on the keyboard and released when an object capable of receiving keyboard events has the focus. The **KeyUp** event passes the same arguments as the **KeyDown** event.

USER-DEFINED EVENTS   With Visual Basic 5.0, developers can define custom events that are triggered from standard Windows events. For example, there's no intrinsic mouse event that occurs when a user moves his or her mouse outside a control such as a **PictureBox**. This kind of event might be useful if the **PictureBox** is used to respond to mouse input, like "toolbar" style buttons found on most Web browsers now. By intelligently interpreting where standard mouse messages come from and what their arguments are, we can simulate that event. This is called *raising* an event. Although events can be used with traditional VB applications, they are more relevant when discussing control creation.

To raise an event, we must first declare the scope of the event, as well as any arguments we want to pass. Let's suppose we have a control, **TestControl**, containing a **CommandButton** called **Command1**.

The first line is the **Event** declaration. The first word is **Public**, indicating that the control will be available to external applications. Next we have **AppClick**, which will be the name we use to refer to the event. Finally, we reach the arguments that will be passed through the event. Event sinks must be able to confirm that only the proper information, and no less than the proper information, was passed. To confirm this, the event arguments must be explicitly declared. In this instance, we're going to pass three arguments: **Button**, **X**, and **Y**. These arguments will correspond to the **Button**, **X** ,and **Y** arguments passed by the **MouseDown** events of standard objects.

```
Public Event AppClick(Button As Integer, X As Single, Y
     As Single)

Private Sub Command1_MouseDown(Button As Integer, Shift
     As Integer, X As Single, Y As Single)
   RaiseEvent AppClick(Button, X, Y)
End Sub

Private Sub UserControl_MouseDown(Button As Integer, Shift
     As Integer, X As Single, Y As Single)
   RaiseEvent AppClick(Button, X, Y)
End Sub
```

We're not going to bother passing the **Shift** argument; we simply decide that information won't be relevant to the developer using the control.

We envision **AppClick** as being used to indicate that a mouse button was pressed anywhere on the control. To do this, we have placed sinks in two different locations: The **MouseDown** events of both the **UserControl** object and the **Command1** button. With an event sink in both of the control's objects, the control is unified; that is, to the end developer, it will appear that the control responds to mouse events as one control. Events don't need to have arguments. This arrangement would be just as valid:

```
Public Event AppClick()

Private Sub Command1_Click()
   RaiseEvent AppClick
End Sub

Private Sub UserControl_Click()
   RaiseEvent AppClick
End Sub
```

In this instance, the **AppClick** event signals only that the mouse activity has occurred. It doesn't pass any more information about that event. To the end developer, these user-defined events look like any other event. Using our control, the first implementation of **AppClick** would look like this:

```
Private Sub TestControl1_AppClick(Button As Integer, X As
     Single, Y As Single)

End Sub
```

Any code we place in this event would be executed when the user clicked anywhere on the control. The second implementation would look like this:

```
Private Sub TestControl1_AppClick()

End Sub
```

GRAPHICAL METHODS   Within your program, you're eventually going to encounter a situation where a simple **PictureBox**, **Line** control, or **Label** won't be enough. When the graphics demands of your program exceed what's automatically handled by VB, you need to use the inherent graphical methods supplied by the graphical controls. The following objects support graphical methods:

▓ **Form**

▓ **UserControl**

▓ **PictureBox**

Other controls support graphical methods, too, but these three are the ones on which we will concentrate.

NOTE   *Just a quick note on the Windows coordinate system: Conventional graphical coordinates are organized with (0,0) in the very middle of the object and the X and Y axes forming a cross. In Windows, the point (0,0) is in the upper-left corner. The X and Y axes run along the top and left. Coordinates are specified, in fact, with the properties* **Top** *and* **Left**. *If an object has a* **Left** *of 0, it's flush with the left side of its container. If it has a* **Top** *equal to 0, it's vertically flush with the top of its container.*

There are four major graphical methods, explained in the following sections.

CIRCLE   The **Circle** method draws a circle on a graphical control. It takes the following arguments:

▓ **X, Y**: These are the X and Y coordinates of the center of the circle.

▓ **Radius**: This is the radius of the circle or the distance from the center that the circle is drawn.

▓ **Color**: This optional argument defines the circle's color. If omitted, the color will match the control's **ForeColor** property.

▓ **Start, End**: Optional radian values that define where the circle begins and ends. If omitted, their values are **0** and **2** π (a complete circle).

```
Private Sub Form_Click()
    Dim I As Integer
    Dim X As Single

    picPrintBox.DrawWidth = 3
    For I = 1 To 12
        picPrintBox.Circle (picPrintBox.ScaleWidth / 2,
            picPrintBox.ScaleHeight
            /2),picPrintBox.ScaleWidth_
        / 4, , , , I
        For X = 1 To 100000
        Next X
        picPrintBox.Cls
    Next I
End Sub
```

▦ **Aspect**: This value defines the aspect ratio of the vertical to the horizontal component. More simply stated, if we have an **Aspect** of 10, the width of the circle is one tenth as wide as it is high. This property is useful for drawing ellipses.

The preceding example illustrates some of the ways we can work with a circle. We declare two loop counters, **I** and **X**. Then we set the **DrawWidth** property of the **picPrintBox** control to **3** so that the circle is 3 pixels thick; now we can see the circle a bit more clearly. We then begin a loop, using **I** from 1 to 12. This represents the aspect ratio of the circle we'll draw. Within the loop, we draw the circle, placing its center at the center of the control with **(picPrintBox.ScaleWidth / 2 and picPrintBox.ScaleHeight /2)**. We set its radius to one fourth of the width of the control. We omit a number of arguments by simply putting commas where the arguments would be, since they don't relate to what we want to do in this procedure.

Finally, we have reached the argument we're interested in—the aspect ratio. As we loop through this, the value will go from **1** to **12**. Next, we stick in a loop that does nothing. Why? Without this time-consuming loop, the procedure executes so fast that it's invisible. The last line in the loop clears the **PictureBox** in preparation for the next drawing of the circle. The result of this procedure? A rough image of a spinning coin (see Figure 15-9).

LINE The **Line** method draws a line on the graphical control. Given the **B** argument, it can also draw a rectangle. The **Line** method accepts the following arguments:

Figure 15-9.
Circle method.

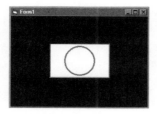

- **x1, y1**: This argument defines the first endpoint of the line.
- **x2, y2**: This argument defines the second endpoint of the line.
- **Color**: This optional argument defines the color of the line. If this argument is omitted, the line will be same color as the color specified in the control's **ForeColor** property.
- **B, F**: These optional arguments control the display of the line. If the **B** argument is included, the line represents the diagonal of a box that will be drawn on the graphical control. If the **F** argument is included, the box drawn will be a solid box rather than just an outline.

The **Line** and **Print** functions are the workhorses of the graphical methods. About 98 percent of what you see in Windows is composed of text and straight lines or rectangles.

The following procedure will be executed when the user moves his or her mouse over the **picPrintBox** PictureBox:

```
Private Sub picPrintBox_MouseMove(Button As Integer, Shift
     As Integer, X As Single, Y As Single)
   picPrintBox.Cls
   If Button = 1 Then
       picPrintBox.Line (picPrintBox.ScaleWidth / 2,
           picPrintBox.ScaleHeight / 2)-(X, Y)
   End If
End Sub
```

Continuing the procedure, we clear the **PictureBox** in preparation for drawing the line. Then, if the user is pressing the left mouse button, we proceed to draw the line. The first endpoint of the line is in the center of the control. This is expressed by **picPrintBox.ScaleWidth / 2**, the X coordinate, and **picPrintBox.ScaleHeight / 2**, the Y coordinate. The next endpoint is at the point of the cursor, so we simply pass it the **x** and **y** arguments that were passed to us through the event. When completed and run, a line will follow the mouse pointer from the center whenever the left mouse button is pressed (see Figure 15-10).

If we wanted it to draw a box, we need to add only one argument:

```
picPrintBox.Line (picPrintBox.ScaleWidth / 2,
        picPrintBox.ScaleHeight / 2)-(X, Y),,BF
```

This has the effect of drawing a larger or smaller box, depending on how far away from the center you are.

PSET The **PSet** method draws a point on the graphical control. It accepts the following arguments:

- **x**, **y**: These arguments define the X and Y coordinates of the point.

- **Color**: This optional argument defines the color of the point. If this argument is omitted, the point will be same color as the color specified in the control's **ForeColor** property.

Again, we have placed the following procedure in the **MouseMove** event of the **picPrintBox PictureBox**:

```
Private Sub picPrintBox_MouseMove(Button As Integer, Shift
As Integer, X As Single, Y As Single)
    picPrintBox.Cls
    If Button = 1 Then
        picPrintBox.PSet (X - 100, Y - 100)
    End If
End Sub
```

We first clear the **PictureBox** in preparation for printing the point. Then, if the left button is pressed, a point is drawn 100 twips (a *twip* is one twentieth of a point, or 1/1440 of an inch) to the left of and above the mouse cursor (see Figure 15-11).

Figure 15-10.
Line example.

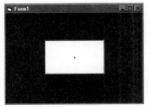

Figure 15-11.
PSet example.

PRINT   Although they aren't directly properties of the **Print** method, there are two properties of graphical objects that relate closely to the **Print** method:

▪ **CurrentX**: This is the current horizontal position on the graphical control in question.

▪ **CurrentY**: This is the current vertical position on the graphical control in question.

When the **Print** method is executed, the graphical control behaves like a typewriter, returning the **CurrentX** property to zero and moving the **CurrentY** property down one line. The height of that line is determined by the **Font** property, which leads us to a discussion of two important functions in the following sections.

TEXTHEIGHT   The **TextHeight** function returns the height of a specified string. It accepts the following argument:

▪ **Text**: This is the text whose height we want to know.

TEXTWIDTH   The **TextWidth** function returns the width of a specified string. It accepts the following argument:

▪ **Text**: This is the text whose width we want to know.

By combining these functions, you can perform some powerful printing and text formatting. Listing 15-14 is an example of using these functions and methods in tandem.

We begin by defining a left margin of 100 (twips). The next line sets the **CurrentX** property to **100**. This means that whatever we print starts at 100 twips over. The next line prints our first line of text. After this line is printed, **CurrentX** is set back to **0** by VB, and **CurrentY** has been set down one line. The exact height of this line is determined by the height of the text we just printed. Next, we set the **CurrentX** property equal to our

Listing 15-14.
Form graphical
methods example.

```
Private Sub Form_Click()
    Dim Margin As Integer

    Margin = 100
    picPrintBox.CurrentX = Margin
    picPrintBox.Print "This is a test"
    picPrintBox.CurrentX = Margin +
        picPrintBox.TextWidth("This is a test")
    picPrintBox.Print "This is a test"
End Sub
```

Margin plus the width of the text we just printed. The output of this function is shown in Figure 15-12.

The net effect here is that our second line starts horizontally where the first line left off.

Visual Basic is not a graphics development language: It was never intended to be. However, although you might not be able to develop Doom in VB, you can create highly complex formatting for reports, create graphical effects, and create attractive user interfaces.

The Windows API

As much as you can do in Visual Basic, sometimes it's better to let Windows do it. Windows does some things better than VB does, and it can do some things that VB can't do at all. To use a Windows function, we must access the Windows *Application Programming Interface* (API) and become familiar with the function. The Windows API is vast, and there are probably only 10 or 12 people on earth who know every single function and procedure. However, knowing a few functions can put you light years ahead of someone who doesn't. Visual Basic, unfortunately, is quite lacking in documentation. Without much documentation on the Windows API, VB programmers are forced to wander the development world looking for information.

TIP *Two good sources we can recommend are the UseNet newsgroup* **microsoft.public.vb.winapi** *and the book considered the definitive text, The Visual Basic Programmer's Guide to the Win32 API by Daniel Appleman.*

Once you know the function you want to use, you must include an API declaration in a code module. This declaration tells VB where to look for the information on the function when it appears in the code. A declaration generally looks something like this, typed all on one line:

Figure 15-12.
Text functions
example.

```
Declare Function FloodFill Lib "gdi32" Alias "FloodFill"
        (ByVal hdc As Long, ByVal x As Long, ByVal y As Long,
        ByVal crColor As Long) As Long
```

You're looking at the **FloodFill** function, which is used to fill a bounded area, much like the paint bucket tool in Paintbrush. First, we state that it's a function; it will return a value. In this case, as with most API functions, the return value will indicate success or failure. The first argument we must pass to the function is the **hDC**, or *device context*, of the graphical control that this function will be performed on. The second and third arguments indicate the point to start flooding from. The final argument is a color that indicates "stop" when the color of the fill reaches that shade. Using the function in code looks something like this:

```
Private Sub Form_Click()
    Dim Ret As Long
    Me.DrawWidth = 4
    Me.Circle (Me.ScaleWidth / 2, Me.ScaleHeight / 2),
        Me.Width / 4
    Me.FillStyle = 0
    Ret = FloodFill(Me.hdc, Me.ScaleWidth / 2,
        Me.ScaleHeight / 2, Me.ForeColor)
End Sub
```

As you can see, once you're past the declaration stage, Windows API functions work pretty much like any other VB function.

Putting it All Together

Now that we have all this cool stuff we've created, how do we make it into something that can be used outside VB? That depends on what we want it to do.

If we've created a simple code library using classes and modules, we need to compile it into a *Dynamic Link Library* (DLL). To do this, choose File | Make DLL to open a dialog box where you can specify the location of the DLL. The name of the DLL should match the name of the project. If you haven't specified a project name, do that now by clicking on Project | Project Properties. When you expose this DLL to other VB applications, you can access the classes and other elements by adding their names to the end of the project name, like so:

```
MyProject.MyClass
```

If we've created an actual program, we need to compile it into a executable program. To do this, choose File | Make EXE. Again, the EXE name should match the name of the project. Use the resulting dialog box to specify where the EXE goes.

Now that you've created your program or DLL, you should create a package for distributing it to others. VB includes the Application Setup Wizard for this purpose. To run it, select it from the Visual Basic menu block on the Start menu. The Wizard takes you through several self-explanatory steps, ending with the location of your new program setup package.

OLE Programming with VB

Visual Basic can access OLE objects (and, therefore, ActiveX objects) by using several special methods described in the following sections.

CreateObject

CreateObject is the most fundamental of the OLE creation functions. It takes a local class and creates a new instance of it. As mentioned, **CreateObject** is a function; its return value is a reference to the new object. **CreateObject** accepts only one argument:

■ **Class**: This is an identifier that defines where the object comes from and what it is. It follows a format like this:

```
CreateObject("Finance.AmortizationObject")
```

Because **CreateObject** returns a reference to another object, we must use the **Set** keyword to assign our blank object:

```
Dim Temp As Object
Set Temp = CreateObject("Finance.AmortizationObject")
```

At this point, **Temp** is an **AmortizationObject**. To execute a function **ComputePrincipal** of this object, we use the following syntax:

```
Princpal = Temp.ComputePrincipal(100,000, .05)
```

The return value of **ComputePrincipal** is assigned to our **Principal** variable.

GetObject

GetObject is like **CreateObject**, except that it returns a reference to a particular ActiveX object rather than a new instance of one. For example, if we use **GetObject** on an Excel XLS file, we would have an ActiveX object with that particular spreadsheet as the object.

The **GetObject** function takes one or more arguments. Either or both can be specified:

- **Filename**: This is the fully qualified path (for example, C:\WINDOWS\ TEST.XLS) to the file containing the object you want to create.

- **Class**: As with **CreateObject**, this is the application and class name of the object you want to assign.

The syntax for the **GetObject** function is as follows:

```
Dim Temp As Object
Set Temp = GetObject("C:\WINDOWS\TEST.XLS")
```

If the **Filename** argument is omitted, the **Class** argument is required:

```
Dim Temp As Object
Set Temp = GetObject(, "Excel.Sheet")
```

In this case, the system will look for an instance of the **Excel.Sheet** object and assign it to the object. If no object of this type exists, an error occurs.

In short, use **GetObject** when the object you want to work with already exists or when you want to load an object from a file.

The following is a simple way to create new ActiveX objects in your application:

```
Dim Object As New [class]
```

We simply declare that we're going to have a new object of the class we specify. The syntax looks like this:

```
Dim Temp As New AmortizationObject
Dim Principal As Single
Principal = Temp.ComputePrincipal(100000, .05)
```

References

The key to all that we have just covered is references. If you're a C++ programmer, you're familiar with the **Import** statement, which creates a reference to an external file and makes its functions and methods available to your application. Visual Basic handles this by supplying an Available References list in the References dialog box, opened by choosing Project | References on the main menu bar.

In Figure 15-13, you can see the references we have for Project1. Adding a reference to a project makes the project "aware" of the existence of this external library. Once this reference is created, the methods, functions, constants, and classes in the library are available.

Another way that VB makes ActiveX objects available to applications is through the OCX format. *OCX* stands for *OLE Control Extension*, although some people who work for Microsoft say it actually stands for *OCX Control Extension*.

OCXs can be accessed by creating references to them, but because of their format, there's an easier way to access them. It's called the Components dialog box, shown in Figure 15-14.

You've probably noticed that this dialog box looks a lot like the References dialog box. It's really just a derivation of the References dialog box. Although the References dialog box can list DLLs, OCXs, and several

Figure 15-13.
Project references.

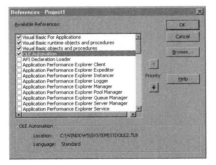

Figure 15-14.
Project components.

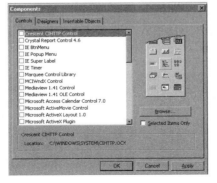

other file formats, the Components menu can access only OCX files. Once an item is selected, its icon appears in the toolbox, and it can be placed on a **Form** just like any other object.

CONCLUSION

We've covered a lot of ground in this chapter: OLE, ActiveX, and a lot of Visual Basic. You should have a basic grasp of Visual Basic, although there's much more to learn. Visual Basic is designed to be as user-friendly and easy as possible, yet still remains a powerful, capable language. We hope you're now comfortable with the concepts of OLE and how they apply to the Internet, and you should be comfortable enough with the basic concepts of programming that we can proceed a little further in the next chapter, where we create an OCX.

16

Creating ActiveX Controls with VB5

With the advent of the Internet, the focus of all development has changed. The great aspect of the Internet, as a communications medium, is its interactivity. *Common Gateway Interface* (CGI) applications, scripting, and similar technologies have extended this interactivity somewhat, but what's really needed is a way to implement the functions of a true application within a Web page. This is where Java and ActiveX come in.

Although Java is a powerful language, it's limited by necessity for security reasons—one approach to the problem of security violations in Web pages. When you request a Web page and its associated embedded application, like a Java applet or ActiveX control, it could be a malicious program, like a virus. Java, as we noted, solves this by placing limitations on what the applet can do. ActiveX controls take another approach. ActiveX controls simply accept the danger of these malicious controls, but make sure, through what's called *code signing*, that if a control is malicious, you will know who attacked your computer. It's important to understand that an ActiveX control can do anything, good or bad, that a traditional application can do.

In spite of the risk, interactivity through the Internet is inevitable. The benefits are simply too great; the Internet will eventually subsume radio, television, and print media as the bandwidth permits. Why? The Internet can present all these media in a processed form at a vastly lower cost, with the increased benefit of user interactivity.

Now, getting to control creation: In Chapter 15, "Visual Basic and OLE," we got a pretty good feel for *Visual Basic 5.0* (VB5). One of the biggest innovations of VB5 is its capability to create ActiveX controls. We'll go over this new capability in detail in this chapter.

This chapter will cover the following topics:

- The nature of Visual Basic
- The Visual Basic 5.0 *Integrated Development Environment* (IDE)
- ActiveX control design considerations
- Creation of an ActiveX control: **LATextBox**

The Nature of Visual Basic

When programmers create a program in a compiled language, C++ for example, they first link the necessary files for the program, and then direct the compiler to transform the code into a language their machine (and operating system) can understand. Visual Basic is a little bit different. Visual Basic versions 1–4 are what's referred to as *interpreted languages*.

This means that what you get isn't "machine language," but something that can be understood by the interpreter.

The Visual Basic Runtime Interpreter

When you execute a program created in Visual Basic, the program issues commands to the VB interpreter, which, in the case of Visual Basic 4.0, is named **VBRUN400.DLL**. The actual machine code lies within the *Dynamic Link Library (DLL)*; it receives commands from the Visual Basic program and then executes the proper machine language instruction. As you can imagine, the step of translating Visual-Basic-created code into machine instructions slows the whole process down (in comparison with compiled code).

In Visual Basic 5.0, all this changes. Visual Basic 5.0 gives the developer the option to create true compiled code (referred to as *native* code). This is a long-awaited change to the Visual Basic landscape. Without the performance penalty introduced by the runtime interpreter, Visual-Basic-created programs will perform on a par with other languages. Because this native code must create a larger file, a developer can still choose to compile to interpret code to minimize file size.

The Visual Basic Virtual Machine

ActiveX controls created with Visual Basic need an interpreter somewhat like the runtime DLL required by Visual Basic programs. This ActiveX interpreter is the Visual Basic 5.0 Virtual Machine (**MSVB50VM.DLL**). A *virtual machine* is a collection of resources that emulates another set of resources, like a hardware device. This allows VB-created ActiveX controls to act within an optimized environment. (You will probably never have to think about this.)

P-code Versus "True Native"

As we mentioned, older versions of Visual Basic didn't create native code. The Visual Basic "compiler" creates instructions in p-code (pseudocode), instructions much smaller than the actual machine instructions. These instructions, however, must be translated and executed indirectly by the interpreter, forcing a performance penalty. The performance penalty isn't as severe as you might think, though. Much of what's being executed by the interpreter is compiled C++ code that resides in Windows DLLs. (Again, this is something you will rarely have to think about.)

The Visual Basic 5.0 Integrated Development Environment

The development environment of Visual Basic 5.0 might differ from other languages with which you're familiar. The general interface concept was developed by user interface pioneer Alan Cooper. The Microsoft Visual C++ environment looks essentially like a souped-up text editor, but the Visual Basic IDE is very, well, visual. Objects like windows, buttons, and textboxes that we're going to write code for are represented, created, and positioned visually as opposed to programmatically. We will begin by looking at the very heart of the VB component collection: The **Form**.

The Form

In terms of Microsoft Windows, a *form* is a window that can contain other objects (these objects technically are windows, but you don't need to worry about that). A Visual Basic 5.0 ActiveX control form is shown in Figure 16-1.

This form looks a little different from a form used to create a regular program: No title bar; no minimize, maximize, or close buttons; and no menus. This is because controls are meant to be contained by other windows that would inherently have these items. The form acts as the "stage" for everything you want to do with your control. You define the appear-

Figure 16.1.
A **UserControl** form.

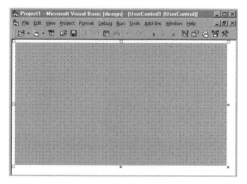

ance of your control by placing buttons, textboxes, and other controls and by using graphical methods. Forms, as you recall from Chapter 15, have 40 properties whose value can be changed to modify the control's behavior. The following sections list some of the important ones and explain how they're used.

Name

The **Name** property is fairly self-explanatory. When you place a control on a form or in a Web page, a number is added to the end of its name. For example, if you name the control **TextBox**, when you place it on a form, its name is **TextBox1**; if you insert another, its name is **TextBox2**.

AutoRedraw

This **True/False** property refers to how Windows handles repainting the control when part of it is covered up by another form. When **AutoRedraw** is set to **True**, the form is repainted automatically when it's revealed again. When **AutoRedraw** is set to **False**, the repainting of the form must be handled programmatically. You might wonder why you would ever want to bother with repainting the form "manually." When the form repaints automatically, if graphics methods have modified the form's appearance, the methods aren't repainted along with the rest of the form. Therefore, it's sometimes better to have more control over this behavior.

BackColor

The **BackColor** property is simply the color of the control's background. The value of this property is an OLE_COLOR data type (this just means it's expecting a value expressed in a certain format). It's best to use the **RGB** function to manipulate this value.

BackStyle

This property has two values: **0 - Transparent** and **1 - Opaque**. When you set **BackStyle** to **Transparent**, the form of the control will be invisible, allowing the background of its container to show through. Also, only nontransparent controls contained by the form can receive mouse events.

When the value is set to **Opaque**, the control's background will appear normally within the container. This property is closely related to the **FontTransparent** property, which we will discuss in the "FontTransparent" section.

CanGetFocus

This **True/False** property determines whether controls in the form can get focus. When **CanGetFocus** is set to **True**, only the main control window can get focus, not the contained controls. When it's set to **False**, the contained controls that normally can get focus will be able to do so. Pay close attention to this property. If you notice your control behaves strangely when using the Tab key to switch between controls on your page, the problem might be related to this property.

Font

This property describes how text will appear when using the control's **Print** method. The **Font** property expects a **Font** object (just think of it as a way of wrapping up several related properties into one package), which has these properties:

- **Bold:** Determines whether the text will be displayed in boldface type, like **this**.
- **Charset:** The character set to be used when displaying this font.
- **Italic:** Determines whether the text will be displayed italicized, like *this*.
- **Name:** The name of the font, like MS Sans Serif or Times New Roman.
- **Size:** The size of the font to be used.
- **Strikethrough:** Determines whether a line will be printed on top of the text, like ~~this~~.
- **Underline:** Determines whether the text is underlined, like <u>this</u>.
- **Weight:** Determines the thickness of the letters (the font's "heaviness"). This attribute is really part of the **Bold** property, and you will probably never use it. I never have.

FontTransparent

This **True/False** property determines whether text and graphics will be invisible when the control form's **BackStyle** property is set to **Transparent**.

ForeColor

Like **BackColor**, this property accepts an **OLE_COLOR** variable. The **ForeColor** property determines what color text will be when it's printed on the form.

Height

This value determines the height of the control when it's first created.

InvisibleAtRunTime

This **True/False** value determines whether the control itself will be visible at runtime. It's useful to make controls invisible when they exist only to create other windows or to handle nongraphical functions.

Picture

This property indicates the image, if any, to be displayed on the control form. This property expects a **StdPicture** object (an object like the **Font** object we talked about before). When set at design time, simply specify the filename requested by the property page. To change this property at runtime, use the **LoadPicture** function.

ToolboxBitmap

This property determines what image will appear on the ToolBox to represent this control. It's a **StdPicture** property, like the **Picture** property.

`Width`

This value determines the width of the control when it's first created.

The ToolBox

The ToolBox, shown in Figure 16-2, is the source of the controls you place in your form.

As you pass your mouse pointer over each item, you see a 3-D box appear around the item, indicating which control you're selecting. If you leave the mouse pointer there for a moment, a ToolTip pops up, telling you what the control is.

Along the top, notice the General tab. It lists all the controls selected for the project. On any given project, you will probably be using only three or four controls, so you might want to create your own Toolbox tab. To do so, right-click on the General tab. You should see a pop-up menu with the choice Add Tab. Click on this tab. You're then prompted to name this tab; name it something that relates to what you will use the tab for, like Graphics Controls or MyControls. Now that you have created the tab, click on it. Notice there are no controls available; only the mouse pointer is present. To add controls, either right-click and choose Components from the menu, or click the General tab and drag controls to this new tab.

To place controls on your control form, click the control you want in the ToolBox. The control should become indented, as though it were pushed into the screen. Now press and hold the left mouse button. Move the mouse cursor as though you were drawing a box. You should see a gray outline appear where you have drawn. After releasing the left mouse button, you should see a control. By pressing and clicking on the control again, you can drag the control around the form and place it where you want. By clicking on the little boxes (called *handles*) surrounding the control, you can adjust the size of the control. Another easier way to create a control is by double-clicking on the control in the ToolBox. This action

Figure 16-2.
The ToolBox.

places a standard-sized control in the center of the form. From here, you can move the control where you want it. Go ahead and place a command button (the sixth item in the ToolBox) on your control form using either method.

The Properties Window

Now that we have a control in our form, we need to manipulate its properties to behave and appear like we want it to. The Properties window, shown in Figure 16-3, allows us to do this easily.

By clicking once on a control and pressing F4, you can view the properties of any control (including a form) in the Properties window. At the top of the window is a drop-down list containing the names and control types of all the controls in your project. You can view the properties of these other controls by clicking on them within the list. Below the Alphabetic and Categorized tabs, you can see the main properties list. In the left column are the names of the properties; in the right column are their values. To change the value of a property, click on the value. What happens next depends on the property. If it's a **Text** value, like **Name** or **Caption**, you can simply type in the box to change the value. If it's a **True/False** or list value, you should see a drop-down arrow appear on the right side, allowing you to select from a list of choices. You might also see an ellipsis (. . .) box to bring up a property page, allowing you to change several subproperties at once. Some properties allow you to change their value simply by double-clicking on the value.

Experiment with this; click on the button we created a moment ago, press F4, and select the **Caption** property. Now click on the value (it should say **Command1**). Change it to read **Click Me!**.

Figure 16-3.
The Properties
window.

The Code Window

By selecting the form and pressing F7, we can reach the very heart of VB: the Code window, shown in Figure 16-4.

The Code window is where we actually make the control do things. As we discussed in the previous chapter, Visual Basic is an event-driven language; when we want a control to do something, we have to figure out what event we want to match to that action and place the code to perform the action with that event. In Figure 16-4, we see several events associated with the **UserControl** object, which is the main window for your control.

Let's say we want to know exactly when control initialization occurs. When the **UserControl_Initialize** event occurs, we will have a message box pop up and say **The control is being initialized!**. The code for this event is simple; we use the **MsgBox** statement under the **UserControl_Initialize** event. As you type **MsgBox**, notice that a window pops up as you're typing (see Figure 16-5).

This window, called an *IntelliSense tip*, provides the syntax for the rest of the function. The first item is the prompt (the text that appears on the message box). The remaining items are surrounded by brackets, which indicates they're optional, so you don't need to enter them if you don't want to. We will enter **The control is being initialized!** and won't bother with the optional arguments.

We then decide that when users move the mouse over the command button we added earlier, we want a message box to pop up with the legend **Don't Click Here!** (which is just about how user interface is handled in some programs). Looking at the Code window, you might notice that the text in the list box at the upper left matches the **UserControl** object whose events we were just coding. By clicking on that list box, we can

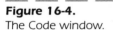

Figure 16-4.
The Code window.

Figure 16-5.
IntelliSense tips.

see a list of all the objects in the control, including **Command1**, the command button we added earlier. Click on **Command1**. You should see now that the **Click** event for **Command1** has popped up, ready for you to enter code that will be executed when the button is clicked. **Click** isn't the event we want to code to, though, so we must select another event from the event list, which is in the second list box at the upper right. By clicking on this list box, you can see a list of all the events associated with the currently selected object (which should be **Command1**). Select the **MouseMove** event from this list (you might have to scroll). You should see the **MouseMove** event pop up, with the cursor at the beginning of the line. We will trigger a message box on this event, so type in the following code:

```
MsgBox "Don't click this button."
```

Project Properties

Along the top of the VB menu bar is the item **Project**. Clicking on this item drops down a sublevel menu, allowing you to add other objects, files, and ActiveX components. At the bottom of this list is **Project Properties**, where you can specify your control's name and description (see Figure 16-6).

After selecting **Properties**, you should see a dialog box with the General tab displayed. In the box labeled Project Name, you specify the name of your control as it will be accessed by others' code. Finally, we see the Project Description box. Enter a brief description of your control here; it will give people using compatible development environments an idea of what your control does. At this point, you should have a good idea of the main components of the Visual Basic 5.0 Control Creation Edition Interface and how they fit together. Next, we'll look at some of the things you should think about before you sit down to program.

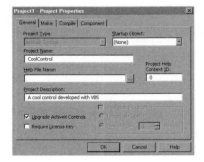

Figure 16-6.
The Project Properties window.

ActiveX Control Design Considerations

As is true with so many things in life, planning is essential to every kind of software development. Before programmers begin any project, there are things they must consider so they can determine the proper course of development. Creating a program is like building a house: You can never plan for every possibility, but it's crazy to simply grab a hammer and nails and start building. Some of the factors you must consider when developing an ActiveX control are shown in Figure 16-7.

Initialization and Termination

Initialization and termination are probably the most important stages your control will have to handle, primarily the processes a control goes through during startup and shutdown. Think of initialization as the birth of the control, and termination as its death. When a control is "born," it's a blank slate, with no properties, no variables initialized, and no behaviors beyond what's handled for you by existing controls you have inserted. Likewise, when a control "dies," it has a "lifetime" of behavior and possibly interaction with other controls to put in order.

INITIALIZATION   When your control is first instantiated, or born, you want to prepare for its purpose. For example, let's say our control is designed to read a file and display it on startup. A useful thing to do at initialization time would be to check for the presence of that file.

Figure 16-7.
A map of
ActiveX control
considerations.

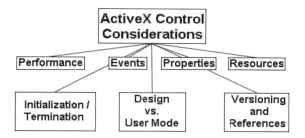

I have included the property statements for completeness. We'll discuss these in detail in the next section. What we have done here is oversimplified; in reality, we would want to actually do something with the information about the presence or absence of the file. We might want to prompt the user for another location, create a new file, or anything else appropriate to the control's operation. Also, you might want to use the initial **Resize** event to position your controls properly. When a control is first instantiated, a **Resize** event occurs that allows you to position your graphics properly. These are the things you should think about when planning your control's initialization.

TERMINATION Luckily for us, Visual Basic handles most of the garbage collection associated with termination. Nevertheless, it's important to take into account what has transpired while a control has been active. It might have created windows that can't simply be blasted out of existence (particularly if a user has entered important data in them). It might have begun processes outside Visual Basic, using the *Windows Application Programming Interface* (API); these need to be closed to avoid problems later on. Most important, a control should terminate in a way that the user expects and can control. For example, if our control managed to find the file, we opened it for use. When the control terminates, the file might or might not be closed. Although Visual Basic closes all file handles in use upon termination, there might be additional activity that we want to be associated with the conclusion of our work with the file. For example, we might want to record the date the file was modified before we close it. The following example assumes we have opened the file and recorded the file handle in a global variable called **FileNum**:

```
Private Sub UserControl_Terminate()
    Print #Filenum, Date$
```

Listing 16-1.
Sample startup code.

```
Private iFileIsPresent As Boolean

Public Property Let FileIsPresent(Val As Boolean)
    iFileIsPresent = Val
End Property

Public Property Get FileIsPresent() As Boolean
    FileIsPresent = iFileIsPresent
End Property

Private Sub UserControl_Initialize()
    If Dir$("C:\Temp\Test.txt") = "" Then
        MsgBox "Cannot find file C:\Temp\Test.txt."
        FileIsPresent = False
    Else
        FileIsPresent = True
    End If
End Sub
```

```
    Close Filenum
    MsgBox "The file is closed."
End Sub
```

In this code, we simply instruct the control to write the current date to the open file with a file handle of **Filenum**. Here is another example, this time assuming we have used a Windows API function and now need to free the resources associated with it:

```
Private Sub UserControl_Terminate()
    FreeConsole()
End Sub
```

Don't worry about what **FreeConsole** really does; it's basically a cleanup function for the **AllocConsole** function we would have perhaps used in the control's **Initialization** event.

Properties and Property Persistence

You might be tempted to sit down and immediately start typing code for your control. This is great for becoming familiar with the environment and the language, but when you're serious about creating a control, you should create a property and variable list. This list will contain all the properties, internal and external, that the control will implement. As we discussed in Chapter 15, you will probably want to have Private variables to store the values of exposed properties. Be sure to include these properties on the list. Also, note the data type of each property to determine whether you use a **Property Let** or **Property Set** statement for it. After you have created this list, determine which properties you want to expose for designers to modify and which will be used only internally. Also, Public properties can be manipulated by JavaScript or VBScript when your control is inserted into the page. This helps you determine whether these properties will be declared Private or Public.

Visual Basic 5.0 also allows you to specify default values for your properties as arguments in the **GetProperty** method of the **PropBag** object that's used in either the **ReadProperties** event (which occurs when we're restoring a control that has already been initialized) or the **InitProperties** event (which occurs the first time a control is inserted by a developer).

Let's take a look at a control with two properties: **Font** and **Title**. The **Font** property defines how text appears, and the **Title** property might be used to identify the control in some way:

```
Private iFont As StdFont
Private iFileIsPresent As Boolean
```

Note we're using an internal **Font** object to keep track of the **Font** property and a simple internal value to keep track of the **FileIsPresent** property.

This is the **Property Set** statement:

```
Public Property Set Font(Ft As StdFont)
    Set iFont = Ft
    PropertyChanged "Font"
End Property
```

It takes a **Font** object as the argument and sets the internal **Font** object (**iFont**) to the same values. It's used when a developer wants to modify the characteristics of our **Font** object.

Here is the **Property Get** statement:

```
Public Property Get Font() As StdFont
    Set Font = iFont
End Property
```

It returns a **Font** object with the same values as our internal **Font** object, **iFont**. It's used when a developer wants information about the characteristics of our **Font** object.

This is a **Property Let** statement:

```
Public Property Let  Title(Val As Boolean)
    iFileIsPresent = Val
    PropertyChanged "FileIsPresent"
End Property
```

The **Property Let** statement is used when we're dealing with simple variables like strings and numbers, rather than objects, which require a **Property Set** statement. This statement assigns the value passed in the property assignment to be stored in the **iFileIsPresent** boolean (true or false) variable.

This is another **Property Get** statement, but with an important difference:

```
Public Property Get FileIsPresent() As Boolean
    FileIsPresent = iFileIsPresent
End Public
```

In the former **Property Get** statement, we needed to use the **Set** keyword to assign the object passed to the property assignment statement to the internal variable. Because we're working with simple variables and not objects here, the **Set** keyword isn't necessary.

This is the most complex part. Because our properties are really just placeholders for the **Font** object, we must actually create a **Font** object to be held. We do this by using the **New** keyword. We then specify the properties we want to be used when the control is first initialized, and then

Listing 16-2.
InitProperties
statement.

```
Private Sub UserControl_InitProperties()
    Dim Temp As New StdFont

    Temp.Name = "MS Sans Serif"
    Temp.Size = 8
    Temp.Underline = False
    Temp.Strikethrough = False
    Set Font = Temp

    FileIsPresent = False
End Sub
```

tell the **Font** property to use the **Font** object we created. As you can see, the **FileIsPresent** property is much easier to work with; we have to assign only a simple **True/False** value to it.

This is how we get started with a control. This code is executed when a developer first inserts the control into a container. When the control's container is activated, the preceding code is executed as well, and the control "loses context." This just means that when the container is shut down, and the program is ended; the control is dead, too. It's not "born again" until the program is run again or until the design environment is refreshed. For example, if we create a control, insert it into a Visual Basic form, and run it, this code executes. When we terminate the form by clicking the Close box on the upper-right corner, the control dies with its container. When we restore the design window with the form containing the control, the control is reborn. A different event, the **ReadProperties** event, is executed (see Listing 16-3).

The first thing you should notice about this code is that it's almost exactly the same code we used for **InitProperties**. In fact, I simply cut and pasted all but the last line and then composed a new last line. Again, we must create a **Font** object; the one we created with **InitProperties** was destroyed along with the rest of the control. After assigning the values as we did before, we come to some new code. Visual Basic 5.0 uses what's called a *property bag*, which is simply an object used to save property values between control instances. I think of the property bag as memories of a past life; the "now-dead" controls are remembering what they were like when "alive." We use the **ReadProperty** method of the **PropBag** object to

Listing 16-3.
ReadProperties
statement.

```
Private Sub UserControl_ReadProperties(PropBag As Property-
Bag)
    Dim Temp As New StdFont

    Temp.Name = "MS Sans Serif"
    Temp.Size = 8
    Temp.Underline = False
    Temp.Strikethrough = False

    Set Font = PropBag.ReadProperty("Font", Temp)

    Title = PropBag.ReadProperty(FileIsPresent, False)
End Sub
```

remember what values we had set for the **Font** object. The second argument is what the control should use for the property if nothing is recalled from the past. We simply use the **Font** object we have created if no "past life" **Font** object can be found, and assign our default **FileIsPresent** value of **False**.

Let's look at the **Property Set** statement again:

```
Public Property Set Font(Ft As StdFont)
    Set iFont = Ft
    PropertyChanged "Font"
End Property
```

Note the second line in the statement: **PropertyChanged "Font"**. It's simply a way of letting the system know that the value of this property has changed, that it should be updated in the Properties window, and that it needs to be persisted for later use. To actually persist the property, use the **WriteProperty** method of the property bag in the **WriteProperties** event:

```
Private Sub UserControl_WriteProperties(PropBag As PropertyBag)
    PropBag.WriteProperty "Font", Font
    PropBag.WriteProperty "FileIsPresent, FileIsPresent
    'you can also specify a default value to be saved as a
third argument
End Sub
```

NOTE *Pay attention here; although we're apparently using the same words twice, they each mean something very different:*

```
PropBag.WriteProperty "FileIsPresent, FileIsPresent
```

The first argument, **"FileIsPresent**, *is the literal name of the property we will store. The second argument refers to the value associated with the first argument we will store. So if we have the value of* **True** *in the* **"FileIsPresent** *property, the preceding line will store the property* **FileIsPresent** *with the value* **True**.

Properties might appear complex at first, but there's actually not too much to their implementation. Once you have done several, there's little variation on the theme. Take a look at the standard values for typical Visual Basic controls; that should give you a good idea of what your properties should be like on startup.

Events

It's useful to plot out what events, both internal and external, you will use in your control. You might decide to use internal events to manage properties or to regulate program flow. If you use separate object modules in your control, or if you want an event to be transmitted from the module to outside the control where a developer can code to it, you need to use internal events to "bubble up" to the control's top level.

Events are typically used by controls to communicate a change in the state of the user. For example, when users click a button, they're indicating they want to change the program's state to the state defined by the button. When users let their mouse pointers hover over a button for a moment, they might be indicating they don't know what it is and want to change the state from passive to informative (with a ToolTip). A good control is designed with this thought in mind. In addition to communicating between the application and the user, events are used to communicate to the developer. If my control downloads a file from the Internet, for example, it might be useful to fire an event letting the developers know that, so they can play a sound, begin another download, or do something with the file.

Now take a look at several user-defined events in a control. The first is an event triggered when users click on a certain area of the control:

```
Public Event ZoneClick(FIP As Boolean)
Public Event MouseClick(Button As Integer)
```

The first event, **ZoneClick**, occurs when users click on the left side of the control. When the event occurs, we pass the **FileIsPresent** value that we defined as a property earlier. The second event occurs when users click anywhere on the control, and passes an argument representing which button was used to click:

```
Private Sub UserControl_MouseDown(Button As Integer, Shift
As Integer, X As Single, Y As Single)
    RaiseEvent MouseClick(Button)
    If X <= UserControl.Width / 2 Then
        RaiseEvent ZoneClick(FileIsPresent)
    End If
End Sub
```

This code represents what happens when users click anywhere on the control. The first line instructs the control to raise the **MouseClick** event for the control, passing the **Button** argument that was passed to it by the main event code. The second line is a bit more complicated. If the value of **x** (that represents the X coordinate of the click on the control) is less than or equal to the width of the control divided by two, then execute the next line. Basically, it says that if we clicked on the left half of the control (less than or equal to the width of the control divided by two), then we will raise the **ZoneClick** event. When we raise the **ZoneClick** event with the **Title** argument, the control retrieves the value of **FileIsPresent** by using the **Property Get** statement we wrote, and passes this value along to the event. All this means that when we insert this control into another container, we will have two events we can use to make things happen:

```
Private Sub TestControl1_MouseClick(Button As Integer)
    MsgBox "You clicked the control with button " & Button
& "."
End Sub

Private Sub TestControl1_ZoneClick(Title As String)
    MsgBox "You clicked on the left hand side of the
control. FileIsPresent is " & FileIsPresent
End Sub
```

This is code that resides in the container into which we have inserted the control. When we execute the program and click on the right side of the container, we should see the message box shown in Figure 16-8.

If we had clicked the control with the right mouse button, it would read **You clicked the control with button 2**. Clicking on the left side of the container yields the same box shown in Figure 16-8, and then a new one, shown in Figure 16-9.

You might wonder why we got the original message box a second time. Keep in mind that we have set it up so that the **MouseClick** event occurs any time users click anywhere on the control, including the left side. If we

Figure 16-8.
A message box.

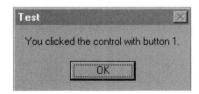

Figure 16-9.
Another message box.

wanted it to occur only when users clicked on the right side, the code would look like this:

```
Private Sub UserControl_MouseDown(Button As Integer, Shift
As Integer, X As Single, Y As Single)
    If X <= UserControl.Width / 2 Then
        RaiseEvent ZoneClick(FileIsPresent)
    Else
        RaiseEvent MouseClick(Button)
    End If
End Sub
```

Here we're checking the coordinates of the click, and then deciding which event we will raise. This should give you an idea of how powerful the **RaiseEvent** statement can be.

Design Versus User Mode

Because your control will be inserted into a container in a development environment, it's important to consider how it will behave in that situation. The control will be in a sort of limbo, between true execution mode and the mode in which we created it. This is called *design mode*. In this mode, the user of your control will be creating, resizing, and manipulating its properties. It's a general convention of control development that when a control is in design mode, it doesn't execute graphical methods or change its appearance in any significant way unless prompted by the user (usually through changing a property). A combo box, for example, doesn't display a list when you click on the drop-down arrow, nor does a checkbox check itself when clicked. This allows the designer to get a better feel for what the form will look like, as well as making it easier for the designer to resize and move the control without aggravation. Your control should follow this convention, if you want it to be user-friendly and taken seriously. In your code, you can easily determine whether the control is in design or user mode (in execution within a program) by using the **Ambient** object, which gives the control developer information about what's going on around the control.

By accessing the **UserMode True/False** property of the **Ambient** object, we can tell which mode the control is in, as shown in this example:

```
Sub Command1_Click()
If Ambient.UserMode = True then 'we're inside a program
    MsgBox "I'm alive!"
Else 'we are being created and modified within a design
environment
```

```
        'do nothing, following the convention
    End If
End Sub
```

With the preceding code, if a designer clicks on your command button while he or she is designing the application using your control, nothing happens. If the control is clicked from within a program, however, a message box bearing the message **I'm alive!** pops up. Carefully consider how you want your control to behave for a developer as opposed to an end user.

NOTE *Although it seems logical to place the detection of the control's user state in the* **Initialization** *code, at that point the* **Ambient** *object hasn't been created. Trying to do this causes an error, and you get the unhelpful message* **Client site not available.** *If you want to perform this kind of global checking, place this code in the* **InitProperty** *and* **ReadProperties** *events. These events are the first ones to occur after initialization, and the* **Ambient** *object will be available then.*

Resources

You might want to include graphics, sound, or other binary format files with your control for multimedia or other purposes. Visual Basic 5.0 has several ways to manage these files, called *resources*. Most of them are handled for you automatically. For example, if you place an image in the control or specify a font, these binary resources are stored in a *Control Cache* (CTX) file before compiling. This file is a companion to the *Control* (CTL) file, which stores information about a control the same way an FRM file stores information about a form. Listing 16-4 shows what a CTL file looks like.

In this code, we have assigned a picture and the Tahoma font to the control. Notice line 16: **Picture = "UserControl1.ctx":0000**. This means "Look at the very beginning of the file named **UserControl1.CTX** and load a picture from it." Very simple. The next line reads **PropertyPages = "UserControl1.ctx":09EC**. It's saying the same thing as the last line, but specifying a different location within that file. The **09EC** is a hexadecimal (base 16) number that specifies an *offset*, or *distance*, from the beginning of the file. It's from this location that you get the dialog box that pops up when you click the ellipsis button to specify font information. If this seems a little confusing, keep in mind that VB does all this for you, so unless you want to manipulate this information at runtime, you don't have to worry about it.

```
VERSION 5.00
Begin VB.UserControl UserControl1
    ClientHeight    =    3600
    ClientLeft      =    0
    ClientTop       =    0
    ClientWidth     =    4800
    BeginProperty Font
        Name         =    "Tahoma"
        Size         =    8.25
        Charset      =    0
        Weight       =    400
        Underline    =    0    'False
        Italic       =    0    'False
        Strikethrough =   0    'False
    EndProperty
    Picture          =       "UserControl1.ctx":0000
    PropertyPages    =       "UserControl1.ctx":09EC
    ScaleHeight      =    3600
    ScaleWidth       =    4800
End
```

You might want to load these binaries at runtime. Visual Basic offers several different ways to do that, depending on exactly what the file is. The easiest of these to work with is the **LoadPicture** function, used to specify a local filename for a new bitmap for use in a graphics control, like a picture box or the **UserControl** control itself. Listing 16-5 shows a simple, if not terribly efficient, way to do a simple 10-frame animation using the **LoadPicture** statement.

In this code, we're looping 100 times through 10 different **LoadPicture**s, each loading a separate frame. Notice how this procedure behaves as though there's an error: It assigns the value of the **UserControl.Picture** property to a **LoadPicture** statement with empty parentheses. This assigns a value of nothing to the picture, clearing the value entirely, which leaves you with a blank **UserControl**.

If you're working with large binary files, or files likely to change between control versions, you might want to consider using a Resource Editor. Resource editors enable you to take several binary files and compile them into one resource file, which you can then access with the **LoadResData** or **LoadResPicture** function. These functions do essentially what **Picture = "UserControl1.ctx":0000** does in the CTL file, except that the resource file takes the place of the CTX file.

Keep in mind that using either the **LoadPicture** or **LoadResData** functions means your project will now reference files outside the ordinary project, which leads us into the next subject.

Listing 16-5.
Animation code.

```
Private Sub UserControl_Click()
    Dim I As Integer
    On Error GoTo ErrHandler

    Do Until I = 100
        UserControl.Picture = LoadPicture("C:\INTERNET\IM-
AGES\DELTAV1.gif")
        UserControl.Picture = LoadPicture("C:\INTERNET\IM-
AGES\DELTAV2.gif")
        UserControl.Picture = LoadPicture("C:\INTERNET\IM-
AGES\DELTAV3.gif")
        UserControl.Picture = LoadPicture("C:\INTERNET\IM-
AGES\DELTAV4.gif")
        UserControl.Picture = LoadPicture("C:\INTERNET\IM-
AGES\DELTAV5.gif")
        UserControl.Picture = LoadPicture("C:\INTERNET\IM-
AGES\DELTAV6.gif")
        UserControl.Picture = LoadPicture("C:\INTERNET\IM-
AGES\DELTAV7.gif")
        UserControl.Picture = LoadPicture("C:\INTERNET\IM-
AGES\DELTAV8.gif")
        UserControl.Picture = LoadPicture("C:\INTERNET\IM-
AGES\DELTAV9.gif")
        UserControl.Picture = LoadPicture("C:\INTERNET\IM-
AGES\DELTAV10.gif")
Loop
Exit Sub
ErrHandler:
    UserControl.Picture = LoadPicture()
End Sub
```

Versioning and External References

When creating a new control, often the easiest way to implement the kind of function you're looking for is to use an external control someone else has created. Also, after you have created a couple of controls, you might want to construct one composed in part of controls you have created. These are called *external references*, which means that when your control tries to create itself, it looks for the files associated with those external components. If these files aren't present or are in a different location than your control expects, the initialization of your component will fail. It's important to look at this from the opposite point of view as well; always think of your control as a component you might want to reuse later on.

In the Project Properties dialog box we looked at earlier is a tab called Make where information about the version, compilation, and application is controlled. Specifying the version is important because it affects how Windows communicates with your control. When your control is compiled, it's assigned a Class ID, which is a unique chain of numbers and letters. This Class ID is then recorded in the Registry along with the information necessary to use your control. With VB5-created controls, one of these items is the version of your control. If you should fail to keep track of versioning information, the information might not match when you implement the control, and the results will be unpredictable (which will almost certainly cause the creation of the control to fail).

On the Make tab is a checkbox labeled AutoIncrement. When it's checked, each time you compile the OCX, the revision of the version (the third digit of 1.01, for example) is incremented. Although this is convenient, you might find that right after you compile a control, you discover an error. When you recompile to correct the error, the version information is incremented again. This automatic increase can lead to ridiculously high, and therefore less useful, version numbers, so I don't recommend using AutoIncrement. It's better to manually increment the control's version when a major aspect of it is changed.

When you form external references, you have no way to know whether the implemented controls exist on the target machine. For example, a control I use often is the Lead Graphics control from LeadTools, an enhanced graphics control allowing for some sophisticated graphics manipulation and creation. This control is extremely unlikely to exist on any given user's machine. It's important, then, to make sure this control will be included in the setup files and package that's distributed with my program, whether it's a standalone application or a CAB file for a Web page.

Performance

In development there's usually an easy way to do things and a right way to do things, and they are seldom the same. In creating controls, you're going to have to balance several factors so that your control behaves as optimally as possible. Even in the smallest of controls, implementing functionality inefficiently can bring about performance penalties. This can frustrate the end user and make your control less useful. There are several general areas in which performance penalties occur, outlined in the following sections.

Graphics

Consider how much memory a wallpaper bitmap occupies. If you're running 640 × 480 resolution, and the wallpaper fills the screen, it can be huge. First, you have 307,200 bits (640 columns by 480 rows = 307,200 pixels, at one bit per pixel) before you even use any color. If the wallpaper is only pure black or pure white, it would use that much. Of course, we want to use colors, so that increases the requirements. To use 256 possible colors requires a byte for each pixel. I think you can see what I mean. Graphics are the traditional grizzly bear of application resources. By way of comparison, you could store a text document 1000 pages long with the same memory requirements as the graphic just described.

Sorting

People usually sort objects by creating two lists—a sort pool and a sorted list. When we note a discrepancy between an unsorted item and the sorted list, we simply insert the item. That's not the case with computers; they can't make the intuitive jump that people can. Therefore, in one way or another, sorting algorithms must approximate this intuition. The big problem with sorting is that as the number of items to be sorted increases, the difficulty and time required to sort them increases exponentially.

File Access

Computers are incredible devices. They mimic the human brain, flashing electrical impulses along silicon neurons at close to the speed of light. This speed allows your computer to perform the miracles it does. Unfortunately, when we want to access the hard disk, we come crashing (excuse the pun) down to earth. The speed of accessing a file is limited by two factors: The distance required for the hard disk head to move from file to file and the speed at which the head can move. Disk defragmentation can minimize the first factor, but little other than buying a faster hard drive can optimize the second.

Graphics are probably the worst offender, at least in Windows environments. Take the `AutoRedraw` property, for example. When you're dealing with a windowed environment, one of the problems you must address is how to handle information that has been obscured and then revealed again. For example, I have a text document open in a word processor and move my Web browser over it, obscuring the text. When I move it away, how does the program know how to rewrite the text that had disappeared? This isn't something most people think about because these environments tend to give the illusion of a three-dimensional world. When one window goes "behind" another, it's really just a function of pixels on a flat video screen being manipulated. There are two main approaches to solving this problem:

- **Persistent bitmapping:** Every image on the screen is stored in memory; when a window is unobscured, the image that pertains to that window is reloaded from memory.

- **Application persistence:** Whenever a window is unobscured, it receives a message from the operating environment, telling it to handle the message itself. The burden of repainting lies on the application with this solution.

Interestingly enough, each of these solutions has been implemented in other operating environments. Microsoft Windows chose to pursue the second solution, but X Windows (for UNIX-based systems) pursued the first. Although the first solution might seem attractive, leaving the not-so-simple work of repainting windows to the operating environment, it requires large amounts of memory devoted strictly to that purpose. Application persistence places a greater workload on the developer, but it's the solution most suited to hardware-challenged machines such as a desktop PC.

The `AutoRedraw` function of graphics controls in Visual Basic gives us a way to slough some of that workload back onto the operating environment. When a control's `AutoRedraw` property is set to `True`, a persistent bitmap is created, but only for that control. This can be convenient, but it places a larger memory load on the system. In addition to this factor, certain programming elements of your control change when you choose to set `AutoRedraw` to `True`. Under normal circumstances, your control receives messages from Windows telling it to paint itself. When `AutoRedraw` is `True`, these `Paint` messages are ignored. If you had planned to use the `Paint` event for something other than painting, this can be a problem. That's not to say that `AutoRedraw` is bad; for small graphics and controls, the performance hit is insignificant, and the code it might save you would be worth it. Larger graphics can lead to visible problems, depending on the system, of course. Consider these factors carefully when planning your control.

Sorting is one of the classic challenges of computer science. Entire books have been written on this seemingly simple subject. An in-depth discussion of sorting is beyond the scope of this book, but we'll discuss a few important principles.

The first step in determining how your control handles sorting is to determine the likely number of items in your sort pool. If you're dealing with less than 50 items, then just about any method will work. For larger sort pools, you need to construct the proper sorting algorithm. One of my favorites is the QuickSort function, a recursive function that sorts items at lightning speed. Any good book on sorting will cover it, and it's widely discussed on the Web. An excellent discussion of sorting is available in *Hard-Core Visual Basic* (McKinney, 1994).

File access can be troublesome for performance, too. When working with programs loaded into memory, you're dealing with electromagnetic energy moving at the speed of light. Access time using this is almost insignificant. When you're dealing with a hard drive, CD-ROM, or floppy drive, you're using mechanical devices that must physically move across the face of disk to access the information. Performance is logically much less impressive.

When we discussed resources, I used an example that loaded frames of an image to display an animation. Using this method, the frames came across at a rate of about six per second, a pleasant speed for animation, but painfully slow compared to the performance of this method. This example assumes we have created a control array of picture boxes named Picture1; we then make them invisible:

```
Private Sub UserControl_Initialize()
    For I = 0 To 19
        Picture1(I).Picture = LoadPicture("C:\INTERNET\IM-
AGES\DELTAV" & (I + 1) & ".GIF")
    Next I
End Sub
```

We loop through the control array, assigning a frame of the animation to it (for example, Picture1(0) contains the frame C:\INTERNET\IMAGES\DELTAV1.GIF). Now that we have loaded all the frames into memory upon initialization, we can play them into the visible picture box, picDisplay:

```
Private Sub UserControl_Click()
Dim Y As Integer
    I = Timer
    Do Until Timer >= I + 1
        For X = 0 To 19
            Frames = Frames + 1
            picDisplay.Picture = Picture1(X).Picture
        Next X
    Loop
End Sub
```

Timer is a Windows function that returns the number of seconds since midnight. Our test says to loop until one second has passed. Within the loop, we cycle through the control array, reading each frame into the visible picture box.

We cycle through the images for only one second, but that's enough. Loading the images from files yielded a frame rate of six frames per second, but this method yields 420 frames per second!

The principle at work here is hiding your work from the end user. Many programs do this by using a *splash screen*, which is an attractive (presumably) window that displays information about the program that's running, its version number, and so on, while initialization is being performed in the background. This is the best example of hiding your work. Sometimes being a good developer calls for a little sleight of hand and misdirection.

The grand scheme of all this is the answer to the question: What is the nature of our control? A command button doesn't have a value property as the checkbox does; its nature isn't to hold data—it's to communicate a change of state from the user. A textbox doesn't have a **Paint** event as a picture box does; its nature is to store text, not to interact with the user in a graphical way. Define what your control does by what it is. Think carefully about what both a developer and an end user are likely to do with your control, and what they are likely to want to do with it. Good user interface design is at the very heart of control creation, and good user interface requires planning and consideration of your audience.

Creating the **LATextBox** Control

In this section we will walk through the creation of a control called **LATextBox**, shown in Figure 16-10. We'll cover the basic considerations first, and then cover the code in detail at the end. I created this control

Figure 16-10.
The **LATextBox**.

for the IntellAgent Control Corporation, which produces a software package for managing sales and contact information. I was in charge of designing the actual pages to display the information. The standard textboxes seemed awfully dull for the clean, Internet look we were shooting for, so with user interface guru Scott Miller, we designed the **LATextBox**. You can pronounce it *El-Lay-Text-Box*, referring to the city in California, or like the French *la*. Either pronunciation gets the message across that we wanted to create a textbox that was chic, cool, and attractive.

The **LATextBox** is a textbox with a colored outline and a drop shadow, giving it a three-dimensional look. We wanted to create list boxes with the same look, too, so we used the functionality of list boxes in the same control. Perhaps the control should be called **LATextListBox**, but by the time we got to the list box elements, the name had stuck. Later on, we decided that the textboxes might be carrying information that could be used by an external program, like an e-mail address or a fax number. We though it would be neat if we could place a button on the textbox that would then fire an event passing the information stored in the textbox up to the container. Then we decided it would be even neater if we could put a custom graphic on the button! Well, this should give you an idea of how the development for this control went.

Obviously, only a few features implemented in the final control were planned; developers rarely have this luxury. When you do, I suggest you take advantage of it because it makes the work three times as easy and ten times as fast. For the purposes of this discussion, however, we'll pretend I was able to plan all the aspects of **LATextBox**.

Control Specifications

LATextBox is similar to a Windows textbox, but it has a colored highlight and a drop shadow (the developer can specify the color for both). **LATextBox** has a **ControlStyle** property with two values: **TextBox** and **ListBox**. When set to **TextBox**, **LATextBox** looks like a standard textbox. When set to **ListBox**, an arrow appears on the right side of the control; when it's clicked, it shows a list of the items in the control's **List** collection. In addition, **LATextBox** has an **Executable** property, which, when set to **True**, causes a clickable button to appear on the left side of the control. When clicked, this button raises the **Execute** event, passing the contents of the textbox or list box along with the event. In addition, this button has an **ExecutableIcon** property that defines the graphic to appear on the button.

LATextBox Considerations

We'll walk through each of the considerations we discussed before and see how they apply to this project.

INITIALIZATION AND TERMINATION Our control consists primarily of three objects—a textbox and two picture boxes. The textbox is the heart of our control, accepting and storing the text the user enters, as well as providing all the normal functionality of a textbox. The two picture boxes function as the highlight and drop shadow. The highlight is a user-defined color, with a default color of pink. The drop shadow is also user-defined, with a default color of light gray. The highlight appears behind and below the main textbox, and the drop shadow is behind and below the highlight, each offset by 15 pixels. To accomplish this visual effect, each of the objects is 30 pixels shorter than the control. The textbox has a **Left** property of 0 so that it's aligned to the very left of the control. The highlight has a **Left** of 30, so that it's to the right of the textbox. Finally, the drop shadow has a **Left** of 60, so that it's aligned to the very right of the control. These figures remain constant, no matter what size the control is.

NOTE *A problem arises when the control is created: We have no idea how wide the control has been made. Because the proportions between the **Left** properties are held constant, when the control is resized wider than the original design, all three objects are too short. After consideration, we realized we needed to ensure the following: All three objects have a length that's 40 pixels shorter than the actual control. Then the textbox will stop 40 pixels short of the end, allowing the highlight and drop shadow to be seen. The highlight will be centered so that it's visible behind the textbox but still allows the drop shadow to be seen. Finally, the drop shadow begins 40 pixels in and travels to the end of the control.*

Furthermore, we need to make sure the controls are positioned properly. There are several controls other than the three objects we have already discussed that need to be dealt with. For example, we use a picture box to implement the drop-down arrow for the list box, and another picture box to implement the button that fires the **Execute** event for the control. These picture boxes should be at the very front, with the drop-down picture box right-aligned in front of the textbox, and the Execute button picture box left-aligned on the picture box. We bring each of these controls to the front in reverse order. First, we bring forward the drop shadow that we want to be in the very back, then the highlight, then the textbox, then the drop-down picture box, and finally the Execute picture box. This procedure ensures that each object is at the proper depth on the screen. This chain of procedures also happens any time the box is resized, so it's a good solution to this particular problem.

PROPERTIES AND PROPERTY PERSISTENCE   We decided that **LATextBox** will have the following properties:

- **ControlStyle:** A value determining whether this control will function as a list box or textbox.
- **DropShadowColor:** A value determining the color of the control's shadow.
- **Enabled:** A value that mirrors the regular textbox **Enabled** property.
- **Executable:** A value that determines whether a button will appear on the left-hand side of the box.
- **EXEPicture:** The picture that would appear in that button.
- **Font:** The font characteristics of the textbox.
- **ForeColor:** The color of the text in the textbox.
- **HighlightColor:** The color of the highlight around the textbox.
- **List:** A value that, when given an index, returns that indexed member of the control's list items.
- **ListCount:** The number of list items in the control.
- **ListIndex:** The currently selected item in the list box.
- **MaxLength:** The greatest allowable number of characters in the textbox.
- **MultiLine:** A value determining whether there can be multiple lines of text in the textbox.
- **Sorted:** A value determining whether the list items will be sorted.
- **Text:** The text in the textbox.
- **TextBoxColor:** The color of the textbox.

It should be clear now that our properties fall into two categories: Those that are stubs for properties of established controls, like **Text** or **MaxLength**, and properties we're creating from the ground up, like **Executable** and **HighlightColor**. Properties in the first category are simple. To get their value, we simply look at the value of the corresponding property in the control we're using for it. To set their value, we just change the value of that property in the control, as in the following example:

```
Public Property Let MaxLength(Val As Integer)
    txtTextBox.MaxLength = Val
    PropertyChanged "MaxLength"
End Property

Public Property Get MaxLength() As Integer
    MaxLength = txtTextBox.MaxLength
End Property
```

Most of our work is already done for us. To retrieve **LATextBox**'s **MaxLength** value, we simply get the **MaxLength** value of **txtTextBox**, which is our main text box. To change it, we reassign the value. All the consequences of changing that value in our control are already handled by the internal code of **txtTextBox**, so it's a snap.

For the second category of properties, however, things are a bit trickier. When we want a change in a property to have a certain effect, we have to handle that entirely ourselves, as shown in Listing 16-6.

Notice that we're referring to an unfamiliar variable: **iHighlightColor**. Without a corresponding control property, we need an internal variable to store the value of the color we're using. Technically, we could use the **BackColor** property of **picHighlight** (the picture box used to provide the outline around the textbox), but it would be poor programming practice. The **BackColor** property of **picHighlight** isn't the same thing as **HighlightColor**. Because of this difference, we might want to do something in the future that would require that internal variable.

Listing 16-6.
HighlightColor
property code.

```
Public Property Let HighLightColor(Col As OLE_COLOR)
    iHighLightColor = Col
    picHighLight.BackColor = Col
    PropertyChanged "HighLightColor"
End Property

Public Property Get HighLightColor() As OLE_COLOR
    HighLightColor = iHighLightColor
End Property
```

When a property doesn't directly correspond to its true nature, use an internal variable. A note on naming conventions here: There's nothing special about naming the internal variable the same as the property it holds, but it does make sense. I name my internals by putting an *i* in front of the variable name (for *internal*, in case you're wondering).

Now that we've decided what are properties are, we need to think about persistence. Saving the properties is simple enough; we just include a **WriteProperty** line for each property. Each line will look like this:

```
PropBag.WriteProperty "ControlStyle", ControlStyle
```

This line states that we're saving the **"ControlStyle"** property with the value contained in **ControlStyle**. As long as we have remembered to include a **PropertyChanged** statement in each **Property Let** or **Set** statement, this should take care of saving the values for future use. Getting the values back is a bit trickier.

Before we get into the thick of **InitProperties** and **ReadProperties**, we need to start thinking about the default values for our properties. Bad default properties can be a real pain; they result in a developer having to change a property every time he or she creates a control. For example, we probably don't want to supply a default color of lime green to the textbox. What we're shooting for is a control whose properties will be modified the fewest times. If we can create a control that's already close to what developers want, then we can reduce their workload and have happy customers.

The **InitProperties** event is simple. As we discussed before, the **InitProperties** event occurs when a control has just been created, and there are no previous properties to be accessed. When this event occurs, we simply assign our default values to the properties, as shown in this example:

```
Private Sub UserControl_InitProperties()
     MaxLength = 0
End Sub
```

Things are a little trickier for the **Font** property. It's expecting an object, not a simple value, so we need to give it one, as shown in Listing 16-7.

We're creating a "blank" **Font** object on the first line, and then populating the desired properties on the following lines. On the next line, we set the **Font** property to the **Font** object we have created.

The **ReadProperties** statement in the **ReadProperties** event is pretty straightforward except for the **Font** property. With all the other properties, we can simply specify the default property in the argument like this:

Listing 16-7.
Font InitProperties
statement.

```
Private Sub UserControl_InitProperties()
        Dim Temp As StdFont
        Temp.Name = "MS Sans Serif"
        Temp.Size = 8
        Temp.Strikethrough = False
        Temp.Underline = False
        Set Font = Temp
        MaxLength = 0
End Sub
```

```
Private Sub UserControl_ReadProperties(PropBag As
PropertyBag)
        MaxLength = PropBag.ReadProperty("MaxLength", 0)
End Sub
```

The trick with **ReadProperties** is the **Font** object. We need to do the same thing we did for the **InitProperties** event: Create a template **Font** object and assign the characteristics, as shown in Listing 16-8.

That's about as tricky as properties get. You might have to deal with different objects, but it probably won't be anything more complicated than what you see here.

EVENTS The primary event consideration for this control is the **Execute** event, although we have to think about exposing certain events of the textbox, as well as mimicking the events of a list box. When an **Execute** event occurs, we want to pass the information that's in the textbox along with the event so that the container can perhaps use the information. For example, if an e-mail address is entered in the box, when the **Execute** event is fired, the container could launch an e-mail program and put the address in the box into the message. We decide to make an event list, shown in Table 16-1, and match each event with the event that will raise it.

As you can see, the **Click**, **MouseUp**, and **MouseDown** events are triggered by clicking on any of our main objects. This helps to create the impression of **LATextBox** being unified as one control. After we have considered what really causes the event, it's pretty simple to implement the event. We have decided that the **Change** event is triggered by the **Change** event of the **txtTextBox** control. We implement the event like this:

```
Private Sub txtTextBox_Change()
    RaiseEvent Change
End Sub
```

Listing 16-8.
Font ReadProperties
statement.

```
Private Sub UserControl_ReadProperties(PropBag As Property-
Bag)
        Dim Temp As New StdFont
        Temp.Name = "MS Sans Serif"
        Temp.Size = 8
        Temp.Strikethrough = False
        Temp.Underline = False
        Set Font = PropBag.ReadProperty("Font", Temp)
        MaxLength = PropBag.ReadProperty("MaxLength", 0)
End Sub
```

Very simple. With events raised by more than one event, like **MouseUp**, we need to place a **RaiseEvent** statement in each of the events. We start with event declarations for each, following them with the **RaiseEvent**s:

```
Public Event MouseUp(Button As Integer, Shift As Integer, x
As Single, y As Single)
```

The four arguments are **Button**, **Shift**, **X**, and **Y**. **Button** indicates which mouse button was pressed, the right or the left. **Shift** indicates whether the Shift, Ctrl, or Alt key was pressed during the click. The **X** and **Y** indicate the position on the control where the button was clicked. We receive this information in the event in which we place the **RaiseEvent** statement, and just pass it on up the line, as shown in Listing 16-9.

Keep in mind we will add **RaiseEvent** statements for the **ExecuteUp** event on **picExecute** later.

DESIGN VERSUS USER MODE   When thinking about design mode, we need to consider what the control does in user mode. One of the more important things the control does graphically is drop down a list of the items. If the control behaves this way in design mode, it could be very irritating. If a developer is trying to move the control and clicks on the drop-down arrow, he or she will get an empty list and have to click on it again to move it. This is an example of something for which we should use mode detection:

```
Private Sub picDropDown_Click()
    If Ambient.UserMode = False Then
        Exit Sub
    End If
    RaiseEvent Click
End Sub
```

Table 16-1.

Table of Events
and Their Event
Triggers.

Our Event	The Source Event
Change	**txtTextBox** (our main textbox) **Change**
KeyPress	**txtTextBox KeyPress**
KeyDown	**txtTextBox KeyDown**
MouseDown	**txtTextBox, picHighlight, picDropShadow, picExecute, picDropDown MouseDown**
MouseUp	**txtTextBox, picHighlight, picDropShadow, picExecute, picDropDown MouseUp**
Click	**txtTextBox, picHighlight, picDropShadow, picExecute, picDropDown Click**
Execute	**picExecute** (our Execute button picture box) **Click**
ExecuteUp	**picExecute MouseUp**
ExecuteDown	picExecute MouseDown

We will put a lot of code in this event later to create the effect of a drop-down list box. This code simply says, "If we're in design mode, exit this procedure and ignore any further code." We'll put the same detection code in the **picDropDown_MouseDown** procedure. We might want to put the same code in other events, like the **picExecute** events, but it's not necessary because they don't really do anything graphical.

RESOURCES The only real resource we use in **LATextBox** is the graphic that appears on the Execute button. As we mentioned earlier, this graphic is defined by the developer at design time. There are several ways we could go about handling this graphic. We could use the **EXEPicture** property as a pointer (in the nontechnical sense) to a file we load at run-time. As we saw earlier, this method isn't very efficient, although it would probably work with just one picture. We do run into a problem, however, with the size of the graphic. The **picExecute** control that contains the picture is about 20 pixels by 20 pixels. Unless we want to use only 20 × 20 pixel graphics, we need to have some kind of resizing mechanism. With

Listing 16-9.
Event statements.

```
Private Sub txtTextBox_MouseUp(Button As Integer, Shift As
Integer, x As Single, y As Single)
    RaiseEvent MouseUp(Button, Shift, x, y)
End Sub

Private Sub picHighLight_MouseUp(Button As Integer, Shift
As Integer, X As Single, Y As Single)
    RaiseEvent MouseUp(Button, Shift, X, Y)
End Sub

Private Sub picDropShadow_MouseUp(Button As Integer, Shift
As Integer, X As Single, Y As Single)
    RaiseEvent MouseUp(Button, Shift, X, Y)
End Sub

Private Sub picExecute_MouseUp(Button As Integer, Shift As
Integer, X As Single, Y As Single)
    RaiseEvent MouseUp(Button, Shift, X, Y)
End Sub

Private Sub picDropDown_MouseUp(Button As Integer, Shift As
Integer, X As Single, Y As Single)
    RaiseEvent MouseUp(Button, Shift, X, Y)
End Sub
```

this kind of overhead, even for just one picture, we don't want to load from a file at runtime. The solution to this problem is a buffering control. We add another picture box, calling it **picHolder**, and use it as a holding and preparation area for the graphic. When the **EXEPicture** property is specified, we load the graphic and paint it properly sized to **picExecute**:

```
Public Property Set EXEPicture(pic As StdPicture)
    If pic Is Nothing Then
        picHolder.Picture = picHolder2.Picture
    Else
        Set picHolder.Picture = pic
    End If
    picExecute.Refresh
End Property
```

We begin by checking to make sure there's actually a picture in the property procedure. You might wonder, how in the world could we get an empty picture? That's exactly what happens when the control is initialized for the first time, in the **ReadProperties** event:

```
Set EXEPicture = PropBag.ReadProperty("EXEPicture")
```

We haven't specified a default value for this property; unless the user has specified one, we have no picture to use. If one is specified, then we don't need a default value because its value will be stored in the property bag. If the picture is empty, we grab the picture stored in the **picHolder2** control(a lightning bolt graphic). If, of course, there's a picture in the variable, we set the buffer's picture equal to it. At this point, we still haven't changed the picture on the actual button. Therefore, we end this property procedure by refreshing the **picExecute** control, triggering the **Paint** event:

```
Private Sub picExecute_Paint()
    picExecute.PaintPicture picHolder.Picture, 0, 0,
picExecute.ScaleWidth, picExecute.ScaleHeight
End Sub
```

This procedure grabs the picture from **picHolder** and slaps it onto the **picExecute** control with the **PaintPicture** method. The principle behind this procedure is buffering. We're using a control that's loaded into memory to hold the image we need to manipulate on the **picExecute** control. Therefore, performance is optimized without going to too much trouble.

VERSIONING AND EXTERNAL REFERENCES Versioning and external references can cause problems that are difficult for Visual Basic developers to detect because the development environment handles these issues at arm's length. When you begin an entirely new project, you already have references to common Windows libraries, including **VBRUN500.DLL**. If these libraries are missing or in the wrong place, errors will occur. Luckily, VB handles most common missing references well, with an error message indicating the missing library. When you begin to create your own references, things can get a little hairy.

We're creating this control to be reused over and over again on a page that displays information from a database. The page itself is an ActiveX control. Now we want to minimize the size of each of these page controls for performance reasons, so each textbox on the page won't actually be part of the control. It will be an external reference, just like adding a reference to any other library. It's critical that when we create the new pages, we must update the page references by recompiling the control, if we need to make any changes to the **LATextBox**. If this isn't done, the errors are particularly cryptic. The control might work properly in some containers, but not others; certain pages containing the control perform when others don't. The only way to get rid of these seemingly unrelated errors is to recompile the control and make sure its latest version resides on the target machine.

PERFORMANCE　　**LATextBox** is a fairly lightweight control, meaning that its effect on system resources is likely to be minimal, but there are still several important considerations. One, in particular, is the performance of sorting the items in the **List** collection of our control. After examining how people use list boxes in Windows, we decide it's unlikely there would ever be more than 50 or so items in the list. This knowledge gives us the freedom to sort the list in absolutely the least efficient way possible: Feed the list into an invisible list box whose **Sorted** property is set to **True**! To avoid guilt over doing this so quickly and easily, we mock up a version of the control that implements the **Quicksort** algorithm, a common, efficient sorting method. In timing tests, we quickly see that the difference is measurable only in microseconds, which makes this method suitable for our control:

LATextBox: From Initialization to Termination

At last, we have arrived: We're ready to begin actual coding. First, we write out our variable and event declarations. We should expect from the outset to modify and add to this list, but a rough outline, shown in Listing 16-10, will do for now.

It would be useful if we could represent the **ControlStyle** property as either a **TextBox** or **ComboBox**, rather than as an integer. Visual Basic 5.0 allows us to do this by using what's called an *Enum*. **Enum**, which is short for *enumeration*, assigns labels to the values, so that it's clearer what the values really mean:

```
Public Enum ControlType
    TextBox = 1
    ComboBox = 2
End Enum
```

With the preceding statement, we can make a property assignment like this:

```
Option Explicit

Public Event Change()
Public Event KeyPress(KeyAscii As Integer)
Public Event KeyDown(KeyCode As Integer, Shift As Integer)
Public Event MouseDown(Button As Integer, Shift As Integer,
x As Single, y As Single)
Public Event MouseUp(Button As Integer, Shift As Integer, x
As Single, y As Single)
Public Event Click()
Public Event Execute(Command As String)
Public Event ExecuteUp(Command As String, Button As Inte-
ger, Shift As Integer, x As Single, y As Single)
Public Event ExecuteDown(Command As String, Button As Inte-
ger, Shift As Integer, x As Single, y As Single)

Private iExecutable As Boolean
Private iMultiLine As Boolean
Private iForeColor As OLE_COLOR
Private iFt As StdFont
Private iText As String
Private iTextBoxColor As OLE_COLOR
Private iHighLightColor As OLE_COLOR
Private iDropShadowColor As OLE_COLOR
Private iSorted As Boolean
Private ControlHeight As Single
```

```
LATextBox1.ControlType = TextBox
```

This not only makes things easier for the programmer to remember when writing this kind of code, it makes the code much easier to read. To refer to the **Enum** we have established, we simply declare a variable with the name of the **Enum**:

```
Private iControlStyle As ControlType
```

The property statements will then look like this:

```
Public Property Let ControlStyle(Val As ControlType)
Public Property Get ControlStyle() As ControlType
```

We also need to create a variable to hold the list items that populate the list box. Furthermore, it would useful to have an internal variable:

```
Private ListItems As New Collection
```

We'll use some unusual property statements to manipulate this collection later. In looking at this list of variables, we come across **MultiLine**, but the **MultiLine** property of a textbox isn't available at runtime. Even though our control is used by a developer in a design environment, it's still "running." **MultiLine** is too important a property for us to just shrug our shoulders and say "Oh, well," so we must come up with a clever solution. What we do is set two controls for the textbox, one with the **MultiLine** property set to **True** and one with the **MultiLine** property set to **False**. To use the property, we're going to have to apply whatever happens to **txtTextBox** to our **MultiLine** control, which we'll call **txtMultiline**. This goes for properties, events, everything. We're lucky we realized this before we wrote any code; it would be a real pain to fix halfway through.

This is a good time to lay out the controls we want onto our control form. We lay them out on the form in a general arrangement of how we need them to be in the final control, as shown in Figure 16-11.

I've made the background of the control black to make things a little clearer. Notice we've added a scrollbar; we'll use it later in the drop-down list box. In addition, there's **lstCheat**, the list control we use to implement the **Sorted** property of the **List** collection.

Next, we tackle initialization:

```
Private Sub UserControl_Initialize()

End Sub
```

Pretty easy, eh? Our primary consideration with initialization is positioning and sizing the controls correctly. Although there's nothing wrong with putting this code here, we're going to have to deal with the same problems whenever the control is resized, so it's smarter to put that code in the **Resize** event, as shown in Listing 16-11.

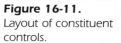

Figure 16-11.
Layout of constituent controls.

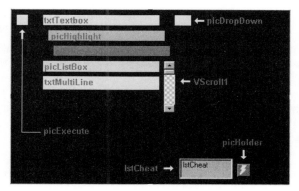

```
Private Sub UserControl_Resize()
    UserControl.ScaleMode = vbTwips
    If Executable Then
        txtTextBox.Left = picExecute.Width
    Else
        txtTextBox.Left = 0
    End If
    txtTextBox.Top = 0
    picHighLight.Left = 15
    picHighLight.Top = 15
    picDropShadow.Left = 30
    picDropShadow.Top = 30
    txtTextBox.Height = UserControl.Height - 30
    txtMultiLine.Height = txtTextBox.Height
    picHighLight.Height = UserControl.Height - 30
    picDropShadow.Height = UserControl.Height - 30
    picDropDown.Height = UserControl.Height - 30
    picDropDown.Left = UserControl.Width -
picDropDown.Width - 30
    picListBox.Height = txtTextBox.Height
    If Not ListMode Then
        Call picDropDown_Paint
    End If
    If Executable Then
        txtTextBox.Width = UserControl.Width - picExe-
cute.Width - 30
    Else
        txtTextBox.Width = UserControl.Width - 30
    End If
    txtMultiLine.Width = txtTextBox.Width
    picHighLight.Width = UserControl.Width - 30
    picDropShadow.Width = UserControl.Width - 30
    picListBox.Width = txtTextBox.Width
    picExecute.Height = txtTextBox.Height
    If ListMode Then
        picListBox.Visible = True
    End If
End Sub
```

We're just restating what we planned in VB code. We know that all three of the main visual controls—**txtTextBox**, **picHighLight**, and **picDropShadow**—need to be 30 pixels shorter than the control, both in width and height. The **picDropDown** control, which we use to draw the arrow to click on for the control, needs to be flush against the edge of the right-hand side of the text box. This is 30 pixels to the left of the right-hand side of the control. Now the **Left** property refers to the position of the left-hand side of the picture box, so we subtract the width of the control. Otherwise, the picture box would be outside the text box, with its left side against the right side of the text box, as shown in Figure 16-12.

When we subtract the width of the control, the **picDropDown** control is then positioned properly, as shown in Figure 16-13 (I've added a border around the control for clarity).

Because we want the sizes to line up, we make the **picExecute** control height the same as the **txtTextBox** control. We actually did the same thing in a different way for **picDropDown**:

```
picDropDown.Height = UserControl.Height - 30
```

If you remember, **txtTextBox** is always 30 pixels smaller than the control, so it's the same thing.

Now that we have established the basic layout of the control, we can use the **InitProperties** event to set up the programmatic elements of our control.

Again, this is a pretty standard procedure; notice that we have created a **Font** template object for the **Font** property, as we discussed earlier. Keep in mind that **InitProperties** is called only when the control is first instantiated; when the control is refreshed, the **ReadProperties** event is called, as shown in Listing 16-13.

We reiterate the **InitProperties** statement, more or less, and grab the old properties from the property bag. At this point, our control is up and running.

Figure 16-12.
LATextBox.

Figure 16-13.
LATextBox.

FOCUS ISSUES   One of the meat-and-potatoes issues to consider with our control is handling focus. *Focus* means just what it sounds like; it's the control we're concentrating on at the moment. A control that has focus is re- acting immediately to the mouse events and keystrokes the user enters. VB- created controls present special challenges with focus because, in general, you're working with a collection of controls that you want to act as one unit.

First, we must make sure the `UserControl` property `CanGetFocus` is set to `True`. If it's set to `False`, the control can't get focus, and we can't pro- gram to the `GotFocus` event. Because we have controls inside the control that will get focus, the control itself can't. If we're going to handle the sit- uation of the control getting the focus, we must address it separately for each of the controls that might get the focus. We need to consider the fo- cus issues of the following controls:

- `txtTextBox` (this control, along with `txtMultiLine`, will be the one we have to think about)
- `txtMultiline`
- `picExecute`
- `picDropDown`
- `picHighLight` and `picDropShadow` (in the unlikely event the user clicks on either)

You might say at this point, "But wait! A user could click on the list box once it has dropped down, or on the list box scrollbar, or even on the `UserControl` itself!" True, but to access either of the first two, they would have had to click on `picDropDown`, which is where we're handling those issues. As far the `UserControl` object itself, we set its `BackStyle` property to `Transparent`, which means it won't receive mouse events. Mouse clicks in the area where the background would be are just passed to the con- tainer behind it.

```
Private Sub txtTextBox_GotFocus()
    UserControl.Extender.ZOrder 0
End Sub

Private Sub txtMultiLine_GotFocus()
    UserControl.Extender.ZOrder 0
End Sub
```

The `Extender` object is defined in the VB5 Help File as an object that holds properties of the control that are actually controlled by the control's container rather than by the control itself.

Listing 16-12.
LATextBox Init-
Properties code.

```
Private Sub UserControl_InitProperties()
        Dim Temp As StdFont

        ControlStyle = TextBox
        DropShadowColor = &H808080
        Enabled = True
        Executable = False
        ForeColor = &HFF0000
        Temp.Name = "MS Sans Serif"
        Temp.Size = 8
        Temp.Strikethrough = False
        Temp.Underline = False
        Set Font = Temp
        HighLightColor = &HFFC0C0
        MaxLength = 100
        MultiLine = False
        PasswordChar = ""
        Sorted = False
        TextBoxColor = &HE0E0E0
        Text = ""
End Sub
```

This definition is a little confusing. The way I think of the **Extender** object is as the actual control that I drop onto a Web page or a form. For example, if I drop an **LATextBox** into a Web page and name it **Text1**, the **Extender.Name** property is **Text1**. The second part of the previous statement, **ZOrder**, is a method used to bring a control to the front or send it to the back. **ZOrder 0** means "Bring this control to the front." So this statement means: "When a user clicks on the textbox, bring the control to the front of the form." This means that if anything was overlapping the textbox, like a drop-down window of another control, it will end up behind this control.

As you can see, all we're doing here is passing the focus to the appropriate textbox control. This particular statement brings me to a point about **If** statements. When you're evaluating an expression, such as **MultiLine = True**, you can leave off **= True**. Without going into too much unnecessary technical detail, every **If** statement evaluates to either **True** or **False**, and boolean values (like **MultiLine**) are already fully qualified as **True** or **False**. It might seem a little confusing at first, but it will save you a lot of keystrokes in the long run.

What we're doing here is centralizing the code that defines the focus behavior. It's best to have the code in a centralized point (or in this case, two places). Changes are inevitable, so when they happen, it's good to

```
Private Sub UserControl_ReadProperties(PropBag As Property-
Bag)
    Dim Temp As New StdFont
        ControlStyle = PropBag.ReadProperty("ControlStyle",
TextBox)
        DropShadowColor = PropBag.ReadProperty("DropShadow-
Color", &H808080)
        Enabled = PropBag.ReadProperty("Enabled", True)
        Executable = PropBag.ReadProperty("Executable",
False)
        Set EXEPicture = PropBag.ReadProperty("EXEPic-
ture")
        ForeColor = PropBag.ReadProperty("ForeColor",
&HFF0000)
        Temp.Name = "MS Sans Serif"
        Temp.Size = 8
        Temp.Strikethrough = False
        Temp.Underline = False
        Set Font = PropBag.ReadProperty("Font", Temp)
        HighLightColor = PropBag.ReadProperty("HighLight-
Color", &HFFC0C0)
        MaxLength = PropBag.ReadProperty("MaxLength", 0)
        MultiLine = PropBag.ReadProperty("MultiLine",
False)
        PasswordChar = PropBag.ReadProperty("PasswordChar",
"")
        Sorted = PropBag.ReadProperty("Sorted", False)
        TextBoxColor = PropBag.ReadProperty("TextBoxColor",
&HE0E0E0)
        Text = PropBag.ReadProperty("Text", "")
End Sub
```

have to edit as few codes as possible. Also, we're going to have a list box that drops down to display the items we've placed in the list of the control. When we click another control, that list has to pop back up and behave like a proper list box. We need to react to the loss of focus, too.

After a bit of thought, we decide to treat the lost focus the same way we handled the user clicking on the list box. In fact, we directly trigger that event by calling the procedure and passing the arguments as though it were a real **MouseDown**:

```
Private Sub picListBox_LostFocus()
    Call picListBox_MouseDown(1, 0, 0, -100)
End Sub
```

Remember that the arguments for the **MouseDown** event are: **Button**, **Shift, X,** , and **Y**. We're passing a **Y** argument of **-100**, which is impossible

Listing 16-14.
Focus issues code.

```
Private Sub picExecute_MouseDown(Button As Integer, Shift
As Integer, X As Single, Y As Single)
    If MultiLine Then
        txtMultiLine.SetFocus
    Else
        txtTextBox.SetFocus
    End If
End Sub

Private Sub picDropDown_Click()
    If MultiLine Then
        txtMultiLine.SetFocus
    Else
        txtTextBox.SetFocus
    End If
End Sub

Private Sub picHighLight_GotFocus()
    If MultiLine Then
        txtMultiLine.SetFocus
    Else
        txtTextBox.SetFocus
    End If
End Sub

Private Sub picDropShadow_GotFocus()
    If MultiLine Then
        txtMultiLine.SetFocus
    Else
        txtTextBox.SetFocus
    End If
End Sub
```

under a normal click. This is our cue in the **MouseDown** event that this is the special case of a lost focus rather than a "legitimate" click. That's about the size of it for **Focus**; no other element needs any particular behavior on losing its focus.

PROPERTY CONSIDERATIONS   As we discussed, properties are going to boil down to one of two categories. Some properties clearly map to another control's property, like the **HighlightColor** property maps to the **BackColor** property of **picHighlight**. Others, like **ControlStyle** and **Executable**, have more complex behavior.

ControlStyle defines whether the control acts like a simple textbox or like a list box. If **ControlStyle** is set to **TextBox**, our work is pretty simple; we don't need to worry about the list, scrolling, or **picDropArrow**,

```
Public Property Let ControlStyle(Val As ControlType)
    Dim PropBag As PropertyBag
    iControlStyle = Val
    If Val = TextBox Then
        picDropDown.Visible = False
    Else
        picDropDown.Visible = True
    End If
    PropertyChanged "ControlStyle"
End Property
```

which supplies the little arrow to click on to access the list. If **ControlStyle** is set to **ListBox**, things are more complicated.

This procedure is deceptively simple. If **ControlStyle** is set to **TextBox**, we make **picDropDown** invisible; otherwise, we make it visible. The complexity is hidden in the **picDropDown.Visible** statement. When **picDropDown** is made visible, its **Paint** event occurs. This is the event we must use to paint the arrow. The code in the **Paint** event is shown in Listing 16-16.

The first line clears the picture box entirely so it can start with a clean slate. The second line addresses the **ScaleMode** property of the **picDropDown** control. In Visual Basic, there are several units we can use when discussing graphics. We can use *pixels*, which refer to the physical ability of the user's monitor to display, or twips, points, characters, or several other units. It's the same thing as talking about feet, inches, or meters. This line just makes sure that when we assign numbers, VB knows we're talking about pixels. The next line assigns the **DrawWidth** property of the control. **DrawWidth** determines how wide a line (or point) drawn on the control is.

The next **Line** statement is simple; we specify two points, giving X and Y coordinates for each, and it draws a line between them. In addition, at the end of the line, we can tell it what color to draw the line.

What we're doing is drawing the top of the arrow on the control. We want it to start just inside the control's left side, so we assign a value of one tenth of the control's width to the **x** argument of the first point. If the control were 10 units wide, this number would be (.1 * 10) = 1. Second, we want to have this arrow drawn one third of the way down the control; we pick this number because it looks about right. Halfway down looks too far; one quarter of the way down looks too short. The second point is nine tenths of the way across, so that the line goes almost all the way across. Because it's a horizontal line, the **y** argument of the second point is the same. Finally, we want the arrow to be light gray, so we give it an **RGB**

Listing 16-16.
DropDown Paint
code.

```
Private Sub picDropDown_Paint()
    picDropDown.Cls 'clear the old image
    picDropDown.ScaleMode = vbPixels
    picDropDown.DrawWidth = 1
    picDropDown.Line (0.1 * picDropDown.ScaleWidth, pic-
DropDown.ScaleHeight / 3)-(0.9 *_
    picDropDown.ScaleWidth, picDropDown.ScaleHeight / 3),
RGB(190, 190, 190)
    picDropDown.Line (0.1 * picDropDown.ScaleWidth, pic-
DropDown.ScaleHeight / 3)_
    -(picDropDown.ScaleWidth / 2, picDropDown.ScaleHeight *
0.9), RGB(190, 190, 190)
    picDropDown.Line (0.9 * picDropDown.ScaleWidth, pic-
DropDown.ScaleHeight / 3)_
    -(picDropDown.ScaleWidth / 2, picDropDown.ScaleHeight *
0.9), RGB(190, 190, 190)
    picDropDown.PSet (picDropDown.ScaleWidth / 2, picDrop-
Down.ScaleHeight * 0.9), RGB(190, 190,_
    190)
    picDropDown.ForeColor = RGB(190, 190, 190) 'the color
of the arrow
    picDropDown.FillStyle = vbFSSolid 'a solid, as opposed
to hatched or whatever fill
    picDropDown.FillColor = RGB(190, 190, 190) 'the color
of the arrow
    FloodFill picDropDown.hdc, picDropDown.ScaleWidth / 2,
picDropDown.ScaleHeight / 2, FillColor
End Sub
```

value of (190, 190, 190). This is equal parts red, green and blue, so it makes a dusty gray. The next line starts from the same point; we're drawing the line from the top left to the bottom of the arrow. The second point is halfway across the control (so that the arrow looks centered) and nine tenths of the way down. The color is obviously the same. The final line starts from the second point of the first line, which is the upper-right corner of the arrow, and goes to the bottom point of the arrow we just defined with the second line.

The next line puts a point at the very bottom of the arrow. It would seem that with the three lines we just drew, we would have a closed triangle. Because of a quirk in how VB draws graphics, however, there's a tiny opening one pixel wide at the bottom. We need this triangle to be closed so that we can fill it with the color gray in the next couple of lines. So far, what we have is shown in Figure 16-14. I've blown up the image and added a border for clarity.

Figure 16-14.
The drop-down
arrow.

```
    picDropDown.ForeColor = RGB(190, 190, 190) 'the color of
the arrow
    picDropDown.FillStyle = vbFSSolid 'a solid, as opposed
to hatched or whatever fill
    picDropDown.FillColor = RGB(190, 190, 190) 'the color
of the arrow
    FloodFill picDropDown.hdc, picDropDown.ScaleWidth / 2,
picDropDown.ScaleHeight / 2, FillColor
```

In the preceding code, we're filling the triangle, much like using the paint bucket in Paint. The last line is the most important one. As you recall from Chapter 15, we're using the **FloodFill** API function. **FloodFill** is a graphics function that does what the paint bucket in Paint does (in fact, **FloodFill** is how Paint does it). **Floodfill** needs several arguments:

- ▒ **hdc:** This is the device context for the control, which just means what graphics area we're dealing with

- ▒ **x, y:** The point we start flooding from; it's like the point you clicked on in Paintbrush with the paint bucket tool

- ▒ **FillColor:** This is the boundary color that the "paint" stops flooding at. In this case, it's going to be the color of the triangle we've drawn.

To set **FloodFill** up to fill the triangle properly, there are a couple of other properties we need to get into place. We need to define what color the arrow will be flooded with the **ForeColor** property. We set this value to be the same as the dusty gray we used earlier. VB allows us to use some custom fill styles, like cross-hatching, dotted, diagonal lines, and so on. We just want a plain-Jane, solid fill, so that's what we set it to. Finally, we need to set the color used as the border color with the **FillColor** property. Again, we set it to the color of the triangle we've drawn. Finally, we pick the smack-dab center of the triangle we've drawn to start the **FloodFill**.

You might wonder why we didn't just create a bitmap of the arrow and put it on the **picDropDown** control. This is much easier, and works great as long as the **LATextBox** remains the same size as you anticipated. If the control is resized, the arrow won't fit correctly in the size of the textbox. Using this method in the **Paint** event, the arrow resizes along with the control.

LISTBOX CONSIDERATIONS   We've covered a lot of ground so far. Our control now handles focus correctly and functions pretty well as a simple text box. It's now time to dig into the hard part of the control: Implementing the list functionality. What we have to do with this control is reverse-engineer the Windows **ComboBox**. If we can create a similar development interface to the common control, users of our control will need to learn nothing new and will be much happier.

The first step is to create the ability of manipulating list items in the same way that **ComboBox** allows. The **ComboBox** has several straightforward ways to do this:

- **AddItem:** Allows you to add a list item
- **RemoveItem:** Allows you to remove a list item
- **ListCount:** Returns the number of items in the list
- **List(Index):** Returns the list item at position index in the list
- **ListIndex:** Returns the current position of the selected item in the list

These are the basic elements we need to implement in our control.

The **AddItem** method allows the developer to add items to the list that will appear when the list drops down. The **AddItem** method is a procedure that accepts the item as a string argument, and adds the item to an internal collection we call **ListItems**. This is one of the simpler of these elements, and it looks like this:

```
Public Sub AddItem(Itm As String)
    ListItems.Add Itm
End Sub
```

Furthermore, we want to implement the **Sorted** property later. We will write a procedure that sorts the list later; for now, we'll just add a call to that procedure:

```
Public Sub AddItem(Itm As String)
    ListItems.Add Itm
    If Sorted Then
        SortList
```

```
        End If
End Sub
```

RemoveItem is even simpler:

```
Public Sub RemoveItem(Index As Integer)
    ListItems.Remove Index
End Sub
```

ListCount is about as simple:

```
Public Property Get ListCount() As Integer
    ListCount = ListItems.Count
End Property
```

Here we're implementing a **Property Get** statement, but no **Property Let** statement. We don't want users manipulating this value directly, only through the **AddItem** method. The **List(Index)** property is used to return whatever list item is at the position in the list defined by the **Index** argument:

```
Public Property Get List(Index As Integer) As String
    List = ListItems.Item(Index)
End Property
```

We're using the **Item** method of the **Collection** object to get results. The **Collection** object has a lot of the behavior we want to include in our list, so we need not reinvent the wheel. **ListIndex**, however, has no direct companion in the **Collection** object, so we need to do a little more work on it, as shown in Listing 16-17.

This procedure cycles through the elements in the list until it finds one that matches what's in the textbox. We use **I** as a counter and return whatever value the counter is at when we get a hit.

Listing 16-17.
Implementing the
ListIndex
property.

```
Public Property Get ListIndex() As Integer
    Dim I As Integer
    For I = 1 To ListItems.Count
        If ListItems.Item(I) = txtTextBox.Text Then
            ListIndex = I
    Exit For
        End If
    Next I
End Property
```

We're now at the at the heart of the most complex behavior of the control. What we handle next is what happens when the user clicks on the drop-down arrow. Because we're emulating a Windows control, all we need to do is examine how that control behaves. There are several specific behaviors we need to implement here:

- When a user clicks on the drop-down arrow for the Windows control, a list containing the list items drops down.
- When the user passes his or her mouse over the list, a gray box surrounding the selected item appears.
- When the user clicks on an item, that item appears in the textbox, and the list disappears.
- If the user clicks on something else while the list is dropped, no new selection is made and the list disappears.
- When there's a greater number of list items than can be displayed, a scrollbar appears along the side.

Each event has a clear point at which it happens: The first and last occur on **picDropDown_Click**, and the second on pic**ListBox_MouseMove**. The third occurs on **picListBox_MouseDown**, and the fourth on **UserControl_LostFocus**. Listing 16-18 shows how we'll handle **picDropDown_Click**.

This might be a little bit intimidating. It's the most complex procedure in the control, so once we're through it, it's mostly smooth sailing. Notice that we put the **UserMode** test at the beginning of this procedure. On the next line, we raise the **Click** event for the control for the end developer. Next, we have a test to see whether we should bother displaying the list. If there's only one list item, we won't; we'll just set the focus back to the text box. Otherwise, we'll begin the display process. Like a standard Windows list box, the box is never any taller than six items and is smaller if there are fewer than six. We use a variable, **Temp**, to store the value we use. We'll assign the number of list items to **Temp** if it's less than six, and six if the list items total is equal to six or more. Next we'll figure out the height of the list box to be dropped by cycling through the first **Temp** items and adding up how tall they are. So that the list doesn't bump up against the control, we add 10 more pixels. Next, if there are more than six items, we put a scrollbar on the control.

We set the **Max** value of the scrollbar equal to the number of **ListItems** minus five. The **ListItems** collection is zero-based, so we need to be one off in using the scrollbar. If we're handling fewer than six items, we ignore

```
Private Sub picDropDown_Click()
    Dim Temp As Integer
    Dim I As Integer
    If Ambient.UserMode = False Then
        Exit Sub
    End If
    RaiseEvent Click
    ControlHeight = UserControl.Height

    Dim THeight As Single
    If ListItems.Count > 1 Then
        ListMode = True
        If ListItems.Count > 6 Then
            Temp = 6
        Else
            Temp = ListItems.Count
        End If
        For I = 1 To Temp
            THeight = THeight + picListBox.TextHeight(Lis-
tItems(I))
        Next I
        UserControl.Height = THeight + 10
        If ListItems.Count > 6 Then
            VScroll1.Height = UserControl.Height
            VScroll1.Top = 0
            VScroll1.Left = UserControl.ScaleWidth -
VScroll1.Width
            VScroll1.Max = ListItems.Count - 5
            VScroll1.Value = 1
            VScroll1.Visible = True
        Else
            picListBox.Width = UserControl.Width - 30
        End If
        picDropDown.Visible = False
        txtTextBox.Visible = False
        picListBox.Visible = True
        picDropShadow.ZOrder 0
        picHighLight.ZOrder 0
        picListBox.ZOrder 0
        VScroll1.ZOrder 0
    Else
        If txtTextBox.Enabled = True Then
            txtTextBox.SetFocus
        End If
    End If
End Sub
```

the scrollbar and make the list box as wide as the control minus the two **picHighlight** and **picDropShadow** controls. Next, we'll make the textboxes and the **picDropDown** controls invisible and make the list box visible.

In the next couple of lines, we're just getting everything into the proper **zOrder**. We cycle through the controls in reverse order, so that the last item, **Vscroll1**, ends up on top, as it should be.

Hidden within this complex procedure is **picListBox_Paint**. It occurs when **picListBox** is made visible. This procedure, shown in Listing 16-19, is used to display the list items on the list box.

This procedure is a little less intimidating. We start by setting the **CurrentX** and **CurrentY** properties of the **picListBox** control to zero. This just means that when we start printing, we start in the control's upper-left corner. We use a variable called **Temp** for something a little different this time. Remember that the list box displays only six items at a time; which six depends on the value of the scrollbar. To figure out which items need to be displayed, we check the value of the scrollbar and add six. If that number is greater than the total, we're near the end of the list on the scrollbar, and we just assign the list items total to the variable. Otherwise, we assign the value plus six. Now that we know the first and last items to be printed, we can cycle through them and print them on the box.

This takes care of the initial painting quite well, but we need to account for the user utilizing the scrollbar. We'll reproduce the last portion of the procedure on the **Change** event of the scrollbar, as shown in Listing 16-20.

As you can see, it's exactly the same procedure, with the deletion of several initial (and unnecessary) lines. Now that we have the list displayed, we need to write code to handle the behavior of the mouse over the list box. We'll put this code in the **picListBox_MouseMove** event, as shown in Listing 16-21.

What we're doing here is taking the Y coordinate passed to us in the procedure and figuring out, based on the height of the list items, which

Listing 16-19.
ListBox Paint
code.

```
Private Sub picListBox_Paint()
    Dim Temp As Integer
    Dim I As Integer
    picListBox.CurrentY = 0
    picListBox.CurrentX = 0
    If VScroll1.Value + 6 > ListItems.Count Then
        Temp = ListItems.Count
    Else
        Temp = VScroll1.Value + 6
    End If
    For I = VScroll1.Value To Temp
        picListBox.Print ListItems(I)
    Next I
End Sub
```

Listing 16-20.
Scrolling code.

```
Private Sub VScroll1_Change()
    Dim I As Integer
    Dim Temp As Integer
    picListBox.Cls
    If VScroll1.Value + 6 > ListItems.Count Then
        Temp = ListItems.Count
    Else
        Temp = VScroll1.Value + 6
    End If
    For I = VScroll1.Value To Temp
        picListBox.Print ListItems(I)
    Next I
End Sub
```

item the mouse is over. We cycle through the items, and if **y** is less than or equal to the present position in the loop times the height of the current item, then we go to the next step. We're storing the present position of the selection rectangle that we'll paint in a variable called **PresentY**. If we're at the same position, we won't bother to repaint the rectangle; otherwise, we paint the rectangle using our **PaintRectangle** procedure:

```
Sub PaintRectangle(Level As Integer)
    picListBox.Cls
    picListBox.Line (0, (Level - 1) * picListBox.Tex-
tHeight(ListItems(Level)) + 30)_-(picListBox.ScaleWidth,
    (Level) * picListBox.TextHeight(ListItems(Level)) - 30),
    RGB(160, 160, 160), BF
End Sub
```

All we're doing here is clearing the box, and then painting a line from the upper-left corner of the current level (where a rectangle needs to be painted) to the lower-left corner. The next argument is the color, which we make a slightly darker gray than the arrow. The next argument is used to draw a box (the **B** argument), which is filled (the **F** argument). So we end up with a filled rectangle. Going back to the previous procedure, now that we have finished painting the rectangle, we tell the **picListBox** control to repaint itself, displaying the appropriate list items. This procedure has the net effect of drawing a "selection box" around the current item, shown in Figure 16-15.

Finally, there are several **RaiseEvent** statements to place in the code. we could show you these directly, but they're straightforward and we will leave it as an exercise for the reader.

Listing 16-21.
ListBox Mouse-
Move code.

```
Private Sub picListBox_MouseMove(Button As Integer, Shift
As Integer, x As Single, y As Single)
    Static PresentY As Integer
    Dim I As Integer
    For I = 1 To ListItems.Count
        If y <= I * picListBox.TextHeight(ListItems(I))
Then
            If PresentY <> I Then
                PaintRectangle I
                picListBox_Paint
            End If
            PresentY = I
            Exit For
        End If
    Next I
End Sub
```

Other VB5 Features

As much as we've covered in this chapter, there are still a lot of cool things we haven't covered. Several of our favorites are described in the following sections.

WithEvents

The **WithEvents** keyword is used when you declare a variable. Use of the **WithEvents** keyword tells VB that the variable being declared is an object with event sinks. For example, we might create a control that uses a **Form** object internally:

```
Dim Test   As Form
```

This allocates a variable we can use to manipulate a **Form** object we've loaded. We could allocate the variable like this:

```
Load frmTest
Set Test = frmTest
```

In this code, **frmTest** is a **Form** we've created and modified so that it suits my purposes within the control. A problem arises when we want to respond to events on that form, however. Although we know **Test** is a **Form**

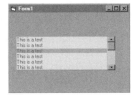

Figure 16-15.
Selection box on list.

variable full of events like **Click**, **MouseDown**, and so on, VB treats it as any other variable. If we want to be able to respond to events within the form, we must declare it like this:

```
Dim WithEvents Test  As Form
```

This tells VB to look for event sinks in the object and display them within the two drop-downs in the code editor. Now that we have declared **Test** with the **WithEvents** keyword, we should see the **Test** variable in the left drop-down list, as though it were any other object we had placed on our **Form**.

NOTE *We can also create our own object variables and use the* **WithEvents** *keyword. This method allows us to either code to events of internal objects or expose these objects to the developer outside the project.*

Property Pages

When you're developing your control, you might find you have many properties that don't relate to any properties other than each other. Additionally, some properties might be irrelevant, based on the other properties. For example, if we were developing a control that had a property like **ForSale**, if the value is **False**, then the **Price** property is irrelevant. It would be nice if this property were grayed out, indicating it's not available. What would be useful here would be a sheet like the **Font** property sheet, where several different properties that are dependent upon each other are combined on one sheet. These are called, accurately enough, *property sheets*. To create a property sheet, choose Project | Add Property

Figure 16-16.
Sample property
page.

Sheet from the menu to insert a blank property sheet into your project (see Figure 16-16). You can then place controls on this sheet and code to them.

In Figure 16-16 you see a property page implementing the properties **ForSale**, **Price**, **Number**, and **Available**. When the value in **ForSale** changes, we can disable or enable the **Price** and **Number** boxes, like so:

```
Private Sub chkForSale_Click()
    txtPrice.Enabled = (chkForSale.Value = vbChecked)
    txtNumber.Enabled = (chkForSale.Value = vbChecked)
    chkAvailable.Enabled = (chkForSale.Value = vbChecked)
End Sub
```

What's going on here is fairly simple. To change the value, the user must click on the checkbox, triggering the **Click** event. If the checkbox is now checked, then each of the other controls become enabled. If not, they are disabled. We get this with a little logic trick; the checkbox's **Value** property doesn't return **True** or **False**; it returns numbers represented by constants, one of which is **vbChecked**. Knowing this, we just test whether the value of **chkForSale.Value** equals **vbChecked**. This yields the **True** or **False** value we're looking for.

The **Property Page** object has a few unfamiliar events:

- **ApplyChanges:** This event occurs when either the Apply or OK button is clicked on a property page.

- **SelectionChanged:** This occurs when the selection of the controls on the property page has changed.

- **SelectedControls:** This is a collection of controls that are presently selected on the property page.

Property pages are very simple once you get the hang of them. They are nothing more than forms with a couple of special properties and events. The best way to learn how to implement property pages is to use the Property Page Wizard. This wizard takes the properties of a control you have created and creates one or more property sheets for it. Once they are created, you can examine the code and figure out exactly what's going on. After you've done this a couple of times, you won't need to use the Wizard anymore.

Friend

The **Friend** keyword gives a new and useful scope for our variables. When dealing with objects, it quickly becomes difficult to separate the outside of the object from the outside of the project. For instance, we might want to expose a certain variable to other objects in the project for internal management. On a form, we have a textbox that process text when the user presses a button. We have a class in the project for processing the text. We might want to expose a variable holding the contents of the textbox to the class, but not to objects outside the application. As what scope do we declare it? Public? Private? Neither of these satisfies both criteria. If it's declared Public, it's available to the class, but also to other applications. If it's declared as Private, it's available only within the object it's declared. When we declare the variable as **Friend**, it works perfectly:

```
Friend iText As String
```

The **iText** variable is visible to the class and to other objects within the application, but not to external applications. This allows more perfect encapsulation of your objects. When an object has to expose a piece of itself, it can select information it's willing to share only with its **Friends** in the project.

CAB Files

Although much has been done to minimize the size of ActiveX controls for download, they can still be pretty hefty. This translates into download time, which is the sludge of the wonderful information-transportation system we call the Internet. Another way you can minimize this speed bump is by creating and using CAB files. *CAB* stands for *cabinet*, which is just a compression format Microsoft has adopted. We spoke briefly about creating a setup package in Chapter 15, and this same process can be used to create CAB files. When running the setup wizard, choose Internet

Download Setup. You then go through several steps that culminate in the creation of CAB files. In addition to the CAB file, the wizard creates a sample HTML file containing an instance of the control and specifying the **CODEBASE** tag for the control. This tag is critical for Web-deployed controls, and we'll cover that separately.

Code Signing

Remember that ActiveX controls grew out of OLE, which is used to develop traditional Windows applications. Because of this, ActiveX controls have none of the security restrictions Java has. An ActiveX control can send nasty e-mails to your boss, delete your files, and if you have a sound card, it could swear at you. The only protection you have against these kinds of things is what's called *code signing*. When Internet Explorer downloads a CAB file, it scans the physical file and determines whether the file contains a digital signature. If it does, then Internet Explorer proceeds happily and prepares the control for execution. If not, depending on your security level, it either aborts the download altogether or prompts the user for instructions.

What is a digital signature? A *digital signature* is a binary file that uniquely identifies the holder of the signature. By requiring this signature, you can be sure that when and if someone does attack your computer using an ActiveX control, you can determine who did it. You can get digital signatures through a trusted third party, which certifies that the signature is genuine. These signatures are encoded with hypercomplex cryptography and are devilishly difficult to crack or fake. It's possible, however, although it would likely take several years, after which a new signature would probably have been obtained. Currently, the main company issuing digital signatures is VeriSign (**http://www.verisign.com**).

The **HyperLink** Object/Property

HyperLink is a property of the **UserControl** that returns a **HyperLink** object. If the control is in a Web page within a Web browser, or any other container that can display pages, the **HyperLink** object can use its methods to navigate.

The **Hyperlink** object has the following methods:

- **GoBack:** This causes the container to navigate back one page.
- **GoForward:** This causes the container to navigate forward one page.
- **NavigateTo:** This method navigates the browser to the page specified in the **Target** argument.
- **Target:** This string represents the URL the container should navigate to.
- **Location**: This optional argument is added to the end of the URL to specify a location on the server specified by the target argument.

FrameName

This optional argument determines the target frame in which the container navigates. It's useful if, for example, a navigation frame is driving navigation within another frame.

Figure 16-17 is an example of using the **HyperLink** object. This control consists of an array of three command buttons; it resides in a frame called **fraNavigation** and drives the navigation of the **fraClient** frame.

cmdNavigate is the array of command buttons. **URL1**, **URL2**, and **URL3** are set up as properties the user could modify through script in the page. When the user clicks on one of the buttons, depending on the index of the button, the container navigates to the specified URL. Because the entire Internet address would be specified in the **URL** property, we omit the **Target** argument. Because we're navigating within the **fraNavigation** frame, we specify that as the final argument.

Figure 16-17.
Sample control.

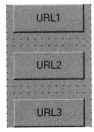

Listing 16-22.
HyperLink
navigation code.

```
Private Sub cmdNavigate_Click(Index As Integer)
    Select Case Index
    Case 0
        UserControl.Hyperlink.NavigateTo URL1, , "fraNavi-
gation"
    Case1
        UserControl.Hyperlink.NavigateTo URL2, , "fraNavi-
gation"
    Case 2
        UserControl.Hyperlink.NavigateTo URL3, , "fraNavi-
gation"
    End Select
End Sub
```

More Information

We live in a world awash in information. It might seem there's too much to absorb. Even the most hard-core developers are overwhelmed from time to time. The best cure for this is to leap into the fray. We strongly urge you to communicate with other developers in one way or another. In most major cities in America, there's a VB developer's group. Or, if that's not your cup of tea, join us on the Microsoft news server (**msnews.microsoft.com**). We generally hang out on **vb.control.creation** and **vb.syntax**. At first, you might feel that everything is over your head, but hang in there. After a couple of days, things will start making sense, and you can take part in the terrific exchange of information there.

CONCLUSION

Now you've had the grand tour of a Visual Basic-created ActiveX control. There are plenty of nooks and crannies in this control to explore, and an entire universe to explore in creating your own controls. Keep in mind that Java and ActiveX have very different starting points, capabilities, and advantages. Being informed about these technologies can help you make the intelligent development decisions required to produce a first-class application or Web page. We advise you to experiment and have fun with this process. Programming can be as tedious as bookkeeping or as rapturous as composing a symphony—it's up to the developer.

Technology
Integration

Beans and ActiveX Convergence

So far we have discussed JavaBeans and ActiveX, the two dominant component architectures. JavaBeans, based on Java, provides a network-oriented framework in the hottest language today. ActiveX, based on Windows, supplies a desktop-oriented framework in today's dominant operating system. There are many reasons to write for one or the other, but ideally we would like to take advantage of both. In this chapter, we explore two options: How to migrate from Beans to ActiveX and how to migrate from ActiveX to Beans.

This chapter will cover the following topics:

- Why do the migration?
- Beans to ActiveX migration
- ActiveX to Beans migration

Why Do the Migration?

These tools allow us to convert our controls from one component architecture to another. An implementer converts the control as part of the implementation process. JavaSoft and Taligent can provide utilities to move between Beans and ActiveX.

The Packager creates an ActiveX type library and Registry entries, installs them in the Registry, adds a set of Java classes to the Bean's JAR file, and wraps the Bean within a `beans.ocx` file. The Migration Assistant produces a Beans framework, which the developer fills in with Java code. The Packager and the Migration Assistant provide a powerful one-two punch to allow interoperability between Beans and ActiveX. Figure 17-1 shows the round-trip process using the Packager and the Migration Assistant.

Figure 17-1.
JavaBeans and
ActiveX conversion.

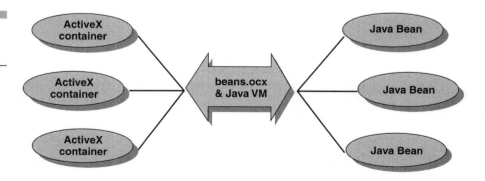

Beans to ActiveX Migration

Let's examine the JavaBeans to ActiveX conversion first. Every Windows desktop has ActiveX built-in. It therefore provides an extensive platform for Beans to leverage. The ActiveX Packager effectively transforms a Bean into an ActiveX control. A Bean can be used in all the same places that an ActiveX control can, such as the following:

- It can be inserted into an ActiveX container, such as Word, Excel, Internet Explorer
- It can be scripted from an ActiveX interpreted language, such as VBScript or JavaScript
- It can be called from an ActiveX language, such as C++ or Visual Basic

ActiveX Packager Description

The Packager is a set of Java classes that produce OLE stub Java classes, a Registry file, and a type library for the Java class. The Packager uses an ActiveX control, called **beans.ocx**, to wrap the generated OLE stub Java classes (see Figure 17-2).

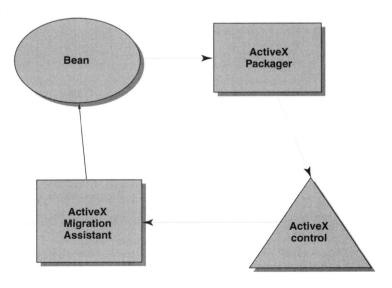

Figure 17-2.
The bridge over the river ActiveX.

These are the files generated by the Packager:

- A Windows Registry (.REG) file, supplying locations of the OCX, class files, and type library
- Java class files, which do the ActiveX to Beans conversions
- A Windows type library (.TLB) file, describing the methods, events, and properties of the class

Packager uses the Java 1.1 introspection feature to determine Bean's methods, properties, and events (see Figure 17-3).

The Registry file contains approximately 20 Registry entries. These are the most important entries:

- A **CLSID** (class ID) for the Bean
- Location of the **beans.ocx** file
- Class name
- JAR location
- TypeLib ID for the Bean data types
- TypeLib location

The Java class files are stub files, which provide the link between the ActiveX control and the Bean. The stub files listen for OLE-style events and method calls, converting them to the appropriate Bean method, and returning OLE-style values. This includes emitting events such as property changes.

Figure 17-3.
Doorway to ActiveX.

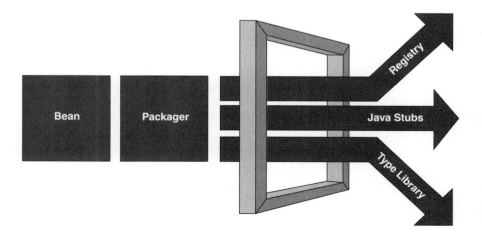

> **NOTE** *Note that the stubs are added to the JAR file, leaving the Java class files intact. Therefore, the JAR file can be used as a Bean or an ActiveX control, using the same code. This assumes that the* **beans.ocx** *and* **sun.beans.ole** *classes are available on the machine viewing the JAR as an ActiveX control. This also means that the Bean knows nothing about the world of ActiveX — or any other component. JavaSoft has also promised a bridge for LiveConnect.*

The type library provides a list of all the methods, properties, and events of the Bean. The Dispatch interface lists every method of the object, including all parent class methods. The Event interface lists all the Bean's events.

We'll take a look at the details of what the Packager does after we run a simple demonstration.

Beans to ActiveX Bridge Demonstration

To demonstrate the Beans to ActiveX bridge from JavaSoft, we will package our **Timer** component as an ActiveX control. We will then create an HTML page that has buttons to start, stop, and reset the timer, and finally, view the HTML page in *Internet Explorer* (IE).

We use the example from Chapter 12, but with a few additions. The Beta 3 version of the ActiveX bridge doesn't work correctly when the class name is the same as the package name, such as our **VisibleTimer.VisibleTimer** example. Changing the package name solves this problem.

In addition, the **run()** method must be modified to correctly render the graphics. The **repaint()** call doesn't result in a call to the **update()** method when used under the ActiveX bridge. Therefore, we must modify the **run()** method to call the **paint()** method with a valid graphics context as a parameter. During the ActiveX packaging stage, the **getGraphics()** method will return a null **Graphics** object, so we can't call **paint()** with a null value.

PACKAGING THE BEAN We now package the visible **Timer** as an ActiveX control. First, we install the JDK 1.1.1 and the ActiveX Packager. Verify that the **PATH** environment variable contains **c:\jdk\bin;c:\bdk\bridge\bin** and that the **CLASSPATH** contains **c:\jdk\lib;c:\bdk\bridge\classes**.

Next, we create the JAR file from the .JAVA files. At the command prompt, we type the following:

```
c:\>nmake -f timer.mk
```

```java
package Timer;

import java.beans.*;
import java.awt.*;
/**
* VisibleTimer, a class to implement a visible Timer that
       has bound properties,
* emits an event when zero seconds is reached.
*
*/
public class VisibleTimer extends java.awt.Canvas
       implements Runnable {
    private          int timeLeft = 40;
    private          int maximumTime = 30;
    private          boolean send0SecondsEvent = true;
    private  transient     Thread timerThread = null;
    private          boolean timerEnabled = false;
    private          PropertyChangeSupport
           send0SecondsEventList = new
           PropertyChangeSupport(this);
    private          PropertyChangeSupport
           propertyListenerList =
           new PropertyChangeSupport(this);

    public VisibleTimer()
    {
        super();
        setFont(new Font("TimesRoman", Font.PLAIN, 14));
        setBackground(Color.lightGray);
        setSize(100,100);
        startTiming();

    }
    public void addFireAt0SecondsListener
        (java.beans.PropertyChangeListener
        a0SecondListener) {
        send0SecondsEventList.addPropertyChangeListener
             (a0SecondListener);
        return;
    }
    public void addPropertyChangeListener
        (PropertyChangeListener newListener) {
        propertyListenerList.addPropertyChangeListener
             (newListener);
        return;
    }
    protected void finalize()
    {
        stopTiming();
        timerThread = null;
    }
```

```
public boolean getFireAt0Seconds(){
    return send0SecondsEvent;
}
public int getFontSize() {
    return getFont().getSize();
}
public synchronized int getMaximumTime(){
    return maximumTime;
}
public synchronized int getTimeLeft(){
    return timeLeft;
}
public synchronized boolean isTimerEnabled()
{
    return timerEnabled;
}
public void paint(Graphics g)
{
    int width = getSize().width;
    int height = getSize().height;

    g.draw3DRect(0, 0, width - 1, height - 1, false);
    g.setFont(getFont());

    g.drawRect(2, 2, width - 4, height - 4);

    FontMetrics fm = g.getFontMetrics();
    Integer Time = new Integer(timeLeft);
    String timeString = new String( Time.toString());
    g.drawString( timeString,
        (width - fm.stringWidth(timeString)) / 2,
            (height + fm.getMaxAscent() -
                fm.getMaxDescent()) / 2);
}
public void removeFireAt0SecondsListener
    (PropertyChangeListener 1) {
    send0SecondsEventList
        .removePropertyChangeListener(1);
}
public void removePropertyChangeListener
    (PropertyChangeListener 1) {
    propertyListenerList.removePropertyChangeListener
        (1);
}
public void resetTimeLeft()
{
    setTimeLeft(maximumTime);
}
public void run()
{
    try {
```

Continues

Listing 17-1.
Continued.

```
                while(true) {
                    // A classic poll/sleep combo
                    // Could be done by a wait
                    while ( !isTimerEnabled()) {
                        Thread.sleep(100);
                    }
                    timerThread.sleep(1000);
                    setTimeLeft( getTimeLeft() - 1 );
                    Graphics g = getGraphics();
                    // During packaging, g will be null
                    if( g != null )
                    {
                        update(g);
                    }
                    else
                    {
                        repaint();
                    }
                }
        } catch (InterruptedException e) {
        }
        timerThread = null;
    }

    public void setFireAt0Seconds( boolean newValue )
    {
        boolean oldValue = send0SecondsEvent;
        send0SecondsEvent = newValue;
        propertyListenerList.firePropertyChange
            ("send0SecondsEvent",
            new Boolean(oldValue),
                new Boolean(newValue) );
    }
    /**
    * Set the current font
    */
    public void setFont(Font newFont) {
        Font oldFont = getFont();
        super.setFont(newFont);
        propertyListenerList.firePropertyChange("font",
            oldFont, newFont);
    }
    /**
    * Set current font's size.
    */
    public void setFontSize(int newFontSize) {
        Font oldFont = getFont();
        setFont(new Font(oldFont.getName(),
            oldFont.getStyle(), newFontSize));
        propertyListenerList.firePropertyChange("fontSize",
            new Integer(oldFont.getSize()), new
                Integer(newFontSize));
```

Listing 17-1.
Continued.

```
    }
    public void setMaximumTime( int newMaxTime )
    {
        Integer oldMaxTime = new Integer(maximumTime);
        maximumTime = newMaxTime;
        propertyListenerList.firePropertyChange
            ("maximumTime", oldMaxTime, new
            Integer(maximumTime));

    }
    /**
    * Set the time left. If 0 seconds is reached at there
        are listeners, fire
    * the 0 seconds left event
    */
    public synchronized void setTimeLeft(int timeRemaining)
        {
        int oldTime = timeLeft;
        timeLeft = timeRemaining;

        if( timeRemaining == 0 && getFireAt0Seconds() )
        {

send0SecondsEventList.firePropertyChange("0SecondsLeft",
    null, null);
        }
        // fire time change to any interested parties

propertyListenerList.firePropertyChange("TimeLeft", null,
    null );
        return;

    }
    /** Enable/Disable the timer. If the timer changes
        state, the thread needs to
    * be either suspended or resumed, depending on the
        original and new state.
    */
    public synchronized void setTimerEnabled(boolean
        isEnabled)
    {
        timerEnabled = isEnabled;

    }
    public synchronized void startTiming() {

        if (timerThread == null) {
            timerThread = new Thread(this);
            timerThread.start();
        }
        timerEnabled = true;
```

Continues

Listing 17-1.
Continued.

```
    }
    /**
     * Stop the timer thread.
     */
    public synchronized void stopTiming() {
        timerEnabled = false;
        repaint();
    }
}
```

Figure 17-4.
ActiveX Packager first step.

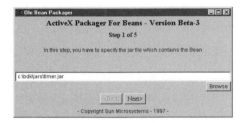

Then we run the ActiveX Packager (see Figure 17-4) by typing this:

`c:\>java sun.beans.ole.packager`

You now see the Packager wizard displayed; it takes you through a series of steps to produce the ActiveX control. We specify the JAR file, **timer.jar**, by either typing or browsing for the file; then click the Next button.

Then we select the Bean to package; the **timer.visibletimer** is selected by default. JAR files can contain multiple Beans, and the Packager enables you to select the appropriate Bean. After selcting the Bean, click the Next button.

Next, select the name of the control. **visibleTimer** is acceptable. The Packager adds a "Bean Control" suffix for Registry entries to the name you specify. Click the Next button after selecting the control name.

Then specify the output directory for the generated TypeLib and Registry files, as well as the **beans.ocx** file. The default directory, c:\bdk\bridge\classes, is acceptable. Click the Next button.

Finally, click the Start Generation button. Figure 17-5 shows the last step of the Packager. We will discuss the generation process in the "Packager Details and ActiveX Trade-Offs" section.

The Bean is now packaged as an ActiveX control. We can check the Registry and see the entries corresponding to the bridge.

Figure 17-5.

ActiveX Packager's
last step.

Table 17-1.

Packager Options.

Option	Description
-jar <*file path*>	Required; the directory and filename of the JAR
-n <*bean in JAR file*>	Optional; the Packager uses the first Bean in the JAR
-ax <*Control Name*>	Optional; the Packager uses the Bean name
-o <*output directory*>	Optional; the output directory for the type library and .REG file
-awt	Optional; specifies uncracking AWT events

COMMAND LINE PACKAGER The Packager has the following command line options for automated execution (see also Table 17-1):

```
c:>java sun.beans.ole.packager -jar <file path> -n <bean
    in JAR file> -ax <Control name> -o <output
    directory> -awt
```

You will see the text output from the Packager as the standard output of the Packager, usually the command prompt.

Displaying ActiveX Control

Any ActiveX container can now use the **VisibleTimer** ActiveX control. Microsoft's Internet Explorer is an interesting container because the ActiveX Packager allows developers to use Beans functionality in Explorer. Developers don't need to rely on the Bean implementation Microsoft chooses for Internet Explorer.

We will create an HTML page that references the ActiveX control by using three buttons: Stop, Start, and Reset Time. First, we find the **CLSID** of the ActiveX control. We can search the Registry for **VisibleTimer Bean**

Control **CLSID** in the CLSID section or read the **VisibleTimer.REG** file created in step 10, probably named c:\bdk\classes. The **CLSID** is in the fifth line of the .REG file. Copy the **CLSID** to the Clipboard. It will look like this:

    C0889300-7176-11D0-B880-0004ACF377A6

Next, create a **timer.html** file containing the ActiveX control reference and three buttons to interact with it. Copy the **CLSID** from the previous step into the **<OBJECT>** tag in the HTML file in Listing 17-2.

When you load the HTML page in Internet Explorer (see Figure 17-6), you will see the Potential Safety Violation dialog box. Click the Yes to All button. Then test the ActiveX control by clicking the Start, Stop, and Reset Time buttons.

Listing 17-2.
Timer.html.

```
<H1>The Visible Timer Bean Page</H1>
<P>
This page shows a Visible Timer bean driven by three HTML
    buttons through Visual Basic Script code.
<P>
<HR>
<CENTER>
<FORM NAME="Form1">
<OBJECT CLASSID="clsid:C0889300-7176-11D0-B880-
    0004ACF377A6" id="VisibleTimer"
      HEIGHT=150 WIDTH=150>
</OBJECT>
<P>
    <input type="button" name="Button1" value="Reset"
       onClick="resetTimeLeft" language="VBScript">
    <input type="button" name="Button2" value="Start"
       onClick="startTiming" language="VBScript">
    <input type="button" name="Button3" value="Stop"
       onClick="stopTiming" language="VBScript">
</CENTER>
<HR>
</FORM>
<SCRIPT language="VBScript">
    sub resetTimeLeft
        document.Form1.VisibleTimer.resetTimeLeft()
    end sub
    sub startTiming
        document.Form1.VisibleTimer.startTiming()
    end sub
    sub stopTiming
        document.Form1.VisibleTimer.stopTiming()
    end sub
</script>
```

Figure 17-6.
Beans in Internet
Explorer.

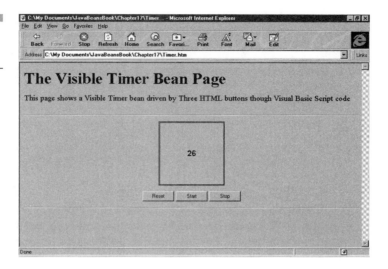

Navigator Versus IE

An interesting idea is embedding a Java component as a Bean in
Netscape Navigator and as an ActiveX control in Internet Explorer. Unfortunately, Beans aren't supported in Navigator 4.0, the latest available
version from Netscape, so we can't try this idea out.

However, it should be possible to use the Java component as a Bean in
Navigator when Navigator supports Beans, while using the component as
an ActiveX control in IE, because the ActiveX Packager doesn't modify the
.CLASS files in the JAR file that's downloaded to Navigator. Therefore,
the JAR can be installed for use in IE or downloaded to Navigator.

Packager Details and ActiveX Trade-Offs

When converting from one component model to another, the conversion
isn't seamless between the properties, events, methods, classes, threading,
and other metadata of each model. Control creators and users know the
differences and the mappings between the component models. We will discuss the following important differences:

- Event model, including AWT events
- Class and type conversion
- Properties

- Threading
- Methods

EVENT MODELS   ActiveX containers must use the single ActiveX interface to access the Bean events. The Packager uses introspection by getting the array of **EventSetDescriptors** to find the events emitted by the Bean. ActiveX containers can always access the default source interface, so the Packager includes all the Bean events in the default source interface. In effect, the Packager converts all Bean event interfaces into a single ActiveX event interface.

ActiveX containers, which receive events from an ActiveX control, usually receive the event as a number of parameters to a method. The delivery of events is slightly different in the ActiveX architecture than it is in Beans. In ActiveX, events are delivered as parameters to a method. The parameters are native types, representing the event properties, and an **Idispatch** reference. In Java, event information is encapsulated in a single event object.

Developers creating Beans and packaging the Beans should "uncrack" all Beans events to make them available to containers. The uncrack AWT events option specifies that the **beans.ocx** file will convert AWT events from a single object to the "uncracked," or separate, elements of the object. The Packager's default is to uncrack the events. To make events available to the widest number of containers, specify outputting uncracked events, ActiveX style. The AWT event is delivered as several parameters, rather than a single object.

There are differences between the ActiveX parameter passing and the Beans parameter passing models. Java data types are *immutable* objects, also known as *pass by value* or *unchangeable*. The ActiveX native types can be *mutable*—also known as *pass by reference* or *changeable*—or immutable. The ActiveX container and the JavaBean must be coded so they agree that the parameters are not changed.

Another issue for developers is naming events. The ActiveX container uses the type library to find the default source interface. The container then invokes the method found. The Packager uses introspection to find the event, then uses a simple algorithm to specify the ActiveX event name. Each Bean event will have a method in a listener interface. The Packager then extracts the method names of the Bean's listener interfaces. The ActiveX event name is set to be the method name. For example, the java.awt.event.ActionListener interface declares the method **actionPerformed()**. Therefore, the ActiveX event name is **actionPerformed**, and this is defined in the default source interface.

Table 17-2.

Java to ActiveX
Type Conversion.

Java Type	ActiveX Equivalent
boolean	VT_BOOL
char	VT_UI1
byte	VT_I2
short	VT_I2
int	VT_I4
long	truncated VT_I4
float	VT_R2
double	VT_R4
java.lang.String	VT_BSTR
java.awt.Color	VT_COLOR
java.awt.Font	VT_FONT
Arrays (one dimension)	VT_ARRAY | type
Everything else	VT_DISPATCH

Events can be connected from one Bean to another by using OLE automation, which avoids the overhead of conversion to and from OLE
events by using the regular Bean event listener interfaces. The ActiveX
container adds one Bean as a listener to events of the other Bean in order to connect the two Beans directly.

CLASS AND TYPE CONVERSION   A significant difference between
ActiveX and JavaBeans is that ActiveX doesn't support classes—only interfaces. The concept of inheriting implementation is completely missing
from ActiveX. This lack of support has many important effects on the
Packager.

Any class packaged into an ActiveX control has its entire class and interface inheritance hierarchy flattened and removed. The resulting
ActiveX control simply implements all the methods and events defined in
the class and interface hierarchy. The Packager doesn't create an ActiveX
control for each class in the hierarchy.

A significant side effect is that only simple types are converted to
ActiveX native types. Objects—classes inheriting from **Object**—are not
converted, but are passed as **Idispatch** values. Methods requiring objects
will have access to the **Idispatch** interface, which is not supported by the

current ActiveX Packager (Beta 3). The ability to access objects through the **Idispatch** interface will be added in later versions of the Packager.

NOTE *A final note on types and objects: ActiveX has mutable types, and Java primitive types are immutable. Any ActiveX container that's expecting a value to be changed by a packaged Bean won't function properly. We must make sure containers don't expect parameters to be changed.*

PROPERTIES   Bindable properties have the **[bindable]** flag set, and constrained properties have the **[requestedit]** flag set in the **OLE** property description. Bean-generated **PropertyChangeEvents** are sunk by using the ActiveX InotifyPropertySink interface. If a container vetoes the property change, the **beans.ocx** generates the expected **PropertyVetoException**.

THREADING   ActiveX containers can be single or multithreaded. Currently, Internet Explorer is one of the few multithreaded containers. In a multithreaded container, each Bean runs in the same Java VM but in different threads. Beans can share objects and communicate directly, so they need to deal with concurrency issues.

METHODS   Any methods a Bean exports publicly are included in the generated interface. These methods are available to OLE automation controllers. Another OLE design decision is that overloaded methods are not supported. The bridge offers a compromise by exporting the method with the most parameters.

Arguments and return values are marshaled by the **beans.ocx** bridge, according to Table 17-1. Bean-generated exceptions are converted to an **EXCEPINFO** structure, then returned to the calling container.

Packager-Generated Files

Users of ActiveX controls, ActiveX containers, and ActiveX scripts need to know how to find the *metadata*, or infomation about the ActiveX control. The Registry entries, OLE interface .CLASS files, and type library supply the bulk of the metadata for the ActiveX control. ActiveX containers access the Registry and type library for interface information, and the **beans.ocx** calls the OLE interface .CLASS files when the control is accessed.

REGISTRY   The Packager created a **VisibleTimer.REG** Registry file, which it then added to the Registry. ActiveX containers using the control can access the Registry for the control information. If we're creating a container to use the control or scripting inside a container, such as Internet Explorer, the Registry entries define the interface.

The Packager enters the **VisibleTimer.REG** file into the Registry by using the **regedit** command. If we modify the Registry file for any reason, we can also enter the Registry information by executing the following:

```
regedit VisibleTimer.reg
```

The .REG file contains many entries. The CLSID and name of the Bean is specified by:

```
[HKEY_CLASSES_ROOT\VisibleTimer.Bean\CLSID]
@= "{C0889300-7176-11D0-B880-0004ACF377A6}"
[HKEY_CLASSES_ROOT\CLSID\{C0889300-7176-11D0-B880-
    0004ACF377A6}]
@= "VisibleTimer Bean Control"
```

The location of the **beans.ocx** file is specified by the following:

```
[HKEY_CLASSES_ROOT\CLSID\{C0889300-7176-11D0-B880-
    0004ACF377A6}\InprocServer32]
@= "c:\\bdk\\bridge\\classes\\beans.ocx"
```

The Bean name, location of the JAR file containing the Bean, and the class responsible for interfacing ActiveX code to the Bean is specified by the following:

```
[HKEY_CLASSES_ROOT\CLSID\{C0889300-7176-11D0-B880-
    0004ACF377A6}\JarFileName]
@= "c:\\bdk\\jars\\timer.jar"
[HKEY_CLASSES_ROOT\CLSID\{C0889300-7176-11D0-B880-
    0004ACF377A6}\JavaClass]
@= "Timer.VisibleTimer"
[HKEY_CLASSES_ROOT\CLSID\{C0889300-7176-11D0-B880-
    0004ACF377A6}\InterfaceClass]
@= "sun/beans/ole/OleBeanInterface"
```

The type library ID, type library version, and type library location information is specified by the following:

```
[HKEY_CLASSES_ROOT\CLSID\{C0889300-7176-11D0-B880-
    0004ACF377A6}\TypeLib]
@= "{C0889301-7176-11D0-B880-0004ACF377A6}"
[HKEY_CLASSES_ROOT\TypeLib\{C0889301-7176-11D0-B880-
    0004ACF377A6}]
@= "VisibleTimer Bean Control Type Library"
[HKEY_CLASSES_ROOT\TypeLib\{C0889301-7176-11D0-B880-
    0004ACF377A6}\1.0]
@= "VisibleTimer Bean Control "
```

```
[HKEY_CLASSES_ROOT\TypeLib\{C0889301-7176-11D0-B880-
    0004ACF377A6}\1.0\0\win32]
@= "c:\\bdk\\bridge\\classes\\VisibleTimer.tlb"
```

The Registry file can be modified and reentered in the Registry, but this is recommended only for experienced Java and ActiveX developers.

ACTIVEX INTERFACES   The **beans.ocx** file provides 14 interfaces to ActiveX containers. The interfaces show the extent of the mapping between ActiveX and Beans. ActiveX container developers can access these interfaces, but no others. We can see that much of the OLE control functionality is provided, but not all. Interfaces such as licensing are missing, so they can't be used by an ActiveX container. The following interfaces are provided:

- IConnectionPointContainer
- IDataObject
- IDispatch
- IOleControl
- IOleInPlaceActivation
- IOleInPlaceObject
- IOleObject
- IPersistPropertyBag
- IPersistStorage
- IPersistStreamInit
- IProvideClassInfo
- IUnknown
- IViewObject
- IViewObject2

Type Library

Three type info interfaces are made visible by the **beans.ocx** wrapper. ActiveX containers use the type libraries to send events to the control, to invoke methods, and to access properties. The first, VisibleTimerSource, provides an interface for every event described in the previous event section. The second, VisibleTimerDispatch, supplies an interface for every method on the object, including all parent classes. The third, VisibleTimer, provides no interfaces.

OLE Stub Files

The Packager generates a number of .JAVA files to map between ActiveX and Beans. These files are compiled and then added to the Bean's JAR file. The Bean creator reads these files in the JAR file. Every time the JAR file is rebuilt, the Packager must be executed to add the .JAVA files to the JAR. The generated .JAVA files are compiled, and then deleted. The generated file contents are of interest only to very experienced developers who want to understand the end-to-end flow of control and data.

These are the files generated as part of the VisibleTimer packaging:

- OleEventListener
- OleComponentListener
- OleMouseListener
- OleKeyListener
- OleActionListener
- OleFocusListener
- OleMouseMotionListener
- OlePropertyChangeListener
- OleVisibleTimerInterface

The listener classes handle mapping ActiveX events to Beans events. For example, the **OleComponentListener** calls the **fireAction()** method with an ActiveX connection point whenever the component is resized, moved, shown, or hidden. This is its declaration:

```
OleComponentListener.java extends OleEventListener
        Implements ComponentListener
```

The **OleVisibleTimerInterface** is an interesting file because it contains many of the functions that deal with events and property changes. It defines the following methods:

- **bindOleStubsTo()**: Creates a Listener vector, with an element for each type of listener (such as **OleComponentListener**) based on the connection point.
- **toggleOleListeners()**: Adds or removes event listeners depending on an input boolean.
- **togglePropertyListeners()**: Adds or removes property change listeners.

▨ **invoke():** An impressively large switch (100+ cases) statement depending on the **dispid** parameter. It handles getting and setting properties, parent class properties, adding and removing event listeners, waiting, **addNotify**, and many more functions.

▨ **getProperty() and setProperty():** The get and set methods for **Timer**-specific properties.

▨ **getPropertyName():** Returns property names defined by Bean info.

Comparing Packager, Microsoft VM, and Visual J++

As described in previous chapters, the Microsoft VM allows bidirectional interaction between Beans and ActiveX. With J++, Java components are converted to ActiveX controls by creating an ODL file, compiling to a type library, and then registering the library.

SIMILARITIES   The Microsoft VM and Visual J++ combination and the Packager are similar in some regards. Both mechanisms require a Java VM, type library generation from Java classes, and registration of a COM component, which wraps the Java component.

DIFFERENCES   There are many differences between using the Packager and using the Microsoft VM to convert Java to ActiveX controls:

▨ The Packager permits Java classes to use any Java VM, not solely the Microsoft VM.

▨ The Java VM can fully use Java 1.1, including Beans and JAR, unlike Java 1.02.

▨ Use of ActiveX functionality, such as event uncracking.

▨ Ease of type library (ODL) generation.

The Packager enables you to use any Java VM, instead of just Microsoft's. There are several reasons why the Microsoft VM might not be appropriate; Microsoft has made many design decisions in the VM that might not be desirable. For example, garbage collection is subtly different between the Microsoft VM and most other Java VMs. The Microsoft VM provides fast, short-term performance but could run out of memory because of a fragmented heap. If we don't rely on the Microsoft VM, we can create Java components that can be used as ActiveX components any-where ActiveX and Java are available, such as UNIX and Macintosh. Re-lying on the Microsoft VM to support both ActiveX and Java means we're locked into a single VM implementation.

It's unclear how Microsoft will support Java 1.1. Microsoft might not provide all the Beans class libraries. The current Microsoft VM supports only Java 1.02, and there's no conversion of Java 1.1 events to ActiveX events. Also, Microsoft VM doesn't support packaging Java components in JAR files. Microsoft will offer some level of Java 1.1 class library support in upcoming VMs, but there's no need to wait.

The Bean Packager is available in Beta 3 and might be more reliable and configurable because of a separation of the ActiveX functionality and the VM. The Packager has more control over functionality conversion, such as uncracking AWT events and having a wizard-style interface to the Packager.

The Packager is simpler to use than J++ 1.0, which requires genera-tion of an ODL file and then a type library. Creating an ODL file is a non-trivial task for large classes, and the Packager completely hides this process from the user.

ActiveX to Beans Migration

The other conversion, causing an ActiveX control to behave as a Bean, gives more control over how to map ActiveX functionality to Beans. Taligent, a subsidiary of IBM, will soon release an ActiveX Migration Assistant. It's currently in beta version, but will eventually become part of the JDK.

Taligent's Migration Assistant doesn't convert the code from C++ to Java, nor does it wrap the ActiveX control. It provides a JavaBean source skeleton corresponding to the ActiveX control. The Migration Assistant examines the ActiveX control to determine the interfaces and methods it supports, and then provides JavaBeans with stubs that contain all classes and interfaces. The Migration Assistant exports an implementation of the property change routines. You then convert the ActiveX C++, C, or VB code to Java to flesh out the functions.

In many ways, the Migration Assistant is a much simpler program than the ActiveX Packager. The Migration Assistant is really a tool to generate stubs for the ActiveX control. It does no runtime cracking of properties, handling of events, and so forth that the ActiveX Packager does.

Using Migration Assistant

The Migration Assistant examines the type library or Registry entries of an ActiveX control to determine its methods, events, and properties. The tool is a Java application that displays the interfaces of a specified ActiveX control. The GUI of the Migration Assistant shows three different aspects of the ActiveX control—methods and properties, events, and enums. The user specifies some or all of the interfaces to appear in the generated JavaBean.

These are the generated output files:

- **VisibleTimer.java:** A large file with simple implementations for every method.
- **VisibleTimerBeanInfo.java:** A trivial implementation of the BeanInfo.
- **VisibleTimerEvent.java:** A single event object containing properties for every event.
- **VisibleTimerListener.java:** An interface declaring all the event-handling methods.
- **build.bat:** A batch file to build a JAR from the .JAVA files.

ActiveX to Beans Migration Assistant Demonstration

The Migration Assistant is a set of Java classes that produces a set of stubs corresponding to a specified ActiveX control.

To package the **VisibleTimer** ActiveX control as a Bean, first install the JDK 1.1.1 and the ActiveX Packager. Verify that the **PATH** environment variable contains **c:\jdk\bin;c:\bdk\bridge\bin** and the **CLASSPATH** contains **c:\jdk\lib;c:\bdk\bridge\classes**.

Then run the ActiveX Packager and package the **VisibleTimer** control, as described earlier in the chapter. Install and execute the Migration Assistant; you will see it listed in the Start Menu under Programs | JavaBeans Migration Assistant.

Choose the File | Open menu item. You will see a list of installed OLE controls. The **VisibleTimer** OCX can't be migrated, so we need to use the type library. Click the Browse button and choose the **VisibleTimer.tlb** file in the \bdk\bridge\classes directory. Click the OK button. The VisibleTimerSource and VisibleTimerDispatch typelibs are displayed in the available interfaces section.

Now click the Add All button. Both typelibs will be listed in the selected interfaces section, as shown in Figure 17-7.

Choose the File | Save As menu item to open the File dialog box. Enter a directory in which to save the .JAVA files, and click the Save button.

The .JAVA and **build.bat** files have now been generated. The skeleton has no real functionality, so we have to modify the .JAVA files to contain the code needed for each class, such as methods and event handlers.

A Detailed Look at the Migration Assistant

As described earlier, the Migration Assistant produces some skeleton Java files and a build batch file. To create a completely functional Bean, we need to fill in the function skeletons with behavior. These functions could be from migrated C++ code or from Java code written from scratch.

VISIBLETIMER The **visibleTimer** file generated by the Migration Assistant is fairly large, approximately 30K. It has stubs for all functions, as well as implementations for all property setters and getters, event handling, adding event listeners, and removing event listeners.

Figure 17-7.
The Migration Assistant ready to export all interfaces.

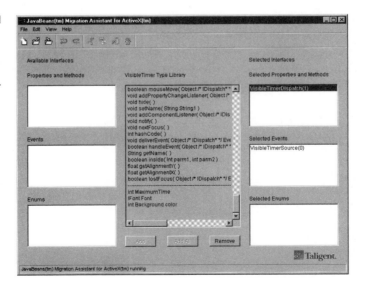

VISIBLETIMEREVENT   The `VisibleTimerEvent` object encapsulates the state information about every possible event. In effect, the `VisibleTimerEvent` is a union of the attributes of every event emitted by the `VisibleTimer`. The type library created by the ActiveX Packager moved every event into a single interface. The Migration Assistant completed that flattening of the hierarchy by combining all events into one. Here's a subset of the `VisibleTimerEvent.JAVA` file:

```
package ocx;
import java.util.*;
public class VisibleTimerEvent extends
     java.util.EventObject
{
  VisibleTimerEvent( Object source ){ super( source ); }
  public int gety() { return m_y; }
  public void sety( int y ) { m_y = y; }
     private int m_y;
}
```

VISIBLETIMERLISTENER   The VisibleTimerListener interface provides a method signature for every event handler method. The following code is a shortened version of the `VisibleTimerListener.JAVA` file, with the `handlemouseClicked()` method signature:

```
package ocx;
import java.util.*;
public interface VisibleTimerListener extends
     java.util.EventListener
{
     public void handlemouseClicked( VisibleTimerEvent evt
     );
     // Remaining handle routines
}
```

VISIBLETIMERBEANINFO

The `VisibleTimerBeanInfo.JAVA` supplies a skeleton for the `BeanInfo` file:

```
package ocx;
import java.beans.*;
// ─────────────────────
// Bean Info for VisibleTimer
// ─────────────────────

public class VisibleTimerBeanInfo extends SimpleBeanInfo
{
}
```

```
package ocx;

import java.awt.*;
import java.awt.event.*;
import java.util.*;
import java.beans.*;

public class VisibleTimer
{
  public VisibleTimer() {}
  // Accessors
    public int getMaximumTime() { return m_MaximumTime; }
    public void setMaximumTime( int MaximumTime )
    {
        m_MaximumTime = MaximumTime;
        m_changes.firePropertyChange( "MaximumTime", new
            Integer( m_MaximumTime ) , new Integer(
            MaximumTime ) ));
    }

    // Declarations
    private int m_MaximumTime;      // MaximumTime
    // isTimerEnabled
    public boolean isTimerEnabled( )
    {
        boolean retVar = false;
        return retVar;
    }

    // run
    public void run( )
    {
    }

    // ----------------------------
    // Custom Events
    // ----------------------------

  protected void firemouseMoved( int y, int x,
        int clickCount,
        Object /* IDispatch* */ point,
        boolean popupTrigger,
        int when, int modifiers,
        boolean altDown, boolean metaDown,
        boolean shiftDown, boolean controlDown,
        boolean consumed,
        Object /* IDispatch* */ component,
        int ID, Object /* IDispatch* */ source )
    {
        // make an event object
        VisibleTimerEvent evt = new VisibleTimerEvent(
```

Continues

Listing 17-3.
Continued.

```
                this );
      evt.sety( y );
      evt.setx( x );
      evt.setclickCount( clickCount );
      evt.setpoint( point );
      evt.setpopupTrigger( popupTrigger );
      evt.setwhen( when );
      evt.setmodifiers( modifiers );
      evt.setaltDown( altDown );
      evt.setmetaDown( metaDown );
      evt.setshiftDown( shiftDown );
      evt.setcontrolDown( controlDown );
      evt.setconsumed( consumed );
      evt.setcomponent( component );
      evt.setID( ID );
      evt.setsource( source );

      // clone the listener list in order to freeze the
          state
      Vector l;
      synchronized(this) { l =
          (Vector)m_VisibleTimerListeners.clone(); }

      // deliver the events
      for( int i=0; i<l.size(); i++ )
          ((VisibleTimerListener)l.elementAt(i))
              .handlemouseMoved(evt);
  }

  private PropertyChangeSupport m_changes = new
      PropertyChangeSupport( this );

  public void addPropertyChangeListener(
      PropertyChangeListener l )
  {
      m_changes.addPropertyChangeListener( l );
  }

  public void removePropertyChangeListener(
      PropertyChangeListener l )
  {
      m_changes.removePropertyChangeListener( l );
  }
}
```

Migration Assistant Compared to Microsoft VM and Visual J++

The Java environment has many benefits that don't translate directly from
ActiveX. The main benefit is that Java is a true object-oriented framework,

with implementation and interface reuse. Only AWT components can be added to AWT containers. An ActiveX control converted to a Bean by J++ always extends **Object**. We saw this in the **visibleTimer.JAVA** class generated by the Migration Assistant. Therefore, the ActiveX control generated by J++ can't be used as an AWT component without modifying the code.

The ActiveX design doesn't allow for implementation reuse, which means that a large ActiveX control might be a much smaller JavaBean. Our **visibleTimer** reused much of the **Canvas** functionality. ActiveX controls converted to Beans by the Migration Assistant can be customized to make use of the extensive class hierarchy, so they should be much smaller.

CONCLUSION

In the first part of this chapter, we saw that the ActiveX Packager from JavaSoft is a flexible, easy-to-use tool for packaging Beans as ActiveX components. It allows ActiveX developers to use JavaBeans components in addition to other ActiveX controls. Beans developers can reach ActiveX developers as well as the platform-independent, 100 percent pure Java developers.

Later in this chapter, we discussed two different products that promote JavaBeans and ActiveX interoperability: JavaSoft's ActiveX Packager and Taligent's ActiveX Migration Assistant. The Packager creates an ActiveX type library and Registry entries, installs them in the Registry (a set of Java classes added to the Bean's JAR file) and wraps the Bean with a **beans.ocx** file. The Migration Assistant produces a Beans framework, which the developer fills in with Java code. The Packager and the Migration Assistant offer a powerful one-two punch to allow interoperability between Beans and ActiveX.

The Migration Assistant generates a JavaBeans skeleton framework corresponding to an ActiveX control. Although it doesn't provide a packaging or wrapper function to keep the ActiveX control intact, this is desirable in many cases because of the Java language's object-oriented nature. By using the Migration Assistant, developers can take advantage of Java functionality, such as class hierarchies and polymorphism—which doesn't exist in ActiveX.

18

VRML and JavaBeans

In Chapter 17, we discussed how to use JavaBeans with ActiveX. Now we will see how to take our existing Java-Beans knowledge and learn some ways to create and manipulate three-dimensional reusable components with behavior—VRML Beans using *Virtual Reality Modeling Language* (VRML) version 2.0. VRML gives Web developers a choice of how to create 3-D worlds on the Web. VRML 2.0 allows you create truly dynamic, interactive environments, where users can interact with animated objects and experience sounds and movies.

This chapter will cover the following topics:

- A brief introduction to VRML 2.0
- Definition of a VRML Bean
- VRMLBeans architecture and design
- Introduction to VRML scripting with Java
- Conversion of script to transitional VRML Beans

A Brief Introduction to VRML 2.0

The purpose of this introduction is to give you a general idea what VRML is. For a complete description of VRML, we recommend that you turn to a good book on VRML and study other resources, some of which are given at the end of this section.

VRML File Syntax

A VRML world is described in a text file that you can create with any text editor. A VRML file can also be created with VRML authoring tools that allow you to edit worlds in three dimensions. Other graphics formats can be converted to VRML with special utilities.

A VRML browser reads a VRML file, whose name ends with the .WRL extension, and builds the world described in the file. Then you can navigate and interact with the world that the browser displays.

VRML 2.0 files must begin with the following VRML header:

```
#VRML V2.0 utf8
```

This header is the only component that's required in every VRML 2.0 file. The browser displays a blank screen if the header is the only item the VRML file contains. Besides the header, a VRML file can contain the following main components of the language:

- Comments
- Prototypes

- Nodes
- Routes

The following VRML world includes a VRML header, a comment, and a Shape node that defines a cone with a default bottom radius and height:

```
#VRML V2.0 utf8
Shape {                        # simple shape
   geometry Cone{}
}
```

A world author might add notes to the VRML file by using comments. Comments begin with # and end at the end of the line. The browser ignores everything on the line after the # symbol.

Nodes

The building blocks of VRML are *nodes* that describe objects in virtual worlds. Nodes describe shapes, their position and orientation, color, lights, sensors and interpolators, animation timers, and so on—everything the VRML world contains. Nodes consist of the following:

- Node type (required)
- A pair of curly brackets (required)
- Fields and their values (optional)
- Events that nodes can receive and send (optional)
- Exposed fields (optional)

If a node has any fields, events, or exposed fields, all of them are grouped within curly brackets. The order of these attributes within a node doesn't matter. Fields define node properties and have types, names, and default values, as shown in this example:

```
Sphere {
   field SFFloat radius   1
}
```

The Sphere node has one field called **radius** of type SFFloat with a default value of **1**. When the field is not specified, its default value is used. So you can specify a default sphere just like this:

```
Sphere {}
```

Fields

Fields are private attributes of a node and can never be changed in the VRML world. VRML defines a set of field types that describe the kind of values those fields might have. Most field types can be grouped in single-value types and multiple-value types. *Single-value types* are used for fields that store a single value, such as a single number or color; *multiple-value types* can be used for a set of values, such as lists of colors or numbers. For single-value types, VRML defines field type names starting with the SF prefix, and multiple-value type names start with the MF prefix, such as SFColor and MFColor for fields describing node color. For example, the following declaration specifies a **fooColor** field value as a triple of floating point numbers in ANSI C floating point format, in the range 0.0 to 1.0, for an RGB (red-green-blue) color triple:

```
SFColor fooColor 1.0 0.0 0.0
```

Values of multiple-value types are written as a set of values enclosed in square brackets and separated by white space (such as commas):

```
MFString url    ["http://www.deepblue.net/-
    avatar-lib/duke.wrl", "
    http://java.moon.com/gallery/human.wrl "]
```

In the preceding example, the **url** field uses the field type MFString to indicate multiple locations for the browser to look for data, in decreasing order of preference.

Events and Exposed Fields

Nodes in the VRML world can exchange events. Event values have the same types that fields have. VRML has naming conventions to specify which events the node can receive and send. Input events that the node receives—**eventIns**—should have names starting with the **set_** prefix. Names of events that the node outputs—**eventOuts**—end with the **_changed** suffix. For example, the PositionInterpolator node shown in Listing 18-1 specifies one **eventIn** and one **eventOut** event.

The PositionInterpolator node is used for interpolating a translation. When this node receives input from the **set_fraction** event, which is specified as a single float value (SFFloat), PositionInterpolator outputs the **value_changed** event whose value is linearly interpolated among a set of SFVec3f values.

```
PositionInterpolator {
    eventIn       SFFloat set_fraction
    exposedField MFFloat key              []
    exposedField MFVec3f keyValue         []
    eventOut      SFVec3f value_changed
}
```

The PositionInterpolator node also has two **exposedField** properties—**keyValue** and **value_changed** of type MFVec3f, and SFVec3f respectively. The **exposedField** keyword is used as a shorthand for specifying that a given field has a **set_ eventIn** that's directly wired to a field value and generates a **_changed eventOut** event. So the following declaration

```
exposedField MFFloat key     []
```

is equivalent to this declaration:

```
eventIn set_key
MFFloat key
eventOut key_changed
```

The **set_** prefix and the **_changed** suffix are recommended conventions, not strict rules. You can use any legal identifier names for the **eventIns** and the **eventOuts** when creating prototypes or scripts. Note, however, that **exposedField** implicitly defines **set_xxx** as a name for **eventIn**, **xxx_changed** as a name for **eventOut**, and **xxx** as a field name for a given **exposedField** named *xxx*. To improve readability, the VRML specification recommends the following conventions:

- For events of SFBool and MFBool types named Foo, **eventIns** and **eventOuts** are named **isFoo** (for example, **isActive**).
- For events of SFTime and MFTime types named Foo, **eventIns** and **eventOuts** are named **fooTime** (for example, **enterTime**).
- The **eventIns** used in groups for adding and removing child nodes are named **addChildren** and **removeChildren**, respectively.

Scene Graph

When building a VRML world, you can group together any number of nodes by using special grouping nodes and then manipulate those groups as a whole. Nodes grouped into hierarchical graphs compose a *scene graph* of a VRML world. Scene graphs provide the general model for viewing and interacting in a VRML world and allow reusing nodes within VRML files.

GROUPING AND CHILDREN NODES   Each grouping node has a `children` field that contains a list of the child nodes and defines a coordinate space for them in relation to itself. Relative coordinate space implies children transformations accumulating down the scene graph hierarchy. VRML uses a Cartesian, right-handed, three-dimensional coordinate system. By default, objects are projected onto a two-dimensional display device in the direction of the positive Z-axis, with the positive X-axis to the right and the positive Y-axis up.

To group abilities that every grouping node provides, each node adds its own additional features. VRML specifies the following grouping nodes:

- **Group node:** Provides basic node-grouping features.

- **Switch node:** Extends grouping by using the group of children as a list of choices, which allows the browser to render only one child at a time. This node can be useful in worlds that have, for example, different versions of one shape.

- **Transform node:** Extends grouping by creating a new coordinate system for its children. The new coordinate system is created with Transform node fields that specify the new origin by translating, rotating, and scaling the parent coordinate system.

- **Billboard node:** Creates a special-purpose coordinate system for its children that automatically shows all shapes in the group always facing the viewer, even as the viewer moves around the group.

NODE INSTANCING   `DEF` and `USE` keywords allow you to reference any node in a VRML file multiple times. The `DEF` keyword defines a node's name and creates a node of that type. Once the node has a name, you can use that node again later in the same file with the `USE` keyword. The `DEF` and `USE` name scope is limited to a single file; the scope allows sharing the same node in different locations in the scene graph. So if the `DEF`ed node is modified, then all references to that node are modified, too. All grouping nodes, as well as any other VRML nodes, can be given a defined name with the `DEF` keyword and then repeatedly referenced later in the file with the `USE` construct.

The simple Group shown in Listing 18-2 consists of two child nodes specified by the Group node's `children` field: Shape and Transform nodes. In this example, the Shape node describes a blue cone positioned in the center of our VRML world's coordinates. After naming this cone `MyShape` with the `DEF`

Listing 18-2.
A simple group.

```
#VRML V2.0 utf8

#
# Listing 18-2. Simple group
#

Group {
  children [
    DEF MyShape Shape {
      geometry Cone { bottomRadius 0.5 height 1 }
      appearance Appearance {
        material Material {
          diffuseColor      0.0 0.0 1.0  # set cone
                 color to blue
        }
      }
    }

    # Build new coordinate system
    Transform {

      # Move cone coordinate system along Y-axis down
          one unit
      translation 0.0 -1.0 0.0

      # Rotate cone coordinate system 180 degrees around
          X-axis
      rotation 1.0 0.0 0.0 3.142

      # Use predefined shape
      children USE MyShape
    }
  ]
}
```

keyword, we can use it in the Transform node that goes next in the scene graph. With Transform node, we can specify a new coordinate system for **MyShape** by translating the old coordinate system along the Y-axis down one unit and then rotating it 180 degrees around the X-axis. Then we can use **MyShape** in the new scene graph location with the **USE MyShape** construct.

Creating New Node Types with Prototypes

VRML 2.0 allows you create new node types with a prototyping mechanism. New node types can be used to encapsulate and assign boundaries to the geometry, attributes, and behaviors of the objects your VRML world consists of. As well as standard VRML node types (over 50 in VRML 2.0), new node types have a node-type name, a node interface, and a node body. Node-type names for new node types can be any text string, except for keywords reserved by VRML. The node interface specifies the interface to a node type and consists of node fields, exposed fields, **eventIns** and **eventOuts**. The body of a node describes what the node does and how it does it. A node body can encapsulate any VRML nodes, including grouping nodes, shape nodes, and any other standard nodes, as well as other node types previously defined with the **PROTO** keyword.

Both for standard node types and new node types created with **PROTO**, VRML has rules about where they can be used in a scene graph. For instance, a Material node can't be used as a value for the **geometry** field of a Shape node. The rules for the new node types are determined automatically—a new node type is considered to be an extension of the node type that appears first in the node body–base node type. Therefore, a new node type follows the same rules of use that its base node does.

To create a new node type, a **PROTO** definition is used. **PROTO** definitions can be placed in separate VRML files to build up a library of new node types. To reference **PROTO** definitions placed in a separate file, the **EXTERNPROTO** declaration is used in referencing a VRML world file.

A **PROTO** definition has the following form:

```
PROTO nodeTypeName [ nodeInterface ] { nodeBody }
```

The **EXTERNPROTO** declaration has a similar syntax: It specifies a node-type name and an interface declaration, but doesn't supply default values for interface fields and exposed fields. Besides, instead of a node body, the **EXTERNPROTO** declaration specifies a URL referencing an external file with the **PROTO** definition, as follows:

```
EXTERNPROTO nodeTypeName [ nodeInterface ] [ urls]
```

We can convert the example of a simple group, explained in Listing 18-2, to a new node type, **MyNode**, as shown in Listing 18-3.

The node interface, in this case, contains a declaration of one field: **MyColor** of type SFColor. We want to use this field to set the different colors of **MyShape** that **MyNode** contains. To make an automatic connection between an interface item and the appropriate field, exposed field, **eventIn**, or **eventOut** in the node body, VRML uses the **IS** syntax:

```
AnyNode {
  xxxField IS xxxInterfaceItem
}
```

```
#VRML V2.0 utf8

#
# Listing 18-3. New node type
#

PROTO MyNode [
    field SFColor MyColor 0.0 0.0 0.1
] {
Group {
  children [
    DEF MyShape Shape {
        geometry Cone { bottomRadius 0.5 height 1 }
        appearance Appearance {
            material Material {
              diffuseColor IS MyColor
              diffuseColor        0.0 0.0 1.0   # set cone
                    color to blue
            }
        }
    }

    # Build new coordinate system
    Transform {

        # Move cone coordinate system along Y-axis down
            one unit
        translation 0.0 -1.0 0.0

        # Rotate cone coordinate system 180 degrees around
            X-axis
        rotation 1.0 0.0 0.0 3.142

        # Use predefined shape
        children USE MyShape
    }
  ]
} # Group ends here
 # New node body ends here
```

In our case, we connect the Material node's **diffuseColor** field with the **IS** syntax to the **MyColor** field in the MyNode interface:

```
PROTO MyNode [  field SFColor MyColor 0.0 0.0 0.1] {...}
...
material Material { diffuseColor IS MyColor ...}
```

Now, with the new node type declared, we can use its instances in our VRML worlds anywhere the **MyNode** type can be used. As long as the first node in the **MyNode** body is the Group node, we can use **MyNode** anywhere the Group node can be inserted in the scene graph. For example, in Listing 18-4, we create a VRML world consisting of three instances of **MyNode** translated along the X-axis, with each instance having its own color: Red, blue, and green.

EVENT MODEL AND TIME   To propagate events among nodes in a VRML world, the connection between the node generating the event and the node that receives the event is specified with the **ROUTE** syntax. **ROUTE** is a syntactic construct describing how to wire nodes together, so that events of a given type can be sent from one node to another node receiving events of the same type. The wiring is specified with the following syntax:

```
ROUTE xxxNodeName.eventOutName_changed TO
yyyNodeName.set_eventInName
```

When specifying routes, the types of the **eventIn** and the **eventOut** must match exactly. You can define routes only from **eventOuts** to **eventIns**. Because **exposedField**'s declaration implicitly defines a field, an **eventIn**, and an **eventOut**, you can route events to and from **exposedField**

Listing 18-4.
Using the
MyNode type.

```
#VRML V2.0 utf8

#
# Listing 18-4. Using MyNode type
#

EXTERNPROTO MyNode [ field SFColor MyColor ] "lis1803.wrl"

Group {
  children [
    MyNode {} # use default node color
    Transform {
      # translate 2.0 units along X axis
      translation 2.0 0.0 0.0
      # set node color to red
      children [ MyNode { MyColor 1.0 0.0 0.0 } ]
    }
    Transform {
      # translate -2.0 units along X axis
      translation -2.0 0.0 0.0
      # set node color to green
      children [ MyNode { MyColor 0.0 1.0 0.0 } ]
    }
  ]
}
```

instead of using corresponding **eventIn** and **eventOut** names in the **ROUTE** declaration.

In a VRML world, the browser controls the passage of time and gives a time stamp to every event written to an **eventOut** and received by an **eventIn** of a node. For a browser, the time starting point is at 00:00:00 GMT January 1, 1970. The event time stamp is the absolute time at which the event is created and sent with a route. The browser automatically creates event time stamps each time an event is sent. Events arriving at a node's **eventIn** are always sorted in time order.

As a rule, events originate in Sensor nodes. VRML provides geometry sensor nodes, such as TouchSensor, PlaneSensor, Collision group, and TimeSensor. Geometry sensor nodes generate events resulting from user actions, such as a mouse click or navigating close to a particular object. TimeSensor nodes generate events as time passes.

TimeSensor events allow you to animate your world by changing the position, orientation, and scale of any coordinate system as time progresses. As a result, shapes built within the coordinate system that changes in time start to animate. TimeSensor acts as a clock and controls animation by generating events that indicate changes in time. To translate, rotate, and scale coordinate systems, VRML supplies a set of interpolator nodes.

In the following example, we use a TimeSensor node, named **Clock**, and an OrientationInterpolator node, named **SpinDrive**, to animate the **MyNode** we discussed in previous examples. A Transform node, named **Spin**, creates the coordinate system for **MyNode**. **Clock**, **SpinDrive**, and **Spin** nodes are wired together with these **ROUTE** instructions:

```
ROUTE Clock.fraction_changed  TO SpinDrive.set_fraction
ROUTE SpinDrive.value_changed TO Spin.set_rotation
```

The TimeSensor ticks through four cycles and produces fractional time events with values from **0.0** to **1.0**. These events travel from the **fraction_changed eventOut** of the TimeSensor node **Clock** to the **set_fraction eventIn** of the OrientationInterpolator node **SpinDrive**. Interpolator uses the values of these events to compute a new rotation. The new rotation is routed from the interpolator **SpinDrive.value_changed eventOut** to the **Spin.set_rotation eventIn** of the Transform node. As a result, **MyNode**'s coordinate system is rotated to a new angle. As you might have already noticed, the **Clock** loop field is set to **TRUE**, which tells TimeSensor to create a time loop that cycles from fractional time **0.0** to **0.1** and then starts over again after each interval. This results in an endless flow of **Clock** events and continuous animation of **MyNode** in 360-degree spin.

Listing 18-5.
MyNode animation.

```
#VRML V2.0 utf8

#
# Listing 18-5. MyNode Animation
#

EXTERNPROTO MyNode [ field SFColor MyColor ] "lis1803.wrl"

Group {
  children [
  # Rotating node
    DEF Spin Transform {
      # Initial position
      rotation 0.0 0.0 1.0 0.0
      children [
      MyNode {}
      ]
    }
    # Animation clock
    DEF Clock TimeSensor {
    cycleInterval 4.0
      loop TRUE
    }
    # Animation sampler
    DEF SpinDrive OrientationInterpolator {
      key [ 0.0, 0.50, 1.0 ]
      keyValue [
        0.0 0.0 1.0  0.0,
        0.0 0.0 1.0  3.14,
        0.0 0.0 1.0  6.28
      ]
    }
  ]
}
ROUTE Clock.fraction_changed   TO SpinDrive.set_fraction
ROUTE SpinDrive.value_changed TO Spin.set_rotation
```

Scripting

For complex animation and behaviors, VRML provides general-purpose
Script nodes. A Script node can have any number of fields, **eventIns**, and
eventOuts, and allows you to provide your own program script to process
these events. The Script node's **url** field references this program or script.
The Script program can be written in any programming language the
browser supports. At the time of this writing, the VRML 2.0 specification
provides APIs for scripting in Java and JavaScript.

The Script node can receive events from other nodes, process them, and send events to other nodes, while keeping its internal state up to date over time between executions. The Script node gets control when it receives an event. The browser executes the program in the Script node's **url** field or passes the program to an external interpreter, if necessary. Script programs can perform a wide variety of actions, such as sending out events to other nodes in the scene graph that might result in complex scene animations or sending events to other entities of some virtual world on the Internet, to name just a few possible examples.

In the following sections of this chapter, we will discuss scripting in more detail as one of the VRML tools that can be used in implementing VRML Beans.

What Is a VRML Bean?

A VRML Bean is a reusable VRML component that can be used in design-time or runtime JavaBeans environments. To the outside world, the VRML Bean looks like a 3-D object with well-defined properties and behaviors. VRML Beans fully support all the core features that the JavaBeans architecture provides, such as introspection, customization, persistence, events, and a properties model. Complete support of JavaBeans architecture should allow design-time environments, such as Bean builders, to operate VRML Beans in exactly the same way as other Beans. This should make constructing different applets and applications with VRML and other Beans as building blocks possible in Bean builders. In a runtime environment, VRML Beans—as part of an applet or application—gives the user a visual 3-D interface. When used in Bean builders, VRML Beans can provide their own 3-D *Graphical User Interface* (GUI) to customize their properties visually.

Another approach is to use a special VRML Bean builder—a sophisticated Bean that allows the user to group a set of "simple" VRML Beans and then connect and customize individual Beans in the group. Next, the VRML Bean builder can generate all the necessary "hookup" code and, finally, save the customized state of the Bean group along with Bean classes and hookup code in the newly born persistent instance of the VRML Bean. This new instance can then be used in a VRML Bean builder tool.

In this section, we evaluate the advantages of JavaBeans architecture for creating visual 3-D components that can be reused in different applications or applets.

VRML Beans Architecture and Design

The VRML Beans framework is based on JavaBeans, the Sun software component model for Java. The framework performs all operations with the VRML scene graph using the Java External Authoring Interface, the JavaScript Authoring Interface, and (in the future) the new Java/VRML API.

VRML Beans should be able to provide different levels of VRML scene graph abstraction, from a complete scene to separate nodes, so every VRML node should have a corresponding **VRMLNodeBean** class encapsulating its functionality.

A VRML Bean consists of some or all of the following components:

■ Classes implementing the VRMLBean interface; at least one such class is required.

■ An optional VRML file; if present, this file contains a VRML scene graph corresponding to the **VRMLNodeBean** classes that form this VRML Bean.

■ Optional (.SER) file with the serialized state of the VRML Bean.

Packaging

All VRML Bean components are contained in a JAR file. The VRML scene graph is loaded by means of a custom URL from the JAR file.

Persistent Storage

The VRML Bean's internal state is defined by property values of the **VRMLNodeBean** classes it includes and by a corresponding VRML file, if present. To store its state, a VRML Bean can do the following:

■ Use a Java-based serialization mechanism to store property values of the **VRMLNodeBean** classes it includes.

■ Use a special stream-based mechanism to store its scene graph. In the future, an "externalization" stream mechanism that JavaBeans will provide might be used.

■ Use encapsulated multiuser technology API. In this case, the Bean can have properties whose values are shared among users on the

Internet. To serialize or deserialize such properties, a VRML Bean can use the multiuser technology it contains.

Events and Properties

Events that a VRML Bean generates range from very high-level, such as "correct combination to open bank vault is entered," to low-level, such as **translation_changed** events.

The same range is true for VRML Bean properties. No matter what level of abstraction a property has, it can be accessed with getter and setter methods conforming to JavaBeans design patterns for read-only, read/write, or write-only properties:

```
public <PropertyType> get<PropertyName>();
public void set<PropertyName>(<PropertyType>
      propertyValue);
```

For example, the read/write property dexterity in an Avatar Bean encapsulating both a 3-D representation of an avatar and its behaviors might be presented by this pair of methods:

```
public Skill getDexterity();
public void setDexterity(Skill s);
```

VRMLNodeBean exports its **eventIns**, **eventOuts**, and fields as distinct JavaBeans properties. It also provides standard JavaBeans property accessor methods for the fields of the corresponding VRML node, with the signatures discussed in the following sections.

FIELDS VRML node fields define the initial values for the node's state. Field values can't be changed in runtime and are considered private. Fields in VRML are designed so that browsers perform scene graph optimization in runtime. Optimization algorithms might choose to replace some nodes with different geometry when node fields are meaningless and useless, which can be done only when node fields are private and handled internally.

To address this VRML limitation, **VRMLNodeBean** doesn't provide any field access methods in runtime.

To customize **VRMLNodeBean**, we need full access to fields in design time:

```
public <FieldType> get<FieldName>();
public void set< FieldName >(< FieldType > fieldValue);
```

After field values have been changed, new VRML code is generated from the corresponding **VRMLNodeBean** object. To see the effect of field customization, this new VRML is loaded in the browser Bean.

EXPOSED FIELDS

```
public <ExposedFieldType> get<ExposedFieldName>();
public void set<ExposedFieldName>(<ExposedFieldType>
    fieldValue);
```

Setting an exposed field in **VRMLNodeBean** automatically sets the value of the corresponding field in a VRML node and generates an **<ExposedFieldName>_changed eventOut**.

EVENTINS   VRML **EventIns** are write-only because they don't store any data; reading them isn't possible. Browsers use this as another opportunity for scene graph optimization. When an **eventIn** setter method of some **VRMLNodeBean** class is called, an input event is sent to the **eventIn** of the corresponding node:

```
public void set<EventInName>(<EventInType> eventInValue);
```

EVENTOUTS   To access the current value of the **eventOut** of a node, the getter method of the corresponding **VRMLNodeBean** class should be used:

```
public <EventOutType> get<EventOutName>();
```

The setter access method for **eventOut**s is not defined, so **eventOut**s are read-only properties.

TRANSFORMBEAN CLASS   For each VRML node, the VRMLBeans framework provides a subclass of the **VRMLNodeBean** class encapsulating the functionality of this node. Therefore, the Sphere node has the **SphereBean** class, TimeSensor has the **TimeSensorBean** class, PositionInterpolator has the **PositionInterpolatorBean** class, and so on.

The **TransformBean** class for the Transform node is shown in Listing 18-6.

VRML Beans Framework

The VRMLBeans framework provides the base classes and interfaces described in the following sections.

```
public class TransformBean extends VRMLNodeBean {

    // * Accessing eventIns *

    // eventIn        MFNode        addChildren
    public void setAddChildren(MFNode eventInValue);

    // eventIn        MFNode        removeChildren
    public void setRemoveChildren(MFNode eventInValue);

    // * Accessing exposedFields *

    //    exposedField SFVec3f        center          0 0 0
    public SFVec3f getCenter();
    public void setCenter(SFVec3f fieldValue);

    //    exposedField MFNode         children         []
    public MFNode getChildren();
    public void setChildren(MFNode fieldValue);

    //    exposedField SFRotation    rotation         0 0 1  0
    public SFRotation getRotation();
    public void setRotation(SFRotation fieldValue);

    //    exposedField SFVec3f        scale           1 1 1
    public SFVec3f getScale();
    public void setScale(SFVec3f fieldValue);

    //    exposedField SFRotation    scaleOrientation 0 0 1  0
    public SFRotation getScaleOrientation();
    public void setScaleOrientation(SFRotation fieldValue);

    //    exposedField SFVec3f        translation      0 0 0
    public SFVec3f getTranslation();
    public void setTranslation(SFVec3f fieldValue);

    // * Accessing fields in design time only *

    //    field        SFVec3f        bboxCenter       0 0 0
    public SFVec3f getBboxCenter();
    public void setBboxCenter(SFVec3f fieldValue);

    //    field        SFVec3f        bboxSize        -1 -1 -1
    public SFVec3f getBboxSize();
    public void setBboxSize(SFVec3f fieldValue);

}
```

VRML BEAN INTERFACE   VRMLBean is an interface that all VRML
Beans must implement:

```
public interface VRMLBean extends java.io.Serializable
```

VRMLNODEBEAN CLASS. The `VRMLNodeBean` class, shown in Listing 18-7, is the base class that all VRML node Beans must extend. This class implements VRMLBean, EventInChangeListener, and EventOutChange-Listener interfaces.

Listing 18-7.
VRMLNodeBean
class.

```java
public class VRMLNodeBean extends vrml.BaseNode
    implements VRMLBean,  EventInChangeListener,
        EventOutChangeListener {

// This method gets called when some eventIn of the VRML
    node has changed.
// Node bean classes may override this. Default
    operation: nop
// Parameters:
//        evt - A EventInChangeEvent object describing
    the eventIn that has changed.
public void eventInChanged(EventInChangeEvent evt);

// This method gets called when some eventOut of the
    VRML node has changed.
// Node bean classes may override this. Default
    operation: nop
// Parameters:
//        evt - A EventOutChangeEvent object describing
    the eventOut that has changed.
public void eventOutChanged(EventOutChangeEvent evt);

// Multicast event listener registration methods for
    PropertyChangeListeners
public void addPropertyChangeListener
    (PropertyChangeListener x);
public void removePropertyChangeListener
    (PropertyChangeListener x);

// May be called to report a bound property update to
    any registered listeners.
// No event is fired if old and new are equal and
    non-null.
// Parameters:
//        propertyName - The programmatic name of the
    property that was changed.
//        oldValue - The old value of the property.
//        newValue - The new value of the property.

public void firePropertyChange(String propertyName,
                               Object oldValue,
                               Object newValue)
```

```
// Link this VRMLNodeBean to corresponding VRML node with
//    "DEFed" node name.
// Parameters :
//       nodeName - "DEFed" node name
public void setNode(String nodeName) throws
    InvalidVRMLNodeException;

// Link this VRMLNodeBean to corresponding VRML *group*
//    node with "DEFed" node name.
// This method allows create "group" VRMLNodeBean object
//    from custom "children" VRMLNodeBean
// objects.
// Parameters :
//       nodeName - "DEFed" group node name
//          children - custom instances of VRML node
//    children beans
public void setNode(String nodeName, VRMLNodeBean[]
    children) throws InvalidVRMLNodeException;

// Set name of the VRML node
public void setNodeName(String nodeName);

// Get name of the VRML node
public String getNodeName();
}
```

The EventInChangeListener interface is used by **VRMLBrowserBean** to notify **VRMLNodeBean** that one of the **eventIns** in the corresponding VRML node has received an input event. An **EventInChangeEvent** object is delivered whenever a **VRMLBrowserBean** detects an input event sent to an **eventIn** of this VRML node. An **EventInChangeEvent** object is sent as an argument to the EventInChangeListener **eventInChanged** method. The **EventInChangeEvent** object supplies methods to access the name and the old and new values of the changed **eventIn**. A null value can be provided for the old value if its true value isn't known.

Respectively, the EventOutChangeListener interface is used by **VRMLBrowserBean** to notify **VRMLNodeBean** that one of the **eventOuts** in the corresponding VRML node has sent an output event. An **EventOutChangeEvent** object is delivered whenever a **VRMLBrowserBean** detects that an output event was sent by an **eventOut** of this VRML node. An **EventOutChangeEvent** object is sent as an argument to the EventOut-ChangeListener **eventOutChanged** method. The **EventOutChangeEvent** object supplies methods to access the name and the old and new values of the changed **eventOut**. A null value can be provided for the old value if its true value isn't known.

Listing 18-8.
EventInChange-
Listener interface
and **EventIn-
ChangeEvent** class.

```
public interface EventInChangeListener {

    // This method gets called when some eventIn of the VRML
    //    node has changed.
    // Parameters:
    //       evt - A EventInChangeEvent object describing
    //       the eventIn that has  changed.
    public abstract void eventInChanged(EventInChangeEvent
        evt);

}

public class EventInChangeEvent extends java.util.
    EventObject {

    /**
        Constructor parameters:
            source - The VRMLBrowserBean that fired the
                event.
            eventInName - name of the eventIn in VRML node
                that has changed.
            oldValue - The old value of the property.
            newValue - The new value of the property.
     */
    public EventInChangeEvent(Object source,
                                String eventInName,
                                Object oldValue,
                                Object newValue);

    public String getEventInName(); // returns the eventIn
        name of the eventIn that has changed.
    public Object getNewValue(); // returns the new value for
        the eventIn
    public Object getOldValue(); // returns the old value for
        the eventIn

}
```

VRMLNodeBean provides a change notification service for some or all of its properties—**eventIns**, **eventOuts**, and fields. Such properties are known as *bound properties* and allow other components to bind special behavior to property changes. When node Bean classes want to report a bound property update to any registered listeners, they should call **VRMLNodeBean**'s **firePropertyChange** method.

The PropertyChangeListener event listener interface is used to report updates to the **VRMLNodeBean** bound properties. **VRMLNodeBean** supports bound properties by a pair of multicast event listener registration methods for PropertyChangeListeners:

```
public interface EventOutChangeListener {

    // This method gets called when some eventOut of the
        VRML node has changed.
    // Parameters:
    //          evt - A EventOutChangeEvent object describing
        the eventOut that has  changed.
    public abstract void eventOutChanged(EventOutChangeEvent
        evt);

}

public class EventOutChangeEvent extends java.util.
    EventObject {

    /**
        Constructor parameters:
            source - The VRMLBrowserBean that fired the
                    event.
            eventOutName - name of the eventOut in VRML node
                    that has changed.
            oldValue - The old value of the property.
            newValue - The new value of the property.
     */

    public EventOutChangeEvent(Object source,
                                String eventOutName,
                                Object oldValue,
                                Object newValue);

    public String getEventOutName(); // returns the eventOut
        name of the eventOut that has changed.
    public Object getNewValue(); // returns the new value for
the eventOut
    public Object getOldValue(); // returns the old value for
        the eventOut

}
```

```
public void addPropertyChangeListener
    (PropertyChangeListener x);
public void removePropertyChangeListener
    (PropertyChangeListener x);
```

VRMLNodeBean fires a **PropertyChangeEvent** event to registered listeners whenever any of its fields, eventIns, or **eventOuts** are changed.

VRMLNodeBean fires a **PropertyChangeEvent** event *after* updating its internal state. Any Bean, not just a VRML Bean, can register itself as a PropertyChangeListener with a source **VRMLNodeBean** to be notified of its property updates.

When a property change occurs on a bound property, the **VRMLNodeBean** calls the PropertyChangeListener's **propertyChange(PropertyChangeEvent)** method on any registered listeners, passing a **PropertyChangeEvent** that encapsulates the property's **eventIn**, **eventOut**, and field name and its old and new values.

The method **setNode(String nodeName)** links this **VRMLNodeBean** object to the corresponding VRML node with the **DEF**ed name. There are two different cases when this method is called:

- When the **VRMLNodeBean** object corresponding to the *existing* VRML node with the **DEF**ed node name is created by **VRMLBrowserBean**. If successful, the **VRMLBrowserBean** calls **VRMLNodeBean.setNodeName(String nodeName)**, setting the VRML node name in this instance of **VRMLNodeBean**. When resolving group nodes, the browser Bean calls this function for each node in all groups, including nested ones in the scene graph.

- When a new VRML node is inserted in the scene graph with the call of **VRMLBrowserBean.createVrmlFromBean(VRMLBean Bean)** method. In this case, you should call **VRMLNodeBean.setNodeName (String nodeName)** first to name the new VRML node, which the browser will insert in the scene graph.

In both cases, this method is called only once for each **VRMLNodeBean** object.

The method **setNode(String nodeName, VRMLNodeBean[] children)** links this **VRMLNodeBean** object to the corresponding VRML group node with the **DEF**ed name. This method allows the creation of group **VRMLNodeBean** objects from custom children **VRMLNodeBean** objects. Custom node Beans extend their base node Bean classes. For example, the **MySensor** class extends the **TouchSensorBean** base class. The advantage of creating group Beans from customized node Beans is that you can override event notification methods in your custom Bean, as shown in Listing 18-10.

Having this custom **MySensor** node Bean defined, you can create a group node Bean, as shown in Listing 18-11.

MyGroup node Bean will be linked with the following scene graph:

```
DEF MyGroup Group {
    children [ DEF MySensor TouchSensor {}  ]
}
```

VRMLBROWSERBEAN INTERFACE   **VRMLBrowserBean** is the interface that any browser Bean must implement:

```
public class MySensor extends TouchSensorBean {

   public MySensor() {
     try {
       setNode("MySensor");
     } catch (InvalidVRMLNodeException e) {}
   }

   public void eventInChanged(EventInChangeEvent evt) {
     System.out.println("MySensor node just received event :
         "+evt.toString());
   }

   public void eventOutChanged(EventOutChangeEvent evt) {
     System.out.println("MySensor node just sent event :
         "+evt.toString());
   }
}
```

```
public class MyGroup extends GroupBean {

   private  transient VRMLNodeBean[] children;

   public MyGroup() {
     children[0] = new MySensor();
     try {
       setNode("MyGroup", children);
     } catch (InvalidVRMLNodeException e) {}
   }

}
```

```
public interface VRMLBrowserBean implements VRMLBean {
   public abstaract void createVrmlFromBean(VRMLBean bean)
       throws invalidVRMLBeanException;
}
```

VRMLBrowserBean performs all operations with a scene graph using the
Java External Authoring Interface, JavaScript Authoring Interface, and,
in the future, a new Java/VRML API, when it becomes available.

VRMLBrowserBean's **createVrmlFromBean(VRMLBean Bean)** method allows
creating a scene graph by using introspection of the parameter Bean.
VRMLNodeBean methods are implemented by the **VRMLBrowserBean** class.

VRMLBEANS CLASS This class provides some general-purpose
VRML Bean control methods:

```
public class VRMLBeans {
  public static VRMLBrowserBean getBrowserBean();
}
```

Example

To understand how the VRMLBeans framework can be used, let's create node Beans for the given scene graph and manipulate them.

For this scene graph, we can create the following node Beans in Listing 18-13.

The **Clicker** Bean informs about TouchSensor events, and the **TimeSource** Bean reports the time when TimeSensor was started. The **AnimationMonitor** class, a non-VRML Bean, listens for any bound property change. The **Animation** Bean reports changes of its bound property rotation to all registered listeners, calling the **firePropertyChange**

Listing 18-12.
Xform.

```
#VRML V2.0 utf8

DEF XForm Transform { children [

  DEF BoxShape Shape {

    appearance DEF BoxAppearance Appearance {
        material DEF BoxMaterial Material {
            diffuseColor 1.0 0.0 0.0
        }
    }

    geometry Box {}
  }

  DEF Clicker TouchSensor {}
  DEF TimeSource TimeSensor { cycleInterval 2.0 } # Run
      once for 2 sec.
  # Animate one full turn about Y axis:
  DEF Animation OrientationInterpolator {
      key       [ 0,       .33,       .66,        1.0 ]
      keyValue [ 0 1 0 0, 0 1 0 2.1, 0 1 0 4.2, 0 1 0 0
          ]
  }
]}
ROUTE Clicker.touchTime TO TimeSource.startTime
ROUTE TimeSource.fraction_changed TO Animation.set_fraction
ROUTE Animation.value_changed TO XForm.rotation
```

```
public class Clicker extends TouchSensorBean {

  public Clicker() {
    try {
      setNode("Clicker");
    } catch (InvalidVRMLNodeException e) {}
  }

  public void eventInChanged(EventInChangeEvent evt) {
    System.out.println("Clicker : 'enabled' changed
!"+evt.toString());
  }

  public void eventOutChanged(EventOutChangeEvent evt) {
    System.out.println("Clicker : just sent event :
        "+evt.toString());
  }

}

public class TimeSource extends TimeSensorBean {

  public TimeSource() {
    try {
      setNode("TimeSource");
    } catch (InvalidVRMLNodeException e) {}
  }

  public void eventInChanged(EventInChangeEvent evt) {

    if(evt.getEventInName().equals("set_startTime"))
      System.out.println("TimeSource started at : "+
          evt.getNewValue());
  }

}
```

method defined in its **VRMLNodeBean** base class. The new rotation value is the value of the **value_changed eventOut** that OrientationInterpolator generates. **AnimationMonitor** receives a new rotation value passed in by the **PropertyChangeEvent** event to its **propertyChange()** method.

The **XForm** node Bean first creates custom **Clicker**, **TimeSource**, and **Animation** node Beans. After that, it links itself to the **XForm** Transform node with its customized child node Beans. Next, it creates the **AnimationMonitor** Bean and adds it as a bound change listener to the **Animation** Bean. Finally, **XForm** starts the animation by setting the exposed field **startTime** in the **TimeSensor** node.

```
public class Animation extends OrientationInterpolatorBean
    {

  private transient SFRotation oldRotation;

  public void eventOutChanged(EventOutChangeEvent evt) {

    if(evt.getEventOutName().equals("value_changed")) {
      SFRotation newRotation = (SFRotation)evt.
          getNewValue();
      firePropertyChange("value_changed", oldRotation,
          newRotation);
    }
  }

}

public class AnimationMonitor implements
    PropertyChangeListener {

  public void propertyChange(PropertyChangeEvent evt) {

    System.out.println("Received changed property from :"+
        evt.getSource());
    if(evt.getPropertyName().equals("value_changed")) {
      System.out.println("Rotation changed from : "+
          evt.getOldValue()+" to :
"+evt.getNewValue());
    }
  }

}
```

Transitional VRML Beans

The VRMLBeans architecture relies on the communication model with a
VRML browser that provides an event notification mechanism for user-
defined classes observing VRML node and scene events. At the time of this
writing, there is no standard defining such a communication model. However, to understand the applicability of VRMLBeans architecture, you can
begin initial development of VRMLBeans components with Transitional
VRML Beans.

The Transitional VRML Bean implementation is based on VRML
scripting with Java, as defined in the JavaScript Authoring Interface. The
general mechanism provided makes a **script** class a VRML event source
for other JavaBeans. Any Bean can register as a listener for VRML events
by using a Transitional VRML Bean.

```
public class XForm extends TransformBean {

  // Create custom node beans

  private  transient VRMLNodeBean[] children;
  private Clicker clicker = new Clicker();
  private TimeSource timeSource = new TimeSource();
  private Animation animation = new Animation();
  private AnimationMonitor monitor = new
        AnimationMonitor();

  public XForm() {

    children[0] = clicker;
    children[1] = timeSource;
    children[2] = animation;

   // link XForm bean to Transform node with DEFed name
        XForm
    try {
      setNode("XForm", children);
    } catch (InvalidVRMLNodeException e) {}

    // add bound property change monitor to animation bean
    animation.addPropertyChangeListener(monitor);

    // get current time
    SFTime startNow = new SFTime
        (System.currentTimeMillis());

    // set exposed field "startTime" in TimeSensor node
        and start animation now
    timeSource.setStartTime(startNow);
  }

}
```

A Transitional VRML Bean identifies itself as a VRML event source by defining registration methods that conform to specific JavaBean design patterns. These registration methods accept references to instances of particular VRMLEventListener interfaces.

To register for VRML events, the listener should implement distinct interfaces, extending the **VRMLEventListener** interface for each VRMLEvent type. **VRMLEventListener**, in turn, inherits from **java.util.EventListener**.

Beans that implement the VRMLEventListener interfaces receive VRML event objects defined as the following:

```
public class VrmlEventObject extends java.util.EventObject;
```

VRML event objects extend `java.util.EventObject` and encapsulate a scene state. A VRML event object is passed as the sole argument to the event method defined in the **VRMLEventListener** class:

```
public interface VrmlListener extends java.util.
    EventListener {
  public void handleVrmlEvent(VrmlEventObject veo);
}
```

A **VRMLEvent** class provides setter and getter methods to access the **vrml.Event** object it contains as a member:

```
public void setVrmlEvent(vrml.Event ve)
public vrml.Event getVrmlEvent()
```

The **vrml.Event** class is defined in the VRML2.0 Java Scripting Reference and provides access methods for its members:

```
public String getName() - returns event name string;
public double getTimeStamp() - returns the timestamp when
the event has occurred;
public ConstField getValue() - returns event value;
```

Introducing VRML Scripting with Java

This section focuses on the communication model that allows a VRML Bean to interact with the browser with the help of a VRML Script node. The Script node implements behavior in the scene that results in animation.

The VRML Bean implementation discussed here uses the *Liquid Reality* (LR) Java/VRML toolkit—a comprehensive Java package, giving you the ability to create your own VRML2.0 browser and scene classes and manipulate them according to the Liquid Reality (LR) API from a Java applet or application.

Making Your World Active

Before describing the VRMLBean framework, you must understand the way your Java code can communicate with Liquid Reality's browser and script classes.

The example shown in Figure 18-1 demonstrates a simple world with a red sphere in the center of the scene, a blue box to the left, and a green cone to the right. Listing 18-16 shows the VRML file that describes our simple world. When you hold down the right mouse button in the LR browser window and drag it sideways, the red sphere moves across the scene.

Figure 18-1.
A simple world.

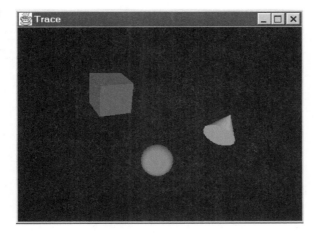

Listing 18-16.
VRML file of a simple world.

```
#VRML V2.0 utf8

WorldInfo {
   title "Simple Interactive World"
}

NavigationInfo {
 type   "WALK"
 speed 2.0
}

DEF MyView Viewpoint {
 position 0 2 15
 #orientation 0 1 0 0.785
 description "First view - From Front"
}

Group {
    children [

            Transform {
```

Continues

Listing 18-16.
Continued.

```
            translation -3.0 4.0 0.0
            rotation 1.0 1.0 0.0 0.785
                children Shape {
                    appearance Appearance {
                            material Material {
                                diffuseColor 0.0 0.0 1.0
                            }
                    }
                    geometry Box {}
                }
        }

        Transform {
            translation 4.0 2.0 0.0
            rotation 1.0 0.0 1.0 -0.785
                children Shape {
                    appearance Appearance {
                            material Material {
                                diffuseColor 0.0 1.0 0.0
                            }
                    }
                    geometry Cone {}
                }

        }

        DEF Mover Transform {
            children Shape {
                appearance Appearance {
                    material Material {
                                diffuseColor 1.0 0.0 0.0
                        }
                }
                geometry Sphere { }
            }
        }

        DEF Sensor PlaneSensor { }

        DEF Trace Script {
            url         "file://c:/vrmlbox/classes/
                vrmltest/trace/Trace.class"
            eventIn         SFVec3f set_translation
            }

    ]
}

ROUTE Sensor.translation_changed TO Mover.set_translation
ROUTE Sensor.translation_changed TO Trace.set_translation
```

Let's have a closer look at our simple world scene. The moving sphere effect is achieved with the help of PlaneSensor and Transform nodes included in the scene. The PlaneSensor node detects viewer actions and converts them to output events that can be used for translating shapes along a 2-D plane. In our example, the PlaneSensor node is a child of the top main group, which includes Sphere, Box, and Cone nodes as well. This allows the PlaneSensor node to sense viewer actions, such as mouse movement with the right button held down, for any shape built in our main group or in any of our main group descendants. Mouse movement causes PlaneSensor to generate translation outputs, as though the shape were sliding across the X-Y plane of our main group's coordinate system.

It would be great if we could use these translation outputs to translate the red sphere across the scene and bring life to our simple world! To do so, we first need to give names to our PlaneSensor node and Transform node that will move the sphere. By having these nodes named, we can specify the PlaneSensor node outputs we want to connect to the corresponding Transform node inputs.

Nodes in VRML are named with the **DEF** keyword, which has the following syntax:

```
DEF node-name node-type {...}
```

Therefore, by having the following lines in our VRML file, we define the name **Sensor** for our PlaneSensor node and the name **Mover** for our Transform node that will move the red sphere across the screen:

```
DEF Sensor PlaneSensor { }
DEF Mover Transform {...}
```

Now we're ready to do the "wiring" of our nodes. Once a route or path between two nodes is wired, the **Sensor** node can start sending messages to the **Mover** node. Such a message or event contains a value, similar to field values within nodes.

Among other fields, the PlaneSensor node has a **translation_changed eventOut** with the following format:

```
PlaneSensor {
   ...
   eventOut        SFVec3f translation_changed
}
```

This **eventOut** has a new 3-D coordinate value each time the viewer changes the *track point*—a changing location on an imaginary flat-track plane, parallel to the X-Y plane, that passes through the hit point.

On the other hand, the Transform node has a `translation` field that specifies the distances in X, Y, and Z directions between the initial coordinate system origin (0, 0, 0) and the origin of the new coordinate system:

```
Transform {
  ...
  exposedField SFVec3f      translation      0 0 0
}
```

In VRML, the `exposedField` type implies two implicit jacks associated with the field: One input jack to set field values and one output jack to send the field value each time the field value changes. The naming convention is to give the names `set_XXX` and `XXX_changed` for input and output jacks respectively; `XXX` is the exposed field's name. Therefore, the `exposedField translation` in the Transform node has the input jack `set_translation` and the output jack `translation_changed`.

`Mover` is a Transform node, so we will use its `set_translation` input to set the new origin for the red sphere coordinate system, which is a child of our `Mover` node. Changing the 3-D coordinate value of `Mover`'s `translation` field each time the viewer changes the track point makes the red sphere move.

To do so, we wire our `Sensor` node's output `translation_changed` to the `Mover` node's input `set_translation` as follows:

```
ROUTE Sensor.translation_changed TO Mover.set_translation
```

Now we have a live world with a red sphere you can drag between the blue box and the green cone. But why should we need a Script node and associated `JavaScript` class? Good question. We need Java scripting in case we want to do something with our world beyond the functionality the browser provides. In this example, our task is simple—we just want to trace VRML events. That's why we add another route from our `Sensor` node to the Script node, which we called `Trace`:

```
ROUTE Sensor.translation_changed TO Trace.set_translation
```

This route delivers events with new 3-D coordinate values from the `Sensor` node to our `Trace` Script node. The Script node has the syntax shown in Listing 18-17.

The Script node receives events from other nodes and performs a custom behavior algorithm. The Script algorithm might decide to change the scene by sending output events or by writing values of exposed fields of other nodes directly. The Script node has associated programming language code, referenced by the `url` field. This code implements node behavior.

```
Script {
    exposedField MFString url              []
    field           SFBool    directOutput   FALSE
    field           SFBool    mustEvaluate   FALSE
    # And any number of:
    eventIn         eventTypeName eventName
    field           fieldTypeName fieldName initialValue
    eventOut        eventTypeName eventName
}
```

We use Java byte code as the programming language for our Script nodes, which we refer to as the *Script class* in the rest of this chapter. We also use *Script* when speaking about the Script node and the **Script** class together, in situations when they're used as an entity.

At the time of this writing, the Java API for Script Authoring Interface was officially defined in *The Virtual Reality Modeling Language*, Appendix C (Java Scripting Reference, Version 2.0, ISO/IEC WD 14772. August 4, 1996).

When creating a Script node, you should define its interface by specifying the Script fields, **eventIns**, and **eventOuts**. VRML has a special syntax for defining a Script interface:

```
Script {
    ...
    field fieldType fieldName initialValue
    ...
    eventIn eventInType eventInName
    ...
    eventOut eventOutType eventOutName
    ...
}
```

A Script node doesn't allow exposed fields in its interface definition. The equivalent of an exposed field can be created by providing an **interface** field and **eventIn** and **eventOut** definitions that work together. For instance, you can define the following Script node:

```
Script {

    field       SFVec3f       translation
    eventIn     SFVec3f       set_translation
    eventOut    SFVec3f       translation_changed
}
```

The Script node's **directOutput** and **mustEvaluate** fields have special meaning for the VRML browser. Having the **mustEvaluate** field set to

FALSE allows the browser to postpone the evaluation of our Script node. The browser might need this to optimize its work on the scene, especially when it's busy drawing our VRML world. In this case, the browser can queue our incoming events until it finds a more convenient time to pass them to the Script node. Otherwise, when the **mustEvaluate** field is set to **TRUE**, the browser is forced to evaluate our Script node every time incoming events for the Script node are pending. This might considerably degrade browser performance when there are a lot of scripts performing intensive computations. Because we don't have intensive computations in this example, we can safely leave this field set to its default **FALSE** value.

The **directOutput** field is set to **TRUE** when the Script node needs to change the values of fields in other nodes in our VRML world. We don't need this now, so we also leave this field set to its default **FALSE** value.

Writing Java Program Scripts

When a Script node receives an event, the VRML browser executes the class in the Script node's **url** field. In our example, we use a Script node with a simple interface:

```
DEF Trace Script {
    url
"file://c:/vrmlbox/classes/vrmltest/trace/Trace.class"
    eventIn          SFVec3f set_translation
}
```

The **url** field of our Script node contains the URL of the Java class that performs a trace of incoming events. We use an **eventIn** of type SFVec3f VRML that we named **set_translation**. The type SFVec3f defines a 3-D floating-point vector that we use here to specify 3-D coordinates in our VRML world. We don't define any other fields or **eventOuts** for our Script node because we don't need them in this example. Finally, we give our Script node the **DEF**ed name **Trace**.

We also use default values for the **directOutput** and **mustEvaluate** fields of our Script node, both of them set to **FALSE**.

Now we're ready to examine the Java class that will perform our script. To make sure a VRML browser will work with our class correctly, the following conditions must be met:

■ Our class must be a subclass of the **Script** class in the vrml.node package.

■ Our **Script** class must contain the class definition whose name is exactly the same as the body of the filename.

That condition explains why our Java class is called **Trace**—the same name as the Script node in our VRML file, as well as why we provide a subclass of the **vrml.node.Script** class:

```
public class Trace extends Script {
...
}
```

The **Script** class in the vrml.node package provides **initialize()** and **shutdown()** methods, which are supposed to be redefined by you in your custom **Script** class. These methods have the following prototypes:

```
public void initialize();
public void shutdown();
```

The **initialize()** method is called before any event is passed to your **Script** class by the browser. You can use it to get references to Script node fields, **eventIns**, and **eventOuts** and then save these references in variables of the **Script** class.

The browser calls the **shutdown()** method when the corresponding Script node is deleted. Default implementation of these methods is "no operation."

In our sample code, we just print a debugging message to standard output, which tells the name of the method being called in both of these methods.

To pass incoming events from the browser to the **Script** class, the *Java Scripting Reference* (Appendix C) of the VRML 2.0 specification defines the following methods:

```
public void processEvent (Event e);
public void processEvents(int count, Event events[]);
public void eventsProcessed();
```

All these methods pass the **Event** object as an argument to the **Script** class. The **Event** class is defined in the vrml package. VRML classes are divided into three packages—vrml, vrml.field, and vrml.node. All VRML data types have an equivalent class in Java, as shown in Listing 18-18.

The **Event** object has three properties—name, value, and timestamp of the **eventIn**. You can get the values of these properties by using the corresponding method on the **Event** object:

```
class Event {
  public String getName();
  public ConstField getValue();
  public double getTimeStamp();
}
```

```
java.lang.Object
    |
    +- vrml.Event
    +- vrml.Browser
    +- vrml.Field
    |        +- vrml.field.SFBool
    |        +- vrml.field.SFColor
    |        +- vrml.field.SFFloat
    |        +- vrml.field.SFImage
    |        +- vrml.field.SFInt32
    |        +- vrml.field.SFNode
    |        +- vrml.field.SFRotation
    |        +- vrml.field.SFString
    |        +- vrml.field.SFTime
    |        +- vrml.field.SFVec2f
    |        +- vrml.field.SFVec3f
    |        |
    |        +- vrml.MField
    |        |        +- vrml.field.MFColor
    |        |        +- vrml.field.MFFloat
    |        |        +- vrml.field.MFInt32
    |        |        +- vrml.field.MFNode
    |        |        +- vrml.field.MFRotation
    |        |        +- vrml.field.MFString
    |        |        +- vrml.field.MFTime
    |        |        +- vrml.field.MFVec2f
    |        |        +- vrml.field.MFVec3f
    |        |
    |        +- vrml.ConstField
    |                 +- vrml.field.ConstSFBool
    |                 +- vrml.field.ConstSFColor
    |                 +- vrml.field.ConstSFFloat
    |                 +- vrml.field.ConstSFImage
    |                 +- vrml.field.ConstSFInt32
    |                 +- vrml.field.ConstSFNode
    |                 +- vrml.field.ConstSFRotation
    |                 +- vrml.field.ConstSFString
    |                 +- vrml.field.ConstSFTime
    |                 +- vrml.field.ConstSFVec2f
    |                 +- vrml.field.ConstSFVec3f
    |                 |
    |                 +- vrml.ConstMFField
    |                          +- vrml.field.ConstMFColor
    |                          +- vrml.field.ConstMFFloat
    |                          +- vrml.field.ConstMFInt32
    |                          +- vrml.field.ConstMFNode
    |                          +- vrml.field.Const
    |                                   MFRotation
    |                          +- vrml.field.ConstMFString
    |                          +- vrml.field.ConstMFTime
    |                          +- vrml.field.ConstMFVec2f
    |                          +- vrml.field.ConstMFVec3f
```

```
    |
+- vrml.BaseNode
            +- vrml.node.Node
            +- vrml.node.Script

java.lang.Exception
        java.lang.RuntimeException
                vrml.InvalidRouteException
                vrml.InvalidFieldException
                vrml.InvalidEventInException
                vrml.InvalidEventOutException
                vrml.InvalidExposedFieldException
                vrml.InvalidNavigationTypeException
                vrml.InvalidFieldChangeException
        vrml.InvalidVRMLSyntaxException
```

There might be situations when multiple events with the same time-stamp are sent to a single Script node. To process them effectively, a VRML browser calls the **processEvents()** method, passing multiple events as an event array to the **Script** class. When events have different timestamps, each coming event invokes separate **processEvents()** methods. If you don't override this method yourself, the **vrml.node.Script** class provides the following implementation of the **processEvents()** method:

```
public void processEvents(int count, Event events[]) {
   for (int i = 0; i < count; i++) {  processEvent(
events[i] );   }
}
```

When writing your **Script** class, you can also override the **eventsProcessed()** method. The default behavior for the method is no operation. A browser calls this method after a set of events has been received. This method can be useful when the latest event received by the Script node is of interest and when you can safely ignore all intermediate events received before. Using this method, you can devise Scripts that generate fewer events than an equivalent Script that generates a new output event each time it receives an incoming event. A browser calls the **eventsProcessed()** method after every invocation of **processEvents()**.

In our **Script** class, we use the **processEvent(Event e)** method, which is called when any event is received by our **Trace** Script node. All we want to do in this example is extract from an incoming event its value, which is a 3-D coordinate, and print out its X, Y, and Z components. As long as we translate the sphere parallel to the X-Y plane, our Z coordinate will always be equal to zero.

First, get the name of the received event:

```
String eventName = e.getName();
```

Next, check whether we want to process the event:

```
if (eventName.equals("set_translation" )) {
...
}
```

Of course, we can't receive any other **eventIn** but **set_translation** in this example, as long as we don't define any other **eventIns** in our **Trace** Script node interface. Still, this piece of code might be useful when you use one **processEvents()** method for different **eventIns** defined in your Script node.

To get the 3-D coordinate value from the incoming event, use the **getValue()** method of the **vrml.Event** class:

```
public ConstField getValue();
```

As you can see from its prototype, this method returns an object of type vrml.ConstField as defined in the vrml package.

The **vrml.Field** class defined in the vrml package is the root of all field types. It has two types of subclasses: Read-only field classes and writable field classes. At the time of this writing, read-only field classes had a common **vrml.ConstField** parent class defined in the vrml package, but writable field classes didn't have a common parent class. This inconsistent approach will change, we hope, in the next version of VRML. Read-only, restricted versions of field types are used only in a Script node's **eventIns**. Unless the read-only field class has an exception explicitly defined, these classes are guaranteed not to generate exceptions. Read-only field classes support the **getValue()** method as well as some other methods to get a value from the field. There's no way to set values in read-only fields. On the other hand, writable field classes support both **getValue()** and **setValue()** methods to get and set field values.

Our 3-D coordinate is a floating-point vector defined in the Java Scripting Reference as a **vrml.field.ConstSFVec3f** class. This class is a subclass of the **vrml.ConstField** class, which is a base class for all read-only field types. That's why we can cast a **getValue()** return type to the type we need:

```
ConstSFVec3f translation = (ConstSFVec3f)e.getValue();
```

Finally, to print out X,Y and Z coordinates we use the handy **getX()**, **getY()**, and **getZ()** methods provided by the **ConstSFVec3f** class. To structure our work, we put this simple **Script** class in a vrmltest.trace package, as the first line of **Trace.java** (Listing 18-19) instructs.

Listing 18-19.
The **Trace Script** class.

```java
package vrmltest.trace;

import java.util.*;

import vrml.*;
import vrml.field.*;
import vrml.node.*;

public class Trace extends Script {

  public void initialize() {

    dbgOut("initialize");
  }

  // This method is called when any event is received
  public void processEvent(Event e) {

    String eventName =     e.getName();

    dbgOut("Event name : "+e.getName());
    dbgOut("Value : "+e.getValue());
    dbgOut("TimeStamp : "+e.getTimeStamp());

    if (eventName.equals("set_translation")) {

      ConstSFVec3f translation =
          (ConstSFVec3f)e.getValue();

      dbgOut("X : "+ translation.getX()+
             " Y : "+ translation.getY()+
             " Z : "+ translation.getZ());
    }

  }


  public void shutdown(){
    dbgOut("shutdown");
  }

  public void dbgOut(String s){
    System.out.println("Trace : "+s);
  }

}
```

Putting Script Code and a VRML Browser Together

Now that we have a VRML file describing our world and a `Script` class animating it, what should we do to bring life to it?

We need a VRML browser to play our VRML and launch our Script. We chose the Liquid Reality Toolkit as the only Java/VRML toolkit currently available that allows you launch and control a VRML2.0 browser, scene, and node classes, as well as many other VRML mechanics, right from your own Java code. At the time of this writing, Liquid Reality is the only toolkit that makes VRML Beans possible.

Liquid Reality Toolkit fully supports not only standard vrml.* packages but also provides a powerful proprietary interface between Java and VRML. In the following examples, we will use only standard vrml.* packages in `Script` classes, and use dnx.*—proprietary LR packages—elsewhere in our code.

No matter how you start your browser—from your own code or command line—your script code gets control after the VRML browser:

■ Loads and processes a VRML file specified in the URL you provide

■ Parses the Script node's `url` field and loads your `Script` class from the URL

In our case, we start the LR browser and load our VRML file right from our Java application. We put all the code related to this task in a separate vrmlbean.vbview package.

The VRML Bean Viewer—`VBViewer.vrmlbean.vbview`—is the main class in this package. The VRML Bean Viewer is based on SimpleViewer, which the LR Toolkit provides as an example of a minimal VRML browser. The inner workings of LR Toolkit are not the focus of this chapter, so we will just skim through the main steps you should take when creating your own working instance of a VRML browser. As you might have already noticed, VRML Bean Viewer does most of its work in its constructor, which has the following signature:

```
public VBViewer (String title, Dimension dim, URL url);
```

The constructor string parameter title is set in VBViewer's `java.awt.Frame` superclass as the title of the window that VRML Bean Viewer creates. The `Dimension` object, also passed to the constructor, determines the window size and URL of the VRML file to be loaded and displayed.

```java
package vrmlbean.vbview;

/**
 *
 * VBViewer.java
 *
 * VBViewer is a VRML Bean viewer based on minimal VRML
 *     browser written using the
 * Liquid Reality toolkit. It loads a VRML file specified
 *     in URL
 * passed as parameter to constructor.
 */

import dnx.lr.*;
import dnx.lr.node.*;
import dnx.lr.app.*;

import java.awt.*;
import java.awt.Toolkit;
import java.awt.Image;
import java.applet.AudioClip;
import java.net.URL;
import java.net.MalformedURLException;
import java.io.File;

public class VBViewer      extends Frame {

  public VBViewer (String title, Dimension dim, URL url) {

      super(title);
      try {
         scene_ = new Scene (new ReadAction (url));
      } catch (VRMLSyntaxException e) {
         System.out.println ("Unable to load: " + e);
         return;
      } catch (java.io.IOException e) {
         System.out.println ("Unable to load: " + e);
         return;
      }

      // Create a document and a view.
      ApplicationDocument document = new
           ApplicationDocument(scene_);

      // If you don't set the layout manager to one that
      //     calls reshape() on
      // its components, you will have explicitly called:
      // view.getComponent().reshape(0,0,width,height)
      // after creating it below.
      setLayout(new FlowLayout());          // Set its layout
        manager
```

Continues

Listing 18-20.
Continued.

```
    View3D view = new BrowserView3D(document);

    setLayout(new BorderLayout());
    add("Center", view.getComponent());             // Add the
        view's canvas
    resize(dim);                                     // Resize
        and show the frame
    show();
    // Run the document, causing periodic "scene frames"
        (event
    // dispatching and redisplay)
    document.start();

    }

/**
 * Get DEFed node by name
 *
 * @param nodeName - node name
 * @result Node instance on success or null if not found
 */
public Node getNode(String nodeName) {

    Node      rootNode = scene_.getRootNode();
    Node      foundNode = null;
    //TransformNode tn = null;

    // Get the node with nodeName in the scene
    NameSearchTraversal t = new NameSearchTraversal
        (nodeName);
    rootNode.traverse (t);
    if (t.foundMatch ()) {
       foundNode = t.getFirstNode ();

       // Print out the VRML of the node
       // System.out.print("Node = ");
       // foundNode.print(new PrintAction(System.out));
       return foundNode;
    } else {
       return null;
    }

}

public static void main(String args[]) {

    URL url = null;

    try {
        url = new URL(args[0]);
    } catch (MalformedURLException e) {
        System.out.println("Bad URL : "+e);
```

Listing 18-20.
Continued.

```
        }
        Dimension dim = new Dimension(440, 340);
    new VBViewer ("VRML Bean Viewer", dim, url);
  }

  private Scene scene_ = null;

}
```

After setting the title in its window, the viewer first creates the **dnx.lr.Scene** object, which is a master object for the VRML world in LR Toolkit. The **Scene** object holds a VRML scene graph, which consists of **node** objects describing the scene contents. To display a scene and interact with it, the viewer needs an **LR Document** and any **View** objects. It creates an instance of **dnx.lr.app.ApplicationDocument**—the subclass of the **LR Document** class—defined in the lr.app package, which encapsulates a **Scene** object:

```
ApplicationDocument document = new
    ApplicationDocument(scene_);
```

The **LR Document** runs in its own thread to display the VRML scene graph that the **Scene** object contains with the help of a set of **Views**. Each **View** is responsible for managing a subtree of the scene graph. This responsibility includes processing input events sent to the subtree and its display. To give the document a **View** class, we use **dnx.lr.app.BrowserView3D** from the same LR package:

```
View3D view = new BrowserView3D(document);
```

A **BrowserView3D** is a particular kind of **View** that **LR Document** needs to display and interact with the scene. Now that we have all the browser components ready, we can start it just by starting the **LR Document** thread:

```
document.start();
```

This statement runs the browser, causing periodic scene frames. Frames update the scene display and dispatch VRML events. If our **Script** class is successfully loaded and initialized, it finally gets input events defined by corresponding **eventIns** in our **Trace** Script Node interface. These events are passed to the **processEvent(Event e)** function defined in the **Trace** class. The debugging output of our **Trace** script is shown in Listing 18-21.

```
Trace : Event name : set_translation
Trace : Value : vrml.field.ConstSFVec3f@13a4e90
Trace : TimeStamp : 8.60581e+008
Trace : X : 0.960341 Y : 1.48291 Z : 0
...
Trace : Event name : set_translation
Trace : Value : vrml.field.ConstSFVec3f@13a78e8
Trace : TimeStamp : 8.60581e+008
Trace : X : 0.962955 Y : 1.36317 Z : 0
...
```

VRML Script node provides a mechanism for creating custom behaviors in a VRML scene. The Java API for Script Authoring Interface allows you access fields, **eventIns**, and **eventOuts** of your Script node and use them to manipulate the scene. A browser-centered approach implies the following execution model for VRML worlds that use Java for script authoring:

■ Starting the browser from the command line or creating its runtime instance in your application with the LR Toolkit.

■ Loading a VRML file specified by its URL and processing it in the browser.

■ Loading the **Script** class specified in the Script node's **url** field.

■ Passing control to the **Script** class the first time the browser calls its **initialize()** method.

■ Passing control to the **Script** class callback functions to process input events as needed.

■ Unloading your **Script** class at the browser's discretion after calling its **shutdown()** method.

Converting the Script to a Transitional VRML Bean

Now that you have some idea of what a VRML script is, we can start building our first Transitional VRML Bean. As you might remember, a Transitional VRML Bean implementation is based on VRML scripting with Java. To make life easier, we will skip the word *Transitional* from now on in the text.

A browser-centered VRML execution model, discussed in the previous section, doesn't conform to the Java software component model, JavaBeans. This means that a VRML scene as a whole, as well as nodes and groups of nodes, can't be used as reusable components in Java design-time or runtime environments.

In this section, we examine some ways to work around this limitation. The JavaScript Authoring Interface, with some extra help from LR Toolkit, can be used as one such workaround. We will use a `Script` class that the VRML Script node specifies in its `url` field as a gateway to the VRML world in a JavaBeans environment. Before going further, let's summarize the most important features that distinguish a VRML Bean, as well as any JavaBean, from other classes:

- **Properties:** Discrete, named attributes that other Beans can access pragmatically by calling their getter and setter methods.
- **Methods:** Public Bean methods exposed as external methods in a Beans environment for access by other Beans.
- **Events:** Mechanisms for propagating state change notifications between a source Bean that's generating events and one or more target listener Beans.

In the following discussion, we will focus on the event mechanism for VRML Beans because it's the core feature of the JavaBeans architecture. A VRML Bean should be a VRML event source for other JavaBeans. Any Bean should be able to register as a listener for VRML events with the VRML Bean. When discussing VRML events in a JavaBeans context, we mean any event that comes from a VRML node or group and inherits from java.util.EventListener. In this particular case, the event object can contain as a member an instance of the `vrml.Event` class, defined in the VRML 2.0 Java Scripting Reference. This assumption is important because it allows us to encapsulate all VRML-specific code inside the VRML Bean so that design-time and runtime Bean environments can operate the VRML Bean transparently without any knowledge of VRML internals.

Defining Transitional VRML Bean Components

To build a VRML Bean with the help of a Script node and associated `Script` class, we will convert the `Script` class we discussed earlier to be a source of VRML events for other Beans. The VRML browser loads the

Script class with its own custom class loader, which makes the **Script** class instance inaccessible from the Bean environment used, such as BeanBox. BeanBox simply doesn't know that the class was loaded; as a result, it can't inspect this class and create a **BeanInfo** object describing its methods and properties.

To create the VRML Bean, we need a special adapter class that Bean-Box will instantiate and treat as a regular Bean. This VRML **Adapter** class should be exactly like any other Bean that BeanBox works with. The main idea of the JavaBeans event adapter is to provide an intermediary class to be interposed between an event source and the real event listener. In the case of our VRML Bean, the event source is the VRML Script node propagating events by means of the **Script** class. The main difference between the VRML event source and other event sources is that BeanBox can't register listeners with the VRML event source directly because BeanBox has no access to the **Script** class. Instead, BeanBox registers VRML event listeners with the VRML **Adapter** class. The VRML **Adapter** class contains a reference to the **Script** class and redirects listener registration calls from its own **add()** and **remove()** methods to corresponding methods in the **Script** class. In other words, the VRML **Adapter** class works like a registration redirector, which makes it different from a JavaBeans event adapter. BeanBox can introspect the VRML **Adapter** class correctly and generate the necessary hookup code for the listeners.

The VRML **Adapter** object starts communicating with the **Script** object after the **Script** object is loaded by the browser. To ensure efficient event delivery, the **Script** class maintains its own list of registered VRML event listeners. When the Script node receives an event from one of its **eventIn** inputs, the **Script** class fires this event directly to target listeners from its internal list.

Now we can define the main execution components of a VRML Bean:

- VRML Script node
- **Script** class
- VRML scene viewer/browser classes
- VRML **Adapter** class

To redirect listener registration to the Script, the VRML **Adapter** must have a reference to the **Script** object as soon as browser has loaded the scene. At the time of this writing, the Java Script Authoring Interface didn't provide an API that allowed you to get references to VRML nodes of the loaded scene as references to the corresponding Java objects. The External Authoring Interface proposed by Silicon Graphics addresses the need for such an API, providing an explicit method to get a pointer to the node named in the scene graph with **DEF** syntax. This interface, implemented in the Silicon Graphics Cosmo Player VRML browser, allows an applet on the Web page access to **DEF**ed nodes in a VRML scene, using the existing VRML event model.

In our discussion, we will use the Liquid Reality Toolkit as the most powerful tool for interfacing with VRML from Java. As long as our goal is to construct a VRML Bean architecture that conforms to the existing standards as closely as possible, we will use the proprietary LR Toolkit API to the smallest extent necessary to create the missing functionality in today's standards. In fact, the **getNode()** method provided by the VRML Bean Viewer that we discussed earlier in this chapter gives us the same functionality as an analogous method from External Authoring Interface. For now, **getNode()** is the only method implemented in the VRML Bean prototype with specific links to LR Toolkit functionality. It has the following signature:

```
public Node getNode(String nodeName);
```

Having explained this, we can finally turn to the real example of a VRML Bean. This time we want VRML events that our simple world generates when we drag the red sphere across the scene to be sent to any other Bean interested in them. In other words, our VRML Bean will propagate new 3-D coordinates resulting from translation along the X-Y plane to target listener Beans registered with it. First, let's look at the VRML event object defined in **VrmlEventObject** class. We could have designed our event object to hold a 3-D coordinate value, but in this example we want to demonstrate the more general case, when a Bean event object encapsulates a VRML event object as a member. The general event object can be processed by different listeners, in contrast to a more specialized event object. Event listeners know the interface to access event members and process them accordingly.

The definition of the VRML event class, shown in Listing 18-22, strictly follows the JavaBeans design pattern. **VrmlEventObject** extends the base event object defined in **java.util.EventObject** and provides a constructor that passes the event source to its base class:

```
public class VrmlEventObject extends java.util.EventObject
    {
  public VrmlEventObject(Object o) {
    super(o);
  }
```

▨▨▨ ▨▨▨ ▨▨▨ ▨▨
Listing 18-22.
VRMLEventObject
class.

```
package vrmlbean.vrmlscript;

import java.util.EventObject;
import vrml.Event;

public class VrmlEventObject extends java.util.EventObject
    {

  public VrmlEventObject(Object o) {
    super(o);
  }

  public void setVrmlEvent(vrml.Event ve) {
    vrmlEvent_ = ve;
  }

  public vrml.Event getVrmlEvent() {
    return vrmlEvent_;
  }

  private vrml.Event vrmlEvent_ = null;

}
```

Listing 18-23.
VRML Event Listener
interface.

```
package vrmlbean.vrmlscript;

import java.util.EventListener;

public interface VrmlListener extends java.util.
    EventListener {

  public void handleVrmlEvent(VrmlEventObject veo);

}
```

Encapsulated VRML events can be accessed with the following methods:

```
public void setVrmlEvent(vrml.Event ve);
public vrml.Event getVrmlEvent();
```

Now that we have defined the event class, we should provide the interface class that listeners interested in VRML events will implement. We define this interface in the **VrmlListener** class shown in Listing 18-23.

As with **VrmlEventObject**, we follow the JavaBeans design pattern, which requires a VRML listener interface to extend java.util.EventListener. We also require listeners to implement a method to process the VRML event object:

```
public void handleVrmlEvent(VrmlEventObject veo);
```

The VRML event object passed as a parameter to this method will be handled differently by different listeners. Later in this chapter, we use one of these listeners—the **EventTrace** Bean—to produce VRML events.

Listing 18-24.
VRML event echo
Script class.

```
package vrmlbean.vrmlscript;

import java.util.*;

import vrml.*;
import vrml.field.*;
import vrml.node.*;

public class VrmlEvtEchoScr extends Script
                                implements VrmlEventSource {

  public void initialize() {
    dbgOut("initialize");
  }

  // This method is called when any event is received
  public void processEvent(Event e) {

    notifyListeners(e);
  }


  //VRML Bean will call these methods to add and remove
       registered listeners
  public synchronized void addVrmlListener(VrmlListener l)
       {
    dbgOut("Adding listener : "+l.toString());
    vrmlListeners_.addElement(l);
  }

  public synchronized void removeVrmlListener(VrmlListener
       l) {

    dbgOut("Removing listener : "+l.toString());
    vrmlListeners_.removeElement(l);
  }

  //Send a VRML event to registered listeners
  private void notifyListeners(vrml.Event ve) {

    Vector l;
    VrmlEventObject veo = new VrmlEventObject(this);
    veo.setVrmlEvent(ve);
```

Continues

Listing 18-24.
Continued.

```
    synchronized(this) {
      if(vrmlListeners_.isEmpty()) {
        dbgOut("No listeners");
        return;
      }
      dbgOut("Notifying listeners");
      //you must copy the vector before sending the event
           to avoid a timing race
      l = (Vector)vrmlListeners_.clone();
    }

    for (int i = 0; i < l.size(); i++) {
      VrmlListener vl = (VrmlListener) l.elementAt(i);
      vl.handleVrmlEvent(veo);
    }

  }

  public void shutdown(){
    dbgOut("shutdown");
  }

  public void dbgOut(String s){
    System.out.println("<<<*** VrmlEvtEchoScr : "+s);
  }

  private Vector vrmlListeners_ = new Vector();
}
```

Before explaining how the VRML **Adapter** works we need to tune the VRML scene and Script components of our Bean. For this example, we use a VRML scene similar to the one used in our previous example. This time, the Script node's **url** field references the **Script** class defined in the **VrmlEvtEchoScr** class, customized for use as a VRML event source. Our VRML Event Echo **Script** class, shown in Listing 18-24, should have the same name as the corresponding Script node in the VRML file. The **VrmlEvtEchoScr** class should also extend its **vrml.node.Script** base class. All these requirements need to be met for the browser to process our Script correctly. The **VrmlEvtEchoScr** class also implements our custom VrmlEventSource interface to be discussed later in this section. As a result, we have the following **Script** class constructor:

```
  public class VrmlEvtEchoScr extends Script implements
VrmlEventSource {
    ...
  }
```

As you can see from the listing, our `Script` class not only provides `initialize()`, `shutdown()`, and `processEvents()` methods, as all VRML `Script` classes normally do, but also has a method to notify registered listeners:

```
private void notifyListeners(vrml.Event ve) {
    ...
}
```

The fact that we make the `notifyListeners()` method private is important because it shouldn't be called from outside the `Script` class. We call this method immediately, as soon as `vrml.Event` is available:

```
public void processEvent(Event e) {

    notifyListeners(e);
}
```

The notification method creates a VRML event object, setting the `Script` class as an event source:

```
VrmlEventObject veo = new VrmlEventObject(this);
```

This way, those listeners interested in the VRML event source will get a reference to the loaded `Script` object calling the `getSource()` method in the VRML event object. The notification method also sets a `vrml.Event` value received from the `processEvents()` method in the VRML event object:

```
veo.setVrmlEvent(ve);
```

When the listener receives the event, it can extract the `vrml.Event` value from the VRML event object with a corresponding `getVrmlEvent()` method as defined in `VrmlEventObject` class.

Our `Script` class maintains a list of registered listeners in a private variable called `vrmlListeners_`. The notification method uses this list to fire a VRML Event Object to registered listeners. When the list is empty, no event processing is performed. Before dispatching an event to the listeners, the notification method makes a copy of the vector that implements the listener list. This is done to avoid a timing race that otherwise might happen when new listeners are added or removed from the list simultaneously with the event dispatch.

As you already know, a VRML `Adapter` class provides `add()` and `remove()` methods for listener registration. To provide for registering these listeners, the `Script` class implements the VrmlEventSource interface shown in Listing 18-25. After the VRML `Adapter` gets a reference to the `Script` object, the adapter redirects registration requests to it by using this interface.

Listing 18-25.
VrmlEventSource
interface.

```
package vrmlbean.vrmlscript;

public interface VrmlEventSource {

  //VRML Adaptor class will call these methods to add and
      remove registered listeners
  public /*synchronized*/ void addVrmlListener(VrmlListener
      l);

  public /*synchronized*/ void removeVrmlListener
      (VrmlListener l);

}
```

In our example, the **VrmlEvtMonitor** class, shown in Listing 18-26, performs VRML **Adapter** functions. Let's have a look at the constructor of this class.

As long as we want our adapter to behave as a standard component in the BeanBox frame, we derive this class from java.awtCanvas. To make it visible, we resize the **Adapter** component and give it a background color. Next, in the **paint()** method, we write VRMLBean inside the blue oval we draw. These are the steps almost every Bean component takes in its constructor. Now, we want our VRML Bean to be as self-contained as possible, so we put the VRML file (**eventmon.wrl**) describing our world in the same JAR file as we put our **VrmlEvtMonitor** adapter class. Great! But what shall we do to get it back and load it when BeanBox starts our VRML viewer? We need to pass the URL of the VRML file that it will read and display in a separate window. The following code in the **VrmlEvtMonitor** constructor creates the URL we need:

```
URL url= getClass().getResource("eventmon.wrl");
```

To create the URL, we use the **getResource()** method defined in **java.lang.Class** with this signature:

```
public URL getResource(String name);
```

This method finds out which class loader was used to load the class and then calls the corresponding method in the class loader. BeanBox loads all resources specified in the JAR manifest to its internal storage. To do this, BeanBox uses its own class loader, which overrides the **getResource()** method defined in **java.lang.ClassLoader**.

When this method is called in the BeanBox class loader, it first checks whether it has a resource with the given name already loaded; in our case,

Listing 18-26.
VRML event monitor
Adapter class.

```
package vrmlbean.vrmlmon;

package vrmlbean.vrmlmon;

import java.awt.*;
import java.io.*;
import java.util.Vector;
import java.net.URL;
import java.net.MalformedURLException;

import vrml.Event;
import vrml.node.Script;

import dnx.lr.*;
import dnx.lr.node.*;

import vrmlbean.vbview.*;
import vrmlbean.vrmlscript.*;

public class VrmlEvtMonitor extends Canvas implements
    Runnable {

  public VrmlEvtMonitor() {

    resize(width_, height_);
    font_ = new Font("Helvetica", Font.BOLD, height_/3);
    setBackground(bgColor_);

    URL url= getClass().getResource("eventmon.wrl");
    Dimension dim = new Dimension(440, 340);
    vrmlView_ = new VBViewer ("VRML Bean Viewer", dim,
        url);
    initThread();
  }

  private void initThread() {

    if(thread_ == null) {
      thread_ = new Thread(this);
      thread_.start();
    }
  }

  public void run() {

    try {
      while(!loadedScriptObject()) {
        thread_.sleep(1000);
        dbgOut("Script node not found yet...");
      }
      thread_.suspend();
```

Continues

Listing 18-26.
Continued.

```
    } catch (Exception e) {
      dbgOut(e.toString());
    }
  }

  private boolean loadedScriptObject() {

    //Get DEFed node "VrmlEvtEchoScr"
    foundNode_ = vrmlView_.getNode("VrmlEvtEchoScr");

    if(foundNode_ == null) {
      dbgOut("VrmlEvtEchoScr - not found");
      return false;
    }

    if (foundNode_ instanceof ScriptNode) {
      scriptNode_ = (ScriptNode)foundNode_;
    } else {
      dbgOut("Not a ScriptNode node!");
      return false;
    }

      // get reference to instance of Java script class
      scriptObject_ = scriptNode_.getLoadedJavaObject();
      if(scriptObject_ == null) {
        dbgOut("Can't get instance of Java script class
            !");
        return false;
      } else {
        dbgOut("Got instance of Java script class ");
      }
      return true;
  }

  //BeanBox will call these methods to add and remove
      registered listeners
  public synchronized void addVrmlListener(VrmlListener l)
      {
    if(scriptObject_ == null) {
      dbgOut("Can't add listener");
      return;
    }
    ((VrmlEventSource)scriptObject_).addVrmlListener(l);
  }

  public synchronized void removeVrmlListener(VrmlListener
      l) {

    if(scriptObject_ == null) {
      dbgOut("Can't remove listener");
      return;
    }
```

Listing 18-26.
Continued.

```
      ((VrmlEventSource)scriptObject_).removeVrmlListener(1);
   }


   public void paint(Graphics g) {

      //the blue oval
      g.setColor(fgColor_);
      g.fillOval(0,0,width_, height_);
      g.setColor(Color.black);
      g.setFont(font_);
      g.drawString("VRMLBean", 4, 2*height_/3);
   }

   public Dimension getMinimumSize() {
      return new Dimension(width_, height_);
   }

   public static void dbgOut(String s){
      System.out.println("***VrmlEvtMonitor : "+s);
   }

   private Font font_;
   private int width_ = 120;
   private int height_ = 60;
   private Color bgColor_ = Color.darkGray;
   private Color fgColor_ = Color.blue;
   private transient Thread thread_;        // will not
          serialize this
   private VBViewer vrmlView_ = null;
   private TransformNode moverNode_ = null;
   private ScriptNode scriptNode_ = null;
   private Script scriptObject_ = null;
   private Node foundNode_ = null;

}
```

this resource is **eventmon.wrl**. If it finds such a resource in its internal storage, the class loader constructs and returns a custom URL for this resource. Otherwise, **NULL** is returned.

Having the URL to our scene ready, we can start the VRML Bean Viewer that will display our world in a separate window:

```
vrmlView_ = new VBViewer ("VRML Bean Viewer", dim, url);
```

Besides the URL, we pass the window title and its dimension to the constructor of the **VBViewer** class, which implements the VRML viewer/browser for VRML Beans that we discussed earlier.

The **VrmlEventMonitor** class, which works as the VRML adapter, implements the java.lang.Runnable interface. We implement this interface to let instances of the **VrmlEventMonitor** class be executed in a separate thread. In the **run()** method, the **VrmlEventMonitor** thread periodically queries VBViewer to find out when the **Script** class is loaded. We need this to handle the situation when the **Script** class specified in the Script node's **url** field is loaded asynchronously from some remote host, which requires additional time. When the **Script** class is loaded, **VrmlEventMonitor** is ready to add and remove any VRML event listeners. To find out if the **Script** class has been loaded, we call the **loadedScriptObject** method every second. After the **Script** class object is loaded, the thread suspends itself:

The **loadedScriptObject** method first calls the **getNode()** method defined in the **VBViewer** class. This method provides the same functionality as an analogous function defined in the External Authoring Interface mentioned previously. In our case, the **getNode()** method uses a proprietary scene traversal algorithm for Liquid Reality to find Java objects corresponding to the scene nodes with **DEF**ed names:

```
foundNode_ = vrmlView_.getNode("VrmlEvtEchoScr");
```

After the **VrmlEvtEchoScr** Script node is found, the **loadedScriptObject** function verifies that the correct instance of the **ScriptNode** class was found with an **instanceof** operator. It's important to understand that what we have just found is the reference to the object corresponding to the **ScriptNode** in the scene graph. What we really need to communicate with the Script code is the reference to the **Script** object itself, as soon as this object implements our VRML event source. Currently, the existing standard for VRML/Java API doesn't have any feature that returns a reference to the loaded **Script** object, so to get the reference we need, we

Listing 18-27.
Waiting for the Script node to be loaded.

```
public void run() {

    try {
        while(!loadedScriptObject()) {
            thread_.sleep(1000);
            dbgOut("Script node not found yet...");
        }
        thread_.suspend();
    } catch (Exception e) {
        dbgOut(e.toString());
    }
}
```

have to use the proprietary LR functionality. The **getLoadedJavaObject()** method that the Liquid Reality **ScriptNode** class provides does exactly what we need:

```
scriptObject_ = scriptNode_.getLoadedJavaObject();
```

The VrmlEvtMonitor listener registration methods **addVrmlListener()** and **removeVrmlListener()** both check whether the **Script** object is already loaded. This is true when **scriptObject_** gets a non-null value. The only thing that registration methods do, as soon as they have a valid **scriptObject_** reference, is pass the registration request to the **Script** object, which internally handles listeners.

Class Name Space and Class Loaders

Now we have everything ready to run our VRML Bean in the BeanBox. To do so, we want to put all the components of our Bean in a single JAR file. As soon as the BeanBox class loader gives us a URL to any resource we put in the JAR file, we also put our VRML file there. We use this URL later as a parameter to the VRML Bean Viewer (**VBViewer**), which displays the VRML world this URL refers to. The BeanBox class loader loads and resolves all classes it finds in the JAR file.

On the other hand, our **VBViewer** class uses its own class loader to load and resolve the **Script** class. As long as **VBViewer** uses Liquid Reality browser classes that do all the work with the scene graph, we can't rewrite **VBViewer** so it could use the same class loader that BeanBox uses. We therefore have to deal with two different class loaders in our VRML Bean. The class loader that the browser provides to load the **Script** class doesn't know anything about classes loaded from the JAR file. For our **Script** class to be successfully loaded and resolved, we have to put the **Script** class and all the classes it refers to in the **CLASSPATH** variable. In our example, we put all these classes in one vrmlbean.vrmlscript package:

```
vrmlbean.vrmlscript.VrmlEvtEchoScr
vrmlbean.vrmlscript.VrmlEventSource
vrmlbean.vrmlscript.VrmlListener
vrmlbean.vrmlscript.VrmlEventObject
```

We put the VRML **Adapter** class in the JAR file, which in our case is the **vrmlbean.vrmlmon.VrmlEvtMonitor** class. We also put the file with the VRML for our world (**eventmon.wrl**), as well as all browser classes from the vrmlbean.vbview.* package, in the same JAR file. Before BeanBox can load the **VrmlEvtMonitor** class, it needs to resolve all classes that **VrmlEvtMonitor** refers to. In our example, **VrmlEvtMonitor** uses the Vrml-EventSource interface to add and remove listeners in the **VrmlEvtEchoScr** class. Here we have a cross-ClassLoader interface, which is Vrml-EventSource. This interface is successfully resolved by both class loaders with the **ClassLoader.findSystemClass** function that searches our **CLASSPATH**.

This solution doesn't look very neat, though, because we can't put interface classes for all possible Beans in the **CLASSPATH**. The better policy is the one suggested by Larry Cable from JavaSoft. The main idea is to allow the class loader to delegate classes to the class loader that was used to load the first class loader. For example, when the Liquid Reality browser class loader can't resolve a class, it can delegate this class to the BeanBox class loader, as shown in Listing 18-28.

Listing 18-28.
Delegating a class.

```
// Liquid Reality ClassLoader should be modified like this
     :
public class LRClassLoader extends ClassLoader {

protected Class loadClass(String name, boolean resolve) {
    // try to find if class already loaded
    Class clazz = findLoadedClass(name);

    if (clazz == null) {
    // get reference to BeanBox class loader
    ClassLoader p = getClass().getClassLoader();

    // delegate class to BeanBox class loader
    if (p != null) clazz = p.loadClass(name);

    if (clazz == null) clazz = findSystemClass(name);

    if (clazz == null) {
    // implement LRClassLoader specific
    // semantics here ....
    }

    if (clazz == null)
       throw new ClassNotFoundException(name);

    if (resolve) resolveClass(clazz);
    }

    // ...

    return clazz;
}
```

Running in BeanBox

We will run our **VRMLBean** in BeanBox connected to the **EventTrace** Bean, shown in Listing 18-29. This simple Bean implements a generic java.util.EventListener interface. The **EventTrace** class defines a **traceEvent()** method that accepts as a parameter **java.util.EventObject**. This method allows us to use **EventTrace** as a generic listener of any events derived from **java.util.EventObject**. **EventTrace** converts the received event object to a string and displays it in a popup **TraceFrame** window.

**Listing 18-29.
EventTrace** class.

```
package bdktest.trace;

import java.awt.*;
import java.io.Serializable;

public class EventTrace extends Canvas
                implements Serializable,
                        java.util.EventListener {

  public EventTrace(){
    resize(width_, height_);
    font_ = new Font("Helvetica", Font.BOLD, height_/3);
    setBackground(bgColor_);
        win_ = new TraceFrame("EventTrace", 6, 40);
  }

  public void traceEvent(java.util.EventObject e) {

    win_.addString(e.toString());
  }

  public void paint(Graphics g) {
    g.setFont(font_);
    g.drawString("EventTrace", 0, 2*height_/3);
  }

  public Dimension getMinimumSize() {
    return new Dimension(width_, height_);
  }

  private TraceFrame win_ = null;
  private Font font_;
  private int width_ = 120;
  private int height_ = 60;
  private Color bgColor_ = Color.green;

}
```

After starting BeanBox, load the **vrmlmon.jar** file, which contains our **VRMLBean**, by choosing File | LoadJar . . . from the BeanBox menu. Load the **EventTrace** Bean from **Trace.jar** file in the same way. In the Tool-Box panel, we now have both the **VrmlEvtMonitor** and the **TraceEvent** Beans. Right after selecting **VrmlEvtMonitor** in the ToolBox panel, Bean-Box creates an instance of the **VrmlEvtMonitor** class, which in turn creates a **VBViewer** object that displays our simple VRML world in a popup window, as shown in Figure 18-2.

Having both components dragged to the BeanBox panel, we select **VRMLBean** to connect to **EventTrace**. From the BeanBox Edit menu, choose Events | vrml | handleVrmlEvent and connect it to the **traceEvent()** method exposed by the **EventTrace** Bean (see Figure 18-3).

After BeanBox has generated hookup code, we can start playing with our first **VRMLBean**. Let's drag the red sphere and place it over the top of the blue box. As you drag, you might see the **EventTrace** window outputting text strings. Each line in this output is a **VrmlEventObject** converted to a string. **EventTrace** calls the **toString()** method on every event it receives. As you can see from Figure 18-4, the **VrmlEventObject.toString** method prints the name of the event source, which in our case is the **VrmlEvtEchoScr Script** class.

Figure 18-2.
Selecting **VRMLBean**
events in BeanBox.

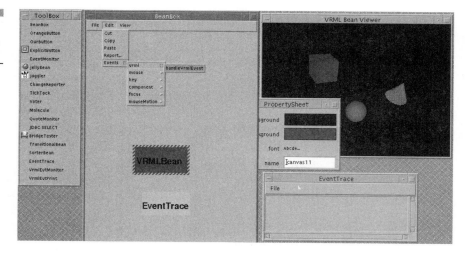

Figure 18-3.
Connecting
VRMLBean to
EventTrace.

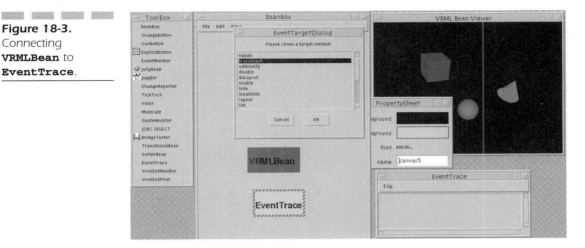

Figure 18-4.
Red Sphere Meets
Blue Box.

CONCLUSION

Well, that's it, folks! This book has been written with a lot of hard work from people all over the world, and we hope you enjoyed our journey through component-based computing. As you can see, now the Web is ready for distributed, reusable software development that can be used to create building blocks for large projects such as electronic commerce. Happy computing!

Appendix A

JavaBeans API Reference

The JavaBeans API consists of the `java.Beans` package, as well as three classes in the `java.util` package. It is not necessary to use this package to create Beans, as any java class is a Bean. However, these classes and interfaces allow application developers to create sophisticated Beans that are truly portable and reusable.

Package java.beans

The `java.beans` package consists of six interfaces. These interfaces provide a framework for Bean developers to describe their Beans' properties to developers and to other tools. Many of the interfaces, such as PropertyEditor, are complex and are only for sophisticated Beans. For easier implementation, several of the classes in this package run the interfaces using no-op methods. In any case, these interfaces allow truly customizable Beans. The six interfaces are

- BeanInfo
- Customizer
- PropertyChangeListener
- PropertyEditor
- VetoableChangeListener
- Visibility

The package also consists of 15 classes. These classes are

- `BeanDescriptor`
- `Beans`
- `EventSetDescriptor`
- `FeatureDescriptor`
- `IndexedPropertyDescriptor`
- `Introspector`
- `MethodDescriptor`

- `ParameterDescriptor`
- `PropertyChangeEvent`
- `PropertyChangeSupport`
- `PropertyDescriptor`
- `PropertyEditorManager`
- `PropertyEditorSupport`
- `SimpleBeanInfo`
- `VetoableChangeSupport`

The classes provide implementations of many of the interfaces to allow Bean developers to easily disseminate information about their Beans. Other classes help with the management of bound and constrained properties. And other classes allow low-level introspection of classes, as well as the ability to efficiently determine the abilities of a Bean. Throughout these classes one will notice an incredible effort on JavaSoft's part to allow Beans to inform both application developers and tools, in real-time, about their various characteristics.

Also, there are two exception classes:

- `IntrospectionException`
- `PropertyVetoException`

Both of these exceptions are important, especially `PropertyVetoException`. The `PropertyVetoException` is extremely powerful as it allows constrained properties to exist and allows Beans to hold a two-way conversation, as we will discuss in more detail later.

Interface java.beans.BeanInfo
public interface BeanInfo

This interface allows a Bean developer to provide specific information about a specific Bean, which the `BeanInfo` class describes. The `BeanInfo` interface is provided so the Bean developer can decide which information he or she wants to provide to the application builder or tool. The rest of the information will be obtained via automatic analysis from low-level reflection. This interface is normally used through its implementation in the `SimpleBeanInfo` class. By overriding the `SimpleBeanInfo` classes the Bean developer can decide exactly which properties, events, and methods he or she wishes to describe.

public final static int ICON_COLOR_16x16

This is a constant that indicates a 16x16 color icon.

public final static int ICON_COLOR_32x32

This is a constant that indicates a 32x32 color icon.

public final static int ICON_MONO_16x16

This is a constant that indicates a 16x16 monochrome icon.

public final static int ICON_MONO_32x32

This is a constant that indicates a 32x32 monochrome icon.

public abstract BeanDescriptor getBeanDescriptor()

RETURNS: A **BeanDescriptor** that provides information about the Bean's customizer class if it has one. The **BeanDescriptor** class currently does little more.

public abstract EventSetDescriptor[] getEventSetDescriptors()

This method determines the events that this Bean fires.

RETURNS: An array of **EventSetDescriptors** that describes the events this Bean fires. It will return null if the information should be obtained by automatic inspection.

public abstract int getDefaultEventIndex()

The default event is the event that will be used the most by application builders when using the Bean.

RETURNS: An index number of the default event in the array returned by `getEventSetDescriptors`. If there is no default event this method returns `-1`.

public abstract PropertyDescriptor[] getPropertyDescriptors()

This method determines the Bean's properties.

RETURNS: An array of `PropertyDescriptors` that describes the events this Bean fires. It will return null if the information should be obtained by automatic inspection. If an indexed property exists, then it will be a subclass of the `IndexedPropertyDescriptor` class. Use `instanceof()` to check if this is indeed the case.

public abstract int getDefaultPropertyIndex()

The default property is the property that will be updated most commonly by application builders who are using the Bean.

RETURNS: An index number of the default property in the array returned by `getPropertyDescriptors`. If there is no default property this method returns `-1`.

public abstract MethodDescriptor[] getMethodDescriptors()

This method determines the methods the Bean supports. These are the methods which are accessible to tools and application builders.

RETURNS: An array of **MethodDescriptors** that describe the methods supported by the Bean. It will return **null** if the information should be obtained by automatic inspection.

public abstract BeanInfo[] getAdditionalBeanInfo()

This method allows a BeanInfo object to return a collection of other **BeanInfo** objects that provide more information about the Bean. The **BeanInfo** objects returned are usually objects related to parent classes, and allow, in effect, an application builder to step up the Bean tree. The current **BeanInfo** takes precedence over the **getAdditionalBeanInfo** objects if there are conflicts between sets of information. Additionally, the closer a **BeanInfo** object is to the current Bean, the higher its precedence.

RETURNS: An array of **BeanInfo** objects. If there are no more it will return **null**.

public abstract Image getIcon(int iconKind)

This method returns an image object that is used to represent the Bean in tools and application builder environments. Beans are not required to provide icons. Though a Bean may support all four types of icons (16x16 color, 16x16 mono, and so on) it is recommended that Bean developers support 16x16 color if only one color is supported.

PARAMETERS:
- **iconKind**—This is the kind of icon requested. It should be one of the constant values listed above.

RETURNS: An image object representing the requested icon. If the requested icon does not exist then this method returns **null**.

Interface java.beans.Customizer
public interface Customizer

This interface allows Bean developers to build a custom GUI for customizing each Bean. Each customizer should have a null constructor.

Because the customizer is not informed of the Bean to be customized (its constructor is null) the constructor does not have access to the Bean's properties. Keep this in mind.

`public abstract void setObject(Object bean)`

This informs the customizer which Bean instance will be customized. It should be called before the customizer has been added to any parent AWT container.

PARAMETERS:

▓ `bean`—This is the object instance to be customized.

`public abstract void addPropertyChangeListener (PropertyChangeListener listener)`

This method registers a listener for a `PropertyChange` event. The customizer fires this event whenever it changes the Bean in a way that might require the displayed properties to be refreshed.

PARAMETERS:

▓ `listener`—An object to be informed when a PropertyChange event is fired.

`public abstract void removePropertyChangeListener (PropertyChangeListener listener)`

This method removes a `listener` for a `PropertyChange` event.

PARAMETERS:

▓ `listener`—The object to be removed from the list of listeners.

Interface java.beans.PropertyChangeListener
public interface PropertyChangeListener
extends EventListener

This interface must be implemented by any object which wishes to listen to `PropertyChange` events being fired. Whenever a Bean changes a bound property a `PropertyChange` event is fired.

public abstract void propertyChange (PropertyChangeEvent evt)

This method is called when a bound property is changed.

PARAMETERS:
- `evt`—A `PropertyChangEvent` object that describes the event source and the property that has been changed.

Interface java.beans.PropertyEditor
public interface PropertyEditor

This interface allows an application builder to create a class that provides support for setting the property value of a given type. The `PropertyEditor` helps make this editing possible in the most intuitive manner. This interface is long and confusing, and this should be implemented through the `PropertyEditorSupport` class which implements each method through no-ops. The simplest `PropertyEditors` will provide support only for the `getAsText()` and `setAsText()` methods, while more complex `PropertyEditors` will provide a GUI through `paintValue()`, or even `getCustomEditor()`. If a `PropertyEditor` does not support a custom editor it must support the `getAsText()` method and all `PropertyEditors` must support the `setValue()` method. Because the `PropertyEditor` cannot access the value (except through `setValue()`), the constructor should be null.

public abstract void setValue(Object value)

This method is used to to set or update the object that this `PropertyEditor` manages. Primitive types must be wrapped with their respective `java.lang.*` object type.

PARAMETERS:
- **value**—The object to be edited. **PropertyEditor** should not modify this object, but should create a new object to hold any modified value.

public abstract Object getValue()

This gets the value of the value **PropertyEditor** is managing.

RETURNS: The value of the property. Primitive types will be wrapped according to their respective object types.

public abstract boolean isPaintable()

This informs the user, or tool, if this **PropertyEditor** is associated with a GUI.

RETURNS: "**true**" if the **PropertyEditor** has a valid **paintValue()** method.

public abstract void paintValue (Graphics gfx,Rectangle box)

This paints a representation of the value on the screen. The **PropertyEditor**'s space is limited to the area described by the parameters. A **paintValue()** method that is not used should be implemented as a silent no-op.

PARAMETERS:
- **gfx**—The graphics object in which to paint.
- **Box**—A rectangle within **gfx** in which the **PropertyEditor** should paint.

public abstract String getJavaInitializationString()

This method can be used to generate Java code to set the value of the property. It returns a string fragment of Java code that can be used to initialize the property value.

RETURNS: A string representing Java code to initialize the value.

public abstract String getAsText()

This method allows the application builder to simply retrieve the value of a property. Note that not all PropertyEditors will support this method.

RETURNS: A string, usable by humans, that is the property value. If the property value cannot be represented as a string this method returns **null**.

public abstract void setAsText(String text) throws IllegalArgumentException

This method sets the property value by parsing a String. **setAsText()** should be able to parse the string returned by **getAsText()**. If this property cannot be expressed as text then the **IllegalArgumentException** may be thrown.

PARAMETERS:
■ **text**—The String to be parsed.

public abstract String[] getTags()

This method can be used to represent **enum** values. If the property must be one of a known set of values, then this method returns those values. If a **PropertyEditor** supports this method, then it should support the two **xxxAsText()** methods, using the tags.

RETURNS: The tag values for this property, if they exist. Otherwise this method returns **null**.

public abstract Component getCustomEditor()

A **PropertyEditor** may choose to make available a full custom Component that edits its property value. It is the responsibility of the **PropertyEditor** to hook itself up to its editor Component and to report property value changes by firing a **PropertyChange** event.

RETURNS: A `java.awt.Component` that allows an application builder to directly edit the current property value. If this is not supported, this method returns `null`.

public abstract boolean supportsCustomEditor()

RETURNS: "`true`" if the `PropertyEditor` provides a custom editor.

public abstract void addPropertyChangeListener (PropertyChangeListener listener)

`PropertyEditors` are required to inform any listeners of changes to the value, if they are registered. Thus, when a `PropertyEditor` changes its value, it should fire a `PropertyChangeEvent` to all registered listeners.

PARAMETERS:
- `listener`—A listener to be informed when a `PropertyChangeEvent` is fired.

public abstract void removePropertyChangeListener (PropertyChangeListener listener)

Parameters:
- `listener`—The listener to be removed.

Interface java.beans.VetoableChangeListener public interface VetoableChangeListener extends EventListener

This interface must be implemented by any object which wishes to listen to `VetoableChange` events being fired. Whenever a Bean changes a constrained property a `VetoableChange` event is fired. A Bean must register itself as a `VetoableChangeListener` with a source Bean to be informed of constrained property updates.

public abstract void vetoableChange (PropertyChangeEvent evt) throws PropertyVetoException

This method is called when a constrained property is changed. Each `VetoableChangeListener` must implement this method. If a listener does not agree with a property change it may throw a `PropertyVetoException`.

PARAMETERS:
- `evt`—A `PropertyChangeEvent` object informing the listener about the event source and the updated property.

Interface java.beans.Visibility
public interface Visibility

This interface allows the environment to query the Bean as to its need for a GUI, and allows the Bean to inform the environment of its GUI needs. When JavaBeans are deployed in embedded applications, the host operating system may not have a GUI available. This interface allows Beans the ability to determine this information and act accordingly. This interface is only for expert developers and most Beans will never need it.

public abstract boolean needsGui()

This method is used by the environment to query the Bean about its needs.

RETURNS: "`true`" if the Bean requires a GUI to complete its task.

public abstract void dontUseGui()

This method is used by the run-time environment to inform the Bean not to use the GUI.

public abstract void okToUseGui()

This method is used by the run-time environment to inform the Bean that it is acceptable to use the GUI.

public abstract boolean avoidingGui()

This method is used by the environment to query the Bean about its current state.

RETURNS: "true" if the Bean is currently not using the GUI, because of a call to dontUseGui().

Class java.beans.BeanDescriptor
public class BeanDescriptor
extends FeatureDescriptor

The BeanDescriptor class can provide information about a Bean such as its class or displayName (through FeatureDescriptor). It also keeps track of a Bean's customizer class. BeanDescriptor, as well as other descriptors, are returned by BeanInfo objects to describe Beans.

public BeanDescriptor(Class beanClass)

If a Bean doesn't have a customizer, use this constructor.

PARAMETERS:
▪ beanClass—The Class object that implements the Bean. For example, sun.beans.Button.class.

public BeanDescriptor
(Class beanClass,Class customizerClass)

If a Bean has a customizer, use this constructor.

PARAMETERS:

■ **beanClass**—The **Class** object that implements the Bean. For example, **sun.beans.Button.class**.

■ **customizerClass**—The **Class** object that implements the Bean's **Customizer**.

public Class getBeanClass()

RETURNS: The **class** object of the Bean.

public Class getCustomizerClass()

RETURNS: The **class** object of the Bean's customizer. If the Bean has no customizer the method returns **null**.

Class java.beans.Beans
public class Beans
extends Object

The **Beans** class provides methods to instantiate Beans, determine if objects are Beans, and a few other things. Both Beans and tools may find this class useful.

public Beans()
public static Object instantiate
(ClassLoader cls,String beanName)
throws IOException,
ClassNotFoundException

This is used to instantiate a Bean. The **beanName** may represent either a serialized object or a class. **Beans.instantiate()** first converts the name to a resource pathname and adds a **".ser"** suffix. It then tries to read the serialized object from that file. If successful, it then attempts to load the **beanName** class and create an instance of it. For example, if you gave the **beanName** of **"foo.bar.etc"** **Beans.instantiate()** tries to read a serialized object from **"foo/bar/etc.ser"**. If it fails, it then loads and instantiates **"foo.bar.etc"**.

PARAMETERS:

- **classLoader**—If you want to use the default system class loader, set this to **null**.
- **beanName**—The fully qualified class name of the Bean to create.

public static Object getInstanceOf (Object bean,Class targetType)

This returns an instance of an object from the Bean passed in as the first parameter with the type view of **targetType**. The return value may be the object passed in or another object. If the specified **targetType** for that Bean is not present, the Bean is returned.

PARAMETERS:

- **bean**—The object from which you want a view.
- **targetType**—The view that you want.

public static boolean isInstanceOf (Object bean,Class targetType)

This is similar to **getInstanceOf()**, and returns **true** if a Bean contains a **targetType** type view.

PARAMETERS:

- **bean**—The object from which you want a view.
- **targetType**—The view that you want.

RETURNS: "**true**" if the given Bean is of the given **targetType**.

public static boolean isDesignTime()

This tells if the Bean has been instantiated in a design tool.

RETURNS: "**true**" if the Bean is running in a development tool.

`public static boolean isGuiAvailable()`

This tells if the Bean is an environment that supports an interactive GUI.

RETURNS: "`true`" if the Bean is running in a environment that supports an interactive GUI to provide dialog boxes, buttons, and so on. Usually this returns `true` in a Windows-based environment.

`public static void setDesignTime (boolean isDesignTime) throws SecurityException`

This sets a global flag indicating that the Bean is in an application builder environment. Applets are not allowed to set this flag.

PARAMETERS:
▓ `isDesignTime`—"true" if the Bean is in a development tool.

`public static void setGuiAvailable (boolean isGuiAvailable) throws SecurityException`

This sets a global flag indicating that the Bean is in an environment that supports an interactive GUI. Applets are not allowed to set this flag.

PARAMETERS:
▓ `isGuiAvailable`—"`true`" if GUI interaction is possible.

`Class java.beans.EventSetDescriptor public class EventSetDescriptor extends FeatureDescriptor`

This class describes a group of events that a Bean fires. Each `EventSetDescriptor` object describes the events for a single listener interface, as a listener interface can have several event target methods.

public EventSetDescriptor (Class sourceClass,String eventSetName,Class listenerType, String listenerMethodName) throws IntrospectionException

This constructor creates an **EventSetDescriptor** properly only if you are following the JavaBeans conventions in which each event "X" delivers the call to interface **Xlistener** that has a single argument of type **XEvent**, registers the **XListener** via **addXListener** at the source component, and removes it via the **removeXListener** method.

PARAMETERS:

▒ **sourceClass**—The class that can fire the event.

▒ **eventSetName**—The internal program name of the event.

▒ **listenerType**—The events will be delivered to the class of the target interface.

▒ **listenerMethodName**—The method called when the event is delivered to **listenerType**.

public EventSetDescriptor(Class sourceClass, String eventSetName,Class listener-Type,String listenerMethodNames[],String addListenerMethodName,String removeListenerMethodName) throws IntrospectionException

This constructor creates the object based purely on the string names given as parameters.

PARAMETERS:

▒ **sourceClass**—The class that can fire the event.

▒ **eventSetName**—The internal program name of the event.

- **listenerType**—The events will be delivered to the class of the target interface.
- **listenerMethodNames**—The methods called when the event is delivered to listenerType.
- **addListenerMethodName**—The method name on the event source used to register an event listener object.
- **removeListenerMethodName**—The method name on the event source used to remove an event listener object from the queue of listening objects.

public EventSetDescriptor (String eventSetName, Class listenerType,Method listenerMethods[],Method addListenerMethod,Method removeListenerMethod) throws IntrospectionException

This constructor creates an **EventSetDescriptor** from scratch.

PARAMETERS:

- **eventSetName**—The internal program name of the event.
- **listenerType**—The events delivered to the class of the target interface.
- **listenerMethods**—Array of **Method** objects which describes the event handling methods in the listener object.
- **addListenerMethodName**—The method name on the event source used to register an event listener object.
- **removeListenerMethodName**—The method name on the event source used to remove an event listener object from the queue of listening objects.

```
public EventSetDescriptor
(String eventSetName,Class
listenerType,MethodDescriptor
     listenerMethodDescriptors[],Method
     addListenerMethod,Method
     removeListenerMethod) throws
     IntrospectionException
```

This constructor creates an **EventSetDescriptor** from scratch.

PARAMETERS:
- **eventSetName**—The internal program name of the event.
- **listenerType**—The events delivered to the class of the target interface.
- **listenerMethodDescriptors**—Array of **MethodDescriptor** objects which describes the event handling methods in the listener object.
- **addListenerMethodName**—The method name on the event source used to register an event listener object.
- **removeListenerMethodName**—The method name on the event source used to remove an event listener object from the queue of listening objects.

public Class getListenerType()

RETURNS: The **class** object for the target interface invoked when an event is fired.

public Method[] getListenerMethods()

RETURNS: All the **Method** objects for the methods within the target listener interface that will be invoked when an event is fired.

public MethodDescriptor[] getListenerMethodDescriptors()

RETURNS: All the **MethodDescriptor** objects for the methods within the target listener interface that will be invoked when an event is fired.

public Method getAddListenerMethod()

RETURNS: The method signature for the method used to register a listener.

public Method getRemoveListenerMethod()

RETURNS: The method signature for the method used to de-register a listener.

public void setUnicast(boolean unicast)

Used to set an event group as unicast.

PARAMETERS:
▧ unicast—"true" if unicast.

public boolean isUnicast()

Event sources are generally multicast.

RETURNS: "true" if the event group is unicast. Default is "false".

public void setInDefaultEventSet (boolean inDefaultEventSet)

The default is "true". This allows you to mark an event set as being in the default set.

PARAMETERS:

■ `inDefaultEventSet`—`"true"` if the event set is in the default set.

public boolean isInDefaultEventSet()

This tells if an event set is in the default set.

RETURNS: Defaults to `"true"`. True if the event set is in the default set.

Class java.beans.FeatureDescriptor
public class FeatureDescriptor
extends Object

This class is the `baseclass` for the `PropertyDescriptor`, `EventSetDescriptor`, `MethodDescriptor`, and `BeanDescriptor` classes. It allows a common set of information to be sent and retrieved for each Bean and is often used in conjunction with the `BeanInfo` class.

public FeatureDescriptor()
public String getName()

RETURNS: The internal program name of the feature (be it `property`, `event set`, or method). This name is for internal use only.

public void setName(String name)

This sets the internal name of the feature.

PARAMETERS:

■ `name`—The internal program name of the feature.

public String getDisplayName()

RETURNS: The localized display name for the feature. If no `displayName` is set then the same name from `getName()` is returned.

public void setDisplayName(String displayName)

PARAMETERS:
■ displayName—The localized name for the feature. This name is meant for humans.

public boolean isExpert()

If a feature is "expert," it is intended only for expert users, and application builder tools in beginner mode should hide the feature.

RETURNS: "true" if the feature is only for experts.

public void setExpert(boolean expert)

If a feature is "expert," it is intended only for expert users, and application builder tools in beginner mode should hide the feature.

PARAMETERS:
■ expert—"true" if the feature is only for experts.

public boolean isHidden()

If a feature is "hidden," it is only to be used by tools, and should not be exposed to humans.

RETURNS: "true" if the feature is not to be shown to humans.

public void setHidden(boolean hidden)

If a feature is "hidden," it is only to be used by tools, and should not be exposed to humans.

PARAMETERS:
■ hidden—"true" if the feature is not to be shown to humans.

public String getShortDescription()

This is useful for understanding the use of a feature.

RETURNS: A localized short description of a feature. If it is not set, it defaults to the display name, which if also not set, defaults to the internal program name.

public void setShortDescription (String text)

The localized string to describe a feature should not exceed 40 characters in length.

PARAMETERS:
- text—A localized String to describe the feature.

public void setValue (String attributeName,Object value)

This is an extension mechanism to associate attribute-value pairs for the feature.

PARAMETERS:
- attributeName—The locale-independent attribute name.
- value—The value.

public Object getValue (String attributeName)

This is an extension mechanism to retrieve an associated attribute and value pair for the feature.

PARAMETERS:
- attributeName—The locale-independent attribute name

RETURNS: The value of the attribute. If the attribute is not defined, null is returned.

public Enumeration attributeNames()

This retrieves all of the attributes of the feature at one time.

RETURNS: An object of type `java.util.Enumeration` that consists of all of the attributes that exist for the feature.

Class java.beans.IndexedPropertyDescriptor public class IndexedPropertyDescriptor extends PropertyDescriptor

This class is a subclass of `PropertyDescriptor` and thus functions similarly. However, it allows the added functionality of describing indexed properties, or properties that are arrays and have indexed read and/or indexed write methods. Indexed properties may also provide more traditional non-indexed read and write methods. If they do so, then they must read and write arrays of the same type returned by the indexed read method.

public IndexedPropertyDescriptor (String propertyName, Class beanClass) throws IntrospectionException

This constructor creates an `IndexedPropertyDescriptor` for a property that follows the JavaBeans convention of having `getX` and `setX` accessor methods for indexed access and array access. It assumes there are two `getX` methods and two `setX` methods.

PARAMETERS:
- `propertyName`—The internal program name of the property.
- `beanClass`—The `Class` object for the target Bean.

public IndexedPropertyDescriptor (String propertyName,Class beanClass, String getterName,String setterName,String indexedGetterName,String indexedSetterName) throws IntrospectionException

This constructor uses the name of the property and a complete set of accessor method names to construct the **IndexedPropertyDescriptor**.

PARAMETERS:

- **propertyName**—The internal program name of the property.

- **beanClass**—The **Class** object for the target Bean.

- **getterName**—The method name for reading property values as an array. If the property must be indexed or is write-only this parameter should be null.

- **setterName**—The method name for writing property values as an array. If the property must be indexed or is read-only this parameter should be null.

- **indexedGetterName**—The method name for reading indexed property values. If the property is write-only this parameter should be null.

- **indexedSetterName**—The method name for writing indexed property values. If the property is read-only this parameter should be null.

public IndexedPropertyDescriptor (String propertyName,Method getter,Method setter,Method indexedGetter,Method indexedSetter) throws IntrospectionException

This constructor takes the program name and four accessor **Method** objects for both reading and writing.

PARAMETERS:

▨ `propertyName`—The internal program name of the property.

▨ `getter`—The method for reading property values as an array. If the property must be indexed or is write-only this parameter should be null.

▨ `setter`—The method for writing property values as an array. If the property must be indexed or is read-only this parameter should be null.

▨ `indexedGetter`—The method for reading indexed property values. If the property is write-only this parameter should be null.

▨ `indexedSetter`—The method for writing indexed property values. If the property is read-only this parameter should be null.

public Method getIndexedReadMethod()

RETURNS: The `Method` object containing the method for reading indexed property values. If the property is not indexed or write-only this function will return `null`.

public Method getIndexedWriteMethod()

RETURNS: The `Method` object containing the method for writing indexed property values. If the property is not indexed or read-only this function will return `null`.

public Class getIndexedPropertyType()

RETURNS: The `class` for the indexed properties type. The `class` may describe a primitive such as `"boolean"`.

Class java.beans.Introspector
public class Introspector
extends Object

This class provides a way for tools or applications to learn about a JavaBean and have a comprehensive understanding of the properties, fired events, and public methods of a Bean. The Introspector analyzes the Bean's class and superclasses to build a **BeanInfo** object, which describes the target Bean. If the Bean has an accompanying **BeanInfo** class, this **BeanInfo** object is returned. For a class "**x**," a corresponding **BeanInfo** class should be entitled "**XBeanInfo**". If no **BeanInfo** class is found in this way, the **Introspector** class takes the final classname component of the name ("**XBeanInfo**") and searches for it in each package in the **BeanInfo** package search path. If none is found, the **Introspector** class will create a **BeanInfo** object on the fly. If no explicit **BeanInfo** exists, **Introspector** will use low-level reflection to examine the Bean and the Bean class's superclass and construct **BeanInfo** on the fly. **Introspector** will continue to analyze up the superclass chain and add this new information to **BeanInfo**. One more note: All of **Introspector**'s methods are static, so **Introspector** objects never need to be instantiated.

public static BeanInfo getBeanInfo (Class beanClass) throws IntrospectionException

This introspects on a JavaBean and merges all **BeanInfo** descriptions of every parent of the Bean. Information collected involves properties, public methods, and events.

PARAMETERS:
■ **beanClass**—The Bean class to be introspected upon.

RETURNS: A **BeanInfo** object describing beanClass and its parents.

public static BeanInfo getBeanInfo (Class beanClass,Class stopClass) throws IntrospectionException

This introspects on a JavaBean and merges **BeanInfo** descriptions of each superclass below a given stop point. Information collected involves properties, public methods, and events.

PARAMETERS:

- **beanClass**—The Bean class to be introspected upon.

- **stopClass**—The **baseclass** at which the analysis stops. Any features in the **stopClass** or its **superclasses** will not be included in the returned **BeanInfo**.

RETURNS: A **BeanInfo** object.

public static String decapitalize(String name)

This helps a string conform to Java name conventions. In Java, the first character of a variable is normally lower-case. In addition, if the first two characters are upper-case then the string is left as is. So "JavaBean" becomes **"javaBean"**, but "URL" remains **"URL"**.

PARAMETERS:

- **name**—The string to be decapitalized.

RETURNS: The decapitalized **string** instance.

public static String[] getBeanInfoSearchPath()

RETURNS: The array of package names that will be searched in order to find **BeanInfo** classes if there is no accompanying **BeanInfo** class. Defaults to {**"sun.beans.infos"**}.

public static void setBeanInfoSearchPath(String path[])

This changes the list of package names that will be used for finding **BeanInfo** classes. It defaults to {**"sun.beans.infos"**}.

PARAMETERS:

- **path**—Array of package names to be searched on Introspection.

Class java.beans.MethodDescriptor
public class MethodDescriptor
extends FeatureDescriptor

This class describes which public methods a JavaBean has available in its interface to other components. The primary use of **MethodDescriptor** objects comes in **overriding BeanInfo.getMethodDescriptors()**.

public MethodDescriptor(Method method)

PARAMETERS:
- **method**—A **Method** object describing the method to be added to the public interface.

public MethodDescriptor (Method method, ParameterDescriptor parameterDescriptors[])

PARAMETERS:
- **method**—A **Method** object describing the method to be added to the public interface.
- **parameterDescriptors**—Descriptive information for each of the method's parameters.

public Method getMethod()

This is used to determine the method to which the **MethodDescriptor** applies.

RETURNS: The **Method** object representing the method.

public ParameterDescriptor[] getParameterDescriptors()

RETURNS: The locale-independent descriptions of the parameters. If the parameter names aren't known the method will return a null array.

Class java.beans.ParameterDescriptor
public class ParameterDescriptor
extends FeatureDescriptor

This class allows Bean developers to disseminate additional information about each parameter in a method. This information augments the low-level type information provided by the `java.lang.reflect.Method` class. This class derives all of its functionality from its super class `FeatureDescriptor`.

public ParameterDescriptor()
Class java.beans.PropertyChangeEvent
public class PropertyChangeEvent
extends EventObject

This class represents the new event model in AWT 1.1 and is the event model for JavaBeans 1.0. Whenever a bound or constrained property changes, a `PropertyChange` Event is delivered to either `propertyChange()` or `vetoableChange()`. These two methods are the sole methods of the `PropertyChangeListener` and VetoableChangeListener interfaces, respectively. `PropertyChangeEvents` contains a number of properties, such as event name, old value, and new value, that allow event handlers to effectively manage the events that are fired. If either the new or old value is a primitive, it must be wrapped using the `java.lang.*` Object type. If the values of the old and new values are not known, null values may be provided. An event source may send a null object as the name to signal that an arbitrary set of its properties have changed.

public PropertyChangeEvent(Object source, String propertyName, Object oldValue, Object newValue)

Each time an event is fired a PropertyChangeEvent is constructed.

PARAMETERS:
- `source`—The Bean that fired the event.
- `propertyName`—The internal program name of the property that was changed.

- **oldValue**—The property's old value.
- **newValue**—The property's new value.

public String getPropertyName()

RETURNS: The internal program name of the property that was changed. May be null if multiple properties have changed.

public Object getNewValue()

RETURNS: The property's new value. If the value is a primitive it will be wrapped in an equivalent object representation. May be null if multiple properties have changed.

public Object getOldValue()

RETURNS: The property's old value. If the value is a primitive it will be wrapped in an equivalent object representation. May be null if multiple properties have changed.

public void setPropagationId (Object propagationId)

If a listener receives an event and then fires its own, it must call this method to ensure that the **propagationId** value is passed from the incoming event to the outgoing event.

PARAMETERS:
- **propagationId**—The propagationId object for the event.

public Object getPropagationId()

The **"propagationId"** field is primarily being reserved for future use. However, JavaBeans 1.0 requires that a listener that catches a **PropertyChangeEvent** and then proceeds to fire a **PropertyChangEvent** of its own is required to pass on the same **propagationId** value from the incoming event to the outgoing event.

RETURNS: The **propagationId** object associated with a bound/constrained property update.

Class java.beans.PropertyChangeSupport
public class PropertyChangeSupport
extends Object
implements Serializable

This class is provided to help Beans manage their bound properties. This class can manage the registration and notification of the listeners of various bound properties. To use this class, a Bean can be subclassed from it, or an instance of this class can exist as a member field of your Bean. We recommend the latter option.

public PropertyChangeSupport
(Object sourceBean)

PARAMETERS:
- **sourceBean**—The Bean for which the **PropertyChangeSupport** class will manage bound properties.

public synchronized void
addPropertyChangeListener
(PropertyChangeListener listener)
Adds a PropertyChangeListener to the
list of listeners.

PARAMETERS:
- **listener**—The PropertyChangeListener to be added. Usually adds this pointer as the object implements the PropertyChangeListener interface.

public synchronized void removePropertyChangeListener (PropertyChangeListener listener)

Removes a PropertyChangeListener to the list of listeners.

PARAMETERS:

■ `listener`—The PropertyChangeListener to be removed

public void firePropertyChange (String propertyName,Object oldValue, Object newValue)

Fires event to all registered listeners. If `oldValue` and `newValue` are equal and non-null, no event is fired.

PARAMETERS:

■ `propertyName`—The internal program name of the property that was changed.

■ `oldValue`—The property's old value. Primitive types must be wrapped as objects.

■ `newValue`—The property's new value. Primitive types must be wrapped as objects.

Class java.beans.PropertyDescriptor public class PropertyDescriptor extends FeatureDescriptor

This class fully describes one property that a Bean exports through the `get`/`set` methods.

```
public PropertyDescriptor(String propertyName,Class
    beanClass) throws IntrospectionException
```

This constructor assumes that the property follows standard Java conventions and has the `getX` and `setX` accessor methods.

PARAMETERS:

- **propertyName**—The internal program name of the property.

- **beanClass**—The **Class** object for the Bean which has the property. For example, **sun.beans.Button.class**.

public PropertyDescriptor (String propertyName,Class beanClass,String getterName,String setterName) throws IntrospectionException

PARAMETERS:

- **propertyName**—The internal program name of the property.

- **beanClass**—The **Class** object for the Bean which has the property. For example, **sun.beans.Button.class**.

- **getterName**—The **String** name of the method used for reading the property value. If the property is write-only this parameter should be null.

- **setterName**—The **String** name of the method used for writing the property value. If the property is read-only this parameter should be null.

public PropertyDescriptor(String propertyName,Method getter,Method setter) throws IntrospectionException

PARAMETERS:

- **propertyName**—The internal program name of the property.

- **getter**—The method (**Method** object) used for reading the property value. If the property is write-only this parameter should be null.

- **setter**—The method (**Method** object) used for writing the property value. If the property is read-only this parameter should be null.

public Class getPropertyType()

This is used to determine the **class** of the property.

RETURNS: The type information for the property. The **class** object may also indicated a primitive type such as **"boolean"**. The result may be null if the property is an indexed property that doesn't support non-indexed access.

public Method getReadMethod()

RETURNS: The **Method** object that should be used to read the **property** value—the **getter** method. If the property can't be read it should return null.

public Method getWriteMethod()

RETURNS: The **Method** object that should be used to write the **property** value—the **setter** method. If the property can't be written it should return null.

public boolean isBound()

Only updates to bound properties will cause a **PropertyChangeEvent** to be fired when the property is changed. This method determines if the property can expect that sort of behavior.

RETURNS: **"true"** if the property is bound.

public void setBound(boolean bound)

Only updates to bound properties will cause a **PropertyChangeEvent** to be fired when the property is changed. This method allows this sort of behavior to be defined for the property.

PARAMETERS:
■ bound—**"true"** if this property is bound.

public boolean isConstrained()

Only updates to constrained properties will cause a **VetoableChangeEvent** to be fired when the property is changed. This method determines if the property can expect that sort of behavior.

RETURNS: "**true**" if the property is constrained.

public void setConstrained (boolean constrained)

Only updates to constrained properties will cause a **VetoableChangeEvent** to get fired when the property is changed. This method allows this sort of behavior to be defined for the property.

PARAMETERS:
- **constrained**—"**true**" if this property is constrained.

public void setPropertyEditorClass (Class propertyEditorClass)

PropertyEditors usually use the **PropertyEditorManager**. But if you want to associate a certain **PropertyEditor** with a given property use this method.

PARAMETERS:
- **propertyEditorClass**—The **Class** for the desired **PropertyEditor**.

public Class getPropertyEditorClass()

RETURNS: A **PropertyEditor** Class that has been registered for this property with this **PropertyDescriptor** class. Usually the **PropertyEditorManager** is used by **PropertyEditors**, so this method will return **null**.

Class java.beans.PropertyEditorManager
public class PropertyEditorManager
extends Object

This class can be used to both register and find property editors for any given type names. The property editors must support the **java.beans.PropertyEditor** interface to be valid.

To locate an editor for a given type, the **PropertyEditorManager** goes through three steps: First, it has a **registerEditor** method that allows a programmer to specifically link a type to a property editor class. Second, it adds **"Editor"** to the fully qualified classname and searches for it. Finally, it takes the simple classname, appends **"Editor"** and looks in a search-path of packages. Default **PropertyEditors** are provided for all the primitive types, as well as the classes **java.lang.String**, **java.awt.Color**, and **java.awt.Font**. A final note: All the methods of this class are static, so there is no need to instantiate it.

public PropertyEditorManager()
public static void registerEditor
(Class targetType, Class editorClass)

This registers an editor class to edit values of a certain type of class.

PARAMETERS:

- **targetType**—the **Class** object of the type to be edited
- **editorClass**—the **Class** object of the **editor** class. If this is null, then any existing definition will be removed.

public static PropertyEditor
findEditor(Class targetType)

This finds an editor for a given class type.

PARAMETERS:

- **targetType**—The **Class** object for the type to be edited

RETURNS: An editor object that conforms to the **PropertyEditor** interface. A null result means no editor was found.

public static String[] getEditorSearchPath()

RETURNS: An array of package names that will be searched in order to find property editors. Defaults to `"sun.beans.editors"`.

public static void setEditorSearchPath (String path[])

This allows the programmer to change the set of package names that will be searched for property editors.

PARAMETERS:

■ **path**—Array of package names.

Class java.beans.PropertyEditorSupport

public class PropertyEditorSupport extends Object implements PropertyEditor

This class is a skeleton class that provides an implementation of the **PropertyEditor** interface. The current implementation of each method uses no-ops, so you can override only specific methods. Please see the **PropertyEditor** interface to see the definition of each method. There are several ways of using the **PropertyEditorSupport** class. If you create a property editor as a direct subclass of the **PropertyEditorSupport** class, then you simply use the default constructor. However, you can also use an instance of the **PropertyEditorSupport** class in the editor you create and delegate most of the work to this instance. If you do this, you should use the second constructor. Also, the **firePropertyChange()** method is called whenever **setValue()** is called.

protected PropertyEditorSupport()

This constructor is used by derived **PropertyEditor** classes.

protected PropertyEditorSupport(Object source)

This constructor is used when a `PropertyEditor` is delegated to use.

PARAMETERS:
- `source`—The source to use for any events fired.

Class java.beans.SimpleBeanInfo
public class SimpleBeanInfo
extends Object
implements BeanInfo

This class is a skeleton class that provides an implementation of the `BeanInfo` interface. The current implementation of each method uses no-ops, so you can override only specific methods. Every method that is not overriden results in an action being denied to anyone querying the Bean about its properties. Please see the `BeanInfo` interface to see the definition of each method. One item to notice is the method `loadImage()`, which makes overriding `getIcon()` much easier.

public SimpleBeanInfo()
public Image loadImage(String resourceName)

This is a simple utility method used in conjunction with `getIcon()` to help load icon images. It takes the name of a resource file associated with the current object's class file and loads an image object (usually a GIF).

PARAMETERS:
- `resourceName`—A pathname that is relative to the directory holding the `.class` file of the current class.

RETURNS: An image object is returned. If the load failed it returns null.

Class java.beans.VetoableChangeSupport
public class VetoableChangeSupport
extends Object
implements Serializable

This class is a support class for Beans that support constrained properties. This class, similar to **PropertyChangeSupport**, manages the low-level details of registering listeners of a property, as well as informing them when a change takes place. Most importantly, this class also manages the chain reaction which occurs when a listener vetoes a change. You can either use a subclass of this class or you can use an instance of this class as a member of your Bean. Be careful not to use the **getter** method of a constrained property because this method will not reflect the new value until all listeners have agreed, even though the value has changed.

public VetoableChangeSupport
(Object sourceBean)

Constructor method

PARAMETERS:
- **sourceBean**—the Bean for which **VetoableChangeSupport** will manage a property.

public synchronized void
addVetoableChangeListener
(VetoableChangeListener listener)

Adds a **VetoableListener** to the list of listeners.

PARAMETERS:
- **listener**—The **VetoableChangeListener** to be added to the list.

public synchronized void removeVetoableChangeListener (VetoableChangeListener listener)

This removes a `VetoableChangeListener` from the list of listeners.

PARAMETERS:
▨ `listener`—The `VetoableChangeListener` to be removed from the list.

public void fireVetoableChange (String propertyName,Object oldValue,Object newValue) throws PropertyVetoException

This informs all registered listeners of a vetoable property update. If someone vetoes the change this method then fires a new event informing all listeners to reregister the old value, and then rethrows the `PropertyVetoException`. If the old and new event are both equal and non-null then no event is fired.

PARAMETERS:
▨ `propertyName`—The internal program name of the property that has changed.
▨ `oldValue`—The property's old value.
▨ newValue—The property's new value.

Class java.beans.IntrospectionException public class IntrospectionException extends Exception

This class represents the exception thrown when an exception happens during the process of introspection. Some of the typical reasons for this exception being thrown include failure to map a string class name to a `Class` object, failure to resolve a string method name, or specifying a method name that has the wrong type signature for its intended use.

public IntrospectionException(String mess)

PARAMETERS:

▨ **mess**—A message printed when an **IntrospectionException** is thrown.

Class java.beans.PropertyVetoException public class PropertyVetoException extends Exception

This class represents the exception thrown when a proposed change to a property is unacceptable to a listener. The **PropertyChangeEvent** that caused the exception to be thrown is required by the constructor, but this can simply be passed down from **VetoableChangeListener.vetoableChange()**, which must be implemented by each listener in order to veto a property change.

public PropertyVetoException (String mess,PropertyChangeEvent evt)

PARAMETERS:

▨ **mess**—A message printed when a **PropertyVetoException** is thrown.

▨ **evt**—A **PropertyChangeEvent** describing the vetoed change.

public PropertyChangeEvent getPropertyChangeEvent()

This returns the **PropertyChangeEvent** that caused the exception to be thrown.

Partial Package java.util

Though the interfaces and classes below are not a part of the **java.beans** package, they are heavily utilized by the JavaBeans model and are a part of the new event model for JDK 1.1.

Interface java.util.EventListener
public interface EventListener

This interface is the prototypical interface from which all event listener interfaces are derived. This interface has no methods, and represents merely a way to identify event listeners. Convention states that all derived `EventListener` interfaces specify their event notification methods according to the following method signature: `public void eventNotificationMethodName(EventType e);`.

Class java.util.EventObject
public class EventObject
extends Object

The `Event` class is the abstract root class from which all event state objects are derived. Events are constructed with reference to an object source, or the object which fired the event.

public EventObject(Object source)

Constructs a prototypical event.

PARAMETERS:
- `source`—The object that fired the Event.

public Object getSource()

RETURNS: The object that fired the Event.

Class java.util.TooManyListenersException public class TooManyListenersException extends Exception

This class represents the exception thrown when the application developer desires a unicast special case of a multicast **Event Source**. Simply put this exception allows only one concurrently registered event listener for a given event listener source

public TooManyListenersException()

This is a constructor for a **TooManyListenersException** with no descriptive message.

public TooManyListenersException(String s)

This is a constructor for a **TooManyListenersException** with a descriptive message.

PARAMETERS:
- **s**—The message to describe the exception.

Appendix B

Adobe Acrobat Control for ActiveX

Adobe Systems, Inc.
http://www.adobe.com/
345 Park Avenue
San Jose, CA 951102704

This control will enable you to view an Acrobat file (PDF extension) in Internet Explorer. If you embed the PDF file in an HTML file and you have the control installed, then you will be able to see the PDF file's contents without any hassle. With Microsoft Internet Explorer 3.0 and 3.01, this control is automatically downloaded and installed. With Microsoft Internet Explorer 3.02 , the control will automatically download and install only if your security in MSIE is checked as medium or none.

At the time of this writing, a new version of the Adobe Acrobat Control for ActiveX was to be released in July 1997 for Microsoft Internet Explorer 4.0.

QuantumChess

Brilliance Labs, Inc.
http://www.brlabs.com
700 SW 62nd Blvd.
Suite H105
Gainesville, FL 32607

Do you like to play chess? Try out **QuantumChess**, one of the first ActiveX Controls available for playing free head-to-head games on the Internet. The **QuantumChess** control allows players to stay in their Web browser and play chess with people from anywhere from the world. The players are connected via the lobby server component in the company's Web page.

CyberGO ActiveX Control

Brilliance Labs, Inc.

http://www.brlabs.com

700 SW 62nd Blvd.

Suite H105

Gainesville, FL 32607

CyberGO (based on the world's oldest game, GO) is a control that lets you play games against opponents from anywhere in the world. All you need is an ActiveX enabled browser.

VR Scout Control

Chaco Communications, Inc.

http://www.chaco.com/

10164 Parkwood Drive, Suite 8

Cupertino, CA 950141533

You can explore 3-D worlds using the **VR Scout** ActiveX control in the Web browser. Using this control, you can fly through a 3-D scene and rotate or walk through 3-D objects. Some VRML 2.0 animation can be viewed using this control.

Light Lib Images

DFL Software, Inc.

http://www.dfl.com

55 Eglinton Avenue East

Suite 208

Toronto, ON M4P 1G8 CANADA

Light Lib Images is a high-performance document and image management ActiveX control. It not only supports all popular image file formats, but also has capabilities such as advanced compression and dithering.

Light Lib Magic Menus

DFL Software, Inc.

http://www.dfl.com

55 Eglinton Avenue East

Suite 208

Toronto, ON M4P 1G8 CANADA

The **Light Lib Magic Menus** control provides innovative menuing and user interfaces. These menus are alternatives for applications, Web sites, and intranets. There are two versions available: Standard and Pro.

Light Lib Multimedia

DFL Software, Inc.

http://www.dfl.com

55 Eglinton Avenue East, Suite 208

Toronto, ON M4P 1G8 CANADA

The **Light Lib Multimedia** control also has two editions. The Standard Edition includes video and sound file managing, processing, and playback capabilities. The Pro edition includes the ability of Optimized BLOB Support (with compression).

Citrix WinFrame ICA control

Citrix Systems, Inc.

http://www.citrix.com

210 University Drive

Suite 700

Coral Springs, FL 33071

With Citrix' **WinFrame ICA** control, you can run a Windows application anywhere and execute the user interface somewhere else. This control allows 16/32-bit and client/server applications to perform at high speed over slow connections. The control supports any application such as Microsoft Access, Excel, Word, and Lotus Notes.

Cal32

DameWare Development

`http://www.dameware.com/`

1024 Live Oak Loop

Mandeville, LA 70448

DameWare's **Cal32** ActiveX control is a calendar custom control that can be used with Visual Basic, Visual C++, or a Web page. Many of the properties of the control have a date range between January 1, 100 through December 31, 9999. You can change the text colors, font styles, tool tips, context menu, and more.

ChkList

DameWare Development

`http://www.dameware.com/`

1024 Live Oak Loop

Mandeville, LA 70448

Check List-Box is another control that can be used with VB, Visual C++, WEB, and so on. Compared to the old multiple select list-box, this control is very user-friendly and customizable. Some of its customizable properties are fonts, colors, and 3-D.

InfoTick

DameWare Development

`http://www.dameware.com/`

1024 Live Oak Loop

Mandeville, LA 70448

DameWare's **InfoTick** ActiveX control is a 32-bit Information Ticker that can be used with VB, Visual C++, Web Page, and so on. You can customize the ticker to suit your needs.

NetList

DameWare Development

http://www.dameware.com/

1024 Live Oak Loop

Mandeville, LA 70448

The **NetList** ActiveX control is a 32-bit Network Resource Browser custom control that can also be used with VB, Visual C++, Web, and so on. Some of its customizable properties are resource type, comments, and context menu.

RasDial

DameWare Development

http://www.dameware.com/

1024 Live Oak Loop

Mandeville, LA 70448

DameWare's **RasDial** ActiveX control is a 32-bit Remote Access Service custom control that can be used with VB, Visual C++, and so on. This control is great for applications that need a specific network connection. If the application is already on a network, you can work on the application and disconnect.

TapiDial

DameWare Development

http://www.dameware.com/

1024 Live Oak Loop

Mandeville, LA 70448

DameWare's **TapiDial** ActiveX control is a 32-bit phone-dialing custom control that can be used with VB, Visual C++, Web, and so on. This easy-to-use control makes it simple to add phone dialing to any application or Web page.

DynamiCube

Data Dynamics, Ltd.

http://www.datadynamics.com

2600 Tiller Lane

Columbus, OH 43231

DynamiCube is a 32-bit ActiveX control that provides high-speed data analysis as well as dynamic OLAP views. It supports DAO, RDO, BDE &and ODBC, and it stores multi-dim data views to a summarized microCube. This can be used for Web publishing and E-Mail.

V-Active ActiveX Control

Ephyx Technologies, Ltd.

http://www.ephyx.com

P.O.Box 12503

9 Maskit St.

Herzliya, IL 46733 Israel

If you have created movies combining CD-ROM or Broadband with updated Web information by using the V-Active Authoring Tool, this control will play them.

Look@Me

Farallon Communications, Inc.

http://www.farallon.com

2470 Mariner Square Loop

Alameda, CA 94501

Look@Me is a free component of Farallon real-time Internet collaboration software Timbuktu Pro. By using Internet Explorer with this control, you can view another user's screen anywhere in the world in real time. Now you can check out the work of a consultant far away from you.

Boolean

FarPoint Technologies, Inc.

`http://www.fpoint.com`

133 Southcenter Court

Suite 1000

Morrisville, NC 27560

This control lets you add true/false functionality to your application. You can customize the control by accessing the property pages.

Mask

FarPoint Technologies, Inc.

`http://www.fpoint.com`

133 Southcenter Court

Suite 1000

Morrisville, NC 27560

The **Mask** control restricts data from being entered into the control. With this control, you can force users to input numbers only, letters only, any character, hexadecimal, upper- or lower-case letters and literal characters in the application.

Text

FarPoint Technologies, Inc.

`http://www.fpoint.com`

133 Southcenter Court

Suite 1000

Morrisville, NC 27560

This control displays text strings in an application. With this control, you can force upper- or lower-case display, validate passwords, display a place-holding character, or limit the number of characters that can be entered.

Daily PlanIt

FarPoint Technologies, Inc.
`http://www.fpoint.com`
133 Southcenter Court
Suite 1000
Morrisville, NC 27560

`Daily PlanIt` adds flexible scheduling capabilities to your application. You can connect the control to a company-wide scheduling database or verify company-wide appointments. You can even activate an optional alarm alerting you to appointments or password-protect tasks for private viewing. This control works the same as a daily scheduler and you can schedule multiple appointments or tasks across any time interval.

fpCalendar Control

FarPoint Technologies, Inc.
`http://www.fpoint.com`
133 Southcenter Court
Suite 1000
Morrisville, NC 27560

`Calendar Control` allows users to generate fully-customizable calendars for any time period. Yearly, monthly, weekly, and daily display formats are available. The display is completely customizable with menus, fonts, colors, dimensions, text, and pictures.

fpClock Control

FarPoint Technologies, Inc.
`http://www.fpoint.com`
133 Southcenter Court
Suite 1000
Morrisville, NC 27560

`Clock Control` allows time display using default, digital, and analog style clocks. Clock and hand shapes can be user-defined. Different shadows, menu bars, fonts, colors, and so on can be applied.

fpPoster Control

FarPoint Technologies, Inc.

`http://www.fpoint.com`

133 Southcenter Court

Suite 1000

Morrisville, NC 27560

`Poster Control` allows users to display a picture in the control and provide scroll bars if necessary. Picture tints, or bleed-throughs, can be applied, as well as matte and overlay effects.

fpCurrency

FarPoint Technologies, Inc.

`http://www.fpoint.com`

133 Southcenter Court

Suite 1000

Morrisville, NC 27560

The `fpCurrency` control displays monetary values in numerous currency formats with unique currency symbols. Maximum and minimum values can be specified, as well as management of negative values. Different button styles are also provided.

fpDateTime

FarPoint Technologies, Inc.

`http://www.fpoint.com`

133 Southcenter Court

Suite 1000

Morrisville, NC 27560

The `fpDateTime` control displays and formats date and time values. Short and long dates, as well as international options and pop-up and drop-down calendars, are available.

fpDoubleSingle

FarPoint Technologies, Inc.

`http://www.fpoint.com`

133 Southcenter Court

Suite 1000

Morrisville, NC 27560

The `fpDoubleSingle` control displays floating-point numbers. Maximum and minimum values can be set, as well as negative number formats. You can choose from four different button styles.

fpLongInteger

FarPoint Technologies, Inc.

`http://www.fpoint.com`

133 Southcenter Court

Suite 1000

Morrisville, NC 27560

The `fpLongInteger` control displays integers and long integer values. You can specify the format for negative numbers, define maximum and minimum values, and choose from four different button styles.

fpMask

FarPoint Technologies, Inc.

`http://www.fpoint.com`

133 Southcenter Court

Suite 1000

Morrisville, NC 27560

The **fpMask** control restricts the manner in wich data is entered or displayed in the control. Virtually any mask can be created,—social security numbers, ID numbers, zip codes, phone numbers, and so on. Alphanumeric masks are also supported.

fpText

FarPoint Technologies, Inc.

http://www.fpoint.com

133 Southcenter Court

Suite 1000

Morrisville, NC 27560

The fpText control displays text strings. Password support is available and the number of characters can be restricted. You can choose from four button styles.

fpMemo

FarPoint Technologies, Inc.

http://www.fpoint.com

133 Southcenter Court

Suite 1000

Morrisville, NC 27560

The **fpMemo** control displays large text strings. Strings greater than 64K are perfect. Text can be wrapped and the length of a text line can be limited.

Button Control

FarPoint Technologies, Inc.

http://www.fpoint.com

133 Southcenter Court

Suite 1000

Morrisville, NC 27560

Button Control allows the user to create completely customizable buttons. Bitmaps, 3-D styles, and various fonts and colors are available. Button designs can be saved as templates to facilitate future use.

Balloon Control

FarPoint Technologies, Inc.

http://www.fpoint.com

133 Southcenter Court

Suite 1000

Morrisville, NC 27560

Balloon Control displays a bubble when the mouse pointer is over a specified control. Four different balloon shapes and three tail shapes are supported. Text and background colors of the balloons are customizable.

Tab Control

FarPoint Technologies, Inc.

http://www.fpoint.com

133 Southcenter Court

Suite 1000

Morrisville, NC 27560

Tab Control creates user-defined tabs with numerous options. Various styles are predefined or proprietary styles can be created. The tabs can be bound to other objects, or rotated, annotated and so on.

Controlling the Tab's Behavior

FarPoint Technologies, Inc.

http://www.fpoint.com

133 Southcenter Court

Suite 1000

Morrisville, NC 27560

`Tab Behavior` allows programmers to change tab aspects at design or run-time. Its appearance can be set to automatically reflect the current operating system environment (Windows 3.1, Windows 95, Windows NT, etc.). Unique colors and fonts can be applied to the tabs as well.

Imprint Control

FarPoint Technologies, Inc.

`http://www.fpoint.com`

133 Southcenter Court

Suite 1000

Morrisville, NC 27560

`Imprint Control` allows the creation of three-dimensional frames. The control can be sized to its parent object, rotated, or bound to a database field.

Spreadsheet/Grid Control

FarPoint Technologies, Inc.

`http://www.fpoint.com`

133 Southcenter Court

Suite 1000

Morrisville, NC 27560

The `Spreadsheet/Grid` control supports large grids of up to 2 billion rows by 2 billion columns. Unique cells, rows, or columns can be locked. Clipboard shortcut controls (Ctrl-V, etc.) are supported and 33 action properties are predefined to perform various tasks within the spreadsheet.

Fulcrum Document Viewer

Fulcrum Technologies Inc.

`http://www.fulcrum.com`

785 Carling Ave.

Ottawa, ON K1s 5H4 Canada

The **Fulcrum Document Viewer**, along with Fulcrum Surfboard™, permits users to search, navigate, and view non-HTML documents while still in their Web browser. **The Fulcrum Document Viewer** control can display and highlight search results inside a non-HTML document without document conversion.

PhotoPRO

ImageFX

http://www.imagefx.com

3021 Brighton Henrietta Rd.

Rochester, NY 14623

With **PhotoPRO**, you can easily add powerful imaging features to your 32-bit Windows Applications. PhotoPRO can be used with VB, VC++, Delphi, or any 32-bit environment that hosts ActiveX controls.

PlanetFX Image

ImageFX

http://www.imagefx.com

3021 Brighton Henrietta Rd.

Rochester, NY 14623

The **PlanetFX Image** control emulates the standard Visual Basic image control, except that it displays BMP, DIB, GIF, JIF, JPG, PCX, PNG, RLE, TGA, TIF (uncompressed only), WMF, and WPG (raster only) images. Countless variations and effects are available, including resizing, tiling, flipping, rotating, and cropping.

PlanetFX URL

ImageFX

http://www.imagefx.com

3021 Brighton Henrietta Rd.

Rochester, NY 14623

The `PlanetFX URL` control enables users to download files located at any given URL address, abort any download while in progress, and keep track of download progress and error events.

PlanetFX Timer

ImageFX

`http://www.imagefx.com`

3021 Brighton Henrietta Rd.

Rochester, NY 14623

The `PlanetFX Timer` control allows users to create high-frequency periodic-delay events. Both single and periodic events are supported.

PlanetFX Shape

ImageFX

`http://www.imagefx.com`

3021 Brighton Henrietta Rd.

Rochester, NY 14623

The `Shape` control renders a graphical emulation of the VB shape control. This control provides 113 effects, six background styles, 16 predefined shapes, unlimited composition features, and unlimited custom shapes in addition to the VB shape controls.

PlanetFX Rotating Text

ImageFX

`http://www.imagefx.com`

3021 Brighton Henrietta Rd.

Rochester, NY 14623

The `PlanetFX Rotating Text` control provides 113 effects, 16 colored backgrounds and text gradient styles, and 360 degrees of text rotation for True Type fonts.

PlanetFX Label

ImageFX

`http://www.imagefx.com`

3021 Brighton Henrietta Rd.

Rochester, NY 14623

The `PlanetFX Label` control is a VB label control emulation. This control adds 113 main and transition effects, allows for screen image capture, 103 multipass dissolve effects, five text foreground styles, and much more.

Surround Video

Black Diamond Consulting, Inc.

`http://www.bdiamond.com`

195 Hanover Street, Suite 22

Portsmouth, NH 03801

The `Surround Video` control (`SVControl`) is designed to function both as a standard control (it can reside within an OLE container application), and as an Internet control (it knows how to retrieve data by way of the Internet and can be sponsored on a Web page). The `Surround Video Control` processes both `Surround Video Image` files (`*.svi`) and `Surround Video Link` files (`*.svh`). If the user wishes to use the control's ability to perform progressive rendering over the Internet, the file to be downloaded and displayed must be of type `.svh`.

TextX

Intranet 2001, Inc.

`http://www.inet2001.com`

9220 SW Barbur Blvd., #119-282

Portland, OR 97291

`TextX` displays a title (text) and then allows the user to interactively define the shape of the title. The user must specify a path that will be used in defining the shape of the title.

ClearFusionX

Iterated Systems, Inc.

http://www.iterated.com

3525 Piedmont Road

Suite 600, Seven Piedmont Center

Atlanta, GA 30305

`ClearFusionX` allows users to view standard AVI video on demand from any Web site. There are no unique server or firewall configurations required. Windows NT is not currently supported.

ClearVideo Decoder

Iterated Systems, Inc.

http://www.iterated.com

3525 Piedmont Road

Suite 600, Seven Piedmont Center

Atlanta, GA 30305

`ClearVideo Decoder` prevents the hassle of downloading and installing the ClearVideo VFW decoder by using ActiveX technology to automate these tasks. Windows NT is not currently supported.

Fractal ViewerX

Iterated Systems, Inc.

http://www.iterated.com

3525 Piedmont Road

Suite 600, Seven Piedmont Center

Atlanta, GA 30305

`Fractal ViewerX` allows the user to view interactive, photo-quality images on the Web. The user will be able to zoom in and out and view full-screen fractal images with download speeds comparable to traditional JPEG images.

Crescendo and Crescendo PLUS

LiveUpdate

`http://www.liveupdate.com`

400 Research Drive

Wilmington, MA 01887

`Crescendo` and `Crescendo` `PLUS` are Web-enabled music players. `Crescendo` `PLUS` utilizes streaming technology, thereby allowing music to play immediately.

MBED Player

mBED Software

`http://www.mbed.com`

185 Berry Street

Suite 3807

San Francisco, CA 94107

`mBED` `Player` is the only provider of open and high-level solutions for rich media and Web-smart interactivity. Using any text editor and a standard Web format, such as GIF, JPEG, or WAV, administrators can add multimedia enhancements to their Web sites immediately.

Carbon Copy

Microcom, Inc.

`http://www.microcom.com`

500 River Ridge Drive

Norwood, MA 02062

`Carbon` `Copy` allows users to remotely control, access, and administer another PC from anywhere. Users can run applications, transfer files, edit documents and more, as if they were using the remote PC itself.

Label

Microsoft

`http://www.microsoft.com`

One Microsoft Way

Redmond, WA 98052

The **Label** control displays text at any user-specified angle. In addition, the control can render the text along a user-defined curve. **Label** supports Click, Change, MouseDown, MouseOver, and MouseUp events.

Marquee

Microsoft

http://www.microsoft.com

One Microsoft Way

Redmond, WA 98052

The **Marquee** control allows users to scroll any HTML file either horizontally or vertically. The control can also change the amount and delay of scrolling. The control is built into Microsoft's Internet Explorer.

MCSiGrid ControlB

Microsoft

http://www.microsoft.com

One Microsoft Way

Redmond, WA 98052

The **MCSiGrid** control allows users to display data or information in a grid format. The control is intended for use with shopping baskets and other similar applications.

MCSiLabel

Microsoft

http://www.microsoft.com

One Microsoft Way

Redmond, WA 98052

The **Label** control allows users to rotate text (any size, color, or font)in 90 degree increments.

MCSiMenu Control

Microsoft

http://www.microsoft.com

One Microsoft Way

Redmond, WA 98052

The **Menu** control allows users to add Windows pop-up or hierarchical menus to any page. Users can enhance their menus with font sizes, colors, icons, and so on.

MCSiTimer Control

Microsoft

http://www.microsoft.com

One Microsoft Way

Redmond, WA 98052

The **Timer** control initiates events at user-defined intervals.

MCSiTree Control

Microsoft

http://www.microsoft.com

One Microsoft Way

Redmond, WA 98052

The **Tree** control allows users to display navigational information in a hierarchical or Windows Explorer style format. Users can select colors, icons, font sizes, and so on to customize their information.

Menu

Microsoft

http://www.microsoft.com

One Microsoft Way

Redmond, WA 98052

The **Menu** control allows users to place a traditional menu button on any page. The menu control initiates events to which the author can respond to VBScript code.

Microsoft Agent

Microsoft

http://www.microsoft.com

One Microsoft Way

Redmond, WA 98052

Microsoft **Agent** supports animated interactive characters. It requires Windows 95 or Windows NT 4, IE 3.0, Pentium 100 or faster, 16 MB RAM, 650K disk space, and a compatible sound card for optional speech support.

Microsoft Chat Control

Microsoft

http://www.microsoft.com

One Microsoft Way

Redmond, WA 98052

Microsoft **Chat Control** allows users who are connected to a chat server to communicate with text and data. The control is a default user interface that is entirely customizable; Web authors can design their own interfaces.

Microsoft Interactive Music Control

Microsoft

http://www.microsoft.com

One Microsoft Way

Redmond, WA 98052

Microsoft **Interactive Music Control** plays original music dynamically on your Web pages. This includes "riffs" associated with hyperlinks. The control is invisible to the user at runtime. It also provides software wavetable synthesis, which features the Roland GS sound set.

Microsoft Wallet

Microsoft

`http://www.microsoft.com`

One Microsoft Way

Redmond, WA 98052

Microsoft `Wallet` can securely store your payment (that is, credit card) and address information. `Wallet` makes shopping on the Internet safe, easy, and expedient.

Pop-up Menu

Microsoft

`http://www.microsoft.com`

One Microsoft Way

Redmond, WA 98052

The `Pop-up Menu` control displays a user defined pop-up menu on demand. This control initiates an event when a menu item is selected.

Pop-up Window

Microsoft

`http://www.microsoft.com`

One Microsoft Way

Redmond, WA 98052

The Pop-up window displays specified HTML documents within a pop-up window, allowing users to view tool tips or preview links, for example.

Preloader

Microsoft

`http://www.microsoft.com`

One Microsoft Way

Redmond, WA 98052

`Preloader` downloads files at a specified URL and puts them in the cache. The control is invisible at runtime and only begins downloading when enabled. Upon completion of the download, the control initiates a `Complete` event.

Stock Ticker

Microsoft

`http://www.microsoft.com`

One Microsoft Way

Redmond, WA 98052

This control is used to display changing data (that is, stock prices) continuously. The control downloads information from the specified URL at regular intervals and displays the data. The data can be in a text or XRT format.

Timer

Microsoft

`http://www.microsoft.com`

One Microsoft Way

Redmond, WA 98052

The `Timer` control initiates an application periodically. At runtime, the control is invisible to the user.

Enliven Viewer for ActiveX

Narrative Communications

`http://www.narrative.com`

204 Second Avenue

Waltham, MA 02154

The **Enliven Viewer** delivers interactive CD-quality multimedia over the Internet to the end-user's desktop. Some firewall restrictions apply.

ComponentWorks User Interface Controls

National Instruments

http://www.natinst.com

6504 Bridge Point Parkway

Austin, TX 78730

ComponentWorks supplies controls for displaying technical data including graphs, meters, gauges, thermometers, and so on. The controls include advanced options such as autoscaling, zooming, and label/value pairs.

BillBoard

NCompass Labs Inc.

http://www.ncompasslabs.com

3rd Floor 321 Water Street

Vancouver, BC V6B1B8 Canada

BillBoard showcases images, in any user-defined order, using various 2-D transitional effects. **BillBoard** is designed for advertising purposes.

Cube

NCompass Labs Inc.

http://www.ncompasslabs.com

3rd Floor 321 Water Street

Vancouver, BC V6B1B8 Canada

Cube is a 3-D spinning cube, displaying different images on each of its sides. Users can interact with the cube as it spins.

LightBoard

NCompass Labs Inc.

`http://www.ncompasslabs.com`

3rd Floor 321 Water Street

Vancouver, BC V6B1B8 Canada

LightBoard enables users to graphically display messages using artificial light bulbs. **LightBoard** also includes numerous transformational effects.

MessageMorph

NCompass Labs Inc.

`http://www.ncompasslabs.com`

3rd Floor 321 Water Street

Vancouver, BC V6B1B8 Canada

MessageMorph, a member of the **CaptiveX** control family, manipulates text to make mesmerizing mixes of messages morphing together.

PowerLabels

NCompass Labs Inc.

`http://www.ncompasslabs.com`

3rd Floor 321 Water Street

Vancouver, BC V6B1B8 Canada

PowerLabels makes text rush at "high speeds" towards the viewer. The text is in a 3-D configuration and can also be spun on several axes.

PowerPanels

NCompass Labs Inc.

`http://www.ncompasslabs.com`

3rd Floor 321 Water Street

Vancouver, BC V6B1B8 Canada

PowerPanels displays a series of images on a 3-D tile set, sequencing them by using dramatic flipping, swiping, and venetian blind transitions.

OnLive! Talker

OnLive! Technologies

`http://www.onlive.com`

10131 Bubb Rd.

Cupertino, CA 95014

OnLive! Talker enables general socialization, communication, and collaboration via voice controls. **OnLive!** allows groups of users to talk, using their own voices, while simultaneously viewing Web content. **OnLive!** has not been tested on Windows NT.

Outrider ButtonTool

Outrider Systems

`http://www.outrider.com`

3701 Kirby Drive

Suite 1196

Houston, TX 77098

ButtonTool is a customizable command button for ActiveX that includes the ability to display both text and graphics and place them in any location on the button. **ButtonTool** also allows for the creation of special checkboxes through a toggle mode.

Outrider CheckList

Outrider Systems

`http://www.outrider.com`

3701 Kirby Drive

Suite 1196

Houston, TX 77098

`CheckList` enhances the existing functionality of a Window list box control while adding checkboxes to list items. User-defined checkbox pictures can be created.

Outrider Enhanced SpinButton

Outrider Systems

`http://www.outrider.com`

3701 Kirby Drive

Suite 1196

Houston, TX 77098

`SpinButton` is an enhanced version of the original `SpinButton` that shipped with Visual Basic. An accelerator function and built-in counter with range-checking functions have been added.

RealAudio Player/Control

Progressive Networks, Inc.

`http://www.realaudio.com/`

1111 3rd Ave.

Seattle, WA 98101

`RA Player/Control` allows users to play audio in real-time over modems. No downloads are necessary. `Control` for ActiveX allows users to incorporate RA controls directly into Web pages or Visual Basic applications.

Calendar Control

ProtoView Development Co.

`http://www.protoview.com`

2540 Route 130

Cranbury, NJ 08512

Create enhanced calendars of any time period— single month, quarter, half year, or full year. Different days can be displayed in different colors or fonts.

Currency Control

ProtoView Development Co.

http://www.protoview.com

2540 Route 130

Cranbury, NJ 08512

Currency Control contains 26 international currency settings. Features include auto scrolling, read-only, both positive and negative values, automatic currency symbol changes, decimals and separators, and editable font sizes and colors.

Data Explorer

ProtoView Development Co.

http://www.protoview.com

2540 Route 130

Cranbury, NJ 08512

Data Explorer is a programmable control for accessing and editing data in the traditional Windows Explorer-like interface. Features include drag-and-drop, sorting, searching, saving, loading, and filters.

DataTable Grid Component

ProtoView Development Co.

http://www.protoview.com

2540 Route 130

Cranbury, NJ 08512

`DataTable` is a grid component that interfaces with database applications. Its virtual memory and robust API features make it both compact and powerful.

DateEdit Control

ProtoView Development Co.

`http://www.protoview.com`

2540 Route 130

Cranbury, NJ 08512

`DateEdit` allows both direct date input and drop-down calendar input. `DateEdit` also provides century support, so users will be protected after the 20th century.

Font Selection Control

ProtoView Development Co.

`http://www.protoview.com`

2540 Route 130

Cranbury, NJ 08512

`Font Selection` adds two combination boxes to an application, allowing users to change both fonts and font sizes with a simple click of the mouse. The control is optimal for use with toolbars.

InterAct

ProtoView Development Co.

`http://www.protoview.com`

2540 Route 130

Cranbury, NJ 08512

InterAct is a diagramming metaphor embedded within an ActiveX control. **InterAct** can be customized, programmed, and edited using methods, properties, and events.

Line 3-D-Control

ProtoView Development Co.

http://www.protoview.com

2540 Route 130

Cranbury, NJ 08512

Line 3-D allows users to add 3-D lines to their applications. Lines can be edited for thickness, style, and color. **Line 3-D** is perfect for adding depth to applications.

Marquee Control

ProtoView Development Co.

http://www.protoview.com

2540 Route 130

Cranbury, NJ 08512

Marquee combines a title (text), color, fonts, and font sizes to create a powerful and exciting display.

MaskEdit Control

ProtoView Development Co.

http://www.protoview.com

2540 Route 130

Cranbury, NJ 08512

MaskEdit allows quick and easy methods for inputting formatted data. Default masks exist for common data types, such as social security numbers, telephone numbers, data, and so on). Customizable masks can also be created using the built-in property pages.

Multi-Directional Button Control

ProtoView Development Co.

`http://www.protoview.com`

2540 Route 130

Cranbury, NJ 08512

`Multi-Directional Button` adds four-directional movement. Four hot spots are incorporated into the application. These hot spots allow users to navigate in any direction in a two-dimensional plane.

Numeric Edit Control

ProtoView Development Co.

`http://www.protoview.com`

2540 Route 130

Cranbury, NJ 08512

`Numeric Edit` allows users to quickly and easily define and edit numbers. Data can be aligned in numerous ways; arrow and spin control can also be added where desired.

Percent Bar Custom Control

ProtoView Development Co.

`http://www.protoview.com`

2540 Route 130

Cranbury, NJ 08512

`Percent Bar` control is perfect for showing users the status of an ongoing process, such as a download or installation. Web authors have complete control over colors, grid lines, notifications, and so on.

Picture Control

ProtoView Development Co.

`http://www.protoview.com`

2540 Route 130

Cranbury, NJ 08512

Picture displays various picture types in the user's application, including icons, metafiles, and bitmaps. **Picture** provides a 3-D frame with beveled edges in order to highlight specified images.

Shape 3-D Control

ProtoView Development Co.

http://www.protoview.com

2540 Route 130

Cranbury, NJ 08512

Shape 3-D allows users to create 3-D shapes within an application. The control features a variety of shapes to choose from. The color and offset of the shadow are completely and easily customizable.

Text 3-D Control

ProtoView Development Co.

http://www.protoview.com

2540 Route 130

Cranbury, NJ 08512

Text 3-D is perfect for creating dynamic, exciting, headers or titles in applications. The control features 3-D frames for outlining key sections of the application.

TimeEdit Control

ProtoView Development Co.

http://www.protoview.com

2540 Route 130

Cranbury, NJ 08512

TimeEdit displays and edits time values. Users can enter a specified time or a standard 24-hour clock dynamically displays the time.

TreeView Control

ProtoView Development Co.

`http://www.protoview.com`

2540 Route 130

Cranbury, NJ 08512

`TreeView` displays data in a hierarchical format. The control can be sized, multiple columns can be set, and scrollbars can be added; filtering and sorting features are included.

Volume Control

ProtoView Development Co.

`http://www.protoview.com`

2540 Route 130

Cranbury, NJ 08512

`Volume` control is an alternative to the Windows volume control. The control features a mouse-controlled volume dial that can be tuned to the desired volume level.

WinX Button Control

ProtoView Development Co.

`http://www.protoview.com`

2540 Route 130

Cranbury, NJ 08512

`WinX Button` allows programmers to customize buttons within applications. A bitmap, color code box, or icon can be added next to the text of the button.

EasyMail Object

Quiksoft Corporation

`http://www.quiksoft.com`

501 Abbott Drive

Broomall, PA 19008

EasyMail generates Internet e-mail. Applications include server-side processing in ASP files and Perl scripts. Other ActiveX compatible applications are also supported, including IE, VB, and Delphi.

FileAccess Control

Quiksoft Corporation

`http://www.quiksoft.com`

501 Abbott Drive

Broomall, PA 19008

FileAccess allows Web programmers to code HTML that can safely and securely read and write to a specified area of the client's local file system. Uploading and background downloading tasks can also be performed.

HtmlShow Control

Quiksoft Corporation

`http://www.quiksoft.com`

501 Abbott Drive

Broomall, PA 19008

HtmlShow creates a window within a Web page which can load and display ordinary HTML documents. The control contains cycling features on a timed basis, creating a slide show effect.

SiteMapper Tree Control

Quiksoft Corporation

`http://www.quiksoft.com`

501 Abbott Drive

Broomall, PA 19008

SiteMapper Tree is a navigation control for a Web site. It allows users to interact with a graphic map of the Web site and jump back and forth within the site.

Sax Canvas Control

Sax Software Corporation

`http://www.saxsoft.com`

950 Patterson Street

Eugene, OR 97401

`Sax Canvas` allows VBScript or JScript code to automatically draw on the canvas. The control contains a variety of drawing instructions. From within Internet Explorer, the user can draw various shapes and lines in any color or size.

Crystal Reports Viewer Control

Seagate Software

`http://www.img.seagatesoftware.com`

4th Floor

1095 West Pender St.

Vancouver, BC V6E 2M6 Canada

`Crystal Reports Viewer` allows Web programmers to include Crystal Reports in their page content. Crystal Reports are a royalty/license-free report format.

Softholic OGL Control

Softoholic

`http://www.softoholic.bc.ca/`

4739 Driftwood Place

Burnaby, BC V5G 4E2 Canada

`Softholic OGL` allows developers to use OpenGL implementation for both Windows NT and Windows 95 operating systems.

Chart FX

Software FX, Inc.

`http://www.softwarefx.com`

7100 W Camino Real. Suite 117

Boca Raton, FL 33433

Chart FX is one of the fastest and most powerful charting controls available. Features include business, financial, statistical, and scientific chart support. MFC libraries are not required, which allows for less download time, enhanced performance, and easy deployment.

ASAP Webshow

Software Publishing Corporation

http://www.spco.com

111 North Market St.

San Jose, CA 95113

ASAP Webshow allows users to view, download, and print WordPowerT Web presentations. WordPowerT is an award-winning presentation software program by Software Publishing Corporation.

EarthTime ActiveX Lite

Starfish Software, Inc.

http://www.starfishsoftware.com

1700 Green Hills Road

Scotts Valley, CA 95066

EarthTime enables users to track time for communications applications across different time zones using a world map. It includes clocks for eight different cites or time zones, a time difference calculator and a database of telephone codes, currencies, and more.

Viscape

Superscape VR Plc

http://www.superscape.com/

Cromwell House,

Bartley Wood Business Park,

Hook, Hampshire, RG27 9XA UK

`viscape` allows users to interact with rich virtual reality worlds over the Internet.

Image and Animation

TegoSoft Inc.

`http://www.tegosoft.com`

404 Front St.

Bellmore, NY 11710

`Image and Animation` allows users to design HTML pages that are flicker-free. Sound can also be synchronized with the images and animations. Various formats of pictures can be used, including 24-bit, 16.8 million colors, and so on.

TegoSoft WAV and MIDI

TegoSoft Inc.

`http://www.tegosoft.com`

404 Front St.

Bellmore, NY 11710

WAV and MIDI control allows WAV and MIDI sound files to be played from within HTML pages. Random selections can be played, sounds can be synchronized with animation, and MIDI Tempos can be changed. MIDI and WAV files can be played simultaneously.

Visual 3Space Control

Template Graphics Software, Inc.

`http://www.tgs.com`

9920 Pacific Heights Blvd. Suite 200

San Diego, CA 92121

`Visual 3Space` is a 3-D/VRML component that supports various file formats including VRML, DXF, and Open Inventor 3-D geometry. The control exposes over 400 interfaces to VB, VBScript, and JavaScript applications.

Sizzler

Totally Hip Software

`http://www.totallyhip.com`

Suite #301

1224 Hamilton Street

Vancouver, BC V6B-2S8 Canada

`Sizzler` uses streaming technology to deliver animation to Web site viewers through their own Web browser.

Envoy Control

Tumbleweed Software Corp.

`http://www.tumbleweed.com`

2010 Broadway

Redwood City, CA 94063

`Envoy` allows users to create, embed, and edit a customized envoy viewer in any HTML Web page.

VDOLive Video Player

VDOnet Corp

`http://www.vdo.net`

4009 Miranda Ave

Suite 250

Palo Alto, CA 94304

`VDOLive Video Player` allows users to view live or on-demand video over the Internet. ISDN is not necessary.

VivoActive Player

Vivo Software, Inc.

`http://www.vivo.com`

411 Waverley Oaks Road

Suite 313

Waltham, MA 02154

VivoActive Player allows users to view on-demand video over the Internet. Special server software is not required. Slow modems behind corporate firewalls can also be utilized.

WIRL

VREAM, Inc.

http://www.vream.com

223 W. Erie Street

Suite 600

Chicago, IL 60610

WIRL enables users to interact with virtual reality on the Internet. **WIRL** supports VRML 1.0 and extends it with robust support for object behaviors, cause-and-effect relationships, and multimedia capabilities, including sound.

Index

W

X

ABOUT THE AUTHORS

REAZ HOQUE is an author, Web developer, and a speaker. Recently he finished working on a three-month project as a fellow technology evangelist for Netscape Corporation. He contributes Web-related articles for online and print magazines around the world. Some of his articles have been seen in *ZD Internet Magazine*, *Web Techniques*, *Internet World* and *NetscapeWorld*. His last book was *Practical Javascript Programming* (`http://rhoque.com/book`) published by MIS press. Reaz spoke at Dev-Con Conference '97 in San Jose, CA, Software Development '97 and Web '97 at Washington, D.C. and many other conferences around the United States. For more information, please visit Reaz's personal homepage at `http://rhoque.com`.

TARUN SHARMA is a Technology Advisor to the CEO of EC Cubed, a technology leader in e-commerce component development. His experience includes software development for artificial intelligence, client/server and Web-based systems, with specific proven expertise in e-commerce component technology. He has written several articles for *ZD Internet* and has taught classes in client/server and object-oriented technologies in India. Tarun is scheduled to speak at several international seminars on the topic of e-commerce application components. JavaBeans seems to be a dream come true for him.

About the Contributing Authors

CHRIS BEHRENS is a writer, speaker, and programmmer focusing on the subjects of Visual Basic and Internet Application development. He is the Vice President in charge of Development of DELTA V, a Level II Microsoft Sitebuilder, and a frequent guest speaker at technology conferences around the world.

AMAR GOEL is the president of Chip Shot Golf , a leading Internet retailer of golf products (`http://www.chipshotgolf.com`). He founded the company in 1995 as the first major golf retailer on the Web. Formerly at Netscape Communications, where he worked as a software engineer in the Internationalization group on Java technologies, Amar is now focused on the burgeoning Internet commerce space.

NAUSHAD KAPASI is a technologist par excellence. He is a Product Leader at EC Cubed, a technology leader in e-commerce component development. Naushad has successfully delivered many systems built upon core technologies like artificial intelligence, client/server and e-commerce application components. Naushad's interests lie in software component development based upon state-of-the-art technology.

DMITRI KONDRATIEV is a senior software engineer at ParaGraph International. He started to program in Java when Alpha 3 was released. Dmitri is an accomplished JavaBeans developer with his "Beans Unlimited" page registered in the Gamelan collection as well as his "VRMLBeans" proposal. In addition, Dmitri has more than 11 years experience with network programming. Before ParaGraph, Dmitri took part in developing software for Russian heterogeneous LAN ALISA+—original Adaptive Local Area Network Architecture, based on the ISO OSI Reference model.

JEFFREY KRAUSE AND JULIA OGRYDZIAK are the Managing Partners at Blacksquare, a firm providing custom corporate Intranet software. While running Blacksquare's Hawaiian office, Jeffrey is also an Assistant Professor of Architecture at the University of Hawaii. Julia holds a B.S. in Physics and a B.S. in Music from the Massachusetts Institute of Technology. Before coming to Blacksquare, Julia conducted physics and music computer research at the MIT Center for Theoretical Physics and the MIT Media Laboratory.

STEPHEN PETSCHULAT is the CEO and the cofounder of OpenRoad Communications. In between running the business and managing OpenRoad's Java projects, he writes about Java and related technologies, teaches courses, and speaks at conferences around the world.

DAVE ORCHARD is a network computing architect at IBM's Pacific Development Center, located in Vancouver, Canada. In his spare time, he does extensive public speaking, writing, and teaching. Dave specializes in writing and teaching JavaBeans technology.

JOHN SMALL is the president of Rogare Scope, a software consulting company specializing in distributed workflow and data-mining applications written in C/C++, Smalltalk, and Java. His software is in use at such places as NYNEX, Shell Oil, the eastern Canadian Air Traffic Control system, military satellites, nuclear power plants, and automated warehouses throughout the world.